Paul McFedries

D1105868

Microsoft® Windows®
Home Server

UNLEASHED

Second Edition

SAMS | 800 East 96th Street, Indianapolis, Indiana 46240 USA

Microsoft® Windows® Home Server Unleashed, Second Edition

ISBN-13: 978-0-672-33106-0
ISBN-10: 0-672-33106-3

Library of Congress Cataloging-in-Publication Data:

McFedries, Paul.

 Microsoft Windows Home Server unleashed / Paul McFedries.—2nd ed.

   p. cm.

 Includes index.

 ISBN 978-0-672-33106-0

 1. Microsoft Windows server. 2. Operating systems (Computers) 3. Home computer networks—Computer programs. I. Title.

 QA76.76.063M398173 2010

 005.4'476—dc22

                                        2010007840

Printed in the United States of America

First Printing March 2010

Trademarks

Warning and Disclaimer

Bulk Sales

Pearson offers excellent discounts on this book when ordered in quantity for bulk purchases or special sales. For more information, please contact:

U.S. Corporate and Government Sales
1-800-382-3419
corpsales@pearsontechgroup.com

For sales outside of the U.S., please contact:

International Sales
international@pearson.com

Associate Publisher
Greg Wiegand

Acquisitions Editor
Rick Kughen

Managing Editor
Patrick Kanouse

Senior Project Editor
Tonya Simpson

Copy Editor
Water Crest
Publishing, Inc.

Indexer
Ken Johnson

Proofreader
Williams Woods
Publishing Services,
LLC

Technical Editor
Tim Barrett

**Publishing
Coordinator**
Cindy Teeters

Book Designer
Gary Adair

Compositor
Mark Shirar

Reviewers
Tim Barrett
Kevin Royalty

Contents at a Glance

Table of Contents

About the Author

Paul McFedries is a Windows expert and full-time technical writer. Paul has been author-ing computer books since 1991 and has more than 70 books to his credit, which combined have sold more than three million copies worldwide. His recent titles include the Sams Publishing book *Windows 7 Unleashed* and the Que Publishing books *Networking with Microsoft Windows Vista* and *Tweak It and Freak It: A Killer Guide to Making Windows Run Your Way*. Paul is also the proprietor of Word Spy (www.wordspy.com), a website devoted to lexpionage, the sleuthing of new words and phrases that have entered the English language. Please drop by Paul's website at www.mcfedries.com or follow Paul on Twitter at twitter.com/paulmcf.

Dedication

For Karen

Acknowledgments

That's why editors and publishers will never be obsolete: a reader wants someone with taste and authority to point them in the direction of the good stuff, and to keep the awful stuff away from their door. —Walter J. Williams

Windows Home Server, like all versions of Windows, is loaded with good stuff, but it also comes with its share of awful stuff, too. One of the goals of *Microsoft Windows Home Server Unleashed* is to help you find the good portions of Windows Home Server and avoid the bad bits. I was helped tremendously in this by the editors at Sams, who not only bring terrific technical know-how to their jobs, but who can also spot chaff in a field of written wheat and aren't shy about separating the two. The result of all their efforts is a book that I think reads better, flows more logically, and has the best content possible.

My name may be the only one that adorns the cover, but tons of people had a big hand in creating what you now hold in your hands. You'll find a list of all the people who worked on this book near the front, but there are a few I'd like to thank personally:

Rick Kughen: Rick is the acquisitions editor for this book, and he was kind enough to electronically tap me on the shoulder and ask if I wanted to tackle this project. I immediately said yes (I've got to learn to be more coy about these things), and I'm glad I did because I had a blast writing this book.

Tonya Simpson: Tonya is the project editor, which means she's responsible for helping the book out of its relatively casual editorial clothes and into its more formal production duds. Coordinating the work of multiple editors, graphic artists, the production team, and, of course, the always fretful author is not easy. And to pull all that off with competence, aplomb, and a sense of humor, as Tonya did with this book, is a rare and remarkable feat.

Sarah Kearns: The job of copy editor requires a remarkable range of skills: a saint-like patience, an obsessive attention to detail, a prodigious memory, and the ability to hold your nose and type at the same time (when you come across a technical writer whose talents lie more toward the technical end of the authorial spectrum). Sarah possesses all those skills in abundance, and this book became much better thanks to her editorial ministrations.

Tim Barrett: As the book's technical editor, it was Tim's job to double-check my facts, try out my techniques, and implement my tips and tricks. This is a crucial step in the editing process because it ensures that you get a book that's accurate, easy to follow, and won't lead you astray. Tim's patience in the face of this daunting work and his unparalleled Windows knowledge make him a tremendous asset and a joy to work with. Any book he tackles becomes better thanks to his helpful suggestions and tactful corrections. This book was no exception.

Thanks to all of you for another outstanding effort. And, of course, I'd be remiss if I didn't thank you, dear reader, for purchasing this book and letting me be your guide to unleashing Windows Home Server.

Paul McFedries

March 2010

We Want to Hear from You!

As the reader of this book, *you* are our most important critic and commentator. We value your opinion and want to know what we're doing right, what we could do better, what areas you'd like to see us publish in, and any other words of wisdom you're willing to pass our way.

You can email or write me directly to let me know what you did or didn't like about this book—as well as what we can do to make our books stronger.

Please note that I cannot help you with technical problems related to the topic of this book, and that due to the high volume of mail I receive, I might not be able to reply to every message.

When you write, please be sure to include this book's title and author as well as your name and phone or email address. I will carefully review your comments and share them with the author and editors who worked on the book.

E-mail: feedback@samspublishing.com

Mail: Greg Wiegand
        Associate Publisher
        Sams Publishing
        800 East 96th Street
        Indianapolis, IN 46240 USA

Reader Services

Visit our website and register this book at informit.com/register for convenient access to any updates, downloads, or errata that might be available for this book.

Introduction

When you think of the word *server*, you probably first imagine either a massive mainframe hulking behind locked doors in the bowels of some large corporation, or a powerful and very expensive desktop-like device full of esoteric hardware that helps it—and perhaps a few others like it—run the network of a medium-sized company. The common thread here is that we've always thought of servers as *business* machines. With the exception of a few hardcore geeks and technical writers (not that the two designations are mutually exclusive), having a server in your home seemed, well, *excessive*. What home needs the power of a server? What home can afford the expense of such a high-end device?

But then a funny thing happened: times changed. All those one-computer households suddenly became two-, three-, and even four-computer households. Broadband became nearly ubiquitous, and of course every family member wanted a piece of the new pipe. We began digitizing our media en masse; we wanted to share that media with other members of the family and with other devices scattered around the house, and we discovered wireless computing and became addicted to working and playing anywhere we wanted. The result has been an explosion of home networks over the past few years.

However, it didn't take long for amateur network administrators to learn something that their professional counterparts have known for many years: the larger the network, the more you need some device in the middle of it all to coordinate activities and offer a central repository for data. And our home networks have started to become quite large, with multiple computers, multiple devices such as wireless access points and network attached storage drives, and increasingly massive files, from multiple-megabyte digital audio files to multi-gigabyte digital video files. Suddenly we, too, needed a powerful machine in the middle of it all to keep things humming.

It helped significantly that extremely powerful computers had became extremely inexpensive, but one big problem remained: A server computer needs a server operating system. Unfortunately, the only choices here simply weren't reasonable or practical choices for the home: the powerful but expensive Windows Server 2003 or Windows Server 2003 Small Business Edition, or the various flavors of Linux, all of which are far too complex and arcane for the average home network.

However, the last piece of the puzzle fell into place when Microsoft announced Windows Home Server to the world in January 2007. Now we all had access to a server operating system that was designed specifically for home networks; we had access to a server OS that was easy to configure, simple to use, inexpensive, and could run on a variety of hardware; we had a server OS that not only did the usual server tasks—store data and manage users—but that also went much further with automatic backups for every computer, streaming media, and easy-to-configure access to any desktop from the network or from the Internet.

Welcome, then, to *Microsoft Windows Home Server Unleashed*, Second Edition. My goal in this book is to take you beyond the basic Windows Home Server Console interface and into the tremendously powerful behind-the-scenes features that enable you to get the most out of your investment without requiring an advanced networking degree.

This book also covers the new and changed features in Power Packs 1, 2, and 3, including the following:

▶ Windows 7 libraries support

▶ Windows Search 4.0

▶ Recorded TV archiving

▶ Windows Media Center Console Quick View

▶ Windows Media Center Connector

▶ Server Backup

▶ Drag-and-drop remote file uploading

▶ Options for downloading remote files

▶ Wake up to back up

▶ Remote Access Configuration Wizard

▶ User-based remote access options

Who Should Read This Book?

For a book like this, it doesn't make much sense to have a "typical reader" in mind when writing. First, there's just no such thing as a typical reader, so you'd be writing for an audience of none. Second, home networks are as varied and unique as the families who use them. There are simple two-computer homes; there are large one-computer-per-person households; there are families who qualify as media powerhouses who create, share, and play audio and video incessantly; there's the home-office crowd who use their network for work as well as play; and finally there's the Alpha Geek family with one person who's juiced not so much about Windows Home Server itself, but about getting his hands on the powerful Windows Server 2003 engine that comes with it.

In this book, I've tried to keep all these different families and situations in mind, and there's lots of content here for everyone. As a general rule, this book is for anyone who wants more from Windows Home Server. If you want to learn more about how Windows Home Server works, if you want to get more out of the unique features in Windows Home Server, and if you want to know how to use the powerful but hidden server features that are also part of the Windows Home Server package, this book is most definitely for you.

How This Book Is Organized

To help give you a sense of the overall structure of the book, the next few sections offer a brief summary of the five main parts of the book.

Part I: Unleashing Windows Home Server Configuration

The five chapters in Part I show you how to get everything configured and connected so that you can start to take full advantage of what Windows Home Server has to offer. You learn how to set up Windows Home Server for networking and how to troubleshoot basic network woes (Chapter 1). You learn how to set up and manage user accounts (Chapter 2), and I show you how to add various computer types—Windows 7, Vista, and XP, as well as Mac and Linux—and various devices—including Windows Mobile and Xbox 360—to the Windows Home Server network (Chapter 3). You learn how to configure various Windows Home Server settings, including the computer name, the password, and various startup options (Chapter 4), and I delve deep into the new Windows Home Server storage system to show you how the system works, how to add, repair, and remove storage, and more (Chapter 5).

Part II: Unleashing Windows Home Server Networking

Part II is the biggest section of the book, with eight chapters focused on various aspects of networking with Windows Home Server. You learn how to share files and folders (Chapter 6); connect to other computers, both over the network and over the Internet (Chapter 7); stream and share digital image, audio, and video (Chapter 8); use Windows Home Server's computer backup and restore features (Chapter 9); monitor your network (Chapter 10); and implement network security (Chapter 11). I close this section with two chapters that take you well beyond Windows Home Server's core capabilities: Chapter 12 shows you how to use the built-in web server to create powerful and flexible websites, and Chapter 13 shows you how to download, install, configure, and use Windows SharePoint Services to run collaborative sites for your family.

Part III: Unleashing Windows Home Server Performance and Maintenance

Part III takes you into some of the features of Windows Home Server that are less glamorous but are still crucially important: performance tuning (Chapter 14), system maintenance (Chapter 15), interface customization (Chapter 16), and problem troubleshooting (Chapter 17).

Part IV: Unleashing Windows Home Server Advanced Tools

The four chapters in Part IV take your Windows Home Server knowledge to a higher level with in-depth looks at some advanced tools and features. You learn how to use the Windows Home Server Registry (Chapter 18); how to use the command-line tools (Chapter 19); how to use power tools such as the Control Panel, the Group Policy Editor, and the Computer Management snap-ins (Chapter 20); and how to create Windows Home Server scripts, including scripts that control the incredibly powerful Windows Management Instrumentation (WMI) interface (Chapter 21).

Part V: Appendixes

To round out your Windows Home Server education, Part V presents a few appendixes that contain extra goodies. You'll find a glossary of Windows Home Server terms (Appendix A), a complete list of Windows Home Server shortcut keys (Appendix B), and a list of online resources for Windows Home Server (Appendix C).

Conventions Used in This Book

To make your life easier, this book includes various features and conventions that help you get the most out of this book and out of Windows Home Server:

Steps	Throughout the book, I've broken many Windows Home Server tasks into easy-to-follow step-by-step procedures.
Things you type	Whenever I suggest that you type something, what you type appears in a **bold monospace** font.
Filenames, folder names, and code	These things appear in a monospace font.
Commands	Commands and their syntax use the monospace font as well. Command placeholders (which stand for what you actually type) appear in an *italic monospace* font.
Pull-down menu commands	I use the following style for all application menu commands: *Menu*, *Command*, where *Menu* is the name of the menu that you pull down and *Command* is the name of the command you select. Here's an example: File, Open. This means that you pull down the File menu and select the Open command.
Code continuation character	When a line of code is too long to fit on only one line of this book, it is broken at a convenient place and continued to the next line. The continuation of the line is preceded by a code continuation character (➥). You should type a line of code that has this character as one long line without breaking it.

This book also uses the following boxes to draw your attention to important (or merely interesting) information:

NOTE

The Note box presents asides that give you more information about the current topic. These tidbits provide extra insights that offer a better understanding of the task.

TIP

The Tip box tells you about Windows Home Server methods that are easier, faster, or more efficient than the standard methods.

CAUTION

The all-important Caution box tells you about potential accidents waiting to happen. There are always ways to mess up things when you're working with computers. These boxes help you avoid those traps and pitfalls.

CHAPTER 1

Setting Up Your Windows Home Server Network

You're almost ready to put Windows Home Server to good use storing files, sharing media, and backing up the other machines on your network. Before you get to all that, however, you need to make sure that Windows Home Server is ready to do the networking thing. To that end, this chapter takes you through a few network configuration chores that you might require to get Windows Home Server and the rest of your network on speaking terms. If you have problems, this chapter also includes an extensive network troubleshooting section that should help.

In this chapter, I assume that the basics of your home network are already in place: You have wired or wireless network interface cards (NICs) installed in each machine, you have the necessary routers and switches, you have a router or wireless access point connected to your broadband Internet service, the wired machines have the correct cable connections, and so on.

> **NOTE**
>
> If your network is either nonexistent or a work in progress, you might want to check out my book, *Networking with Microsoft Windows Vista*, to get things going.

Configuring Windows Home Server for Networking

Windows Home Server's default networking setup creates a basic configuration that should work without a hitch on most home networks. However, you should know about a few small tweaks that can make Windows Home Server a bit easier to work with and that are required for certain features to work properly. For example, setting up remote access to the Windows Home Server machine is much easier if you give the computer a static IP address. These next few sections take you through this and other network modifications.

Changing the Windows Home Server Workgroup Name

Home networking works best when all the computers on the network use the same workgroup name. By default, Windows Home Server installs with the name WORKGROUP, which is also the default workgroup name used by Windows 7, Windows Vista, and Windows XP Professional. Therefore, if you're using any of those operating systems and you've set up your network using the default settings, all your machines should reside in the WORKGROUP group.

However, if your client machines are using some other workgroup name, you need to modify the Windows Home Server workgroup name to match. The steps to do that follow:

1. Log on to Windows Home Server either locally or by using a Remote Desktop connection (see "Making a Remote Desktop Connection to the Server," later in this chapter).
2. Click Start, right-click My Computer, and then click Properties. (You also can press Windows Logo+Pause/Break.) The System Properties dialog box appears.
3. Display the Computer Name tab.

> **TIP**
>
> Another way to open the System Properties dialog box with the Computer Name tab displayed is to select Start, Run (or press Windows Logo+R), type **control sysdm.cpl,,1** in the Run dialog box, and then click OK.

4. Click Change. The Computer Name Changes dialog box appears, as shown in Figure 1.1.
5. Make sure the Workgroup option is selected.
6. Type the common workgroup name.
7. Click OK. A dialog box welcoming you to the new workgroup appears.
8. Click OK. Windows Home Server tells you that you must restart the computer to put the changes into effect.
9. Click OK to return to the System Properties dialog box.
10. Click OK. Windows Home Server prompts you to restart your computer.
11. Click Yes.

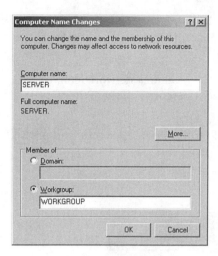

FIGURE 1.1   Use this dialog box to change the Windows Home Server workgroup name.

Displaying the Network Icon in the Notification Area

You can save yourself a bit of time when working with some networking settings on Windows Home Server by adding the network icon to the notification area. This gives you quick access to the current network speed and status, the network repair tool, the Network Connections window, and more. Follow these steps to add the network icon to the notification area in Windows Home Server:

1. Log on to Windows Home Server either locally or by using a Remote Desktop connection (see "Making a Remote Desktop Connection to the Server," later in this chapter).

2. Select Start, All Programs, Accessories, Communications, Network Connections to open the Network Connections window.

3. Right-click the icon for the connection to your local area network (this icon is named Local Area Connection as the default), and then click Properties. Windows opens the connection's property sheet.

4. Click to activate the Show Icon in Notification Area When Connected check box.

5. Click OK. Windows Home Server adds the network icon to the notification area, as shown in Figure 1.2.

Configuring Windows Home Server with a Static IP Address

Every computer on your network requires a unique designation so that packets can be routed to the correct location when information is transferred across the network. In a default Microsoft peer-to-peer network, the network protocol that handles these transfers is TCP/IP, and the unique designation assigned to each computer is the Internet Protocol (IP) address.

By default, Windows Home Server obtains its IP address via Dynamic Host Configuration Protocol (DHCP). This requires a server, and in the vast majority of home broadband networks, that server is the router or wireless access point. (If you have no DHCP server on your network, you can convert Windows Home Server into one; see the next section.) To find out the current IP address of the Windows Home Server machine, log on to the server and then use either of the following methods:

▶ In the Network Connections window, right-click the local area network icon, click Status, and then display the Support tab. As shown in Figure 1.3, the IP Address value appears in the Connection Status group.

▶ Select Start, All Programs, Accessories, Command Prompt, type **ipconfig**, and press Enter.

Default Local Area Connection

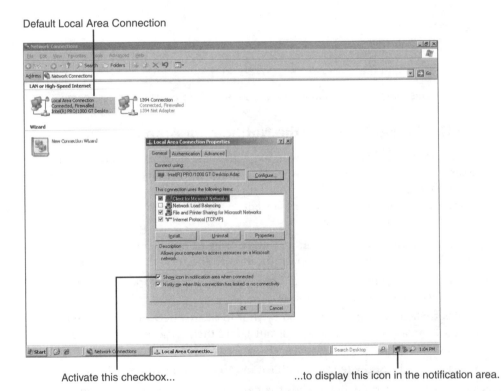

Activate this checkbox...   ...to display this icon in the notification area.

FIGURE 1.2   Display the network icon in the notification area for easier access to some networking features and tools.

The DHCP server offers each client a lease on the IP address, and in most cases that lease expires after 24 hours. When the expiration time approaches, the client asks for a new IP address. In small networks, the DHCP server often assigns each client the same IP address each time, but that's not guaranteed. A changing IP address is no big deal for client computers, but it can be a problem for the Windows Home Server machine. Most importantly, remote access sessions require that you set up your router to forward remote requests to the Windows Home Server computer. You do that by specifying the server's IP address, so if that address changes, the remote access sessions won't work.

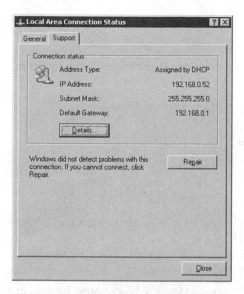

FIGURE 1.3   In the network connection's Status dialog box, the Support tab displays the server's current IP address.

▶ **SEE** For the details on setting up your router for remote access sessions, **see** "Setting Up Port Forwarding on the Router," **P. 195**.

Therefore, it's a good idea to assign a static IP address to your Windows Home Server machine. Here's how:

1. Log on to Windows Home Server either locally or by using a Remote Desktop connection (see "Making a Remote Desktop Connection to the Server," later in this chapter).

2. Select Start, All Programs, Accessories, Communications, Network Connections to open the Network Connections window.

TIP

If you added the network icon to the notification area as described earlier, you can display the Network Connections window much faster by right-clicking the network icon and then clicking Open Network Connections.

3. Right-click the icon for the connection to your local area network, and then click Status. The connection's Status dialog box appears.

4. Display the Support tab, and then click Details.

5. Make a note of the following values:

   ▶ **Subnet Mask**—On home networks, this is usually 255.255.255.0.

   ▶ **Default Gateway**—On home networks, this is the IP address of your router or access point.

   ▶ **DNS Servers**—These are the IP addresses of the preferred and alternate Domain Name System servers that your ISP uses.

6. Click Close to return to the Status dialog box.

7. On the General tab, click Properties. The connection's property sheet appears.

8. On the General tab, click Internet Protocol (TCP/IP), and then click Properties.

9. Click the Use the Following IP Address option.

10. Type the IP address you want to use. Be sure to use an address that won't conflict with the other DHCP clients on your network. A good idea is to use the highest possible address, such as 192.168.1.254 (if your network uses 192.168.1.* addresses) or 192.168.0.254 (if your network uses 192.168.0.* addresses).

11. Type the IP addresses for the Subnet Mask (Windows Home Server should fill this in automatically), Default Gateway, Preferred DNS Server, and Alternate DNS Server that you noted in step 5. Figure 1.4 shows a completed version of the dialog box.

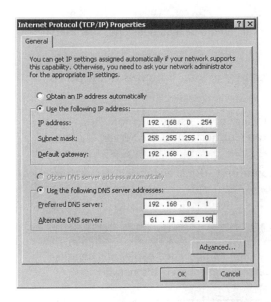

FIGURE 1.4   It's a good idea to assign a static IP address to the Windows Home Server machine.

12. Click OK to return to the connection's property sheet.

13. Click Close to return to the Status dialog box.

14. Click Close.

TIP

When you specify a static IP address, you must also specify static DNS servers. This shouldn't cause a problem with most ISPs because their DNS server addresses are constant. However, you might have trouble if your ISP changes its DNS settings. You can work around this problem by first returning Windows Home Server to getting its IP address dynamically. Then log in to your router and look for an option that enables you to map a static IP address to the server's Media Access Control (MAC; see the next Note) address. This means that each time the server requests a new DHCP lease, the router supplies the server the same IP address each time. Note that not all broadband routers offer this option.

NOTE

To find out your server's MAC address, open the Network Connections window, right-click the local area network icon, click Status, display the Support tab, and then click Details. (Alternatively, select Start, Command Prompt, type `ipconfig/all`, and press Enter.) The MAC address is given by the Physical Address value.

Setting Up Windows Home Server as a DHCP Server

If your home network doesn't have a device that acts as a DHCP server, or if you want more control over DHCP on your network, you can convert Windows Home Server into a DHCP server. (The next three sections assume that you're logged on to Windows Home Server either locally or by using a Remote Desktop connection; see "Making a Remote Desktop Connection to the Server," later in this chapter.)

CAUTION

Windows Home Server's DHCP Server service will not work if it detects another DHCP server on the network. If you have a router or access point that currently has DHCP enabled, you must first disable DHCP on that device.

Installing the DHCP Service

To set up a DHCP server, you must start the DHCP Server service. This service comes with Windows Home Server, but it's not installed by default. Follow these steps to install it:

1. Select Start, All Programs, Accessories, Communications, Network Connections. Alternatively, right-click the network icon in the notification area (if you displayed it as described earlier), and then click Open Network Connections.

2. Select Advanced, Optional Networking Components to launch the Windows Optional Networking Components Wizard.

3. In the Components list, click Networking Services, and then click Details.

4. Click to activate the Dynamic Host Configuration Protocol (DHCP) check box, and then click OK.

5. Click Next. Windows Home Server installs the DHCP Server service. (If you didn't assign a static IP address to the home server earlier, you'll see an error message at

this point warning you not to use a dynamic address on the server. Follow the prompts to assign a static IP to the server.)

6. Click Finish.

Starting the DHCP Server Service

After it's installed, Windows Home Server should start the DHCP Server service automatically, but it might not. To make sure, follow these steps:

1. Select Start, All Programs, Administrative Tools, Services.

2. In the Services window, find DHCP Server and check the Status column. If it says Started, skip the rest of these steps; otherwise, proceed with step 3.

3. Click the DHCP Server service.

4. Click the Start link or the Start Service button. After a few seconds, you should see Started in the Status column.

NOTE

The DHCP Server service should start automatically each time you reboot Windows Home Server. To confirm this, open the Services snap-in and double-click the DHCP Server service. In the Startup Type list, select Automatic, and then click OK.

Specifying Windows Home Server as the DHCP Server

You're now ready to configure the DHCP service and set up Windows Home Server to act as a DHCP server. This involves (primarily) defining a scope for the DHCP server, which is a range of IP addresses that the server can dole out to the clients. Here are the steps to follow:

1. Select Start, All Programs, Administrative Tools, DHCP. Windows runs the Microsoft Management Console application and displays the DHCP snap-in.

2. Select Action, Add Server. (If you already see the home server listed, skip to step 4.)

3. In the This Server text box, type the name of the Windows Home Server machine, and then click OK. The server appears in the DHCP branch.

4. Right-click the server, and then click New Scope. The New Scope Wizard appears.

5. Click Next.

6. Type a name and optional description for the scope, and then click Next. The IP Address Range dialog box appears.

7. Fill in the following two IP address boxes, and then click Next:

   ▶ **Start IP Address**—Type the starting address for the IP address range you want the server to use (for example, 192.168.1.100).

   ▶ **End IP Address**—Type the ending address for the IP address range you want the server to use (for example, 192.168.1.150). Make sure this address is higher than the Start IP Address value.

8. If you want certain addresses excluded from being used by the server, use the Add Exclusions dialog box to specify the Start IP Address and End IP Address, and then click OK. The Lease Duration dialog box appears.

9. Specify the time in hours, days, and minutes that you want to use as the duration for each DHCP lease, and then click Next. (A lease duration of one day is standard.) The Configure DHCP Options dialog box appears.

10. Click Next.

11. The New Scope Wizard runs through a series of dialog boxes that don't apply to Windows Home Server, so click Next in each until you see the Activate Scope dialog box.

12. Click Next.

13. Click Finish.

Viewing the Windows Home Server Network

With your Windows Home Server networking tweaks done, you can now check to make sure that the rest of the network can see the server:

▶ In Windows 7, click the Windows Explorer taskbar icon, and then click Network.

▶ In Vista, select Start, Network.

▶ In XP, select Start, My Network Places, and then click View Workgroup Computers. (If you have the Folders list displayed, open the My Network Places, Entire Network, Microsoft Windows Network branch, and then click your workgroup.)

Figure 1.5 shows Windows 7's Network window, which displays icons for the computers, devices, and shared media connections on the network (as does the Network window in Vista). (XP just displays icons for the workgroup computers.)

Notice that for the Windows Home Server machine, you might see as many as three icons:

▶ **Server device icon**—Double-click this icon to see data about the server as a network device. The data includes the server's IP address and MAC address.

▶ **Server shared folders icon**—Double-click this icon to see the server's shared folders.

▶ **Server shared media icon**—Double-click this icon to open Windows Media Player, which then lets you access the server's shared media. This icon appears only when you configure Windows Home Server to share its Music, Photos, or Videos folders.

▶ **SEE** To learn how to share Windows Home Server media folders, **see** Chapter 8, "Streaming and Sharing Digital Media."

Server Shared Folders Icon

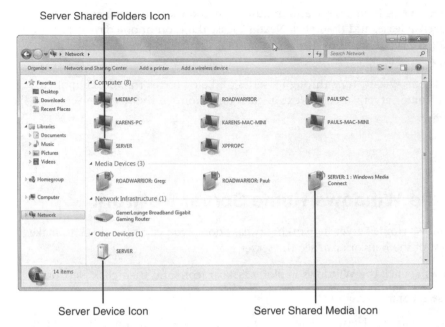

Server Device Icon   Server Shared Media Icon

FIGURE 1.5   Windows 7's Network window may have as many as three icons for Windows Home Server.

Troubleshooting Network Problems

Big-time corporate networking is a complex, arcane topic that taxes the patience of all but the most dedicated *wireheads* (an affectionate pet name often applied to network hackers and gurus). There are so many hardware components to deal with (from the network adapters to the cables to the routers to the hubs) and so many layers of software (from the device drivers to the protocols to the redirectors to the network providers) that big networks often seem like accidents looking for a place to happen.

Home networks are much simpler beasts, and more often than not they work well right out of the box. That's not to say that home networks are bulletproof—not by a long shot. If your network has become a *notwork* (some wags also refer to a downed network as a *nyetwork*), this section offers a few solutions that might help. I don't make any claim to completeness here, however. Most network ills are a combination of several factors and are therefore relatively obscure and difficult to reproduce. Instead, I go through a few general strategies for tracking down problems and offer solutions for some of the most common network afflictions.

Checking Connection Status

A good starting point for diagnosing network problems is to check the status of the Windows Home Server network connection. This shows you things such as your connection status, connection speed, current IP address, network's default gateway addresses,

DHCP server, DNS servers, and so on. Invalid entries for these and other status items could provide a hint as to where the network problem might lie.

To display the connection status, log on to Windows Home Server, and then use either of the following techniques:

► If you added the network connection icon to the notification area, double-click the icon.

► Select Start, All Programs, Accessories, Communication, Network Connections. In the Network Connections window, double-click the connection.

Figure 1.6 shows the Status dialog box that appears. In the General tab are two groups to check out, as follows:

► **Connection**—This group shows the connection's current status: Connected or Disconnected. If the status value shows Connected, the Duration value shows how long the connection has been active, and the Speed value shows the connection speed in Mbps or Gbps.

► **Activity**—This group shows the number of network packets that the connection has sent and received. A low number for either value gives you a hint about the direction of the problem. For example, a low Sent value might indicate that Windows Home Server can't communicate with the client computers.

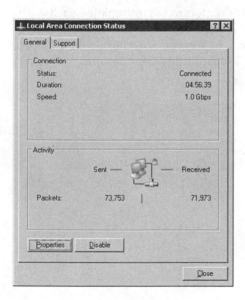

FIGURE 1.6   In the Status dialog box, the General tab offers basic connection details and activity metrics.

NOTE

On most Windows Home Server networks, the Sent and Received values should be fairly balanced, with one or the other being perhaps 10 to 40 higher than the other. On networks that do a lot of media streaming, however, the Sent value may be significantly higher than the Received value.

The Support tab displays basic connection data, including your IP address, subnet mask, and default gateway address (see Figure 1.3, earlier in this chapter). The Address Type value will be one of the following:

▶ **Assigned by DHCP**—A DHCP server assigns your IP address automatically.

▶ **Manually Configured**—You entered a static IP address in the Internet Protocol (TCP/IP) Properties dialog box, as described earlier in this chapter. (See "Configuring Windows Home Server with a Static IP Address.")

▶ **Automatic Private Address**—Your network uses the Automatic Private Internet Protocol Addressing (APIPA). This is unlikely on a home network.

▶ **Invalid IP Address**—An invalid IP address (0.0.0.0) usually indicates that either your network's DHCP server is down or that the static IP address you entered conflicts with another IP address on the network.

For other network connection data, click the Details button to see information such as the addresses of the DHCP server (this appears only if you're using a dynamically allocated IP address), DNS servers, and WINS server (see Figure 1.7). You can also click Repair to initiate the Windows Home Server network connection repair utility. See "Repairing a Network Connection," later in this chapter.

FIGURE 1.7   Use the Details dialog box to see extra information about your network connection.

Checking Network Utilization

If your network feels sluggish, it could be that the computer you're working with is sharing data slowly or that network traffic is exceptionally high. To see whether the latter situation is the cause of the problem, you can check out the current *network utilization* value, which is the percent of available bandwidth that your network adapter is currently using.

To check network utilization, follow these steps:

1. Log on to Windows Home Server either locally or by using a Remote Desktop connection (see "Making a Remote Desktop Connection to the Server" later in this chapter).

2. Right-click an empty section of the taskbar, and then click Task Manager.

3. Display the Networking tab, shown in Figure 1.8.

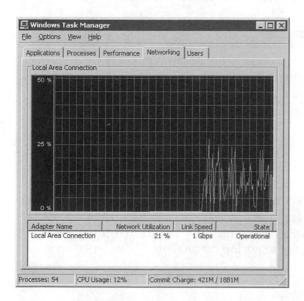

FIGURE 1.8   Use Task Manager's Networking tab to check the current network utilization percentage.

4. If you have multiple adapters, click the one you want to check in the Adapter Name list.

5. Use the graph or the Network Utilization column to monitor the current network utilization value.

Repairing a Network Connection

When a user calls Microsoft Support to resolve a networking issue, the support engineer has a list of troubleshooting steps that he takes the user through. For example, if there's a problem with a DHCP network, the engineer usually starts by telling the user to use IPCONFIG to release (`ipconfig /release`) and then renew (`ipconfig /renew`) the IP address. Other steps include running specific commands with the ARP (Address Resolution Protocol) and NBTSTAT (NetBIOS over TCP/IP Statistics) utilities.

Someone at Microsoft realized that all these steps could be automated by creating a script that runs the various `ipconfig`, `arp`, and `nbstat` commands. The result is the network connection repair tool, which runs the following six troubleshooting steps:

1. **Broadcasts a request for the renewal of the computer's DHCP lease**—A *DHCP lease* is a guarantee that the DHCP client computer will have the IP address supplied by the DHCP server for a specified period. To avoid lease expiration, the DHCP client usually sends a request—a `DHCPREQUEST` message—for lease renewal to the original DHCP server after 50% of the lease time has expired. If 87.5% of its lease time has expired, the DHCP client sends a lease renewal request to all available DHCP servers. This broad request for a lease renewal is what the repair tool does.

NOTE

Why send a `DHCPREQUEST` message instead of just using IPCONFIG to release and renew the IP address? Because if the current address is functioning properly, releasing that address could cause extra problems if a new address cannot be obtained from a DHCP server. With a lease renewal request, the DHCP client keeps its current address.

---

2. **Flushes the ARP cache**—The *ARP* (*Address Resolution Protocol*) handles the conversion of an IP address to the MAC address of a network adapter. To improve performance, Windows Home Server stores resolved addresses in the *ARP cache* for a short time. Some networking problems are caused by ARP cache entries that are obsolete or incomplete. The cache is normally flushed regularly, but the repair tool forces a flush. This is the same as running the following command:

```
arp -d
```

TIP

To see the contents of the ARP cache, run the following command:

```
arp -a
```

You'll see output similar to the following, which lists IP addresses and their corresponding MAC addresses:

```
Interface: 192.168.1.254 --- 0x10003
  Internet Address      Physical Address      Type
  192.168.1.101         00-c0-a8-b2-e0-d3     dynamic
  192.168.1.102         00-11-11-ce-c7-78     dynamic
  192.168.1.108         00-0f-66-ea-ea-24     dynamic
  192.168.1.111         00-0d-4b-04-27-2f     dynamic
```

3. **Flushes the NetBIOS name cache**—NetBIOS handles the conversion between the network names of computers and their IP addresses. To improve performance, Windows Home Server stores resolved names in the *NetBIOS name cache*. To solve problems caused by NetBIOS name cache entries that are obsolete or bad, this step clears the cache. This is the same as running the following command:

```
nbtstat -R
```

4. **Reregisters the computer with the network's WINS server**—The repair tool asks the WINS server to release the computer's NetBIOS names that are registered with the server and then reregister them. This is useful if you're having problems connecting to other computers using their network names. This is the same as running the following command:

```
nbtstat -RR
```

5. **Flushes the DNS cache**—DNS handles the conversion of domain names to IP addresses. To improve performance, Windows Home Server stores resolved domain names in the DNS cache. To solve problems caused by DNS cache entries that are obsolete or bad, this step clears the cache. This is the same as running the following command:

```
ipconfig /flushdns
```

6. **Reregisters the computer with the DNS server**—This is useful if you're having trouble resolving domain names or if you're having trouble with a dynamic DNS server. This is the same as running the following command:

```
ipconfig /registerdns
```

To launch the repair process, log on to Windows Home Server, and then use one of the following techniques:

▶ In the Support tab of the connection's Status dialog box, click Repair.

▶ In the Network Connections window, right-click the connection, and then click Repair.

▶ Right-click the network icon in the notification area (see "Displaying the Network Icon in the Notification Area," earlier in this chapter), and then click Repair.

The Repair *Connection* dialog box appears (where *Connection* is the name of the connection you're repairing) and shows you the progress of the repair, as shown in Figure 1.9. When the repair is complete, click Close.

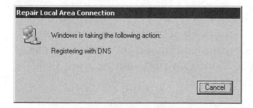

FIGURE 1.9   The network connection repair tool runs through six common network troubleshooting steps in an attempt to resolve the problem.

Working with Network Diagnostics

If you suspect you're having network trouble—such as computers on the network not being able to see each other or file transfers or other network activity behaving erratically—but you aren't sure, one easy way to find out is to run the Network Diagnostics utility. This is a Help and Support Center connectivity troubleshooting tool that can aid you in isolating network problems.

To get started, log on to Windows Home Server, and then use any one of the following techniques:

▶ Select Start, Run, type **helpctr**, and click OK to open the Help and Support Center. Click Tools, Help and Support Center Tools, Network Diagnostics.

▶ In the System Configuration Utility (select Start, Run, type **msconfig**, and click OK), display the Tools tab, click Network Diagnostics, and then click Launch.

▶ In the System Information utility (Start, All Programs, Accessories, System Tools, System Information), select Tools, Net Diagnostics.

▶ In a Command Prompt window, enter the following command:

```
netsh diag gui
```

Network Diagnostics operates by performing three different actions:

▶ **Ping**—Pings various objects to check for basic connectivity. For example, Network Diagnostics pings the loopback address (127.0.0.1), your IP address, the default gateway, the DHCP and DNS servers, and more.

▶ **Connect**—Attempts to connect to certain servers, such as your Internet mail and news servers.

▶ **Show**—Displays information about various objects, including your network adapters, network clients, DHCP servers, IP addresses, modems, and more.

Setting Scanning Options

To specify which of these actions are performed on which objects, click the Set Scanning Options link in the Network Diagnostics window. You see the Network Diagnostics window shown in Figure 1.10. You have two ways to proceed:

▶ In the Actions section, activate the check box beside each action that you want Network Diagnostics to perform.

▶ In the Categories section, activate the check box beside each object that you want the actions performed on. (Note, however, that not all actions are performed on all objects. For example, the Connect action is performed only on the mail and news server and the Internet Explorer proxy server, if one exists on your network.)

Running Network Diagnostics

To start the Network Diagnostics scan, click the Scan Your System link. Network Diagnostics displays the progress of the scan. When the scan has finished, you'll see the results in a window similar to the one shown in Figure 1.11. Open the branches to see more detailed objects and the actions that Network Diagnostics performed on them. Look for FAILED in red type to see where possible problems occurred.

FIGURE 1.10   Click the Set Scanning Options link to see the list of Network Diagnostics options.

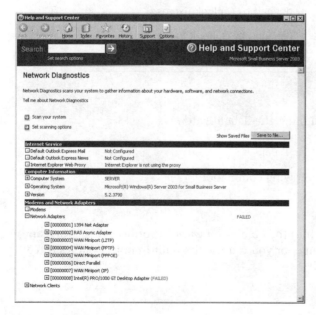

FIGURE 1.11   The results of a Network Diagnostics scan.

Running Network Diagnostics from the Command Line

You can also run network diagnostics during a Command Prompt session using the NETSH (Net Shell) utility.

For the `ping` action, you use the following command:

```
netsh diag ping object
```

Here, `object` is a parameter that specifies the object you want to ping. You can either specify an IP address or hostname, or you can use the built-in object names listed in Table 1.1.

TABLE 1.1   The **object** Parameter's Built-In Names for the **ping** Action

Name	Pings
adapter	The network adapter
dhcp	The DHCP server
dns	The DNS server
gateway	The default gateway
ieproxy	The Internet Explorer proxy server
ip	The computer's IP address
loopback	The loopback address (127.0.0.1)
mail	The default mail server defined by Outlook Express
news	The default news server defined by Outlook Express
wins	The WINS server

For example, the following command pings the default gateway:

```
netsh diag ping gateway
```

For the `connect` action, you use the following command:

```
netsh diag connect object
```

Here, `object` is a parameter that specifies the object you want to connect with. You can either specify an IP address or hostname, or you can use the built-in object names listed in Table 1.2.

TABLE 1.2   The **object** Parameter's Built-In Names for the **connect** Action

Name	Connects With
ieproxy	The Internet Explorer proxy server
mail	The default mail server defined by Outlook Express (if one is defined)
news	The default news server defined by Outlook Express (if one is defined)

For example, the following command attempts to connect to the mail server:

```
netsh diag connect mail
```

For the show action, you use the following command:

```
netsh diag show object
```

Again, *object* is a parameter that specifies the object you want to display information about. You can use the built-in object names listed in Table 1.3.

TABLE 1.3   The **object** Parameter's Built-In Names for the **show** Action

Name	Shows Information For
adapter	The network adapter
all	All the objects in this list
client	The installed network clients
computer	The computer
dhcp	The DHCP server
dns	The DNS server
gateway	The default gateway
ieproxy	The Internet Explorer proxy server
ip	The computer's IP address
mail	The default mail server defined by Outlook Express
modem	All installed modems
news	The default news server defined by Outlook Express
os	The operating system
test	All the objects in this list; also performs all the actions in the Ping and Connect categories
version	The Windows and *WMI* (*Windows Management Instrumentation*) versions
wins	The WINS server

For example, the following command shows information for the network adapter:

```
netsh diag show adapter
```

Troubleshooting Cables

If one of the problems discussed so far isn't the cause of your networking quandary, the next logical suspect is the cabling that connects the workstations. This section discusses cabling, gives you a few pointers for preventing cable problems, and discusses some common cable kinks that can crop up.

Although most large-scale cabling operations are performed by third-party cable installers, home setups are usually do-it-yourself jobs. You can prevent some cable problems and simplify your troubleshooting down the road by taking a few precautions and "ounce of prevention" measures in advance:

- ▶ First and foremost, always buy the highest-quality cable you can find (for example, Category 5e or higher for twisted-pair cable). With network cabling, you get what you pay for.

- ▶ Good-quality cable will be labeled. You should also add your own labels for things such as the source and destination of the cable.

- ▶ To avoid electromagnetic interference, don't run cable near electronic devices, power lines, air conditioners, fluorescent lights, motors, and other electromagnetic sources.

- ▶ Try to avoid phone lines because the ringer signal can disrupt network data carried over twisted-pair cable.

- ▶ To avoid the cable being stepped on accidentally, don't run it under carpet.

- ▶ To avoid people tripping over a cable (and possible damaging the cable connector, the NIC port, or the person doing the tripping!), avoid high-traffic areas when laying the cable.

- ▶ If you plan to run cable outdoors, use conduit or another casing material to prevent moisture damage.

- ▶ Don't use excessive force to pull or push a cable into place. Rough handling can cause pinching or even breakage.

If you suspect cabling might be the cause of your network problems, here's a list of a few things to check:

- ▶ **Watch for electromagnetic interference**—If you see garbage on a workstation screen or experience random packet loss or temporarily missing nodes, the problem might be electromagnetic interference. Check your cables to make sure they are at least 6 to 12 inches from any source of electromagnetic interference.

- ▶ **Check your connections**—Loose connections are a common source of cabling woes. Be sure to check every cable connection associated with the workstation that's experiencing network difficulty, including connections to the network adapter, router, switch, and so on.

▶ **Check the lay of the line**—Loops of cable could be generating an electrical field that interferes with network communication. Try not to leave your excess cable lying around in coils or loops.

▶ **Inspect the cable for pinching or breaks**—A badly pinched cable can cause a short in the wire, which could lead to intermittent connection problems. Make sure that no part of the cable is pinched, especially if the back of the computer is situated near a wall. A complete lack of connection with the network might mean that the cable's copper core has been severed completely and needs to be replaced.

Troubleshooting the Network Interface Card

After cabling, the NIC is next on the list of common sources of networking headaches. Here's a list of items to check if you suspect that Windows Home Server and your NIC aren't getting along:

▶ **Make sure that Windows Home Server installed the correct NIC**—Windows Home Server usually does a pretty good job of detecting the network card. However, a slight error (such as choosing the wrong transceiver type) can wreak havoc. Double-check that the NIC listed in Device Manager (see the next section) is the same as the one installed in your computer. If it's not, click Remove to delete it, run the Add Hardware Wizard, and choose your NIC manually.

▶ **Perform a physical check of the NIC**—Open the case and make sure the card is properly seated in its slot.

CAUTION

Before touching any component inside a computer case, ground yourself to prevent electrostatic discharge. To ground yourself, touch any metal surface, such as the metal of the computer case.

▶ **Try a new NIC**—Try swapping out the NIC for one that you know works properly. (If the existing NIC is on the computer's motherboard, insert the working NIC in an open bus slot.) If that fixes the problem, you'll have to remove the faulty interface card (if possible) and insert a new one.

▶ **Get the latest driver**—Check with the manufacturer of the NIC to see whether it has newer Windows Home Server or Windows Server 2003 drivers for the card. If so, download and install them, as described in the next section.

Viewing the NIC in Device Manager

Windows Home Server stores all its hardware data in the Registry, but it provides Device Manager to give you a graphical view of the devices on your system. To display Device

Manager, log on to Windows Home Server, click Start, right-click My Computer, click Manage in the shortcut menu, and then click Device Manager.

TIP

A quick way to go directly to the Device Manager snap-in is to select Start, Run, type **devmgmt.msc**, and click OK. Note, too, that you can also press Windows Logo+Pause/Break to display the System Properties dialog box, click Hardware, and then click Device Manager.

Device Manager not only provides you with a comprehensive summary of your system's hardware data, but it also doubles as a decent troubleshooting tool. To see what I mean, check out the Device Manager tab shown in Figure 1.12. See how the icon for the Marvell Yukon 88E8056 PCI-E Gigabit Ethernet Controller device has an exclamation mark superimposed on it? This tells you that there's a problem with the device.

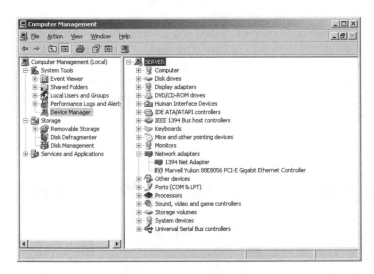

FIGURE 1.12   The Device Manager uses icons to warn you if there's a problem with a device.

If you examine the device's properties, as shown in Figure 1.13, the Device Status area tells you a bit more about what's wrong. As you can see in Figure 1.13, the problem here is that the device won't start. Either try Device Manager's suggested remedy or click the Troubleshoot button to launch the hardware troubleshooter.

NOTE

Device Manager has several dozen error codes. See the following Microsoft Knowledge Base article for a complete list of the codes, as well as solutions to try in each case: http://support.microsoft.com/kb/310123/. (This page shows codes for XP, but they also apply to Windows Home Server.)

FIGURE 1.13   The Device Status area tells you if the device isn't working properly.

Device Manager uses three different icons to indicate the device's current status:

▶ A black exclamation mark (!) on a yellow field tells you that there's a problem with
   the device.

▶ A red X tells you that the device is disabled or missing.

▶ A blue i on a white field tells you that the device's Use Automatic Settings check box
   (on the Resources tab) is deactivated and that at least one of the device's resources
   was selected manually. Note that the device might be working just fine, so this icon
   doesn't indicate a problem. If the device isn't working properly, however, the manual setting might be the cause. (For example, the device might have a DIP switch or
   jumper set to a different resource.)

Updating the NIC Device Driver

If a device is flagged on your system but you don't notice any problems, you can usually
get away with just ignoring the flag. I've seen lots of systems that run perfectly well with
flagged devices, so this falls under the "If it ain't broke..." school of troubleshooting. The
danger here is that tweaking your system to try and get rid of the flag can cause other—
usually more serious—problems. Otherwise, a good next step is to get an updated device
driver from the manufacturer and then install it.

Follow these steps to update a device driver:

1. If you have a floppy disk or CD with the updated driver, insert the disk or CD. If you
   downloaded the driver from the Internet, decompress the driver file, if necessary.

2. In Device Manager, click the device you want to work with.

3. Select Action, Update Driver. (You can also open the device's property sheet, display
   the Driver tab, and click Update Driver.)

Handling Multiple Network Subnets

By default, Windows Home Server assumes that all the computers on your home network lie within the same *subnet*, which is a subsection of a network that uses related IP addresses. For example, suppose that your Windows Home Server computer uses the IP address 192.168.1.254 and a subnet mask of 255.255.255.0. This means that the subnet that Windows Home Server can "see" is the IP address range 192.168.1.1 to 192.168.1.254. Working from client to server, any computer on your network that has an IP address within that range can therefore "see" Windows Home Server and connect to it. Windows Home Server allows this because its Windows Firewall is configured to allow only traffic that comes from the local subnet.

This works fine in the vast majority of home networks. However, you may have clients on your network that aren't on the same subnet as Windows Home Server. For example, you might have clients that use IP addresses in the range 192.168.0.2 to 192.168.0.254. (The default address in some routers is 192.168.0.1, so if you have clients that get IP addresses assigned from that router, the addresses will be in the 192.168.0.*x* subnet.) This represents a different subnet, so those clients won't be able to see Windows Home Server and won't be able to connect to it.

To handle this problem, you need to configure the Windows Home Server firewall to allow traffic from the other subnet. Follow these steps:

1. Log on to Windows Home Server either locally or by using a Remote Desktop connection (see "Making a Remote Desktop Connection to the Server" later in this chapter).

2. Select Start, Control Panel, Windows Firewall to launch the Windows Firewall dialog box.

3. Click the Exceptions tab.

4. In the Programs and Services list, click Windows Home Server Transport Service.

5. Click Edit to open the Edit a Port dialog box.

6. Click Change Scope to open the Change Scope dialog box.

7. Click the Custom List option.

8. In the Custom List text box, type the IP address and subnet mask for your main subnet (the one that contains Windows Home Server). Here's an example:

   ```
   192.168.1.1/255.255.255.0
   ```

9. In the Custom List text box, type a comma (,) and then add the data for the other subnet. You have two choices:

   ▶ If you have just one or two clients on the other subnet and they use static IP addresses, type the specific IP address followed by the 255.255.255.255 subnet mask, as in this example:

   ```
   192.168.0.10/255.255.255.255
   ```

▶ If you have several clients on the other subnet or if the clients on the other subnet have their IP addresses assigned dynamically, use the 255.255.255.0 subnet mask to specify the entire range, as in this example (see Figure 1.14):

`192.168.0.1/255.255.255.0`

10. Click OK to return to the Edit a Port dialog box.

11. Click OK to return to the Windows Firewall dialog box.

12. Repeat steps 5–11 for the following services:

▶ Windows Home Server Computer Backup

▶ Remote Desktop

13. Click OK to close the Windows Firewall dialog box.

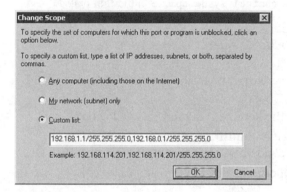

FIGURE 1.14   In the Change Scope dialog box, handle multiple subnets by specifying all your network subnets in the Custom List text box.

Making a Remote Desktop Connection to the Server

Windows Home Server's Remote Desktop feature enables you to connect to the server from a workgroup computer and use the server's desktop just as though you were sitting in front of it. This is handy if you can't leave your desk but need to tweak a setting or run a program on the server.

▶ **SEE** This section gives you just a bare-bones look at remote desktop connections. For an in-depth treatment, **see** "Connecting via Remote Desktop Connection," **P. 181**.

Making Sure That Windows Home Server Is Ready to Host

Out of the box, Windows Home Server is configured to host remote desktop sessions using the Administrator account. However, just to be safe, you should run through the following steps to make sure that Windows Home Server is configured properly:

1. Select Start, right-click My Computer, and then click Properties to open the System Properties window.
2. Click the Remote tab.

> **TIP**
>
> To open the System Properties dialog box with the Remote tab displayed directly, select Start, Run (or press Windows Logo+R), type `control sysdm.cpl,,5` in the Run dialog box, and then click OK.

3. In the Remote Desktop group, make sure that the Enable Remote Desktop on This Computer check box is activated.
4. Click Select Remote Users to display the Remote Desktop Users dialog box.
5. Above the Add button, you should see Administrator Already Has Access. If not, click Add to display the Select Users dialog box, type `Administrator`, and click OK.
6. Click OK to return to the System Properties dialog box.
7. Click OK.

Making the Connection to the Server

On the client computer, you can now connect to the host computer's desktop. Follow these steps:

1. Select Start, All Programs, Accessories, Remote Desktop Connection. (In Windows XP, select Start, All Programs, Accessories, Communications, Remote Desktop Connection.) The Remote Desktop Connection dialog box appears.
2. In the Computer text box, type the name or the IP address of the Windows Home Server computer.
3. Click Connect. Windows Vista prompts you to enter your security credentials.
4. In Windows Vista, type `Administrator` in the User Name box and the Administrator account password in the Password box, and then click OK. (Note that in subsequent logons, you'll only need to type the password.)

The remote desktop then appears on your computer. If you're working in full-screen mode, move the mouse to the top of the screen to see the connection bar, shown in Figure 1.15.

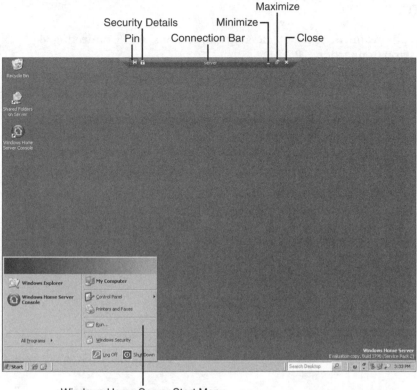

FIGURE 1.15   After you've connected and the remote computer's desktop appears on your screen, move the mouse to the top of the screen to see the connection bar.

If you want the connection bar to appear all the time, click to activate the Pin button. If you need to work with your own desktop, you have two choices:

▶ Click the connection bar's Minimize button to minimize the Remote Desktop window.

▶ Click the connection bar's Restore button to display the Remote Desktop window.

Disconnecting from the Server

When you finish with the Remote Desktop session, you have two choices for disconnecting:

▶ Using the Windows Home Server desktop and selecting Start, Log Off.

▶ Clicking the Close button in the connection bar. Windows displays a dialog box to let you know that your remote session will be disconnected. Click OK.

From Here

▶ For an in-depth treatment of remote desktop connections, **see** "Connecting via Remote Desktop Connection," **P. 181**.

▶ For the details on setting up your router for remote access sessions, **see** "Setting Up Port Forwarding on the Router," **P. 195**.

▶ To learn how to share a Windows Home Server media folder, **see** Chapter 8, "Streaming and Sharing Digital Media."

CHAPTER 2

Setting Up and Working with User Accounts

Windows Home Server doesn't really do much until you connect one or more client machines to the network by installing the Windows Home Server Connector software (as described in Chapter 3, "Adding Devices to the Windows Home Server Network"). However, the Connector software won't install properly unless Windows Home Server recognizes the current user account on the client computer. Because, out of the box, Windows Home Server really has only one working user account—the Administrator account (there are a few other built-in accounts that you can ignore)—you won't be able to connect any machines to the network right away. Instead, you need to set up user accounts for each person who'll be accessing Windows Home Server. This chapter shows you how to set up user accounts using the Home Server Console. It also takes you through a few useful techniques for managing those accounts.

> ▶ **SEE** For the details on running the Connector software, **see** "Installing Windows Home Server Connector on the Client Computers," **P. 63.**

Understanding Security Groups

Security for Windows Home Server user accounts is handled mostly (and most easily) by assigning each user to a particular security group. For example, the default Administrator account is part of the Administrators group. Each security group is defined with a specific set of access and rights, and any user added to a group is automatically granted that group's access and rights.

Windows Home Server has four main security groups:

▶ **Administrators**—Members of this group have complete control over the server, meaning they can access all folders and files; install and uninstall programs (including legacy programs) and devices; create, modify, and remove user accounts; install Windows updates, service packs, and fixes; use Safe mode; repair Windows; take ownership of objects; and more. For safety, only the Administrator account should be a member of this group.

▶ **Remote Desktop Users**—Members of this group have access to log on to the server remotely (from inside or outside the LAN) using the Remote Desktop feature.

▶ **SEE** To learn how to start a remote session from inside the LAN, **see** "Connecting via Remote Desktop Connection," **P. 181.**

▶ **SEE** For the details on making remote connections via the Internet, **see** "Connecting via the Internet," **P. 194.**

▶ **Users**—Members of this group can access files only in their own folders and in the server's shared folders, change their account's password, and run programs that don't require administrative-level rights.

▶ **Windows Home Server Users**—Members of this group can be managed by Windows Home Server. For example, Windows Home Server can check the password on the client account to see if it differs from the password on the server account. If they are different, Windows Home Server can then (with your access) change the password on the client account to match the password on the server account. (See "Synchronizing the Client and Windows Home Server Passwords" later in this chapter.)

Besides these main security groups, Windows Home Server also defines a long list of groups that specify access to the server's shared folders. For the default shares, Windows Home Server defines 10 security groups:

▶ **RO_3**—Members of this group have Read access to the shared Photos folder.

▶ **RO_4**—Members of this group have Read access to the shared Music folder.

▶ **RO_5**—Members of this group have Read access to the shared Videos folder.

▶ **RO_6**—Members of this group have Read access to the shared Software folder.

▶ **RO_7**—Members of this group have Read access to the shared Public folder.

▶ **RW_3**—Members of this group have Full access to the shared Photos folder.

▶ **RW_4**—Members of this group have Full access to the shared Music folder.

▶ **RW_5**—Members of this group have Full access to the shared Videos folder.

▶ **RW_6**—Members of this group have Full access to the shared Software folder.

▶ **RW_7**—Members of this group have Full access to the shared Public folder.

In this context, *Full access* means that the user has read/write permissions on the share: he can traverse subfolders, run programs, open documents, make changes to documents, create new files and folders, and delete files and folders. By contrast, *Read access* means that the user has read-only permission on the shared folder: He can traverse subfolders, run programs, and open documents, but he can't make changes to the shared folder or any of its contents. (A third type is *None access*, which prevents users from even viewing a shared folder.)

Windows Home Server also adds new security groups as you add users—each of whom gets a personal shared folder on the server—and extra shared folders that you add to the server. For each new user share or server share, Windows Home Server creates two groups: RO_*X* and RW_*X*, where *X* is a letter (such as D or E), RO_*X* is the group with Read access, and RW_*X* is the group with Full access.

MORE WINDOWS HOME SERVER SECURITY GROUPS

For the sake of completeness, here's a list of the other security groups defined by Windows Home Server:

▶ **Backup Operators**—Members of this group can access the Backup program and use it to back up and restore folders and files, no matter what access is set on those objects.

▶ **Distributed COM Users**—Members of this group can start, activate, and use Distributed COM (DCOM) objects.

▶ **Guests**—Members of this group have the same privileges as those of the Users group. The exception is the default Guest account, which is not allowed to change its account password.

▶ **Network Configuration Operators**—Members of this group have a subset of the Administrator-level rights that enables them to install and configure networking features.

▶ **Performance Log Users**—Members of this group can use the Performance snap-in to monitor performance counters, logs, and alerts, both locally and remotely.

▶ **Performance Monitor Users**—Members of this group can use the Performance snap-in to monitor performance counters only, both locally and remotely.

▶ **Power Users**—Members of this group have a subset of the Administrator group privileges. Power Users can't back up or restore files, replace system files, take ownership of files, or install or remove device drivers. In addition, Power Users can't install applications that explicitly require the user to be a member of the Administrators group.

▶ **Print Operators**—Members of this group can administer network printers.

▶ **Replicator**—Members of this group can replicate files across a domain.

▶ **DHCP Administrators**—Members of this group have full control of the DHCP service.

> ▶ **DHCP Users**—Members of this group have read-only access on the DHCP service.
>
> ▶ **HelpServicesGroup**—Members of this group (generally, Microsoft and OEM personnel) can connect to your computer to resolve technical issues using the Remote Assistance feature.
>
> ▶ **IIS_WPG**—Members of this group can start a worker process (that is, an ASP.NET application) on the IIS (Internet Information Server) web server.
>
> ▶ **Telnet Clients**—Members of this group can access the Telnet Server.
>
> ▶ **Windows Media Center**—Members of this group can access Windows Media Center on network clients as part of Power Pack 3's new Media Center Connector technology.

When you add a new user, Windows Home Server creates a new shared folder:

`D:\shares\users\user`

Here, *user* is the account's user name. The user is given read/write access to this folder, while subsequent accounts that you create will be assigned no access to the share.

The rest of this chapter shows you the various methods Windows Home Server offers to create, modify, disable, and remove user accounts.

Adding a New User

As I mentioned earlier, you can't connect a client computer to Windows Home Server until you configure Windows Home Server with a user account that has the same logon name as a user account on the client computer. You have two ways to go about this:

> ▶ If the user account already exists on the client, create a new account on Windows Home Server that uses the same username.
>
> ▶ If the user account doesn't exist on the client, create the account both on the client and on Windows Home Server. (It doesn't matter which order you do this; just make sure that both accounts have the same username and password.)

Before getting to the specifics of creating a user account on Windows Home Server, the next few sections take you through some important password-related material.

Setting the Password Length and Complexity

Windows Home Server maintains several password policies that determine the length and complexity of the passwords you can assign to the Windows Home Server accounts. Before creating an account, you should specify the policy you want to use. You have three choices:

> ▶ **Weak**—This policy has no restrictions on password length or complexity. You can specify any password you want for most users (with the exception of users granted

Remote Access; see the Strong policy, which follows). Note that this policy implies that you can set up accounts without any password.

▶ **Medium**—This is the default policy, and it requires that all passwords be at least five characters long. This policy has no restrictions on password complexity.

▶ **Strong**—This policy requires that all passwords be at least seven characters long and that they contain three out of the following four character types: lowercase letters, uppercase letters, numbers, and symbols (!, @, #, $, and so on). Note that every user who gets Remote Access must have a strong password, even if you've configured Windows Home Server to use the Weak or Medium policy.

Follow these steps to specify the Windows Home Server password policy:

1. Select Start, All Programs, Windows Home Server Console.

2. If you're configuring the server from a client machine, type the Windows Home Server password and then click Connect.

3. Click Settings to display the Windows Home Server Settings dialog box.

4. Click the Passwords tab, shown in Figure 2.1.

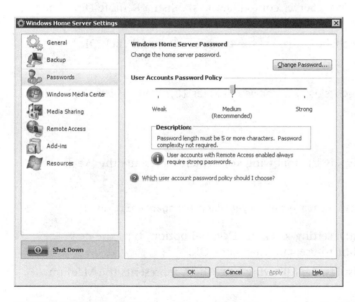

FIGURE 2.1   In the Windows Home Server Console, use the Passwords tab to set the user accounts password policy.

5. Click and drag the User Accounts Password Policy slider to the policy setting you want: Weak, Medium, or Strong.

Customizing the Password Length Requirement

You saw in the previous section that each Windows Home Server password policy has a length component:

▶ **Weak**—Passwords can be any length.

▶ **Medium**—Passwords must be at least five characters.

▶ **Strong**—Passwords must be at least seven characters.

To increase security on your Windows Home Server, you might want to bump up these minimums. For example, you might want to change the minimum length of the Weak password policy to at least 1 to ensure that all users have some kind of password. Similarly, you might want to increase the length minimum of the Strong password policy (which is automatically applied to users given Remote Access permission) to 8 or more to make your network even safer from potential Internet-based intrusions.

You can adjust these minimums by modifying some settings in the Windows Home Server Registry. Follow these steps:

1. Log on to the Windows Home Server computer, or establish a Remote Desktop connection to the server.

2. Select Start, Run to open the Run dialog box, type regedit, and click OK.

▶ **SEE** To learn how to use the Registry Editor, **see** Chapter 18, "Working with the Windows Home Server Registry."

3. In the Registry Editor, display the following key, which represents the Weak password policy:

   HKLM\Software\Microsoft\Windows Home Server\User Manager\Policies\1

4. Double-click the MinLength setting, click the Decimal option, type the new minimum length you want to use, and then click OK.

5. In the Registry Editor, display the following key, which represents the Medium password policy:

   HKLM\Software\Microsoft\Windows Home Server\User Manager\Policies\2

6. Double-click the MinLength setting, click the Decimal option, type the new minimum length you want to use, and then click OK.

7. In the Registry Editor, display the following key, which represents the Strong password policy:

   HKLM\Software\Microsoft\Windows Home Server\User Manager\Policies\3

8. Double-click the `MinLength` setting, click the Decimal option, type the new minimum length you want to use, and then click OK.

9. Close the Registry Editor.

Building a Strong Password

If you just use your home network locally, the passwords you assign to each user account aren't that important from a security point of view. Your goal should be to make them easy to remember and avoid those "I forgot my password!" tech support calls. The security landscape changes drastically when you add users to the Remote Desktop Users group, and thus enable them to connect to the network via the Internet. In this case, it's crucial to supply remote users with strong passwords. Ideally, when you're creating such a password, you want to pick one that that provides maximum protection without sacrificing convenience. Follow these guidelines when choosing a password:

TIP

The password guidelines I provide will ensure that your passwords exceed Windows Home Server's Complex password policy. For an extra challenge, submit the password (or, ideally, text that's similar to your password) to an online password complexity checker. Microsoft runs such a checker at www.microsoft.com/athome/security/privacy/password_checker.mspx. You can also run a Google search on "password complexity checker" to see others.

▶ **Use passwords that are at least eight characters long**—Shorter passwords are susceptible to programs that just try every letter combination. You can combine the 26 letters of the alphabet into about 12 million different five-letter word combinations, which is no big deal for a fast program. If you bump things up to eight-letter passwords, however, the total number of combinations rises to 200 *billion*, which would take even the fastest computer quite a while. If you use 12-letter passwords, as many experts recommend, the number of combinations goes beyond mind-boggling: 90 *quadrillion*, or 90,000 trillion!

▶ **Mix up your character types**—The secret to a strong password is to include characters from the following categories: lowercase letters, uppercase letters, numbers, and symbols. If you include at least one character from three (or, even better, all four) of these categories, you're well on your way to a strong password.

▶ **Don't be too obvious**—Because forgetting a password is inconvenient, many people use meaningful words or numbers so that their password will be easier to remember. Unfortunately, this means that they often use extremely obvious things such as their name, the name of a family member or colleague, their birth date or Social Security number, or even their system username. Being this obvious is just asking for trouble.

CAUTION

After going to all this trouble to create an indestructible password, don't blow it by writing it on a sticky note and then attaching it to your notebook keyboard! Even writing it on a piece of paper and then throwing the paper away is dangerous. Determined crackers have been known to go through a company's trash looking for passwords. (This is known in the trade as *dumpster diving*.) Also, don't use the password itself as your Windows 7, Vista, or XP password hint. Finally, if you've thought of a particularly clever password, don't suddenly become unclever and tell someone. Your password should be stored in your head alongside all those "wasted youth" things you don't want anyone to know about.

Changing the Password on the Client

If you already have a user account on the client computer, you might want to adjust the account password before adding the account to Windows Home Server. For example, if you'll be accessing the network remotely with the account, you might want to specify a strong password when you set up the account in Windows Home Server. If you know the new password you want to use, it makes sense to update the client account with the new password in advance.

If you're running Windows 7 or Vista on the client, or if you're running XP with the Welcome screen disabled, follow these steps to change an account password:

1. Log on to the account you want to modify.
2. Press Ctrl+Alt+Delete.
3. Click Change a Password. (Click Change Password in XP.)
4. Type the old password in the appropriate box.
5. Type the new password in the appropriate box and then type it again in the Confirm Password text box. (It's Confirm New Password in XP.)
6. Press Enter. Windows changes the password.
7. Click OK.

If your client is running XP with the Welcome screen enabled, follow these steps to change an account password:

1. Log on to the account you want to modify.
2. Select Start, Control Panel, User Accounts.
3. Click the account you want to work with.
4. Click Change My Password.
5. Use the text boxes provided to type your old password, then your new password (twice), as well as an optional password hint.
6. Click Change Password.

Adding the User Account

Here are the steps to add an account to Windows Home Server:

1. Select Start, All Programs, Windows Home Server Console.

2. If you're configuring the server from a client machine, type the Windows Home Server password and then click Connect. The Windows Home Server Console appears.

3. Click the User Accounts tab. If you see the User Accounts Setup window at this point, click to activate the Do Not Show This Message Again check box, and then click OK.

4. Click Add. The Add User Account Wizard appears, shown in Figure 2.2.

FIGURE 2.2   The Add User Account Wizard takes you through the process of setting up a new account on Windows Home Server.

5. Type the user's first name and last name in the appropriate boxes. (The latter is optional.)

6. Type the user's logon name.

> **NOTE**
>
> The logon name can consist of only letters, numbers, spaces, periods (.), hyphens (-), or underscores (_). The name can't end with a period, and you must use at least one letter or number. Also, the name must be unique among the Windows Home Server accounts.

7. If you want to give this user access to the network over the web, click to activate the Enable Remote Access for This User check box, and then use the list to choose what you want the user to be able to access remotely: shared folders, home computers, or both.

8. Click Next. The Add User Account Wizard prompts you for the account password.

9. Type the password and then type it again in the Confirm Password text box. As you type the password, watch the Password Requirements section (see Figure 2.3; note that this section doesn't appear if you're using the Weak password policy and you didn't enable remote access for the user):

   ▶ If the password meets or exceeds the length requirements specified by the Windows Home Server password policy, a check mark appears beside the Length item. You see this item if you're using the Medium or Strong password policy, or if you enabled remote access for this user.

   ▶ If the password meets or exceeds the complexity requirements specified by the password policy, a check mark appears beside the Complexity item. You see this item only if you're using the Strong password policy, or if you enabled remote access for this user.

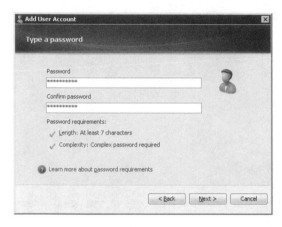

FIGURE 2.3   The password you enter must meet or exceed the length and complexity requirements of the current Windows Home Server password policy.

10. Click Next. The Add User Account Wizard prompts you to specify the user's access to the shared folders (see Figure 2.4).

11. For each shared folder, click the option that corresponds to the access you want to give: Full, Read, or None.

12. Click Finish. Windows Home Server adds the user account, sets the shared folder access, and creates a shared folder for the user. If you left the Enable Remote Access for This User check box activated, Windows Home Server adds the user to the Remote Desktop Users group.

13. Click Done. The account appears in the Windows Home Server Console's User Accounts tab, as shown in Figure 2.5.

NOTE

Remember that you can add a maximum of 10 user accounts to Windows Home Server.

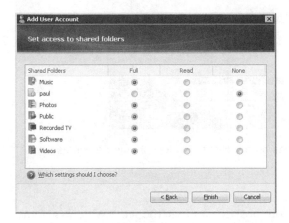

FIGURE 2.4   You can give the new user Full, Read, or None access to the shared folders.

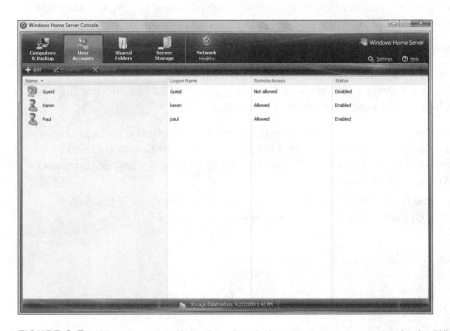

FIGURE 2.5   When you complete the wizard, the new account appears in the Windows Home Server Console's User Accounts tab.

Synchronizing the Client and Windows Home Server Passwords

After you add an account to Windows Home Server, you may later change the account password on the client computer. This means that the passwords for the client account and the Windows Home Server account are no longer in synch. Almost as soon as you make the password change, the Windows Home Server Tray application displays the message shown in Figure 2.6.

FIGURE 2.6   If the account password changes on the client, Windows Home Server displays this message.

You can put the client and server accounts out of synch and see the same Windows Home Server Tray application message in two other circumstances:

▶ You create a new account where the server account password is different from the client account password.

▶ You change the password on the Windows Home Server account.

In all these cases, if you want to be able to access the Windows Home Server shares without entering your server username and password, you need to synchronize the passwords on the client and server. Here are the steps to follow:

1. Click the Windows Home Server Tray application message. (If the message is no longer visible, right-click the Windows Home Server icon in the notification area and then click Update Password.) Windows Home Server asks whether you want to update your password now.

2. Select the Update Password option, and then click OK. Windows Home Server displays the Update Password dialog box, shown in Figure 2.7.

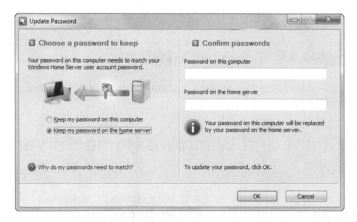

FIGURE 2.7   Use the Update Password dialog box to synchronize the account password on the client PC and Windows Home Server.

3. Click one of the following options to decide which password you want to use for the account:

   ▸ **Keep My Password on this Computer**—Click this option to update the account password on Windows Home Server to match the account password on the client.

   ▸ **Keep My Password on the Home Server**—Click this option to update the account password on the client machine to match the account password on Windows Home Server.

4. Use the Password on This Computer text box to enter the password of the client account.

5. Use the Password on the Home Server text box to enter the password of the Windows Home Server account.

6. Click OK. Windows Home Server synchronizes the passwords.

7. Click Close.

> ▸ **SEE** You can use Windows Home Server's monitoring tools to monitor each user's network activity. **See** "Monitoring Users via Task Manager," **P. 281.**

Automating Client Logons

Many people run their home networks with at least one computer that doesn't use a password—that is, they have a computer that contains no personal or confidential data, just common documents (such as media files) and web access. Anyone in the family can use that PC just by starting it up. Because there's no password, Windows boots right to the desktop without prompting for a logon. That's convenient, but if you have Windows Home Server configured to use the Normal or Complex password policy, you've got a problem because these policies require accounts to have nonblank passwords.

How do you maintain the convenience of a no-logon startup and still get Windows Home Server connectivity? One solution would be to configure Windows Home Server to use the Simple password policy, which allows blank passwords. However, that won't work if the user account is configured for remote access, which requires a strong password. The best workaround I know is to set up the client machine with a password that Windows Home Server is happy with, and then configure the client with an automatic logon.

After you add a password to the client machine's user account, use these steps to automate the logon:

1. Press Windows Logo+R (or select Start, Run) to open the Run dialog box.

2. Type **control userpasswords2**, and then click OK. (If the client is running Windows Vista, enter your UAC credentials.) Windows opens the User Account dialog box.

3. If multiple accounts are on the computer, click the account you want to use for the automatic logon.

4. Click to deactivate the Users Must Enter a User Name and Password to Use This Computer check box.

5. Click OK. Windows displays the Automatically Log On dialog box, shown in Figure 2.8.

FIGURE 2.8   Use this dialog box to set up an automatic logon for a client computer.

6. Type the account's password in the Password and Confirm Password text boxes.

7. Click OK. Windows configures the automatic logon.

TIP

You can temporarily bypass the automatic logon and display the Windows logon screen by holding down the Shift key while Windows boots.

TIP

If the version of Windows 7 or Windows Vista running on the client doesn't support the User Accounts dialog box, you can still set up an automatic logon by hand using the Registry. Open the Registry Editor (see Chapter 20) and head for the following Registry key:

`HKLM\Software\Microsoft\Windows NT\CurrentVersion\Winlogon\`

Double-click the `AutoAdminLogon` setting and change its value to 1. Double-click the `DefaultUserName` setting and change its value to the username you want to log on automatically. Finally, create a `String` setting named `DefaultPassword` and change its value to the password of the default user.

Modifying User Accounts

After you've added a user to Windows Home Server, you can modify the account as needed via the Windows Home Server Console. You can view the current account properties, change the account password, disable the account, and remove the account. These next few sections take you through these and other account chores.

Before continuing, I should point out that Windows Home Server does come with other tools for modifying user accounts. The server's Windows Server 2003 underpinnings mean that two advanced user account tools are available:

▶ **The User Accounts dialog box**—Select Start, Run, type **control userpasswords2**, and click OK (see Figure 2.9). You saw in the previous section that you can use this dialog box to set up an automatic logon. You can do the same thing for the Windows Home Server machine. You can also display the Advanced tab and then click Advanced to display the Local Users and Groups snap-in, discussed next. Other than that, however, to avoid breaking Windows Home Server's user accounts, you shouldn't use the User Accounts dialog box for any other account-related chores.

FIGURE 2.9   In Windows Home Server, you can do only a limited number of things with the User Accounts dialog box.

CAUTION

Set up Windows Home Server with an automatic logon only if security is absolutely not a problem in your house. Otherwise, you won't be able to lock out unauthorized users from the server, and the results could be catastrophic (depending on the age and rebelliousness of the users in your house).

▶ **The Local Users and Groups snap-in**—Select Start, right-click My Computer, click Manage, click Local Users and Groups, and then click Users (see Figure 2.10). This snap-in plays a bit nicer with Windows Home Server than it does the User Accounts dialog box. For example, you can use this snap-in to disable or enable an account, change an account's full name, and give a user access to remotely access the server. You can also make an account a member of a group not used by Windows Home Server. (See "Adding a User to a Group" later in this chapter.) However, some actions—such as renaming an account—can break the account in Windows Home Server, so again you're mostly better off using the Home Server Console.

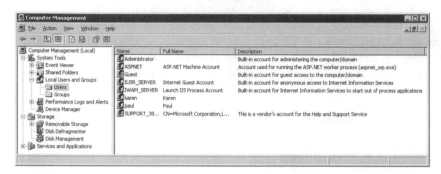

FIGURE 2.10   You can use the Local Users and Groups snap-in for some account-related chores, but caution is required.

Viewing Account Properties

When you open the Home Server Console and click the User Accounts tab, you see a list of users with accounts on the server. For each user, you see the full name, the logon name, whether the user has remote access (Allowed or Not Allowed), and the current account status (Enabled or Disabled). To see more properties, click the account and then click Properties. Windows Home Server displays the accounts property sheet, as shown in Figure 2.11.

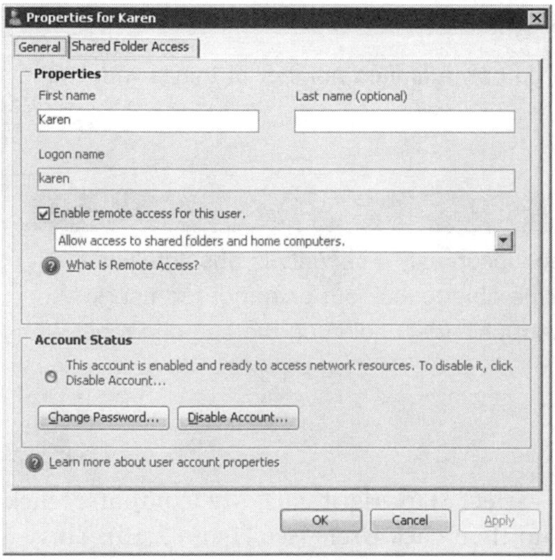

FIGURE 2.11   The property sheet for a Windows Home Server user account.

TIP

For faster service, you can also display the user's property sheet either by double-clicking the account or by right-clicking the account and then clicking Properties.

The next few sections take you through some of the tasks you can run from this dialog box, but here's a quick look at some of the more basic chores:

▶ **Changing the full name**—Edit the First Name and Last Name text boxes.

▶ **Configuring remote access**—Click the Enable Remote Access for This User check box, and then use the list to choose what you want the user to be able to access remotely: shared folders, home computers, or both.

▶ **Apply shared folder access**—Display the Shared Folder Access tab and then use the option buttons beside each available share to set the access to Full, Read, or None.

Changing the Account Password

If you want to change a user's password, here are the steps to follow:

1. In the Home Server Console, display the property sheet for the user account you want to work with.
2. In the General tab, click Change Password. Windows Home Server displays the Change Password for *User* dialog box (where *User* is the user account's full name).

TIP

To go directly to the Change Password for *User* dialog box, right-click the user in the User Accounts tab and then click Change Password.

3. Type the new password in the Password text box. When you're done, make sure that you see check marks in the Password Requirements area for both the Length and Complexity, meaning that your new password meets or exceeds the Windows Home Server password policy requirements.
4. Retype the password in the Confirm Password dialog box.
5. Click OK. Windows Home Server displays a dialog box to let you know that it changed the password.
6. Click OK to return to the account's property sheet.
7. Click OK.
8. Synchronize the new password with the client user account, as described earlier. (See "Synchronizing the Client and Windows Home Server Passwords.")

TIP

Somewhat unusually, when you change a user's password in the Windows Home Server Console, the program doesn't ask you to first enter the user's current password. That may be unusual, but it can also come in handy if you (and the user) forget an account's password. Just follow the steps in this section to create a new password for the account. On the downside, note that you won't be able to synchronize the new password with the user's client account because Windows Home Server requires you to provide the forgotten client account password to perform the synchronization.

Disabling a User Account

If you want to prevent an account from accessing the network temporarily, you can disable it by following these steps:

1. In the Home Server Console, display the property sheet for the user account you want to disable.
2. In the General tab, click Disable Account. Windows Home Server displays the Disable User Account dialog box to ask you to confirm.
3. Click Yes. Windows Home Server disables the account.
4. Click OK.

TIP

A faster way to get to the Disable User Account dialog box is to right-click the account in the User Accounts tab and then click Disable Account.

When the user tries to access the Windows Home Server shares, he sees the message shown in Figure 2.12.

FIGURE 2.12   Disabled users see this message when they try to access the Windows Home Server shared folders.

Disabling All User Accounts with a Script

Sometimes you might want to prevent all users from accessing the server's shares. For example, you might be performing maintenance on the shares or running a task that requires all the server's resources. Rather than disabling each user account individually, Listing 2.1 presents a script that disables all the user accounts at once.

> **NOTE**
>
> You can find the VBS files containing this book's scripts on my website at www.mcfedries.com/HomeServerUnleashed2E.

LISTING 2.1   A Script That Disables All the User Accounts on the Home Server

```
'
' Use WMI to get the collection of user accounts on the local machine
'
compName = "localhost"
Set wmi = GetObject("winmgmts:{impersonationLevel=impersonate}!//"& _
          compName & "\root\cimv2")
Set users = wmi.ExecQuery("SELECT * FROM Win32_UserAccount")
'
' Initialize the display string
'
disabledUsers = "Here is the list of disabled user accounts:"
'
' Run through the collection of user accounts
'
For Each user In users
    '
    ' Is the account a user?
    '
    If user.Description = "" Then
        '
        ' If so, disable the account and add the account name to the string
        '
        user.Disabled = True
        disabledUsers = disabledUsers & vbCrLf & user.Name
    End If
Next 'user
'
' Display the string
'
If disabledUsers = "Here is the list of disabled user accounts:" Then
    WScript.Echo "No accounts to disable."
Else
    WScript.Echo disabledUsers
End If
```

This script accesses the Windows Management Instrumentation (WMI) interface to return the collection of all user accounts on the local computer. A For Each...Next loop runs through all the users, looking for those where the Description property is blank. This identifies the Windows Home Server client user accounts, because all the built-in accounts have descriptions and the client user accounts don't. (The Home Server Console doesn't give you any way to add a description.) For each client user account, the script sets the Disabled property to True. The script finishes by displaying a string that lists the accounts that were disabled.

▶ **SEE** To learn more about WMI scripting, **see** "Programming the Windows Management Instrumentation Service," **P. 688.**

Viewing Disabled Accounts

If you want to know whether any accounts are currently disabled and, if so, which ones those are, you can always load the Home Server Console, click the User Accounts tab, and then examine the Account Status column. Or, for slightly quicker access, you can run the script shown in Listing 2.2.

LISTING 2.2   A Script That Displays a List of Disabled User Accounts

```
'
' Use WMI to get the collection of user accounts on the local machine
'
compName = "localhost"
Set wmi = GetObject("winmgmts:{impersonationLevel=impersonate}!//"& _
          compName & "\root\cimv2")
Set users = wmi.ExecQuery("SELECT * FROM Win32_UserAccount")
'
' Initialize the display string
'
disabledUsers = "Here is the list of disabled user accounts:"
'
' Run through the collection of user accounts
'
For Each user In users
    '
    ' Is the account disabled?
    '
    If user.Description = "" And user.Disabled Then
        '
        ' If so, add the account name to the string
        '
        disabledUsers = disabledUsers & vbCrLf & user.Name
    End If
```

```
Next 'user
'
' Display the string
'
If disabledUsers = "Here is the list of disabled user accounts:" Then
    WScript.Echo "There are no disabled accounts."
Else
    WScript.Echo disabledUsers
End If
```

Enabling a User Account

If you've disabled a user account in Windows Home Server, here are the steps to follow to enable the account and once again allow it to access the network:

1. In the Home Server Console, display the property sheet for the user account you want to enable.

2. In the General tab, click Enable. Windows Home Server enables the account.

3. Click OK.

TIP

The fastest way to enable an account is to right-click the account in the User Accounts tab and then click Enable Account.

Enabling Users Accounts with a Script

Earlier you learned how to disable all the Windows Home Server user accounts with a script. When you're ready to give those users access to the network shares once again, use the script in Listing 2.3 to enable them all at once.

LISTING 2.3   A Script That Enables All the User Accounts on the Home Server

```
'
' Use WMI to get the collection of user accounts on the local machine
'
compName = "localhost"
Set wmi = GetObject("winmgmts:{impersonationLevel=impersonate}!//"& _
          compName & "\root\cimv2")
Set users = wmi.ExecQuery("SELECT * FROM Win32_UserAccount")
'
' Initialize the display string
'
enabledUsers = "Here is the list of enabled user accounts:"
'
' Run through the collection of user accounts
```

```
'
For Each user In users
    '
    ' Is the account a user?
    '
    If user.Description = "" Then
        '
        ' If so, enable the account and add the account name to the string
        '
        user.Disabled = False
        enabledUsers = enabledUsers & vbCrLf & user.Name
    End If
Next 'user
'
' Display the string
'
If enabledUsers = "Here is the list of enabled user accounts:" Then
    WScript.Echo "No accounts to enable."
Else
    WScript.Echo enabledUsers
End If
```

Enabling the Guest Account

What do you do if you have someone visiting your place and that person wants to, say, access some media on Windows Home Server with his computer? You could allow the person to log on using an existing account, but that might not be reasonable due to privacy or security concerns. You could set up a user account for that person, but that seems like overkill, particularly for a person on a short visit.

A better solution is to enable the Guest account and allow your visitor to log on under that account. Here are the steps to follow:

1. In the Home Server Console, display the property sheet for the Guest user account.

2. In the General tab, click Enable Account. Windows Home Server starts the Enable Guest Account Wizard.

> **TIP**
>
> You can also launch the Enable Guest Account Wizard by right-clicking the Guest account in the User Accounts tab and then clicking Enable Guest Account.

3. Click Next. The Choose a Password dialog box appears.

4. You have two choices:

   ▶ **No Guest Password**—Click this option to do without a password for the Guest account.

▶ **Create a Guest Password**—Click this option to add a password to the Guest account. This is probably the best idea because it makes your network that much more secure. Type the password in the Password and Confirm Password text boxes.

5. Click Next. The wizard prompts you to specify the Guest account's access to the shared folders. By default, the Guest account gets None access to the user shared folders and Read access to the Windows Home Server shared folders.

6. For each shared folder, click the option that corresponds to the access you want to give: Full, Read, or None.

7. Click Finish. Windows Home Server enables the Guest account, sets the password (if any), and applies the access permissions.

8. Click Done.

9. Click OK.

Removing a User Account

Windows Home Server supports up to 10 user accounts, which ought to be plenty for most households, with only the odd Brady Bunch-like clan bumping up against this ceiling. Still, that doesn't mean you should just leave unused accounts lying around the Windows Home Server Console. Dormant accounts clutter the interface and waste space on the server's shares.

If you have a Windows Home Server user account that you no longer need, follow these steps to delete it:

1. Select Start, All Programs, Home Server Console.

2. If you're configuring the server from a client machine, type the Windows Home Server password and then click Connect. The Windows Home Server Console appears.

3. Click the User Accounts tab.

4. Click the user you want to delete.

5. Click Remove. The Remove a User Account Wizard appears.

TIP

A quicker way to launch the Remove a User Account Wizard is to right-click the account in the User Accounts tab and then click Remove.

6. You have two options related to the user's shared folder on the server:

▶ **Keep the Shared Folder**—Click this option to leave the user's shared folder on the server. This is useful if you know (or suspect) that the shared folder contains useful data that you want to preserve.

▶ **Remove the Shared Folder**—Click this option to delete the user's shared folder from the server.

7. Click Next. Windows Home Server warns you that you're about to remove the account and its shared folder (if you chose the Remove the Shared Folder option in step 6).

8. Click Finish. Windows Home Server removes the user's access on the shared folders, deletes the account, and deletes the account's shared folder (if applicable).

9. Click Done.

Changing the Account Name

If you need to change the logon name for an account, I'm afraid that Windows Home Server doesn't offer any straightforward way to do this. In the Home Server Console, when you open the property sheet for a user account, the Logon Name text box is visible but disabled, so you can't edit it.

CAUTION

You might be tempted to change the account name via either the User Accounts dialog box (select Start, Run, type **control userpasswords2**, and click OK) or the Local Users and Groups snap-in (select Start, right-click My Computer, click Manage, and then click Local Users and Groups). Unfortunately, neither technique works properly in Windows Home Server. You see the new username in the Home Server Console, but the name of the user's shared folder remains unchanged. Even worse, changing the name outside the Console means that you break the user's access beyond repair. The only solution is to delete and re-create the user, as described in this section.

The only way to rename a user account is to follow these steps:

1. Remove the user account as described in the previous section. When prompted, be sure to activate the Save the Shared Folder That Is Associated with This User option.

2. Create a new user account using the logon name you prefer.

3. Move the user's files from the old account's shared folder to the new account's shared folder.

4. Delete the old account's shared folder.

Adding a User to a Group

You learned earlier that Windows Home Server adds each user to the Users group and to the Windows Home Server Users group. An account is also added to the Remote Desktop Users group if you give that person remote access to the network. It's unlikely that you'll need to add a user to any other group defined by Windows Home Server, but it's not unheard of. For example, if you want to script the Windows Home Server machine from a client machine on the network using WMI, you need to add that user to the Administrators group. (See Chapter 21, "Scripting Windows Home Server.")

Just in case it comes up, here are the steps to follow to add a user to a security group:

1. On the server, select Start, right-click My Computer, and then click Manage to open the Computer Management snap-in.

2. Select Local Users and Groups, Users to display the list of users on the server.

3. Double-click the user you want to work with to open that user's property sheet.

4. Display the Member Of tab.

5. Click Add to display the Select Groups dialog box.

6. Type the name of the group to which you want the user added.

TIP

If you're not sure of the exact group name, click Advanced and then click Find Now to display a complete list of the available groups. Click the group you want to use and then click OK.

---

7. Click OK. Windows Home Server returns you to the user's property sheet and adds the group to the Member Of list.

8. Click OK.

Allowing a User to Log On to the Windows Home Server Desktop

For security purposes, it's a good idea to allow just the Administrator account to access the Windows Home Server desktop. (Other users can log on to Windows Home Server remotely, but they only see the Windows Home Server Console.) However, if you really need to allow another user to access the desktop, you can configure Windows Home Server to allow this. You can configure the user for a local logon (sitting at the Windows Home Server computer) or a remote logon (from another computer or over the Internet).

CAUTION

If you're going to allow a user access to the Windows Home Server desktop, be sure to assign a strong password to that user's account.

Technically, it's the Administrators group that has permission to log on to Windows Home Server locally and remotely. Therefore, the easiest way to give someone the same permissions is to add that account to the Administrators group (see "Adding a User to a Group" earlier in this chapter).

Allowing a User to Log On Locally

To give a user permission to log on locally, follow these steps:

1. Log on to Windows Home Server.

2. Select Start, Control Panel, Administrative Tools, Local Security Policy. The Local Security Settings snap-in appears.

TIP

You can also open the Local Security Setting snap-in by selecting Start, Run to open the Run dialog box, typing **secpol.msc**, and then clicking OK.

3. Open the Security Settings, Local Policies, User Rights Assignment branch.

4. Double-click the Allow Log On Locally policy.

5. Click Add User or Group to display the Select Users or Groups dialog box.

6. Type the user's name and then click OK to return to the policy's property sheet.

7. Click OK.

Allowing a User to Log On Remotely

To give a user permission to log on remotely, you have two choices:

▶ Follow steps 1 through7 from the previous section, but instead of adding the user to the Allow Log On Locally policy, add the user to the Allow Log On Through Terminal Services policy.

▶ Add the user via the Terminal Services Configuration tool.

For the latter, here are the steps to follow:

1. Log on to Windows Home Server.

2. Select Start, Control Panel, Administrative Tools, Terminal Services Configuration.

3. Click the Connections branch.

4. Double-click RDP-Tcp to open the connection's property sheet.

5. Display the Permissions tab.

6. Click Add to open the Select Users or Groups dialog box.

7. Type the user's name and then click OK to return to the property sheet.

8. At this point, the user can log on with Guest access. If you want to give the user more permissions, activate either the User Access check box or (if you *really* trust the user) the Full Control check box. (In both cases, use the check box in the Allow column.)

9. Click OK.

From Here

▶ For details on running the Connector software, **see** "Installing Windows Home Server Connector on the Client Computers," **P. 63**.

▶ To learn how to start a remote session from inside the LAN, **see** "Connecting via Remote Desktop Connection," **P. 181**.

▶ For the details on making remote connections via the Internet, **see** "Connecting via the Internet," **P. 194**.

▶ You can use Windows Home Server's monitoring tools to monitor each user's network activity. **See** "Monitoring Users via Task Manager," **P. 281**.

▶ To learn how to use the Registry Editor, **see** Chapter 18, "Working with the Windows Home Server Registry."

▶ To learn more about WMI scripting, **see** "Programming the Windows Management Instrumentation Service," **P. 688**.

CHAPTER 3

Adding Devices to the Windows Home Server Network

A network consisting of just a single Windows Home Server box isn't much of a "network" at all, it goes without saying. To make things interesting, you need to add one or more devices to the network. By "devices," I mean other computers, first and foremost. As you'll see, Windows 7, Windows Vista, and Windows XP machines can participate in the full extent of the Windows Home Server experience by accessing the Windows Home Server shares, streaming media, and getting backed up nightly. However, that doesn't mean these are the only computers you can insert into your network. Older Windows boxes, Macs, and Linux machines can also get in on the action by accessing the Windows Home Server shared folders. In some cases, with the right software installed, you can connect remotely to the network from these machines.

By "devices," I also mean noncomputer equipment, including Xbox consoles, Zune media players, and other media devices such as network media players and digital picture frames. This chapter gives you the details on connecting these other devices to your Windows Home Server network.

Installing Windows Home Server Connector on the Client Computers

Your key to the riches of Windows Home Server from a client computer's point of view is a program called Windows Home Server Connector, which does the following:

▶ Locates the Windows Home Server on the network.

▶ Registers your computer with Windows Home Server.

▶ Configures Windows Home Server to automatically back up your computer every night.

▶ Installs the Backup Now component that enables you to back up your computer manually at any time.

▶ Installs the client version of the Restore Wizard, which enables you to restore backed-up files and folders.

▶ Adds a desktop shortcut for the Windows Home Server shared folders.

▶ Installs the Home Server Tray application, a notification area icon that tells you the current network status and gives you access to Windows Home Server features.

▶ Installs the client version of the Windows Home Server Console.

Supported Operating Systems

The good news is that it's the Connector program that lets your client machine get in on the complete Windows Home Server experience. The bad news is that the Connector software only works on clients running newer versions of Windows, as follows:

▶ Windows 7 Home Basic

▶ Windows 7 Home Premium

▶ Windows 7 Professional

▶ Windows 7 Enterprise

▶ Windows 7 Ultimate

▶ Windows Vista Home Basic

▶ Windows Vista Home Premium

▶ Windows Vista Business

▶ Windows Vista Enterprise

▶ Windows Vista Ultimate

▶ Windows Vista Home N (European Union only)

▶ Windows Vista Business N (European Union only)

▶ Windows XP Home with Service Pack 2

▶ Windows XP Professional with Service Pack 2

▶ Windows XP Media Center Edition 2005 with Service Pack 2 and Rollup 2

▶ Windows XP Media Center Edition 2005 with Service Pack 2

▶ Windows XP Media Center Edition 2004 with Service Pack 2

▶ Windows XP Tablet Edition with Service Pack 2

Note that Microsoft has posted no other system requirements for Windows Home Server Connector. In other words, if your system is capable of running any of the preceding operating systems and can make a wired or wireless connection to your network, you can install and run Windows Home Server Connector.

Preparing to Install Windows Home Server Connector

Before installing Windows Home Server connector, you should make sure that your client is ready for the installation and for joining the Windows Home Server network. Here's a checklist:

- ▶ Set up a wired or wireless connection to your network.

- ▶ Make sure the client's computer name is unique on the network.

- ▶ Make sure the client's workgroup name is the same as the workgroup name used by Windows Home Server.

- ▶ Make sure you can see the Windows Home Server on your network. (In Windows 7, click Windows Explorer on the taskbar, and then click Network; in Windows Vista, select Start, Network; in Windows XP, select Start, My Network Places, and then either click the View Workgroup Computers link or select Entire Network, Microsoft Windows Network, and then click your workgroup.)

- ▶ On the client, set up the user account you want to use with Windows Home Server (if you don't want to use an existing account).

- ▶ On Windows Home Server, set up a user account with the same username and password as the client user account.

Running the Windows Home Server Connector Setup Program on Windows 7 and Windows Vista

With your Windows 7 or Windows Vista client PC ready, here are the steps to follow to install the Windows Home Server Connector:

1. Launch the installation program:

   - ▶ **Via the network**—Access your workgroup, open the Windows Home Server computer to view its shares, double-click Software, double-click Home Server Connector Software, and then double-click setup.exe.

   - ▶ **Via a web browser**—Launch the browser and navigate to http://*server*:55000, where *server* is the name of your Windows Home Server machine. When the Windows Home Server Connector Setup page loads, click Download Now.

   - ▶ **Via CD**—Insert the Windows Home Server Connector CD. If you see the AutoPlay window, click the Run setup.exe link. Otherwise, use Windows Explorer to open the CD and double-click SETUP.EXE.

2. Enter your User Account Control credentials to authorize the installation.

3. In the initial Windows Home Server Connector dialog box, click Next.

4. Accept the license agreement and click Next. The Windows Home Server Connector installation begins. When the install is complete, you're prompted for the Windows Home Server password, as shown in Figure 3.1.

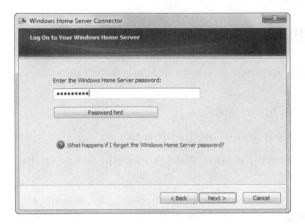

FIGURE 3.1   When the Windows Home Server Connector software is installed, you need to log on to Windows Home Server.

5. Type the Windows Home Server password. If you're not sure of the correct password, click Password Hint to display the hint text that was entered during the Windows Home Server install.

6. Click Next. Windows Home Server Connector asks if you want to wake up the computer to back it up.

7. Leave the Yes option activated to have Windows Home Server wake up your sleeping computer. If you'd prefer to leave your computer in sleep mode, click the No option instead.

8. Click Next. Windows Home Server Connector joins your computer to the network and configures Windows Home Server to back up your computer nightly.

9. Click Next to complete the Windows Home Server Connector installation.

10. Click Finish. Windows Home Server Connector adds a shortcut to the server shares on your desktop. Note that this shortcut appears on the desktop for all users of the computer.

11. The Home Server Tray application icon appears in the notification area. If your client user account password doesn't match your server user account password, the icon displays a message letting you know. Synchronize the passwords as described in Chapter 2, "Setting Up and Working with User Accounts."

▶ **SEE** For the details on getting your client and server user account passwords in synch, **see** "Synchronizing the Client and Windows Home Server Passwords," **P. 45.**

Running the Windows Home Server Connector Setup Program on Windows XP

Installing Windows Home Server Connector on Windows XP is similar to installing it on Vista, but the two are different enough that the XP process deserves a separate set of steps. Follow these steps to install the Windows Home Server Connector on a Windows XP client:

1. Log on to Windows XP with an Administrator-level account. Administrator rights are required to install the Connector software. If you don't want to use this Administrator-level account with Windows Home Server, that's okay. After Windows Home Server Connector is installed, you can log off and then log back on using the account you want to use with Windows Home Server.

NOTE

If you're logged on to Windows XP with a Standard user account when you insert the Windows Home Server Connector CD, you see the Install Program As Other User dialog box. Normally, you use this dialog box to run an installation program under a different user account by selecting an Administrator-level account and password. That won't work with Windows Home Server Connector, however, because it requires that the Administrator-level user be logged on.

You might think that you can log on to XP with a Standard user account and then use the Run As command to run Setup under the elevated privileges of an Administrator-level account. (The usual way to do this is to right-click the file you want to run and then click Run As in the shortcut menu.) That won't work, however, because Windows Home Server Connector's install program doesn't support the Run As command or any kind of privilege elevation.

---

2. Insert the Windows Home Server Connector CD.
3. The Setup program should start automatically. If not, use Windows Explorer to open the CD and double-click SETUP.EXE.
4. Depending on the configuration of your XP machine, Windows Home Server Connector may install Microsoft .NET Framework 2.0. If so, follow the onscreen instructions to install the framework.
5. In the initial Windows Home Server Connector dialog box, click Next.
6. Accept the license agreement and click Next. The Windows Home Server Connector installation begins. When the install is complete, you're prompted for the Windows Home Server password.
7. Type the Windows Home Server password. If you're not sure of the correct password, click Password Hint to display the hint text that was entered during the Windows Home Server install.
8. Click Next. Windows Home Server Connector asks if you want to wake up the computer to back it up.

9. Leave the Yes option activated to have Windows Home Server wake up your sleeping computer. If you'd prefer to leave your computer in sleep mode, click the No option, instead.

10. Click Next. Windows Home Server Connector joins your computer to the network and configures Windows Home Server to back up your computer nightly.

11. Click Next to complete the Windows Home Server Connector installation.

12. Click Finish. Windows Home Server Connector adds a shortcut to the server shares on your desktop. Note that this shortcut appears on the desktop for all users of the computer.

13. The Home Server Tray application icon appears in the notification area. If your client user account password doesn't match your server user account password, the icon displays a message letting you know. Synchronize the passwords as described in Chapter 2.

▶ **SEE** For the details on getting your client and server user account passwords in synch, **see** "Synchronizing the Client and Windows Home Server Passwords," **P. 45.**

14. If the Administrator-level account you're using for the installation doesn't have a corresponding account in Windows Home Server, you see a dialog box similar to the one shown in Figure 3.2. Click Close.

FIGURE 3.2   You see this dialog box if the current client user account doesn't have a corresponding user account on Windows Home Server.

15. If you are using the current Administrator-level user account only for installing Windows Home Server Connector, log off the account and then log back on using the account you want to use with Windows Home Server.

Rediscovering the Windows Home Server

If you change certain aspects of Windows Home Server—for example, if you change or modify the computer name or give the server a different IP address—your client computer will almost certainly lose its connection to Windows Home Server, and it probably won't be able to find the server again. The next time you log on to the client, the Windows Home Server Tray icon will be grayed out, and hovering your mouse over the icon will display a Not connected to server message, as shown in Figure 3.3.

FIGURE 3.3   Changing the server name or IP address can cause a client computer to lose its connection to the server.

If that happens, one solution is to uninstall and then reinstall the Windows Home Server Connector software. However, an easier solution is to run the Discovery program that installs with Windows Home Server Connector. This is the program that the Windows Home Server Connector uses to find the server in the first place when you initially install the Connector software. However, you're free to reuse it any time to rediscover the server. Here are the steps to follow:

1. On the client computer, use Windows Explorer to open the following folder:

    %ProgramFiles%\Windows Home Server

NOTE

%ProgramFiles% is an environment variable that holds the location of the PROGRAM FILES folder, which is usually C:\Program Files.

2. Double-click Discovery.exe.

TIP

You can combine steps 1 and 2 by opening the Run dialog box (press Windows Logo+R or select Start, Run in XP), typing the following command, and then clicking OK:

%ProgramFiles%\Windows Home Server\Discovery.exe

3. If the client is running Windows 7 or Windows Vista, enter your User Account Control credentials. The Windows Home Server Connector then attempts to locate the server, as shown in Figure 3.4. If the Discovery program locates Windows Home Server, it prompts you for the server password.

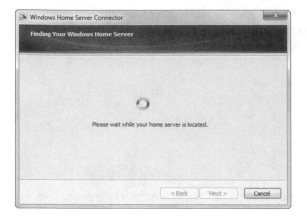

FIGURE 3.4   Run Discovery.exe on the client to attempt to locate the Windows Home Server.

4. Type the password and then click Next. Windows Home Server Connector rejoins your computer to the network.

5. Click Next to complete the discovery portion of Windows Home Server Connector.

6. Click Finish.

Using a Mac on Your Windows Home Server Network

One of the important networking layers used by all Microsoft networks—including, of course, your Windows Home Server network—is called Server Message Block (SMB). It is via SMB that Windows PCs can share folders on the network and access folders that other Windows PCs have shared. In a very real sense, SMB *is* the network.

SMB's central role in Windows networking is good news if you have a Mac in your household. That's because all versions of OS X support SMB natively, so you can use your Mac not only to view the Windows Home Server shares, but also to open and work with files on those shares (provided, of course, that you have permission to access the share and that OS X has an application that's compatible with whatever file you want to work with). You can even switch things around and view your Mac shares from within Windows. The next few sections provide you with the details.

Connecting to the Windows Home Server Network

First, connect your Mac to the Windows Home Server network. If the Mac is near your network's switch (or router, depending on your configuration), run a network cable from the device to the Mac. If you're using a wireless connection, instead, follow these steps to connect your Mac to the wireless portion of your Windows Home Server network:

1. Click the System Preferences icon in the Dock.

2. Click Network to open the Network preferences.

3. Click AirPort.

4. Use the Network Name list to select your Windows Home Server wireless network ID.

TIP

OS X normally shows the AirPort status icon in the menu bar. If you see that icon, a faster way to initiate a wireless connection is to click the icon and then click the name of the network you want to join.

5. If your network is secure, make sure the Wireless Security list displays the correct security type.

6. Type the security key in the Password text box and then click OK to return to the Network window. As shown in Figure 3.5, the Status should show connected.

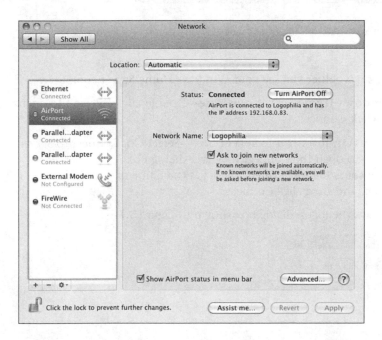

FIGURE 3.5   When you connect your Mac to the Windows Home Server network via wireless, the AirPort tab shows the connection status.

7. Close the Network preferences window.

Mounting a Windows Home Server Shared Folder

You're now ready to access the Windows Home Server shares. Before you get started, check that your Mac can see the Windows Home Server computer. Open Finder and then select Go, Network (or press Shift+Command+K). In the Network folder that appears, you see an icon for each network computer that your Mac can see (see Figure 3.6).

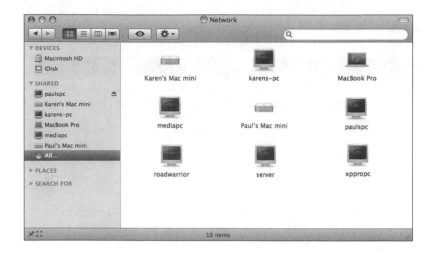

FIGURE 3.6   Check out Finder's Network folder and see if there's an icon for your Windows Home Server computer.

How you proceed depends on whether you see your Windows Home Server computer:

▶ **If you see your Windows Home Server machine**—Double-click the icon to open the server, and then click Connect As.

▶ **If you don't see your Windows Home Server box**—Select Go, Connect to Server (or press Command+K) to open the Connect to Server dialog box. In the Server Address text box, type **smb://server**, where *server* is the name of your Windows Home Server computer, and then click Connect.

Either way, Mac OS X displays the logon dialog box shown in Figure 3.7.

FIGURE 3.7   You need to enter your Windows Home Server Administrator password to access the shares from OS X.

Here are the steps to follow from here:

1. Make sure the Registered User option is selected.

2. Type **Administrator** in the Name text box.

3. Type your Administrator account password in the Password text box.

4. If you want OS X to remember your credentials, activate the Remember This Password in My Keychain check box.

5. Click Connect. OS X asks you to select which shared volume you want to connect to.

6. In the list, select the Windows Home Server share you want to access (Music, Photos, and so on).

7. Click OK. OS X mounts the share and displays the folder's contents, as shown in Figure 3.8.

Windows Home Server's Music Share

Click the server to access the other shared folders.

FIGURE 3.8 When you connect to a Windows Home Server share, OS X mounts it on the desktop, and an icon appears in the sidebar.

8. Work with the folder contents using the OS X tools. In the Music share, for instance, you could play compatible music files using iTunes.

Backing Up Mac Data to a Windows Home Server Shared Folder

Besides working with the files on a Windows Home Server share in an OS X application, you can use a Windows Home Server share to store OS X backups. This is handy if you don't have a second hard drive attached to your Mac, or if your backups are too big to burn to a DVD. The easiest way to do this in OS X is to use the Disk Utility to archive a folder or the entire system to an image file on a Windows Home Server share. Here's how it's done:

1. In Windows Home Server, create a share to store the OS X backup.

▶ **SEE** For the details on setting up a new share in Windows Home Server, **see** "Creating a New Shared Folder," **P. 149.**

2. Follow the steps in the previous section to mount the new share in OS X.

3. Click the Finder icon in the Dock.

4. Select Applications, Utilities, and then double-click Disk Utility. OS X launches the Disk Utility application.

5. If you want to back up your entire system, click Macintosh HD in the Disk Utility window.

6. Select File, New and then select either Disk Image from Folder or Disk Image from *disk* (Macintosh HD), where *disk* is the name of your Mac's hard disk.

7. If you selected Disk Image from Folder, the Select Folder to Image dialog box appears. Select the folder you want to back up and then click Image.

8. In the New Image dialog box, use the Save As text box to edit the filename, if desired.

9. Select the Windows Home Server share that you mounted in step 2.

10. Click Save. OS X creates the disk image on the Windows Home Server share. (Depending on the amount of data you're archiving, this may take several hours.)

11. When the image creation is done, select Disk Utility, Quit Disk Utility.

Using a Mac to Make a Remote Desktop Connection to Windows Home Server

You learn in Chapter 7, "Making Connections to Network Computers," how to use Windows' Remote Desktop Connection program to connect to the desktop of another computer on your network. However, it's also possible to make Remote Desktop connections to Windows computers from your Mac.

▶ **SEE** For the details on connecting via Remote Desktop, **see** "Connecting via Remote Desktop Connection," **P. 181.**

To do this, you need to install on your Mac the Remote Desktop Connection Client for Mac, which is available from Microsoft. Go to www.microsoft.com/downloads and search for *Remote Desktop Mac*. (Note that as I write this, the latest version of the Remote Desktop Connection Client for Mac is 2.0.1.)

After you have the Remote Desktop Connection Client installed on your Mac, mount it and then follow these steps:

1. Ensure that the Windows PC to which you'll be connecting is configured to accept Remote Desktop connections.

► **SEE** To learn how to get a computer set up for Remote Desktop connections, **see** "Getting the Client Computer Ready," **P. 181.**

2. In Finder, open the Applications folder, and then launch the Remote Desktop Connection icon.

3. In the Computer text box, type the IP address of the host computer.

4. If you don't want to customize Remote Desktop, skip to step 7. Otherwise, select RDC, Preferences to open the Remote Desktop Connection preferences dialog box, shown in Figure 3.9.

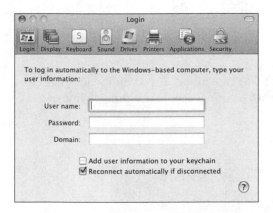

FIGURE 3.9   Use the preferences dialog box to customize Remote Desktop Connection for Mac.

5. The Login tab offers the following options:

   ► **User Name**—This is the username you want to use to log in to the host computer.

   ► **Password**—This is the password to use to log on to the host computer.

   ► **Domain**—Leave this text box blank.

   ► **Add User Information to Your Keychain**—Activate this check box to have OS X remember your logon data.

   ► **Reconnect Automatically if Disconnected**—Leave this check box activated to enable automatic reconnections.

6. Fill in the options in the Display, Keyboard, Sound, Drives, Printers, Applications, and Security tabs, as required, and then close the preferences dialog box.

▶ **SEE** For a complete look at the various Remote Desktop Connection options, **see** "Making the Connection to the Remote Desktop," **P. 182.**

TIP

The default number of colors that Remote Desktop Connection Client for Mac uses is Thousands, which can make most Windows screens look hideous. In the Display tab, use the Colors list to select Millions.

---

7. Click Connect. Remote Desktop Connection Client for Mac connects to the Windows PC and prompts you for your login credentials, if you didn't add them to the Login tab. Figure 3.10 shows OS X with a connection to a Windows Home Server computer.

FIGURE 3.10   A Mac connected to a Windows Home Server PC using the Remote Desktop Connection Client for Mac software.

When you're done, select RDC, Quit RDC, and then click OK when the program warns you that you're about to disconnect from the Windows PC.

Letting Windows Computers See Your Mac Shares

SMB not only lets your Mac see shares on the Windows Home Server network, it also can let Windows PCs see folders shared by the Mac. This feature is turned off by default in OS X, but you can follow these steps to turn it on:

1. Click the System Preferences icon in the Dock.
2. Click Sharing to open the Sharing preferences.
3. Click to activate the File Sharing check box.
4. Click Options to open the Options sheet.
5. Click to activate the Share Files and Folders Using SMB (Windows) check box, as shown in Figure 3.11.

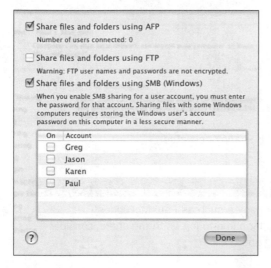

FIGURE 3.11   Activate the Share Files and Folders Using SMB check box to enable your Mac to share folders with Windows machines.

6. Click to activate the check box beside a user to enable SMB sharing for that user, enter the user's password when prompted, and then click OK.

TIP

For easiest sharing, enable SMB sharing for accounts that also exist on the Windows machines.

7. Click Done. The Sharing window shows you the address that Windows PCs can use to access your Mac shares directly, as shown in Figure 3.12.

FIGURE 3.12   The Sharing window with Windows Sharing activated.

TIP

Macs often end up with long-winded computer names such as Paul McFedries' Computer. Because you need to use the computer name to log on to the share, consider editing the Computer Name field to something shorter.

8. Select System Preferences, Quit System Preferences.

One way to access the Mac shares from a Windows PC is to enter the share address directly, using either the Run dialog box or Windows Explorer's address bar. You have two choices:

```
\\IP\user
\\Computer\user
```

Here, *IP* is the IP address shown in the OS X Sharing window (see Figure 3.13), *Computer* is the Mac's computer name (also shown in the OS X Sharing window), and in both cases, *user* is the username of the account enabled for Windows Sharing. For example, I can use either of the following addresses to access my Mac:

```
\\192.168.0.54\paul
\\Pauls-Mac-mini\paul
```

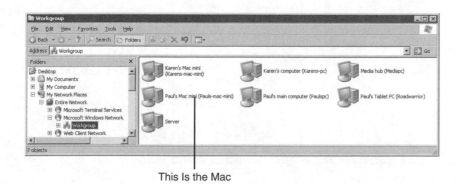

This Is the Mac

FIGURE 3.13   Look for the icon that has the same name as your Mac.

Alternatively, open your workgroup as shown in Figure 3.13 and look for the icon that has the same name as the Mac's computer name (shown in Figure 3.12). Double-click that icon.

> **NOTE**
>
> If you don't see the icon for your Mac, it could be that the Mac isn't set up to use the same workgroup as your Windows Home Server network. (Both OS X and Windows Home Server use the name Workgroup by default, but you never know.) To check this, open System Preferences, click the Network icon, click the network interface you're using (usually either Ethernet or AirPort), and then click Advanced. Click the WINS tab, make sure the Workgroup value is the same as your Windows Home Server workgroup name, click OK, and then click Apply.

Either way, you're prompted for the username and password of the Mac account that you enabled for SMB sharing. (If your Windows user account uses the same username and password, you go directly to the Mac share.) For the username, use the form *Computer\UserName*, where *Computer* is the name of your Mac and *UserName* is the name of the SMB sharing account. Figure 3.14 shows a Mac share opened in Windows Home Server.

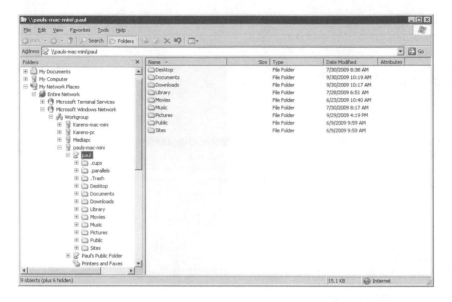

FIGURE 3.14   A shared Mac folder opened in Windows Home Server.

> **TIP**
>
> If you have trouble logging on to your Mac from Windows Vista, the problem is likely caused by Vista's use of NT LAN Manager version 2 (NTLMv2) authentication, which doesn't work properly when negotiated between some versions of Vista and some versions of OS X. To fix this, on the Vista PC, press Windows Logo+R (or select Start, All Programs, Accessories, Run), type **secpol.msc**, click OK to open the Local Security Policy snap-in, and enter your UAC credentials. Open the Security Settings, Local Policies, Security Options branch. Double-click the Network Security: LAN Manager Authentication Level policy, change the authentication level to Send LM & NTLM - Use NTLMv2 Session Security If Negotiated, and then click OK.
>
> If your version of Vista doesn't come with the Local Security snap-in (it's not available in Home and Home Premium), open the Registry Editor (press Windows Logo+R, type **regedit**, and click OK), and navigate to the following key:
>
> HLM\SYSTEM\CurrentControlSet\Control\Lsa\
>
> Change the value of the LMCompatibilityLevel setting to 1.

Using a Linux Client on Your Windows Home Server Network

Until recently, it was a rare household that included a Linux box as part of its computer collection. That is changing rapidly, however, thanks to easy-to-use and easy-to-install Linux distributions such as Ubuntu and new Linux-based offerings from mainstream computer manufacturers such as Dell.

The good news is that Linux, like OS X, supports SMB natively (via Samba, a free implementation of the SMB protocols), so it's possible for Linux machines to coexist on your Windows Home Server network. In the sections that follow, I use the Ubuntu distribution (specifically, Ubuntu 9.04, also known as Jaunty Jackalope) to access the Windows Home Server network. The procedures for your Linux distribution should be similar.

Viewing the Windows Home Server Network in Ubuntu

Ubuntu isn't set up out-of-the-box to view and work with Windows shares that use NTFS. This is a problem for Windows Home Server because all your shares are NTFS. To fix this problem, you need to install the NTFS Configuration tool in Ubuntu:

1. Select Applications, Add/Remove to open the Add/Remove Applications window.
2. In the Show list, select All Available Applications.
3. Type **ntfs** in the Search box. You should see NTFS Configuration Tool appear in the Application list.
4. Activate the check box beside NTFS Configuration Tool and then click Apply Changes.
5. Click OK. Ubuntu asks you to confirm the changes.
6. Click Apply Changes, click Apply, and then enter your administrative password.

Here are the steps to follow to open your workgroup and view the Windows Home Server shares:

1. Select Places, Network. The File Browser program opens and displays the Network folder. If you see your network computers, skip to step 4.
2. Double-click the Windows Network icon. You should now see the icon for your Windows Home Server workgroup.
3. Double-click the workgroup icon. You should now see icons for each computer in your workgroup, as shown in Figure 3.15.
4. Double-click the icon for the Windows Home Server computer. File Browser prompts you for your username and password.
5. Type your username and password, clear the Domain field, and then click Connect. File Browser displays the Windows Home Server shares, as shown in Figure 3.16.

Letting Windows Computers See Your Ubuntu Shares

The Linux support for SMB cuts both ways, meaning that not only can you see and work with Windows shares in Ubuntu, but you can also configure Ubuntu as a file server and enable Windows computers to see and work with Ubuntu shares. The next few sections show you how to set this up in Ubuntu.

Installing Samba in Ubuntu

Your first step is to install Samba by following this procedure:

1. Select System, Administration, Synaptic Package Manager.
2. In the Quick Search text box, type **samba**. You see a list of packages that include "samba" in the name.

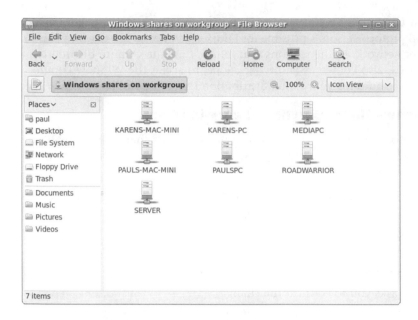

FIGURE 3.15   In Ubuntu's File Browser, open the workgroup icon to see your workgroup computers.

FIGURE 3.16   In Ubuntu's File Browser, open the Windows Home Server icon to see the server's shared folders.

3. In the Package list, click the check box beside samba and then click Mark for Installation. Synaptic Package Manager displays a list of packages that must be upgraded.

4. Click Mark.

5. Click Apply.

6. Synaptic Package Manager displays a list of the changes that will be applied.

7. Click Apply and then click Apply again. Synaptic Package Manager downloads and installs the software.

8. Click Close.

Defining Samba Users in Ubuntu

Next, you need to define one or more users who can access Samba shares. For this to work, you need to set up the same username and account on both the Ubuntu box and the Windows PC.

Assuming you already have your Windows users configured, follow these steps to add a user in Ubuntu:

1. Select System, Administration, Users and Groups.

2. Click Unlock, type your administrative password, and click Authenticate.

3. Click Add User.

4. Type the username. Again, make sure this is a username that exists on the Windows PC you'll be using to access the Ubuntu shares.

5. Type the user password and the password confirmation.

6. Fill in any other user settings as you see fit.

7. Click OK to add the user.

8. Repeat steps 3–6 to add other users.

9. Click Close.

Now you can add these users to Samba. Here are the steps to follow:

1. Select Applications, Accessories, Terminal to launch a terminal session.

2. Type the following command (where *user* is the username) and then enter your administrative password when prompted:

```
sudo smbpasswd -a user
```

3. Ubuntu displays the following prompt:

```
New SMB password:
```

4. Type the user account's password (you won't see characters onscreen while you type), and then press Enter. Ubuntu displays the following prompt:

```
Retype new SMB password:
```

5. Type the user account's password again and press Enter. Ubuntu adds the user.

6. Reload Samba by typing the following command and pressing Enter:

   ```
   sudo /etc/init.d/samba reload
   ```

7. Repeat steps 2–6 to add the other users to Samba.

You need the terminal session for the next setup task, so leave the session running for now.

Changing the Samba Workgroup Name in Ubuntu

In the latest versions of Samba, the default Samba workgroup name is WORKGROUP, which is likely to be the same as the workgroup name you use for your Windows Home Server network. However, older versions of Samba used MSHOME as the default workgroup name. If you're running an older version of Samba, or if your Windows Home Server workgroup name is something other than Workgroup, then for easier access to the Ubuntu shares, you should configure Samba to use the same workgroup name that you use for your Windows network. Here are the steps to follow:

1. If you don't already have a terminal session running from the previous section, select Applications, Accessories, Terminal.

2. Type the following command and press Enter:

   ```
   sudo gedit /etc/samba/smb.conf
   ```

3. If you see the Password prompt, type your Ubuntu password and press Enter. The gedit text editor loads and opens smb.conf, which is the configuration file for Samba.

4. Locate the workgroup line and change the value of the workgroup parameter to the name of your Windows Home Server workgroup. For example, if your network uses the name workgroup, the line should appear as follows:

   ```
   workgroup = workgroup
   ```

5. Select File, Save (or press Ctrl+S or click the Save button).

6. Select File, Quit (or press Ctrl+Q) to return to the terminal session.

7. Select File, Close Window (or press Ctrl+Shift+Q).

TIP

If you want to change the name of the Ubuntu computer, you must install the gnome-network-admin package using Synaptic Package Manager. (For the general steps, see "Installing Samba in Ubuntu," earlier in this chapter.) Once that's done, select System, Administration, Network to open the Network Settings dialog box. Click Unlock and then enter your administrative password. Display the General tab, modify the Host Name setting, and then click Close.

Sharing a Folder in Ubuntu

You're now ready to share a folder or two for Windows users to access. Use these steps:

1. Select Places, Home Folder to open File Browser and display your Ubuntu home folder.

2. Display the icon for the folder you want to share.

3. Right-click the icon and then click Sharing Options. Ubuntu displays the Folder Sharing dialog box.

4. Click to activate the Share This Folder check box, as shown in Figure 3.17.

FIGURE 3.17   Use the Folder Sharing dialog box to set up a folder to share with your Windows Home Server network.

5. Modify the name, if necessary.

6. If you want Windows users to be able to change the contents of the folder, activate the Allow Other People to Write In This Folder check box.

7. Click Create Share. Ubuntu lets you know that it needs to add some permissions.

8. Click Add the Permissions Automatically.

To work with the Ubuntu machine, open your workgroup as shown in Figure 3.18 and look for the icon that has the same name as the Ubuntu computer. Double-click that icon and then enter the username and password of a Samba account on the Ubuntu box. Windows displays the Ubuntu shares, as shown in Figure 3.19.

Connecting Other Devices to the Windows Home Server Network

Getting other devices to access your Windows Home Server network always begins with making the initial network connection:

▶ If the device has an RJ-45 jack, run a network cable from the jack to a port on your network's switch or router.

▶ If the device supports Wi-Fi, turn on the Wi-Fi option, if necessary. (Some devices have a physical switch that you must set to activate Wi-Fi.) Then use the device interface to display a list of the available wireless networks, select your Windows Home Server network, and enter the security key.

When that's done, you can usually access the Windows Home Server shares directly using the device interface.

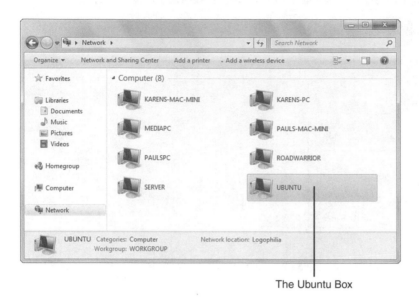

The Ubuntu Box

FIGURE 3.18   Look for the icon that has the same name as your Ubuntu box.

FIGURE 3.19   Open the Ubuntu box icon to see the folders it's sharing via Samba.

To give you some idea how this works on various devices, the rest of this chapter looks at connecting three different devices to a Windows Home Server network: a Windows Mobile Pocket PC or Smartphone, an Xbox 360, and a Wi-Fi digital picture frame.

Connecting a Windows Mobile Device

If you have a Windows Mobile 5.0 or 6.0 Pocket PC or Smartphone that supports Wi-Fi, you can use that wireless connection to access the Windows Home Server network. You can then access documents to work on with the mobile version of Word or Excel, download music or images for Windows Media Player, and so on.

Connecting to Your Windows Home Server Wireless Network

Your first task is to connect your Windows Mobile device to the wireless portion of your Windows Home Server network.

First, make sure you have Wi-Fi enabled:

1. Tap Start, Programs, Comm Manager.
2. If you see an X over the Wi-Fi icon, tap that icon.
3. Tap Exit.

Now here are the steps to follow to connect to the Windows Home Server network:

1. Tap the Wi-Fi icon that appears at the top of the Windows Mobile screen (see Figure 3.20). Windows Mobile displays a list of available wireless networks, as shown in Figure 3.20.

The Wi-Fi Icon

FIGURE 3.20   When you activate Wi-Fi in Windows Mobile, clicking the Wi-Fi icon displays a list of available wireless networks.

2. Tap your Windows Home Server wireless network to select it.

3. Tap OK.

4. Tab Work.

5. Tap Connect. Windows Mobile prompts you to enter the network's security key.

6. Tap the key and then tap Connect.

Access the Windows Home Server Network Shares

With the wireless network connection established, you can now connect to a Windows Home Server shared folder:

1. Tap Start, Programs.

2. Tap File Explorer.

3. Tap Menu, Go To, Open Path, New Path to display the Open dialog box.

4. Type **server**, where *server* is the name of your Windows Home Server computer.

5. Tap OK. The Logon to Server dialog box appears.

6. Type a Windows Home Server username and password. If you want Windows Mobile to store your logon data, tap to activate the Save Password check box.

7. Tap OK. Windows Mobile displays the Windows Home Server shares, as shown in Figure 3.21.

FIGURE 3.21   Windows Mobile showing the Windows Home Server shared folders.

Adding an Xbox 360 to the Network

The Xbox 360 and Windows Home Server go together well because the Xbox can access and play media streamed from the server. First, you need to get the Xbox 360 connected to your network. Follow these steps:

1. Connect your Xbox 360 to the network. If you have physical access to the network, you can plug a network cable into the Xbox 360's network port. Otherwise, you need to attach a wireless networking adapter (sold separately) to the Xbox 360.

2. Turn on the Xbox 360.

3. When the Dashboard appears, display the System blade.

4. Highlight Network Settings and press Select.

5. Highlight Edit Settings and press Select.

6. In the Basic Settings tab, if the IP Settings field isn't set to Automatic, highlight the IP Settings section, press Select, highlight the Automatic setting, and then press Select.

7. If the DNS Settings field isn't set to Automatic, highlight the DNS Settings section, press Select, highlight the Automatic setting, and then press Select.

8. Highlight the section that includes the Network Name (SSID) field and press Select. The Xbox 360 displays a list of available wireless networks. (I'm assuming here that you have a wireless card plugged in to your console.)

9. Highlight your network and press Select. (Tip: If you don't see your network listed, press X to rerun the network search.)

10. If your network uses WEP or WPA security, use the onscreen keyboard to enter the security key. When you're finished, select Done. The Xbox 360 updates the network settings.

11. Highlight Test Media and press Select. You should see Connected in the Wireless Network field and Confirmed in the IP Address field. (If not, highlight Edit Settings, press Select, and repeat steps 6–10.)

Connecting a Kodak Wi-Fi Digital Picture Frame

A *digital picture frame* is a standalone device that displays digital images, usually in a slideshow format and often accompanied by music. Most digital picture frames accept one or more memory card formats, and you supply the frame with images by inserting a card that contains digital photos or pictures. Other digital picture frames have a USB port for direct connections to computers.

Most new digital picture frames also support Wi-Fi. If you have a wireless component to your Windows Home Server network, this means that you can connect one of these digital picture frames to your network, and the frame can then pick up images streamed from a Windows Media Connect device, such as Windows Home Server's Photos share.

An example of a digital picture frame that supports wireless connection is the Kodak Wi-Fi Digital Picture Frame. Here are the steps to follow to connect this frame to your Windows Home Server network when you start up the device for the first time:

1. Turn on the Kodak Wi-Fi Digital Picture Frame. On the frame, the Setup - Network Connection window appears and asks if you want to connect to a wireless network.

2. Select Yes and then press OK on the remote. The frame scans for and then displays a list of the available wireless networks.

3. Select your Windows Home Server network and then press OK on the remote. The frame prompts you to enter your wireless network security key.

4. Use the remote to enter the security key characters, select Done, and then press OK. The frame connects to your network and then displays a list of computers that have media sharing activated.

5. Select the Windows Home Server media sharing item, which appears as follows (where *SERVER* is the name of your Windows Home Server computer):

   SERVER: 1 : Windows Media Connect

6. Press OK on the remote. The frame completes the network setup.

7. Press OK. The frame appears in the Network window, as shown in Figure 3.22.

Kodak Wi-Fi Digital Picture Frame

FIGURE 3.22   After you set up the Kodak Wi-Fi Digital Picture Frame, it appears with your other network devices.

If you've already connected the frame to a different network, follow these steps to change the frame to your Windows Home Server network:

1. Turn on the Kodak Wi-Fi Digital Picture Frame.

2. On the frame's remote, press the Home button.

3. Select the Settings icon and then press OK. The frame displays the Setup window.

4. Select Network and then press OK.

5. Select Scan for Wireless Networks and then press OK.

6. Follow steps 3–7, earlier in this section, to select your Windows Home Server network and make the connection.

From Here

▶ To learn how to add a user to Windows Home Server, **see** "Adding the User Account," **P. 43**.

▶ For the details on getting your client and server user account passwords in synch, **see** "Synchronizing the Client and Windows Home Server Passwords," **P. 45**.

▶ For the details on setting up a new share in Windows Home Server, **see** "Creating a New Shared Folder," **P. 149**.

▶ To learn how to get a computer set up for Remote Desktop connections, **see** "Getting the Client Computer Ready," **P. 181**.

▶ For the details on connecting via Remote Desktop, **see** "Connecting via Remote Desktop Connection," **P. 181**.

▶ For a complete look at the various Remote Desktop Connection options, **see** "Making the Connection to the Remote Desktop," **P. 182**.

▶ For the details on the Registry and using the Registry Editor, **see** Chapter 18, "Working with the Windows Home Server Registry."

CHAPTER 4

Configuring Windows Home Server

W indows Home Server isn't meant to be constantly tweaked in the same way that you might always find yourself fiddling with settings in Windows 7, Windows Vista, or even Windows Server 2003. After you get through the setup (which nearly qualifies as a *forehead install*—that is, an installation so simple that theoretically you could run through each step by just hitting the spacebar with your forehead) and the simple and straightforward *OOBE* (out-of-box experience—that is, what you must do to get a computer running after you take it out of the box), there isn't much you're supposed to do with the machine. You set up your users and permissions, perhaps add a few extra shared folders, and your Windows Home Server is good to go.

Of course, this only applies to the nongeek users that Microsoft is truly targeting with Windows Home Server. For the rest of us, adjusting the settings of *any* operating system (OS) is a must because there has never been an OS made that satisfies and is set up for everyone. We tweak; therefore, we are.

In a sense, this book is all about tweaking Windows Home Server to get the most out of it. However, this chapter in particular takes you through some essential configuration tasks. You can accomplish most of these tasks via the Windows Home Server Console (meaning that you can adjust the server's settings from any client machine), but some of the techniques in this chapter run outside the Console (and so require either a direct login or a Remote Desktop connection to the server). Be sure to also see Chapter 16, "Customizing the Windows Home Server Interface," for some tweaks on the look-and-feel front.

Changing the Name of the Home Server

The default computer name in a Windows Home Server install is SERVER, but you may decide to change the name after Windows Home Server is up and running. For example, you might simply be bored with the prosaic name SERVER, or you might be adding a second Windows Home Server machine to your network and you want them to have names such as SERVER1 and SERVER2.

Whatever the reason, here are the steps you need to follow to change the server's name:

1. Log on to the Windows Home Server computer, or establish a Remote Desktop connection to the server.

   ▶ **SEE** For the details on connecting to Windows Home Server via Remote Desktop, **see** "Making a Remote Desktop Connection to the Server," **P. 31.**

2. Click Start, right-click My Computer, and then click Properties. The System Properties dialog box appears.

3. Display the Computer Name tab.

TIP

You can open the System Properties dialog box with the Computer Name tab displayed directly. Select Start, Run (or press Windows Logo+R), type **control sysdm.cpl,,1** in the Run dialog box, and then click OK.

---

4. Click Change. The Computer Name Changes dialog box appears.
5. Use the Computer Name text box to type the new name for the server.
6. Click OK. Windows Home Server tells you that you must restart the computer to put the change into effect.
7. Click OK to return to the System Properties dialog box.
8. Click OK. Windows Home Server prompts you to restart your computer.
9. Click Yes. Windows Home Server restarts. If you connected via Remote Desktop, the connection ends.

Running the Windows Home Server Console

Most of the Windows Home Server configuration chores are most easily accomplished via the Windows Home Server Console application. To ensure that you can always access this program easily, here's a list of the various methods you can use to launch it:

▶ On the Windows Home Server machine, select Start, Windows Home Server Console.

- ▶ On the Windows Home Server machine or a client, double-click the Windows Home Server Console desktop icon.

- ▶ On a client machine, select Start, All Programs, Windows Home Server Console.

- ▶ On the client machine, right-click the Windows Home Server icon in the notification area and then click Windows Home Server Console.

- ▶ On the server, select Start, Run (or press Windows Logo+R) to open the Run dialog box, type `%ProgramFiles%\Windows Home Server\HomeServerConsole.exe`, and then click OK.

- ▶ On a client, select Start, Run (or press Windows Logo+R) to open the Run dialog box, type `%ProgramFiles%\Windows Home Server\WHSConsoleClient.exe`, and then click OK.

If you're running Windows Home Server Console on a client, you see the logon screen shown in Figure 4.1. Type the Windows Home Server password (that is, the password for Windows Home Server's Administrator account) in the text box and then press Enter or click the arrow. The Windows Home Server Console appears, as shown in Figure 4.2.

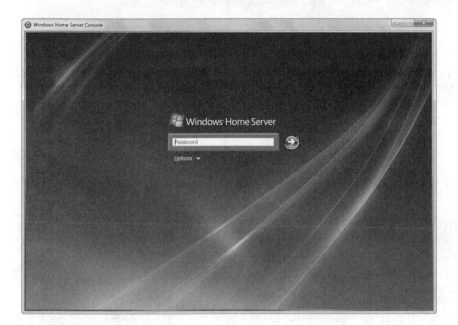

FIGURE 4.1 When you run the client version of Windows Home Server Console, you must first log on to the server.

TIP

If you want to avoid entering the Windows Home Server password each time, display the logon screen and then select Options, Remember the Windows Home Server Password.

FIGURE 4.2   Use the Windows Home Server Console program to configure most common server settings.

NOTE

If you can't recall the Windows Home Server password, select Options, Password Hint to see some text that gives you a hint about the password.

Changing the Date and Time on Windows Home Server

Windows Home Server runs the client backups each night starting around midnight. This is usually ideal because it's late enough that you or anyone in your family won't be working on a client machine, but early enough that the server has sufficient time to complete all the client backups (which it performs one client at a time). So it's important that the time is set up correctly on Windows Home Server.

The server's internal date is important, too, because Windows Home Server uses the date to organize backups. If you need to restore a file or folder, you need the date to be accurate so you can tell which version of the file or folder to restore.

Setting the Current Date and Time

If the Windows Home Server date or time is off, follow these steps to make a correction:

1. Launch the Windows Home Server Console.
2. Click Settings to open the Windows Home Server Settings dialog box.

3. In the General tab's Date & Time section, click Change to display the Date and Time Properties dialog box, shown in Figure 4.3.

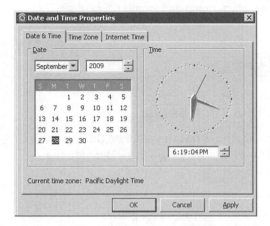

FIGURE 4.3   Use the Date and Time Properties dialog box to set the server's internal date and time.

TIP

If you're logged in to the server, a faster way to display the Date and Time Properties dialog box is to double-click the time in the taskbar's notification area. Alternatively, select Start, Control Panel, Date and Time.

4. In the Date & Time tab, use the controls in the Date group to specify the current month, year, and day.

5. Use the spin box in the Time group to specify the current hour, minute, second, and AM or PM. These four items are separate "sections" within the text box. Either edit each section directly, or click within a section and use the up and down arrows to increase or decrease the section value.

6. To change the time zone, display the Time Zone tab, and then use the list to select your time zone.

7. If you want Windows Home Server to adjust the time during daylight saving time changeovers, leave the Automatically Adjust Clock for Daylight Saving Changes check box activated. (Note that you only see this check box if your time zone uses daylight saving time.)

8. Click OK to put the new settings into effect.

TIP

If you're working with a client machine and you just want to know the current time on the server, use the NET TIME command. Start a command prompt session on the client machine (select Start, All Programs, Accessories, Command Prompt), type the following, and press Enter:

net time *server*

Replace *server* with the name of your Windows Home Server.

Synchronizing the Date and Time with a Time Server

If you want to ensure that Windows Home Server always has the accurate time, you can configure the system to synchronize with an Internet-based time server. Here are the steps to follow:

1. Launch the Windows Home Server Console.
2. Click Settings to open the Windows Home Server Settings dialog box.
3. In the General tab's Date & Time section, click Change to display the Date and Time Properties dialog box.
4. In the Internet Time tab, make sure the Automatically Synchronize with an Internet Time Server check box is activated.
5. Use the Server list to choose a time server.
6. Click Update Now to synchronize the time manually. (Windows Home Server schedules the next synchronization for a week later.)
7. Click OK to put the new settings into effect.

Unfortunately, the time synchronization in Windows Home Server (and, indeed, in all versions of Windows that support this feature) isn't very reliable. On my Windows machines, I usually have to configure a different time server by hand either using a command prompt session or by modifying the list of servers in the Internet Time tab. I most often use one of the time servers operated by the U.S. Navy:

tick.usno.navy.mil
tock.usno.navy.mil

NOTE

You can find a long list of time servers at http://ntp.isc.org/bin/ view/Servers/WebHome.

Specifying the Time Server at the Command Prompt

To configure a time server via the command prompt, follow these steps:

1. In Windows Home Server, select Start, All Programs, Accessories, Command Prompt.

2. Enter the following command to specify the time server you want to use. (Replace *TimeServer* with the domain name of the time server.)

   ```
   net time /setsntp:TimeServer
   ```

3. Stop the Windows Time service by entering the following command:

   ```
   net stop w32time
   ```

4. Restart the Windows Time service by entering the following command:

   ```
   net start w32time
   ```

When you restart the Time service, it automatically synchronizes with the time server you specified.

Adding Time Servers to the Internet Time Tab

Rather than working with the command prompt, you can customize the list of servers that appears in the Internet Time tab. Follow these steps:

1. Select Start, Run (or press Windows Logo+R) to open the Run dialog box, type **regedit**, and click OK to open the Registry Editor.

2. Display the following key:

   ```
   HKLM\SOFTWARE\Microsoft\Windows\CurrentVersion\DateTime\Servers
   ```

   ▶ **SEE** To learn how to get around in the Registry, **see** "Navigating the Registry," **P. 525.**

3. Select Edit, New, String Value.

4. Type the number that represents the next highest value among the settings in the Servers key, and then press Enter. For example, the default Servers key contains the settings 1 through 5, so for your first server, you'd type **6** (and press Enter).

5. Press Enter or double-click the new setting to open the Edit String dialog box.

6. Type the domain name (or IP address) of the time server, and then click OK.

7. Repeat steps 3–6 to add other time servers.

8. If you want one of your custom time servers to be the default server for synchronization, double-click the (Default) setting and change its value to the number that corresponds to the server you want to use as the default.

9. Exit the Registry Editor.

The next time you open the Date and Time Properties dialog box and display the Internet Time tab, you see your custom time servers in the Server list, as shown in Figure 4.4.

Time servers added to the Servers key...

...appear in the Server list.

FIGURE 4.4   When you add time server settings to the Registry's Servers key, the servers appear in the Internet Time tab's Server list.

Customizing the Synchronization Interval

By default, Windows Home Server synchronizes with the default time server once a week. If you'd prefer that Windows Home Server synchronize more often—for example, once a day—you can follow these steps to customize the synchronization interval:

1. Select Start, Run (or press Windows Logo+R) to open the Run dialog box, type **regedit**, and click OK to open the Registry Editor.

2. Display the following key:

   HKLM\SYSTEM\CurrentControlSet\Services\W32Time\TimeProviders\NtpClient

3. Double-click the SpecialPollInterval setting to open the Edit DWORD Value setting.

4. Click the Decimal option.

5. In the Value Data text box, type the number of seconds you want to use as the synchronization interval. For example, to synchronize every 24 hours, type **86400.**

6. Click OK.

7. Exit the Registry Editor.

To put the new setting into effect, you have two choices:

▶ In the Date and Time Properties dialog box, display the Internet Time tab and then click Update Now.

▶ Stop and then restart the Windows Time service. One way to do this is to use the net stop w32time and net start w32time commands I mentioned earlier. Alternatively, select Start, Control Panel, Administrative Tools, Services to open the Services snap-in. Click the Windows Time service, click the Stop link (see Figure 4.5), and then click the Start link.

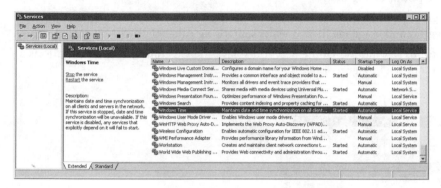

FIGURE 4.5   You can use the Services snap-in to stop and start the Windows Time service.

▶ **SEE** For more information on the Services snap-in, **see** "Controlling Services with the Services Snap-In," **P. 636.**

Selecting the Windows Home Server Region

In Windows Home Server, you can specify the region you're in. This determines how Windows Home Server formats data such as numbers, currency values, dates, and times. For example, depending on the region, Windows Home Server would display August 7, 2010 in the short date format as 8/7/2010 or as 7/8/2010.

Changing the Region in the Windows Home Server Console

Here are the steps to follow to use the Windows Home Server Console to change the current region setting:

1. Launch the Windows Home Server Console.

2. Click Settings to open the Windows Home Server Settings dialog box.

3. In the General tab, use the Region list to select the region and the language within that region.

4. Click OK to put the new setting into effect.

Customizing the Region Formats

The Windows Home Server Console only enables you to switch from one region setting to another. However, you might need to customize a particular region's formats. For example, you may select a region where the short date format is d/m/yyyy but you'd rather use m/d/yyyy. Windows Home Server enables you to customize the format not only of dates, but also of times, numbers, and currency values. Follow these steps:

1. Log in to the Windows Home Server machine and select Start, Control Panel, Regional and Language Options. Windows Home Server displays the Regional and Language Options dialog box.

2. In the Regional Options tab, use the list in the Standards and Formats group to select a region and language, if you want something other than the displayed value.

3. Click Customize. Windows Home Server displays the Customize Regional Options dialog box, shown in Figure 4.6.

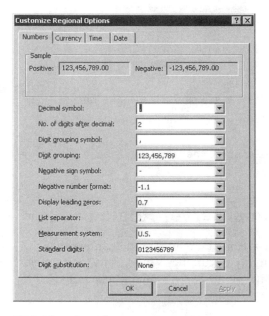

FIGURE 4.6   Use the Customize Regional Options dialog box to set up custom formats for numbers, currency values, dates, and times.

4. Use the lists in the Numbers tab to customize how Windows Home Server displays numeric values.

5. Use the lists in the Currency tab to customize how Windows Home Server displays monetary values.

6. Use the lists in the Time tab to customize how Windows Home Server displays time values.

7. Use the lists in the Date tab to customize how Windows Home Server displays date values.

8. Click OK to return to the Regional and Language Options dialog box.

9. Click OK to put the new settings into effect.

Configuring Windows Update

Windows Update is a feature that keeps Windows Home Server up-to-date by offering power packs, operating system fixes, security patches, enhancements, and new features for download. You can check for new updates at any time by selecting Start, All Programs, Windows Update to load the Microsoft Windows Update website into the browser.

Rather than you remembering to check for updates and then trying to figure out which ones to download and install, Windows Home Server offers the Automatic Updates feature. This takes the guesswork out of updating the server by automatically checking to see whether updates are available, downloading those that are, and then installing them, all without intervention on your part. The next few sections show you how to configure Windows Update and Automatic Updates and how to check for updates from within Windows Home Server.

Configuring Windows Update via the Windows Home Server Console

When you first started Windows Home Server, the OOBE program asked you to choose a Windows Update setting. If you want to change that setting, you can do it using the Windows Home Server Console, as described in the following steps:

1. Launch the Windows Home Server Console.

2. Click Settings to open the Windows Home Server Settings dialog box.

3. In the General tab, click one of the following options:

   ▸ **On**—Click this option to enable the Automatic Updates feature.

   ▸ **Off**—Click this option to prevent Windows Home Server from checking for new updates.

4. Click OK to put the new setting into effect.

CAUTION

I strongly recommend that you *not* choose to turn Windows Update off. All recent versions of Windows have been plagued with security vulnerabilities, and Windows Home Server (or, more accurately in this case, Windows Server 2003, which underlies Windows Home Server) isn't an exception. You need to keep your server updated to avoid having your system—and, almost certainly, your entire home network—compromised or damaged by malicious hackers.

Configuring Windows Update via the Automatic Updates Control Panel

The Windows Home Server Console only gives you two choices for the Automatic Updates feature: on or off. If this all-or-nothing choice seems too restrictive, you can give yourself more choices by accessing the server and using the Control Panel's Automatic Updates icon. Here are the steps to follow:

1. Log in to the server and select Start, Control Panel, Automatic Updates. Windows Home Server displays the Automatic Updates dialog box, shown in Figure 4.7.

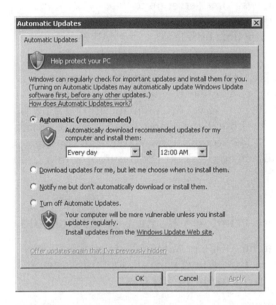

FIGURE 4.7   Use the Automatic Updates dialog box to configure Windows Home Server's automatic updating.

NOTE

The Automatic Updates options are also available in the System Properties dialog box. A quick way to get there is to select Start, Run to open the Run dialog box, type `control sysdm.cpl,,4`, and then click OK.

---

2. Activate one of the following options to determine how Windows Home Server performs the updating:

   ▶ **Automatic**—This option tells Windows Home Server to download and install updates automatically. Windows Home Server checks for new updates on the date (such as Every Day or Every Sunday) and time you specify. For example, you might prefer to choose a time when you won't be using your computer.

CAUTION

Some updates require your server to be rebooted to put them into effect. In such cases, if you activate the Automatic option, Windows Home Server automatically reboots your system. This might lead to problems if you have a particular program that you need to be running at all times. You can work around this problem by setting up an automatic logon and by setting up the program to run automatically at startup. (Refer to "Launching Applications and Scripts at Startup," later in this chapter.)

▶ **SEE** To learn how to set up an automatic logon, **see** "Automating Client Logons," **P. 47.**

- ▶ **Download Updates for Me, but Let Me Choose When to Install Them—** If you activate this option, Windows Home Server checks for new updates and then automatically downloads any updates that are available. Windows Home Server then displays an icon in the notification area to let you know that the updates are ready to install. Click the icon to see the list of updates. If you see an update that you don't want to install, deactivate its check box. Click Install to install the selected updates.

- ▶ **Notify Me but Don't Automatically Download or Install Them—**If you activate this option, Windows Home Server checks for new updates and then, if any are available, displays an icon in the notification area to let you know that the updates are ready to download. Click the icon to see the list of updates. If you see an update that you don't want to download, deactivate its check box. Click Start Download to initiate the download. When the download is complete, Windows Home Server displays an icon in the notification area to let you know that the updates are ready to install. Click the icon and then click Install to install the updates.

- ▶ **Turn Off Automatic Updates—**Activate this option to prevent Windows Home Server from checking for new updates.

   3. Click OK to put the new setting into effect.

Updating Windows Home Server

If you elected not to use automatic updating, you need to watch out for available updates and install the ones you want by hand. How do you watch for updates? The easiest method is to watch the Network status icon in the Windows Home Server Console. When updates are ready for download, that icon reads Critical. On a client machine, you can also monitor the Windows Home Server Tray icon in the notification area, which turns red when the network status is critical.

You then have two choices in Windows Home Server Console, as follows:

▶ Click the Network status icon to open the Home Network Health dialog box, shown in Figure 4.8. If you see an item that says Windows Home Server Updates Are Ready, click Install Updates.

FIGURE 4.8   If updates are available, you can install them via the Home Network Health dialog box.

▶ Click Settings to open the Windows Home Server Settings dialog box, and then, in the General tab, click Update Now.

Windows Home Server then downloads and installs the updates.

Changing the Windows Home Server Password

The Windows Home Server password—that is, the password associated with the Administrator account—must be strong, which means it must be at least seven characters, and those characters must come from three out of the following four sets: lowercase letters, uppercase letters, numbers, and symbols. This means that Windows Home Server passwords are quite secure. However, you may still feel that you could make the password even more secure by making it longer or by including characters from all four sets. Similarly, you might want to enhance security by changing the password regularly, as security experts urge us to do. Either way, here are the steps to follow to change the password using the Windows Home Server Console:

1. Launch the Windows Home Server Console.
2. Click Settings to open the Windows Home Server Settings dialog box.
3. Display the Passwords tab.
4. Click Change Password to display the Windows Home Server Password Change dialog box.
5. Type the new password in the Password and Confirm Password text boxes.
6. Edit the password hint, as necessary.
7. Click OK to put the new password into effect. Windows Home Server tells you that the password has been changed.
8. Click OK to return to the Windows Home Server Settings dialog box.
9. Click OK.

TIP

If you just want to change the password hint, follow the steps in this section, but enter the current password in the Password and Confirm Password text boxes. Then enter the new hint in the Password Hint text box. Alternatively, you can edit the hint via the Registry Editor. Log on to the server and select Start, Run to open the Run dialog box, type **regedit**, and click OK. In the Registry Editor, open the following key: HKLM\ Software\Microsoft\Windows Home Server\install. Double-click the PasswordHint setting, type the new hint, and then click OK.

Restarting or Shutting Down Windows Home Server

The Windows Home Server is meant to run as an always-on appliance that should rarely need to be restarted or shut down. However, if you find that Windows Home Server is performing sluggishly or is acting flaky, the standard Windows troubleshooting advice— reboot the machine!—might be in order. Similarly, if you need to add an internal circuit board or hard drive, or if you'll be going on vacation for an extended time, you need to shut down the server.

If you're logged on to the Windows Home Server, you can use the normal Windows technique of selecting Start, Shut Down to display the Shut Down Windows dialog box, choosing Restart or Shut Down in the list, and then clicking OK.

If you're on a client, you can restart or shut down the server remotely using the Windows Home Server Console. Here are the steps to follow:

1. Launch the Windows Home Server Console.
2. Click Settings to open the Windows Home Server Settings dialog box.
3. Click Shut Down.
4. Click either Restart or Shut Down.

TIP

On the client machine, you probably want to know when Windows Home Server restarts. One way to do this is to select Start, All Programs, Command Prompt to open a command prompt session. Enter the following command (replace the IP address shown with the IP address of the server):

`ping 192.168.1.254 -t.`

This tells Windows to repeatedly ping the server's IP address. While the server is restarting, Windows will display the following result for each ping:

`Request timed out.`

When the server is back up and running, you'll know because the ping result will change to something like the following:

`Reply from 192.168.1.254: bytes=32 time=1ms TTL=128`

Press Ctrl+C to stop the pinging.

Configuring an Uninterruptible Power Supply

Windows Home Server is a crucial component in your home network, so you want to protect it (and its precious contents) as much as possible. For example, as with any computer, you never want to shut off the server without going through the proper interface channels (that is, by first selecting Start, Shut Down on the server, or by using the Windows Home Server Console's Shut Down button, as explained in the previous section).

Unfortunately, power failures happen, so despite your best efforts, the Windows Home Server may get shut off abruptly. To avoid this fate, it's a good idea to run the server off an uninterruptible power supply (UPS), which provides battery-based backup power should the AC suddenly disappear. Depending on the battery capacity of the UPS and the number of devices attached to it, this gives you a few minutes or more to shut down the server properly.

The better UPS devices come with monitoring software that enables you to view the current status of the UPS, warn you when a power failure has occurred, and let you know how much time you have to shut down the devices attached to the UPS. For this software to work properly, you need to run a monitoring cable (use the cable that came with the UPS or is available from the manufacturer) from the UPS to a USB or serial port on the computer.

If you don't have a UPS monitoring program, or if the program that came with your UPS isn't compatible with Windows Home Server, you may still be able to monitor the UPS and receive power failure alerts. Windows Home Server's Power Options come with a UPS feature that enables you to connect and monitor a UPS connected to your computer. Here are the steps to follow to configure the UPS monitor:

1. Log in to the server and select Start, Control Panel, Power Options to open the Power Options Properties dialog box.
2. Display the UPS tab.
3. In the Details group, click Select to open the UPS Selection dialog box.
4. In the Select Manufacturer list, choose either American Power Conversion or Generic.
5. If you chose American Power Conversion in step 4, use the Select Model list (see Figure 4.9) to choose the UPS model you're using.

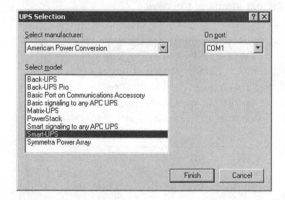

FIGURE 4.9   Use the UPS Selection dialog box to tell Windows Home Server what type of uninterruptible power supply is connected to the server.

6. Use the On Port list to select the server port that you're using to connect to the UPS.
7. Click Finish.
8. Click OK.

Windows Home Server establishes a link to the UPS over the port and then displays the current status of the UPS (such as the estimated UPS runtime should the power fail) in the UPS tab (see Figure 4.10).

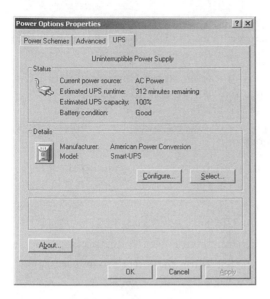

FIGURE 4.10 With a connection established between Windows Home Server and the uninter-ruptible power supply, the UPS tab shows the current status of the device.

NOTE

If the UPS tab tells you that the Uninterruptible Power Supply service is not started, select Start, Control Panel, Administrative Tools, Services. In the list of services, click Uninterruptible Power Supply and then click the Start link. To ensure this service starts automatically in the future, double-click the service, use the Startup Type list to select Automatic, and then click OK.

If you want to customize the UPS, click the Configure button to display the UPS Configuration dialog box, shown in Figure 4.11.

You have the following options:

- ▶ **Enable All Notifications**—Leave this check box activated to have Windows Home Server alert you when the power fails. You can use the two spin boxes to set when the alerts appear: the number of seconds after the power failure for the first alert, and the number of seconds between subsequent alerts.

- ▶ **Minutes on Battery Before Critical Alarm**—Activate this check box to have Windows Home Server display a critical alarm after the UPS has been on battery power for the number of minutes you specify. (If you leave this check box deacti-vated, Windows Home Server displays the critical alarm when it detects that the UPS battery power is almost used up.)

- ▶ **When the Alarm Occurs, Run This Program**—Activate this check box and then click Configure to set up a program to run after the critical alarm occurs.

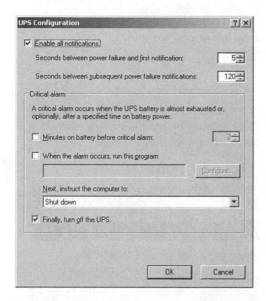

FIGURE 4.11   Use the UPS Configuration dialog box to customize how Windows Home Server interacts with the UPS.

▶ **Next, Instruct the Computer To**—Use this list to specify what you want the server to do after the critical alarm occurs (and after the program you specified in the previous item runs). In Windows Home Server, the only choice here is Shut Down.

▶ **Finally, Turn Off the UPS**—Leave this check box activated to also have the UPS turned off if a critical alarm occurs.

Configuring the Windows Home Server Startup

One day, not long after I installed a prerelease version of Windows Home Server, I also installed a screen capture program so that I could capture some screen shots for this book. Unfortunately, the Windows Home Server beta and that screen capture program did *not* get along. The machine crashed, and I mean *hard*: It wouldn't boot into Windows Home Server, nor would it boot to the Windows Home Server DVD or to *any* bootable medium I added to the machine. The server was simply dead in the water.

Fortunately, I know a few startup tricks, and I was able to use one of those tricks to get the machine back on its feet. (Hint: I ran a startup command called Last Known Good Configuration, which I'll tell you about shortly.) I hope you never have any serious (or even minor) startup problems with your Windows Home Server machine. However, just in case you do, there are a few startup tips and techniques you should know about.

The next few sections take you through the most important of these startup tricks, and they involve two components used in the Windows Home Server startup:

▶ **BOOT.INI**—This is a text file that contains some Windows Home Server startup options. You can edit this file to modify the way Windows Home Server starts up.

▶ **Advanced Options menu**—This is a menu of startup commands that you can invoke to load Windows Home Server with different configurations.

Editing BOOT.INI Directly

BOOT.INI is a hidden text file that resides in the root folder of your system's bootable partition. (On Windows Home Server systems, this is always drive C.) Before you work with this file, you need to tell Windows Home Server to display hidden files:

1. Log on to the server and then select Start, Windows Explorer.
2. Select Tools, Folder Options to display the Folder Options dialog box.

TIP

You can also display the Folder Options dialog box by selecting Start, Control Panel, Folder Options.

---

3. Display the View tab.
4. Click to deactivate the Hide Protected Operating System files check box. Windows Home Server asks you to confirm the change.
5. Click Yes.
6. Make sure the Show Hidden Files and Folders option is activated (as it is by default in Windows Home Server).
7. Click OK.

You can now run Windows Explorer and display the C:\ folder. Double-click the BOOT.INI icon to open the file. (Alternatively, select Start, Run, type **c:\boot.ini**, and click OK.)

Windows Home Server loads the file into Notepad, and you see text similar to the following:

```
[boot loader]
timeout=30
default=multi(0)disk(0)rdisk(0)partition(1)\WINDOWS
[operating systems]
multi(0)disk(0)rdisk(0)partition(1)\WINDOWS="Windows Server 2003 For Small
➥Business Server" /noexecute=optout /fastdetect
```

There are two sections in BOOT.INI: [boot loader] and [operating systems]. The [boot loader] section always has two values:

▶ timeout—This value determines the number of seconds after which NTLDR boots the operating system that's highlighted in the menu by default.

▶ default—This value determines which item listed in the [operating systems] section is loaded by default at startup.

The [operating systems] section lists the operating systems to which the system can boot. (In Windows Home Server setups, there is always just one operating system listed.) The Windows Home Server line has a strange configuration, to say the least. The part up to the equal sign (=) is called an Advanced RISC Computer (ARC) pathname, and its purpose is to let a startup program called NT Loader know how to find the Windows Home Server kernel.

Let's run through the various parts so you understand what you're seeing:

NOTE

%SystemRoot% refers to the folder into which Windows Home Server was installed, which is C:\Windows.

---

multi(*n*)	This is a reference to the drive controller that's used to access the Windows Home Server installation. The value *n* is 0 for the first controller, 1 for the second, and so on. On systems that use a SCSI controller, you might see scsi(*n*) instead of multi(*n*). (The exception is on systems that have the SCSI BIOS disabled.)
disk(*n*)	This is a reference to the SCSI ID of the device on which Windows Home Server is installed. For multi devices, the value of *n* is always 0.
rdisk(*n*)	This is a reference to the hard disk on which Windows Home Server is installed. This disk is attached to the controller specified by multi(*n*). The value of *n* is 0 for the first hard disk, 1 for the second hard disk, and so on.
partition(*n*)	This is a reference to the partition on which Windows Home Server is installed. This partition is part of the disk specified by rdisk(*n*).
WINDOWS	This is the name of the folder into which Windows Home Server was installed.

You also see a couple of switches—/noexecute and /fastdetect—that set a couple of startup parameters. The ARC pathname syntax supports more than 30 different switches that enable you to control various aspects of the Windows Home Server startup. Here's a summary of the switches that are most useful:

/basevideo   Boots Windows Home Server using the standard VGA mode: 640×480 with 256 colors. This is useful for troubleshooting video display driver problems. Use this switch if Windows Home Server fails to start using any of the safe mode options, if you recently installed a new video card device driver and the screen is garbled or the driver is balking at a resolution or color depth setting that's too high, or if you can't load the Windows Home Server GUI. After Windows Home Server has loaded, you can reinstall or roll back the driver, or you can adjust the display settings to values that the driver can handle.

/bootlog   Boots Windows Home Server and logs the boot process to a text file named NTBTLOG.TXT that resides in the %SystemRoot% folder. Move to the end of the file, and you might see a message telling you which device driver failed. You probably need to rein-stall or roll back the driver. Use this switch if the Windows Home Server startup hangs, if you need a detailed record of the startup process, or if you suspect (after using one of the other Startup menu options) that a driver is causing Windows Home Server startup to fail.

/debug   Enables remote debugging of the Windows Home Server kernel. This sends debugging information to a remote computer via one of your computer's serial ports. If you use this switch, you can specify the serial port by also using the \debugport=port switch, where port is one of com1, com2, com3, com4, or 1394. If you use a COM port, you can specify the transmission speed of the debugging information by also using the \baudrate= speed switch, where speed is one of the following: 300, 1200, 2400, 4800, 9600, 19200, 38400, 57600, or 115200. If you use an IEEE 1394 (FireWire) connection, you can also add the /channel=number switch, where number is a channel value between 1 and 62.

/fastdetect   Tells Windows Home Server not to enumerate the system's serial and parallel ports during startup. These ports aren't needed during the boot process, so this reduces the system startup time.

/maxmem=MB   Specifies the maximum amount of memory, in megabytes, that Windows Home Server can use. Use this value when you suspect a faulty memory chip might be causing problems.

/noexecute =level   Sets the *Data Execution Prevention* (*DEP*) policy level. DEP prevents malicious code from executing in protected memory locations. There are four levels, as follows:

OptIn—Windows system programs are protected by DEP, as well as any applications that have been programmed to take advantage of (opt into) DEP protection.

OptOut—Provides DEP protection for the entire system, except for programs that have been specified not to use (opt out of) DEP.

AlwaysOn—Provides DEP protection for the entire system.

AlwaysOff—Provides no DEP protection for the system.

NOTE

If you think that DEP isn't something to worry about, I have a tale of woe (and embarrassment) to relate. Remember that nasty screen capture program that crashed my Windows Home Server machine? After installing it, Windows Home Server displayed a message telling me that the program was a potential DEP hazard and that it had disabled the program. It also gave me an option to opt the program out of DEP protection and, somewhat densely, I did just that. The major crash that followed taught me a valuable lesson on just how important it is to respect an OS when it tells you that a program is a potential DEP problem.

`/noguiboot`	Tells Windows Home Server not to load the VGA display driver that is normally used to display the progress bar during startup. Use this switch if Windows Home Server hangs while switching video modes for the progress bar, or if the display of the progress bar is garbled.
`/numproc=`*n*	In a multiprocessor (or multicore) system, specifies the maximum number of processors that Windows Home Server can use. Use this switch if you suspect that using multiple processors is causing a program to hang.
`/pcilock`	Tells Windows Home Server not to dynamically assign hardware resources for PCI devices during startup. The resources assigned by the BIOS during the POST are locked in place. Use this switch if installing a PCI device causes the system to hang during startup.
`/safeboot:minimal`	Boots Windows Home Server in *safe mode*, which uses only a minimal set of device drivers. Use this switch if Windows Home Server won't start, if a device or program is causing Windows Home Server to crash, or if you can't uninstall a program while Windows Home Server is running normally.
`/safeboot:minimal` `(alternateshell)`	Boots Windows Home Server in safe mode but also bypasses the Windows Home Server GUI and boots to the command prompt instead. Use this switch if the programs you need to repair a problem can be run from the command prompt or if you can't load the Windows Home Server GUI.

NOTE

The shell loaded by the `/safeboot:minimal(alternateshell)` switch is determined by the value in the following Registry key:

`HKLM\SYSTEM\CurrentControlSet\Control\SafeBoot\AlternateShell`

The default value is `CMD.EXE` (the command prompt).

`/safeboot:network`	Boots Windows Home Server in safe mode but also includes networking drivers. Use this switch if the drivers or programs you need to repair a problem exist on a shared network resource, if you need access to email or other network-based communications for technical support, or if your computer is running a shared Windows Home Server installation.
`/safeboot:dsrepair`	This option applies only to domain controllers, so you won't use it with Windows Home Server. It boots the OS in safe mode and restores a backup of the Active Directory service.
`/sos`	Displays the path and location of each device driver (using the ARC pathname syntax) as it is loaded, as well as the operating system version and build number and the number of processors.

Using the System Configuration Editor to Modify BOOT.INI

Rather than edit the BOOT.INI file directly, you can modify the file indirectly by using the System Configuration Editor. To start this program, log on to the server, select Start, Run, type **msconfig** in the Run dialog box, and then click OK. When the System Configuration Window appears, select the BOOT.INI tab, shown in Figure 4.12.

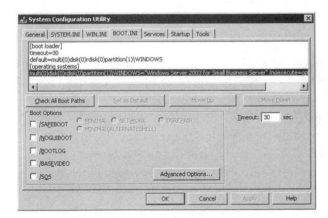

FIGURE 4.12   In the System Configuration Utility, use the BOOT.INI tab to modify the BOOT.INI startup file.

The large box near the top of the tab displays the current BOOT.INI text. You can't edit this text directly, however. All you can do is use the check boxes in the Boot Options. You can add other switches (such as /maxmem and /debug) by clicking the Advanced Options button, which takes you to the BOOT.INI Advanced Options dialog box shown in Figure 4.13.

FIGURE 4.13   In the BOOT.INI tab, click Advanced Options to display the dialog box shown here.

TIP

If you modify BOOT.INI using the System Configuration Utility, Windows Home Server maintains a copy of the original BOOT.INI. If you want to revert to that copy, display the General tab in the System Configuration Utility and activate the Use Original BOOT.INI option. If you need to use the edited version of BOOT.INI again, activate the Use Modified BOOT.INI option instead.

Configuring Startup with the Advanced Options Menu

After you start your computer, wait until the Power On Self Test (POST) is complete (this is usually signaled by a beep), and then press F8 to display the Advanced Options menu. (If your computer is set up to "fast boot," it might not be obvious when the POST ends. In that case, just turn on your computer and press F8 repeatedly until you see the Advanced Options menu.) Here's the menu you see:

```
Windows Advanced Options Menu
Please select an option:

    Safe Mode
    Safe Mode with Networking
    Safe Mode with Command Prompt

    Enable Boot Logging
    Enable VGA Mode
    Last Known Good Configuration (your most recent settings that worked)
    Directory Services Restore Mode (Windows domain controllers only)
    Debugging Mode
```

```
Disable automatic restart on system failure

Start Windows Normally
Reboot
```

Use the up and down arrow keys to move the highlight to your choice.

The Start Windows Normally option loads Windows Home Server in the usual fashion. You can use the other options to control the rest of the startup procedure:

▶ **SEE** To learn how to use the Advanced Options menu to troubleshoot startup woes, **see** "Troubleshooting Startup," **P. 513.**

▶ **Safe Mode**—If you're having trouble with Windows Home Server—for example, if a corrupt or incorrect video driver is mangling your display, or if Windows Home Server won't start—you can use the Safe Mode option to run a stripped-down version of Windows Home Server that includes only the minimal set of device drivers that Home Server requires to load. You could reinstall or roll back the offending device driver and then load Home Server normally. When Windows Home Server finally loads, the desktop reminds you that you're in Safe mode by displaying Safe Mode in each corner. Choosing the Safe Mode option is the same as using the following BOOT.INI switches:

```
/safeboot:minimal /bootlog /noguiboot /sos
```

NOTE

If you're curious to know which drivers are loaded during a Safe mode boot, see the subkeys in the following Registry key:

HKLM\SYSTEM\CurrentControlSet\Control\SafeBoot\Minimal\

▶ **Safe Mode with Networking**—This option is identical to plain Safe mode, except that Windows Home Server's networking drivers are also loaded at startup. This enables you to log on to your network, which is handy if you need to access the network to load a device driver, run a troubleshooting utility, or send a tech support request. Choosing this option is the same as using the following BOOT.INI switches:

```
/safeboot:network /bootlog /noguiboot /sos
```

▶ **Safe Mode with Command Prompt**—This option is the same as plain Safe mode, except that it doesn't load the Windows Home Server GUI. Instead, it runs CMD.EXE to load a command prompt session. Choosing this option is the same as using the following BOOT.INI switches:

```
/safeboot:minimal(alternateshell) /bootlog /noguiboot /sos
```

▶ **Enable Boot Logging**—This option is the same as the Boot Normally option, except that Windows Home Server logs the boot process in a text file named NTBTLOG.TXT that resides in the system root. Choosing this option is the same as using the following BOOT.INI switch:

`/bootlog`

▶ **Enable VGA Mode**—This option loads Windows Home Server with the video display set to 640×480 and 256 colors. Choosing this option is the same as using the following BOOT.INI switch:

`/basevideo`

▶ **Last Known Good Configuration**—This option boots Windows Home Server using the last hardware configuration that produced a successful boot. This is the option I used to get my Windows Home Server machine back on its feet after it was cut off at the knees by the screen capture program.

▶ **Directory Services Restore Mode**—This option is the same as using the following BOOT.INI switch:

`/safeboot:dsrepair`

▶ **Debugging Mode**—This option is the same as using the following BOOT.INI switch:

`/debug`

▶ **Disable Automatic Restart on System Failure**—This option prevents Windows Home Server from restarting automatically when the system crashes. Choose this option if you want to prevent your system from restarting so that you can troubleshoot the problem.

▶ **Boot Normally**—This options loads Windows Home Server normally.

▶ **Reboot**—This option reboots the computer.

TIP

For those advanced options that have equivalent BOOT.INI switches, you can use those switches to place individual advanced options choices on the OS Choices menu. You do this by adding an item to BOOT.INI's [operating systems] section that starts Windows Home Server with the appropriate switches. For example, to add an option to the OS Choices menu to start Windows Home Server in Safe mode, you'd add the following to BOOT.INI's [operating systems] section:

`multi(0)disk(0)rdisk(0)partition(1)\WINDOWS="Safe Mode" /safeboot:minimal /bootlog /noguiboot /sos`

Launching Applications and Scripts at Startup

Two key features of Windows Home Server are that it's always on and that it's always available to computers and devices on the network. Many people take advantage of these features to run programs and scripts on the server. For example, one common Windows Home Server application is a home automation system. Another is a program that sends random images to a digital photo frame.

Because you want these and similar programs to be always running, you can save yourself the hassle of launching these programs manually by getting Windows Home Server to do it for you automatically at startup. Similarly, you can also get Windows Home Server to automatically launch scripts or batch files at startup. As the next few sections show, you can set up a program or script for automatic startup launch using the Startup folder, the Registry, the Group Policy snap-in, and the Scheduled Tasks folder.

Launching Items Using the Startup Folder

The Startup folder is a regular file folder, but it has a special place in Windows Home Server. You can get a program or script to run automatically at startup by adding a shortcut for that item to the Startup folder. (Adding shortcuts to the Startup folder is part of the Start menu customizations that I discuss in more detail in Chapter 16, "Customizing the Windows Home Server Interface.")

Note that the Startup folder appears twice in the Windows Home Server interface:

> ▶ **SEE** To learn how to modify the Windows Home Server Start menu, **see** "Making the Start Menu More Efficient," **P. 460.**

- ▶ Via the Start menu. (Click Start, All Programs, Startup.)

- ▶ Via Windows Explorer as a subfolder in `%SystemDrive%:\Documents and Settings`. Actually, there are three different subfolders you can work with, as follows:

    - ▶ `\user\Start Menu\Programs\Startup`—Here, *user* is the name of a user defined on the system, which in Windows Home Server will almost always be Administrator. A shortcut placed in this folder runs automatically when this user logs on to the system.

    - ▶ `\All Users\Start Menu\Programs\Startup`—A shortcut placed in this folder runs automatically when any user logs on to the system.

    - ▶ `\Default User\Start Menu\Programs\Startup`—A shortcut placed in this folder (which is normally hidden) is automatically copied to a user's Startup folder when you create a new user account.

Note that only users who have Administrator-level rights can access all three of these subfolders. Users with lesser privileges can work only with their own Startup folder. They can see the All Users version of the Startup folder, but Windows Home Server prevents them from adding files to it.

TIP

You can prevent the Startup items from running by holding down the Shift key while Windows Home Server loads. (Hold down Shift after logging on.)

Launching Items Using the Registry

The Startup folder method has two drawbacks: Users can easily delete shortcuts from their own Startup folders, and users can bypass Startup items by holding down the Shift key while Windows Home Server loads. These aren't likely to be major problems on Windows Home Server because you'll probably only ever log on with the Administrator account. However, should the need arise, you can work around both problems by using the Registry Editor to define your startup items.

Assuming that you're logged in as the user you want to work with, the Registry offers two keys:

▶ HKCU\Software\Microsoft\Windows\CurrentVersion\Run—The values in this key run automatically each time the user logs on.

▶ HKCU\Software\Microsoft\Windows\CurrentVersion\RunOnce—The values in this key run only the next time the user logs on; then they are deleted from the key. (This key might not be present in your Registry. In that case, you need to add this key yourself.)

If you want an item to run at startup no matter who logs on, use the following keys:

▶ HKLM\Software\Microsoft\Windows\CurrentVersion\Run—The values in this key run automatically each time any user logs on.

▶ HKLM\Software\Microsoft\Windows\CurrentVersion\RunOnce—The values in this key run only the next time any user logs on; then they are deleted from the key. Don't confuse this key with the RunOnceEx key. RunOnceEx is an extended version of RunOnce that developers use to create more robust startup items that include features such as error handling and improved performance.

To create a startup item, add a string value to the appropriate key, give it whatever name you like, and then set its value to the full pathname of the executable file or script file that you want to launch at startup.

CAUTION

Placing the same startup item in both the HKCU and the HKLM hives results in that item being started twice: once during the initial boot and again at logon.

TIP

If the program is in the %SystemRoot% folder, you can get away with entering only the name of the executable file. Also, if the program you want to run at startup is capable of running in the background, you can load it in this mode by appending /background after the pathname.

Launching Items Using Group Policies

If you prefer not to edit the Registry directly, or if you want to place a GUI between you and the Registry, Windows Home Server's Group Policy snap-in can help. Note, however, that Group Policy doesn't work directly with the Run keys in the HKLM and HKCU hives. Instead, these are considered to be *legacy keys*, meaning they're mostly used by older programs. The new keys (new as of Windows 2000, that is) are the following:

```
HKLM\Software\Microsoft\Windows\CurrentVersion\policies\Explorer\Run
HKCU\Software\Microsoft\Windows\CurrentVersion\Policies\Explorer\Run
```

These keys do not appear in Windows Home Server by default. You see them only after you specify startup programs in the Group Policy editor, as discussed in the next section. Alternatively, you can add these keys yourself using the Registry Editor.

NOTE

The startup items run in the following order:

```
HKLM\Software\Microsoft\Windows\CurrentVersion\RunOnce
```

```
HKLM\Software\Microsoft\Windows\CurrentVersion\policies\Explorer\Run
```

```
HKLM\Software\Microsoft\Windows\CurrentVersion\Run
```

```
HKCU\Software\Microsoft\Windows\CurrentVersion\Run
```

```
HKCU\Software\Microsoft\Windows\CurrentVersion\Policies\Explorer\Run
```

```
HKCU\Software\Microsoft\Windows\CurrentVersion\RunOnce
```

Startup folder (all users)

Startup folder (current user).

Adding Programs to the Run Keys

As mentioned, you can either add values to these keys via the Registry Editor, or you can use the Group Policy snap-in. To open the Group Policy window in Windows Home Server, select Start, Run, type **gpedit.msc**, and then click OK. In the Group Policy window, you have two choices:

▶ To work with startup programs for all users, select Computer Configuration, Administrative Templates, System, Logon. The items here affect the Registry keys in the HKLM (all users) Registry hive.

▶ To work with startup programs for the current user, select User Configuration, Administrative Templates, System, Logon. The items here affect the Registry keys in the HKCU (current user) hive.

Either way, you see at least the following three items:

▶ **Run These Programs at User Logon**—Use this item to add or remove startup programs using the \Policies\Explorer\Run keys in the Registry. To add a program, double-click the item, select the Enabled option, and then click Show. In the Show Contents dialog box, click Add, enter the full pathname of the program or script you want to run at startup, and then click OK.

▶ **Do Not Process the Run Once List**—Use this item to toggle whether Windows Home Server processes the RunOnce Registry keys (which I discussed in the previous section). Double-click this item and then activate the Enabled option to put this policy into effect; that is, programs listed in the RunOnce key are not launched at startup.

▶ **Do Not Process the Legacy Run List**—Use this item to toggle whether Windows Home Server processes the legacy Run keys. Double-click this item and then activate the Enabled option to put this policy into effect; that is, programs listed in the legacy Run key are not launched at startup.

Specifying Startup and Logon Scripts

You also can use the Group Policy snap-in to specify script files to run at startup. You can specify script files at two places, as follows:

▶ **Computer Configuration, Windows Settings, Scripts (Startup/Shutdown)**— Use the Startup item to specify one or more script files to run each time the computer starts (and before the user logs on). Note that if you specify two or more scripts, Windows Home Server runs them synchronously. That is, Windows Home Server runs the first script, waits for it to finish, runs the second script, waits for it to finish, and so on.

▶ **User Configuration, Windows Settings, Scripts (Logon/Logoff)**—Use the Logon item to specify one or more script files to run each time any user logs on. Logon scripts are run asynchronously.

Finally, note that Windows Home Server has policies dictating how these scripts run. For example, you can see the startup script policies by selecting Computer Configuration, Administrative Templates, System, Scripts. Three items affect startup scripts:

▶ **Run Logon Scripts Synchronously**—If you enable this item, Windows Home Server runs the logon scripts one at a time.

▶ **Run Startup Scripts Asynchronously**—If you enable this item, Windows Home Server runs the startup scripts at the same time.

▶ **Run Startup Scripts Visible**—If you enable this item, Windows Home Server makes the startup script commands visible to the user in a command window.

For logon scripts, a similar set of policies appears in the User Configuration, Administrative Templates, System, Scripts section.

CAUTION

Logon scripts are supposed to execute before the Windows Home Server interface is displayed to the user. However, Windows Home Server's new Fast Logon Optimization can interfere with that by displaying the interface before all the scripts are done. The Fast Logon Optimization feature runs both the computer logon scripts and the user logon scripts asynchronously, which greatly speeds up the logon time since no script has to wait for another to finish.

To prevent this, select Computer Configuration, Administrative Templates, System, Logon and enable the Always Wait for the Network at Computer Startup and Logon setting.

Using the Scheduled Tasks Folder

Yet another way to set up a program or script to run at startup is to use the Scheduled Tasks folder. (Select Start, All Programs, Accessories, System Tools, Scheduled Tasks, or use Windows Explorer to display the `%SystemRoot%\Tasks` folder.) When you create a new task, two of the startup options you'll see are the following:

- ▶ **When My Computer Starts**—Choose this option to run the program when your computer boots, no matter which user logs in. Note that only someone logged in under the Administrator account can use this option. The tasks run otherwise, but they don't display.

- ▶ **When I Log On**—Choose this option to run the program only when you log on to Windows Home Server. This is the option to use for accounts other than Administrator.

From Here

- ▶ To learn how to set up an automatic logon, **see** "Automating Client Logons," **P. 47**.

- ▶ For details on running the Connector software, **see** "Installing Windows Home Server Connector on the Client Computers," **P. 63**.

- ▶ For tweaks that customize Windows Home Server's look and feel, **see** Chapter 16, "Customizing the Windows Home Server Interface."

- ▶ To learn how to use the Advanced Options menu to troubleshoot startup woes, **see** "Troubleshooting Startup," **P. 513**.

- ▶ For details on the Registry and using the Registry Editor, **see** Chapter 18, "Working with the Windows Home Server Registry."

- ▶ For more information on the Services snap-in, **see** "Controlling Services with the Services Snap-In," **P. 636**.

- ▶ To learn more about WMI scripting, **see** "Programming the Windows Management Instrumentation Service," **P. 688**.

Setting Up and Using Home Server Storage

Windows Home Server offers the home network a wide range of capabilities that include monitoring the health of network PCs (for example, detecting whether the clients have their firewalls turned on), establishing a central fax server, and enabling remote access to any computer from outside the network. I'll go into all of these features in a satisfying amount of detail later in the book. However, just about every other Windows Home Server feature is related to storage: shared folders, media streaming, centralized backup and restore, data duplication, an expandable data pool, and backups of the home server itself. In other words, it's no stretch to say that storage is at the heart of Windows Home Server and is the source of much of what makes Windows Home Server such a useful package.

With that in mind, this chapter takes you on a complete tour of all the Windows Home Server storage features. You learn some background on the technologies behind Windows Home Server storage, and you learn techniques such as adding, configuring, and removing storage, turning on folder duplication, repairing storage, and much more.

Understanding Windows Home Server Storage

When the Windows Home Server developers and designers were putting together the storage portion of the new operating system, it appears that they asked themselves three fundamental questions:

▶ How can we simplify storage management?

▶ How can we make storage more flexible?

▶ How can we ensure that the data on the server is always safe?

The next three sections show you how the Windows Home Server team answered these questions.

Simplicity: Saying Goodbye to Drive Letters

In other versions of Windows, storage is a complex bit of business because drive letters tend to proliferate. Each hard drive gets its own drive letter, and it's not unusual to split a drive into two or more partitions, each of which usually gets its own drive letter. Add an external hard drive, and there goes *another* drive letter. Throw in removable media devices such as USB floppy drives, DVD drives, USB flash drives, and multiport memory card readers, toss in a few mapped network drives, and you soon find yourself eyeballing the 26-letter limit.

The sheer number of drive letters is bad enough to keep track of, but then you actually have to find the data you want among all those drives. It's complicated, and it gets worse every year as hardware manufacturers pump out more devices for storing our data.

Windows Home Server solves this dilemma in a radical (for Windows) way: It does away with drive letters entirely! For example, when you display the Server Storage tab in the Windows Home Server Console, as shown in Figure 5.1, there are no drive letters in sight. Instead, Windows Home Server presents a single data space (represented graphically by the pie chart) that's broken down not into unintuitive letters, but into easily grasped categories: Shared Folders, Duplication, PC Backups, System, and Free Space. That's so simple and so intuitive that it's hard to believe this is a Windows OS we're dealing with.

Technically, I should point out that Windows Home Server hasn't entirely broken the drive letter habit. If you log on to Windows Home Server and then select Start, My Computer, you see that drive letters are still under the hood. However, as you can see in Figure 5.2, the Windows Home Server system has far fewer driver letters than most Windows systems. Besides the DVD drive (drive X), there are only two other drives on any Windows Home Server system:

▶ **Drive C (SYS)**—This is the system drive that stores the operating system files and any programs you install. The size of this drive is fixed at 20GB.

▶ **Drive D (DATA)**—This single drive represents all the remaining storage on the system, and it's where Windows Home Server stores its shared folders and client backups. If you add another hard drive to the system, it doesn't get its own drive letter, as it would in other versions of Windows. Instead, the drive's storage space gets added to drive D.

You might be wondering why in Figure 5.1 the Server Storage tab reports that the system has 2.5TB total space (the sum of the three hard drive capacities: 931.51GB, 931.51GB, and 698.64GB), whereas Figure 5.2 shows only 931GB total space (20GB for the system drive and 911GB for the Data drive). That has to do with Windows Home Server's folder duplication feature, which I'll discuss a bit later. (See "Safety: Using Duplication to Ensure No Data Is Lost.")

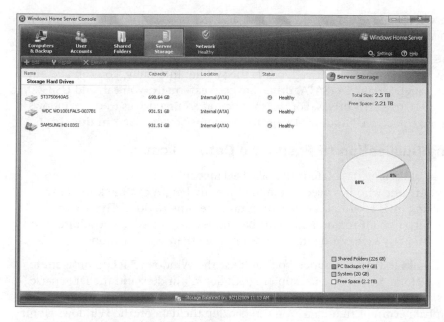

FIGURE 5.1   Windows Home Server does away with drive letters and instead combines all available storage into a single data space.

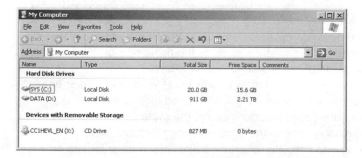

FIGURE 5.2   Opening My Computer shows that, under the hood, Windows Home Server does use drive letters, although in a unique way.

Flexibility: Expanding (or Contracting) the Data Pool

In Figure 5.1, earlier in this chapter, you saw that the Server Storage tab in the Windows Home Server Console showed a data pie chart along with a simple list of the hard drives installed on the system. That list of hard drives is really the extent of Windows Home Server's treatment of disk drives from your perspective. That is to say, your job is simply to manage that list: When you install a new disk drive, you add it to the list; when you uninstall a disk drive, you remove it from the list. As you do this, Windows Home Server expands or contracts the data pool seamlessly and without any need on your part to reconfigure the storage, move data, make backups, and any of the other hassles normally associated with adding and removing hard drives.

Windows Home Server takes this admirably flexible approach even further by allowing you to add a fairly wide variety of hard drive types to the system: Internally, you can add any type of drive, although Serial ATA (SATA) drives are best; externally, you can add USB 2.0, FireWire (IEEE 1394), or eSATA drives. For the specifics on adding drives to the Windows Home Server storage pool, see "Adding Storage to the Home Server," later in this chapter.

Safety: Using Duplication to Ensure No Data Is Lost

The standard way of keeping data safe is to make backup copies of that data—the more often, the better. Anyone who has used a computer for any length of time knows the reasons why backing up is essential, yet few of us take the time to do it. That's why Windows Home Server's built-in and automatic backup feature is a welcome addition to our homes and will likely save our digital bacons on more than one occasion.

Unfortunately, thanks to Drive Extender, you can't use the Windows Backup program to back up Windows Home Server. The Backup program doesn't understand the DE reparse point functions, so although you can use it to make backups, *restoring* anything from those backups will probably corrupt that data. You can back up the data on the Windows Home Server shared folder by adding another drive to the server, but leaving that drive out of the storage pool. You can then use Windows Explorer to copy the shares to the new drive.

CAUTION

If you want to copy data from the shared folder to some other location, *always* access the shares via the *server**share* address, where *server* is the name of your Windows Home Server and *share* is the name of the shared folder (for example, \\Server\Music). If you try to work with the shares directly using Windows Explorer on the server, you'll likely mess up Drive Extender. In fact, it's a good idea to avoid moving and copy files in *all* Windows Home Server partitions except the system partition (drive C). For the latter, you should probably stick to the Documents and Settings folder (although you'll be fine if you have to copy files or create subfolders in other folders on C, such as Inetpub\wwwroot or Program Files; don't mess with anything in C:\fs, however, because that's where Drive Extender mounts the secondary partitions. See "Understanding Drive Extender," later in this chapter).

Copying the shared folders by hand to another drive is a quick-and-dirty backup solution, but Windows Home Server offers an easier way to protect your shared data. If you have at least two drives in the storage pool, Windows Home Server enables a feature called *folder duplication*. When you activate this feature for a shared folder, Windows Home Server always maintains two copies of every file in that folder, and these copies always reside on separate hard drives. This means that if one of your hard drives dies, you won't lose any data because copies of each file still exist on the other drive.

> ▶ **SEE** By default, Windows Home Server turns on folder duplication for existing shares. To learn how to turn off this feature, **see** "Toggling Duplication for a Shared Folder," **P. 151.**

Understanding Drive Extender

Earlier you saw that Windows Home Server uses the data drive (drive D) to store its shared folders and client backups, and that each time you install a hard drive on the server, that drive's capacity is added to the data drive's storage pool. This nifty bit of storage legerdemain is handled by a piece of technology new to Windows Home Server: *Drive Extender* (DE).

If you have two hard drives on your system, DE divides the storage pool into two partition types: a primary partition and a secondary partition. (It's worth noting here that Microsoft often uses the term *volume* as a synonym for partition.) DE uses the secondary partition to store the actual data, and it uses the primary partition to store pointers that specify where the actual data is stored. (The Windows Home Server developers call these pointers *tombstones*, for reasons unknown. They are, in fact, NTFS reparse points that make it appear as though the files are stored on the D drive. The actual files are called *shadows*, again for mysterious reasons.)

NOTE

If you have duplication turned on for one or more folders, the program that performs the duplication—Drive Extender Migrator—waits until the CPU is free before writing the file duplicates. (This is called a *lazy write* or a *delayed write*.)

NTFS Reparse Points

A *reparse point* is an ingenious bit of NTFS technology. It's a kind of tag or marker that is associated with a file system object. Each reparse point implements some kind of custom file system function. When the file system goes to access an object with an associated reparse point, it looks up the custom function and performs that instead of the default action. (The file system "reparses" the request, hence the name of this feature.)

A good example of a reparse point function is the ability (available in Windows 2000 and later) to mount drives so that they display their contents in a folder instead of a drive letter. (Select Start, right-click My Computer, and then click Manage. In the Computer Management snap-in, click Disk Management, right-click a drive, click Change Drive Letters and Paths, click Add, click Mount in the Following Empty NTFS Folder, and then select the folder.) Windows Home Server uses this type of reparse point to mount secondary partitions in the `C:\fs` folder.

When all the files are in the secondary partition, their duplicates have been created (if any), and their corresponding tombstones have been set up, the Windows Home Server Console shows Storage Balanced on *Date* at the bottom of the window, where *Date* is the date and time that Drive Extender completed its labors. If Drive Extender is currently at work moving files to the secondary partition, duplicating files, or preparing a new hard drive, the Windows Home Server Console shows Balancing Storage at the bottom of the window.

Server Storage on a One-Drive System

If you have just one hard drive on your system, Windows Home Server has no choice but to store all of its files on that one drive, as shown in Figure 5.3. The hard drive is divided into two partitions: one—named SYS—for the Windows Home Server system files (seen as drive C in My Computer) and another—named DATA—for the primary partition. There is no secondary partition—the folder `C:\fs` doesn't exist—so no tombstones are used as pointers to data. Instead, Windows Home Server loads all the data onto drive D.

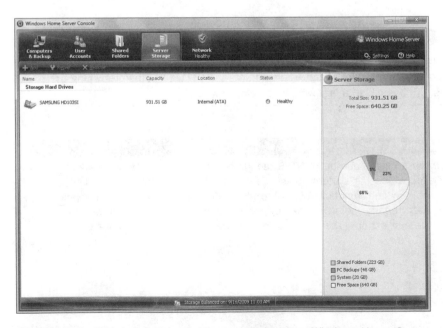

FIGURE 5.3   With just one hard drive on your system, Windows Home Server must store all your data on the single drive.

Perhaps most importantly, a one-drive system means that Windows Home Server doesn't have a second drive on which to create duplicate copies of the files in the shared folders. Therefore, Windows Home Server disables folder duplication on the single drive.

Server Storage on a Two-Drive System

If you install a second hard drive on your system and then add that drive to the storage pool, Windows Home Server responds by setting up the drive as the secondary partition (like the primary partition, the secondary is also named DATA). The secondary partition is mounted to a subfolder of C:\fs (for example, C:\fs\E). The DE Migrator then moves all the data off the primary partition and onto the secondary partition. The primary partition gets a collection of tombstones that point to the locations of the data files on the secondary partition.

Adding a second drive to your system also means that Windows Home Server can now use folder duplication. If you activate duplication for a folder, Windows Home Server maintains copies of the folder's files on both the primary and secondary partitions.

Server Storage on a Multi-Drive System

Windows Home Server lets you add as many drives as you can either fit inside the case or plug into your system's USB 2.0, FireWire, and eSATA ports. After you install a third drive and add it to the storage pool, Windows Home Server sets up the drive as another secondary partition, which is mounted to a subfolder of C:\fs (such as C:\fs\G). If you have folder duplication activated for at least one folder, DE Migrator moves all the duplicates onto the secondary partitions—leaving behind only tombstone pointers on the primary partition—and ensures that the original files and the duplicates are stored on different partitions.

With three or more drives in the storage pool, Windows Home Server can also start *load balancing*, which means optimizing how data is stored and retrieved by writing or reading data using a hard drive that's not currently busy. This is possible because every data file exists on two (and only two) hard drives. For example, suppose Windows Home Server needs to read a file that has copies stored on drive 1 and drive 2. If drive 1 is busy, say, writing data, Windows Home Server can always read the file from drive 2. Load balancing can greatly improve performance because Windows Home Server should spend far less time waiting for a hard drive to become available.

Setting the Primary Hard Drive

All computers define a primary hard drive, which is the hard drive the system boots from. When you install Windows Home Server, it uses the primary hard drive for the system partition (drive C) and the primary data partition (drive D). If you have multiple internal hard drives, how do you know which one is the primary drive? The easiest way to tell is to run Windows Home Server Console, select the Server Storage tab, and look for the hard drive that has the Windows logo superimposed on the drive icon. (The primary drive is also the only drive where the Remove button is disabled.)

When configuring your storage in Windows Home Server, it's important to understand that using a relatively small hard drive as the system's primary drive can lead to problems. For example, suppose your system uses a 50GB drive as the primary. Windows Home Server sets asides 20GB for the system partition, leaving you with 30GB as the primary data partition. However, when you copy data to any Windows Home Server share, the data always lands first on the primary partition, and then DE Migrator farms it out to the secondary partitions using lazy writes. This means that, even if your secondary partitions have hundreds of gigabytes free, you can't copy more than 30GB at one time, because that's the most that fits (however temporarily) on the primary data partition.

Therefore, always install Windows Home Server with the largest hard drive as the primary drive. If you installed Windows Home Server on a relatively small drive, you can still switch to a larger primary drive, although you lose some settings in the process. I tell you how to replace your primary hard drive in Chapter 17, "Troubleshooting Windows Home Server."

> ▶ **SEE** To learn how to replace your primary hard drive, **see** "Replacing Your System Hard Drive," **P. 490.**

In the old days, setting up a drive as the primary (that is, the "master" rather than the "slave") involved configuring jumpers on the drive, using the right kind of cable, and using the correct connector on the cable. Fortunately, the Serial ATA (SATA) drives recommended for use with Windows Home Server don't have master/slave configurations, which makes life much easier. To set a drive as the primary, you have two choices:

- ▶ Shut down your computer, open the case, and find the SATA ports on the motherboard. The ports are usually orange or red, but the easiest way to find them is to follow the SATA cables from your hard drives to the motherboard. On most systems, the order that the hard drives are plugged into the ports determines the hard drive boot sequence. Some motherboards label the SATA ports (SATA1, SATA2, and so on), so plug the largest drive into the first port. If there are no port labels, note that on many tower system motherboards, the SATA boot sequence runs from the bottom port to the top, so plug the cable of the largest hard drive into the bottom port. If the ports are arranged in a square or rectangle, determine which port is used by the hard drive that's currently the primary, and then swap ports with the largest drive.

- ▶ Reboot the computer and then look for a message telling you how to enter the computer's BIOS setup utility. You usually do this by pressing a key such as F2 or Delete. BIOS setup interfaces vary, so finding the setting you want may take some time. You want to change the boot order of the hard drives. On many systems, you first need to select the "Advanced" (or "Advanced BIOS") section, and then select the "Boot" or "Startup" section. Some systems also have a separate "Hard Drive Boot Priority" section. Locate the utility's instructions for changing the boot sequence, and then move the largest hard drive up in the order so that it's the first hard drive to boot.

> **NOTE**
>
> If the boot sequence setting in your BIOS utility includes all boot devices (not just hard drives), remember that the largest hard drive doesn't have to be first of *all* the devices in the sequence, just the first hard drive in the sequence. Just in case you need it down the road (for example, if you have to reinstall Windows Home Server), it's best to have your DVD drive first in the boot sequence.

Adding Storage to the Home Server

Parkinson's Law of Data nicely encapsulates a computing truism: data expands to fill the space available. You've no doubt experienced this on your own systems, so just think how much more acute this problem is on a Windows Home Server system that's being used to store data from a number of computers. If your family regularly generates music, video, and recorded TV files—an all-too common scenario these days—that are stored on the Windows Home Server shares, and you combine all those fat files with multiple backups from each computer, even a system with several hundred gigabytes of storage will fill up alarmingly quickly.

Fortunately, Windows Home Server was designed to handle such scenarios and enable you to solve space problems in the most straightforward way possible: by adding more space. You can cram as many Serial ATA drives inside the case as can fit, and if you need more space, you can start adding USB 2.0, FireWire, and eSATA drives externally. As a bonus, adding a second hard drive to Windows Home Server enables you to take advantage of folder duplication, and adding a third drive improves performance by allowing Windows Home Server to implement load balancing.

> **NOTE**
>
> When you're adding secondary hard drives to your system, bear in mind that the minimum hard drive capacity required by Windows Home Server is 8GB. If you add a hard drive that's smaller than 8GB, Windows Home Server prohibits you from adding it to the storage pool.

When you add either an internal or external hard drive to your system, that drive is not added to the store pool automatically. The drive does appear in the Server Storage tab of the Windows Home Server Console, but it's shown in the Non Storage Hard Drives section, as shown in Figure 5.4.

FIGURE 5.4   When you first install a hard drive, Windows Home Server does not automatically add it to the storage pool.

In some cases, you might want to leave the new hard drive out of the storage pool, at least temporarily:

▶ You might want to use the new hard drive to store files such as downloads and drivers.

▶ You might have useful data on the new hard drive that you want to preserve. Before adding the drive to the storage pool (which wipes out all the data because Windows Home Server formats the drive), you can copy the data to your My Documents folder or to a network share.

Otherwise, you can either add the hard drive to the Windows Home Server storage pool or set it up as the Windows Home Server backup drive. The next two sections take you through both procedures.

Adding a Drive to the Storage Pool

If you want to add the drive to the storage pool, follow these steps:

1. Open the Windows Home Server Console.
2. Display the Server Storage tab.
3. In the Non Storage Hard Drives section, click the drive you want to add.
4. Click Add. Windows Home Server launches the Add a Hard Drive wizard.
5. Click Next in the wizard's initial dialog box. The wizard asks how you want to use the hard drive (see Figure 5.5).

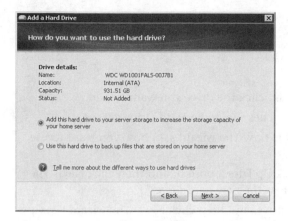

FIGURE 5.5   The Add a Hard Drive Wizard lets you set up a hard drive for storage or backups.

6. Make sure the Add This Hard Drive to Your Server Storage... option is selected, and then click Next. The wizard warns you that it will format the new hard drive.

7. Click Finish. The Add a Hard Drive Wizard formats the drive. If you added to a single-drive system, Windows Home Server also sets up the primary and secondary partitions and enables folder duplication.

8. Click Done.

Adding a Drive for Windows Home Server Backups

If you want to add the new drive for use as the Windows Home Server backup location, you must first ensure that the drive has at least one partition. If the drive is new and so doesn't contain a partition, follow these steps to create one:

1. Select Start, right-click My Computer, and then click Manage. The Computer Management snap-in appears.

2. Click Disk Management.

3. Right-click the new hard drive and then click New Partition. Windows Home Server launches the New Partition Wizard.

4. Click Next. The wizard asks you to select a partition type.

5. Select the Primary Partition option, and then click Next. The wizard prompts you for a partition size.

6. Make sure the Partition Size in MB is equal to the maximum size, and then click Next. The wizard prompts you to choose a drive letter.

7. Select a drive letter and then click Next. The wizard prompts you to format the drive.

8. Click Next.

9. Click Finish. Windows Home Server formats the drive.

10. Restart Windows Home Server.

With your new drive ready for action, follow these steps to add it as the Windows Home Server backup drive:

1. Open the Windows Home Server Console.
2. Display the Server Storage tab.
3. In the Non Storage Hard Drives section, click the drive you want to add.
4. Click Add. Windows Home Server launches the Add a Hard Drive wizard.
5. Click Next in the wizard's initial dialog box. The wizard asks how you want to use the hard drive.
6. Select the Use This Hard Drive to Back Up Files... option, and then click Next. The wizard asks whether you want to format the new hard drive.
7. Select Yes, if you want to format the drive, and then click Next. The wizard prompts you for a drive name.
8. Type a name for the drive, and then click Next.
9. Click Finish.
10. Click Done. Windows Home Server Console creates a new section in the Server Storage tab called Server Backup Hard Drives, and it displays your new drive in that section, as shown in Figure 5.6. (Your Windows Home Server machine also now appears in the Computers & Backup tab.)

FIGURE 5.6   Windows Home Server creates a new Server Backup Hard Drives section in the Server Storage tab, and adds your backup drive to the section.

Viewing Storage Status

One of the nice features of Windows Home Server is that it gives you visual and text feedback on the status of certain components of your network. For example, on the client computers, the Windows Home Server Tray icon in the notification area changes color to reflect the current network status. That status also appears in the Windows Home Server Console program, via the Network status icon. Windows Home Server also displays the current status of each hard drive on your system. Open the Windows Home Server Console and display the Server Storage tab. This tab lists the manufacturer's name for the drive (this only applies to drives in the storage pool), the drive's capacity, the drive's location—Internal (ATA), External (USB), or External (FireWire)—and the drive's current status (see Figure 5.7).

FIGURE 5.7   In the Server Storage tab, the Status column tells you the current status of each hard drive installed on the server.

The Status column will almost always show Healthy (fingers crossed!) or, if the drive is being used for backups, the percentage of free space, but five other states are possible, as follows:

▶ **Not Added**—This means that the drive is installed on the Windows Home Server system, but you haven't yet added it to the storage pool.

▶ **Initializing**—This status appears while the Add a Hard Drive Wizard is formatting a new drive to prepare it for use in the storage pool.

▶ **Healthy**—This means that the hard drive is part of the Windows Home Server storage pool and is functioning correctly.

▶ **Missing**—You see this status if Windows Home Server can't locate a hard drive that's part of the storage pool. (In Figure 5.7, see the status of the first hard drive.) This most often happens with external hard drives that have either been turned off or unplugged.

▶ **Failing**—This means that Windows Home Server has detected signs of corruption or other problems on the hard drive. You should run the Windows Home Server Repair feature on the drive. (See the section "Repairing Storage," next.)

▶ **Removing**—This status appears while the Remove a Hard Drive Wizard is moving data off the hard drive in preparation for removing the drive from the Windows Home Server storage pool.

Repairing Storage

You saw in the previous section that Windows Home Server can detect data corruption and other hard drive problems. When this happens, Windows Home Server changes the drive's status to Failing. In that case, you should run Windows Home Server's Repair feature on the drive. Here's how it works:

1. Launch the Windows Home Server Console.
2. Display the Server Storage tab.
3. Click the drive you want to repair.
4. Click Repair. Windows Home Server starts the Repair a Hard Drive Wizard.
5. Click Next.
6. Follow the wizard's prompts to repair the hard drive.
7. Click Done.

Removing Storage from the Home Server

If you have a hard drive that you no longer want to use with Windows Home Server, you can remove it from the storage pool. Before I show you how it's done, consider these notes:

▶ Always go through the Windows Home Server Console to remove a hard drive. Drive Extender needs to reconfigure the storage pool and redistribute the drive's data to other disks before allowing you to physically remove the drive. If you just yank out the drive, you could lose data.

▶ You can't remove a hard drive if Windows Home Server is currently storing more data than can be redistributed to the remaining drives. For example, suppose you have a 100GB drive and a 50GB drive, and Windows Home Server is storing 75GB of data. You won't be able to remove the 100GB drive because the 75GB of data won't fit on the 50GB drive. In this case, you'd need to remove enough data from Windows Home Server to allow the remaining data to fit on the smaller drive.

▶ If you currently have a two-drive system with duplication turned on for at least one folder, removing a drive automatically turns off duplication for all folders.

▶ Windows Home Server doesn't allow you to remove the hard drive that it's using as the primary partition.

Removing a Storage Hard Drive

With all that in mind, here are the steps to follow to remove a hard drive from the Windows Home Server storage pool:

1. Launch the Windows Home Server Console.

2. Display the Server Storage tab.

3. Click the drive you want to remove from the system.

4. Click Remove. (If the Remove button is disabled, it means that Windows Home Server won't allow you to remove that drive.) Windows Home Server starts the Remove a Hard Drive Wizard.

5. Click Next. If you have any shared folders open on the server or any client, the wizard displays a list of the open folders and asks you to close them to avoid losing data (see Figure 5.8). Note the Used On column, which tells you which home computer has the file open.

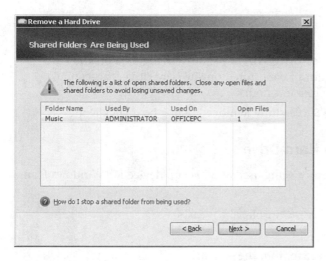

FIGURE 5.8   The Remove a Hard Drive Wizard warns you if any shared folders are open.

6. Close the open shared folders, if any, and then click Next. The Remove a Hard Drive Wizard calculates the disk space required by your data to see if the removal can proceed. It then displays the Hard Drive Removal Consequences dialog box. Figure 5.9 shows an example.

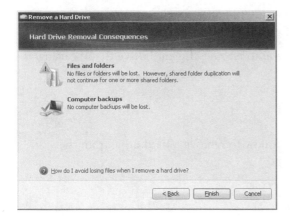

FIGURE 5.9   The Remove a Hard Drive Wizard lets you know the consequences of removing a hard drive from the Windows Home Server storage pool.

CAUTION

If the Remove a Hard Drive Wizard's Hard Drive Removal Consequences dialog box tells you that you might permanently lose files or backups, believe it. You should cancel the wizard and move data off Windows Home Server and onto a client drive. If you plan on adding another hard drive after the removal, you'd be much better off by adding the other hard drive first, if possible.

---

7. Click Finish. The Remove a Hard Drive Wizard begins moving data off the hard drive. Depending on the amount of data stored on the hard drive, this can take anywhere from a few minutes to a few hours.

8. When you see the Hard Drive Successfully Removed dialog box, click Done.

Removing a Server Backup Hard Drive

If you have a hard drive that's currently being used as a backup device for Windows Home Server, follow these steps to remove it:

1. Launch the Windows Home Server Console.

2. Display the Server Storage tab.

3. Click the drive you want to remove from the system.

4. Click Remove. Windows Home Server starts the Remove a Hard Drive Wizard, which asks what you want to do with the hard drive.

5. Select one of the following options, and then click OK.

> **Temporarily Remove It From My Home Server**—Select this option if you only want to remove the hard drive temporarily and will be adding it back as a backup hard drive later.

> **Stop Using It For Server Backups**—Select this option if you no longer want to use the hard drive for backing up Windows Home Server.

From Here

> To learn how to add shared folders to Windows Home Server, **see** "Creating a New Shared Folder," **P. 149**.

> To learn how to disable duplication on a Windows Home Server share, **see** "Toggling Duplication for a Shared Folder," **P. 151**.

> For details on copying data to a Windows Home Server share, **see** "Copying Files to a Shared Folder," **P. 159**.

> For information on using the Windows Home Server media shares, **see** Chapter 8, "Streaming and Sharing Digital Media."

> To learn how to replace your primary hard drive, **see** "Replacing Your System Hard Drive," **P. 490**.

Sharing Folders and Files on the Home Server

Sharing data with other people is one of the principal benefits of networking. Whether you want to collaborate with someone on a document or just make a document accessible for reference purposes, you can place that file in a shared network folder. Unfortunately, network file sharing is marred by the time and complexity it entails. You have to set up the shared folder, give users secure access to that folder, and upload the data to the folder. IT types are old pros at this, but the average user—particularly the average home user—usually doesn't want to bother with such geeky chores.

Fortunately, Windows Home Server takes almost all of the geekiness out of sharing files over the network. Windows Home Server comes with several predefined shares for common file types such as music and photos, it automatically adds shares for each new user, and it presents a simple interface for giving users secure access to each share. And if your local username and password are the same as your Windows Home Server username and password, logging in to Windows automatically logs you in to Windows Home Server, so you can access the shared folders with just a few clicks. Best of all, everything happens on the server, so you don't have to bother creating separate shares on the users' computers, which could leave your home network vulnerable to possible security threats.

This chapter takes you through Windows Home Server's file sharing features. You learn about the predefined shares, how to create your own shares, how to set user permissions, how to access shares, how to search the shared folders, and much more.

Examining the Predefined Windows Home Server Shares

You learn how to create new shares on Windows Home Server a bit later in this chapter. (See "Creating a New Shared Folder.") However, it's entirely possible (albeit unlikely) that you won't have to create new shares. That's because Windows Home Server comes with quite a few predefined shared folders. Here's a summary of what's on the system by default:

▸ **Music**—Use this shared folder for music and other digital audio files.

▸ **Photos**—Use this shared folder for digital photos, images, artwork, and other graphics files.

▸ **Public**—Use this shared folder for miscellaneous documents and files that don't fit with any of the other shared folder themes.

▸ **Recorded TV**—Use this shared folder to store TV shows that you've recorded.

▸ **Software**—Use this shared folder to store the installation files for programs and Windows Home Server add-ins. (These are usually the setup files for programs you've downloaded from the Internet.)

▸ **Users**—This shared folder contains a subfolder for each user defined on the Windows Home Server system. The name of each subfolder is the same as the account's username. By default, users (along with the Windows Home Server Administrator account) have Full access to their own subfolder; users have None access to folders other than their own.

▸ **Videos**—Use this shared folder to store digital video files, movies, and animations.

Setting User Permissions on Shared Folders

The first thing you should do with the existing Windows Home Server shared folders is set user permissions on those shares. Permissions specify the level of access that each user has to the folder. As you learned in Chapter 2, "Setting Up and Working with User Accounts," Windows Home Server defines three types of access, as follows:

▸ **SEE** To learn about security groups and their associated permissions, **see** "Understanding Security Groups," **P. 35.**

▸ **Full**—This level of access means that the user has both read and write permission on the share. The user can open subfolders, launch programs, open documents, edit documents, create new files and folders, and delete files and folders.

▸ **Read**—This level of access means that the user has read-only permission on the shared folder. The user can open subfolders, launch programs, and open documents, but he can't make changes to the shared folder or any of its contents. If a user with Read access changes a file and then attempts to save it, an error message appears, and what that message says depends on the editing program. For example, Notepad displays the unhelpful Cannot Create the *file* File error (where *file* is the pathname of

the remote file), as shown in Figure 6.1. WordPad displays the more to-the-point
Access to *file* was Denied error, as shown in Figure 6.2.

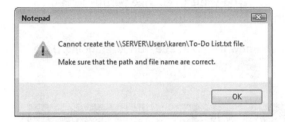

FIGURE 6.1   Notepad displays this error message when you attempt to save a file in a read-
only folder.

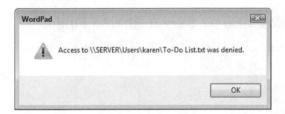

FIGURE 6.2   WordPad's error message is a bit more helpful.

▶ **None**—This level of access means that the user can't view a shared folder. If the user
   double-clicks the shared folder to open it, he receives an Access is Denied error (see
   Figure 6.3).

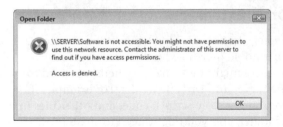

FIGURE 6.3   If a user's access level for a folder is set to None, Windows Home Server doesn't
even let the user open the folder.

If you've ever worked with shared folders in Windows, you probably know that you
usually modify share permissions via the Sharing tab in the folder's property sheet (that is,
you right-click the folder, click Sharing and Security, and then click Permissions in the

Sharing tab). However, recall from Chapter 5, "Setting Up and Using Home Server Storage," that thanks to Windows Home Server's Drive Extender technology, you no longer have direct access to the server's shared folders. This means, as well, that you no longer have direct access to a shared folder's permissions, either at the user level or at the group level. (More accurately, you can change permissions using the old method, but Windows Home Server ignores those changes.) If you want to change permissions on a shared server folder, you must do it through the Windows Home Server Console program.

▶ **SEE** For the details on Drive Extender and how it works, **see** "Understanding Drive Extender," **P. 129.**

NOTE

Just because you can't set permissions on the Windows Home Server shares doesn't mean that you can't set up permissions the "old-fashioned" way on other server folders. See "Sharing Server Folders Outside of Drive Extender," later in this chapter.

Modifying Permissions for a Windows Home Server Shared Folder

Here are the steps to follow to modify the user access levels for a shared Windows Home Server folder:

1. Launch Windows Home Server Console.
2. Display the Shared Folders tab.
3. Click the folder you want to work with and then click Properties. (You can also double-click the folder.) The folder's property sheet appears.
4. Display the User Access tab.
5. For each user, click the option that corresponds to the access level you want to apply: Full, Read, or None (see Figure 6.4).
6. Click OK. Windows Home Server sets the new permissions.

Sharing Server Folders Outside Drive Extender

As I mentioned at the beginning of this chapter, the shared folders that Windows Home Server maintains will in most cases mean that home users need not share any other folders, particularly on the server. However, there might be scenarios where you need to share a server folder outside Windows Home Server and Drive Extender. For example, if you use the server for development work, you might store scripts, code, and other files in the Administrator account's My Documents folder, and you might need to share those files with one or more client machines. Because you can't include My Documents with the Drive Extender shares, you need to set up a regular share for that folder.

Follow these steps to share a folder outside Drive Extender:

1. Log on to the server.

FIGURE 6.4   In Windows Home Server Console, open a shared folder's property sheet and use the User Access tab to set the permissions.

2. Select Start, Windows Explorer, right-click the drive or folder, and then click Properties. Windows Home Server displays the object's property sheet.

3. Select the Sharing tab and activate the Share This Folder option, as shown in Figure 6.5.

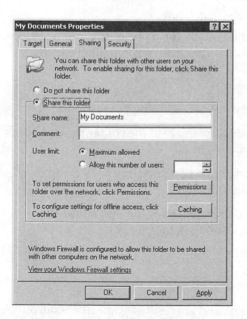

FIGURE 6.5   Activate the Share This Folder option to enable sharing on the folder.

4. Edit the Share Name, if desired, and add a comment. (The latter is optional.)

5. Click Permissions to display the Permissions dialog box, shown in Figure 6.6.

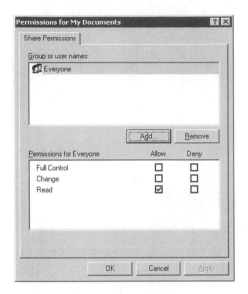

FIGURE 6.6   Use the Permissions dialog box to specify file permissions for the shared resource.

6. Select the Everyone group in the Group or User Names list and then click Remove.

7. Click Add to display the Select Users or Groups dialog box.

8. In the Enter the Object Names to Select text box, type the name of the user or group you want to give permission to access the shared resource. (Separate multiple user-names or group names with semicolons.) Click OK when you're done.

9. Select an item in the Group or User Names list.

10. Using the Permissions list, you can allow or deny the following permissions:

    ▶ **Read**—Gives the group or user the ability only to read the contents of a folder or file. The user can't modify those contents in any way.

    ▶ **Change**—Gives the group or user Read permission and allows the group or user to modify the contents of the shared resource.

    ▶ **Full Control**—Gives the group or user Change permission and allows the group or user to take ownership of the shared resource.

11. Repeat steps 7 through10 to add and configure sharing for other users and groups.

12. Click OK to return to the folder's property sheet.

13. Display the Security tab.

14. Repeat steps 7 through 9 to add the same users and groups that you earlier added to the Sharing tab.

15. Using the Permissions list, you can allow or deny the following permissions:

> ▶ **Full Control**—Gives the group or user the ability to perform any of the actions listed. The group or user can also change permissions.

> ▶ **Modify**—Gives the group or user the ability to view the folder contents, open files, edit files, create new files and subfolders, delete files, and run programs.

> ▶ **Read and Execute**—Gives the group or user the ability to view the folder contents, open files, and run programs.

> ▶ **List Folder Contents**—Gives the group or user the ability to view the folder contents.

> ▶ **Read**—Gives the group or user the ability to open files but not edit them.

> ▶ **Write**—Gives the group or user the ability to create new files and subfolders, and open and edit existing files.

> ▶ **Special Permissions**—Gives the group or user advanced settings for permissions, auditing, ownership, and effective permissions.

16. Repeat steps 14 and 15 to add and configure security for other users and groups.

17. Click OK to share the resource with the network.

Creating a New Shared Folder

Windows Home Server's predefined shared folders should suit most needs, but you might require other folders to hold different file types. For example, you might want a folder for scripts, a folder for downloaded programs, or a folder to hold user calendars. (See "Publishing a Windows Vista Calendar to the Server," later in this chapter.) Windows Home Server allows you to create as many shared folders as you need. Again, it's possible to create and share folders outside of Drive Extender, but if you want the safety of duplication and the simple permissions, you need to create and share the folder within the Windows Home Server Console.

Follow these steps to create a new shared folder:

1. Launch Windows Home Server Console.

2. Display the Shared Folders tab.

3. Click Add. Windows Home Server launches the Add a Shared Folder Wizard.

4. Type a name for the folder.

NOTE

The folder name must consist of only letters, numbers, spaces, hyphens (-), underscores (_), or periods (.), and it must end with a letter or number.

5. Type an optional description. (This text appears in the Description column of the Shared Folders tab.)

6. If you want Windows Home Server to maintain duplicate copies of the folder's files, leave the Enable Folder Duplication check box activated, as shown in Figure 6.7.

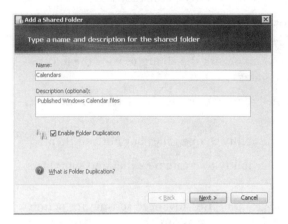

FIGURE 6.7   In the initial Add a Shared Folder wizard dialog box, type a name and description for the new shared folder.

TIP

If you plan to copy a large amount of data to the new shared folder, deactivate the Enable Folder Duplication check box. This speeds up the file transfer because Drive Extender doesn't attempt to duplicate the files as they're being copied. When the file transfer is complete, you can then turn on folder duplication. (See the next section, "Toggling Duplication for a Shared Folder," for the details.)

---

7. Click Next. The wizard asks you to set the access level for the users.

CAUTION

Note that the default access level for all users is Read (except for the Guest user, which is set to None). If you want a particular user to have full control over the new share, be sure to change that user's access level to Full.

---

8. For each user, click the option that corresponds to the access level you want to apply: Full, Read, or None.

9. Click Finish. Windows Home Server creates the folder, applies the access permissions, and then enables folder duplication, if applicable. The new folder appears in the Shared Folders tab.

10. Click Done.

Toggling Duplication for a Shared Folder

As you saw in the previous section, the Add a Shared Folder Wizard activates the Enable Folder Duplication check box when you create a new share. This is not surprising because folder duplication is a simple but effective way to keep your shared folder data safe. (Note, however, that Windows Home Server initially has folder duplication turned off for the default shares. This, too, makes sense, because it's common to copy lots of data to the shares at first, and it's better to have duplication turned off for any massive file transfers.) However, sometimes you don't want to use folder duplication:

▶ **SEE** For more information about folder duplication, **see** "Safety: Using Duplication to Ensure No Data Is Lost," **P. 128.**

▶ If you have a folder with extremely large files. A good example is a media folder that contains recorded TV shows or ripped DVD movies. Forcing Drive Extender to constantly duplicate such behemoth files can slow down the server.

▶ If you plan on copying a large amount of data to a folder, you'll speed up the file transfer if you turn off folder duplication temporarily.

▶ If you're running low on drive space on the server, you might want to free up some space by turning folder duplication off on some larger folders. This is especially attractive for folders where the contents already exist elsewhere on the network. You can always turn folder duplication back on later if you add more storage to the system.

Here are the steps to follow to toggle duplication on and off for a folder:

1. Launch Windows Home Server Console.
2. Display the Shared Folders tab.
3. Click the folder you want to work with.
4. Click Properties. (You can also double-click the folder.) Windows Home Server displays the folder's property sheet.
5. Click the Enable Folder Duplication check box.
6. Click OK to put the new setting into effect.

> **NOTE**
>
> If you're not sure whether a folder has duplication turned on, open the Windows Home Server Console, display the Shared Folders tab, and then examine the Duplication column, which displays either On or Off for each folder.

Accessing the Windows Home Server Shared Folders

To add files to a shared folder, or to open and edit files in a shared folder, you first need to access the share from a client PC. You have several choices:

▶ In Windows 7, Vista, or XP clients that have the Windows Home Server Connector software installed, double-click the desktop's Shared Folders on Server icon (where Server is the name of the Windows Home Server machine).

▶ In Windows 7, click Windows Explorer in the taskbar, click Network, and then double-click the icon for the Windows Home Server.

▶ In Windows Vista, select Start, Network and then double-click the icon for the Windows Home Server.

▶ In Windows XP, select Start, My Network Places. If you don't see the server shares, click View Workgroup Computers and then double-click the icon for the Windows Home Server.

▶ In Windows XP or Windows Me, launch Windows Explorer and, in the Folders list, select My Network Places, Entire Network, Microsoft Windows Network. Click your workgroup, and then double-click the icon for the Windows Home Server.

▶ In Windows 2000, double-click the desktop's My Network Places icon, double-click the Computers Near Me icon, and then double-click the icon for the Windows Home Server.

▶ In Windows 98, double-click the desktop's Network Neighborhood icon and then double-click the icon for the Windows Home Server.

TIP

On a Windows 7, Windows Vista, or Windows XP client with the Windows Home Server Connector installed, an often easier way to open a server share is to run Windows Home Server Connector, click the Shared Folders tab, click the shared folder you want to work with, and then click Open. You can also right-click the Windows Home Server icon in the notification area, and then click Shared Folders.

NOTE

Windows Home Server doesn't have a limit on the number of users who can access a shared folder. However, because Windows Home Server only allows you to add up to 10 user accounts, the practical limit on share access is 10 users (plus the Guest account, if you activate it). The Sharing tab (see "Sharing Server Folders Outside of Drive Extender," earlier in this chapter) has a User Limit feature but, like the other options in this tab, this has no effect on shares controlled by Drive Extender.

In all cases, you end up with a folder window that displays the Windows Home Server shared folders, as shown in Figure 6.8. (Note that this figure includes an extra Calendars folder that I added to my Windows Home Server.) From here, you double-click the icon of the shared folder you want to work with.

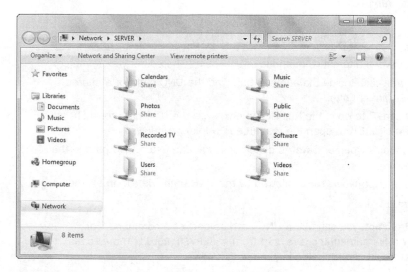

FIGURE 6.8   When you access the Windows Home Server over the network, the resulting folder window displays the server's shared folders.

Understanding the Universal Naming Convention

If you examine the address bar with a share open, you see an address that uses the following format:

*SERVER**Share*

Here, *SERVER* is the name of the server and *Share* is the name given to the shared resource. This is the universal naming convention (UNC). For example, the following UNC path refers to a shared resource named Public on a computer named SERVER:

SERVER\Public

> **NOTE**
>
> The Windows 7 and Windows Vista address bars show a "breadcrumb" path to the server share: Network > *SERVER* > *Share*. To see the UNC address, either right-click the address and then click Edit Address, or click the icon that appears on the left side of the address bar (or click an empty spot within the address bar).

(UNC paths aren't case sensitive, so you can enter a path using any combination of uppercase and lowercase letters; however, it's traditional to write computer names in all-uppercase.) If the UNC path refers to a drive or folder, you can use the regular path conventions to access subfolders on that resource. For example, if the resource Public on SERVER has a Downloads subfolder, you can refer to that subfolder as follows:

\\SERVER\Public\Downloads

TIP

The UNC offers you several alternative methods of accessing shared network resources:

▶ In Windows Explorer, click inside the address bar, type the UNC path for a shared resource, and then press Enter.

▶ Press Windows Logo+R to open the Run dialog box. Type the UNC path for a shared resource and then click OK to open the resource in a folder window.

▶ In a 32-bit application's Open or Save As dialog box, you can use a UNC path in the File Name text box.

▶ At the command prompt, type **start** followed by the UNC path. Here's an example:

start \\SERVER\Public

▶ At the command prompt, you can use a UNC path as part of a command. For example, to copy a file named archive.zip from \\SERVER\Public\Downloads\ to the current folder, you'd use the following command:

COPY "\\SERVER\Public\Downloads\archive.zip"

Mapping a Shared Folder to a Local Drive Letter

One networking conundrum that comes up repeatedly is the problem of referencing network resources (in, say, a script or command). You can reference UNC paths, but they're a bit unwieldy to use. To avoid the hassle, you can map a Windows Home Server shared folder to your own computer. Mapping assigns a drive letter to the server share so that it appears to be just another disk drive on your machine.

NOTE

Another good reason to map a Windows Home Server share to a local drive letter is to give certain programs access to the shared folder. Some older programs aren't network aware, so if you try to save files to a Windows Home Server share, the program might display an error or tell you that the location is out of disk space. In most cases, you can solve this problem by mapping the folder to a drive letter, which fools the program into thinking it's dealing with a local folder.

To map a Windows Home Server shared folder, follow these steps:

1. Select Start, right-click Computer (in Windows 7), Network (in Vista) or My Network Places (in XP), and then click Map Network Drive. (In any folder window, you can also select Tools, Map Network Drive; in Windows 7 and Vista, you need to first press Alt to display the menu bar.) The Map Network Drive dialog box appears.

2. The Drive drop-down list displays the last available drive letter on your system, but you can pull down the list and select any available letter.

CAUTION

If you use a removable drive, such as a memory card or Flash drive, Windows assigns the first available drive letter to that drive. This can cause problems if you have a mapped network drive that uses a lower drive letter. Therefore, it's good practice to use higher drive letters (such as X, Y, and Z) for your mapped resources.

---

3. Use the Folder text box to type the UNC path to the Windows Home Server shared folder, as shown in the example in Figure 6.9. (Alternatively, click Browse, select the shared folder in the Browse for Folder dialog box, and then click OK.)

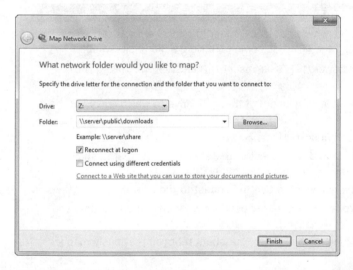

FIGURE 6.9   Use the Map Network Drive dialog box to assign a drive letter to a Windows Home Server shared folder.

4. If you want Windows to map the server share each time you log on to the system, leave the Reconnect at Logon check box activated.

5. If you prefer to log on to the server share using a different account, use one of the following techniques:

> ▶ **Windows 7**—Click to activate the Connect Using Different Credentials link. After you click Finish in step 6, Windows 7 prompts you to enter the username and password.

> ▶ **All other versions of Windows**—Click the Different User Name link, type the username and password, and click OK.

Either way, make sure you specify a username and password that corresponds to an existing Windows Home Server account.

6. Click Finish. Windows adds the new drive letter to your system and opens the shared folder in a new folder window.

CAUTION

In certain situations, a bug in Windows 7 and Windows Vista causes Explorer to show any Windows Home Server shared folder mapped to a drive letter as full. (That is, when you clicked the mapped drive, the Space Used bar shows that the drive is full.) Explorer also shows the free space as greater than the available space! (For example, 2.4TB free of 900GB.)

To open the mapped server folder later, select Start, Computer (or My Computer in XP), and then double-click the drive in the Network Location group.

Mapping Folders at the Command Prompt

You can also map a shared Windows Home Server folder to a local drive letter by using a Command Prompt session and the NET USE command. Here's the basic syntax:

```
NET USE [drive] [share] [password] [/USER:user] [/PERSISTENT:[YES ¦ NO]] ¦
     /DELETE]
```

▶ *drive*—The drive letter (following by a colon) of the local drive to which you want the shared folder mapped.

▶ *share*—The UNC path of the Windows Home Server shared folder.

▶ *password*—The password required to connect to the shared folder (that is, the password associated with the username, specified next).

▶ /USER:*user*—The username you want to use to connect to the shared folder.

▶ /PERSISTENT:—Add YES to reconnect the mapped network drive the next time you log on.

▶ /DELETE—Deletes the existing drive letter for the share that you previously mapped to *drive*.

For example, the following command maps the shared folder \\SERVER\Public\Downloads to drive Z:

```
net use z: \\server\public\downloads \persistent:yes
```

Disconnecting a Mapped Network Folder

If you no longer need to map a Windows Home Server share, you should disconnect it by following these steps:

1. Select Start, Computer (or My Computer in XP).

2. Right-click the mapped drive and then click Disconnect.

3. If there are files open from the server share, Windows displays a warning to let you know that it's unsafe to disconnect the share. You have two choices:

   ▶ Click No, close all open files from the mapped folder, and then repeat steps 1 and 2.

   ▶ If you're sure there are no open files, click Yes to disconnect the share.

Creating a Network Location in Windows 7 and Windows Vista

When you map a Windows Home Server shared folder to a drive on your computer, Windows 7 and Windows Vista create an icon for the mapped drive in the Computer folder's Network Locations group. You can also add your own icons to this group. These are similar to the network places you can create in Windows XP (as described in the next section). That is, after you create a network location, you can access that location by double-clicking the icon. This is usually a lot faster than drilling down through several layers of folders on the server, so create network locations for those Windows Home Server shares you access most often.

Follow these steps to create a network location in Windows 7 and Vista:

1. Select Start, Computer to open the Computer window.
2. Right-click an empty section of the Computer folder and then click Add a Network Location. Windows launches the Add Network Location Wizard.
3. Click Next in the initial wizard dialog box.
4. Click Choose a Custom Network Location and then click Next.
5. Type the UNC address of the Windows Home Server shared folder (see Figure 6.10; you can also click Browse to use the Browse for Folder dialog box to select it), and then click Next.

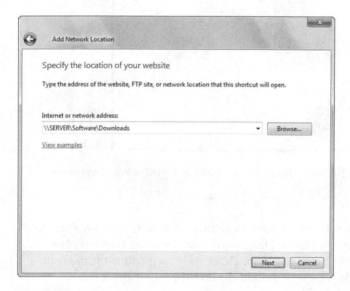

FIGURE 6.10   In Windows 7 and Vista, you can create network locations for Windows Home Server shares that you use frequently.

6. Type a name for the network location and click Next.
7. Click Finish.

Creating a Network Place in Windows XP

In Windows XP, a network place is a shared folder on a network computer. (It can also be a location on a web or FTP server.) The name of each network place uses the following format:

Share on *Description* (*Computer*)

Here, *Share* is the name of the shared resource, *Description* is the description of the computer where the network place resides, and *Computer* is the name of that computer. Windows Home Server machines don't have descriptions, so these network places appear as *Share on Server*, as shown in Figure 6.11. (Again, I created the extra Calendars share on my Windows Home Server.)

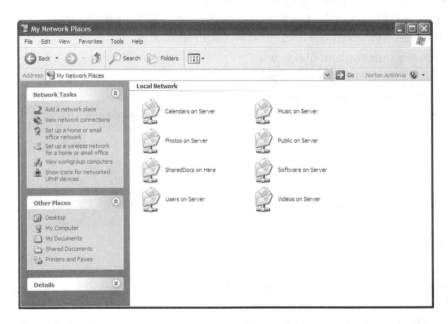

FIGURE 6.11   Windows XP's My Network Places folder showing icons for Windows Home Server shared folders.

Whenever a workgroup computer shares a folder, Windows XP detects the new share and adds it automatically to My Network Places. This means that the main Windows Home Server shares should appear in My Network Places. However, you might want to create a new network place for a subfolder of a server share. To do this, follow these steps:

TIP

You can tell Windows XP not to add new shared resources to My Network Places automatically. To do this, launch Control Panel's Folder Options icon, display the View tab, and then deactivate the Automatically Search for Network Folders and Printers check box.

---

1. In the My Network Places (or any network folder) task pane, click Add a Network Place to launch the Add Network Place Wizard.

2. Click Next.

3. Click Choose Another Network Location and click Next.

4. Either use the Internet or Network Address text box to type the UNC address of the shared Windows Home Server folder, or click Browse to select the folder using the Browse for Folder dialog box. Click Next.

5. Modify the name in the Type a Name for this Network Place, if desired, and then click Next.

6. To open the network place in a folder window, leave the Open This Network Place When I Click Finish check box activated.

7. Click Finish.

Copying Files to a Shared Folder

Most of the Windows Home Server shares are empty after the initial installation. To make these shares useful, you need to copy (or move) files from a client machine to the server. It's quite common to load up Windows Home Server with a huge number of media files—music, photos, videos, and so on—to give other people on the network access to those files to stream those files to an Xbox 360 or other network media device. Before you initiate such a large copy operation, you need to check the following two things:

▶ Check to see whether the Windows Home Server share has folder duplication turned on. If it's on, Drive Extender might start balancing the data by moving files from the primary partition to a secondary partition, which just slows down the file transfer. You should turn off duplication for the duration of the file transfer, and then turn it back on again. (See "Toggling Duplication for a Shared Folder," earlier in this chapter.)

▶ Check to see whether media sharing is turned on for the destination folder. If it's on, Windows Home Server will start indexing the media while the file transfer is in progress which, again, will only slow everything down. Turn off media sharing before starting the file transfer, and then turn it back on again afterward.

▶ **SEE** For the details on Windows Home Server's media-sharing feature, **see** "Streaming Digital Media to Network Computers and Devices," **P. 214.**

Follow these steps to copy or move files from a client machine to a Windows Home Server shared folder:

1. On the client or server, double-click the desktop's Shared Folders on Server icon (where Server is the name of your Windows Home Server).

2. Open the Windows Home Server shared folder or subfolder you want to use as the file destination.

3. On the client or server, open Windows Explorer and navigate to the client folder that contains the files you want to work with.

4. Select the client files and then either press Ctrl+C (if you're copying them) or Ctrl+X (if you're moving them).

5. Switch to the window containing the Windows Home Server share.

6. Press Ctrl+V to paste the files.

TIP

It's often easier to copy files by selecting them in the client folder, dragging them to the window containing the Windows Home Server share, and then dropping inside the shared folder. (If you want to move the files instead, hold down Shift while dragging and dropping the files.) If you can't see the window containing the Windows Home Server share, first drag the mouse pointer to the taskbar and hover it over the share's taskbar button. After a second or two, the share window will come to the front, and you can then drop the files inside the window. Windows Home Server will ask you to confirm that you want to move or copy the files. Click Yes.

CAUTION

If you have a Windows Home Server shared folder that has duplication turned on, make sure that none of the files you store on that share have the Read-Only attribute set. If this attribute is set, Windows Home Server can't duplicate the files, and it generates a Storage Status error in the Windows Home Server Console. To ensure that all files in a share have the Read-Only attribute turned off, open the share, press Ctrl+A to select every file and folder, right-click the selection, and then click Properties. Click the Read-Only check box to deactivate it, and then click OK.

Publishing a Windows Vista Calendar to the Server

One of the pleasant surprises in Windows Vista was a new program called Windows Calendar. It's not as powerful as Outlook's Calendar feature, but it does all the basic jobs that a calendar should: You can create appointments (one-time and recurring), set up all-day events, schedule tasks, apply reminders to appointments and tasks, and view appointments by day, week, or month. For our purposes, Windows Calendar even does something that Outlook's Calendar can't: It can publish a calendar to a network share. (With Outlook, you need to be on a Microsoft Exchange network to do this.) You can set things up so that the published calendar is updated automatically, so the remote calendar always has current data. Your family members can then subscribe to the calendar to see your appointments (and, optionally, your notes, reminders, and tasks).

This means that you can create a new shared folder—called, say, Calendars—and publish your calendar to that folder. After you've done that, start Windows Calendar using any of the following methods:

▶ Select Start, All Programs, Windows Calendar.

▶ Press Windows Logo+R (or select Start, All Programs, Accessories, Run) to open the Run dialog box, type **wincal,** and click OK.

▶ In Windows Mail, select Tools, Windows Calendar, or press Ctrl+Shift+L.

Publishing Your Calendar

Here are the steps you need to follow in Windows Calendar to publish your calendar:

1. In the Calendars list, click the calendar you want to publish.

2. Select Share, Publish to open the Publish Calendar dialog box.

3. Edit the calendar name, if necessary.

TIP

After the calendar publishes, you have the option of sending an email message that includes the address of the shared calendar. Most email clients display this address as a link. However, if the address includes spaces, the link stops at the first space. Therefore, consider changing the calendar name to remove any spaces.

4. Use the Location to Publish Calendar text box to type the address of the shared folder you created on Windows Home Server (see Figure 6.12).

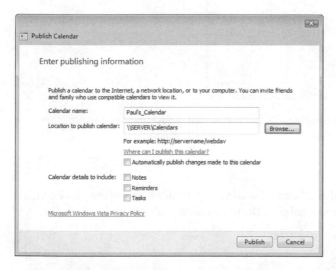

FIGURE 6.12   Use the Publish Calendar dialog box to publish your calendar to a shared Windows Home Server folder.

5. If you want Windows Calendar to update your calendar whenever you make changes to it, activate the Automatically Publish Changes Made to This Calendar check box. (If you leave this option deactivated, you can still publish your changes by hand, as described later; see "Working with Shared Calendars.")

6. In the Calendar Details to Include section, activate the check box beside each item you want in your published calendar: Notes, Reminders, and Tasks.

7. Click Publish. Windows Calendar publishes the calendar to Windows Home Server by creating a file in the iCalendar format (.ics extension) and copying that file to the share. Windows Calendar then displays a dialog box to let you know the operation was successful.

8. To let other people know that your calendar is shared and where it can be found, click Announce. Windows Calendar creates a new email message that includes the following in the body (where *address* is the address of your published calendar; see Figure 6.13 for an example):

   You can subscribe to my calendar at address

9. Click Finish.

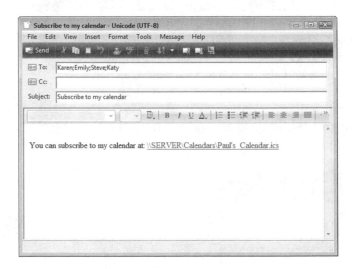

FIGURE 6.13   You can send an email message to let everyone know that you've published your calendar on Windows Home Server.

Subscribing to a Calendar

You can add another person's published calendar to your Calendars list. How you do this depends on whether you've received a subscription invitation via email.

If you have such a message, follow these steps:

1. Open the invitation message.

2. Click the link to the published calendar. Windows Mail asks you to confirm that you want to open the iCalendar file.

3. Click Open. Windows Calendar opens and displays the Import dialog box, shown in Figure 6.14.

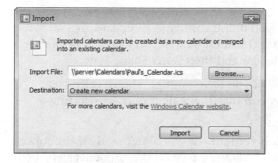

FIGURE 6.14   If you receive an email inviting you to subscribe to a calendar, click the link to import the calendar into Windows Calendar.

4. If you want to merge the published calendar into your own calendar, use the Destination list to select the name of your calendar; otherwise, the published calendar appears as a separate calendar.

5. Click Import. Windows Calendar adds the published calendar.

If you don't have a subscription invitation message, follow these steps instead:

1. Select Share, Subscribe to open the Subscribe to a Calendar dialog box.

2. Use the Calendar to Subscribe To text box to type the address of the published calendar.

3. Click Next. Calendar subscribes you to the published calendar and then displays the Calendar Subscription Settings dialog box.

4. Edit the calendar name, if necessary.

5. Use the Update Interval list to select the interval at which you want Calendar to update the subscribed calendar: Every 15 Minutes, Every Hour, Every Day, Every Week, or No Update.

6. If you want to receive any reminders in the calendar, activate the Include Reminders check box.

7. If you also want to see the published calendar's tasks, activate the Include Tasks check box.

8. Click Finish. The published calendar appears in your Calendars list.

Working with Shared Calendars

After you publish one or more of your calendars and subscribe to one or more remote calendars, Windows Calendar offers a number of techniques for working with these items. Here's a summary:

▶ **Changing a calendar's sharing information**—When you select a published or subscribed calendar, the Details pane displays a Sharing Information section, and you use the controls in that section to configure the calendar's sharing options.

▶ **Publishing calendar changes**—If your published calendar isn't configured to automatically publish changes, you can republish by hand by selecting the calendar and then selecting Share, Sync.

▶ **Updating a subscribed calendar**—If you didn't configure an update interval for a subscribed calendar, or if you want to see the latest data in that calendar before the next update is scheduled, select the calendar and then select Share, Sync.

▶ **Synchronizing all shared calendars**—If you have multiple shared calendars (published and subscribed), you can synchronize them all at once by selecting Share, Sync All.

▶ **Sending a published calendar announcement**—If you didn't send an announcement about your published calendar, or if you want to send the announcement to different people, select the calendar and then select Share, Send Publish E-Mail.

▶ **Stopping a published calendar**—If you no longer want other people to subscribe to your calendar, select it and then select Stop Publishing. When Calendar asks you to confirm, click Unpublish. (Note, however, that if you want your calendar file to remain on the server, you first need to deactivate the Delete Calendar on Server check box.)

▶ **Stopping a subscribed calendar**—If you no longer want to subscribe to a remote calendar, select it and then press Delete. When Calendar asks you to confirm, click Yes.

Viewing Share Storage History

Your Windows Home Server shared folders will likely see a lot of data traffic, depending on the kinds of digital activities your family prefers. Shares such as Music, Photos, and Videos might be constantly getting bigger as people share their media. As the administrator of your home network, you should keep an eye on the Windows Home Server storage, not only to make sure the server doesn't run out of space, but also to look for possible abuse of the system (for example, someone with several months of recorded TV shows languishing in the Recorded TV folder).

To see how much space a shared folder is using, follow these steps:

1. Open the Windows Home Server Console.
2. Display the Shared Folders tab.
3. For the shared folder in question, examine the value in the Used Space column. (You can also double-click the folder and then look at the Used Space value in the property sheet's General tab.)

However, it isn't enough just to know how much space the folder is currently using. To properly manage a shared folder, you need to know the usage history of that folder. Is the current usage historically low or high? Did the usage suddenly and substantially increase recently? For these and similar questions, you need to view the shared folder history. If the folder has been around for at least a week (Windows Home Server won't display a history for any time frame less than that), follow these steps to display its usage history:

1. Open the Windows Home Server Console.
2. Display the Shared Folders tab.
3. Right-click the shared folder and then click View History. Windows Home Server displays the folder history, as shown in Figure 6.15.

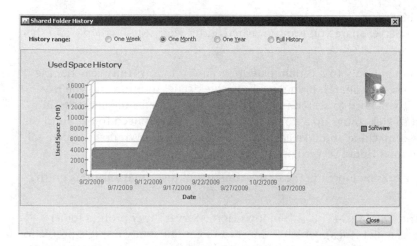

FIGURE 6.15   For a shared folder that's at least a week old, you can view the folder's usage history.

If you want to see the history for all the shared folders in a single graph, right-click an empty section of the Shared Folders tab, and then click View History.

4. Use the History Range options to specify the amount of data you want to see: One Week, One Month, One Year, or Full History.

5. When you're done, click Close.

Searching the Shared Folders

After you've used Windows Home Server for a while, you could easily end up with thousands—heck, even tens of thousands—of files on the server shares. This is particularly true if you have a large Windows Home Server storage pool (remember the old computing law that data expands to fill the space available for storage), several Windows clients, and several users. Of course, it's perfectly acceptable to treat the Windows Home Server shares as a kind of virtual basement where you toss a bunch of files and folders; however, there will almost certainly come a day when you need to actually find a particular file or folder in that mess. Assuming you have a life, you probably don't want to waste valuable chunks of that life by scouring the server shares manually.

One solution is to use the search feature on your Windows client:

▶ In Windows 7 and Windows Vista, open the Windows Home Server share you want to search, and then type your search criteria in the Search box.

▶ In Windows XP's Search Companion, use the Look In list to browse for the Windows Home Server share you want to search, enter your search criteria, and then click Search.

These techniques work, but only to a certain extent because Windows only searches file and folder names on network shares. If you need to delve deeper to find what you're looking for—that is, if you need to search not only filenames, but also file contents and metadata—you need to kick things up a notch or three. That is, you need to log on to the Windows Home Server machine and take advantage of the powerful Windows Search 4.0 that comes with Windows Home Server Power Pack 3.

Windows Search 4.0 works by indexing the entire contents of just three locations on the server:

▶ **Documents and Settings**—This is Windows Home Server's user profiles folder (`C:\Documents and Settings`), which in most cases contains only a single profile for the Administrator user. (By default, Windows Search also indexes the All Users profile.)

▶ **Internet Explorer History**—The Administrator account's list of visited websites.

▶ **Shares**—The Windows Home Server shared folders (`D:\shares`).

These strike me as sensible defaults because there isn't likely to be anything else on your server that you'd want to search. However, you can control what Windows Search indexes and force a rebuild of the index. Log on to the server and select Start, Control Panel, Indexing Options. This displays the Indexing Options dialog box shown in Figure 6.16. To customize the search engine, you have two choices:

► **Modify**—Click this button to display the Indexed Locations dialog box, which enables you to change the locations included in the index. Activate the checkbox for each drive or folder you want to include.

► **Advanced**—Click this button to display the Advanced Options dialog box, which enables you to index encrypted files, change the index location, specify the file types (extensions) that you want include in or exclude from the index, and even add network shares to the index. You can also click Rebuild to re-create the index, which is useful if you find that Windows Search doesn't seem to be returning the correct results.

CAUTION

The Windows Search Engine takes a long time to index even a relatively small amount of data. If you're asking WSE to index dozens of gigabytes of data, wait until you're done working for the day and let the indexer run all night.

FIGURE 6.16   Use Control Panel's Indexing Options to configure Windows Search.

As-You-Type Searches with Desktop Search

When you log on to Windows Home Server, one of the first things you notice is the Windows Search Deskbar, which is a taskbar toolbar that consists of a text box and a search button. As shown in Figure 6.17, as you type characters in the Deskbar's text box, the Windows Search Results window appears with a list that displays the following search links:

▶ A list of shortcuts for programs with names that include the typed characters

▶ A list of files (documents) with content or metadata that include the typed characters

▶ Other data—such as contacts, email messages, and sites from Internet Explorer's Favorites and History lists—with content or metadata that include the typed characters

▶ A Search Desktop link

▶ A Search Web link

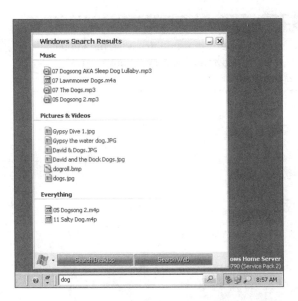

FIGURE 6.17   As-you-type searching using the Windows Search Deskbar.

If you see the program or file you want, click it to open it. Otherwise, you can click Search Desktop to see the complete list of matches from the files in the index. If you prefer to search the Web for your text, click the Search the Web link instead.

Advanced Searches

As-you-type searches are handy and fast, but they tend to return too many results because they look for your search text in documents' metadata and contents. However, to find what you're looking for in a server with dozens or even hundreds of gigabytes of data and many thousands of files, you need a more sophisticated approach. Windows Search can help here, too.

Either run an as-you-type search and then click Search Desktop or, in any folder window, click the Search button. The Windows Search window appears.

Windows Search assumes that you want to search by file type, so click one of the displayed types: Everything (matches any file type), Documents, E-mail, or Other.

To modify the search location, pull down the All Location list and click a location. You can also click Add Location to display the Browse For Folder dialog box.

With your search criteria set up, you can run the search by typing your search criteria in the text box and then clicking the Desktop button. Figure 6.18 shows some example results.

FIGURE 6.18   Use the Windows Search window to perform more advanced searches.

Using Advanced Query Syntax to Search Properties

Simple text searches aren't going to radically boost anyone's productivity or help you find a file needle in a hard disk haystack. To take searching to the next level, you need to know about another powerful search feature: Windows Search syntax.

When you run a standard text search, Windows Search looks for matches not only in the filename and the file contents, but also in the file metadata: the properties associated with each file. That's cool and all, but what if you want to match only a particular property. For example, if you're searching the Music share for albums that include the word Rock in the title, a basic search on "rock" will also return music where the artist's name includes rock and the album genre is Rock. This is not good.

To fix this kind of thing, you can create powerful and targeted searches by using a special syntax in your search queries. You can use this syntax either in the Windows Search Deskbar or in the Windows Search window.

For file properties, you use the following syntax:

```
property:value
```

Here, *property* is the name of the file property you want to search on, and *value* is the criteria you want to use. The property can be any of the metadata categories used by Windows Home Server. For example, the categories in a music folder include Name, Track Number, Title, Artist, Album Title, and Bit Rate. Right-click any column header in Windows Explorer's Details view to see more properties such as Genre and Duration, and you can click More to see the complete list.

Here are a few things to bear in mind:

▶ If the property name is a single word, use that word in your query. For example, the following code matches music where the Artist property is Coldplay:

```
artist:coldplay
```

▶ If the property name uses two or more words, remove the spaces between the words and use the resulting text in your query. For example, the following code matches pictures where the Date Taken property is August 23, 2009:

```
datetaken:8/23/2009
```

▶ If the value uses two or more words and you want to match the exact phrase, surround the phrase with quotation marks. For example, the following code matches music where the Genre property is Alternative & Punk:

```
genre:"alternative & punk"
```

▶ If the value uses two or more words and you want to match both words in any order, surround them with parentheses. For example, the following code matches music where the Album property contains the words Head and Goats in any order:

```
album:(head goats)
```

▶ If you want to match files where a particular property has no value, use empty braces, [], as the value. For example, the following code matches files where the Tags property is empty:

```
tags:[]
```

You can also refine your searches with the following operators and wildcards:

▶ **>**—Matches files where the specified property is greater than the specified value. For example, the following code matches pictures where the Date Taken property is later than January 1, 2009:

```
datetaken:>1/1/2009
```

▶ **>=**—Matches files where the specified property is greater than or equal to the specified value. For example, the following code matches files where the Size property is greater than or equal to 10000 bytes:

```
size:>=10000
```

▶ **<**—Matches files where the specified property is less than the specified value. For example, the following code matches music where the Bit Rate property is less than 128 (bits per second):

```
bitrate:<128
```

▶ **<=**—Matches files where the specified property is less than or equal to the specified value. For example, the following code matches files where the Size property is less than or equal to 1024 bytes:

```
size:<=1024
```

▶ **..**—Matches files where the specified property is between (and including) two values. For example, the following code matches files where the Date Modified property is between and including August 1, 2008 and August 31, 2008:

```
datemodified:8/1/2008..8/31/2008
```

▶ *****—Substitutes for multiple characters. For example, the following code matches music where the Album property includes the word Hits:

```
album:*hits
```

▶ **?**—Substitutes for a single character. For example, the following code matches music where the Artists property begins with Blu and includes any character in the fourth position:

```
artists:blu?
```

For even more sophisticated searches, you can combine multiple criteria using Boolean operators:

▶ **AND (or +)**—Use this operator to match files that meet all of your criteria. For example, the following code matches pictures where the Date Taken property is later than January 1, 2009 and the Size property is greater than 1000000 bytes:

```
datetaken:>1/1/2009 AND size:>1000000
```

▶ **OR**—Choose this option to match files that meet at least one of your criteria. For example, the following code matches music where the Genre property is either Rock or Blues:

```
genre:rock OR genre:blues
```

▶ **NOT (or –)**—Choose this option to match files that do not meet the criteria. For example, the following code matches pictures where the Type property is not JPEG:

```
type:NOT jpeg
```

NOTE

The Boolean operators AND, OR, and NOT must appear with all-uppercase letters in your query.

Deleting a Shared Folder

If you no longer need a shared folder, you should delete it so that it doesn't clutter the Shared Folders tab. Windows Home Server enables you to delete any folder that you've created yourself, as well as any user folder. (You can't remove the predefined shares, such as Music and Software.) Follow these steps to delete a shared folder:

1. If you have any data in the shared folder that you want to preserve, open the folder and copy or move it to another location.
2. If the shared folder is open either on the server or on a client, close the folder. (Technically this step isn't strictly necessary because Windows Home Server closes all open instances of the folder automatically. However, if any files from that folder are open, you must close them.)
3. Run Windows Home Server Console.
4. Display the Shared Folders tab.
5. Click Remove. (If the Remove command is disabled, it means you can't delete the folder.) Windows Home Server warns you that the deletion will be permanent.
6. Click Finish. Windows Home Server deletes the folder.

From Here

▶ To learn about security groups and their associated permissions, **see** "Understanding Security Groups," **P. 35**.

▶ For information on viewing Windows Home Server shared folders using a Mac, **see** "Using a Mac on Your Windows Home Server Network," **P. 70**.

▶ For information on viewing Windows Home Server shared folders using Linux, **see** "Using a Linux Client on Your Windows Home Server Network," **P. 80**.

▶ For more information about folder duplication, **see** "Safety: Using Duplication to Ensure No Data Is Lost," **P. 128**.

▶ For the details on Drive Extender and how it works, **see** "Understanding Drive Extender," **P. 129**.

▶ To learn how to use Windows Home Server's media sharing feature, **see** "Streaming Digital Media to Network Computers and Devices," **P. 214**.

CHAPTER 7

Making Connections to Network Computers

You saw in Chapter 6, "Sharing Folders and Files on the Home Server," that Windows Home Server offers a number of predefined folders that you can use to store your own files as well as media such as music, photos, and videos. Of course, you're also free to share folders on any client computer, and those folders will show up when you open the computer's folder from the Network window (in Windows 7 or Vista) or My Network Places (in XP).

However, having access to shared folders may not be sufficient in some cases:

▶ You want to edit a document, but only another computer on your network has the required application.

▶ You want to read or respond to an email message that you received on another network computer.

▶ You want to access files in *any* folder on another network computer, not just a shared folder.

▶ You want to visit an Internet site that you've set up as a favorite in Internet Explorer on another network computer.

All of these scenarios require a higher level of connection to the network computer: the computer's desktop itself. If you can't physically sit down in front of the computer, or if it's just not convenient to use the computer directly right now, you need to access the computer's desktop remotely. As you learn in this chapter, you actually have three options for getting a network computer's desktop to appear on your screen:

▶ You can connect directly using the Remote Desktop Connection feature found in Windows 7, Windows Vista, and Windows XP.

▶ You can use Windows Home Server Web Site Remote Access to access a network computer's desktop through a web browser and a local area network connection.

▶ You can use Windows Home Server Web Site Remote Access to access a network computer's desktop through a web browser and an Internet connection.

In each case, you get full access to the network computer's desktop, which enables you to open folders, run programs, edit documents, and tweak settings. In short, anything you can do while physically sitting in front of the other computer you can now do remotely from your own computer. The responsiveness of the remote session depends a great deal on the speed of the connection. For a LAN connection, an Ethernet (10Mbps) connection or 802.11b (11Mbps) wireless connection is just too slow, whereas a Fast Ethernet (100Mbps) or 802.11g (54 Mbps) connection will give you adequate performance for most tasks. If you want to play games or perform other graphics-intensive tasks, you really need a Gigabit Ethernet (1Gbps) or 802.11n (248Mbps) connection. Over the Internet, don't even try to connect using dial-up; instead, you need a cable or DSL broadband (1Mbps or better) link, and even then you'll want to avoid large files and heavy-duty graphic tasks.

Configuring a Computer as a Remote Desktop Host

Remote Desktop is easy to configure and use, but it does require a small amount of prep work to ensure trouble-free operation. Let's begin with the remote computer, also called the *host* computer.

The first thing you need to know is that not all versions of Windows 7, Vista, and XP can act as Remote Desktop hosts. The only versions that support this are Windows 7 Professional, Windows 7 Enterprise, and Windows 7 Ultimate; Vista Business, Vista Enterprise, and Vista Ultimate; XP Pro, and XP Media Center Edition 2005. Yes, you read that right: The five versions of Windows most likely to be used in the home and therefore most likely to be clients on a Windows Home Server network—Windows 7 Home Basic, Windows Home Premium, Vista Home Basic, Vista Home Premium, and XP Home—*can't* act as Remote Desktop hosts. This is a mind-numbingly shortsighted move on Microsoft's part, and it may prevent many home users from making the move to Windows Home Server.

All that aside, on machines that *can* act as hosts, by default the user currently logged on to the host machine has permission to connect remotely to the host. Other users with default remote connection permissions are members of the host's Administrators and Remote Desktop Users groups. (In all cases, only users with password-protected accounts can use Remote Desktop.) If you want to connect to the host remotely, you first need to set up an account for the username with which you want to connect from the client. (Again, you must assign a password to this account.)

Configuring a Windows 7 or Vista Host

If the host machine is running Windows 7 Professional, Enterprise, or Ultimate, or Vista Business, Enterprise, or Ultimate, you have to do two things to prepare the computer for its Remote Desktop hosting duties:

▶ Disable Sleep mode.

▶ Activate the Remote Desktop service.

Most Windows 7 and Vista machines are configured to go into Sleep mode after one hour of inactivity. Sleep is a low-power mode that turns everything off except power to the memory chips, which store the current desktop configuration. When you turn the machine back on, the desktop and your open programs and documents appear within a few seconds. However, remote clients won't be able to connect to the host if it's in Sleep mode, so you have to disable this feature. Here are the steps to follow:

1. Select Start, Control Panel, click either System and Security (in Windows 7) or System and Maintenance (in Windows Vista), and then under Power Options click Change When the Computer Sleeps.

2. In the Put the Computer to Sleep list, select Never.

3. Click Save Changes.

Now follow these steps to activate the Remote Desktop service:

1. Select Start, right-click Computer, and then click Properties to open the System window.

2. Click the Remote Settings link. (In Windows Vista, you must enter your UAC credentials at this point.) Windows opens the System Properties dialog box with the Remote tab displayed, as shown in Figure 7.1.

TIP

Another way to open the System Properties dialog box with the Remote tab displayed is to press Windows Logo+R (or select Start, All Programs, Accessories, Run), type `systempropertiesremote` (or `control sysdm.cpl,,5`), click OK, and (in Vista) enter your UAC credentials.

3. In the Remote Desktop group, you have two choices:

▶ **Allow Connections from Computers Running Any Version of Remote Desktop**—Select this option if you want people running previous versions of Remote Desktop to be able to access the host.

▶ **Allow Connections Only from Computers Running Remote Desktop with Network Level Authentication**—Select this option if you only want the most secure form of Remote Desktop access. In this case, Vista checks the client computer to see if its version of Remote Desktop supports Network Level Authentication (NLA). NLA is an authentication protocol that authenticates the user before making the Remote Desktop connection. NLA is built into every version of Windows 7 and Windows Vista, but is not supported on older Windows systems.

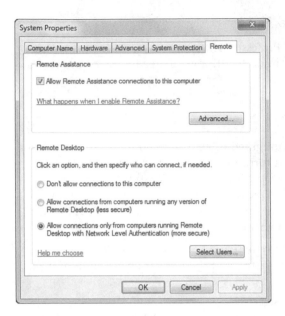

FIGURE 7.1   In Windows 7 or Vista versions that can act as remote hosts, select an option in the Remote Desktop group to enable remote connections to the computer's desktop.

4. If you didn't add more users earlier, skip to step 7. Otherwise, click Select Users to display the Remote Desktop Users dialog box.

5. Click Add to display the Select Users dialog box, type the username, and click OK. (Repeat this step to add other users.)

6. Click OK to return to the System Properties dialog box.

7. Click OK.

Configuring an XP Host

If the host machine is running XP Pro, here are the steps to follow to set it up to host Remote Desktop sessions:

1. Log on to the host as an Administrator.

2. Launch Control Panel's System icon to open the System Properties dialog box. (Alternatively, click Start, right-click My Computer, and then click Properties.)

3. Display the Remote tab.

4. In the Remote Desktop group, activate the Allow Users to Connect Remotely to This Computer check box, as shown in Figure 7.2.

5. If you didn't add more users earlier, skip to step 8. Otherwise, click Select Remote Users to display the Remote Desktop Users dialog box.

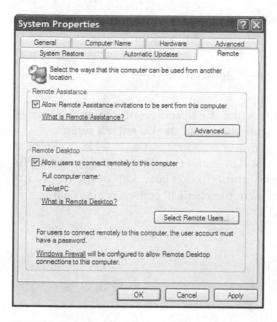

FIGURE 7.2   In XP Pro, the Allow Users to Connect Remotely to This Computer check box must be activated to enable Remote Desktop sessions on the computer.

6. Click Add to display the Select Users dialog box, type the username, and click OK. (Repeat this step to add other users.)

7. Click OK to return to the System Properties dialog box.

8. Click OK.

Restricting the Computers That Can Connect to the Host

When you configure a computer to be a host, Windows adds the Remote Desktop service to Windows Firewall's Exceptions list and, in Windows 7 and Windows Vista, it also creates a Windows Firewall rule that allows incoming connections using the Remote Desktop Protocol (RDP) on port 3389. You can increase the security of the Remote Desktop connection by modifying this rule using Windows Firewall with Advanced Security (WFAS), which is a Microsoft Management Console snap-in. Specifically, you can specify the IP addresses of the computers that are allowed to connect to the host. You might do this, for example, if you want to be able to connect the host from your desktop computer and your notebook, but you don't want the kids' computers to be able to connect.

Here are the steps to follow:

1. Press Windows Logo+R (or select Start, All Programs, Accessories, Run), type `wf.msc`, and then click OK.

2. In Windows Vista, enter your User Account Control credentials. The WFAS snap-in appears.

3. Click Inbound Rules. After a few seconds, the list of Inbound Rules appears.

4. Double-click the Remote Desktop (TCP-In) rule. (If you see two of these rules, double-click the one with the green checkmark.) The rule's property sheet appears.

5. Display the Scope tab.

6. In the Local IP Address group, select These IP Addresses.

7. Click Add to open the IP Address dialog box.

8. In the This IP Address or Subnet text box, enter the IP address of a computer that can connect to the host, as shown in Figure 7.3. (You can also enter a subnet address such as 192.168.0.0/24, which allows any address in the 192.168.0.x subnet; alternatively, you can click This IP Address Range and type the beginning address in the From text box and the ending address in the To text box. Both of these options are useful for networks that use DHCP where the client IP addresses may change over time.)

FIGURE 7.3   Use the property sheet for the Remote Desktop (TCP-In) rule to customize security for incoming Remote Desktop connections.

9. Click OK.

10. Repeat steps 7–9 to add other IP addresses to the Scope tab.

11. If you also want to restrict access to only wired or wireless connections, display the Advanced tab, click Customize in the Interface Types group, and then click These Interface Types. Activate the check box beside the type you want to allow: Local Area Network (wired) or Wireless. Click OK.

12. Click OK.

Connecting via Remote Desktop Connection

Although, as I mentioned earlier, only certain Windows 7, Vista, and XP machines can act as Remote Desktop hosts, *all* Windows 7, Vista, and XP computers can initiate a Remote Desktop connection to a host (that is, they can act as Remote Desktop *clients*). In this section, you learn how to prepare the clients and make the connection.

Getting the Client Computer Ready

You must install the Remote Desktop Connection software on the client computer. This software is already installed in all versions of Windows 7 and Windows Vista. If you're running Windows XP on the client, you can install the Remote Desktop Connection software from the Windows XP CD (if you have one):

1. Insert the Windows XP CD and wait for the Welcome to Microsoft Windows XP screen to appear.
2. Click Perform Additional Tasks.
3. Click Set Up Remote Desktop Connection.

> **TIP**
>
> You can also download the latest client software from Microsoft:
>
> www.microsoft.com/windowsxp/downloads/tools/rdclientdl.mspx
>
> You can also use this client if you're running Windows XP and don't have access to the XP install disc.
>
> If you have a Mac machine running OS X connected to your network, you can initiate a session with any Remote Desktop host and even share files between the two computers. The Remote Desktop Connection Client for Mac is available from Microsoft:
>
> www.microsoft.com/mac/otherproducts/otherproducts.aspx?pid=remotedesktopclient
>
> If you have a Linux box on your network, you can use `rdesktop` as a Remote Desktop Protocol client. You can download the software here:
>
> www.rdesktop.org/

▶ **SEE** For details on Mac-based Remote Desktop connections, **see** "Using a Mac to Make a Remote Desktop Connection to Windows Home Server," **P. 74.**

Making the Connection to the Remote Desktop

On the client computer, you can now connect to the host computer's desktop. Follow these steps:

1. Select Start, All Programs, Accessories, Remote Desktop Connection. (In Windows XP, select Start, All Programs, Accessories, Communications, Remote Desktop Connection.) The Remote Desktop Connection dialog box appears.

2. In the Computer text box, type the name or the IP address of the host computer.

3. If you don't want to customize Remote Desktop, skip to step 10. Otherwise, click Options to expand the dialog box to the version shown in Figure 7.4.

FIGURE 7.4   Clicking the Options button expands the dialog box so that you can customize Remote Desktop.

4. The General tab offers the following additional options:

    ▶ **Computer**—The name or IP address of the remote computer.

    ▶ **User Name**—The username you want to use to log in to the host computer.

    ▶ **Password**—(Windows XP Service Pack 2 or earlier only) The password to use to log on to the host computer.

    ▶ **Domain**—(Windows XP only) Leave this text box blank.

    ▶ **Allow Me to Save Credentials**—(Windows 7 only) Activate this check box to enable the Remember My Credentials option in the login dialog box.

▶ **Save**—(Windows 7 and Vista only) Click this button to have Windows remember your current settings so that you don't have to type them again the next time you connect. This is useful if you only connect to Windows Home Server.

▶ **Save As**—Click this button to save your connection settings to a Remote Desktop (.rdp) file for later use. This is useful if you regularly connect to other hosts.

▶ **Open**—Click this button to open a saved .rdp file.

5. The Display tab offers three options for controlling the look of the Remote Desktop window:

▶ **Remote Desktop Size**—(Display Configuration in Windows 7) Drag this slider to set the resolution of Remote Desktop. Drag the slider all the way to the left for a 640×480 screen size; drag the slider all the way to the right to have Remote Desktop take up the entire client screen, no matter what resolution the host is currently using.

▶ **Colors**—Use this list to set the number of colors used for the Remote Desktop display. Note that if the number of colors on either the host or the client is fewer than the value you select in the Colors list, Windows uses the lesser value.

▶ **Display the Connection Bar...**—When you activate this check box, the Remote Desktop Connection client displays a connection bar at the top of the Remote Desktop window, provided you selected Full Screen for the Remote Desktop Size setting. You use the connection bar to minimize, restore, and close the Remote Desktop window. If you find that the connection bar just gets in the way, deactivate this check box to prevent it from appearing.

6. The Local Resources tab offers three options for controlling certain interactions between the client and host:

▶ **Remote Computer Sound**—(Remote Audio in Windows 7) Use this list to determine where Windows plays the sounds generated by the host. You can play them on the client (if you want to hear what's happening on the host), on the host (if you want a user sitting at the host to hear the sounds), or not at all (if you have a slow connection). In Windows 7, you can also choose to enable remote audio recording.

▶ **Keyboard**—Use this list to determine which computer is sent special Windows key combinations—such as Alt+Tab and Ctrl+Esc—that you press on the client keyboard. You can have the key combos sent to the client, to the host, or to the host only when you're running the Remote Desktop window in full-screen mode. What happens if you're sending key combos to one computer and you need to use a particular key combo on the other computer? For such situations, Remote Desktop offers several keyboard equivalents:

Windows Key Combo—Remote Desktop Equivalent

Alt+Tab—Alt+Page Up

Alt+Shift+Tab—Alt+Page Down

Alt+Esc—Alt+Insert

Ctrl+Esc or Windows Logo—Alt+Home

Print Screen—Ctrl+Alt+– (numeric keypad)

Alt+Print Screen—Ctrl+Alt++ (numeric keypad)

TIP

Here are three other useful keyboard shortcuts you can press on the client computer and have Windows send to the host:

Ctrl+Alt+End	Displays the Windows Security dialog box. This is equivalent to pressing Ctrl+Alt+Delete, which Windows always applies to the client computer.
Alt+Delete	Displays the active window's Control menu.
Ctrl+Alt+Break	Toggles the Remote Desktop window between full-screen mode and a regular window.

- ▶ **Local Devices and Resources**—Leave the Printers check box activated to display the client's printers in the host's Printers and Faxes window. The client's printers appear with the syntax *Printer* (`from` *COMPUTER*), where *Printer* is the printer name and *COMPUTER* is the network name of the client computer. In Windows 7 and Vista, leave the Clipboard check box activated to use the client's Clipboard during the remote session. In XP, you can also connect disk drives and serial ports, which I describe in the next step.

7. In Windows 7 and Vista, click More to see the Remote Desktop Connection dialog box. Use the following check boxes to configure more client devices and resources on the host (click OK when you're done):

   - ▶ **Smart Cards**—Leave this check box activated to access the client's smart cards on the host.

   - ▶ **Serial Ports**—(Ports in Windows 7) Activate this check box to make any devices attached to the client's serial ports (such as a barcode scanner) available while you're working with the host.

   - ▶ **Drives**—Activate this check box to display the client's hard disk partitions and mapped network drives in the host's Computer (or My Computer) window. (You can also open the branch to activate the check boxes of specific drives.) The client's drives appear in the window's Other group with the syntax *D* on *Computer*, where *D* is the drive letter and *Computer* is the network name of the client computer.

   - ▶ **Supported Plug and Play Devices**—Activate this check box to make some of the client's Plug and Play devices, such as media players and digital cameras, available to the host. (You can also open the branch to activate the check boxes of specific devices.)

8. Use the Programs tab to specify a program to run on connection. Activate the Start the Following Program on Connection check box, and then use the Program Path and File Name text box to specify the program to run. After connecting, the user can work with only this program, and when he quits the program, the session also ends.

9. Use the Experience tab (the Windows 7 version is shown in Figure 7.5) to set performance options for the connection. Use the Choose Your Connection Speed to Optimize Performance drop-down list to set the appropriate connection speed. Because you're connecting over a network, you should choose the LAN (10 Mbps or higher) option. Depending on the connection speed you choose, one or more of the following check boxes will be activated (the faster the speed, the more check boxes Windows activates):

   ▸ **Desktop Background**—Toggles the host's desktop background on and off.

   ▸ **Font Smoothing**—(Windows 7, Vista, and XP Service Pack 3 only) Toggles the host's font smoothing on and off.

   ▸ **Desktop Composition**—(Windows 7, Vista, and XP Service Pack 3 only) Toggles the host's desktop composition engine on and off.

   ▸ **Show Windows Contents While Dragging**—Toggles the display of window contents when you drag a host window with your mouse.

FIGURE 7.5   Use the Experience tab to set performance options for the connection.

▶ **Menu and Windows Animation**—Toggles on and off the animations that Windows normally uses when you pull down menus or minimize and maximize windows.

▶ **Visual Styles**—(Themes in Windows Vista and XP) Toggles the host's current visual theme on and off.

▶ **Persistent Bitmap Caching**—Improves performance by not storing frequently used host images on the client computer.

10. Click Connect. Windows Vista prompts you to enter your security credentials.

11. In Windows 7 or Vista, type the username and password of the host account you want to use for the logon, and then click OK. (Note that in subsequent logons, you'll only need to type the password.)

12. If you activated the Disk Drives or Serial Ports check boxes in the Local Resources tab, a security warning dialog box appears. If you're sure that making these resources available to the remote computer is safe, activate the Don't Prompt Me Again for Connections to This Remote Computer check box. Click OK.

The remote desktop then appears on your computer. If you choose to work in full-screen mode, move the mouse to the top of the screen to see the connection bar, shown in Figure 7.6.

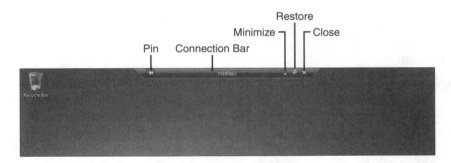

FIGURE 7.6   After you've connected and the remote computer's desktop appears on your screen, move the mouse to the top of the screen to see the connection bar.

If you want the connection bar to appear all the time, click to activate the Pin button. If you need to work with your own desktop, you have two choices:

▶ Click the connection bar's Minimize button to minimize the Remote Desktop window.

▶ Click the connection bar's Restore button to display the Remote Desktop window.

Disconnecting from the Remote Desktop

When you finish with the Remote Desktop session, you have two choices for disconnecting:

- ▶ Using the host desktop, select Start, Log Off.
- ▶ Click the Close button in the connection bar. Windows displays a dialog box to let you know that your remote session will be disconnected. Click OK.

Connecting via Windows Home Server Web Site Remote Access

You can use the Remote Desktop Connection program to connect to *any* Remote Desktop host, even hosts that don't have the Windows Home Server Connector software installed. A second method you can use to connect to Remote Desktop hosts is to go through the Windows Home Server network. With this method, which is a bit easier than running Remote Desktop Connection directly, you can only connect to hosts that have Windows Home Server Connector installed.

This method runs Remote Desktop Connection behind the scenes via Windows Home Server. That is, instead of connecting directly to the remote host, Remote Desktop Connection takes you to the Windows Home Server, which then shows you the remote computer's desktop. Up front, Windows Home Server gives you a simple interface that lists the available computers to which you can connect. This interface is part of Windows Home Server Web Site Remote Access. This is the same interface that you use to connect to your network via the Internet, as described a bit later (see "Connecting via the Internet"). However, you also use it to connect to a Remote Desktop host over your LAN, which is what I discuss in this section.

For this to work, you must enable the Remote Desktop service on the host, as described earlier (see "Configuring a Computer as a Remote Desktop Host"), and then be sure to reboot the host PC.

CAUTION

Windows Home Server's Remote Access feature is *not* compatible with Network Level Authentication. Therefore, when you're setting up a Windows 7 or Windows Vista host, don't select the Allow Connections Only from Computers Running Remote Desktop with Network Level Authentication option. Instead, select the Allow Connections from Computers Running Any Version of Remote Desktop option.

NOTE

It's crucial that you reboot the host PC after you enable Remote Desktop; otherwise, Windows Home Server won't recognize the PC as being configured for Remote Desktop duties.

Configuring Users for Remote Access

You need to configure Windows Home Server to allow remote access for the user account that you'll be using to log on to the Remote Desktop host. Here are the steps to follow:

1. Log in to the Windows Home Server Console.
2. Select the User Accounts tab.
3. Click the user you want to configure and then click Properties (or just double-click the user). The user's property sheet appears.
4. In the General tab, click to activate the Enable Remote Access for this User check box.
5. In the list box, select Allow Access to Shared Folders and Home Computers. (If you don't want the user messing with the shared folders remotely, select Allow Access to Home Computers Only, instead.)
6. Click OK.

Activating Remote Access on the Server

Your final bit of prep involves turning on the Remote Access service in Windows Home Server. Here's how it's done:

1. Log in to the Windows Home Server Console.
2. Click Settings.
3. Click the Remote Access tab.
4. Click Turn On. Windows Home Server configures remote access on your network.
5. Click Next. Windows Home Server prompts you to set up a domain name. I discuss this in detail a bit later (see "Obtaining a Domain Name from Microsoft"), so click Cancel.
6. Click OK.

Displaying the Remote Access Home Page

Before you can connect to a remote computer, you need to log on to Windows Home Server's Remote Access home page. This is a page on the Windows Home Server website that gives you access to the Remote Desktop hosts on your network, as well as to the

Windows Home Server shared folders. Here are the steps to follow to display the Remote Access home page:

1. On the client, launch the Internet Explorer web browser.

TIP

You can use Firefox to display the Remote Access pages, but Firefox doesn't display the Computers tab, so you can't access network computers. To fix this, install the IE Tab add-on (available from ietab.mozdev.org). When you get to the Remote Access logon page, right-click the page and then click View Page in IE Tab.

---

2. Type the following address into the address bar (where *server* is the name of your Windows Home Server):

   `http://server`

3. Press Enter. Windows Home Server redirects you to the Windows Home Server Web Site home page (see Figure 7.7) at the following address:

   `http://server/home/default.aspx`

4. Click Log On. The Windows Home Server Remote Access logon page appears.

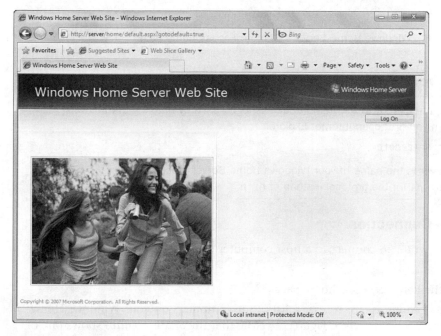

FIGURE 7.7   The home page of the Windows Home Server Web Site.

5. Type the username and password of your Windows Home Server account, and then click Log On. Windows Home Server redirects you to the Windows Home Server Web Site Remote Access page (see Figure 7.8) at the following address:

```
https://server/remote/default.aspx
```

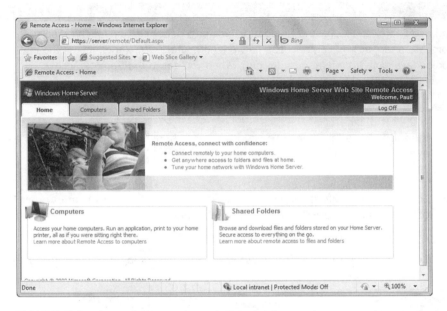

FIGURE 7.8   Windows Home Server's Remote Access home page.

TIP

You can navigate directly to the Remote Access logon page by entering the following address when you first open Internet Explorer:

```
https://server/remote
```

As usual, *server* is the name of your Windows Home Server machine. Note, too, that you specify https for the protocol instead of http.

Making the Connection

With that done, you can connect to a host computer on your network by following these steps:

1. Display the Remote Access home page.

2. Click the Computers tab. You see a list of the computers on your Windows Home Server network, as shown in Figure 7.9. Note that the Status column shows one of the following four values:

   ▶ **Available for Connection**—The computer is capable of acting as a Remote Desktop host, and it has the Remote Desktop service enabled.

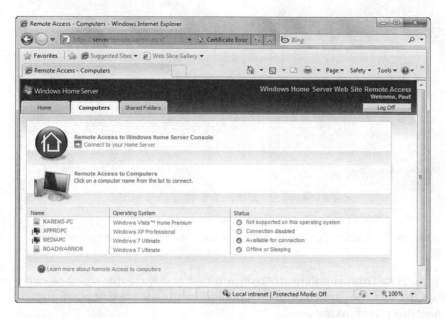

FIGURE 7.9   In the Remote Access site, the Computers tab displays a list of the Windows Home Server clients.

- ▶ **Connection Disabled**—The computer is capable of acting as a Remote Desktop host, but it doesn't have the Remote Desktop service enabled.

- ▶ **Offline or Sleeping**—The computer either is not connected to the network or is in sleep mode.

- ▶ **Not Supported on This Operating System**—The computer is not capable of acting as a Remote Desktop host. That is, the computer is running Windows7 Home Basic, Windows7 Home Premium, Vista Home Basic, Vista Home Premium, or XP Home.

3. If the computer you want to connect to shows Available for Connection in the Status column, click the computer. The Connection Options dialog box appears, as shown in Figure 7.10.

4. Configure the following options:

- ▶ **Connection Speed**—Select Broadband. (You should only select Modem if you're connecting via a dial-up Internet connection, as described in the next section.)

- ▶ **Select a Screen Size for This Connection**—Select either Full Screen or a specific screen size (such as 1024×768 or 1280×1024).

- ▶ **Enable the Remote Computer to Print to My Local Printer**—If you leave this check box activated, if you run the Print command in an application on the remote computer, the document is sent to the printer on your local computer.

FIGURE 7.10   Use the Connection Options to configure some settings for the connection to the remote host.

> **Hear Sounds from the Remote Computer**—If you leave this check box activated, any operating system sounds produced by the remote computer play through your local sound card.

> **Enable Files to Be Transferred from Remote Computer to This Computer**—Activate this check box if you need to upload files from the remote host to your computer.

5. Click OK. Windows Home Server runs the Remote Desktop Connection software to make the connection to Windows Home Server. The Remote Desktop Connection dialog box appears and asks if you trust the computer you're connecting to.

6. Before continuing, note that the Remote Desktop Connection dialog box shows one or more of the following check boxes (if you don't see these check boxes, click Details):

> **Drives**—You see this check box only if you activated the Enable Files to Be Transferred from Remote Computer to This Computer check box in step 4.

> **Clipboard**—If you leave this check box activated, objects that you cut or copy on the remote host are also available on your local computer's Clipboard. This means that you can then paste those objects locally.

> **Printers**—You see this check box only if you activated the Enable the Remote Computer to Print to My Local Printer check box in step 4.

7. Click Connect. Windows Home Server opens a new full-screen browser window, connects to the remote computer, and displays that computer's logon screen in the new window.

8. If you're not displaying the host's desktop full screen, press the spacebar or Enter to enable the ActiveX control that displays the remote desktop in the browser window.

9. Log on to the remote computer.

Figure 7.11 shows a remote computer's desktop displayed in the browser window. Notice that not only do you see the connection bar at the top of the screen, but the connection bar displays the name of your Windows Home Server machine, which indicates that the Remote Desktop connection is going through the server instead of directly to the host PC. Also, in Figure 7.11, I've opened the remote machine's Computer window. Notice that this window now contains a group named Other, and that group contains icons for all the drives on the local computer. Each drive appears with the syntax *Drive* on *COMPUTER*, where *Drive* is the local drive letter and *COMPUTER* is the network name of the local computer (ROADWARRIOR, in this case).

Remote Host's Computer Window

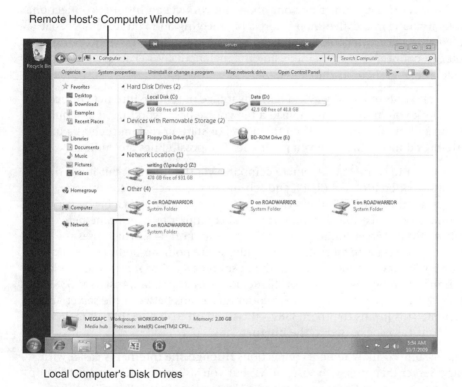

Local Computer's Disk Drives

FIGURE 7.11   The remote host's Computer window displayed in the local computer's browser window.

Disconnecting from the Host

When you finish with the Remote Desktop session, you have three choices for disconnecting:

▶ Using the host desktop, select Start, Log Off.

▶ Display the Connection bar and click the Close button.

▶ Switch to the original browser window (by clicking the minimize button in the connection bar), and then click Disconnect at the top of the window.

When you return to the Windows Home Server Remote Access page, click Log Off to end your session.

Connecting via the Internet

One of the most significant features in the Windows Home Server package is the capability to securely connect to a computer on your home network via an Internet connection. So, for example, if you're in a coffee shop before a big meeting and you remember that you forgot to copy to your notebook the updated presentation file you were working on last night, you can connect to the Internet using the merchant's Wi-Fi access, connect to your home machine, and then download the file.

In fact, there are all kinds of useful ways to take advantage of remote Internet connections: You can check your home email; upload a file you've been working on as a quick-and-dirty backup system; transfer files from the office; or start a program such as a backup or defrag so that it's done by the time you get home. The possibilities are endless.

Windows enables you to connect to a remote computer via the Internet, but it did this using the Remote Desktop Protocol (RDP), and setting up the machines to connect securely wasn't straightforward. Windows Home Server simplifies things a bit by *not* using RDP for the initial Internet connection from the local computer to your home network. Instead, Windows Home Server initiates the connection on port 443, which uses the Secure Sockets Layer (SSL) protocol to create a highly secure point-to-point connection between you and Windows Home Server and then uses port 4125 to set up a secure RDP channel. The port that provides the bulk of the Remote Desktop data transfers is 3389, but Windows Home Server only uses that port for communications between the server and the network client. This means that port 3389—the standard RDP port that all malicious hackers know about—is *not* exposed to the Internet.

Setting up your system to allow remote connections through the Internet is easier with Windows Home Server than it is with Vista or XP, but you still have a few hoops to jump through. Here's a summary of the steps involved. (The sections that follow fill in the details for each step.)

1. Determine the IP address of the Windows Home Server.
2. Configure your network router or gateway to forward data sent on ports 443 and 4125 to the Windows Home Server.
3. Determine your router/gateway's IP address.

Determining the Windows Home Server IP Address

To ensure that the incoming data gets to Windows Home Server, you need to know the server's IP address. Ideally, you configured Windows Home Server with a static IP address, as described in Chapter 1, "Setting Up Your Windows Home Server Network." This is the best way to go because if you use DHCP on the server instead, you have to modify the gateway/router port forwarding (discussed in the next section) every time the server's IP address changes.

> ▶ **SEE** For details on setting a static IP address, **see** "Configuring Windows Home Server with a Static IP Address," **P. 9.**

If you didn't set up Windows Home Server with a static IP address, or if you don't remember the static IP address, you can get the address via the Windows Home Server Console (see the next section) or by following these steps:

1. Log on to Windows Home Server.
2. Select Start, Command Prompt.
3. Type **ipconfig** and press Enter. Windows Home Server displays its current IP address.
4. Write down the address, and then close the Command Prompt window.

Setting Up Port Forwarding on the Router

If your network uses a router, gateway, or other hardware firewall, you need to configure it to forward to the Windows Home Server computer and data sent on the following ports:

- ▶ Port 443 (SSL) using the TCP protocol
- ▶ Port 4125 (RDP) using the TCP protocol

This is *port forwarding*, and you can either get Windows Home Server to configure this for you, or you can do it by hand.

Letting Windows Home Server Configure the Router

If your router or gateway supports Universal Plug and Play (UPnP), Windows Home Server may be able to configure it for you automatically. Here are the steps to follow:

> **NOTE**
>
> Most routers that support UPnP also come with options that enable and disable UPnP. Before asking Windows Home Server to configure your router, access the router's setup pages and make sure that UPnP is enabled.

1. Open the Windows Home Server Console.
2. Click Settings to open the Windows Home Server Settings dialog box.
3. Select the Remote Access tab.
4. In the Remote Access section, click Turn On to launch the Turn On Remote Access wizard. Windows Home Server attempts to configure your router, as shown in Figure 7.12.

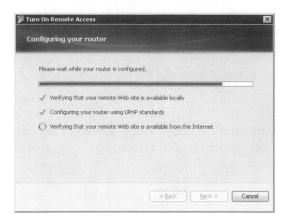

FIGURE 7.12   The Turn On Remote Access wizard configures your router for remote access.

5. The wizard now prompts you to configure a domain name, but we'll skip that here by clicking Cancel. (See "Obtaining a Domain Name from Microsoft," later in this chapter.) If the configuration was successful, the Remote Access tab now displays a Router section that shows the router IP address, the Windows Home Server IP address, and the Windows Home Server physical address (that is, the Media Access Control—MAC, for short—address), as shown in Figure 7.13.

FIGURE 7.13   With Remote Access turned on, Windows Home Server Console shows the router and server addresses.

6. Click OK.

> **TIP**
>
> If Windows Home Server fails to configure your router, consider upgrading the router's firmware. This seems to solve many UPnP problems, particularly with Linksys routers. To upgrade the firmware, go to the router manufacturer's site, find the support or downloads section, and then download the latest firmware version of your device. Then access the router's setup page (use a wired connection, not a wireless one) and look for the page that enables you to apply the new firmware version.

> **TIP**
>
> After Windows Home Server configures the router, it activates the Port Forwarding service, which automatically updates the router every 9,000 seconds, or 2.5 hours. Why does it do this when the configuration is already set? Probably because Windows Home Server assumes the server is getting a dynamic IP address from DHCP on the router. If the server's IP address changes, the router must be updated with the new address.
>
> If you use a static IP address on the server, you can prevent these updates from happening by stopping the Port Forwarding service. Log on to Windows Home Server, select Start, Control Panel, Administrative Tools, Services. Double-click the Windows Home Server Port Forwarding service, change the Startup Type to Manual, and then click Stop.

Configuring the Router By Hand

If Windows Home Server couldn't configure the router, you can always do it yourself, although the steps you follow depend on the device. Figure 7.14 shows the Port Forwarding screen of the router on my system. In this case, I've forwarded the two ports—443 and 4125—so that any data sent to them over TCP is sent automatically to the address 192.168.0.254, which is the static IP address of my Windows Home Server. Consult your device documentation to learn how to set up port forwarding.

Enable	Name	IP Address	Protocol Private Port/Public Port	Inbound Filter	Schedule		
☑	RPD 4125	192.168.0.254	TCP 4125/4125	Allow All	Always		
☑	RDP 443	192.168.0.254	TCP 443/443	Allow All	Always		

FIGURE 7.14   On your router/gateway, forward ports 443 and 4125 to the Windows Home Server IP address.

Determining the Router's External IP Address

To connect to your network via the Internet, you need to specify an IP address instead of a computer name. (You can bypass this if you get a Windows Home Server domain name; see "Obtaining a Domain Name from Microsoft," later in this chapter.) The IP address you use is the address that your ISP assigns to your router when that device connects to the Internet. This is called the router's *external* IP address (to differentiate it from the router's *internal* IP address, which is the address you use to access the router locally). Although some ISPs provide static IP addresses to the router, it's more likely that the address is dynamic and changes each time the gateway connects.

Either way, you need to determine the router's current external IP address. You usually have to log on to the router's setup pages and view some sort of status page. When you set up your remote connection, you'll connect to the router's IP address, which will then forward your connection (thanks to your efforts in the previous section) to Windows Home Server.

TIP

Another way to determine your router's IP address is to navigate to any of the free services for determining your current IP. Here are two:

WhatIsMyIP (www.whatismyip.com)

DynDNS (checkip.dyndns.org)

Using a Dynamic DNS Service

If you want to use Remote Desktop via the Internet regularly, constantly monitoring your router's dynamic IP address can be a pain, particularly if you forget to check it before heading out of the office. A useful solution is to sign up with a dynamic DNS service, which supplies you with a static domain name. The service also installs a program on your computer that monitors your IP address and updates the service's dynamic DNS servers to point your domain name to your IP address. Here are some dynamic DNS services to check out:

DynDNS (www.dyndns.org)
TZO (www.tzo.com)
No-IP.com (www.no-ip.com)

To give you some idea how to go about this, here's a summary of the steps I took to set up dynamic DNS with DynDNS:

1. Sign up for one of the company's services. In my case, I already had a domain name, so I signed up for the Custom DNS service so that DynDNS could handle the DNS duties for my domain. If you don't have a domain, you can sign up for the Domain Registration service.

2. After confirming my account, I used one of the excellent "how-to" articles found on DynDNS to determine the domain names of their DNS servers.

3. With those names in hand, I logged in to my account on the registrar that handles my domain. I then changed the DNS servers for my domain so that they pointed to the DynDNS servers.

4. I downloaded the DynDNS Updater, a program that runs on your local computer and monitors your gateway's dynamic IP address. When that address changes,

DynDNS Updater passes the new address to the DynDNS system so that my domain name always points to the correct IP address.

5. I waited for about a day for the DNS changes to propagate throughout the Internet.

Obtaining a Domain Name from Microsoft

Using a domain name instead of an IP address is better because domain names are easier for everyone in the family to remember, and they don't change the way the IP address assigned by your ISP probably does. Using a dynamic DNS service as described in the previous section enables you to never worry about your router's IP address again. However, if there's a downside to using these services, it's that they cost money (usually around U.S. $25 for a year's subscription), and you can never be sure how long the company might be in business.

If you prefer a service that's free and will almost certainly always be available, you can sign up for a subdomain name from Microsoft. Whereas a domain name takes the form *domain*.com, a subdomain name takes the form *mydomain.domain*.com. Here, *domain*.com is the domain name of the company providing the service, and *mydomain* is a unique name that you provide.

With Windows Home Server, the subdomain takes the form *mydomain*.homeserver.com, and the domain is administered by Microsoft's Windows Live Custom Domains service via the homeserver.com site, the official home of Windows Home Server. The subdomain is free, although it does require you to have a Windows Live ID, such as a Hotmail, Live, or MSN account. This is a dynamic DNS service, so even if your router's IP address changes, your subdomain will be updated to point to the new address. (Windows Home Server periodically polls the router for its current IP address and sends that address to the dynamic DNS server on homeserver.com. The server then updates its DNS database with the current IP address of your router.)

TIP

The default polling interval is 900 seconds, or 15 minutes. If you prefer more frequent polling, log on to Windows Home Server, open the Registry Editor (select Start, Run, type **regedit**, and click OK) and navigate to the following key:

`HKLM\SOFTWARE\Microsoft\Windows Home Server\Dynamic DNS Service`

Double-click the `Ping Time` setting, click the Decimal option, and then enter a value in milliseconds. For example, if you want a polling interval of 5 minutes, enter **300000**.

Follow these steps to set up a Windows Home Server subdomain:

1. Open the Windows Home Server Console.
2. Click Settings to open the Windows Home Server Settings dialog box.
3. Select the Remote Access tab.
4. In the Domain Name section, click Configure to launch the Set Up a Domain Name wizard. (If you don't have Remote Access turned on, click Turn On instead; once

Windows Home Server has configured your router, it will launch the Set Up a Domain Name wizard automatically.)

5. Click Next. The wizard asks you to sign in to your Windows Live ID account.

6. Type your email address and password, and then click Next. The wizard presents a couple of links that display information about Windows Live Custom Domains.

7. Click I Accept and then click Next.

8. Type your subdomain name and then click Confirm to check that it's available. If the name is available, the wizard displays a green check mark and shows you your full domain name.

NOTE

Your subdomain name can be any length, but it must contain only letters, numbers, or hyphens, and it must begin and end with a letter or number.

9. Click Finish. The wizard sets up your subdomain name.

10. Click Done. The wizard returns you to the Windows Home Server Settings dialog box and displays a link for your new domain name. (You can click this link to access your Windows Home Server over the Internet.)

11. Click OK.

Displaying the Remote Access Home Page

As with LAN connections through Windows Home Server, before you can connect to a computer via the Internet, you need to log on to Windows Home Server's Remote Access home page.

If you signed up for a Windows Home Server subdomain, you have two choices:

▶ Log on to the Windows Home Server Console, click Settings, click the Remote Access tab, and then click the link in the Domain Name section.

▶ Run Internet Explorer and enter the address `https://subdomain.homeserver.com`, where *subdomain* is the subdomain you registered with Microsoft.

If you don't have a subdomain, you need to use your router's external IP address. Launch Internet Explorer and enter the following address (where *RouterIP* is the external IP address of your router:

`https://RouterIP`

NOTE

Whether you use a subdomain or an IP address, note that you use `https` as the protocol instead of `http`.

Windows Home Server redirects you to the Windows Home Server website home page at the following address (where *Address* is your homeserver.com subdomain or your router's external IP address):

```
https://Address/home/default.aspx
```

Click Log On to open the Windows Home Server Remote Access logon page, type the username and password of your Windows Home Server account, and then click Log On. Windows Home Server redirects you to the Windows Home Server Web Site Remote Access page (see Figure 7.15) at the following address:

```
https://Address/remote/Default.aspx
```

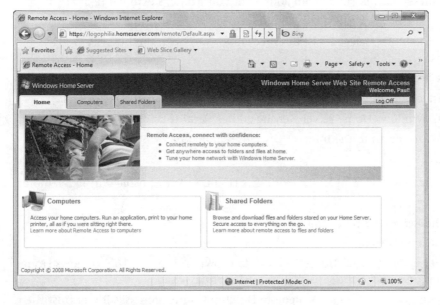

FIGURE 7.15   Windows Home Server's Remote Access home page accessed over the Internet.

Connecting to a Network Computer

After you're logged in to Windows Home Server, connecting to a network computer running the Remote Desktop service is as easy as clicking the Computers tab and then clicking the computer in the list. For the details, see "Making the Connection," earlier in this chapter.

TIP

If you're using Firefox, remember that it doesn't display the Computers tab unless you install the IE Tab add-on (available from ietab.mozdev.org).

Connecting to the Windows Home Server Console

When you display the Windows Home Server Remote Access pages via the Internet, the Computers tab enables you to connect to the Remote Desktop hosts on your network. However, what about Windows Home Server itself? You may need to tweak a setting during the remote session, so it would be nice to have *some* access to Windows Home Server.

Fortunately, the Remote Access pages *do* enable you to get to Windows Home Server. Unfortunately, the default access is limited to the Windows Home Server Console. (However, see the next section for a workaround that enables you to access the Windows Home Server desktop.)

Before you can use this feature, you must add your Windows Home Server website address (either your homeserver.com subdomain address or your router's external IP address) to Internet Explorer's Trusted Sites zone. Here are the steps to follow:

1. In Internet Explorer, select Tools, Internet Options to open the Internet Options dialog box.
2. Select the Security tab.
3. Click Trusted Sites and then click Sites. The Trusted Sites dialog box appears.
4. Type your Windows Home Server website address, and then click Add.
5. Click Close to return to the Internet Options dialog box.
6. Click OK.

Here are the steps to follow to open the Windows Home Server Console during a remote session:

1. Display the Remote Access home page.
2. Click the Computers tab.
3. Click the Connect to Your Home Server link, shown in Figure 7.16. Windows Home Server prompts you for the server's Administrator password.
4. Type the password and click OK. Remote Desktop Connection asks if you trust the computer you're connecting to.
5. Click Connect. The Windows Home Server Console appears in the browser, as shown in Figure 7.17.
6. When you have finished working with the Windows Home Server Console, click Disconnect at the top of the browser page.

Connecting to the Windows Home Server Desktop

Being able to access the Windows Home Server Console via the Internet is handy, to be sure. However, what if you really need access to the Windows Home Server desktop? For example, you might need to launch a program, access the Control Panel, or tweak some other system setting that's not available through the Windows Home Server Console. In such cases, it *is* possible to get to the desktop, although you have to modify one of Windows Home Server's website files.

Click this link to display the Windows Home Server Console.

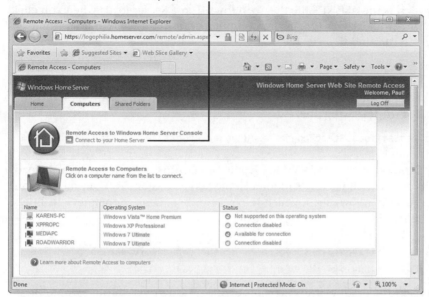

FIGURE 7.16   The Computers tab includes a link to log on to Windows Home Server.

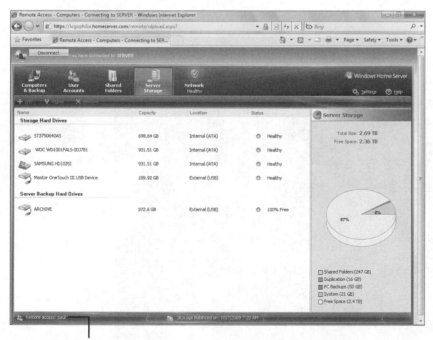

The logged-on user appears here.

FIGURE 7.17   The Windows Home Server Console running in the web browser.

Refer to Figure 7.17 and examine the URL that appears in the address bar. The filename is rdpload.aspx, which is the ASP.NET file that Windows Home Server loads when you click the Connect to Your Home Server link in the Computers tab. On your Windows Home Server machine, you can find that file here:

`C:\Inetpub\remote`

Right-click rdpload.aspx, and then click Edit to load the file into Notepad. Scroll down the file and look for the following line:

`MsRdpClient.SecuredSettings.StartProgram = "HomeServerConsole.exe -b";`

This line specifies the program that Windows Home Server runs when rdpload.aspx loads. This program acts as the shell for the Windows Home Server session. You can modify this line to run the regular Windows shell, which is explorer.exe. Replace the previous line with the following two lines:

```
//MsRdpClient.SecuredSettings.StartProgram = "HomeServerConsole.exe -b";
MsRdpClient.SecuredSettings.StartProgram = "explorer.exe";
```

The two slashes mark the original line as a comment, so it is ignored during execution. Instead, Windows Home Server runs the next line, which loads explorer.exe as the shell. Figure 7.18 shows the Windows Home Server desktop loaded into the browser window.

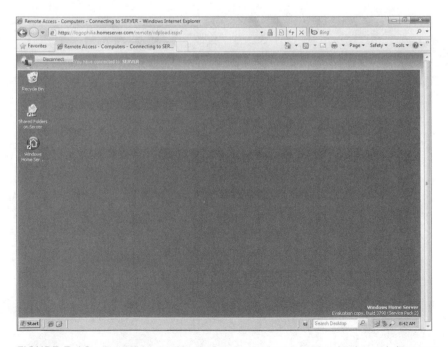

FIGURE 7.18   The Windows Home Server desktop running in the web browser.

> **TIP**
>
> If you don't feel like messing around with a Windows Home Server system file, there's another method you can use to connect directly to the Windows Home Server desktop. On your network, log on to the Windows Home Server computer, select Start, Control Panel, Administrative Tools, Terminal Services Configuration. In the TSCC window, click Connections and then double-click RDP-Tcp to open the connection's property sheet. Select the Environment tab, click the Do Not Allow an Initial Program to be Launched. Always Show the Desktop option, and then click OK. Note, however, that this affects *all* your remote connections, including Windows Home Server Console.

> **NOTE**
>
> When you attempt to log in to the Windows Home Server desktop directly, you might see the following error:
>
> `The terminal server has exceeded the maximum number of allowed connections`
>
> Usually this means that other people are already using Remote Desktop connections to the server, so you're out of luck and need to try again later. However, if you're connected to your network, you may be able to fix the problem. Log in to the Windows Home Server computer, right-click the taskbar, and then click Task Manager. Select the Users tab. If you see a user where the Status column shows `Disconnected`, click that user, click Logoff, and then click Yes when Windows Home Server asks you to confirm. This might be enough to enable you to log in remotely.

Working with Windows Home Server Shares in the Web Browser

Besides connecting to Remote Desktop hosts and to Windows Home Server, you can also use Remote Access to work with the server's shared folders via the Internet. You can access your user account's shared folder, as well as the built-in shares and any nonuser shares that you've created. Within each shared folder, you can create subfolders, rename and delete files, upload files from your computer to the server, and download files from the server share to your computer.

When you log on to the Remote Access pages, click the Shared Folders tab. As you can see in Figure 7.19, this tab displays links for your user account share (paul, in this case), the built-in shares (such as Music and Photos), and the nonuser shares you've created (such as Calendars in Figure 7.19). Click a shared folder link, and you see the file management interface shown in Figure 7.20.

Here's a summary of the actions you can perform in this page:

▶ **Select items**—Use the check boxes to select files and subfolders, or click the Select All check box (the one at the top of the file list) to select all the files shown in the current page.

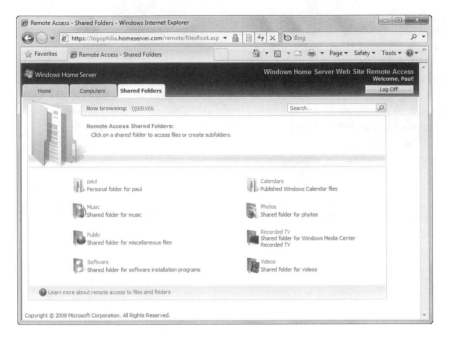

FIGURE 7.19   The Shared Folders tab contains links to the Windows Home Server shared folders that are accessible to your user account.

TIP

If you want to select every item in the shared folder, first click the All Files link to display all the files and subfolders in a single page. Then click the Select All check box to activate all the check boxes.

▶ **Create a subfolder**—Navigate to the folder in which you want the subfolder created and click the New Folder button (see Figure 7.20) to open the Type a Name for This New Folder dialog box. Type the folder name and then click OK.

▶ **Rename a file or folder**—Select the file or folder and then click Rename to open the Type a New Name for This Item dialog box. Type the new name and then click OK.

▶ **Upload items from your computer to the server**—Click Upload to display the Upload Files to Your Home Server page, shown in Figure 7.21. Click Browse to open the Choose File to Upload dialog box, select the file or folder, and then click Open to add the item to the Upload page. Repeat for other items you want to send to the share, and then click Upload.

▶ **Download items from the server share to your computer**—Select the items you want to download and then click the Download button. Windows Home Server asks whether you want the selected items downloaded as a self-extracting executable file or as a compressed ZIP file. Click the option you prefer, and then click OK. Windows Home Server inserts the selected items into a compressed file named either *share*.exe or *share*.zip (where *share* is the name of the shared folder) and then displays the File Download dialog box. Click Save, use the Save As dialog box to choose a download location (and, optionally, rename the download files), and then click Save.

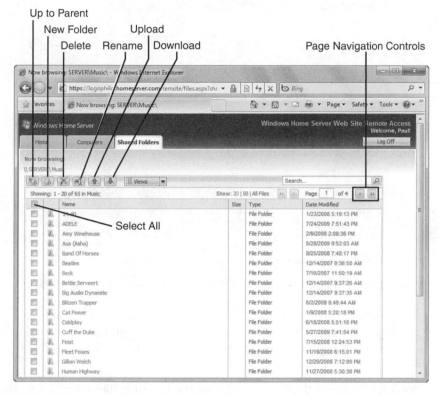

FIGURE 7.20 Use this file management interface to work with the files and folders in the share.

▶ **Delete a file or folder**—Select the objects you want to work with and then click the Delete button (see Figure 7.20). When Windows Home Server asks you to confirm the deletion, click OK.

Enabling Drag-and-Drop Uploading

Windows Home Server's Remote Access Upload page is a decent-enough interface for uploading, but we're used to dragging-and-dropping files in Windows, and the web browser is mouse-oriented, so it would be nice to be able to upload files using drag-and-drop. Happily, that functionality is now built in to Power Pack 3, but it's turned off by default. To enable it, follow these steps:

1. Click the Upload icon to open the Upload Files to Your Home Server page.

2. Click Enable Easy File Uploads. The first time you do this, Internet Explorer prompts you to install an ActiveX control.

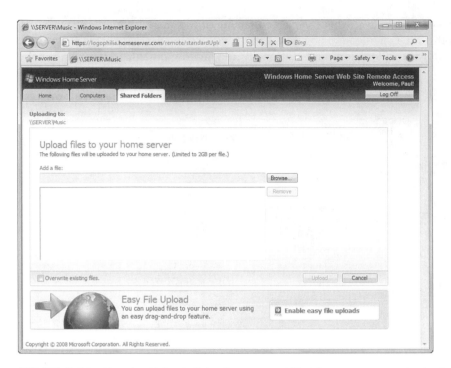

FIGURE 7.21   Use the Upload dialog box to send files from your computer to the server share.

3. Install the control (either by clicking the Information bar message or by clicking the "Click here" message), and then clicking Install this Add-On for All Users on This Computer. In Windows 7 or Vista, enter your User Account Control credentials when prompted.

You now see an upload area in the Upload page, and now you can drag files from Windows Explorer and drop them in the area. Each time you drop a file, Windows Home Server adds it to the list, as shown in Figure 7.22 (which also shows an MP3 file about to be dropped in the upload area). When you're done, click Upload.

Customizing the Remote Access Web Pages

You saw earlier that you can change Windows Home Server's Remote Access shell program by modifying some text in a file named rdpload.aspx (see "Connecting to the Windows Home Server Desktop"). In fact, much of what you see in the Remote Access web pages is ASP.Net code found in text files that reside in the following folder:

%SystemRoot%\Inetpub\remote

If you know ASP.NET, HTML, and cascading style sheets (CSS), you can customize the Remote Access pages in any way you see fit. I won't go into the details here. However, the next three sections take you through a couple of customizations that you can perform easily through the Windows Home Server Console and with a few HTML tweaks.

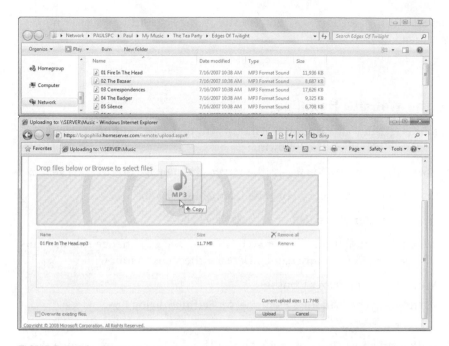

FIGURE 7.22   With drag-and-drop enabled, you can drag files from Windows Explorer and drop them inside the Upload page.

CAUTION

Take some care when modifying the Remote Access files to avoid breaking Windows Home Server. Before modifying anything in the `Inetpub` folder, it's a really good idea to make backups of the files so that you can restore the defaults should anything go awry.

Setting Remote Access as the Default Home Page

As with a LAN connect, you can navigate directly to the Remote Access logon page by entering the following address when you first open Internet Explorer:

`https://Address/remote`

Again, *Address* is either your homeserver.com address or the external IP address of your network's router.

Alternatively, you can set up the Remote Access logon page as Windows Home Server's default home page. This means that accessing `http://Address` automatically redirects you to `https://Address/remote`. Here are the steps to follow:

1. Open the Windows Home Server Console.

2. Click Settings to open the Windows Home Server Settings dialog box.

3. Select the Remote Access tab.

4. In the Web Site Settings section, use the Web Site Home Page list to select Windows Home Server Remote Access.

5. Click OK.

Customizing the Website Headline

The *website headline* is text that identifies the Windows Home Server website. This text appears in several places, including the following:

▶ In the browser title bar when you access the server's home page (`http://server/`).

▶ In the Remote Access logon page, above the Username text box.

▶ In the upper-right corner of the Remote Access pages.

The default headline is Windows Home Server Web Site, but you can change this to something more suitable (such as your family name). Here are the steps to follow:

1. Open the Windows Home Server Console.

2. Click Settings to open the Windows Home Server Settings dialog box.

3. Select the Remote Access tab.

4. In the Web Site Settings section, use the Web Site Headline text box to change the headline (see Figure 7.23).

FIGURE 7.23   In the Remote Access tab, use the Web Site Headline text box to change the headline that appears in Windows Home Server's Remote Access pages.

5. Click OK.

Figure 7.24 shows the main Remote Access with a new headline displayed.

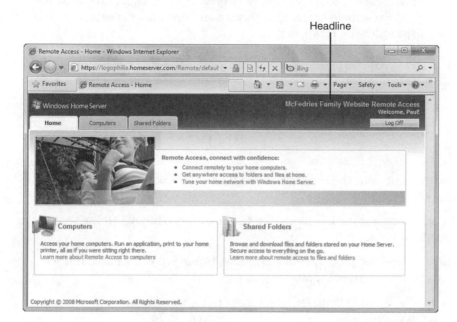

FIGURE 7.24   Windows Home Server's Remote Access home page showing the new headline.

Customizing the Website Images

The home page (`http://server/home/default.aspx`) and the Remote Access page's Home tab (`http://server/remote/default.aspx`) contain images that add visual interest. However, who wants to look at someone *else's* family on your own family's site? Fortunately, you can tweak the website to replace these images with your own.

On the home page, the main image you see is a PNG file named `i_landingpage_main.png`, and it resides in the following folder:

```
C:\Inetpub\home\images
```

One way to replace this image would be to create your own image with the same name (and roughly the same size: 759 pixels wide and 316 pixels high) and copy it to the images folder to replace the existing image file. Alternatively, navigate to `C:\Inetpub\home` and open the `css.css` file for editing. Look for the following style property:

```
background: white url("images/i_landingpage_main.png");
```

Replace the `background` path with the path to your own image.

Replacing the Remote Access Home tab image is similar. The main image you see is a PNG file named `i_default_photo.png`, and it resides in the following folder:

```
C:\Inetpub\remote\images
```

You can create your own image with the same name (and roughly the same size: 263 pixels wide and 148 pixels high) and copy it to the images folder to replace the existing image file. Alternatively, navigate to C:\Inetpub\remote and open the default.aspx file for editing. Look for the following HTML tag:

```
<td width="263" background="images/i_default_photo.png"
style="background-repeat:repeat-x">
```

Replace the background path with the path to your own image.

From Here

Here are some other sections in the book where you'll find information related to the topics in this chapter:

▶ For details on setting a static IP address, **see** "Configuring Windows Home Server with a Static IP Address," **P. 9**.

▶ To learn how to view the properties of a Windows Home Server user account, **see** "Viewing Account Properties," **P. 50**.

▶ For details on Mac-based Remote Desktop connections, **see** "Using a Mac to Make a Remote Desktop Connection to Windows Home Server," **P. 74**.

▶ For information on other ways to take advantage of Windows Home Server's built-in web server, **see** Chapter 12, "Setting Up a Windows Home Server Website."

CHAPTER 8

Streaming and Sharing Digital Media

Windows Home Server comes with support for Windows Media Connect, which is software that streams digital media from (in this case) the server to programs and devices that support Windows Media Connect. Supported programs include digital media players such as Windows Media Player and devices such as the Xbox 360 and Roku SoundBridge. The latter two are examples of *digital media receivers* (DMRs), devices that can access a media stream being sent over a wired or wireless network connection and then play that stream through connected equipment such as speakers, audio receivers, or a TV. Note, too, that Windows Media Connect uses standard protocols—specifically Hypertext Transfer Protocol (HTTP) and Universal Plug and Play (UPnP)—so, theoretically, any device that supports these protocols should also be able to receive Windows Home Server media streams. (Most UPnP devices have options to disable and enable UPnP, or "network control" as it's sometimes called. Access the device settings and make sure that UPnP is enabled.)

Windows Home Server offers three media streams: music, photos, and videos. This chapter shows you how to get your devices ready for streaming and how to activate streaming via Windows Home Server. You also learn nonstreaming techniques for sharing photos, music, and videos via Windows Home Server.

CAUTION

Before purchasing a DMR, check the device's wireless capabilities. Some older and less expensive devices can only connect to wireless networks that use Wired Equivalent Privacy (WEP) security. However, WEP has been superseded by Wi-Fi Protected Access (WPA), which is much more secure than WEP. If you use WPA or WPA2 (a more secure version of WPA) on your wireless network (as you should), make sure any DMR you purchase either supports WPA out of the box or can be updated to support WPA with a firmware upgrade.

Streaming Digital Media to Network Computers and Devices

The ability to stream music over the network is one of Windows Home Server's most attractive features. Yes, you can activate the Media Streaming feature in Windows Media Player 12 (or the Media Sharing feature in Windows Media Player 11) and share your library over the network, but that sharing is limited to the media on your computer. Throw Windows Home Server's centralized storage into the mix, and you suddenly have a much wider variety of media to stream.

Getting Your Devices Ready

Getting a device ready to receive and play streaming media is a fairly straightforward affair that usually encompasses just the following steps:

1. Get the device ready for networking:

   ▶ If the device is physically near a network router or switch, run a network cable from the device to the router or switch.

   ▶ If you need to use a wireless connection, check to see if the device has built-in wireless (at least 802.11b) support. Many devices—including the Xbox 360— require separate wireless components to be plugged in to the device.

2. Turn on the device.

3. If you're using a wireless connection, set up the device to connect to your wireless network.

   ▶ **SEE** For information on connecting various devices to your Windows Home Server network, **see** Chapter 3, "Adding Devices to the Windows Home Server Network."

4. Use audio or video cables to connect the device to the appropriate output equipment, such as powered speakers, a receiver, a display, or a TV set.

After you have the device on the network, you should see an icon for it in Windows 7's Network folder, or Windows Vista's Network window. For example, Figure 8.1 shows a Network window with two media devices: an Xbox 360 and a Roku SoundBridge.

FIGURE 8.1 Devices that support Windows Media Connect should also appear in the Network window.

TIP

Whatever device you use, it's always a good idea to install the latest firmware to ensure that you're using the most up-to-date version of the device interface. See the device documentation to learn how to upgrade the firmware.

NOTE

You can also see many digital media devices in Windows XP with Service Pack 2 or later. Select Start, My Network Places, and then click the Show Icons for Networked UPnP Devices link in the Network Tasks section. (XP may install support for this feature at this point.) The devices appear in My Network Places in a new Local Network group.

Note too that some devices offer a link to their built-in control and settings pages. Right-click the device icon and look for the View Device Webpage command. For example, Figure 8.2 shows the pages that appear for the Roku SoundBridge device.

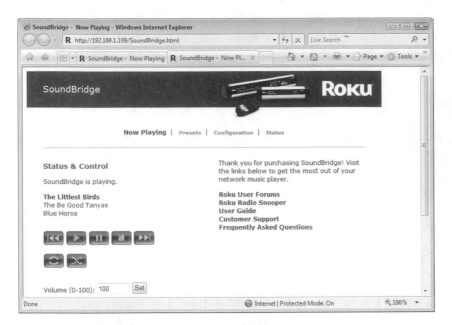

FIGURE 8.2   Right-click a device icon and then click View Device Webpage to open the control and settings pages for the device.

TIP

If you don't see the View Device Webpage command, you can also try opening the device directly in a web browser. Find the device's IP address (right-click the device icon and then click Properties) and then enter *http://address* in the web browser (where *address* is the device's IP address).

Activating Media Sharing in Windows Home Server

The next step in getting media streaming up and running in Windows Home Server is to enable Media Library Sharing for some or all of the shared media folders. You can stream three folders: Music, Photos, and Videos. Before getting to the specifics, here are some notes to bear in mind:

▶ Media Library Sharing doesn't work with most copy-protected media, because generally you can only play that media on the computer or device that you used to purchase the media in the first place. You're still free to place copies of such media on the Windows Home Server shares, but you can only use the purchase device to play back the media stream.

▶ Media Library Sharing isn't related to sharing the files themselves through \\server and the Windows Home Server user accounts. With the latter, you can assign permissions such as Full or Read to tailor the access that a specific user has to the folder contents. When you enable Media Library Sharing on a folder, however, any program or device that supports Windows Media Connect can access the library and play the media it contains.

► As a consequence of the previous point, note that Media Library Sharing overrides any user restrictions that you've placed on a media folder. Even if the folder access level that you've assigned to a particular user is None, after you enable Media Library Sharing for that folder, the user will be able to stream the folder contents to a Windows Media Connect media player on his computer. If you have media in a folder that you don't want others to stream, you must move the files into a folder that doesn't have Media Library Sharing activated.

CAUTION

A further consequence to the open nature of Media Library Sharing is that any computer or device that can access your network can also stream the media. Therefore, if your wireless network is not secured, anyone within range of the network will have access to your streamed media. If you don't want this, secure your wireless network.

Here are the steps to follow to stream some or all of the Windows Home Server shared media folders:

1. Log on to the Windows Home Server Console.
2. Click Settings to open the Windows Home Server Settings dialog box.
3. Click the Media Sharing tab.
4. Activate the On option for each media folder you want to stream, as shown in Figure 8.3.

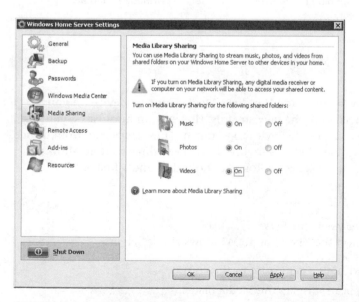

FIGURE 8.3   In the Media Sharing tab, activate the On option for each media share you want to stream over the network.

5. Click OK. Windows Home Server immediately starts sharing the selected media folders.

When you activate Media Library Sharing for at least one media share, Windows Home Server activates a new Windows Media Connect "device," which appears in the list of network devices, as shown in Figure 8.4.

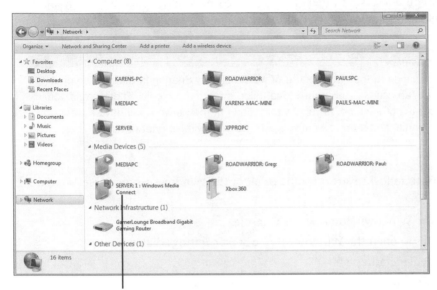

The Server's Windows Media Connect Device

FIGURE 8.4   When you turn on Media Library Sharing, the server's Windows Media Connect device appears in the list of network devices.

Connecting Devices

After you enable Media Library Sharing, any Windows Media Connect device on your network should immediately recognize the new streams. However, in most cases, you must take a few extra steps to connect the device to a stream. These steps vary from device to device. To give you an indication of what's involved, the next three sections show you how to connect three devices: an Xbox 360, a Roku SoundBridge, and a Kodak Wi-Fi digital picture frame.

Connecting an Xbox 360 to Windows Home Server

Just follow these steps to connect the Xbox 360 to Windows Home Server:

1. Turn on the Xbox 360 without a game disc in the console.

2. When the Dashboard appears, display the Media blade.

3. Highlight Music or Photos and press Select.

4. Highlight Computer and press Select. The Xbox 360 asks if you've installed Windows Media Connect on the computer.

5. WMC is already part of Windows Home Server, so highlight Yes, Continue and press Select. The Xbox 360 displays a list of Windows Media Connect computers.

6. Highlight your Windows Home Server and press Select. The Xbox 360 connects to the server and displays a list of media.

7. Use the Xbox 360 interface to play the music or run a slide show.

If you want to play streaming media from another computer on your network, you first need to disconnect from the Windows Home Server. Here are the steps to follow to disconnect from the Windows Home Server:

1. Turn on the Xbox 360.

2. When the Dashboard appears, display the System blade.

3. Highlight Computers and press Select.

4. Highlight Windows-Based PC and press Select.

5. Highlight Disconnect and press Select. The Xbox 360 disconnects from the server.

Connecting a Roku SoundBridge to Windows Home Server

If you have a Roku SoundBridge and you're streaming Windows Home Server's Music share, here are the steps to access the music being streamed from that share:

1. On the SoundBridge remote, press the Home button.

2. Scroll through the list of options until you see one that looks like this (where *SERVER* is the name of Windows Home Server machine):

   Play *SERVER*: 1 : Windows Media Connect

3. Use the arrow buttons to select this item, and then press Select.

4. Use the SoundBridge interface to select the playlist, album, or song you want to hear.

Connecting a Kodak Wi-Fi Digital Picture Frame

If you're streaming Windows Home Server's Photos share and you have a Kodak Wi-Fi Digital Picture Frame, you can set up the frame to display the images being streamed from that share. Assuming you already have the frame connected to your wireless network, follow these steps to access the Photos stream:

> ▶ **SEE** To learn how to connect the Kodak Wi-Fi Digital Picture Frame to a wireless network, **see** "Connecting a Kodak Wi-Fi Digital Picture Frame," **P. 89.**

1. Turn on the Kodak Wi-Fi Digital Picture Frame.

2. On the frame's remote, press the Home button.

3. Select the Network Computer icon and then press OK. The frame displays a list of computers that are streaming media.

4. Select the Windows Home Server media sharing item, which will appear as follows (where *SERVER* is the name of your Windows Home Server computer):

   SERVER: 1 : Windows Media Connect

5. Press OK on the remote. The frame connects to the Windows Home Server Photos share.

Playing Streamed Media in Windows Media Player

After you activate Media Library Sharing on a Windows Home Server share, Windows Media Player (which supports Windows Media Connect in versions 11 and later) immediately recognizes the new streams and adds them to its library.

To play the streamed media, follow these steps:

1. Select Start, All Programs, Windows Media Player (or click the Windows Media Player icon in the taskbar).

2. In Media Player 11, click the Library tab.

3. In Media Player 11, pull down the Library menu and select a media category: Music, Pictures, or Video.

4. In the Navigation pane, click the Windows Home Server shared library, the name of which in Media Player 12 always takes the following form (where *server* is the name of the Windows Home Server computer; see Figure 8.5. In Media Player 11, the library name is *User 1 on server*):

   User 1 (*server*)

5. Use the library properties (such as Artist and Album in the Music category) to open the media you want to view.

6. Play the media.

This all works fine, but it's a bit cumbersome to have to deal with multiple libraries. Fortunately, if you're running Windows Home Server Power Pack 3 and you have Windows 7 on the client PC, the whole multiple library setup is a thing of the past. That's because Power Pack 3 supports Windows 7's libraries, which are virtual folders that can gather content from multiple folders, including (crucially for our purposes here) network shares. When you install the Windows Home Server Connector on your Windows 7 PC, the program automatically adds the server shares to the appropriate Windows 7 libraries. For example, the server's Music folder gets added to Windows 7's Music library (see Figure 8.6), and the Photos share appears in the Pictures library.

Not only does this give you an easy way to access the server's shares, but it also means that Windows Media Center automatically adds the media files to its own library, since the program automatically scours the Music, Pictures, and Videos libraries for media content. In Figure 8.7, for example, I've opened the Artist genre of the Music section of the Media Center library. Of the five artists shown, four are located in Windows Home Server's Music share.

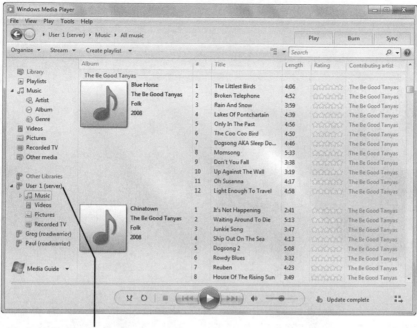

Windows Home Server Media Library

FIGURE 8.5   Windows Media Player automatically adds the shared Windows Home Server media libraries to its own library.

FIGURE 8.6   When you install Windows Home Server Connector for Power Pack 3 on a Windows 7 PC, the server's shares get added automatically to the Windows 7 libraries.

FIGURE 8.7   On a Windows 7 PC, Media Center automatically loads the Windows Home Server media shares into the library for easier access.

Playing Streamed Media in Windows Media Center

As with Windows Media Player, Windows Media Center (another Media Connect application) also automatically recognizes Windows Home Server's shared media libraries and sets them up in the Media Center interface.

NOTE

For some reason, Media Center takes quite a bit longer to add all the Windows Home Server media to its libraries. Whereas Media Player usually populates its libraries with Windows Home Server media within a few minutes (depending on how much media exists on the shares), Media Center can take considerably longer, even a few hours.

To play the streamed media, follow these steps:

1. Select Start, All Programs, Windows Media Center.
2. Select a media library:
   ▶ For Windows Home Server music, select Music, Music Library.

- For Windows Home Server photos, select Pictures + Videos, Picture Library.

- For Windows Home Server videos, select Pictures + Videos, Video Library.

3. Use the Media Center interface to open and play the media you want.

Connecting Windows Media Center to Your Home Server

If you have Windows Home Server Power Pack 3, you can integrate some Windows Home Server functionality into the Media Center interface. Specifically, you can add new Media Center features to archive TV recordings to Windows Home Server, and to view much of the same information that you see in the Windows Home Server Console.

Follow these steps to set this up:

1. Select Start, All Programs, Windows Media Center Connector. The Windows Media Center Connector Setup wizard appears.

2. Click Next. The wizard prompts you for your Windows Home Server password.

3. Type the password and then click Next. The wizard accesses the server and then updates Windows Media Center with the server's media files.

4. If you don't want the wizard to automatically restart your computer to put the changes into effect, click to activate the Do Not Restart Now check box.

5. Click Done.

6. If you didn't have the wizard restart your machine, you need to restart at your earliest convenience to finalize the changes.

The next time you start Windows Media Center, you see a new Home Server item in the main menu. Selecting that item shows two tiles called TV Archive and Console View, as shown in Figure 8.8. You use TV Archive to set up archiving recorded TV programs to the server (more on this later; see "Archiving Recorded TV on Windows Home Server"), and you use Console View (shown in Figure 8.9) to see information similar to what you see when you run the Windows Home Server Console.

Sharing Photos

Whether or not you activate Media Library Sharing for Windows Home Server's Photos folder, you can still use this share as the central repository for some or even all of your family's photos. The next few sections take you through a few techniques that should make the shared Photos folder easier to work with.

Customizing the Photos Share with a Template

When you access your user account's Pictures library (in Windows 7), Pictures folder (in Windows Vista), or My Pictures folder (in Windows XP), you see a few features that aren't part of the regular folder view, as follows:

- You get access to image-related file metadata such as the date an image was taken and the image dimensions.

▶ In Windows 7 and Windows Vista, the task pane includes extra commands such as Slide Show and E-mail.

▶ In Windows XP, the task pane includes a Picture Tasks group with links such as View as a Slide Show, Order Prints Online, and Print Pictures.

FIGURE 8.8   With the Windows Media Center Connector installed, you see a new Home Server item on the main Media Center menu.

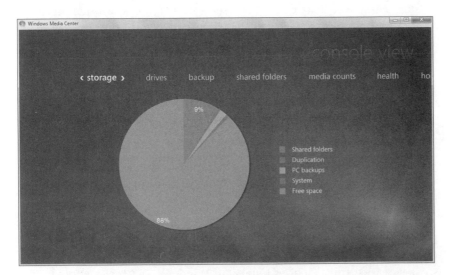

FIGURE 8.9   The Console View shows you server information such as the current storage breakdown, installed drives, backup status, and more.

These extra features come from a special template that Windows applies to this type of folder. However, when you access the Windows Home Server Photos share, Vista and XP treat it just like any other folder. (In Windows 7, if you access the Photos share through the Pictures library, you get the extra image-related features; if you access the share via the Network folder, you don't see those features.) If you want access to the extras that you see in the local Pictures (or My Pictures) folder, follow these steps to customize the Photos share to use a picture folder template:

1. Open the folder containing the Windows Home Server shares.

2. Right-click the Photos folder and then click Properties to open the folder's property sheet.

3. Display the Customize tab.

4. In the list, select the template you want to apply:

   ▶ **Picture and Videos**—(Windows Vista) Choose this template to give the folder the same features as Vista's Pictures folder.

   ▶ **Pictures**—(Windows 7 and Windows XP) Choose this template to give the folder the same features as Windows 7's Pictures library or XP's My Pictures folder.

   ▶ **Photo Album**—(Windows XP only) Choose this template to give the folder the same features as XP's My Pictures folder, and also display the folder in Filmstrip view by default.

5. If you also want Windows to apply this template to all the subfolders in the Photos share, click to activate the Also Apply This Template to All Subfolders check box.

6. (Windows XP only) If you also want to change the image used for the folder icon, click Choose Picture, choose a new picture in the Browse dialog box, and then click Open.

7. Click OK.

Using Server Photos as a Screensaver Slideshow

In the old days (a few years ago) when everyone was still using CRT monitors, you had to be careful to avoid *burn-in*, which is permanent damage to areas of the screen caused by continuously displaying a particular image over a long period. Whatever the image—it could be a menu bar, the Windows taskbar, or an application toolbar—if it was onscreen long enough, it eventually became a permanent part of the screen as a ghostly reflection of the original.

Now that most of us are using LCD monitors, burn-in is a thing of the past, but that doesn't mean that continuously displayed images are no longer a worry. LCDs suffer from a similar problem called *persistence*, where a long-displayed image persists onscreen as a faint version of the original. Fortunately, LCD persistence is usually temporary and can often be remedied just by turning off the monitor for a while (say, half an hour or so). However, persistence does become permanent on occasion, so further preventative measures are necessary.

The best of these measures is configuring a screensaver to kick in after an extended period of computer idleness. Windows 7, Vista, and XP come with built-in screensavers, but you can also set up a screensaver that displays a slideshow of images from a folder. If you have lots of pictures stored on Windows Home Server's Photos share, this folder is perfect for a screensaver. Here are the steps to follow to set this up:

1. Use one of the following methods to display the Screen Saver tab:

   ▶ In Windows 7 and Windows Vista, right-click the desktop, click Personalize, and then click Screen Saver. (Alternatively, select Start, Control Panel, Appearance and Personalization, Change Screen Saver.)

   ▶ In Windows XP, right-click the desktop, click Properties, and then display the Screen Saver tab. (Alternatively, select Start, Control Panel, Display, Screen Saver.)

2. In the Screen Saver list, select Photos (in Windows 7 or Vista) or My Pictures Slideshow (in XP).

3. Click Settings.

4. Click Browse, use the Browse for Folder dialog box to select the \\SERVER\Photos folder, and then click OK.

5. Configure any other screensaver options you want to use (such as the slide show speed), and then click Save (in Windows 7 or Vista) or OK (in XP).

6. Click OK to put the new screensaver into effect.

Adding the Photos Folder to Windows Media Player

If you're not streaming the Photos share, you can still add it to Windows Media Player so that you can access it in the Pictures portion of the Media Player library. Note, however, that you don't have to bother with this in Windows 7 if you have the Windows Home Server Connector software installed, because the Connector automatically adds the \\SERVER\Photos share to Windows 7's Pictures Library.

Here are the steps to follow in Windows Media Player 11:

1. Select Start, All Programs, Windows Media Player.

2. Pull down the Library menu and select Add to Library. Media Player displays the Add to Library dialog box.

3. If you don't see the Monitored Folders list, click Advanced Options to expand the dialog box.

4. Click Add to display the Add Folder list.

5. Select Windows Home Server's Photos share and then click OK. Media Player adds the folder to the Monitored Folders list.

6. Click OK. Media Player begins adding the contents of the Photos share to the library.

7. Click Close. (Note that you don't have to wait until Media Player has added all the pictures to the library; the process continues in the background, although it might take a bit longer than if you had left the dialog box open.)

To view the folder contents in Media Player, pull down the Library menu and select Pictures. In the Navigation pane, click Library, and then double-click the Folder view. You then see an icon for \\SERVER\Photos, as shown in Figure 8.10. Double-click that icon to view the images.

FIGURE 8.10   Double-click \\SERVER\Photos to view the contents of the Photos share in Media Player 11.

Adding the Photos Folder to Windows Live Photo Gallery

By default, Windows Live Photo Gallery includes your user account's Pictures and Videos folders, as well as the Public Pictures and Public Videos folders. If you want to use the extensive Photo Gallery tools—fixing image problems, burning images to DVD, ordering prints online, and so on—with your server images, you need to add the Windows Home Server Photos share to the program's Folders list. Here are the steps to follow:

1. Select Start, All Programs, Windows Live, Windows Live Photo Gallery.
2. Select File, Include a Folder in the Gallery. The Include a Folder in the Gallery dialog box appears.
3. Select Windows Home Server's Photos share. (In Windows 7, you can add the share either via your user account's Pictures library or via the network.)
4. Click OK. Photo Gallery asks you to confirm that you want to add the folder.
5. Click Add. Photo Gallery confirms that it has added the folder.
6. Click OK.

To view the folder contents in Windows Live Photo Gallery, open the Folders branch and click Photos, which has a network icon beside it, as shown in Figure 8.11.

FIGURE 8.11   Click Photos to view the contents of the Photos share in Windows Live Photo Gallery.

Adding the Photos Folder to Windows Photo Gallery

By default, Vista's Windows Photo Gallery program includes your user account's Pictures and Videos folders, as well as the Public Pictures and Public Videos folders. To add the Windows Home Server Photos share to the program's Folders list, follow these steps:

1. Select Start, All Programs, Windows Photo Gallery.
2. Select File, Add Folder to Gallery. The Add Folder to Gallery dialog box appears.
3. Select Windows Home Server's Photos share.
4. Click OK. Photo Gallery asks you to confirm that you want to add the folder.
5. Click Add. Photo Gallery confirms that it has added the folder.
6. Click OK.

Running a Slide Show from the Photos Share

You saw earlier that you can configure a screensaver–based slide show that uses Windows Home Server's Photos share as the image source. If you don't want to wait until the screensaver kicks in, you can run a slide show anytime you like. Windows 7, Vista, and XP give you several ways to run a slide show based on images from the Photos share:

▶ If you added the Photos share to Media Player (see "Adding the Photos Folder to Windows Media Player," earlier), open the User 1 (*server*) branch, select Pictures, and then click Play.

▶ If you added the Photos share to Windows Live Photo Gallery (see "Adding the Photos Folder to Windows Live Photo Gallery," earlier), open Photo Gallery's Folders branch, select Photos, and then click the Slide Show button (you also can press F12 or Alt+S).

▶ If you added the Photos share to Photo Gallery (see "Adding the Photos Folder to Windows Photo Gallery," earlier), open Photo Gallery's Folders branch, select Photos, and then click the Play Slide Show button (you also can press F11).

▶ If you applied a picture template to the Photos share earlier (see "Customizing the Photos Share with a Template"), open the share and either click Slide Show (in Windows 7 or Vista) or View as a Slide Show (XP).

Changing the Default Picture Import Location to Windows Home Server

Both Windows Live Photo Gallery and Windows Photo Gallery come with a feature that enables you to import images from a digital camera or a document scanner (select File, Import from Camera or Scanner). By default, the program imports the images to a subfolder in your user account's Pictures folder. If you prefer to import the images directly to Windows Home Server's Photos share, follow these steps:

1. Select File, Options. The program's Options dialog box appears.
2. Select the Import tab.
3. Use the Settings For list to select the type of import you want to customize: Cameras, CDs and DVDs, or Scanners.
4. Click Browse to open the Browse for Folder dialog box.
5. Select Windows Home Server's Photos share, and then click OK.
6. Repeat steps 3–5 to customize the other import types, if necessary.
7. Click OK to put the new options into effect.

Sharing Music

When you think of the word *streaming*, you probably think about music, because it's the medium that's most closely associated with streaming and that's most easily streamed (because music files generally contain less information than, say, video files). However, even if you don't activate Media Library Sharing for Windows Home Server's Music folder, you can still use this share to store your family's digital music files. To help make this easier, the next few sections show you some techniques for using and managing the Music share.

Customizing the Music Share with a Template

Earlier you learned about the folder template that applies special features to the Pictures folder. There is also a template associated with the Music library (in Windows 7), the Music folder (in Windows Vista), and the My Music folder (in Windows XP). This template gives you a few features that aren't part of the standard folder view:

▶ You get access to music-related file metadata such as the Artists, Album, and Genre.

▶ In Windows 7 and Vista, the task pane includes extra commands such as Play and Play All.

▶ In Windows XP, the task pane includes a Music Tasks group with links such as Play All, Play Selection, and Shop for Music Online.

However, when you access the Windows Home Server Music folder, Vista and XP treat it like a regular folder. (In Windows 7, if you access the Music share through the Music library, you get the extra image-related features; if you access the share via the Network folder, you don't see those features.) If you want to see the extras that are part of the local Music (or My Music) folder, follow these steps to customize the Music share to use a music folder template:

1. Open the folder containing the Windows Home Server shares.

2. Right-click the Music folder and then click Properties to open the folder's property sheet.

3. Display the Customize tab.

4. In the Use This Folder as a Template list, select the template you want to apply:

    ▶ **Music Icons**—(Windows Vista) Choose this template to give the folder the same features as the Music folder. The folder opens in Large Icons view.

    ▶ **Music Details**—(Windows Vista) Choose this template to give the folder the same features as the Music folder. The folder opens in Details view.

    ▶ **Music**—(Windows 7 and Windows XP) Choose this template to give the folder the same features as the My Music folder.

    ▶ **Music Artist**—(Windows XP) Choose this template for a folder that holds music by a single artist. This gives the folder the same features as the My Music folder and opens the folder in Thumbnails view, which displays an album art icon for each folder that holds an album by the artist.

▶ **Music Album**—(Windows XP) Choose this template for a folder that holds music from a single artist. This gives the folder the same features as the My Music folder and opens the folder in Tiles view, which displays an icon for each track from the album.

5. If you also want Windows to apply this template to all the subfolders in the Music share, click to activate the Also Apply This Template to All Subfolders check box.

6. (Windows XP only) If you also want to change the image used for the folder icon, click Choose Picture, choose a new picture in the Browse dialog box, and then click Open.

7. Click OK.

Adding the Music Folder to Windows Media Player

You saw earlier that when you activate Media Library Sharing for Windows Home Server's Music folder, it appears in Media Player's Navigation pane in the User 1 (*server*) branch (or the User 1 on *server* branch), where *server* is the Windows Home Server name (see the earlier section "Playing Streamed Media in Windows Media Player 11"). However, even if you don't stream the Music share, you can still add it to Windows Media Player so that you can access it in the Music portion of the Media Player library. Note, however, that you don't have to bother with this in Windows 7 if you have the Windows Home Server Connector software installed, because the Connector automatically adds the *SERVER*\Music share to Windows 7's Music Library.

Just follow these steps in Windows Media Player 11:

1. Select Start, All Programs, Windows Media Player.

2. Pull down the Library menu and select Add to Library. Media Player displays the Add to Library dialog box.

3. If you don't see the Monitored Folders list, click Advanced Options to expand the dialog box.

4. Click Add to display the Add Folder list.

5. Select Windows Home Server's Music share and then click OK. Media Player adds the folder to the Monitored Folders list.

6. Click OK. Media Player begins adding the contents of the Music share to the library.

7. Click Close. (Note that you don't have to wait until Media Player has added all the songs to the library; the process continues in the background, although it might take a bit longer than if you had left the dialog box open.)

To view the folder contents in Media Player, pull down the Library menu and select Music. In the Navigation pane, click Library, and then double-click the Folder view. You then see an icon for *SERVER*\Music, as shown in Figure 8.12. Double-click that icon to view the music.

FIGURE 8.12   Double-click *SERVER*\Music to view the contents of Windows Home Server's Music share in Media Player.

Changing the Default Rip Location to Windows Home Server

When you rip music from an audio CD in Windows Media Player, the resulting digital audio files are stored in a subfolder of your user profile's Music library (in Windows 7), Music folder (in Windows Vista), or My Music folder (in Windows XP). If you then want to stream those files over your network, you need to copy them to Windows Home Server's Music share.

This two-step process is fine if you always want to maintain a local copy of the audio files. However, if you only access the music on Windows Home Server, having to both rip and move the audio files is a waste of time. A better idea is to rip your audio CDs straight to Windows Home Server.

Here are the steps to follow to change Media Player's rip location to Windows Home Server's Music folder:

1. Select Start, All Programs, Windows Media Player.
2. Select Tools, Options. (If you don't see the Tools menu, press Alt.) The Options dialog box appears.
3. Select the Rip Music tab.
4. In the Rip Music to This Location group, click Change to open the Browse for Folder dialog box.
5. Select *SERVER*\Music and then click OK to return to the Options dialog box.
6. Click OK to put the new setting into effect.

Sharing Videos

The rest of this chapter takes you through a few techniques to make Windows Home Server's shared Videos folder easier to use and manage.

Customizing the Videos Share with a Template

In previous sections of this chapter, you learned about the folder templates that apply special features to the Pictures and Music folders (My Pictures and My Music in Windows XP). There is also a template associated with the Videos library (in Windows 7), the Videos folder (in Windows Vista), and the My Videos folder (in Windows XP). This template provides some features that aren't part of the normal folder view:

▶ You get access to video-related file metadata, such as Date Taken and Duration.

▶ In Windows 7 and Vista, the task pane includes extra commands such as Play and Slide Show.

▶ In Windows XP, the task pane includes a Video Tasks group with links such as Play All and Copy to CD.

However, when you access the Windows Home Server Videos folder, Vista and XP treat it like a normal folder. (In Windows 7, if you access the Videos share through the Videos library, you get the extra video-related features; if you access the share via the Network folder, you don't see those features.) If you want to see the extras that are part of the local Videos (or My Videos) folder, follow these steps to customize the Videos share to use a video folder template:

1. Open the folder containing the Windows Home Server shares.
2. Right-click the Videos folder and then click Properties to open the folder's property sheet.
3. Display the Customize tab.
4. In the Use This Folder as a Template list, select the template you want to apply:

    ▶ **Picture and Videos**—(Windows Vista) Choose this template to give the folder the same features as Vista's Videos folder.

    ▶ **Videos**—(Windows 7 and Windows XP) Choose this template to give the folder the same features as XP's My Videos folder.

5. If you also want Windows to apply this template to all the subfolders in the Photos share, click to activate the Also Apply This Template to All Subfolders check box.
6. (Windows XP only) If you also want to change the image used for the folder icon, click Choose Picture, choose a new picture in the Browse dialog box, and then click Open.
7. Click OK.

Adding the Videos Folder to Windows Media Player

If you turn on Media Library Sharing for Windows Home Server's Videos share, that folder appears in Media Player's Navigation pane as part of the User 1 (*server*) branch (or the User 1 on *server* branch), where *server* is the Windows Home Server name (see "Playing Streamed Media in Windows Media Player 11"). If you're not streaming the Videos share, you can still add it to Windows Media Player's library in the Video section. Note, however, that you don't have to bother with this in Windows 7 if you have the Windows Home Server Connector software installed, because the Connector automatically adds the *SERVER*\Videos share to Windows 7's Videos Library.

Here are the steps to follow in Windows Media Player 11:

1. Select Start, All Programs, Windows Media Player.
2. Pull down the Library menu and select Add to Library. Media Player displays the Add to Library dialog box.
3. If you don't see the Monitored Folders list, click Advanced Options to expand the dialog box.
4. Click Add to display the Add Folder list.
5. Select Windows Home Server's Videos share and then click OK. Media Player adds the folder to the Monitored Folders list.
6. Click OK. Media Player begins adding the contents of the Videos share to the library.
7. Click Close. (Note that you don't have to wait until Media Player has added all the videos to the library; the process continues in the background, although it might take a bit longer than if you had left the dialog box open.)

To view the folder contents in Media Player, pull down the Library menu and select Video. In the Navigation pane, click Library, and then double-click the Folder view. You then see an icon for *SERVER*\Videos, as shown in Figure 8.13. Double-click that icon to view the video files.

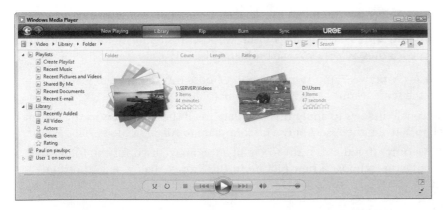

FIGURE 8.13   Double-click *SERVER*\Videos to view the contents of Windows Home Server's Videos share in Media Player.

If the Windows Home Server Videos share contains recorded TV shows, Media Player displays them separately. Pull down the Library menu and select Recorded TV. Figure 8.14 shows a Media Player icon for a Windows Home Server folder that contains some recorded TV content.

FIGURE 8.14   Media Player shows Windows Home Server's recorded TV shows in the Recorded TV section of the library.

Archiving Recorded TV on Windows Home Server

When you record TV in Windows Media Center, the program stores the resulting files—which use the Microsoft Recorded TV Show file type with the .dvr-ms extension—in the following folder:

```
%SystemDrive%\Users\Public\Recorded TV
```

If you want to stream your recorded TV shows to Windows Media Connect programs and devices on your network, you need to move or copy the Recorded TV files to Windows Home Server's Videos share (or the Recorded TV share if you have Windows Home Server Power Pack 3 installed).

As with ripping music (see "Changing the Default Rip Location to Windows Home Server," earlier), this extra step is a hassle, particularly since Recorded TV files are often multi-gigabyte affairs that can take quite a while to transfer. A better solution is to record TV shows directly to Windows Home Server. In versions of Windows Home Server prior to Power Pack 3, this wasn't as simple as tweaking a folder value, because by default Media Center has no such setting. It was possible to work around this problem by modifying some Media Center services and Registry settings (as I explained in the previous edition of this book), but it was a hassle.

Fortunately, it's a hassle that's now history. Power Pack 3 comes with a new Windows Media Center Connector feature, which adds a Home Server menu item to the Media Center interface, as you saw earlier (see "Connecting Windows Media Center to Your Home Server"). The Home Server menu item includes a tile called TV Archive that enables you to configure Media Center to record TV shows directly to the server. Finally!

CAUTION

Recording a TV show is incredibly bandwidth-intensive, so the modification in this section stretches your home network to its limit. So, although it's possible to record shows to Windows Home Server on a 100Mbps wired or 54Mbps wireless connection, for best results, you really should do this only on a network that uses 1Gbps wired or 802.11n (248Mbps) wireless connections.

Assuming you've installed Windows Media Center Connector, follow these steps to configure TV archiving in Media Center:

1. In Windows Media Center, select Home Server and then click TV Archive.

2. Click Settings. Media Center shows the TV archiving settings, as shown in Figure 8.15.

FIGURE 8.15   With Power Pack 3's Windows Media Center Connector installed, use the TV Archive Settings tab to configure TV recording directly to the server.

3. If you want Media Center to archive all of your TV shows—that is, shows you've already recorded and shows you record in the future—to Windows Home Server's Recorded TV share, activate the Archive All Recordings Automatically check box.

4. If you want Media Center to record TV shows directly to Windows Home Server's Recorded TV share, activate the Move Recordings to My Home Server check box.

NOTE

Actually, it's not really accurate to say that, if you activate the Move Recordings to My Home Server check box, Media Center records TV shows "directly" to the server. Instead, Media Center creates a temporary copy of the recorded TV show locally, and it then moves that copy to the server.

---

5. If you want Media Center to also create a compressed version of each recorded TV show, activate the Create a Compressed Copy For check box, and then choose a format and location:

   ▶ **Create a Compressed Copy For**—Use this list to choose one of the following three formats: TV (uses the original resolution of the recording); Windows Mobile (320×240, 500Kbps bitrate); or Zune (720×480, 1,500Kbps). Note that in all cases, the resulting file uses the Windows Media Audio/Video (.wmv) format.

   ▶ **Save Compressed Copy To**—Use this list to select a location for the compressed copies. The default is Home Server Videos folder, and you should leave that as is if you want your compressed copies on the server. Otherwise, you can choose either Public Videos Folder or Let Me Use a Different Folder (the latter requires a path to the save location).

6. Click Save to put the new settings into effect.

If you left the Archive All Recordings Automatically check box deactivated, you can select which of your existing recordings get archived to the server. In Media Center, select the Home Server item, and then click the TV Archive tile. You have two choices from here, as follows:

▶ **Series**—Click this tab to see a list of your recorded TV series. Activate the check box beside each series that you want to archive.

▶ **Programs**—Click this tab to see a list of your recorded TV programs. Activate the check box beside each program that you want to archive.

Click Save to put the settings into effect. Remember that how your existing series and programs get archived depends on the options you configured in the Settings tab:

▶ If you activated the Move Recordings to My Home Server check box, your selected series and programs get moved to the server's Recorded TV share.

▶ If you activated the Create a Compressed Copy For Server check box, Media Center creates compressed copies of your selected series and programs and stores the copies in the server's Videos share.

From Here

▶ To learn how to add a user to Windows Home Server, **see** "Adding a New User," **P. 38**.

▶ For information on connecting various devices to your Windows Home Server network, **see** Chapter 3, "Adding Devices to the Windows Home Server Network."

▶ Recorded TV requires plenty of storage. To learn how to add more storage to Windows Home Server, **see** "Adding Storage to the Home Server," **P. 133**.

▶ For details on changing user permissions, **see** "Modifying Permissions for a Windows Home Server Shared Folder," **P. 146**.

▶ To learn how to work with the Registry, **see** Chapter 18, "Working with the Windows Home Server Registry."

CHAPTER 9

Backing Up and Restoring Network Computers

Backing up your computer is a "spinach" task. By that, I mean that it's a task that, like the vegetable, is good for us but not particularly palatable. (This will no doubt seem a libelous association to anyone who enjoys spinach.) The reasons why people don't like backing up are legion: It's too hard, it's too complicated, it's too time-consuming, my computer will never die, and so on. Whatever the excuse, most people simply don't bother backing up their system, much less their precious and irreplaceable documents. Now apply this backup negativity to your home network, where the difficulty is multiplied by the number of computers on the LAN, and you're left with a major problem.

Fortunately, it's a problem that Windows Home Server was designed to solve. As soon as you connect a computer to the network, Windows Home Server automatically adds the machine to its list of computers to back up. This means that the computer gets backed up every night, no questions asked. It's as simple and as painless as backups can be, and it means you may never have to worry about (or even think about) backing up again.

Of course, this is *Windows* we're talking about, so the initial simplicity is a front that hides a fairly complex bit of technology that you can tweak and tune to fit your needs. This chapter takes you behind the scenes of Windows Home Server's backups and tells you a bit about the underlying technology, how to take advantage of the backup settings, and how to restore files, folders, and even entire systems should something go wrong down the road.

Understanding Windows Home Server's Backup Technology

Backups seem like such straightforward things: You take all the files that exist on a computer and you make copies of them somewhere else. In the case of Windows Home Server backups, however, there's a lot more going on under the hood. This section provides you with a few notes that give you some idea of the efficiencies and power that Windows Home Server implements.

▶ **SEE** If you want to back up Windows Home Server itself, **see** Chapter 15, "Maintaining Windows Home Server."

Single Instance Storage

Unlike almost every other backup system, Windows Home Server does *not* back up at the file level (by, say, storing copies of files on the server). Instead, it backs up data at the *cluster* level. (A cluster, you'll recall, is the fundamental unit of storage in the file system. That is, every file is really a series of clusters, each of which is usually 4KB.) When Windows Home Server backs up a file, it performs a cluster-by-cluster check to see if the same data has already been backed up. If it finds an identical cluster already on the system, it doesn't include the redundant cluster in the backup. Instead, it leaves the existing cluster on the system and makes a note about which files that cluster belongs to. This technology is new to Windows Home Server, and it's called *Single Instance Storage*.

Note that this applies not just to the backups for a single computer, but for *every* machine on the network. For example, suppose that a popular song resides on your computer and on two other computers on your home network. If your computer is the first to be backed up, Windows Home Server will include the song in that backup. When it backs up the other two computers, it will see that song on each one, but it won't add the redundant data to the backup.

You might think the space-savings generated by cluster-level backups will be minimal because, after all, how many songs (or whatever) do multiple computers have in common? However, remember that Windows Home Server doesn't just back up your data. It also backs up the `%SystemRoot%` folder, which contains the Windows system files, many of which are identical across multiple machines (depending on the versions of Windows each is running). It also backs up the `%ProgramFiles%` folder, so popular applications such as Microsoft Office and Internet Explorer also have lots of common files across the network. As a result, the storage space used by the backups on Windows Home Server is a mere fraction of the size of all the original files put together.

No Backup Types

Other backup systems muddy the waters by offering numerous backup types: Full, Incremental, Differential, Daily, and so on. Part of the reluctance many people have to setting up a backup regimen is trying to figure out the differences between these various types.

Windows Home Server does away with all that by having no backup types at all. Instead, Windows Home Server's backups use a simple two-stage system:

▶ For a computer's first backup, Windows Home Server backs up everything on the machine (with a few exceptions, as you'll see a bit later).

▶ On subsequent backups for the same machine, Windows Home Server only backs up data that has been added or that has been changed since the last backup.

This sounds like an incremental (or is it differential?) backup, but that's not the case. Instead, Windows Home Server treats *every* backup as a full backup. So even if Windows Home Server only had to back up a single file last night, if you look at that backup, you see all your files. In other words, with Windows Home Server, you never run into the situation where you need to restore one file from yesterday's backup, a second file from last week's backup, and so on.

The other (not insignificant) advantage to this backup strategy is that although a computer's initial backup may take several hours, subsequent backups for that machine may take just a few minutes.

> **CAUTION**
>
> To avoid an extremely long initial backup for a computer, make sure that the machine has a wired connection to the network. Even a 100Mbps wired connection is twice as fast as the typical 54Mbps wireless connection, and gigabit wired connections are closer to 20 times faster. Of course, that's assuming that your wireless connection can even achieve 54Mbps, which is rare due to interference, shared bandwidth, and so on.

Smarter Backups

Single Instance Storage is a pretty smart technology, but Windows Home Server also implements a few other features for intelligent backups:

▶ To avoid conflicts, Windows Home Server never backs up more than one computer at a time. When the backup time comes around (the default time is midnight), Windows Home Server puts the network clients in a queue and backs them up one at a time. Even if you initiate a manual backup during that time, Windows Home Server still puts that machine in the queue.

▶ Windows Home Server backs up the entire computer by default, but it doesn't back up every last file. Intelligently, it avoids unnecessary files such as the contents of the Temp folder (where Windows and programs store temporary files); the paging file (used by Windows to swap oft-used data to disk rather than having to retrieve it from its original location); the Recycle Bin (where Windows stores your deleted files); the hibernation file (where Windows stores the current contents of memory when the system goes into hibernation mode); and file system shadow copies (the previous versions of files and folders maintained by Windows).

▶ If a computer is in sleep or hibernate mode when the scheduled backup time occurs, Windows Home Server pings the computer to let it know that it's time for backup, and the server puts the machine into the queue. When the backup completes, Windows Home Server tells the computer to put itself back into sleep or hibernate mode. For notebooks, this only happens if the computer is running on AC; if it's on batteries, the machine skips the "wakeup call" to avoid using too much battery life during the backup.

NOTE

Windows Home Server only wakes up the computer if you enabled that option during the Windows Home Server Connector setup process. If you want to change whatever option you chose during setup, you need to run the Windows Home Server Connector Setup program again.

▶ **SEE** "Installing Windows Home Server Connector on the Client Computers," **P. 63.**

Automatic Backup Management

Some backup systems accumulate backups until there's no space left for new ones! Windows Home Server's Single Instance Storage technology means that this is less likely to happen. However, storage is always finite, so even Windows Home Server's backups can't accumulate indefinitely. Fortunately, as part of Windows Home Server's commitment to a fully automated backup system, even the process of removing old backups happens behind the scenes. This is called *Automated Backup Management*, and it means that Windows Home Server deletes old backups after a preset time has elapsed.

For dedicated tinkerers, you can customize the frequency with which Windows Home Server removes old backups (see "Configuring Automatic Backup Management," later in this chapter), and you can even delete old backups manually (see "Cleaning Up Old Backups").

Converting Client Partitions to NTFS

Windows Home Server only supports backing up client partitions that use the NTFS file system. If you have partitions that use FAT16 or FAT32, they won't be included in the backups. If you need such a partition backed up, you must convert it to NTFS. (Doing this has other benefits as well. NTFS is your best choice if you want optimal hard disk performance because, in most cases, NTFS outperforms both FAT16 and FAT32. This is particularly true with large partitions and with partitions that that have lots of files. Also, NTFS enables you to encrypt files for maximum security.)

You can use two methods to convert a partition to NTFS:

- ▶ Format the partition as NTFS.
- ▶ Run the CONVERT utility.

Format the Partition as NTFS

Formatting the partition as NTFS is the best way to go because it maximizes the performance of NTFS, which means faster backups. Note, however, that formatting wipes all the data from the partition, so you need to store any important files in a safe place (say, on a Windows Home Server share) before formatting.

Here are the steps to follow:

1. If the drive contains important files, copy or move those files to another partition, an external drive or memory card, a recordable CD or DVD, or a network share.
2. Select Start, Computer (or My Computer in Windows XP).
3. Right-click the partition you want to work with and then click Format.
4. In Windows Vista, enter your UAC credentials to continue.
5. In the Format dialog box, select NTFS in the File System list.
6. (Optional) Enter a volume label. (This is the partition name that appears in the Computer or My Computer window.)
7. Click Start. Windows warns you that all data on the partition will be erased.
8. Click OK. Windows formats the partition.
9. When you see the Format Complete message, click OK.
10. Click Close to shut down the Format dialog box.

Run the CONVERT Utility

If you have data on the partition that you can't store in a safe place, you can preserve the data and convert the partition to NTFS by using the CONVERT command-line utility:

```
CONVERT volume /FS:NTFS [/V] [/CvtArea:filename] [/NoSecurity] [/X]
```

volume	Specifies the drive letter (followed by a colon) or volume name you want to convert.
/FS:NTFS	Specifies that the file system is to be converted to NTFS.
/V	Uses verbose mode, which gives detailed information during the conversion.
/CvtArea:filename	Specifies a contiguous placeholder file in the root directory that will be used to store the NTFS system files.

| /NoSecurity | Specifies that the default NTFS permissions are not to be applied to this volume. All the converted files and folders will be accessible by everyone. |
| /X | Forces the volume to dismount first if it currently has open files. |

For example, running the following command at the command prompt converts drive G to NTFS:

```
convert g: /FS:NTFS
```

Configuring Windows Home Server Backups

Before I cover the specifics of running backups, you should configure the Windows Home Server backup settings to suit your needs. In keeping with the overall simplicity of the backup feature, there are only two things you can configure: the backup time and when Windows Home Server performs Automatic Backup Management.

Configuring the Backup Time

When the backup time occurs, Windows Home Server does three things:

- ▶ It backs up all the connected computers, one machine at a time.

- ▶ If you have automatic updates turned on, Windows Home Server installs any pending updates and then restarts the system if an update requires a reboot.

  ▶ **SEE** To learn how to enable automatic updating, **see** "Configuring Windows Update," **P. 103**.

- ▶ Every Sunday, Windows Home Server runs the Backup Cleanup feature, which deletes old backups according to the schedule maintained by Automatic Backup Management (discussed in the next section).

Windows Home Server's default backup time runs from midnight to 6:00 AM.

Note that if Windows Home Server hasn't completed its backups or maintenance by 6:00 AM, it finishes whatever task it's currently running, and then it cancels the remaining operations and reschedules them for the next backup period. If this is a problem on your network, you might want to extend the backup time. Windows Home Server supports backup periods as long as 23 hours (or as short as one hour).

Here are the steps to configure Windows Home Server's backup time:

1. Log on to the Windows Home Server Console.

2. Click Settings to display the Windows Home Server Settings dialog box.

3. Display the Backup tab, shown in Figure 9.1.

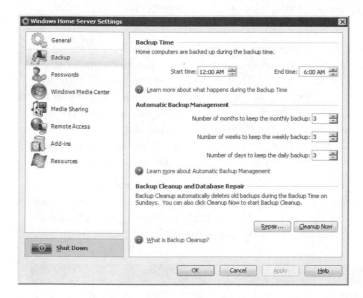

FIGURE 9.1   In the Windows Home Server Settings dialog box, use the Backup tab to configure the start and end time for the backup and maintenance period.

4. Use the Start Time box to set the time you want Windows Home Server to begin its backup and maintenance period.

5. Use the End Time box to set the time you want Windows Home Server to stop its backup and maintenance period.

NOTE

Make sure the End Time value is at least one hour later and at least one hour before the Start Time value. For example, if you leave the Start Time at 12:00 AM, the End Time can't be earlier than 1:00 AM or later than 11:00 PM.

6. Click OK to put the new settings into effect.

Configuring Automatic Backup Management

To avoid the unwelcome scenario of old backups gradually usurping all of your storage space, Windows Home Server regularly deletes old backups. This Automatic Backup Management feature keeps old backups under control by maintaining three deletion schedules:

▶ The number of days to keep the first backup of the day. (There is, by default, just one backup per day, but you can also add backups by running them manually; see "Running a Manual Backup," later in this chapter.) The default value is three days.

▶ The number of weeks to keep the first backup of the week. The default value is three weeks.

▶ The number of months to keep the first backup of the month. The default value is three months.

The default values should be fine for most people, but they could cause you to lose data in some relatively rare scenarios. For example, suppose you create a document on Tuesday and then permanently delete it (by pressing Shift+Delete to bypass the Recycle Bin) on Wednesday. Assuming Tuesday wasn't the first of the month, the file will only reside in the daily backups (since it didn't make it into the first backup of the week on Monday). Windows Home Server's Automatic Backup Management will delete the Tuesday backup on Friday (because, by default, it only keeps three days' worth of daily backups), which means that if you suddenly yearn to have the file back on Saturday (or later), you're out of luck.

If you or your family members generate a lot of new content, and if your Windows Home Server is swimming in storage space, you might want to bump up the default values for extra safety. For example, bumping up the value for the daily backup to, say, 14, and the monthly backup to, say, 12, will make it less likely that you'll lose important information.

CAUTION

Even if you have tons of storage space on the server, bumping up the number of saved backups can eat disk space in a hurry, even with Single Instance Storage doing its duty. If you drastically increase the number of saved backups, be diligent about keeping an eye on how much space the backups are using. In the Windows Home Server Console, display the Storage Space tab and check the PC Backups value.

Follow these steps to configure Windows Home Server's Automatic Backup Management feature:

1. Log on to the Windows Home Server Console.
2. Click Settings to display the Windows Home Server Settings dialog box.
3. Display the Backup tab.
4. In the Automatic Backup Management group, use the following controls to set the number of backups you want to keep (see Figure 9.1, shown earlier):

Number of Months to Keep the Monthly Backup	Specify the number of months to keep the first backup of the month. The maximum number of months is 120.
Number of Weeks to Keep the Weekly Backup	Specify the number of weeks to keep the first backup of the week. The maximum number of weeks is 52.
Number of Days to Keep the Daily Backup	Specify the number of days to keep the first backup of each day. The maximum number of days is 90.

5. Click OK to put the new settings into effect.

Configuring a Computer for Backup

By default, Windows Home Server always backs up all the computer's drives (or, more accurately, it backs up all the computer's NTFS drives). This is ideal because it means that if a computer crashes and can't be recovered, you can still get the machine back on its feet by using the Home PC Restore CD to restore one of the complete backups. (For the details on this, see "Restoring a Computer to a Previous Configuration," later in this chapter.) However, there may be situations where you don't want or need certain parts of a computer included in the backups:

▶ You have a folder that contains some extremely large files (for example, ripped DVDs), and you don't want those files taking up space in the backups.

▶ You have a folder that contains files you're going to delete anyway. For example, most people delete recorded TV shows after viewing them. Because these files tend to be huge, it's a good idea to exclude the Recorded TV folder from the backups to save space. (If you have shows you want to save, consider moving them to a separate folder that *does* get backed up.)

▶ You have an external hard drive that you occasionally bring home from work or borrow from someone else. Because the files on this drive aren't really yours, you probably don't want them backed up.

▶ You have an external hard drive that gets swapped among your family members. This could cause problems with Windows Home Server if it expects the drive to be on one computer and finds it "missing" the next time it tries to back up that machine.

For these and similar scenarios, you can exclude one or more drives and folders from a computer's backup configuration. The next two sections show you how to do this. (Note that Windows Home Server doesn't let you exclude all the drives on a system or all the folders on a drive. If you want to stop Windows Home Server from backing up a client, see "Turning Off Backups for a Computer," later in this chapter.)

Excluding a Disk Drive from a Backup

To exclude one or more hard disk drives or hard disk partitions from a computer's backup configuration, follow these steps:

1. Log on to the Windows Home Server Console.
2. Display the Computers & Backup tab.
3. Click the computer you want to work with.
4. Click Configure Backup. Windows Home Server launches the Backup Configuration Wizard.
5. Click Next in the initial dialog box. The wizard examines the computer and then displays a list of disk partitions, as shown in Figure 9.2.

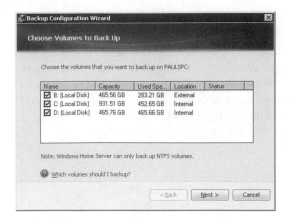

FIGURE 9.2   Use the Backup Configuration Wizard to exclude one or more drives or partitions from a computer's backups.

6. Deactivate the check box for each partition that you want to exclude from the backup. (Note that if you deactivate *all* the check boxes, the wizard disables the Next button.)

7. Click Next. The wizard displays the Choose Folders to Exclude from Backup dialog box.

8. I discuss this dialog box in detail in the next section, so click Next to continue.

9. Click Done to complete the configuration.

Excluding Folders from a Backup

To exclude one or more folders from a computer's backup configuration, follow these steps:

1. Log on to the Windows Home Server Console.

2. Display the Computers & Backup tab.

3. Click the computer you want to configure.

4. Click Configure Backup to run the Backup Configuration Wizard.

5. Click Next. The wizard displays a list of disk partitions.

6. Deactivate the check box for each partition that you want to exclude from the backup. (Note that if you deactivate *all* the check boxes, the wizard disables the Next button.)

7. Click Next to get to the Choose Folders to Exclude from Backup dialog box. As you can see in Figure 9.3, the folders that Windows Home Server automatically excludes from the backup are shown in light gray type.

8. Click Add to display the Exclude a Folder dialog box.

9. Click the plus sign (+) beside the drive that contains the folder or folders you want to exclude. A list of the folders on that drive appears.

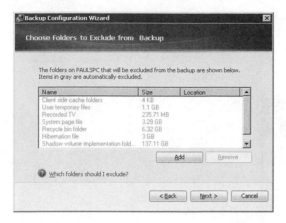

FIGURE 9.3 The folders that Windows Home Server automatically excludes from the backups are shown in light gray type.

10. Select the folder you want to exclude. (You may need to drill down into various levels of subfolders to find the one you want.)

11. Click Exclude. The wizard adds the folder to the list of excluded folders.

12. Repeat steps 8–11 to exclude other folders, as needed.

13. Click Next.

14. Click Done to complete the configuration.

Adding a New Hard Drive to a Backup

If you add a hard drive to a computer, Windows Home Server eventually detects the new drive, changes the network status to At Risk, and displays the Backup Warning shown in Figure 9.4 on each client.

FIGURE 9.4 When you add a hard drive to a computer, Windows Home Server broadcasts a warning to add that drive to the computer's backups.

If you don't want to include this drive in the computer's backups, follow these steps to handle the warning:

1. Log on to the Windows Home Server Console.

2. Click the Network status icon.

3. In the backup warning for the new drive, click to activate the Ignore This Issue check box. Windows Home Server ignores the new drive and returns the network status to Healthy, as shown in Figure 9.5.

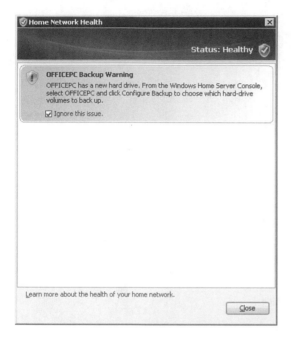

FIGURE 9.5   You can tell Windows Home Server to ignore the new drive.

4. Click Close.

On the other hand, you might prefer to include the new drive in the computer's nightly backups. In that case, you need to work through the following steps to reconfigure the computer:

1. Log on to the Windows Home Server Console.

2. Display the Computers & Backup tab.

3. Click the computer that has the new drive.

4. Click Configure Backup to start the Backup Configuration Wizard.

5. Click Next. The wizard displays a list of partitions on the computer.

6. Make sure that the check box for the new drive is activated (it should be by default), and then click Next.

7. Click Next.

8. Click Done. Windows Home Server adds the new drive to the backup configuration and returns the network status to Healthy.

Turning Off Backups for a Computer

There might be times when you don't want a particular computer to get backed up:

▶ You might know that you'll be using the computer during the backup time, and you don't want the backup process to slow down your work.

▶ You might need the computer to run an all-night job (such as compiling a large application or rendering a 3D image), and you don't want the backup to interfere.

▶ The computer might be a backup or spare with no important information on it.

▶ You might be running out of storage space on the server, and you want to prevent backups until you can add more storage.

For these and similar situations, you can tell Windows Home Server not to back up one or more computers. Here are the steps to follow:

1. Log on to the Windows Home Server Console.
2. Display the Computers & Backups tab.
3. Right-click the computer that you want to work with.
4. Click Turn Off Backups. Windows Home Server changes the computer's backup status to Off. (You can see what this looks like in Figure 9.7.)

To tell Windows Home Server to resume backing up the computer, follow steps 1–3 and then click Turn On Backups.

Running a Manual Backup

Windows Home Server's nightly backups ought to suit the needs of most people. However, at times you may want even more assurance that your data is safe:

▶ You just installed the Windows Home Server Connector on a client PC, and you don't want to wait until midnight to get it backed up.

▶ You spent the morning creating, modifying, or downloading a large number of files, and you want them backed up now.

▶ You turned off backups for a computer the previous night and now you want a backup for the current day.

▶ The previous backup failed for some reason, so you want to try again.

▶ You just installed a major program (such as Microsoft Office), and you want to back it up.

▶ You added a new hard drive full of important files, and you want to get them backed up right away.

▶ You're more paranoid than most.

Whatever the reason, Windows Home Server lets you make as many backups as you want, as long as it has the free space to store them.

Here are the steps to follow to launch a backup manually:

1. Log on to the Windows Home Server Console.
2. Display the Computers & Backups tab.
3. Click the computer that you want to back up.
4. Click Backup Now. Windows Home Server displays the Backup Now dialog box, shown in Figure 9.6.

FIGURE 9.6   Type a description for your manual backup.

TIP

A faster way to launch a manual backup is to log on to the client computer, right-click the Windows Home Server icon in the notification area, and then click Backup Now.

---

5. Type a description for the backup. Just in case you need to use this backup later on to restore some files, make your description useful and unique (for example, Just Installed Microsoft Office or Retrying Failed Backup).
6. Click Backup Now. Windows Home Server begins backing up the computer.

If you're in the Windows Home Server Console, the Status column in the Computers & Backup tab displays the progress of the operation, as shown in Figure 9.7. If you initiated the manual backup from the client, either click the A backup is starting message or right-click the Windows Home Server icon in the notification area, and then click View Backup Status to see the Backup Status dialog box, shown in Figure 9.8.

Cancelling a Running Backup

When a backup starts on your computer, the Windows Home Server Tray application icon turns blue and displays the message A backup is starting, as shown in Figure 9.9.

FIGURE 9.7   In the Computers & Backup tab, the Status column shows the progress of the backup.

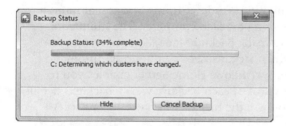

FIGURE 9.8   On the client, the Backup Status dialog box shows the progress of the backup.

FIGURE 9.9   The Windows Home Server icon lets you know when a backup is starting on your computer.

However, you might be busy with the computer and don't want the backup to run just now. In that case, you can cancel the backup:

▶ Right-click the Windows Home Server icon in the notification area, click View Backup Status, and then click Cancel Backup.

▶ In the Windows Home Server Console, display the Computers & Backup tab, right-click the computer that's being backed up, and then click Cancel Backup.

Backing Up Other Systems to Windows Home Server

Because the Windows Home Server Connector software only works on Windows 7, Vista, and XP PCs, the automatic backup feature of Windows Home Server isn't available for other systems on your network. If you need to back up an older Windows machine, a Mac, or a Linux box, you need to do it the old-fashioned way: You need to run the computer's built-in (or third-party) backup software.

The good news is that you don't have to worry about *where* you store the backups for these other systems because you've got your Windows Home Server shares ready to do the job. On my network, I created a `Backups` subfolder in the `Public` share:

\\SERVER\Public\Backups

When configuring backups on your other systems, use this Windows Home Server shared folder as the backup destination.

Working with Backups

As your network computers get backed up nightly, Windows Home Server maintains a database of the backups that it's currently storing for each computer. The number of backups in the database depends on the Automatic Backup Management settings you specified for saving daily, weekly, and monthly backups (see "Configuring Automatic Backup Management," earlier in this chapter). Windows Home Server enables you to access this database of backups and see the status of each backup, view a backup's details, prevent a backup from being deleted, and browse the files in a backup. The next few sections provide the details.

Viewing a Computer's List of Backups

In the Windows Home Server Console, the Computers & Backup tab has a Status column that tells you the current state of the backups for each computer. You can see five values in the Status column:

▶ **Backed Up**—This means that Windows Home Server is currently storing at least one successful backup for the computer.

▶ **No Backups in Last *X* Days**—This means that Windows Home Server has backed up the computer successfully in the past, but it has not been able to back up the computer for the specified number of days.

▶ **Not Backed Up**—This means that Windows Home Server is not currently storing any successful backups for the computer. In this case, the Network status icon also shows At Risk.

▶ **Off**—This means that you've turned off backups for the computer (as explained earlier in the "Turing Off Backups for a Computer" section).

▶ **Backed Up On** *Date Time*—You see this status with your Windows Home Server computer when you've configured the server to back itself up to a non-storage pool hard drive. The status tells you the date and time the server was last backed up.

Note that seeing `Backed Up` for a computer doesn't necessarily mean that the most recent backup was successful; it just means that Windows Home Server does have a successful backup stored, so it's possible to restore the computer if the need arises.

If you want to know the status of the individual backups, you need to display the computer's list of backups. Here are the steps to follow:

1. Log on to the Windows Home Server Console.

2. Display the Computers & Backup tab.

3. Click the computer you want to work with.

4. Click View Backups. The View Backups dialog box appears. Figure 9.10 shows an example.

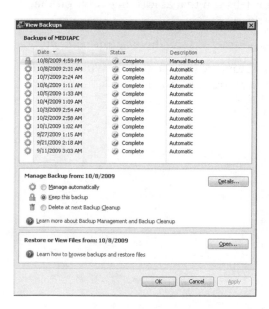

FIGURE 9.10   The View Backups dialog box shows the list of stored backups on the computer.

TIP

You can also double-click a computer to see its list of backups.

The list of backups has four columns:

▶ **Management**—The icons in this column tell you the current Automatic Backup Management status for the backup:

  ▶ **Gear**—Windows Home Server manages the backup according to the settings in Automatic Backup Management.

  ▶ **Lock**—Windows Home Server will not delete the backup (see "Preventing Windows Home Server from Deleting a Backup," later in this chapter).

  ▶ **Trash can**—Windows Home Server will delete the backup the next time it performs a backup cleanup (see the sections "Scheduling a Backup for Deletion" and "Cleaning Up Old Backups," later in this chapter).

▶ **Date**—This column tells you the date of the backup or backup attempt.

▶ **Status**—This column tells you the status of the backup. There are three possibilities (see Figure 9.11):

  ▶ **Complete**—Windows Home Server successfully backed up the entire computer.

  ▶ **Incomplete**—Windows Home Server backed up some, but not all, of the computer. In other words, this status tells you that at least one drive on the computer was not backed up properly.

  ▶ **Failed**—Windows Home Server did not back up any drive on the computer.

▶ **Description**—This column shows either Automatic (for the nightly Windows Home Server backups) or the description of a manual backup you ran.

FIGURE 9.11   The Status column can have three values: Complete, Incomplete, or Failed.

Viewing Backup Details

The View Backups window tells you some useful information about each backup, but there is more data available. For example, it's also possible to see the time it took to perform a backup, the partitions included in the backup, and the files that were excluded from each partition during the backup.

To view this extra detail for a backup, follow these steps:

1. Log on to the Windows Home Server Console and display the Computers & Backup tab.

2. Click the computer you want to work with and then click View Backups to open the View Backups dialog box.

3. Click the backup you want to view.

4. Click Details. The Backup Details dialog box appears, as shown in Figure 9.12.

FIGURE 9.12   The Backup Details dialog box provides extra information about each backup.

TIP

You can also double-click a backup to see its details.

Note that in the Volumes in Backup list, Windows Home Server shows the partition name (drive letter and partition label), capacity, and location (internal or external). It also shows the status for each partition, which will be either Complete or Failed. So if the overall status of the backup is either Incomplete or Failed, you can view the details and see which partition is causing the problem. Click the failed volume backup to see the Failure Details, as shown in Figure 9.13.

FIGURE 9.13   If the overall backup status is Incomplete or Failed, the Backup Details dialog box tells you which partition (or partitions) failed.

> **NOTE**
>
> What should you do if a particular partition is failing routinely? First, just try rebooting the client computer to see if that helps. If it's an external hard drive, make sure the drive is powered up and connected to the PC. It's also possible that a drive error could be causing the problem, so run Windows' Check Disk utility on the drive. (Right-click the partition, click Properties, display the Tools tab, and then click Check Now. Note that this operation requires Administrator credentials in Windows Vista.) If you still can't get Windows Home Server to back up the partition successfully and if the partition doesn't contain important files, exclude it from the backups (see "Excluding a Disk Drive from a Backup," earlier in this chapter).

Preventing Windows Home Server from Deleting a Backup

As I mentioned earlier in this chapter, Windows Home Server routinely deletes old backups every Sunday according to the Automatic Backup Management settings. However, sometimes you might not want Windows Home Server to remove a particular backup during the cleanup process. For example, you may know that a backup contains an important version of a file or folder, and you always want the ability to restore that version if necessary.

> **NOTE**
>
> If you create a backup manually (see "Running a Manual Backup," earlier), Windows Home Server automatically configures that backup not to be deleted during the cleanup.

For such situations, you can tell Windows Home Server not to delete a particular backup. Follow these steps:

1. Log on to the Windows Home Server Console and display the Computers & Backup tab.
2. Click the computer you want to work with, and then click View Backups to open the View Backups dialog box.
3. Click the backup you want to keep.
4. In the Manage Backup section, click the Keep This Backup option. Windows Home Server displays a lock icon beside the backup. The lock icon tells you that Windows Home Server won't delete the backup during the cleanup process.

Cleaning Up Old Backups

Windows Home Server's backup cleanup process should prevent each computer's list of backups from getting unwieldy. Even so, there are situations in which you might want to accelerate the cleanup process:

▶ You have a number of manual backups that you no longer need.

▶ The list of backups includes many failed or incomplete backups that you no longer need to see (because, for example, you've solved whatever problem was causing the unsuccessful backups).

▶ You're running low on storage space in Windows Home Server.

To delete backups, Windows Home Server gives you two choices: you can schedule a backup to be deleted the next time Windows Home Server runs the backup cleanup process, or you can delete one or more backups right away by running the backup cleanup by hand. The next two sections provide the specifics.

Scheduling a Backup for Deletion

Here are the steps to follow to schedule a backup to be deleted the next time Windows Home Server performs the backup cleanup:

1. Log on to the Windows Home Server Console and display the Computers & Backup tab.
2. Click the computer you want to work with, and then click View Backups to open the View Backups dialog box.

3. Click the backup you want to delete.

4. In the Manage Backup section, click the Delete at Next Backup Cleanup option. Windows Home Server displays a trash can icon beside the backup. The trash can icon tells you that Windows Home Server will delete the backup during next Sunday's cleanup process.

5. Repeat steps 3 and 4 to schedule other backups for deletion.

6. Click OK.

Running Backup Cleanup Manually

Follow these steps to delete one or more backups immediately by running the backup cleanup by hand:

1. Log on to the Windows Home Server Console and display the Computers & Backup tab.

2. Click the computer you want to work with, and then click View Backups to open the View Backups dialog box.

3. Click the backup you want to delete.

4. In the Manage Backup section, click the Delete at Next Backup Cleanup option. Windows Home Server displays a trash can icon beside the backup.

5. Repeat steps 3 and 4 to schedule other backups for deletion.

6. Click OK.

7. Click Settings to open the Windows Home Server Settings dialog box.

8. Display the Backup tab.

9. Click Cleanup Now. Windows Home Server performs the backup cleanup.

Browsing Backed-Up Files

If you're curious about which files reside in a backup, you can view the backup contents. Here are the steps to follow:

1. Log on to the Windows Home Server Console and display the Computers & Backup tab.

2. Click the computer you want to work with, and then click View Backups to open the View Backups dialog box.

3. Click the backup you want to view.

4. Click Open. If the backup includes two or more partitions, the Choose a Volume to Open dialog box appears.

5. Choose the partition you want to view, and then click Open.

6. In Windows 7 or Vista, enter your User Account Control credentials.

7. If you see the Windows Security dialog box asking if you want to allow device software to be installed, click Install. Windows Home Server displays the backup files.

Note that Windows Home Server uses a special Z: drive to display the files, as shown in Figure 9.14. (If your system is already using Z:—for example, as a mapped network drive—Windows Home Server uses the highest available drive letter.)

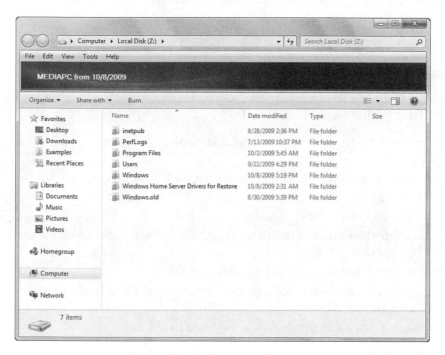

FIGURE 9.14 Windows Home Server displays the backup files in a special Z: drive.

Restoring Network Backups

Like any type of insurance, backups are something you hope you never have to use. Unfortunately, in the real world, stuff happens:

- ▶ Important information inside a document gets deleted or edited.
- ▶ Important files get permanently deleted by accident.
- ▶ Hard drives and entire systems kick the digital bucket.

These and similar situations are when you thank your lucky stars (or your deity of choice) that Windows Home Server has been on the job making nightly backups because now you can restore the file, folder, or system and get back to more important things. The rest of this chapter takes you through various techniques for restoring files via Windows Home Server.

NOTE

One of the remarkable things about Windows Home Server is that you can restore objects from computers other than your own. For example, if an image, song, or video was backed up on your media PC, you can access that PC's backups and then restore the file to a folder on your own computer.

Restoring Backed-Up Files

If the file or folder you want to restore exists in a backup of your computer, you need to follow these steps to restore it:

1. Log on to the Windows Home Server Console and display the Computers & Backup tab.

2. Click the computer you want to work with, and then click View Backups to open the View Backups dialog box.

3. Click the backup you want to view.

4. Click Open. If the backup includes two or more partitions, the Choose a Volume to Open dialog box appears.

5. Choose the partition you want to view, and then click OK.

6. In Windows 7 or Vista, enter your User Account Control credentials. Windows Home Server displays the backup files.

7. Navigate to the folder that contains the data you want to restore.

8. Copy the data you want to restore.

9. Navigate to the folder where you want the data restored.

10. Paste the data. If some or all of the objects already exist in the destination folder, Windows asks how you want to handle the conflict:

    ▶ Windows XP displays a dialog box asking whether you want to replace the existing file or folder. Click Yes to replace the existing file with the backup copy. (If you don't want the existing file replaced, click No, instead.)

    ▶ Windows 7 and Vista display a Copy File dialog box like the one shown in Figure 9.15. You have three choices:

Copy and Replace	Click this option to have the backup copy replace the existing item.
Don't Copy	Click this option to bypass copying the backup version and leave the existing item as is.
Copy, But Keep Both Files	Click this option to leave the existing file as is and to add the backup copy to the folder with (2) appended to the file's primary name.

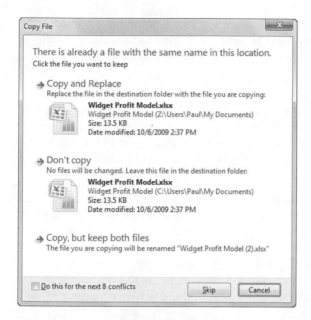

FIGURE 9.15   If one or more of the objects already exist in the destination folder, use the Copy File dialog box to decide which objects you want to restore.

If Windows 7 or Vista detects multiple conflicts, you can save time by activating the Do This for the Next X Conflicts check box (see Figure 9.15) to resolve the conflict in the same way with each file.

Restoring a Computer to a Previous Configuration

Losing a file or two or even an entire folder is no big deal because, as you saw in the previous section, recovering the data requires nothing more than a simple copy-and-paste operation. It's a much more serious problem when your entire system goes south due to a hard drive crash, a virus, or some other major problem.

Before Windows Home Server, restoring a computer would be a day-long affair that involved reinstalling the operating system and all your programs, reconfiguring Windows, recreating email accounts, and salvaging as much of your data as you could.

With Windows Home Server, however, restoring a computer is pretty close to painless because it already has your entire computer backed up, so its main chore is to take that backup and apply it to the computer. Because the backup includes not only your data, but Windows, your applications, and your settings, at the end of the restore you have your computer back up and running. You may lose a bit of work or changes that you made since the most recent backup, but that's a small price to pay for having your system back on its feet without much fuss on your part.

Before attempting the recovery, you should of course remedy whatever problem caused the system crash in the first place. If your hard drive died, replace it with one that's as big or bigger than the original and then set up the same partitions that you had before; if your system was infected by a virus, purchase a good antivirus program and run a scan of your computer after the restore because there's a possibility that restoring the computer could also restore the virus. Also, because the restore process requires access to Windows Home Server, make sure your computer has a physical connection to the network router or switch.

TIP

The recovery will go much faster if you use a wired connection to your network rather than a wireless connection.

With your hardware ready to go, here are the steps to follow to restore your computer:

1. Turn off the computer, if it isn't off already.
2. Start the computer.
3. Insert the Windows Home Server Home Computer Restore CD into the computer's CD/DVD drive.
4. When you see the `Press any key to boot from CD or DVD` message, press a key. The Windows Boot Manager appears.
5. Select either `Restore a Home Computer That Has Less Than 512 MB of RAM` or `Restore a Home Computer That Has 512 MB or More of RAM`, and then press Enter. Windows Home Server loads from the CD and, after a few minutes, displays the Detect Hardware dialog box, which prompts you for the regional and keyboard settings you want to use.
6. Change the settings as needed (the defaults are probably fine for most folks) and then click Continue. The Detect Hardware dialog box next shows you how many network and storage devices were found on the computer.
7. If you don't need to install additional device drivers, click Continue and skip to step 10. Otherwise, click Show Details to view the list of devices.
8. Copy the device driver files to a USB flash drive and then insert the flash drive.

9. Click Install Drivers.

10. Click Scan. Windows Home Server locates the drivers on the flash drive or floppy and then installs them. When you see the message telling you that the drivers were found, click OK.

11. Click Continue. Windows Home Server launches the Restore Computer Wizard.

12. Click Next. The wizard locates Windows Home Server on your network and then prompts you to enter the Windows Home Server password. (If the wizard fails to find your home server, click Find My Home Server Manually, click Next, type the server name, and then click Next.)

13. Type the password and click Next. The wizard logs on to Windows Home Server.

14. How you proceed from here depends on whether the wizard recognizes your computer:

    ▶ If the wizard thinks it recognizes your computer, the option for the computer's name will be activated. If that option is not correct, click Another Computer and then use the list to select the computer you're restoring.

    ▶ If the wizard doesn't recognize your computer, it displays a list of computers that have available backups on Windows Home Server. Select the computer you're restoring and click Next.

15. The wizard now displays a list of the computer's stored backups. Select the backup you want to use for the restore. (If you're not sure, you can click Details to see more information about the selected backup.) Click Next. The wizard asks you to choose the volumes (partitions) that you want to restore.

16. For each item in the Destination Volume section (that is, for each partition currently on the computer), use the lists in the Source Volume section (that is, the partitions available in the backup) to select a corresponding partition to restore. Generally, you'll want to restore drive C on the computer from drive C in the backup, drive D on the computer from drive D in the backup, and so on.

NOTE

There's no rule that says you must restore the entire system. For example, if your computer has two hard drives and only one of them crashed, you only need to restore the crashed drive. To prevent Windows Home Server from restoring a drive, select None in its corresponding Source Volume list.

TIP

If you need to perform disk maintenance of any kind, click the Run Disk Manager button. This loads the Disk Management snap-in, which enables you to format partitions, change partition sizes, delete partitions, change drive letters, and more. Right-click the partition you want to work with, and then click the command you want to run.

17. Click Next. The wizard warns you that all data on the selected partitions will be deleted and asks you to confirm that you want to restore.

18. Click Next. Windows Home Server begins restoring the computer. After a few seconds, it displays an estimate of how long the restore might take. (The length of the restore depends on the size of the partitions and the amount of data you're restoring; it could take as little as 15 minutes and as much as an hour or two.)

When the restore is complete, the wizard shuts down and then restarts your computer.

From Here

▶ To learn how to enable automatic updating, **see** "Configuring Windows Update," **P. 103**.

▶ Windows Home Server Power Pack 3 lets you back up the server itself; **see** "Backing Up Windows Home Server," **P. 454**.

Monitoring Your Network

Even a humble home network with just a few computers is still a fairly large and unwieldy beast that requires a certain amount of vigilance to keep things running smoothly. If you're the one around the house who wears the hat that says "Network Administrator," it's your job to keep an eye on the network to watch for things going awry.

Fortunately, Windows Home Server makes network monitoring about as easy as this kind of chore can get. For one thing, Windows Home Server comes with its own set of features that enable you to quickly monitor the network and be alerted to problems. For another, the Windows Server 2003 code that underlies Windows Home Server means that you have a few other powerful tools at your disposal for monitoring the network.

This chapter takes you through all of these tools and shows you how to use them to keep tabs on various aspects of your home network.

Monitoring the Windows Home Server Status Icon

Before getting to the remote administration tools that you implement yourself, let's take a second to look at Windows Home Server's built-in monitoring tool, the Windows Home Server Status icon, which appears in the Windows notification area. The purpose of this icon is to give you visual indications of the current health status of the Windows Home Server network. There are two types of indications: the icon color and the network health notifications.

Monitoring the Icon Color

The simplest way to monitor your network's health status is to examine the color of the Status icon. Table 10.1 presents the five icon colors and what they mean.

TABLE 10.1   Colors Used by the Windows Home Server Status Icon

Icon Color	Status	Description
Green	Healthy	The network is healthy. All the clients are backed up and have their security settings set up correctly, and Windows Home Server has all available updates installed.
Blue	Backing Up	The client is current being backed up by Windows Home Server.
Orange	At Risk	The network has a problem. For example, one of the client computers might not have any successful backups.
Red	Critical	The network has a serious problem. For example, one of the client computers might not have its firewall turned on, or Windows Home Server might not have an available update installed.
Gray	Not Connected	The client computer can't find Windows Home Server. For example, a network cable might be unplugged, or there might be no wireless connection.

▶ **SEE** If your computer is on the network but you still see the gray Windows Home Server Status icon, run the Windows Home Server Discovery program; **see** "Rediscovering the Windows Home Server," **P. 68**.

Monitoring Network Health Notifications

You can see the network's current status at any time by hovering the mouse pointer over the Windows Home Server Status icon. As you can see in Figure 10.1, Windows Home Server displays a fly-out message that tells you the current status.

FIGURE 10.1   Hover the mouse pointer over the Windows Home Server Status icon to see the current health status of the network.

When the network health status changes from green to any other color, the Windows Home Server Status icon displays a *network health notification,* a fly-out message that tells you why the status changed. Windows Home Server has all kinds of these messages. To give you some idea what to expect, Table 10.2 lists a few of the more common network health notifications that you're likely to see.

TABLE 10.2   Common Network Health Notifications Displayed by the Windows Home Server Status Icon

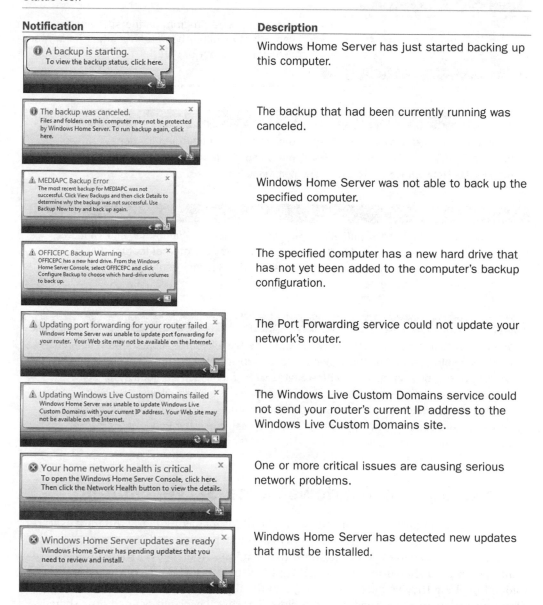

Notification	Description
ℹ️ A backup is starting. To view the backup status, click here.	Windows Home Server has just started backing up this computer.
ℹ️ The backup was canceled. Files and folders on this computer may not be protected by Windows Home Server. To run backup again, click here.	The backup that had been currently running was canceled.
⚠️ MEDIAPC Backup Error The most recent backup for MEDIAPC was not successful. Click View Backups and then click Details to determine why the backup was not successful. Use Backup Now to try and back up again.	Windows Home Server was not able to back up the specified computer.
⚠️ OFFICEPC Backup Warning OFFICEPC has a new hard drive. From the Windows Home Server Console, select OFFICEPC and click Configure Backup to choose which hard-drive volumes to back up.	The specified computer has a new hard drive that has not yet been added to the computer's backup configuration.
⚠️ Updating port forwarding for your router failed Windows Home Server was unable to update port forwarding for your router. Your Web site may not be available on the Internet.	The Port Forwarding service could not update your network's router.
⚠️ Updating Windows Live Custom Domains failed Windows Home Server was unable to update Windows Live Custom Domains with your current IP address. Your Web site may not be available on the Internet.	The Windows Live Custom Domains service could not send your router's current IP address to the Windows Live Custom Domains site.
❌ Your home network health is critical. To open the Windows Home Server Console, click here. Then click the Network Health button to view the details.	One or more critical issues are causing serious network problems.
❌ Windows Home Server updates are ready Windows Home Server has pending updates that you need to review and install.	Windows Home Server has detected new updates that must be installed.

TABLE 10.2   Common Network Health Notifications Displayed by the Windows Home Server Status Icon (*continued*)

Notification	Description
Windows Firewall is off — OFFICEPC has Windows Firewall turned off.	Windows Firewall has been turned off on the specified computer.
No spyware protection — TABLETPC has antispyware software turned off or out of date.	The antispyware program on the specified computer has either been turned off, or its spyware definitions are out of date.

NOTE

If you don't want Windows Home Server to display these health notifications, you can turn them off. Right-click the Windows Home Server Status icon and then deactivate the Display Network Health Notifications command.

NOTE

The security-related health notifications are only available for Windows 7 and Windows Vista PCs. The Windows 7 and Vista Security Center has an internal feature that enables other programs to poll its current status. The Security Center in Windows XP doesn't have this feature.

TIP

You may occasionally find that the Windows Home Server Status icon shows a different network health status than the Windows Home Server Console. The Console status is always correct, so this means that the Status icon has missed an update, for some reason. To fix this, right-click the Status icon and then click Exit. Now select Start, All Programs, Windows Home Server Console. This restores the Status icon, which should now show the correct network health status. (You can close the Windows Home Server Console window at this point.)

Monitoring the Windows Home Server Shares

The Computer Management snap-in is a great tool for managing many different aspects of your system, from devices to users to services and much more. But Computer Management also enables you to monitor the Windows Home Server shared folders. For example, for each shared folder, you can find out the users who are connected to the folder, how long they've been connected, and the files they have open. You can also disconnect users from a shared folder or close files that have been opened on a shared folder. The next few sections provide the details.

Launching the Computer Management Snap-In

To get started, you need to open the Computer Management snap-in. Here are the steps to follow:

1. Log on to Windows Home Server.
2. Select Start, right-click My Computer, and then click Manage. The Computer Management snap-in appears.
3. Open the Shared Folders branch.

> **TIP**
>
> Another way to launch the Computer Management snap-in is to select Start, Run (or press Windows Logo+R) to open the Run dialog box, type `compmgmt.msc`, and click OK.

> **TIP**
>
> If you don't want to work with the entire Computer Management snap-in, you can load just the Shared Folders snap-in. Select Start, Run (or Press Windows Logo+R) to open the Run dialog box, type `fsmgmt.msc`, and click OK.

Viewing the Current Connections

To see a list of the users connected to any Windows Home Server shared folder, select System Tools, Shared Folders, Sessions. Figure 10.2 shows an example. For each user, you get the following data:

User	The name of the user.
Computer	The name of the user's computer. If Windows Home Server doesn't recognize the computer, it shows the machine's IP address instead.
Type	The type of network connection. Windows Home Server always shows this as Windows (even if the user is connected from a Mac or from Linux).
Open Files	The number of open files in the shared folders.
Connected Time	The amount of time that the user has been connected to the remote computer.
Idle Time	The amount of time that the user has not been actively working on the open files.
Guest	Whether the user logged on using the Guest account.

> **NOTE**
>
> To ensure that you're always viewing the most up-to-date information, regularly select the Action, Refresh command or click the Refresh toolbar button (pointed out in Figure 10.2).

Refresh

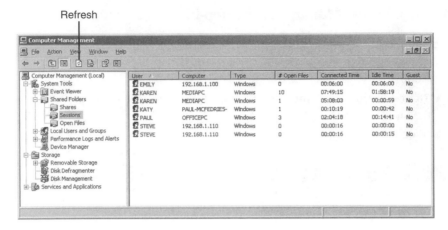

FIGURE 10.2   The Sessions folder shows the users currently connected to shared folders on the remote computer.

Viewing Connections to Shared Folders

The Computer Management snap-in also makes it possible for you to view the connections to Windows Home Server by its shared folders. To get this display, select System Tools, Shared Folders, Shares. As you can see in Figure 10.3, this view provides the following information:

Share Name	The name of the shared folder. Note that the list includes the Windows Home Server hidden shares.
Folder Path	The drive or folder associated with the share.
Type	The type of network connection, which Windows Home Server always shows as Windows.
# Client Connections	The number of computers connected to the share.
Comment	The description of the share.

CAUTION

The Shares branch includes commands that enable you to change the properties of a share, disable sharing for a folder, and create a new shared folder. However, you should not use these commands. In Windows Home Server, always manage shares either via the Windows Home Server Console or by using each share's UNC path (for example, \\SERVER\Photos).

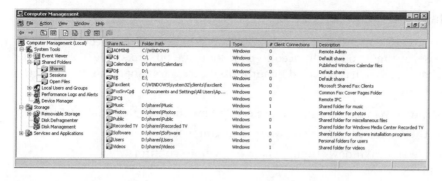

FIGURE 10.3   The Computer Management snap-in can display a server's connections by its shared folders.

Viewing Open Files

The Computer Management snap-in can also display the files that are open on the Windows Home Server shares. To switch to this view, select System Tools, Shared Folders, Open Files. Figure 10.4 shows the result. Here's a summary of the columns in this view:

Open File   The full pathname of the file.

Accessed By   The name of the user who has the file open.

Type   The type of network connection, which Windows Home Server always shows as Windows.

Locks   The number of locks on the file.

Open Mode   The permissions the user has over the file.

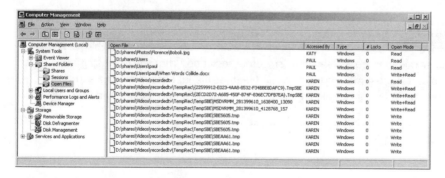

FIGURE 10.4   The Computer Management snap-in can also display a remote computer's open files in its shared resources.

Closing a User's Session or File

Although in the interest of network harmony, you'll want to let users connect and disconnect as they please, at times you might need to boot someone off a machine. For example, you might see that someone has obtained unauthorized access to a share. To disconnect that user, follow these steps:

1. In the Computer Management snap-in, select System Tools, Shared Folders, Sessions.
2. Right-click the name of the user you want to disconnect.
3. Click Close Session. Windows Home Server asks you to confirm.
4. Click Yes.

Similarly, you'll usually want to let users open and close files themselves so that they don't lose information. However, you might find that a user has a particular file open and you would prefer that the user not view that file (for example, because you want to work on the file yourself or because the file contains information you don't want the user to see). To close a file opened by a user, follow these steps:

CAUTION

If you have a file in a shared folder and you don't want other users to see that file, it makes more sense to either move the file to a protected folder or change the permissions on the file's current folder.

1. In the Computer Management snap-in, select System Tools, Shared Folders, Open Files.
2. Right-click the name of the file you want to close.
3. Click Close Open File. Windows Home Server asks you to confirm.
4. Click Yes.

NOTE

The remote user doesn't see a warning or any other indication that you're closing the file. For example, if the user is playing a music file, that file just stops playing and can't be started again (except by closing all open shared files and folders and starting a new session).

Monitoring Remote Desktop Sessions

There are three ways you can connect to Windows Home Server:

- ▶ On a network computer, you can connect to the Windows Home Server desktop via the Remote Desktop Connection feature, as described in Chapter 1, "Setting Up Your Windows Home Server Network."

▶ **SEE** For the specifics of using Remote Desktop to connect to Windows Home Server, **see** "Making a Remote Desktop Connection to the Server," **P. 31**.

- ▶ On a network computer, you can connect to Windows Home Server using the Windows Home Server Console (see Chapter 4, "Configuring Windows Home Server"), which creates a special kind of Remote Desktop session.

▶ **SEE** For information on using the Windows Home Server Console to connect to Windows Home Server, **see** "Running the Windows Home Server Console," **P. 94**.

- ▶ On the Internet, you can connect to Windows Home Server using the Remote Access Home Page, as described in Chapter 7, "Making Connections to Network Computers."

▶ **SEE** To learn how to connect to Windows Home Server from the Internet, **see** "Connecting via the Internet," **P. 194**.

As your network's administrator, you might want to monitor such connections so you know which PC is connected and when that person logged on. You can also send messages to logged on users and disconnect sessions. You do all this using Windows Home Server's Terminal Services Manager, described in the next few sections.

Starting the Terminal Services Manager

To get the Terminal Services Manager onscreen, follow these steps:

1. Log on to Windows Home Server.
2. Select Start, Control Panel, Administrative Tools, Terminal Services Manager.

3. If you see a dialog box telling you that Remote Control and Connect only work from a client session, click OK. (For more on the Remote Control feature, see "Controlling the Administrator's Desktop via Remote Control," later in this chapter.)

TIP

Another way to launch the Terminal Services Manager is to select Start, Run (or press Windows Logo+R) to open the Run dialog box, type **tsadmin**, and click OK.

Viewing Remote Desktop Sessions

In the Terminal Services Manager's This Computer branch, you see an item for your Windows Home Server. Click this item to see three tabs: Users, Sessions, and Processes. The Users tab (shown in Figure 10.5) has the following columns:

User   The name of the user who initiated the session.

Session   The session type. For Remote Desktop connections, the session is RDP Tcp#*n*, where *n* is an integer that increments with each new session. For anyone logged on directly to Windows Home Server, the session is Console.

ID   A number that uniquely identifies each session.

State   The current state of the session: Active (the Remote Desktop session has started), Connected (the client has connected to the server, but the Remote Desktop session hasn't yet started), or Disconnected.

Idle Time   For a disconnected session, the time that the session has been closed.

Logon   For an active session, the time the user logged on.
Time

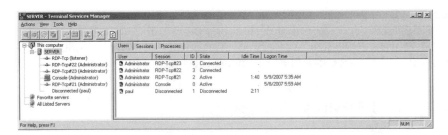

FIGURE 10.5   In Terminal Services Manager, the Users tab shows information about the users with active or disconnected Remote Desktop sessions.

TIP

If you don't want to see a disconnected session in the Terminal Services Manager, right-click the session, click Reset, and then click OK when Terminal Services Manager asks you to confirm.

The Sessions tab (shown in Figure 10.6) has the following columns:

Session   The session type (this is the same as in the Users tab).

User   The name of the session's user.

ID   A number that uniquely identifies each session.

State   The current state of the session: Active, Connected, Disconnected, or Listen. The latter refers to the RDP Listener, a Terminal Services component that detects and processes incoming requests for new RDP sessions.

Type   The session type, which will either be Console (which refers to the local logon session) or Microsoft RDP 5.2 (which refers to any RDP-related session).

Client   The name of the client computer on which the RDP session was initiated.
Name

Idle Time   For a disconnected session, the time that the session has been closed.

Logon   For an active session, the time the user logged on.
Time

Comment   Text that describes the session.

The Processes tab lists the programs and services that are active in each session, as shown in Figure 10.7.

Sending a Message to a Remote Desktop Client

There may be situations where you find it necessary to send a message to a user with an active Remote Desktop session. For example, you may need to shut down the server for maintenance, or restart the server after applying an update. Ideally, it's best if the user disconnects the Remote Desktop session correctly to avoid losing data or damaging open files. This is no big deal if the user is in the next room because you can easily tell the person to disconnect the session. It's a bit more of a hassle if you're in the basement and the user is a floor or two above you.

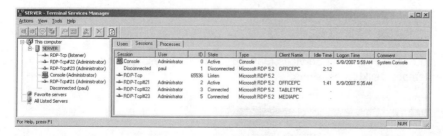

FIGURE 10.6   In Terminal Services Manager, the Sessions tab provides data about the various Remote Desktop sessions.

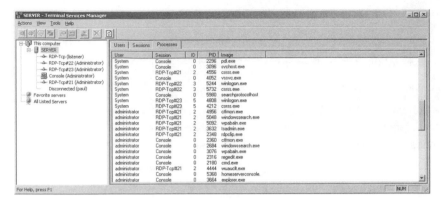

FIGURE 10.7   In Terminal Services Manager, the Processes tab shows you the programs and services in use in each session.

When you need to let connected users know something important, but it's not convenient to convey that information face-to-face, you can do the next best thing: You can send the user a message. Here's how it works:

1. Start Terminal Services Manager and display the list of sessions.

2. In either the Users tab or the Sessions tab, select the user or users to whom you want to send the message. (To select multiple users, hold down Ctrl and click each user.)

3. Right-click the selection and then click Send Message. Terminal Services Manager displays the Send Message dialog box.

4. Type your message (see Figure 10.8) and then click OK. Terminal Services Manager sends the message to each user. The message appears in a dialog box inside the remote session window, as shown in Figure 10.9.

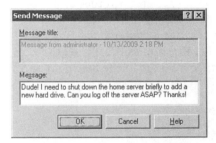

FIGURE 10.8   You can use Terminal Services Manager to send a message to one or more users with active Remote Desktop sessions.

FIGURE 10.9   On the Remote Desktop client computers, the message appears in a dialog box.

Disconnecting a Remote Desktop Session

If you need to shut down or restart Windows Home Server, you should make sure that all Remote Desktop sessions are disconnected. The best way to do this is to send a message to each user with an active session, as described in the previous section. If that doesn't work, you can either access the computer physically (if it's a network session) and log off Windows Home Server, or you can force the session off by disconnecting it from Terminal Services Manager. Here's how you do the latter:

1. Start Terminal Services Manager and display the list of sessions.

2. In either the Users tab or the Sessions tab, select the user or users you want to disconnect. (To select multiple users, hold down Ctrl and click each user.)

3. Right-click the selection and then click Disconnect. Terminal Services Manager asks you to confirm.

4. Click OK. Terminal Services Manager disconnects the sessions.

Controlling the Administrator's Desktop via Remote Control

When you Remote Desktop into Windows Home Server, you start a new session using the Administrator account—that is, you get a fresh desktop that you can use as you like. However, what if you want to work with the Administrator's *actual* desktop? By "actual" desktop, I mean the desktop that appears when you log on to Windows Home Server directly. This is handy if you're using Windows Home Server and you have some programs and documents open, and you want access to those same programs and documents from a remote client.

Terminal Services offers a feature called Remote Control that enables you to work with the Administrator's desktop remotely. When a Remote Control session is running, whatever actions you take on your client computer are also reflected on Windows Home Server. For example, if you click the Start button to open the Start menu, someone working at the Windows Home Server machine would see the whole thing: the mouse moving to the Start button, the click, and the Start menu appearing.

Enabling Remote Control Sessions

For this to work properly, you first need to enable a group policy that allows Remote Control sessions. Here are the steps to follow:

1. Log on to Windows Home Server.

2. Select Start, Run (or press Windows Logo+R) to open the Run dialog box, type **gpedit.msc**, and click OK. The Group Policy Object Editor appears.

3. Select Computer Configuration, Administrative Templates, Windows Components, Terminal Services.

4. Double-click the Sets Rules for Remote Control of Terminal Services User Sessions policy.

5. Select Enabled.

6. In the Options list, select one of the following (see Figure 10.10):

Full Control With User's Permission — Choose this option to allow full interaction with the Windows Home Server desktop. A user sitting at the Windows Home Server machine must give permission to start the session.

Full Control Without User's Permission — Choose this option to allow full interaction with the Windows Home Server desktop. No permission is required to start the session. For your home network, this is most likely the choice you want.

View Session With User's Permission — Choose this option to allow the user only to see the Windows Home Server desktop. A user sitting at the Windows Home Server machine must give permission to start the session.

View Session Without User's Permission — Choose this option to allow the user only to see the Windows Home Server desktop. No permission is required to start the session.

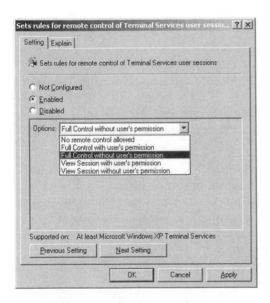

FIGURE 10.10   You need to enable the Sets Rules for Remote Control of Terminal Services User Sessions policy.

7. Click OK to put the policy into effect.

Starting the Remote Control Session

You start a Remote Control session from the Terminal Services client. Specifically, you Remote Desktop into Windows Home Server, display the Terminal Services Manager, and initiate the Remote Control session from there. Here are the steps you need to follow:

1. On the client computer, Remote Desktop into Windows Home Server using the Administrator account.

2. In the Remote Desktop window, select Start, Control Panel, Administrative Tools, Terminal Services Manager.

3. Click the Windows Home Server item, and look for the Console session.

4. Right-click the Console session, and then click Remote Control, as shown in Figure 10.11. The Remote Control window appears.

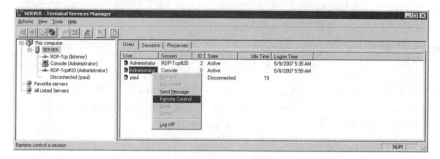

FIGURE 10.11   Select Remote Control on the Console session.

5. Specify the key or key combination you want to press to end the Remote Control session. (The default is Ctrl+* on the numeric keypad.) Select a key from the list and then activate one or more of the Shift, Ctrl, and Alt check boxes. Click OK.

6. If you opted to require permission before starting the Remote Control session, a user sitting at the Windows Home Server computer must click Yes.

The Terminal Services client connects to Windows Home Server and displays the Administrator's current desktop. When you've completed your work on the server, press the key or key combination from step 5 to close the session.

Monitoring Users via Task Manager

Much of the information displayed by Terminal Services Manager's Users tab is also available in Windows Task Manager, which is sometimes more convenient to use. To launch Task Manager, log on to Windows Home Server and use either of the following techniques:

▶ Right-click the taskbar, and then click Task Manager.

▶ Press Ctrl+Alt+Delete, and then click Task Manager.

> **TIP**
>
> You can also open Task Manager directly by pressing Ctrl+Shift+Esc.

The Users tab (shown in Figure 10.12) has the following columns:

User   The name of the user who initiated the session.

ID   A number that uniquely identifies each session.

Status   The current state of the session: Active (the Remote Desktop session has started),
              Connected (the client has connected to the server, but the Remote Desktop session
              hasn't yet started), or Disconnected.

Client   The name of the client computer on which the RDP session was initiated.
Name

Session   The session type. For Remote Desktop connections, the session is RDP Tcp#*n*,
              where *n* is an integer that increments with each new session. For anyone logged on
              directly to Windows Home Server, the session is Console.

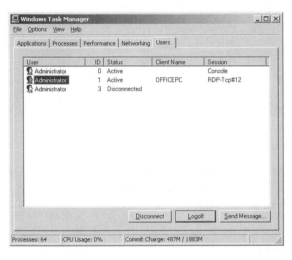

FIGURE 10.12   You can view Remote Desktop sessions from the Task Manager's Users tab.

You can also use the following buttons in the Users tab:

Disconnect   Click this button to disconnect the selected user or users.

Logoff   If the user disconnected the session (so he appears with the status
              Disconnected), click Logoff to remove that user from the list.

Send   Click this button to broadcast a message to the selected users. This is similar to
Message   sending a message from Terminal Services Manager (see "Sending a Message to
              a Remote Desktop Client," earlier in this chapter), except that the Task Manager
              method also enables you to specify the message title, as shown in Figure 10.13.

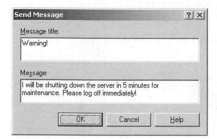

FIGURE 10.13 When you send a message from Task Manager, you can specify both the title and text.

From Here

▶ For the specifics of using Remote Desktop to connect to Windows Home Server, **see** "Making a Remote Desktop Connection to the Server," **P. 31**.

▶ If you see the gray Windows Home Server Status icon, try running the Windows Home Server Discovery program; **see** "Rediscovering the Windows Home Server," **P. 68**.

▶ For information on using the Windows Home Server Console to connect to Windows Home Server, **see** "Running the Windows Home Server Console," **P. 94**.

▶ To learn how to connect to Windows Home Server from the Internet, **see** "Connecting via the Internet," **P. 194**.

▶ For the details on monitoring the performance of Windows Home Server and your network, **see** "Monitoring Performance," **P. 391**.

CHAPTER 11

Implementing Windows Home Server Security

Networking your home computers offers lots of advantages: easy and fast file swapping, simple hardware sharing, a single Internet connection for all computers, the ability to work or play anywhere in your house (if you have a wireless connection), and many more. If networking has a downside, it's that computers that can easily share resources can also easily share malicious resources, such as viruses, Trojan horses, and spyware. Also, cobbling your home PCs into a network—particularly a wireless network—opens up a few extra avenues that nefarious users can take advantage of to try to infiltrate your network.

Fortunately, you don't need a degree in electrical engineering to safeguard your Windows Home Server network from all these threats. As you see in this chapter, all it takes is a healthy dose of paranoia and a few techniques for battening down the hatches on the Windows Home Server and on your network clients.

Enabling Security Auditing on Windows Home Server

A big part of keeping any computer secure involves keeping an eye on what users do with the computer. For Windows Home Server, this means tracking events such as logon failures (repeated failures might indicate a malicious user trying different passwords) and account changes (where someone changes some aspect of a user account). This type of tracking is called *auditing*.

Unfortunately, Windows Home Server only implements a small subset of its auditing features, and even those that it does implement aren't all that useful. For example, Windows Home Server audits logon successes, but not logon failures.

In the next section, I show you how to enable the security auditing policies in Windows Home Server, and then I explain how to track auditing events.

Activating the Auditing Policies

To enable Windows Home Server's security auditing policies, follow these steps:

1. Log on to Windows Home Server.
2. Select Start, Control Panel, Administrative Tools, Local Security Policy. The Local Security Settings window appears.

3. Open the Local Policies branch and click Audit Policy. Windows Home Server displays the audit policies, as shown in Figure 11.1.

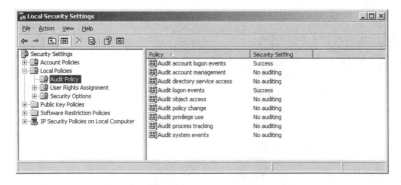

FIGURE 11.1   Windows Home Server's audit policies.

4. Double-click the policy you want to work with.
5. If you want to know when someone uses the policy event successfully, activate the Success check box.

6. If you want to know when someone uses the policy event unsuccessfully, activate the Failure check box.

7. Click OK.

8. Repeat steps 4–7 for the other events you want to audit.

Understanding the Auditing Policies

To help you decide which auditing policies to use, the next few sections give you a bit of detail about some of them. Note that several of these policies require AD to return meaningful or useful results. This means they don't apply to Windows Home Server, so I don't discuss them here.

Audit Account Logon Events

The Audit Account Logon Events policy enables you to track when users log on to their account on the Windows Home Server computer. If you track failures for this policy, the resulting Failure Audit event returns an Error Code value, as shown in Figure 11.2. (To learn how to view these events, see "Tracking Auditing Events," later in this chapter.) Table 11.1 tells you what the various error codes mean.

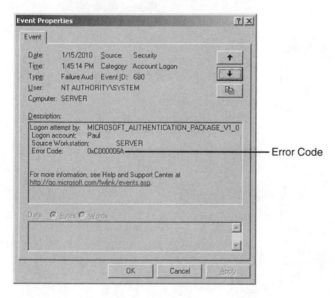

FIGURE 11.2   An example of a failed Account Logon event.

TABLE 11.1   Error Codes Returned for Account Logon Failure Events

Error Code	Description
0xC0000064	The user tried to log on with a misspelled or invalid username.
0xC000006A	The user tried to log on with a misspelled or invalid password.
0xC000006F	The user tried to log on outside of the account's authorized hours.

TABLE 11.1   Error Codes Returned for Account Logon Failure Events *(continued)*

Error Code	Description
0xC0000070	The user tried to log on from an unauthorized computer.
0xC0000071	The user tried to log on with an expired password.
0xC0000072	The user's account is disabled.
0xC0000193	The user's account is expired.
0xC0000224	The user was supposed to change his password at the next logon, but he didn't.
0xC0000234	The user's account is locked.

Audit Account Management

The Audit Account Management policy enables you to track events related to managing groups and user accounts on Windows Home Server. Events include creating new groups or users, modifying or deleting groups or users, changing user passwords, or renaming or disabling users. Figure 11.3 shows a sample event that occurred when a user's account was disabled.

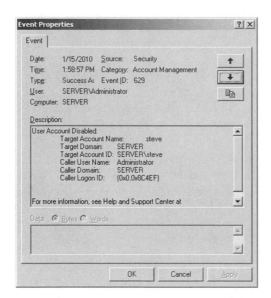

FIGURE 11.3   An example of an Account Management event.

Audit Logon Events

The Audit Logon Events policy enables you to track when users log on to the Windows Home Server network. These events always occur in conjunction with Account Logon events. That is, first Windows Home Server processes the logon to the user's account on the server; then it processes the logon to the network.

If you're auditing failures for this category, each Failure Audit event tells you the reason for the failure, as shown in Figure 11.4.

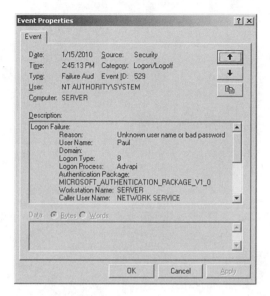

FIGURE 11.4   An example of a failed Logon event.

Audit Policy Change

The Audit Policy Change policy enables you to track when users make changes to group policies. The resulting event shows you what policy was changed and what the new policy setting is. For example, Figure 11.5 shows an event generated by modifying the auditing policies.

Audit Process Tracking

The Audit Process Tracking policy enables you to track the starting and stopping of processes, including programs. For example, you might want to track when scripts run on the server. Most scripts are handled by wscript.exe, so that the program runs each time a script is launched. Figure 11.6 shows an example event created when a script starts. (Note that these events fall under the Detailed Tracking category.)

Audit System Events

The Audit System Events policy enables you to track system events such as shutdown and startup, security changes, and system time changes. Figure 11.7 shows an example event, and Table 11.2 lists the possible event IDs.

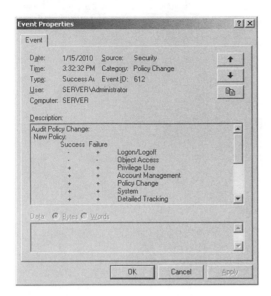

FIGURE 11.5   An example of a Policy Change event.

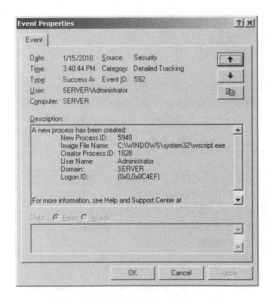

FIGURE 11.6   An example of a Detailed Tracking event.

TABLE 11.2   Event ID Values for System Events

System Event ID	Description
512	Windows Home Server started.
513	Windows Home Server shut down.
514	An authentication package was loaded by the Local Security Authority.
515	A trusted logon process has registered with the Local Security Authority.
516	Internal resources allocated for the queuing of security event messages have been exhausted, leading to the loss of some security event messages.
517	The Windows Home Server audit log was cleared.
518	The Security Accounts Manager loaded a notification package.
519	A process is using an invalid local procedure call (LPC) port in an attempt to impersonate a client and reply or read from or write to a client address space.
520	The Windows Home Server system time was changed.

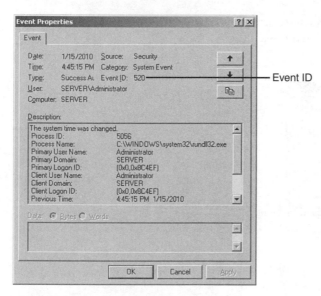

FIGURE 11.7   An example of a System event.

Tracking Auditing Events

After you've enabled the security auditing policies that you want Windows Home Server to monitor, you can start tracking them to look for suspicious behavior. You do this using Windows Home Server's Event Viewer. Unfortunately, the Security event log (which is where the auditing events appear) likely has tens of thousands of items. How do you look for suspicious behavior in such a large database? The trick is to filter the log to show just the events you want. Here are the steps to follow:

1. Log on to Windows Home Server.

2. Select Start, Run, type **eventvwr.msc**, and click OK. Windows Home Server opens the Event Viewer.

3. Click the Security branch.

4. Select View, Filter. Windows Home Server opens the Security Properties dialog box with the Filter tab displayed.

5. In the Event Source list, select Security.

6. In the Category list, select the audit type you want to track (Account Logon, Account Management, and so on).

7. In the Event Types group, activate the check boxes for just the events you want to see (such as Failure Audit).

8. Fill in the Event ID, User, and Computer fields, as necessary. (You'll likely want to leave these blank.)

9. In the From section, select Events On, select today's date, and set the time to 12:00:00 AM.

10. In the To section, select Events On, select today's date, and set the time to 11:59:59 PM. Figure 11.8 shows a completed filter.

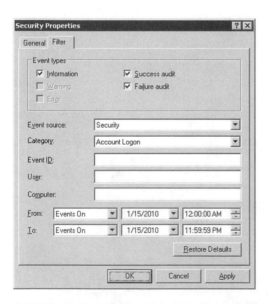

FIGURE 11.8   Use the Filter tab to specify exactly the events you want to see.

11. Click OK. Event Viewer filters the Security log using your criteria. Figure 11.9 shows an example.

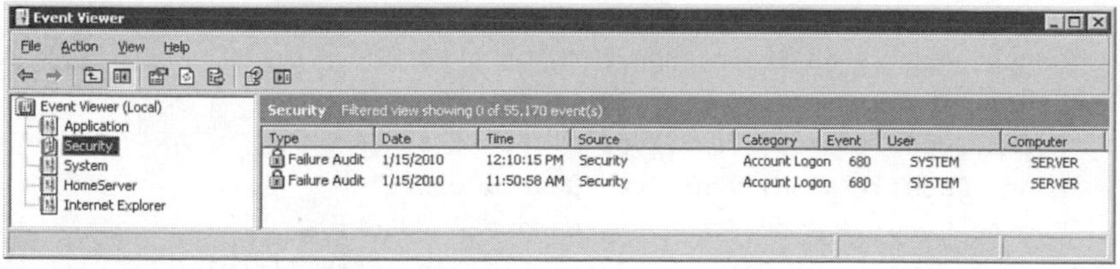

FIGURE 11.9   The results of the filter shown in Figure 11.8.

Viewing Auditing Events with a Script

The only problem with filtering the Security log, as described in the previous section, is that you can't filter based on detailed information such as the account logon error code. To do that, you need to use a script. Listing 11.1 presents a script that extracts just those Security events where the type is Audit Failure and the error code is 0xC000006A (which represents an incorrect password).

> **NOTE**
>
> You can find the VBS files containing this book's scripts on my website at www. mcfedries.com/HomeServerUnleashed2E. See Chapter 21, "Scripting Windows Home Server," to learn how to run scripts on the server.

LISTING 11.1   A Script That Extracts Events from the Security Log

```
'
' Use WMI to extract events from the Security log where:
'   - The type is "Audit Failure" (5)
'   - The date is today
'   - The error code points to an incorrect password (0xC000006A)
'
compName = "localhost"
Set objWMI = GetObject("winmgmts:{impersonationLevel=impersonate}!//" & _
                        compName & "\root\cimv2")
Set colSecLog = objWMI.ExecQuery("SELECT * FROM Win32_NTLogEvent Where " & _
                        "LogFile = 'Security' And " & _
                        "EventType = 5 And " & _
                        "TimeWritten > '" & TodaysDate & "' And " & _
                        "Message Like '%0xC000006A%'")
'
' Run through the returned events
'
i = 0
For Each objEvent in colSecLog
    '
    ' Display the event data
    '
```

```
    WScript.Echo "Category: " & objEvent.CategoryString & VBCrLf & _
                 "Computer: " & objEvent.ComputerName & VBCrLf & _
                 "User: " & objEvent.User & VBCrLf & _
                 "Event Type: " & objEvent.Type & VBCrLf & _
                 "Event Code: " & objEvent.EventCode & VBCrLf & _
                 "Source Name: " & objEvent.SourceName & VBCrLf & _
                 "Time Written: " & ReturnLogDate(objEvent.TimeWritten) & _
                 VBCrLf & VBCrLf & _
                 "Message: " & VBCrLf & VBCrLf & objEvent.Message
    i = i + 1
Next
'
' Check for no events
'
If i = 0 Then
    WScript.Echo "No events found!"
End If
'
' Release objects
'
Set wmi = Nothing
Set secLog = Nothing
'
' This function creates a datatime string based on today's date
'
Function TodaysDate()
    strYear = Year(Now)
    If Month(Now) < 10 Then
        strMonth = "0" & Month(Now)
    Else
        strMonth = Month(Now)
    End If
    If Day(Now) < 10 Then
        strDay = "0" & Day(Now)
    Else
        strDay = Day(Now)
    End If
    TodaysDate = strYear & strMonth & strDay & "000000.000000-000"
End Function
'
' This function takes the event datetime value and converts
' it to a friendlier date and time format
'
Function ReturnLogDate(logTime)
    eventYear = Left(logTime, 4)
    eventMonth = Mid(logTime, 5, 2)
    eventDay = Mid(logTime, 7, 2)
```

```
    eventHour = Mid(logTime, 9, 2)
    eventMinute = Mid(logTime, 11, 2)
    eventSecond = Mid(logTime, 13, 2)
    ReturnLogDate = DateSerial(eventYear, eventMonth, eventDay) & " " & _
                    TimeSerial(eventHour, eventMinute, eventSecond)
End Function
```

The script uses WMI to query the W32_NTLogEvent database, which consists of all the events on the system. The query extracts just those events where the following is true:

▶ The LogFile property equals Security.

▶ The EventType property equals 5, which represents Audit Failure events.

▶ The TimeWritten property contains only today's date. The values in the TimeWritten property use the datetime data type, which uses the general format yyyymmddhhmmss.000000-000. So, the script uses the TodaysDate function to return a datetime value that corresponds to midnight today. The query actually looks for events that were written to the log after that time.

▶ The Message property (which holds the error code, among other data) contains the error code 0xC000006A.

Then a For Each...Next loop runs through all the returned events. For each event, various event properties are displayed in a dialog box, as shown in Figure 11.10. The code calls the ReturnLogDate function to convert the TimeWritten property's datetime value into a more readable format.

FIGURE 11.10   An example of the event data displayed by the script in Listing 11.1.

More Ways to Secure Windows Home Server

Enabling security auditing is a good start for securing Windows Home Server. However, you can take a number of other security measures, such as renaming the Administrator account, hiding the most recent user name, checking the firewall status, and disabling Windows Home Server's hidden administrative shares. The next few sections take you through these and other Windows Home Server security measures.

Renaming the Administrator Account

By default, Windows Home Server sets up one member of the Administrators group: the Administrator account. This account is all-powerful on Windows Home Server (and, by extension, on your home network), so the last thing you want is for some malicious user to gain control of the system with Administrator access. Unfortunately, black-hat hackers have one foot in your digital door already because they know the default account name is Administrator; now all they have to do is guess your password. If you've protected the Administrator account with a strong password, you almost certainly have no worries.

However, you can close the door completely on malicious intruders by taking away the one piece of information they know: the name of the account. By changing the account name from Administrator to something completely unobvious, you add an extra layer of security to Windows Home Server.

Here are the steps to follow to change the name of the Administrator account:

1. Log on to Windows Home Server.
2. Select Start, right-click My Computer, and then click Manage. The Computer Management snap-in appears.
3. Open the System Tools, Local Users and Groups, Users branch.

> **TIP**
>
> You can open the Local Users and Groups snap-in directly by selecting Start, Run to open the Run dialog box, typing **lusrmgr.msc**, and then clicking OK.

4. Right-click the Administrator account, and then click Rename.
5. Type the new account name, and then press Enter.

> **NOTE**
>
> The Guest account also has an obvious and well-known name, so if you've enabled the Guest account, be sure to rename it as well.

Hiding the User Name in the Log On Dialog Box

When you log on locally to Windows Home Server, the Log On to Windows dialog box always shows the name of the most recent user who logged on successfully. It's unlikely that a malicious user would gain physical access to the server in your home, but it's not impossible. Therefore, renaming the Administrator account as described in the previous section is useless because Windows Home Server will just display the new name to anyone who wants to see it.

Fortunately, you can plug this security breach by following these steps:

1. Log on to Windows Home Server.

2. Select Start, Control Panel, Administrative Tools, Local Security Policy. The Local Security Setting snap-in appears.

TIP

You can also open the Local Security Setting snap-in by selecting Start, Run to open the Run dialog box, typing **secpol.msc**, and then clicking OK.

---

3. Open the Security Settings, Local Policies, Security Options branch.
4. Double-click the Interactive Logon: Do Not Display Last User Name policy.
5. Click the Enabled option.
6. Click OK.

Making Sure Windows Firewall Is Turned On

Your Windows Home Server network probably connects to the Internet using a *broadband*—cable modem or DSL—service. This means that you have an always-on connection, so there's a much greater chance that a malicious hacker could find your computer and have his way with it. You might think that with millions of people connected to the Internet at any given moment, there would be little chance of a "script kiddy" finding you in the herd. Unfortunately, one of the most common weapons in a black-hat hacker's arsenal is a program that runs through millions of IP addresses automatically, looking for live connections. The fact that many cable systems and some DSL systems use IP addresses in a narrow range compounds the problem by making it easier to find always-on connections.

When a cracker finds your address, he has many avenues from which to access your computer. Specifically, your connection uses many different ports for sending and receiving data. For example, File Transfer Protocol (FTP) uses ports 20 and 21, web data and commands typically use port 80, email uses ports 25 and 110, the domain name system (DNS) uses port 53, remote connections to the network use ports 443 and 4125, and so on. In all, there are dozens of these ports, and every one is an opening through which a clever cracker can gain access to your computer.

As if that weren't enough, attackers can check your system for the installation of some kind of Trojan horse or virus. (Malicious email attachments sometimes install these programs on your machine.) If the hacker finds one, he can effectively take control of your machine (turning it into a *zombie computer*) and either wreak havoc on its contents or use your computer to attack other systems.

Again, if you think your computer is too obscure or worthless for someone else to bother with, think again. Hackers probe a typical computer connected to the Internet for vulnerable ports or installed Trojan horses at least a few times every day. If you want to see just how vulnerable your computer is, several good sites on the Web can test your security:

▶ **Gibson Research (Shields Up)**—grc.com/default.htm

▶ **DSL Reports**—www.dslreports.com/secureme_go

▶ **HackerWhacker**—www.hackerwhacker.com

The good news is that Windows Home Server comes with Windows Firewall. This program is a personal firewall that can lock down your ports and prevent unauthorized access to your machine. In effect, your computer becomes *invisible* to the Internet (although you can still surf the Web and work with email normally).

Windows Firewall is activated by default in Windows Home Server. However, it pays to be safe, so here are the steps to follow to ensure that it's turned on:

1. Log on to Windows Home Server.
2. Select Start, Control Panel, Windows Firewall. Windows Home Server displays the Windows Firewall dialog box.
3. Make sure the On option is activated, as shown in Figure 11.11.
4. Click OK.

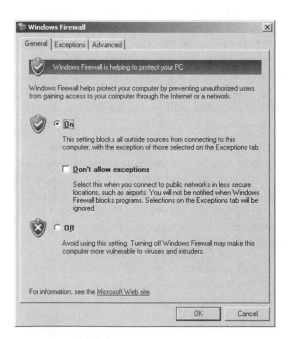

FIGURE 11.11   To ensure safe computing, make sure Windows Firewall is turned on.

CAUTION

Activating Windows Firewall on Windows Home Server only protects the server; it does nothing for the security of your client computers. Therefore, it's a good idea to check your Windows 7, Vista, and XP machines to ensure that Windows Firewall is activated on each. (Note, however, that Windows Home Server will let you know if any Windows 7 or Vista machine has its firewall turned off.)

Disabling the Hidden Administrative Shares

By default, Windows Home Server sets up automatic administrative shares for the root folders of the C: and D: drives, as well as C:\Windows. These shares have a dollar sign ($) at the end of their names (C$, D$, and ADMIN$), so they're hidden from the list of shares you see when you access \\SERVER. To see them, select Start, Command Prompt to open a command prompt session, type **net share**, and press Enter. You'll see a listing similar to this:

```
Share name   Resource             Remark
-------------------------------------------------------------
C$           C:\                  Default share
D$           D:\                  Default share
ADMIN$       C:\WINDOWS           Remote Admin
IPC$                              Remote IPC
Music        D:\shares\Music      Shared folder for music
Photos       D:\shares\Photos     Shared folder for photos
Public       D:\shares\Public     Shared folder for miscellaneous files
Recorded TV D:\shares\Recorded TV Shared folder for Windows Media Center
Software     D:\shares\Software   Shared folder for software installation programs
Users        D:\shares\Users      Personal folders for users
Videos       D:\shares\Videos     Shared folder for videos
```

Although the C$, D$, and ADMIN$ shares are otherwise hidden, they're well known, and they represent a small security risk should an intruder get access to your system. To close this hole, you can force Windows Home Server to disable these shares. Here are the steps to follow:

1. Log on to Windows Home Server.

2. Select Start, Run to open the Run dialog box.

3. Type **regedit** and then click OK. Windows Home Server opens the Registry Editor.

4. Navigate to the following key:

   HKLM\SYSTEM\CurrentControlSet\Services\lanmanserver\parameters

5. Select Edit, New, DWORD Value.

6. Type **AutoShareServer** and press Enter. (You can leave this setting with its default value of 0.)

7. Restart Windows Home Server to put the new setting into effect.

Once again, select Start, Command Prompt to open a command prompt session, type **net share**, and press Enter. The output now looks like this:

```
Share name   Resource          Remark
---------------------------------------------------------------------------
IPC$                           Remote IPC
Music        D:\shares\Music   Shared folder for music
Photos       D:\shares\Photos  Shared folder for photos
Public       D:\shares\Public  Shared folder for miscellaneous files
Recorded TV D:\shares\Recorded TV  Shared folder for Windows Media Center
Software     D:\shares\Software   Shared folder for software installation programs
Users        D:\shares\Users   Personal folders for users
Videos       D:\shares\Videos  Shared folder for videos
```

> **CAUTION**
>
> Some programs expect the administrative shares to be present, so disabling those shares may cause those programs to fail or generate error messages. If that happens, enable the shares by opening the Registry Editor and either deleting the AutoShareServer setting or changing its value to 1.

Securing Network Computers

Implementing security across a network is a "weakest link" proposition. That is, your network as a whole is only as secure as the most vulnerable of the clients. So although you may now have Windows Home Server locked down, you still have to get your security up to snuff on each computer. This section takes you through a few features and techniques that enhance the security of the rest of your network.

Monitoring Home Computer Security

I mentioned in Chapter 10, "Monitoring Your Network," that Windows Home Server displays various network health notifications via the Windows Home Server Status icon, which appears in the notification area. If you have a Windows 7 or Vista PC, the Windows Home Server Status icon can check the current Security Center settings for the computer's firewall, automatic updating, and antispyware and antivirus programs. If any of these is turned off or, in the case of antispyware and antivirus programs, out of date, the Windows Home Server Status icon displays a notification. Table 11.3 shows the four security-related notifications that you might see.

TABLE 11.3   Security-Related Network Health Notifications Displayed by the Windows Home Server Status Icon

Notification	Description
⊗ Windows Firewall is off x MEDIAPC has Windows Firewall turned off.	Windows Firewall has been turned off on the specified computer.
⊗ Windows Updates are turned off x MEDIAPC is configured to never check for Windows Updates.	Automatic updating has been turned off on the specified computer.
⊗ Check your antivirus software status. x Antivirus software is either not installed or is out of date on MEDIAPC.	The antivirus program on the specified computer has either been turned off, or its virus definitions are out of date.
⊗ No spyware protection x MEDIAPC has antispyware software turned off or out of date.	The antispyware program on the specified computer has either been turned off, or its spyware definitions are out of date.

▶ **SEE** To learn more about Windows Home Server's health notifications, **see** "Monitoring Network Health Notifications," **P. 268.**

Thwarting Spyware with Windows Defender

Malware is the generic term for malicious software such as viruses and Trojan horses. The worst malware offender by far these days is *spyware*, which is generally defined as any program that surreptitiously monitors a user's computer activities—particularly the typing of passwords, PINs, and credit card numbers—or harvests sensitive data on the user's computer and then sends that information to an individual or a company via the user's Internet connection (the so-called *back channel*) without the user's consent.

You might think that having a robust firewall between you and the bad guys would make malware a problem of the past. Unfortunately, that's not true. These programs piggyback on other legitimate programs that users actually *want* to download, such as file-sharing programs, download managers, and screensavers. A *drive-by download* is the download and installation of a program without a user's knowledge or consent. This relates closely to a *pop-up download*—the download and installation of a program after the user clicks an option in a pop-up browser window, particularly when the option's intent is vaguely or misleadingly worded.

To make matters even worse, most spyware embeds itself deep into a system, and removing it is a delicate and time-consuming operation beyond the abilities of even some experienced users. Some programs actually come with an Uninstall option, but it's nothing but a ruse, of course. The program appears to remove itself from the system, but what it actually does is a *covert reinstall*—it surreptitiously reinstalls a fresh version of itself when the computer is idle.

All this means that you need to buttress your firewall with an antispyware program that can watch out for these unwanted programs and prevent them from getting their hooks into your system. In early versions of Windows, you needed to install a third-party program. However, Windows 7 and Vista come with an antispyware program named Windows Defender.

TIP

Many security experts recommend installing multiple antispyware programs on the premise that one program may miss one or two examples of spyware, but two or three programs are highly unlikely to miss any. So, in addition to Windows Defender, you might also consider installing antispyware programs such as SuperAntiSpyware (www.superantispyware.com), Lavasoft Ad-Aware (www.lavasoft.com), and PC Tools Spyware Doctor (www.pctools.com).

To open Windows Defender, select Start, type **defender**, and then click Windows Defender in the search results. You end up at the Windows Defender Home screen, shown in Figure 11.12. This window shows you the date, time, and results of your last scan, as well as the current Windows Defender status.

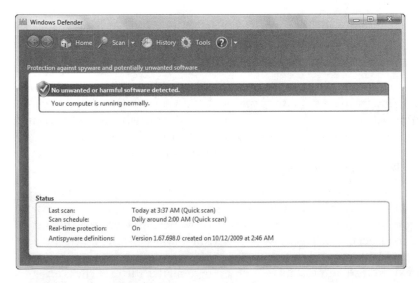

FIGURE 11.12   Windows Defender removes spyware from your system and keeps your system safe by preventing spyware installations.

Spyware Scanning

Windows Defender protects your computer from spyware in two ways. It can scan your system for evidence of installed spyware programs (and remove or disable those programs, if necessary), and it can monitor your system in real time to watch for activities that indicate the presence of spyware (such as a drive-by download or data being sent via a back channel).

For the scanning portion of its defenses, Windows Defender supports three different scan types:

- ▶ **Quick Scan**—This scan checks just those areas of your system where it is likely to find evidence of spyware. This scan usually takes just a couple of minutes. This scan is the default, and you can initiate one at any time by clicking the Scan link.

- ▶ **Full Scan**—This scan checks for evidence of spyware in system memory, all running processes, and the system drive (usually drive C:), and it performs a deep scan on all folders. This scan might take 30 minutes or more, depending on your system. To run this scan, pull down the Scan menu and click Full Scan.

- ▶ **Custom Scan**—This scan checks just the drives and folders that you select. The length of the scan depends on the number of locations you select and the number of objects in those locations. To run this scan, pull down the Scan menu and click Custom Scan, which displays the Select Scan Options page shown in Figure 11.13. Click Select, activate the check boxes for the drives you want scanned, and then click OK. Click Scan Now to start the scan.

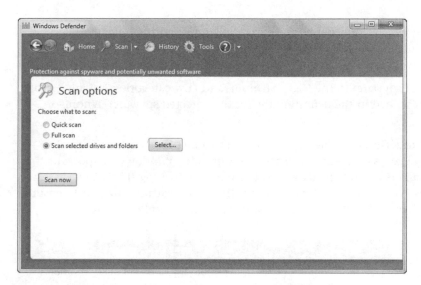

FIGURE 11.13   In the Scan menu, select Custom Scan to see the Select Scan Options page.

Windows Defender Settings

By default, Windows Defender is set up to perform a Quick Scan of your system every morning at 2:00 a.m. To change this, click Tools and then click Options to display the

Options page shown in Figure 11.14. Use the controls in the Automatic Scanning section to specify the scan frequency time and type.

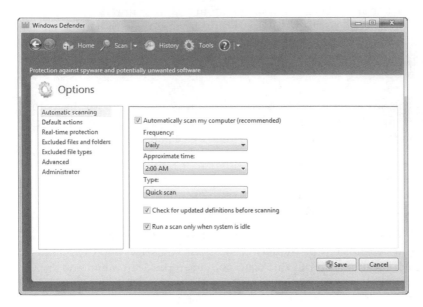

FIGURE 11.14   Use the Options page to set up a spyware scan schedule.

The rest of the Options page offers options for customizing Windows Defender. The remaining options include the following:

▶ **Default Actions**—Set the action that Windows Defender should take if it finds alert items (potential spyware) in the High, Medium, and Low categories: Default Action (the action prescribed in the definition file for the detected spyware), Ignore, or Remove.

▶ **Real-Time Protection**—Enables and disables real-time protection. You can also toggle security agents on and off. *Security agents* monitor Windows components that are frequent targets of spyware activity. For example, activating the Auto Start security agent tells Windows Defender to monitor the list of startup programs to ensure that spyware doesn't add itself to this list and run automatically at startup.

TIP

Windows Defender often warns you that a program might be spyware and asks whether you want to allow the program to operate normally or to block it. If you accidentally allow an unsafe program, click Tools, Allowed Items; select the program in the Allowed Items list; and then click Remove from List. Similarly, if you accidentally blocked a safe program, click Tools, Quarantined Items; select the program in the Quarantined Items list; and then click Remove.

> ▶ **Advanced**—Use these options to enable scanning inside compressed archives. In Windows 7, you can also elect to scan email and removable drives; in Windows Vista, you can prevent Windows Defender from scanning specific folders.

> ▶ **Administrator**—This section has a check box that toggles Windows Defender on and off. In Windows 7, you can activate a check box that lets you see Windows Defender items from other users; in Windows Vista, you see a check box that, when activated, allows all non-Administrators to use Windows Defender.

Protecting Yourself Against Email Viruses

By far the most productive method for viruses to replicate is the humble email message. The list of email viruses and Trojan horses is a long one, but most of them operate more or less the same way: They arrive as a message attachment, usually from someone you know. When you open the attachment, the virus infects your computer and then, without your knowledge, uses your email client and your address book to ship out messages with more copies of itself attached. The nastier versions also mess with your computer by deleting data or corrupting files.

You can avoid infection by one of these viruses by implementing a few common sense procedures:

> ▶ Never open an attachment that comes from someone you don't know.

> ▶ Even if you know the sender, if the attachment isn't something you're expecting, assume that the sender's system is infected. Write back and confirm that the sender emailed the message.

> ▶ Some viruses come packaged as scripts hidden within messages that use the Rich Text (HTML) format. This means that the virus can run just by your viewing the message! If a message looks suspicious, don't open it—just delete it. (Note that you'll need to turn off the Windows Mail Preview pane before deleting the message. Otherwise, when you highlight the message, it appears in the Preview pane and sets off the virus. Select View, Layout, deactivate the Show Preview Pane check box, and click OK. If you're using Windows Live Mail, select View, Layout, deactivate the Show the Reading Pane check box, and click OK.)

CAUTION

It's particularly important to turn off the Preview pane before displaying Windows Mail's Junk E-Mail folder. Because many junk messages also carry a virus payload, your chances of initiating an infection are highest when working with messages in this folder.

> ▶ Install a top-of-the-line antivirus program, particularly one that checks incoming email. In addition, be sure to keep your antivirus program's virus list up-to-date. As

you read this, there are probably dozens, maybe even hundreds, of morally challenged scumnerds designing even nastier viruses. Regular updates will help you keep up. Here are some security suites to check out:

Norton Internet Security (www.symantec.com/index.jsp)

McAfee Internet Security Suite (mcafee.com/us)

AVG Internet Security (free.avg.com/)

In addition to these general procedures, Windows Mail also comes with its own set of virus protection features. Here's how to use them:

1. In Windows Mail, select Tools, Options. (In Windows Live Mail, select Menus, Safety Options, or Tools, Safety Options if you have the menu bar displayed.)

2. Display the Security tab.

3. In the Virus Protection group, you have the following options:

   Select the Internet Explorer Security Zone to Use—Earlier in this chapter, I described the security zone model used by Internet Explorer (refer to "Using Internet Explorer on Windows Home Server"). From the perspective of Windows Mail, you use the security zones to determine whether to allow active content inside an HTML-format message to run:

   ▶ **Internet Zone**—If you choose this zone, active content is allowed to run.

   ▶ **Restricted Sites Zone**—If you choose this option, active content is disabled. This is the default setting and the one I recommend.

   Warn Me When Other Applications Try to Send Mail as Me—As I mentioned earlier, it's possible for programs and scripts to send email messages without your knowledge. This happens by using Simple MAPI (*Messaging Application Programming Interface*) calls, which can send messages via your computer's default mail client—and it's all hidden from you. With this check box activated, Windows Mail displays a warning dialog box when a program or script attempts to send a message using Simple MAPI.

   Do Not Allow Attachments to Be Saved or Opened That Could Potentially Be a Virus—With this check box activated, Windows Mail monitors attachments to look for file types that could contain viruses or destructive code. If it detects such a file, it disables your ability to open and save that file, and it displays a note at the top of the message to let you know about the unsafe attachment.

NOTE

Internet Explorer's built-in unsafe-file list defines the file types that Windows Mail disables. That list includes file types associated with the following extensions: .ad, .ade, .adp, .bas, .bat, .chm, .cmd, .com, .cpl, .crt, .exe, .hlp, .hta, .inf, .ins, .isp, .js, .jse, .lnk, .mdb, .mde, .msc, .msi, .msp, .mst, .pcd, .pif, .reg, .scr, .sct, .shb, .shs, .url, .vb, .vbe, .vbs, .vsd, .vss, .vst, .vsw, .wsc, .wsf, .wsh.

> **TIP**
>
> What do you do if you want to send a file that's on the Windows Mail unsafe file list and you want to make sure that the recipient will be able to open it? The easiest workaround is to compress the file into a `.zip` file—a file type not blocked by Windows Mail, Outlook, or any other mail client that blocks file types.

4. Click OK to put the new settings into effect.

Implementing Parental Controls

On your home network, there's a good chance that you have children who share your computer or who have their own computer. Either way, it's smart to take precautions regarding the content and programs that they can access. Locally, this might take the form of blocking access to certain programs (such as your financial software), using ratings to control which games they can play, and setting time limits on when the computer is used. If the computer has Internet access, you might also want to allow (or block) specific sites, block certain types of content, and prevent file downloads.

All this sounds daunting, but the Parental Controls in Windows 7 and Windows Vista make things a bit easier by offering an easy-to-use interface that lets you set all the afore-mentioned options and lots more. (You get Parental Controls in the Home Basic, Home Premium, and Ultimate editions of Windows 7 and Vista.)

Creating Accounts for the Kids

Before you begin, be sure to create a standard user account for each child that uses the computer. Here are the steps to follow:

1. Select Start, Control Panel, Add or Remove User Accounts, and then enter your UAC credentials. Windows displays the Manage Accounts window.
2. Click Create a New Account. The Create New Account window appears.
3. Type the name for the account. The name can be up to 20 characters and must be unique on the system.
4. Make sure the Standard User option is activated.
5. Click Create Account. Windows returns you to the Manage Accounts window.
6. Repeat steps 2–5 to add standard user accounts for all your kids.

Activating Parental Controls and Activity Reporting

With the kid's accounts in place, you get to Parental Controls using either of the following methods:

▶ If you still have the Manage Accounts window open, click Set Up Parental Controls.

▶ Select Start, Control Panel, Set Up Parental Controls.

In Vista, enter your UAC credentials to get to the Parental Controls window, and then click the user you want to work with to get to the User Controls window.

You should activate two options here (see Figure 11.15):

▶ **Parental Controls**—Click On, Enforce Current Settings. This enables the links in the Settings area.

▶ **Activity Reporting (Windows Vista only)**—Click On, Collect Information About Computer Usage. This tells Vista to track system events such as blocked logon attempts and attempted changes to user accounts, the system date and time, and system settings.

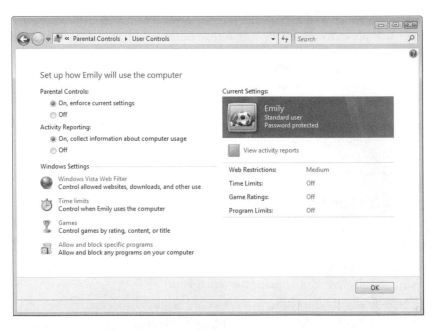

FIGURE 11.15   The User Controls window enables you to set up web, time, game, and program restrictions for the selected user.

The Windows Settings section has links that you use to set up the controls on the selected user. Two of these are security related—Windows Vista Web Filter (available only in Windows Vista) and Allow and Block Specific Programs—so I discuss them in the next two sections.

Controlling Web Use

In the User Controls window, click Windows Vista Web Filter to display the Web Restrictions page, shown in Figure 11.16. Make sure the Block Some Websites or Content option is activated.

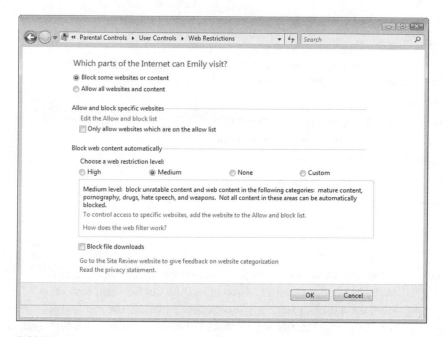

FIGURE 11.16   Use the Web Restrictions window to control web surfing actions for the selected user.

You can control websites, web content, and file downloads:

Allow and Block Specific Websites   Click the Edit the Allow and Block List to open the Allow Block Webpages window. For each safe site that the user can visit, type the website address and click Allow to add the site to the Allowed Websites list; for each unsafe site that the user can't visit, type the website address and click Block to add the site to the Blocked Websites list. Because there are so many possible sites to block, consider activating the Only Allow Websites Which Are On the Allow List check box.

TIP

To make your life easier, you can import lists of allowed or blocked sites. First, create a new text file and change the extension to `Web Allow Block List` (for example, `MyURLs.Web Allow Block List`). Open the file and add the following text to start:

```
<WebAddresses>
</WebAddresses>
```

Between these lines, add a new line for each site using the following format:

<URL AllowBlock="*n*">*address*</URL>

Replace n with 1 for a site you want to allow, or 2 for a site you want to block, and replace address with the site URL. Here's an example:

<WebAddresses>

<URL AllowBlock="1">http://goodcleanfun.com</URL>

<URL AllowBlock="1">http://wholesomestuff.com</URL>

<URL AllowBlock="2">http://smut.com</URL>

<URL AllowBlock="2">http://depravity.com</URL>

</WebAddresses>

Block Web Content Automatically	Select the option you want to use to restrict site content: High, Medium, None, or Custom. If you select the Custom Web restriction level, Vista adds a number of check boxes that enable you to block specific content categories (such as Pornography, Mature Content, and Bomb Making).
Block File Downloads	Activate this check box to prevent the user from downloading files via the web browser.

Allowing and Blocking Programs

In the User Controls window, click Allow and Block Specific Programs to display the Application Restrictions page. Activate the *User* Can Only Use the Programs I Allow option. Windows 7 or Vista then populates the Check the Programs That Can Be Used list with the applications on your computer, as shown in Figure 11.17. Activate the check boxes for the programs you want to allow the person to use.

Avoiding Phishing Scams

Phishing refers to creating a replica of an existing web page to fool a user into submitting personal, financial, or password data. The term comes from the fact that Internet scammers are using increasingly sophisticated lures as they "fish" for users' financial information and password data. The most common ploy is to copy the web page code from a major site—such as AOL or eBay—and use it to set up a replica page that appears to be part of the company's site. (This is why another name for phishing is *spoofing*.) Phishers send out a fake email with a link to this page, which solicits the user's credit card data or password. When a recipient submits the form, it sends the data to the scammer and leaves the user on an actual page from the company's site so that he doesn't suspect a thing.

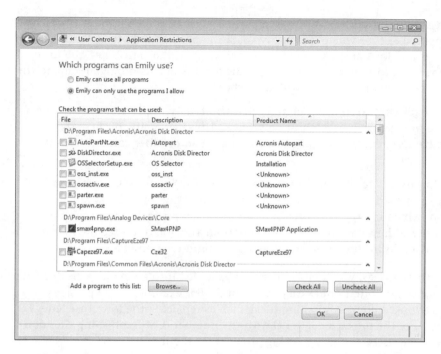

FIGURE 11.17   Use the Application Restrictions window to control the programs that the selected user can run.

A phishing page looks identical to a legitimate page from the company because the phisher has simply copied the underlying source code from the original page. However, no spoof page can be a perfect replica of the original. Here are five things to look for:

▶ **The URL in the address bar**—A legitimate page will have the correct domain—such as aol.com or ebay.com—whereas a spoofed page will have only something similar—such as aol.whatever.com or blah.com/ebay.

NOTE

The URL in the address bar is usually the easiest way to tell whether a site is trustworthy. For this reason, Internet Explorer 8 makes it impossible to hide the address bar in almost all browser windows, even simple pop-ups.

▶ **The URLs associated with page links**—Most links on the page probably point to legitimate pages on the original site. However, some links might point to pages on the phisher's site.

▶ **The form-submittal address**—Almost all spoof pages contain a form into which you're supposed to type whatever sensitive data the phisher seeks from you. Select View, Source, and look at the value of the `<form>` tag's `action` attribute—the form submits your data to this address. Clearly, if the form is not sending your data to the legitimate domain, you're dealing with a phisher.

▶ **Text or images that aren't associated with the trustworthy site**—Many phishing sites are housed on free web hosting services. However, many of these services place an advertisement on each page, so look for an ad or other content from the hosting provider.

▶ **Internet Explorer's lock icon in the status bar and Security Report area**—A legitimate site would transmit sensitive financial data only using a secure HTTPS connection, which Internet Explorer indicates by placing a lock icon in the status bar and in the address bar's new Security Report area. If you don't see the lock icon on a page that asks for financial data, the page is almost certainly a spoof.

If you watch for these things, you'll probably never be fooled into giving up sensitive data to a phisher. However, it's often not as easy as it sounds. For example, some phishers employ easily overlooked domain-spoofing tricks such as replacing the lowercase letter *L* with the number *1*, or the uppercase letter *O* with the number *0*. Still, phishing sites don't fool most experienced users, so this isn't a big problem for them.

Novice users, on the other hand, need all the help they can get. They tend to assume that if everything they see on the Web looks legitimate and trustworthy, it probably is. And even if they're aware that scam sites exist, they don't know how to check for telltale phishing signs. To help these users, Internet Explorer 8 comes with a tool called the *SmartScreen Filter*. This filter alerts you to potential phishing scams by doing two things each time you visit a site:

▶ Analyzes the site content to look for known phishing techniques (that is, to see whether the site is *phishy*). The most common of these is a check for domain spoofing. This common scam also goes by the names *homograph spoofing* and the *lookalike attack*. Internet Explorer 8 also supports Internationalized Domain Names (IDN), which refers to domain names written in languages other than English, and it checks for *IDN spoofing*, domain name ambiguities in the user's chosen browser language.

▶ Checks a global database of known phishing sites to see whether it lists the site. This database is maintained by a network of providers, such as Cyota, Inc., Internet Identity, and MarkMonitor, as well as by reports from users who find phishing sites while surfing. According to Microsoft, this "URL reputation service" updates several times an hour with new data.

Here's how the SmartScreen Filter works:

▶ If you visit a site that Internet Explorer *knows* is a phishing scam, it changes the background color of the address bar to red and displays an `Unsafe Website` message in the Security Report area, as shown in Figure 11.18. It also blocks navigation to the

site by displaying a separate page telling you that the site is a known phishing scam.
A link is provided to navigate to the site, if you so choose.

Security Report Area

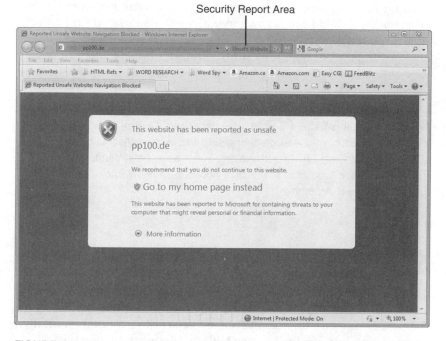

FIGURE 11.18   If Internet Explorer 8 detects a known phishing site, it displays Unsafe
Website in the Security Report area and blocks access to the site.

NOTE

The Security Report area is another Internet Explorer security innovation. Clicking whatever text or icon appears in this area produces a report on the security of the site. For
example, if you navigate to a secure site, you see the lock icon in this area. Click the
lock to see a report that shows the site's digital certificate information.

► If you visit a site that Internet Explorer *thinks* is a potential phishing scam, it
changes the background color of the address bar to yellow and displays a Suspicious·
Website message in the Security Report area.

Sharing a Computer Securely

If you're the only person who uses your computer, you don't have to worry all that much
about the security of your user profile—that is, your files and Windows settings. However,
if you share your computer with other people, either at home or at the office, you need to

set up some kind of security to ensure that each user has his "own" Windows and can't mess with anyone else's (either purposely or accidentally). Here's a list of security precautions to set up when sharing your computer:

▶ **Create an account for each user**—Everyone who uses the computer, even if they use it only occasionally, should have his own user account. (If a user needs to access the computer rarely, or only once, activate the Guest account and let him use that. You should disable the Guest account after the user finishes his session.)

> **NOTE**
>
> To activate the Guest account in Windows 7 or Vista, select Start, Control Panel, Add or Remove User Accounts, and enter your UAC credentials. In the Manage Accounts window, click Guest and then click Turn On. To activate the Guest account in Windows XP, select Start, Control Panel, User Accounts. In the User Accounts window, click Guest and then click Turn On the Guest Account.

▶ **Remove unused accounts**—If you have accounts set up for users who no longer require access to the computer, you should delete those accounts.

▶ **Limit the number of administrators**—Members of the Administrators group can do *anything* in Windows 7 or Vista simply by clicking Continue in the User Account Control dialog box. These powerful accounts should be kept to a minimum. Ideally, your system should have just one (besides the built-in Administrator account).

▶ **Rename the Administrator account**—Renaming the Administrator account ensures that no other user can be certain of the name of the computer's top-level user.

▶ **Put all other accounts in the Users (Standard users) group**—Most users can perform almost all of their everyday chores with the permissions and rights assigned to the Users group, so that's the group you should use for all other accounts.

▶ **Use strong passwords on all accounts**—Supply each account with a strong password so that no user can access another's account by logging on with a blank or simple password.

▶ **SEE** To learn what constitutes a strong password, **see** "Building a Strong Password," **P. 41.**

▶ **Set up each account with a screensaver, and be sure the screensaver resumes to the Welcome screen**—To do this, right-click the desktop, click Personalize (in Windows 7 or Vista) or Properties (in XP), and then click Screen Saver. Choose an item in the Screen Saver list, and then activate the On Resume, Display Welcome Screen check box.

▶ **Lock your computer**—When you leave your desk for any length of time, be sure to lock your computer; either select Start, Lock in Windows 7 or Vista, or press Windows Logo+L in Windows 7, Vista, or XP. This displays the Welcome screen; no one else can use your computer without entering your password.

Implementing Wireless Network Security

Wireless networks are less secure than wired ones because the wireless connection that enables you to access the network from afar can also enable an intruder from outside your home or office to access the network. In particular, *wardriving* is an activity where a person drives through various neighborhoods with a portable computer or another device set up to look for available wireless networks. If the person finds a nonsecured network, he uses it for free Internet access or to cause mischief with shared network resources.

> **NOTE**
>
> If you don't believe that your wireless signals extend beyond your home or office, you can prove it to yourself. Unplug any wireless-enabled notebook and take it outside for a walk in the vicinity of your house. View the available wireless networks as you go, and you'll probably find that you can travel a fair distance (several houses, at least) away from your wireless access point and still see your network.

Here are a few tips and techniques you can easily implement to enhance the security of your wireless network:

▶ **Enable encryption**—First and foremost, enable encryption for wireless data so that an outside user who picks up your network packets can't decipher them. Be sure to use the strongest encryption that your equipment supports. For most home routers, this is usually *Wi-Fi Protected Access (WPA)*, particularly WPA2, which is more secure than regular WPA.

> **NOTE**
>
> If you change your access point encryption method as described in the previous tip, you also need to update each wireless client to use the same form of encryption. In the Network Connections window, right-click your wireless network connection and then click Properties. Display the Wireless Networks tab, click your network in the list, and then click Properties. Change the following three settings, and then click OK:
>
> ▶ Network Authentication—Select WPA-PSK.
>
> ▶ Data Encryption—Select TKIP.
>
> ▶ Network Key—Type your shared key here and in the Confirm Network Key text box.

▶ **Disable network broadcasting**—Windows sees your wireless network because the access point broadcasts the network's SSID. However, Windows remembers the wireless networks that you have successfully connected to. Therefore, after all of your computers have accessed the wireless network at least once, you no longer need to broadcast the network's SSID. Therefore, you should use your AP setup program to disable broadcasting and prevent others from seeing your network.

CAUTION

You disable SSID broadcasting by accessing the wireless access point's configuration page and deactivating the broadcast setting. (Exactly how you do that varies depending on the manufacturer; see your documentation or just poke around in the settings page.) However, when previously authorized devices attempt to connect to a nonbroadcasting network, they include the network's SSID as part of the probe requests they send out to see whether the network is within range. The SSID is sent in unencrypted text, so it would be easy for a snoop with the right software (easily obtained from the Internet) to learn the SSID. If the SSID is not broadcasting to try to hide a network that is unsecure or uses an easily breakable encryption protocol, such as WEP, hiding the SSID in this way actually makes the network *less* secure.

▶ **Change the default SSID**—Even if you disable broadcasting of your network's SSID, users can still attempt to connect to your network by guessing the SSID. All wireless access points come with a predefined name, such as `linksys` or `default`, and a would-be intruder will attempt these standard names first. Therefore, you can increase the security of your network by changing the SSID to a new name that is difficult to guess.

▶ **Change the access point username and password**—Any person within range of your wireless access point can open the device's setup page by entering `http://192.168.1.1` or `http://192.168.0.1` into a web browser. The person must log on with a username and password, but the default logon values (usually `admin`) are common knowledge among wardrivers. To prevent access to the setup program, be sure to change the access point's default username and password.

▶ **Consider static IP addresses**—DHCP makes it easy to manage IP addresses, but it also gives an IP address to *anyone* who accesses the network. To prevent this, turn off DHCP in the access point and assign static IP addresses to each of your computers.

▶ **Enable MAC (Media Access Control) address filtering**—The *MAC address* is the physical address of a network adapter. This is unique to each adapter, so you can enhance security by setting up your access point to allow connections from only specified MAC addresses. (Unfortunately, MAC address filtering isn't a particularly robust form of security. The problem is that wireless network packets use a nonencrypted header that includes the MAC address of the device sending the packet! So any reasonably sophisticated cracker can sniff your network packets, determine the MAC address of one of your wireless devices, and then use special software to spoof that address so that the AP thinks the hacker's packets are coming from an authorized device.)

NOTE

To find out the MAC address of your wireless network adapter, open a Command Prompt session and enter the following command:

`ipconfig /all`

Find the data for the wireless adapter and look for the `Physical Address` value. (Alternatively, right-click the wireless connection, click Status, display the Support tab, and click Details.)

▶ **Avoid windows**—When positioning your access point within your home or office, don't place it near a window, if possible, because otherwise the access point sends a strong signal out of the building. Try to position the access point close to the center of your house or building.

From Here

▶ To learn what constitutes a strong password, **see** "Building a Strong Password," **P. 41**.

▶ To learn more about Windows Home Server's health notifications, **see** "Monitoring Network Health Notifications," **P. 268**.

Setting Up a Windows Home Server Website

Most of the features and techniques that I've talked about thus far in the book have been directly related to Windows Home Server (rightly so, what with the book's title and all). However, it's sometimes easy to forget the powerful server underpinnings upon which Windows Home Server does its thing. I speak, of course, of the Windows Server 2003 code that underlies Windows Home Server and that has, until now, merely lurked in the background.

This chapter changes all that by tackling a subject that takes you well beyond the standard features of Windows Home Server and into brand new territory. Here you get a chance to play with one of Windows Home Server's most useful and most powerful features: Internet Information Services (IIS), the Windows Server 2003 web server. Yes, you can use one of the many thousands of web hosting companies to put up your site, but if you want complete control over the site, you need to roll up your sleeves and get hands on with IIS.

Books bigger than this one have been written on the seemingly endless features and properties of this world-class web server, so I'm under no illusion that a single chapter will be even remotely exhaustive. However, Windows Home Server is designed as a family-oriented product, so my goal here is to show you how to get one or more websites online for you and your family members to put their best digital feet forward on the web.

Understanding the Windows Home Server Default Website

As you saw in Chapter 7, "Making Connections to Network Computers," when you enter the address http://*server* into Internet Explorer (where *server* is the name of your Windows Home Server PC), you're redirected to the Windows Home Server website at https://*server*/home. When you click Log On, you end up at the Windows Home Server Remote Access site at https://*server*/remote.

> ▶ **SEE** For more information on connecting to Windows Home Server's home site and Remote Access site, **see** "Displaying the Remote Access Home Page," **P. 188.**

The folders home and remote comprise the Windows Home Server default website that's created, configured, and started automatically when you install Windows Home Server.

Viewing the Default Website Folders

To view these folders, log on to Windows Home Server, select Start, Windows Explorer, and navigate to the C:\Inetpub folder. This folder contains several subfolders, including home and remote. The other folders—such as upnp and wwwroot—are used internally by IIS and Windows Home Server. Figure 12.1 shows the contents of the home folder.

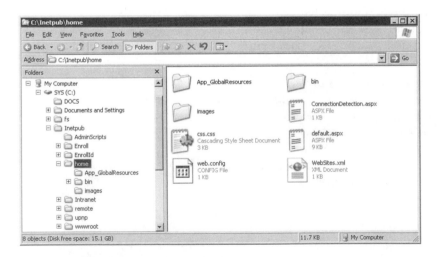

FIGURE 12.1   The contents of the IIS home folder.

The home folder contains the following subfolders and files:

App_GlobalResources   Contains the file GlobalResources.resx, which is an XML file containing references to .NET resources used globally in the Windows Home Server's default application pool.

bin   This folder contains a couple of dynamic-link libraries (DLLs) that contain code used by Windows Home Server.

images   This folder contains the images used on the home page.

css.css   This file is the cascading stylesheet (CSS) used by the home page.

default.aspx   This file contains the HTML tags, CSS properties, and ASP.NET programming code that creates and configures the home page.

web.config   This file contains configuration data for the home site's ASP.NET application.

WebSites.xml   You can use this file to customize the home page with links to internal or external sites. See "Adding Site Links to the Home and Remote Access Pages," later in this chapter.

Figure 12.2 shows the contents of the remote folder. This folder contains quite a few files used internally by Windows Home Server, so I'll just list the most important subfolders and files:

images   This folder contains the images used on the Remote Access pages.

admin.aspx   This file contains the HTML tags, CSS properties, and ASP.NET programming code that creates and configures the Remote Access page's Computers tab.

css.css   This file is the CSS used by the Remote Access pages.

default.aspx   This file contains the HTML tags, CSS properties, and ASP.NET programming code that creates and configures the Remote Access home page.

filesRoot.aspx   This file contains the HTML tags, CSS properties, and ASP.NET programming code that creates and configures the Remote Access page's Shared Folders tab.

logon.aspx   This file contains the HTML tags, CSS properties, and ASP.NET programming code that creates and configures the Remote Access page's logon page.

rdpload.aspx   This file contains the HTML tags, CSS properties, and ASP.NET programming code that creates and configures the Remote Desktop connection page you see when you click the Connect to Your Home Server link in the Remote Access page's Computers tab.

WebSites.xml   You can use this file to customize the Remote Access page with links to internal or external sites. See "Adding Site Links to the Home and Remote Access Pages," later in this chapter.

FIGURE 12.2   The contents of the IIS remote folder.

Viewing the Default Website with Internet Information Services Manager

The C:\Inetpub folder enables you to examine the physical files and subfolders associated with the Windows Home Server default website. However, you probably won't often deal with the C:\Inetpub folder (or any folder) directly when creating and configuring your own web pages and websites. Instead, you'll most often use a Microsoft Management Console snap-in called the IIS Manager.

To display this snap-in, select Start, Control Panel, Administrative Tools, Internet Information Server (IIS) Manager. When the snap-in loads, open the *SERVER*, Web Sites, Default Web Site branch (where *SERVER* is the name of your Windows Home Server PC). You can then click either Home (see Figure 12.3) or Remote to see the site contents.

TIP

You can also launch IIS Manager by selecting Start, Run (or pressing Windows Logo+R) to open the Run dialog box, typing **inetmgr**, and clicking OK.

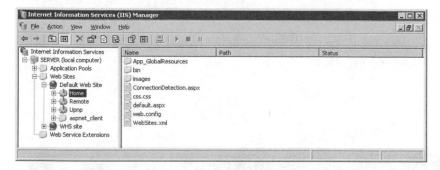

FIGURE 12.3   In the IIS Manager snap-in, the Default Web Site represents the Windows Home Server default site.

The Default Web Site branch also includes a Universal Plug and Play (UPnP) node that represents the Windows Home Server page that enables clients to install the Windows Home Server Connector software via Internet Explorer. See `http://server/upnp/welcome.aspx` (where *server* is the name of your Windows Home Server PC). However, it's easier and quicker just to navigate directly to `http://server:55000/`.

Much of the rest of this chapter shows you how to use IIS Manager to create and configure Windows Home Server website content.

Adding Folders and Files to the Default Website

By far, the easiest way to set up your own web content on Windows Home Server is to add that content to the existing default website. This requires no reconfiguration of the server, of IIS, of the Windows Home Server firewall, of the client computers, or of the router. You simply add the content, and it's ready for browsing.

Adding a File to a Default Website Folder

If you have just a few web content files that you want to add to the Windows Home Server website, you can add them directly to the IIS folders. First, create your web content file (HTML, ASP, or whatever). Here's a sample HTML file—which I've named `HelloWorld.htm`—that I'll use as an example:

```
<html>
<head>
<title>Hello World!</title>
</head>
```

```
<body>
<p>
<font style="size: 20pt; font-family: Verdana; color:DarkBlue">
Hello Windows Home Server World!
<font>
</p>
</body>
</html>
```

> **NOTE**
>
> For a primer on HTML and CSS, check out my book *The Complete Idiot's Guide to Creating a Website*. You can find out more about it at www.mcfedries.com/ CreatingAWebsite/.

> **TIP**
>
> Don't use spaces in the names of files (or folders) that you add to any IIS website. Although Internet Explorer might display such resources successfully, other browsers might not.

Next, save the file to one of Windows Home Server's default website folders:

home   Add your web content to this folder to view the content without having to log on to Windows Home Server. To browse to the content, use Internet Explorer to navigate to `http://server/home/content,` where *server* is the Windows Home Server name and *content* is the name of the web content file.

remote   Add your web content to this folder if you want users to have to log on to Windows Home Server before they can view the content. To browse to the content, use Internet Explorer to first navigate to `https://server/remote/` (where *server* is the Windows Home Server name), log on to Windows Home Server, and then navigate to `https://server/remote/content` (where *content* is the name of the web content file).

> **CAUTION**
>
> If your web content file references other files—for example, an HTML file that uses the `<img>` tag to reference an image file—be sure to copy those files to the home or remote folder (whichever folder you're using for the main file). You can either put the files in the root, or you can store them in a subfolder. For example, you might want to store image files in the `images` subfolder. If you store the files in subfolders, make sure you adjust the path in your code, as required. For example, if you place a file named `HelloWorld.jpg` in the `images` subfolder, you need to add the subfolder to the `<img>` tag, like so:
>
> `<img src="images/HelloWorld.jpg" />`

Figure 12.4 shows the `HelloWorld.htm` file copied to the `home` folder, and Figure 12.5 shows the file displayed with Internet Explorer.

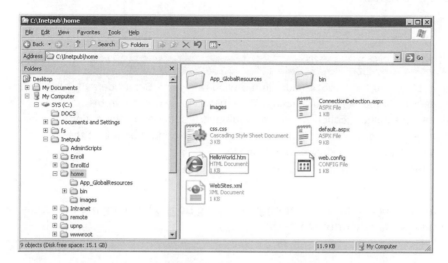

FIGURE 12.4   You can add individual files directly to the `home` or `remote` folder.

FIGURE 12.5   The `HelloWorld.htm` file displayed with Internet Explorer.

Adding a Folder to the Default Website

To add a folder to the Windows Home Server default website, you have two choices:

- ▶ Add the folder manually.
- ▶ Use the Virtual Directory Creation Wizard.

The next two sections provide you with the details.

Adding a Folder Manually

Adding a folder to the Windows Home Server default website is not all that different from adding a file. That is, you can simply create a new subfolder within the `home` or `remote` folder, or copy or move an existing folder and paste it within `home` or `remote`. To access web content within the new folder, tack the folder name and filename to the default website address. For example, if you create a subfolder named photos within the home folder, and the main page is named photos.htm, you access the content by entering the following address into the browser:

```
http://server/home/photos/photos.htm
```

NOTE

If you add the subfolder to the remote folder in the Windows Home Server default website, you can't browse to the subfolder directly. That's because all content in the remote folder requires authentication. Therefore, you must first log on to the main Remote Access page (https://server/Remote/default.aspx), and then adjust the address to browse to your new subfolder (for example, https://server/Remote/photos/photos.htm).

Note that you can save some wear and tear on your typing fingers by changing the name of the main content file to one of the following:

```
default.htm
default.asp
index.htm
default.aspx
```

When you use one of these names, IIS displays the file by default if you don't specify a filename as part of the URL. For example, if you rename the photos.htm file to default.htm, you can access the file just by specifying the folder path in the URL:

```
http://server/home/photos/
```

I discuss default content files in more detail later on in this chapter (see "Setting the Default Content Page").

Adding a Folder Using the Virtual Directory Creation Wizard

When you add a folder manually, IIS Manager detects the new folder and adds it to the folder content. However, you can also use IIS Manager to create a new folder with the default website. This method gives you a few extra options—such as setting permissions on the new folder—that you might find useful. Here are the steps to follow:

1. In IIS Manager, open the *SERVER*, Web Sites, Default Web Site branch (where *SERVER* is the name of your Windows Home Server PC).

2. Click either Home or Remote.

3. Select Action, New, Virtual Directory. IIS Manager launches the Virtual Directory Creation Wizard.

4. Click Next. The wizard asks you to enter an alias for the virtual directory. The alias is the name that appears in IIS Manager, within either the Home branch or the Remote branch. Note that this is *not* the same (nor does it have to be the same) as the name of the directory itself.

5. Type the alias and then click Next. The wizard prompts you for the folder path.

6. You have three choices (click Next when you're done):

   ▶ If the folder exists and you know the full pathname (drive and folders), type it in the Path text box.

   ▶ If the folder exists and you're not sure of the full pathname (or it's too long to type), click Browse, use the Browse for Folder dialog box to select the folder, and then click OK.

   ▶ If the folder doesn't exist, click Browse, use the Browse for Folder dialog box to select the folder within which you want the new folder to appear, click Make New Folder, type the folder name, press Enter, and then click OK.

7. Activate the check boxes for the permissions you want to apply to the new folder (see Figure 12.6; click Next when you're done):

Read	Allows each user to view and download files within the folder. This is the default permission.
Run Scripts	Allows each user to open files that contain scripts, such as Active Server Pages (ASP) or Perl files.
Execute	Allows each user to run programs in the folder, such as Common Gateway Interface (CGI) applications.
Write	Allows each user to upload files to the folder and to modify files within the folder. Obviously, you want to apply this potentially destructive permission only in the rarest circumstances.
Browse	Allows each user to view the contents of the directory. This occurs only if there is no file in the folder that uses one of the default names mentioned earlier.

8. Click Finish.

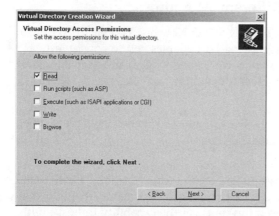

FIGURE 12.6   When you add a folder using IIS Manager, you can set permissions on that folder.

Creating a New Website

With the powerful capabilities of IIS at your disposal, you're not stuck with using just the default Windows Home Server website. For all practical purposes, you can create as many websites as you want: you can create a website for each member of the family; you can create a website to display family photos; or you can create a website that hosts the family blog, which might be a record of your family's activities (a sort of year-round Christmas newsletter).

You can do all this and much more because IIS is capable of hosting multiple sites on a single Windows Home Server PC. The secret behind this is that you can use one or more of the following items to construct a unique address for each site:

IP address   You can assign multiple IP addresses to the Windows Home Server computer and then apply each address to a new website.

Port number   Windows Home Server site uses ports 80 and 88, but you can assign port numbers such as 81, 82, 8080, and so on to each new website. This enables you to host multiple websites on a single IP address.

Host header name   This is a unique name that you assign to each new website. This name enables you to host multiple websites on a single IP address and port number.

You can mix and match these techniques, as needed. For example, you could use nothing but unique IP addresses or port numbers for each website, or combinations of IP addresses and port numbers. The method you use depends on the number of websites you want to set up and the number of computers on your network. As you see over the next few sections, the methods require a varying amount of effort on your part and varying levels of complexity for users to access the sites. Read through and try each method before deciding which one to implement.

Creating a New Website Using a Different IP Address

Back in Chapter 1, "Setting Up Your Windows Home Server Network," you learned how to set up Windows Home Server with a static IP address. This enables you to consistently access the server using an IP address that you know will never change, and it enables you to set up your router to forward ports to the server's IP address.

▶ **SEE** To learn the details on applying a static IP address to the server, **see** "Configuring Windows Home Server with a Static IP Address," **P. 9.**

However, there's nothing to stop you from assigning a second (or a third or a fourth) static IP address to Windows Home Server. This means that you can have the same benefits that come from a static IP address for your own websites (plus get the capability to host multiple sites on a single server in the first place) by adding more IP addresses to Windows Home Server and then using those addresses to define the location of your new websites.

Assigning an Additional IP Address to Windows Home Server

The first step here is to assign another IP address to Windows Home Server. Here are the steps to follow:

1. Select Start, All Programs, Accessories, Communications, Network Connections to open the Network Connections window.

> **TIP**
>
> If you see the network icon in the notification area, you can display the Network Connections window by right-clicking the network icon and then clicking Open Network Connections.

2. Right-click the icon for the connection to your local area network, and then click Properties. The connection's property sheet appears.

3. In the General tab, click Internet Protocol (TCP/IP), and then click Properties to display the Internet Protocol (TCP/IP) property sheet.

4. Make sure the connection is set up to use a static IP address (again, as explained in Chapter 1).

5. Click Advanced to display the Advanced TCP/IP Settings dialog box.

6. In the IP Settings tab, click Add to display the TCP/IP Address dialog box.

7. Type the IP address you want to use. Be sure to use an address that doesn't conflict with an existing static IP address on the server or with the other DHCP clients on your network. A good idea is to start with the highest possible address (usually 192.168.0.254) for the first static IP address and then work down (so the second static IP address would be 192.168.0.253, the third would be 192.168.0.252, and so on).

8. Type the IP addresses for the subnet mask. (Windows Home Server should fill this in automatically.)

9. Click Add. Windows Home Server returns you to the Advanced TCP/IP Settings dialog box and displays the new IP address in the IP Addresses list, as shown in Figure 12.7.

10. Click OK to return to the Internet Protocol (TCP/IP) property sheet.

11. Click OK to return to the connection's property sheet.

12. Click Close.

Note that you can repeat these steps as often as you like (with the only practical limit being the number of available IP addresses) to add more static IP addresses as you need them.

Creating a Website Using a Different IP Address

With your newly minted IP address at the ready, you can now create your website. Here are the steps to follow:

1. In IIS Manager, open the *SERVER*, Web Sites branch (where *SERVER* is the name of your Windows Home Server PC).

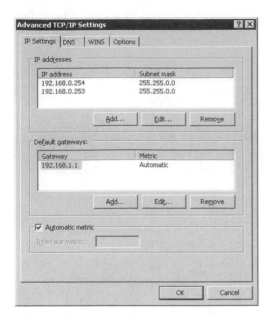

FIGURE 12.7   You can assign two or more static IP addresses to Windows Home Server.

2. Click an existing website, and then select Action, New, Web Site. (You can also right-click any website and click New, Web Site.) IIS Manager launches the Web Site Creation Wizard.

3. Click Next. The wizard asks you to enter a description for the website. The description is the name that appears in IIS Manager, within the Web Sites branch.

4. Type the description and then click Next. The wizard displays the IP Address and Port Settings dialog box.

5. In the Enter the IP Address to Use for This Site list, select the IP address you created in the previous section, as shown in Figure 12.8.

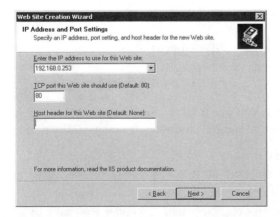

FIGURE 12.8   Select the other static IP address that you assigned to Windows Home Server.

6. Leave the TCP Port This Web Site Should Use value at 80, and click Next. The wizard prompts you to specify the path to the site's home folder.

7. Either type the full pathname (drive and folders) in the Path text box, or click Browse and use the Browse for Folder dialog box to either select the folder or create a new folder.

8. If you don't want to allow anonymous users to view the website, deactivate the Allow Anonymous Access to This Web Site check box. Click Next.

NOTE

If you deactivate the Allow Anonymous Access to This Web Site check box, all users must enter a valid Windows Home Server username and password to enter the site.

---

9. Activate the check boxes for the permissions you want to apply to the new folder (Read, Run Scripts, Execute, Write, or Browse; see "Adding a Folder Using the Virtual Directory Creation Wizard," earlier in this chapter), and then click Next.

10. Click Finish. IIS Manager adds the new site to the Web Sites branch, as shown in Figure 12.9 (see the Family Photos site).

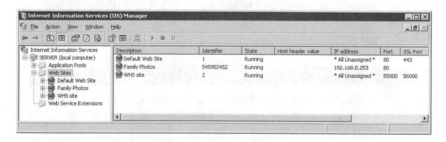

FIGURE 12.9   IIS Manager displays your new site in the Web Sites branch.

From here, add content to the folder you specified in step 7, including a file that uses one of the IIS default names.

Associating the IP Address with a Hostname

Your new website now works, but the only way you can access it is to browse to http://*IP*, where *IP* is the IP address that you created earlier, as shown in Figure 12.10.

That's fine, but you probably don't want some members of your family having to deal with the complexities of IP addresses. To avoid that, you can associate a hostname (such as FamilyPhotos) with the IP address.

On a regular server, you'd use a DNS (domain name system) server or WINS (Windows Internet Name Service) server to do this. Unfortunately, Windows Home Server doesn't come with either of these tools. Fortunately, you can get the same benefit by making a manual adjustment to the hosts file, which you use to map IP addresses to hostnames.

FIGURE 12.10   Enter the IP address into the web browser to access your website.

The only downside to this technique is that you must edit the hosts file on Windows Home Server and every computer that you want to give access to the site.

Before proceeding, note that you can use the hosts file to set up both local and remote (that is, Internet) mappings:

▶ A local mapping associates an IP addresses with a simple hostname, such as FamilyPhotos or KarensWeb.

▶ A remote mapping associates an IP address with a subdomain name. For example, suppose you're using the Windows Live Custom Domains service and your domain name is ourfamily.homeserver.com. You can use the hosts file to map an IP address to a subdomain name, such as photos.ourfamily.homeserver.com or karen.ourfamily.homeserver.com.

NOTE

It's worth pointing out here that this technique of modifying the hosts file is only viable for the computers on your network. Obviously, you can't expect anyone else trying to access your site from the Internet to modify their hosts file.

Follow these steps to open the hosts file on non-Windows 7 and non-Vista computers:

1. Select Start, Run (or press Windows Logo+R) to open the Run dialog box.

2. Type the following command in the Open text box:

   notepad %systemroot%\System32\drivers\etc\hosts

3. Click OK. The hosts file opens in Notepad.

Windows 7 and Vista require elevated permissions to edit any file in the %SystemRoot% folder or any of its subfolders. Therefore, you need to follow these steps to open hosts in Notepad:

1. Select Start, All Programs, Accessories.

2. Right-click Command Prompt, and then click Run as Administrator.

3. Enter your UAC credentials to continue.

4. At the command prompt, type the following:

```
notepad %systemroot%\system32\drivers\etc\hosts
```

5. Press Enter. The `hosts` file opens in Notepad.

With the `hosts` file open, start a new line at the end of the file. Then enter the mapping using the following general format:

```
IP    hostname
```

Here, replace *IP* with the address you assigned to your website, and replace *hostname* with the hostname you want to associate with the IP address. In the following example, I've assigned both a local name and a subdomain name to 192.168.1.253:

```
192.168.0.253    photos
192.168.0.253    photos.ourfamily.homeserver.com
```

Figure 12.11 shows the website from Figure 12.10 being accessed using the local hostname as the address (`http://photos`).

FIGURE 12.11   After you map an IP address to a hostname using the `hosts` file, you can access the website using the hostname.

Creating a New Website Using a Different Port

For IIS, the TCP port is the communications channel that gets set up between the web browser and the web server. The traditional port used for the HTTP protocol is port 80, and that's the port used by the Windows Home Server default website and by any website you create using a different IP address, as described in the previous section. However, you don't have to use port 80. In fact, you can host multiple websites on a single server by assigning each of those websites a different port.

To access a site on a different port, you specify the port number in the address, after the host or domain name, as in the following general case:

```
http://server:port
```

Here, *server* is the hostname or domain name of the website, and *port* is the port number. In most cases, the *server* name is the same as the name you use to access the default site on port 80. In Windows Home Server, this means you specify the name of the server. For example, suppose your Windows Home Server PC is named SERVER, and you set up a new website and assign it to port 81. Then to access that site, you'd use the following address:

`http://server:81`

Similarly, if you have a Windows Live Custom Domains name of
`ourfamily.homeserver.com`, you can access a website on port 81 as follows:

`http://ourfamily.homeserver.com:81`

Note, too, that you can also use an IP address instead of the host or domain name, which means you can set up a website that uses a different IP address *and* a different port. For example, here's the address you'd use to access a website using IP address 192.168.0.253 and port 81:

`http://192.168.0.253:81`

NOTE

It's traditional to use HTTP ports that begin with the number 8. For example, because IIS already uses ports 80 and 88, you can use 81 to 87, and 89; 8080 is a commonly used custom HTTP port number. For a complete list of ports used by Windows Server systems, Microsoft offers an Excel workbook that you can download. Go to the Microsoft Download Center (www.microsoft.com/downloads/en/default.aspx), and search for "Port Requirements for Microsoft Windows Server System."

You can also get information on the ports used by Windows Home Server using the Port Reporter tool. For information and a download link, see the following Microsoft Knowledge Base article at support.microsoft.com/kb/837243.

Creating a Website Using a Different Port

Here are the steps to follow to create a website that uses a different port number:

1. In IIS Manager, open the *SERVER*, Web Sites branch (where *SERVER* is the name of your Windows Home Server PC).
2. Select Action, New, Web Site. IIS Manager launches the Web Site Creation Wizard.
3. Click Next. The wizard asks you to enter a description for the website. The description is the name that appears in IIS Manager, within the Web Sites branch.
4. Type the description and then click Next. The wizard displays the IP Address and Port Settings dialog box.
5. In the Enter the IP Address to Use for This Site list, select the main IP address assigned to your Windows Home Server PC. Leave the TCP Port This Web Site Should Use values as is.
6. Enter a new value in the TCP Port This Web Site Should Use text box, as shown in Figure 12.12.
7. Click Next. The wizard prompts you to specify the path to the site's home folder.

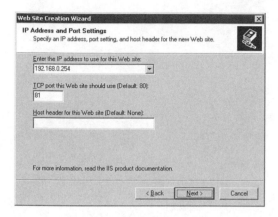

FIGURE 12.12   Type a new value in the TCP Port This Web Site Should Use text box.

8. Either type the full pathname (drive and folders) in the Path text box, or click Browse and use the Browse for Folder dialog box to either select the folder or create a new folder.

9. If you don't want to allow anonymous users to view the website, deactivate the Allow Anonymous Access to This Web Site check box. Click Next.

10. Activate the check boxes for the permissions you want to apply to the new folder (Read, Run Scripts, Execute, Write, or Browse; see "Adding a Folder Using the Virtual Directory Creation Wizard," earlier in this chapter), and then click Next.

11. Click Finish. IIS Manager adds the new site to the Web Sites branch.

From here, add content to the folder you specified in step 7, including a file that uses one of the IIS default names.

Adding a Firewall Exception for the Website Port

As things stand now, your new website will work properly when you access it using a web browser running on the Windows Home Server PC. If you try to access the site on any other computer (or from a location outside your network), you get an error message.

The problem is that the Windows Firewall on Windows Home Server hasn't been configured to allow data traffic using the port you assigned to your new website. For your site to work from any remote location, you need to set up an exception for the port in Windows Firewall. Here are the steps to follow:

1. Log on to Windows Home Server.

2. Select Start, Control Panel, Windows Firewall.

3. Display the Exceptions tab.

4. Click Add Port to display the Add a Port dialog box.

5. In the Name text box, type **TCP Port** *n*, where *n* is the port number you assigned to your website.

6. In the Port Number text box, type the port you assigned to the site.

7. Make sure the TCP option is activated. Figure 12.13 shows the dialog box set up to allow traffic on port 81.

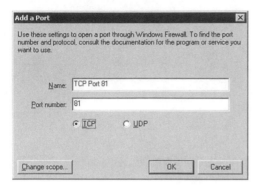

FIGURE 12.13 Configure Windows Firewall on Windows Home Server to allow traffic on the port you assigned to your new website.

8. Click Change Scope to display the Change Scope dialog box.

9. You have three choices:

   ▶ If you want to be able to access this website from the Internet, leave the Any Computer option activated.

   ▶ If you only want computers on your network to access the website, activate the My Network (Subnet) Only option.

   ▶ If you only want specific IP addresses to access the website, activate the Custom List option and use the text box to enter the IP addresses, separated by commas.

10. Click OK to return to the Add a Port dialog box.

11. Click OK.

You can now access the site on port 81, as shown in Figure 12.14.

FIGURE 12.14 With the Windows Firewall exception in place on Windows Home Server, you can now access the site on the different port.

Forwarding the Port in Your Router

In the previous section, you may have set up the Windows Firewall port exception with the Any Computer scope to allow Internet access to your new website. However, users still can't access the site because your network's router doesn't know that it's supposed to allow data to come through the port you assigned to the website.

To allow traffic on that port, you need to configure the router to forward any data that comes in on that port to the IP address of the Windows Home Server PC. How you do this depends on the router. Figure 12.15 shows the Port Forwarding screen of the Linksys router on my system. In this case, I've forwarded TCP port 81 to the address 192.168.0.254, which is the static IP address of my Windows Home Server. Consult your device documentation for information on configuring port forwarding.

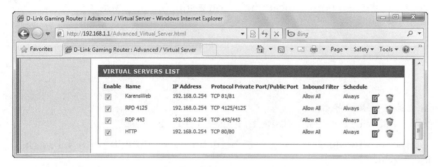

FIGURE 12.15   On your router, you need to forward the port associated with your new website to the Windows Home Server IP address.

Creating a New Website Using a Host Header

When a web browser opens a TCP communications channel with a web server, the HTTP data that gets passed to the server comes with a header that includes information such as the date and a string that identifies the browser. The header also includes a hostname field, which identifies the location of the resource sought by the browser. The host header is usually either a domain name (for an Internet connection) or a network name (for a LAN connection).

Interestingly, it's also possible to simply make up a hostname of your own choosing: KatysBlog, FamilyWeb, or whatever. You can then create a new website and use a custom hostname as the identity of your site.

Associating the Host Header with an IP Address

Custom host headers work because you normally map them to an IP address using either a DNS server or a WINS server. However, as you saw earlier (see "Associating the IP Address with a Hostname"), Windows Home Server doesn't support either of these servers.

Fortunately, as before, you can set up the mapping yourself by editing the hosts file, and you can set up both local and remote mappings. Remember that you must edit the hosts file on Windows Home Server and on every computer that you want to give access to the site. (So, as before, this method only really works for your local computers and not for anyone outside of your network.)

You modify the hosts file in the same way that I described in the earlier section. That is, you open the hosts file, start a new line at the end of the file, and then enter the mapping using the following general format:

```
IP    hostheader
```

In this case, you replace *IP* with the IP address of your Windows Home Server PC, and you replace *hostheader* with the host header name you want to use for the website. In the following example, I've assigned both a local name and a subdomain name to 192.168.0.254:

```
192.168.0.254    katysblog
192.168.0.254    katysblog.ourfamily.homeserver.com
```

Creating a Website Using a Host Header

Here are the steps to follow to create a website that uses a host header:

1. In IIS Manager, open the SERVER, Web Sites branch (where SERVER is the name of your Windows Home Server PC).

2. Select Action, New, Web Site. IIS Manager launches the Web Site Creation Wizard.

3. Click Next. The wizard asks you to enter a description for the website. The description is the name that appears in IIS Manager, within the Web Sites branch.

4. Type the description and then click Next. The wizard displays the IP Address and Port Settings dialog box.

5. In the Enter the IP Address to Use for This Site list, select the main IP address assigned to your Windows Home Server PC. Leave the TCP Port This Web Site Should Use values as is.

6. Use the Host Header for This Web Site text box to type the host header, as shown in Figure 12.16.

7. Click Next. The wizard prompts you to specify the path to the site's home folder.

8. Either type the full pathname (drive and folders) in the Path text box, or click Browse and use the Browse for Folder dialog box to either select the folder or create a new folder.

9. If you don't want to allow anonymous users to view the website, deactivate the Allow Anonymous Access to This Web Site check box. Click Next.

10. Activate the check boxes for the permissions you want to apply to the new folder (Read, Run Scripts, Execute, Write, or Browse; see "Adding a Folder Using the Virtual Directory Creation Wizard," earlier in this chapter), and then click Next.

11. Click Finish. IIS Manager adds the new site to the Web Sites branch.

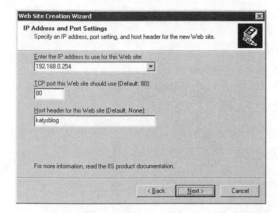

FIGURE 12.16   Type the host header in the Host Header for This Web Site text box.

From here, add content to the folder you specified in step 7, including a file that uses one of the IIS default names. Figure 12.17 shows Internet Explorer displaying a new website using the host header katysblog (http://katysblog).

FIGURE 12.17   A website accessed using a host header name.

Configuring a Website

After you've set up one or more websites—either by adding folders to the Windows Home Server default website or by creating your own websites using the IIS Manager—you may need to adjust certain site properties. For example, you may need to change the website identification (IP address, port number, or host header), modify the website location, adjust the site permissions, and so on. All of these options and many more are available using the website's property sheet. The next few sections take you through some of the more common and useful properties.

Modifying the Website Identity

If you've added your own website to IIS, you may need to adjust the site identity. For example, you may need to specify another IP address, a new port number, a different host header, or any combination of these. Here are the steps to follow:

1. Log on to Windows Home Server and launch IIS Manager.

2. Open the *SERVER*, Web Sites branch (where *SERVER* is the name of your Windows Home Server PC).

3. Click the website you want to work with.

4. Select Action, Properties, or click the Properties button in the toolbar. (You can also right-click the website and then click Properties.) The website's property sheet appears.

5. Display the Web Site tab, shown in Figure 12.18.

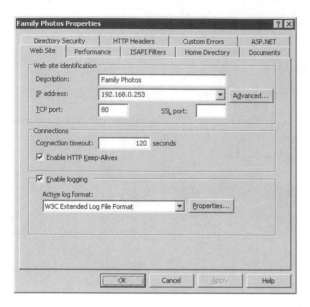

FIGURE 12.18   In the website's property sheet, use the Web Site tab to modify the site's identity.

6. Use one or more of the following techniques to modify the website identity:

   ▶ To change the site's IP address, use the IP Address list to select a different address that has been assigned to Windows Home Server. (See "Assigning an Additional IP Address to Windows Home Server," earlier in this chapter.)

   ▶ To change the site's port, use the TCP Port text box to specify a different port number.

CAUTION

If you assign the site a new port, you also need to set up a Windows Firewall exception on Windows Home Server to allow data through that port; see "Adding a Firewall Exception for the Website Port," earlier in this chapter. If you or others will be accessing the site from the Internet, be sure to configure your router to forward the port to the site's IP address; see "Forwarding the Port in Your Router," earlier in this chapter.

► To change the site's host header, click Advanced to open the Advanced Web Site Identification dialog box. Click the current identity and then click Edit to open the Add/Edit Web Site Identification dialog box, shown in Figure 12.19. Type the new host header in the Host Header Value text box, click OK, and then click OK again to return to the site's property sheet.

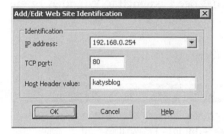

FIGURE 12.19   Use the Add/Edit Web Site Identification dialog box to change a site's host header.

CAUTION

If you give the site a new host header, you must modify the hosts file to map the host header to the site's IP address; see "Associating the Host Header with an IP Address," earlier in this chapter

---

7. Click OK to put the new identity into effect.

Giving a Website Multiple Identities

There's no rule that says a website must use only a single identity. In fact, you can assign as many separate identities as you like to a single website. These identities can be any combination of IP address, TCP port, and host header, although each combination must be unique.

Why use multiple identities for a single website? One common reason is that you want to change the site's current identity, but you don't want to go through the hassle of letting other users know about the change (or reconfiguring their PCs to handle the change). In this case, you can leave the existing identity intact so that users who know that identity can still use it. You can then create a second identity and supply that identity to any new users who need to access the site.

Here are the steps to follow to add another identity to a website:

1. Launch IIS Manager.

2. Open the *SERVER*, Web Sites branch (where *SERVER* is the name of your Windows Home Server PC).

3. Click the website you want to work with.

4. Select Action, Properties, or click the Properties button in the toolbar. (You can also right-click the website and then click Properties.) The website's property sheet appears.

5. Display the Web Site tab.

6. Click Advanced to open the Advanced Web Site Identification dialog box.

7. Click Add to open the Add/Edit Web Site Identification dialog box.

8. Use the IP Address list to select an address that has been assigned to Windows Home Server. (See "Assigning an Additional IP Address to Windows Home Server," earlier in this chapter.)

9. Use the TCP Port text box to specify a port number.

> **CAUTION**
>
> If you specify a new TCP port, be sure to configure Windows Firewall on the Windows Home Server PC to allow traffic through that port; see "Adding a Firewall Exception for the Website Port," earlier in this chapter. If you want to access the site from the Internet, be sure to forward the port to the site's IP address in your router; see "Forwarding the Port in Your Router," earlier in this chapter.

10. Use the Host Header Value text box to type the host header.

> **CAUTION**
>
> If you specify a new host header, be sure to edit the hosts file to map the host header to the IP address you specified in step 8; see "Associating the Host Header with an IP Address," earlier in this chapter.

11. Click OK to return to the Advanced Web Site Identification dialog box. IIS Manager adds the new identity to the Multiple Identities for This Web Site list. Figure 12.20 shows a site with several identities.

12. Click OK to return to the site's property sheet.

13. Click OK.

Changing the Website Location and Permissions

The home folder (or home directory, as IIS calls it) that you specified when you created a website isn't necessarily permanent. You may decide to move a website to a different home folder, or you may decide to rename the existing folder. In either case, you must use IIS Manager to specify the new home folder. While you're at it, you can also modify the IIS permissions on that folder. Here are the steps to follow:

1. Launch IIS Manager.

2. Open the *SERVER*, Web Sites branch (where *SERVER* is the name of your Windows Home Server PC).

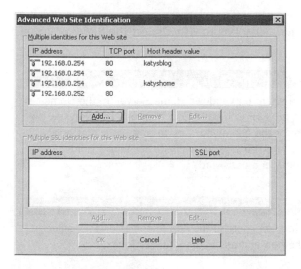

FIGURE 12.20   You can configure a website with multiple identities.

3. Click the website you want to work with.

4. Select Action, Properties, or click the Properties button in the toolbar. (You can also right-click the website and then click Properties.) The website's property sheet appears.

5. Display the Home Directory tab, shown in Figure 12.21.

FIGURE 12.21   Use the Home Directory tab to change the site's home folder and its IIS permissions.

6. Either type the full pathname (drive and folders) in the Local Path text box, or click Browse and use the Browse for Folder dialog box to either select the folder or create a new folder.

7. Set the folder's IIS permissions by activating or deactivating the following check boxes:

Script Source Access	Allows each user to view the source code for scripts such as ASP scripts.
Read	Allows each user to view and download files within the folder. This is the default permission.
Write	Allows each user to upload files to the folder and to modify files within the folder. Obviously, you only want to apply this potentially destructive permission in the rarest circumstances.
Directory Browsing	Allows each user to view the contents of the directory. This only occurs if there is no file in the folder that uses one of the default names mentioned earlier.
Log Visits	Grants permission for IIS to record visits to the folder in a log file.
Index This Resource	Grants permission for the Microsoft Indexing Service to include this folder in the site's full-text index.

8. In the Execute Permissions list, you have three choices:

None	Users can't run scripts or executable files in the folder.
Scripts Only	Allows each user to open files that contain scripts, such as ASP scripts or Perl files.
Scripts and Executables	Allows each user to also run programs in the folder, such as Common Gateway Interface (CGI) applications

9. Click OK.

Setting the Default Content Page

A normal website URL looks like the following:

```
http://name/folder/file
```

Here, *name* is a domain name or hostname, *folder* is a folder path, and *file* is the filename of the web page or other resource. Here's an example:

```
http://server/photos/default.htm
```

Intriguingly, you can view the same web page by entering the following address into the browser:

```
http://server/photos/
```

This works because IIS defines default.htm as one of its default content page filenames. Here are the others:

```
default.asp
index.htm
default.aspx
```

This means that as long as a folder contains a file that uses one of these names, you can view the corresponding page without specifying the filename in the URL.

Note, too, that these default content pages have an assigned priority, with default.htm having the highest priority, followed by default.asp, then index.htm, and finally default.aspx. This priority defines the order in which IIS looks for and displays the default content pages. That is, IIS first looks for default.htm; if that file doesn't exist in a folder, IIS next looks for default.asp, and so on.

For your own websites, you can add new content pages (for example, index.htm and index.asp), remove existing content pages, and change the priority of the content pages. Here are the steps to follow:

1. Launch IIS Manager.
2. Open the *SERVER*, Web Sites branch (where *SERVER* is the name of your Windows Home Server PC).
3. Click the website you want to work with.
4. Select Action, Properties, or click the Properties button in the toolbar. (You can also right-click the website and then click Properties.) The website's property sheet appears.
5. Display the Documents tab, shown in Figure 12.22.

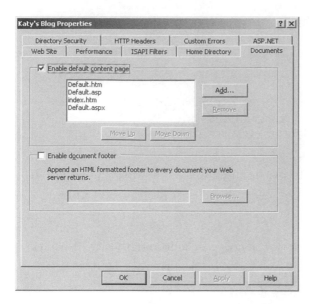

FIGURE 12.22   Use the Documents tab to add, remove, and reorder a site's default content pages.

NOTE

For the default Windows Home Server website, the Enable Default Content Page list shows an HTML file named iisstart.htm. This is an "Under Construction" page, and it appears if none of the files above it in the list are present in the root of the virtual folder or website. If you want to customize this file, you can find it in the C:\Inetpub\wwwroot folder.

TIP

Using a default content page is usually a good idea because it enables users to access your site without knowing the name of any file. However, for security reasons, you might want to allow access to the site only to users who know a specific filename on the site (for example, through a URL that you've provided). In that case, you have two choices: either don't include a file that uses one of the default content page names, or deactivate the Enable Default Content Page check box. Either way, be sure to deny directory browsing permission to all users: In the Home Directory tab, make sure the Directory Browsing check box is deactivated.

6. To specify a new default content page, click Add to open the Add Content Page dialog box, type the filename, and then click OK. IIS Manager adds the new filename to the Enable Default Content Page list.

7. To delete a default content page, select it in the Enable Default Content Page list and click Remove.

8. To change the default content page priority order, click the content page you want to work with and then click either Move Up or Move Down.

NOTE

While you're in the Documents tab, you can also activate the Enable Document Footer check box. This enables you to specify an HTML file that IIS automatically appends to the bottom of every web page that it serves. A footer is an excellent way to display certain data consistently and globally on your site. For example, you can use a footer to display a copyright notice or some links common to all pages. Click the Browse button to specify the HTML file that contains the code you want to use as the footer

9. Click OK to put the new settings into effect.

Disabling Anonymous Access

As you saw earlier, when you create a new site, IIS Manager asks if you want to allow anonymous access to the site, and that option is activated by default. This is desirable for most websites because it enables users to most easily access the site content. IIS provides anonymous access via the IUSR_*SERVER* account (where *SERVER* is the name of the Windows Home Server computer), which is a member of the Guest security group, and so has read-only access to the site.

However, you might have a site with content that you want to restrict to people who have user accounts on Windows Home Server. In that case, you need to disable anonymous access for the website and switch to Windows authentication, which means IIS prompts each user for a username and password before allowing access to the site.

Follow these steps to disable anonymous access:

1. Launch IIS Manager.

2. Open the *SERVER*, Web Sites branch (where *SERVER* is the name of your Windows Home Server PC).

3. Click the website you want to work with.

4. Select Action, Properties, or click the Properties button in the toolbar. (You can also right-click the website and then click Properties.) The website's property sheet appears.

5. Display the Directory Security tab.

6. In the Authentication and Access Control group, click Edit to open the Authentication Methods dialog box.

7. Deactivate the Enable Anonymous Access check box.

8. Activate the Integrated Windows Authentication check box, as shown in Figure 12.23.

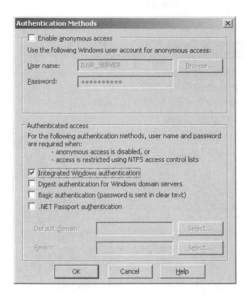

FIGURE 12.23   To secure a website, disable anonymous access and enable Integrated Windows Authentication.

9. Click OK to return to the site's property sheet.

10. Click OK to put the new settings into effect.

TIP

Switching to integrated Windows authentication means that any user with a valid account on Windows Home Server can access the website. What if there are one or more users with Windows Home Server accounts that you do *not* want to view the website? In that case, you must adjust the security of the website's home folder directly. Use Windows Explorer to display the website's home folder, right-click the folder, and then click Sharing and Security. In the Security tab, click Add, type the name of the user, and then click OK. Select the user, and then activate the Full Control check box in the Deny column. This tells Windows Home Server not to allow that user to view the folder, thus barring the user from viewing the website.

> **TIP**
>
> Another way to deny access to your website is to block access based on either an IP address or a computer name. Follow steps 1 to 5 in this section to display the Directory Security tab. In the IP Address and Domain Name Restrictions group, click Edit, and then click Add to open the Deny Access dialog box. (If you see the Grant Access dialog box, instead, click Cancel, click the Granted Access option, and then click Add.) If you know the IP address of the computer you want to deny and that address is static, select the Single Computer option and enter the IP address; if you know the network name of the computer you want to deny, select the Domain Name option and enter the domain name. Click OK in the open dialog boxes.

Adding Site Links to the Home and Remote Access Pages

When you use Internet Explorer to log on to Windows Home Server's Remote Access page, the Home tab normally displays two sections—Computers and Shared Folders—and you use the associated links to display, respectively, a list of computers on the Windows Home Server network and a list of shared folders on the server.

However, it's also possible to customize the Home tab with links to your own Windows Home Server websites. After you customize the page, you end up with a new Websites section that contains the site links. Best of all, if your custom website requires authentication, your users don't need to authenticate themselves twice. That is, using Windows Home Server's Unified Sign On feature, after a user successfully logs on to the Remote Access page, Windows Home Server will then pass along that user's credentials to your secure website.

Windows Home Server also enables you to add custom links to the Home page (http://server/home), which means you can access links before logging on to the Remote Access pages.

You add links to the Home and Remote Access pages by modifying a couple of XML files, each called WebSites.xml. Here are the steps to follow:

1. Use Windows Explorer to open the folder that corresponds to the page you want to modify:

   ▶ To add site links to the Home page, open the following folder:

   `%SystemDrive%\InetPub\home`

   ▶ To add site links to the Remote Access page's Home tab, open the following folder:

   `%SystemDrive%\InetPub\remote`

2. In that folder, right-click WebSites.xml and then click Open With.

3. What you do next depends on whether you've edited an XML file in Notepad previously on Windows Home Server:

   ▶ If you've never edited an XML file, the Open With dialog box appears. Click Notepad, make sure the Always Use the Selected Program to Open This Kind of File check box is deactivated, and then click OK.

   ▶ If you've previously edited an XML file in Notepad, a submenu appears. Click Notepad.

4. The `WebSites.xml` file shows two example sites. Ignore those, and start a new link above the `</WebSites>` tag.

5. Type the tags shown here, and make your replacements for the following placeholders:

LinkText   The text that appears in the Remote Access page's new Web Sites section. This is the link text that users will click to access your site.

folder   This is the name of the virtual root folder that contains your site's pages.

image   This is the name of a 16×16 image that serves as your site's icon. This icon appears beside the link on the Remote Access page:

```
<WebSite name="LinkText" uri="/folder" imageUrl="/folder/image"
➥<absolute="false">
   </WebSite>
```

6. If you also want to include a link to an external site, start a new line and type the tags shown here, making your replacements for the following placeholders:

LinkText   The text that appears in the Remote Access page's Web Sites section. This is the link text that users will click to access the external site.

url   This is the address of the external site.

image   This is the name of a 16×16 image that serves as your site's icon. This icon appears beside the link on the Remote Access page:

```
<WebSite name="LinkText" uri="http://url" imageUrl="http://url/image"
<absolute="true">
</WebSite>
```

7. Save the file and close Notepad.

Figure 12.24 shows an example `WebSites.xml` file with one internal link, an external link to a local website that uses a different server IP address, and another external link to a third-party website. Figure 12.25 shows the Home tab of the Remote Access home page. The custom links appear in the Web Sites section.

FIGURE 12.24 The Remote Access `WebSites.xml` file modified with an internal and an external website.

FIGURE 12.25 Windows Home Server's Remote Access home page displaying the two links shown in Figure 12.24.

From Here

▶ To learn the details on applying a static IP address to the server, **see** "Configuring Windows Home Server with a Static IP Address," **P. 9**.

▶ For more information on connecting to Windows Home Server's home site and Remote Access site, **see** "Displaying the Remote Access Home Page," **P. 188**.

▶ You can also use Windows Home Server to host a SharePoint website; **see** Chapter 13, "Running a SharePoint Site on Windows Home Server."

Running a SharePoint Site on Windows Home Server

One of the major (but hidden) advantages you get with Windows Home Server is the ability to use software that *only* installs and runs on Windows Server 2003. Now, granted, most such software programs and services are high-end tools for network administrators, IT personnel, and developers. However, a few powerful programs are useful for home networks as well as corporate shops. This chapter looks at one of the best examples of such software: Windows SharePoint Services 3.0, which is normally used as a powerful and robust tool for business collaboration. However, SharePoint is loaded with features for sharing data among family members: picture libraries, calendars, contact lists, web page link lists, and more. You can also use SharePoint to set up a blog, run a wiki, and plan an upcoming social event.

As you see in this chapter, it takes a few steps to ensure that Windows Home Server and SharePoint get along well together, but after that's done, the full power of SharePoint is at your disposal. This chapter introduces you to SharePoint and shows you at least a bit of what you can do with it. However, SharePoint is a massive program with tons of features. As a result, this chapter can only really scratch the SharePoint surface. Fortunately, the SharePoint interface is intuitive and easy to use, so after you get up to speed with this chapter's techniques, you shouldn't have trouble figuring out the rest.

Installing and Configuring Windows SharePoint Services

SharePoint Services 3.0 is not difficult to install and configure, but it does break (temporarily) the default Windows Home Server website. The next few sections take you through the steps for downloading, installing, and configuring SharePoint Services 3.0, including how to get the Windows Home Server default website back on its feet.

> **NOTE**
>
> As I was writing this edition of the book, Microsoft was preparing a SharePoint update called Windows SharePoint Services 2010 (or sometimes, Windows SharePoint Services 4.0). This new version of SharePoint requires Windows Server 2008, so it's not compatible with Windows Home Server. I expect that Microsoft will eventually release a version of Windows Home Server that sits on Windows Server 2008, so you'll eventually be able to use the new version of SharePoint. For now, you can stick with SharePoint Services 3.0.

Downloading and Installing SharePoint Services 3.0

To download Windows SharePoint Services, first head for the Microsoft site at www.microsoft.com/sharepoint/default.mspx. In the Downloads section, click the Windows SharePoint Service link, and then follow the download links for the 32-bit version Windows SharePoint Services 3.0. Follow these steps to install SharePoint Services on Windows Home Server:

1. Launch the file that you downloaded and click Run when prompted. After a few moments, the license agreement appears.
2. Click I Accept the Terms of This Agreement and then click Continue. SharePoint asks you to choose the installation you want.
3. Click Advanced.
4. In the Server Type tab, shown in Figure 13.1, make sure the Stand-Alone option is selected.
5. Click Install Now. Windows Home Server installs SharePoint Services 3.0.
6. When the install is complete, leave the Run the SharePoint Products and Technologies Configuration Wizard Now check box activated, and then click Close.

Running the Initial SharePoint Services 3.0 Configuration

When you click the Close button to end the installation, SharePoint launches the Configuration Wizard. This wizard runs through a series of 10 configuration tasks that get SharePoint Services ready to run. Follow these steps to perform this configuration:

1. Click Next. The wizard displays a list of services and asks if these services can be restarted, if necessary, during the configuration.

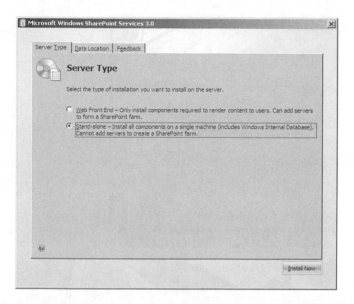

FIGURE 13.1   Make sure you install SharePoint as a stand-alone server.

2. Click Yes. The wizard then runs through the configuration tasks, which takes several minutes.

3. When the configuration is complete, click Finish. SharePoint then attempts to load the default site (http://*server*, where *server* is the name of your Windows Home Server).

4. If you see the Connect to Server dialog box, click Cancel.

5. Close the web browser window.

Creating a New SharePoint Web Application

During the initial SharePoint configuration, two things happen that cause the Windows Home Server default website to go offline and be replaced by the SharePoint default website:

▶ SharePoint stops the Windows Home Server default website.

▶ SharePoint creates its own default website and configures it to use TCP port 80.

This means that the http://*server* now loads the SharePoint default site instead of the Windows Home Server default site, as shown in Figure 13.2.

To fix this, you can't simply configure the default SharePoint site to use a different port or IP address, as you might expect. Instead, the solution is to create a new SharePoint web application that runs through a TCP port other than port 80. (In SharePoint, a *web application* is an object that acts as a container for one or more SharePoint sites.) You then shut down the default SharePoint site and restart the Windows Home Server default site.

For now, here are the steps to create a new SharePoint web application:

1. Select Start, Control Panel, Administrative Tools, SharePoint 3.0 Central Administration. Windows Home Server prompts you to log on.

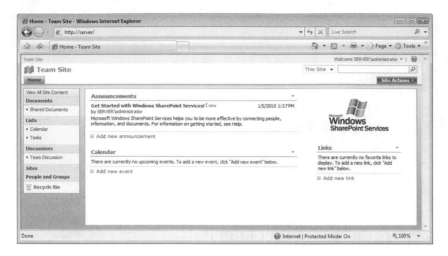

FIGURE 13.2 SharePoint takes over the http://server site.

2. Type your Administrator account username and password, and then click OK. The SharePoint Central Administration site appears, as shown in Figure 13.3. (Note that in the address of this site, the port number you see will be different than the one shown in Figure 13.3 because the port number is assigned randomly at setup.)

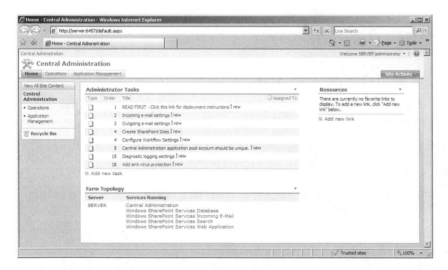

FIGURE 13.3 You use the Central Administration site to configure SharePoint.

3. Click the Application Management tab.

4. Click the Create or Extend Web Application link. SharePoint displays the Create or Extend Web Application page.

5. Click Create a New Web Application. SharePoint loads the Create New Web Application page, shown in Figure 13.4.

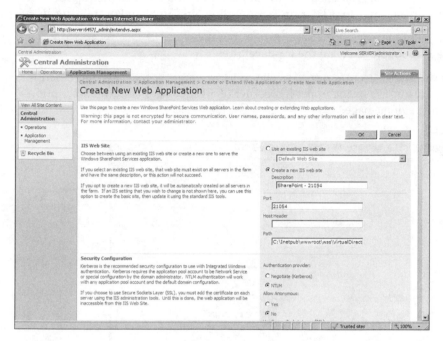

FIGURE 13.4   Use the Create New Web Application page to set up your new SharePoint web application.

6. For the most part, you can (and should) leave the settings as is on this page. If you want, you can make a few tweaks:

▶ **Description**—This is the name that appears in IIS Manager's list of websites, so you can change this to whatever you want.

▶ **Port**—Enter any unused port that you prefer to use.

▶ **Select Windows SharePoint Services Search Server**—Choose your Windows Home Server computer here.

7. In the Application Pool section, click the Predefined option (and leave Network Service chosen in the list).

8. Click OK. SharePoint creates your new site, which might take a minute or two. When that's done, you see the Application Created page.

9. Click the Create Site Collection link to open the Create Site Collection page. You learn how to fill in this page in the next section.

Creating a Top-Level SharePoint Site

With the new SharePoint web application created, your next task is to add a top-level SharePoint site—called a *site collection*—to the application. You can use the top-level site by itself, or you can add sites to it later on (see "Adding Sites to SharePoint," later in this chapter).

Here are the steps to follow to create the top-level site:

1. In the Create Site Collection page (see Figure 13.5), enter the site title and description. The title appears in the upper-left corner of all site pages, and the description appears on the home page.

FIGURE 13.5   Use the Create Site Collection page to set up your new SharePoint site.

2. In the Web Site Address section, use the URL list to define the path used for new sites that you add to the site collection. You have two choices:

   ▶ /—Choose this path if you won't be adding other sites to the collection, or if you want to place all new sites in the root folder of the site collection. For example, if your SharePoint web application address is http://server:21054/, and you later add a site that uses a folder named wedding, that site's URL will be http://server:21054/wedding/.

   ▶ /**sites**/—Choose this path if you want to place all new sites in the sites subfolder of the site collection. SharePoint adds an extra text box so that you can add a folder name for the site collection. If your SharePoint web application address is `http://server:21054/` and you specify the site collection folder name as main, your site's URL will be `http://server:21054/sites/main/`.

TIP

You might prefer to store some or all of your SharePoint sites in a subfolder other than sites. For example, if you'll be creating several blogs, you might want to set up a blogs subfolder. To specify another subfolder, click the Define Managed Paths link to open the Define Managed Paths page. In the Add a New Path section, type / followed by the folder name, click OK, and then click the Back button until you return to the Create Site Collection page. To see the new folder in the URL list, you need to refresh the page. (If you made a long entry in the Description box, copy it before refreshing the page; otherwise, you'll lose the text and have to retype it.)

---

3. In the Template Selection section, select either the Collaboration or Meetings tab, and then select the template you want to use as a starting point for the site. When you click a template, a description of the template appears in the Template Selection section, as shown in Figure 13.6. If you're not sure which template to use, a good all-purpose choice is the Team Site template.

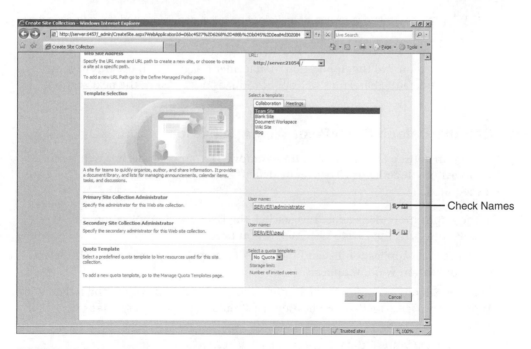

FIGURE 13.6   Select the template you want to use as a starting point for your site.

4. In the Primary Site Collection Administrator section, type the name of the user who will be the main administrator of the site collection. Click the Check Names icon to ensure that you've entered an existing username.

5. (Optional) If you want to designate a second user as an administrator of the site collection, in the Secondary Site Collection Administrator section, type the name of the user. (Again, click Check Names to ensure that you've entered an existing username.)

6. Click OK to create the site collection. When the operation is complete, SharePoint displays the Top-Level Site Successfully Created page, which includes a link to the site, as shown in Figure 13.7.

FIGURE 13.7   You see this page when SharePoint has successfully created the site collection.

7. Click OK to return to the Application Management page. You'll use this page to remove the default SharePoint web application, as described in the next section.

Deleting the Default SharePoint Web Application

The next step in getting SharePoint and the Windows Home Server default website to operate successfully together is to delete the default SharePoint web application. Here are the steps required:

1. In the Application Management page, click the Delete Web Application link. SharePoint opens the Delete Web Application page.

2. Click the Web Application list and then click Change Web Application. The Select Web Application window appears.

3. Click the SharePoint - 80 web application. SharePoint returns you to the Delete Web Application page. The Web Application list should now show http://server/, as it does in Figure 13.8.

4. In the Delete Content Databases option, click Yes.

5. In the Delete IIS Web Sites option, click Yes.

6. Click Delete. SharePoint asks you to confirm.

7. Click OK. SharePoint deletes the default site and its content.

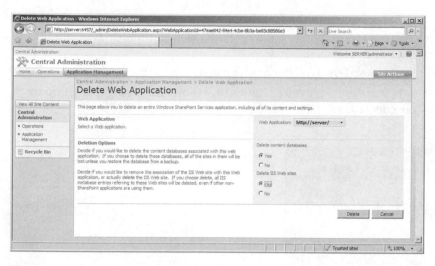

FIGURE 13.8　Before deleting, make sure the Web Application list shows `http://server/`.

Restarting the Windows Home Server Default Website

With SharePoint's default site deleted, you can now restart the Windows Home Server default site. Follow these steps:

1. Select Start, Control Panel, Administrative Tools, Internet Information Server (IIS) Manager.

2. Open the *SERVER*, Web Sites branch (where *SERVER* is the name of your Windows Home Server PC).

3. Click Default Web Site.

4. Select Action, Start, or click the Start button. IIS Manager restarts the Windows Home Server default website.

Adding a Firewall Exception for the SharePoint Web Application Port

You can access your new SharePoint web application on Windows Home Server, but you won't be able to access it from a client computer. The problem is that Windows Home Server's firewall won't let traffic through on the TCP port associated with the web application. To fix this, you must add an exception for the port in Windows Firewall. Here are the steps to follow:

1. Log on to Windows Home Server.

2. Select Start, Control Panel, Windows Firewall.

3. Display the Exceptions tab.

4. Click Add Port to display the Add a Port dialog box.

5. In the Name text box, type **TCP Port** *n*, where *n* is the port number associated with your SharePoint web application.

6. In the Port Number text box, type the port you assigned to the site.

7. Make sure the TCP option is activated. Figure 13.9 shows the dialog box set up to allow traffic on port 21054.

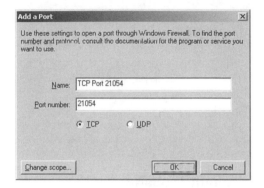

FIGURE 13.9   Set up a Windows Firewall exception to allow traffic on the TCP port associated with your SharePoint web application.

8. Click Change Scope to display the Change Scope dialog box.

9. You have three choices:

   ▶ If you want to be able to access your SharePoint site from the Internet, leave the Any Computer option activated.

   ▶ If you only want computers on your network to access the SharePoint site, activate the My Network (Subnet) Only option.

   ▶ If you only want specific IP addresses to access the SharePoint site, activate the Custom List option and use the text box to enter the IP addresses, separated by commas.

10. Click OK to return to the Add a Port dialog box.

11. Click OK.

Forwarding the SharePoint Port in Your Router

If you configured the Windows Firewall port exception for your SharePoint web application with the Any Computer scope, Internet users won't be able to access the site because your network's router won't forward data through the port you associated with the web application.

You need to configure the router to forward any data that comes in on that port to the IP address of the Windows Home Server computer. The steps for doing this vary depending on the manufacturer of the router. As an example, Figure 13.10 shows the Port Forwarding screen for a D-Link router. Here, I've forwarded TCP port 21054 to the address 192.168.0.254, which is the static IP address of my Windows Home Server. Consult your device documentation for information on configuring port forwarding.

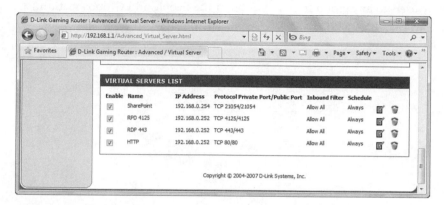

FIGURE 13.10   Configure your network's router to forward the SharePoint web application port to the Windows Home Server IP address.

Adding Users to the Top-Level SharePoint Site

You can now log on to the top-level SharePoint site (as described next in the "Logging On to the Top-Level SharePoint Site" section) using the primary site collection administration account. If you specified a secondary site collection administration account, you can log on to the top-level site under that account, as well. However, if you try to log on using any other Windows Home Server account, you get an Access Denied error.

To solve the problem, you must add users to the top-level SharePoint site. SharePoint enables you to add users to one of the following groups:

▶ **Visitors**—Users in this group have Read permission, which enables them to only view the contents of the site.

▶ **Members**—Users in this group have Contribute permission, which enables them to view, change, add, and delete content.

▶ **Owners**—Users in this group have Full Control permission, which enables them to perform any action on the site, including adding users, changing permissions, and adding sites.

You can also designate a specific permission level for a user: Read, Contribute, Full Control, or Design. (The latter includes the same permissions as the Contribute level but also allows the user to customize the site.)

Here are the steps to follow to add a user to the site:

1. Log on to the top-level SharePoint site using the primary (or secondary) site collection administration account.

2. Click Site Actions and then click Site Settings.

3. In the Site Settings page, click the People and Groups link.

4. Either click a group in the Groups list to see a list of users in that group, or click All People to see a list of all the users on the site. (Note that this step is optional; you can add new users to any group from any page in the People and Groups section.)

5. Click New and then click Add Users to open the site's Add Users page, shown in Figure 13.11.

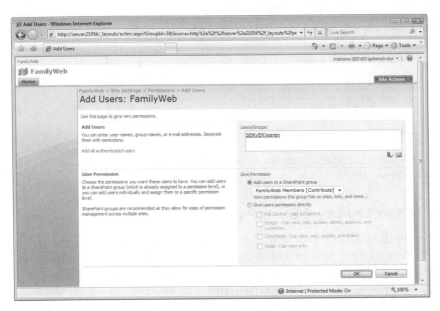

FIGURE 13.11   Use the Add Users page to add users to the SharePoint top-level site.

6. Type the username in the User/Groups box, and then click the Check Name icon to verify the name. (You can also enter the name of a Windows Home Server security group.)

7. Repeat step 6 to specify other users or groups.

TIP

If you have a large number of Windows Home Server user accounts and you want to add them all to the site, you don't have to enter each one by hand. Instead, click the Add All Authenticated Users link. SharePoint adds the NT Authority\Authenticated Users group to the Users/Groups box.

8. In the Give Permission section, you have the following two choices:

▶ **Add Users to a SharePoint Group**—Activate this option and use this list to add the users or groups to a SharePoint group: Visitors, Members, or Owners.

> ▶ **Give Users Permission Directly**—Activate this option and use the check boxes to select the specific permissions you want to apply to the users or groups: Full Control Design, Contribute, or Read.

9. Click OK. SharePoint adds the users or groups to the site.

Logging On to the Top-Level SharePoint Site

With the Windows Firewall exception in place and users added, you can now access the top-level SharePoint site from any network computer by following these steps:

1. Select Start, Internet to launch Internet Explorer.

2. In the address bar, type the URL of the top-level SharePoint site. This is the URL that SharePoint displayed in the Create Site Collection page. (See step 2 in the section "Creating a Top-Level SharePoint Site," earlier in this chapter.) Internet Explorer prompts you to enter your username and password.

3. Type the username and password, and then click OK.

The browser loads the home page of the top-level site. Your username appears in the top-right corner, as shown in Figure 13.12. (Note that the design of your top-level site may be quite different from the one you see in Figure 13.12, depending on the template you chose for the site.)

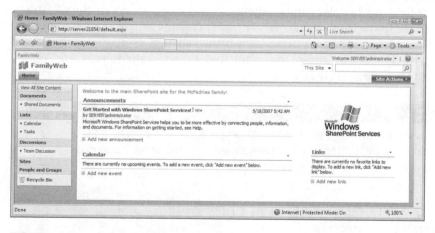

FIGURE 13.12   The home page of a top-level SharePoint site.

Adding Sites to SharePoint

With your SharePoint top-level site in place, you're ready to start using it for sharing, collaborating, and any other tasks you can think of. Before going further, however, you need to decide whether you want a single SharePoint site or multiple sites. SharePoint actually gives you three options:

> ▶ **Single top-level site**—This option means that you add all your content to the top-level site that you just created. Use this setup if your collaboration requirements are

fairly basic. With a single site, you can add content such as a calendar, picture library, discussion boardlists for contacts, announcements, links, web pages, and more. (See "Creating Content for a SharePoint Site," later in this chapter, for the details on adding and working with these SharePoint content types.) In this case, you usually access your SharePoint site using an address of the form `http://server:port/`, where *server* is your Windows Home Server computer name and *port* is the TCP port associated with the SharePoint web application. An example is `http://server:21054/`.

▶ **Multiple top-level sites**—This option means that you create two or more top-level sites, each of which contains different content. Use multiple top-level sites if your collaboration needs are more complex. For example, you might want to create one site for the whole family, separate sites for each of the kids, and another site for your home business. In this case, you access the other top-level sites using an address of the form `http://server:port/sites/folder/`, where *server* is your Windows Home Server computer name, *port* is the TCP port associated with the SharePoint web application, and *folder* is the folder used by the top-level site. An example is `http://server:21054/sites/katysblog/`.

▶ **Single top-level site with subsites**—This option means that you augment the top-level site that you just created with one or more secondary SharePoint sites. Again, this is useful for more elaborate collaboration needs, but navigating between the sites is easier (which I'll explain in a moment). In this case, you access the subsites using an address of the form `http://server:port/folder/`, where *server* is your Windows Home Server computer name, *port* is the TCP port associated with the SharePoint web application, and *folder* is the folder used by the subsite. An example is `http://server:21054/wedding/`.

TIP

If you want to view a SharePoint site on a mobile device such as a handheld PC or smartphone, add `m/` to the URL to see a version suitable for the small screens on most mobile devices. Here are some examples:

`http://server:21054/m/`

`http://server:21054/sites/katysblog/m/`

`http://server:21054/wedding/m/`

In the previous item, I mentioned that using a single top-level site with subsites makes site navigation easier. To see what I mean, you need to know that if you set up multiple top-level sites, the sites can't "see" each other. That is, there's no default method for linking from one site to another. Instead, to navigate to another site, you must enter that site's URL into the browser. This isn't necessarily a bad thing because you (or your family) might *want* to keep the sites separate.

However, when you use a single top-level site with subsites, SharePoint gives you the option of adding links to the subsites in various navigation aids that are part of the top-level site. A good example is the SharePoint Central Administration site, shown earlier in Figure 13.3. Examine the tabs near the top of the page. (This section of the page is called the *top link bar*; see Figure 13.15.) The Home tab represents the top-level Central Administration site, whereas the Operations and Application Management tabs represent subsites within the top-level site. Links to these subsites also appear in Quick Launch, which is on the left side of the home page (again, see Figure 13.15).

Adding a Top-Level Site

Here are the steps to follow to add another top-level site to your SharePoint web application:

1. Select Start, Control Panel, Administrative Tools, SharePoint 3.0 Central Administration. Windows Home Server prompts you to log on.

2. Type your Administrator account username and password, and then click OK to open the SharePoint Central Administration site.

3. Click the Application Management tab.

4. Click the Create Site Collection link to display the Create Site Collection page.

5. Follow the steps I outlined earlier in the "Creating a Top-Level SharePoint Site" section. In this case, when you specify the site URL, you must use the `sites` folder and specify a subfolder for your site. (Again, you can also click Defined Managed Paths to create a folder other than `sites`.)

Adding a Subsite

If you prefer to use a single top-level SharePoint site, follow these steps to add a subsite:

1. Log on to the top-level SharePoint site using the primary (or secondary) site collection administration account.

2. Click Site Actions and then click Create to display the Create page.

3. Under Web Pages, click the Sites and Workspaces link to display the New SharePoint Site page, shown in Figure 13.13.

4. Enter the site title and description.

5. In the Web Site Address section, use the URL Name text box to type the name of the folder you want to use to hold the site's contents. If the name consists of two or more words, separate each word with an underscore (_) instead of a space.

6. Use the Template Selection section to select the template you want to use as a starting point for the site.

7. In the Permissions section (see Figure 13.14), select a User Permissions option:

   ▶ **Use Same Permissions as Parent Site**—Select this option to configure the subsite with the same permissions that are configured on the top-level site.

   ▶ **Use Unique Permissions**—Select this option to configure the secondary site with its own permissions.

8. In the Navigation section, click Yes or No to specify whether you want a link to the subsite to appear in the top-level site's Quick Launch and top link bar.

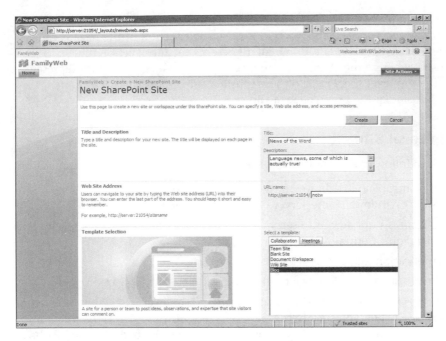

FIGURE 13.13   Use the New SharePoint Site page to set up a subsite.

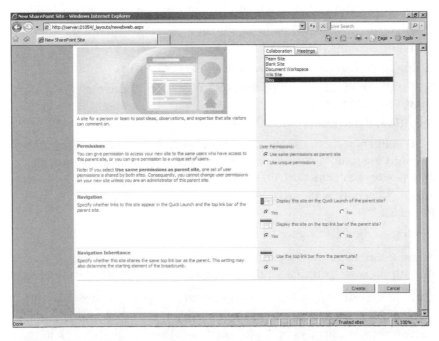

FIGURE 13.14   The rest of the New SharePoint Site page.

9. In the Navigation Inheritance section, click Yes or No to specify whether you want the top-level site's top link bar to remain onscreen when you navigate to the subsite.

10. Click Create to create the subsite.

11. If you selected the Use Unique Permissions option, you see the Set Up Groups for This Site page. To learn how to configure site groups, see "Setting Up Groups for a Site," later in this chapter. Click OK when you're done.

Figure 13.15 shows a top-level site with a subsite added. Note the extra tab in the links bar and the link to the subsite in Quick Launch's Sites section.

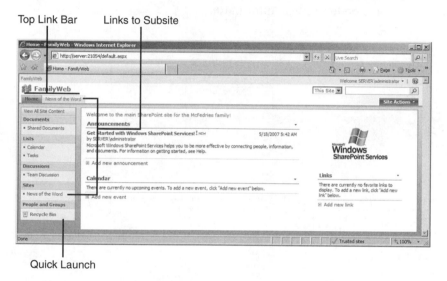

FIGURE 13.15   A top-level site showing links to a subsite.

Working with Site Settings

SharePoint Services 3.0 gives you a tremendous number of settings that you can use to configure almost any aspect of a site. Space limitations prevent me from discussing all of the 30 or so settings, so the next few sections take you through some of the most useful tweaks you can make to a site.

Customizing a Site

The look and feel of a SharePoint site is governed by settings that control the title, the description, the visual theme, the top link bar and Quick Launch, and more. Follow these steps to adjust some or all of these settings:

1. Log on to the top-level SharePoint site as the primary or secondary site administrator, or use an account in the site's Owners group.

> **NOTE**
>
> Logging on as a site administrator or owner is ideal because it gives you access to the full range of customization settings. However, there are also a few aspects of a site that you can customize if you log on as a user with Design permissions (as noted in step 4, which follows).

2. If you want to customize a subsite, navigate to that site.

3. Click Site Actions and then click Site Settings. Figure 13.16 shows the Site Settings page that appears for a top-level site administrator.

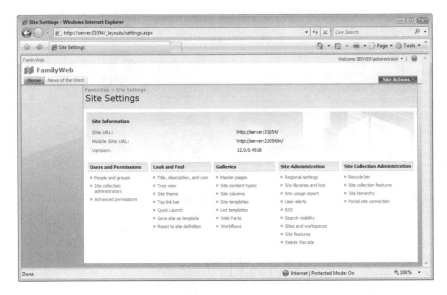

FIGURE 13.16   Use the Site Settings page to customize all aspects of a site.

4. Use the links in the Look and Feel section to customize the site.

The next few sections describe what you can do with each link.

Editing a Site's Title and Description

You specified the site's title and description when you first set up the site, but you're not stuck with the original values if you're tired of them or you feel they no longer reflect the site's content. Follow these steps:

1. In the Site Settings page, click the Title, Description, and Icon link.

2. Use the Title text box to edit the site title.

3. Use the Description text box to edit the site description.

4. Click OK to put the new settings into effect.

Displaying a Custom Site Icon

When you navigate to a site, you see an icon for the site to the left of the site title. This icon is the same for all sites, so you can inject some individuality into a site by specifying a custom icon. The image file (smaller images are better) can reside in a local folder, a shared network folder, or on a website. Here are the steps to follow:

1. In the Site Settings page, click the Title, Description, and Icon link.

2. In the Logo URL and Description section, use the URL text box to enter the address of the image file you want to use as the site's icon. Enter a local pathname, a UNC pathname, or a web URL.

TIP

After you enter the image address, click the Click Here to Test link to open the image in a browser window. If you see the image, you know your address is accurate.

3. Use the Enter a Description text box to type text that describes the image. This text appears when a user points at the image, displays the site with image display turned off in his browser, or views the site using a screen-reading device.

4. Click OK to put the new settings into effect.

Changing a Subsite's Folder

If the name you originally supplied for a subsite's folder is no longer relevant or is too long, you can change it to something more suitable or shorter. Follow these steps:

1. In the Site Settings page for the subsite, click the Title, Description, and Icon link.

2. Use the URL Name text box to enter the new folder name you want to use.

3. Click OK to put the new settings into effect.

Adding a Tree View

A *tree view* is a method of displaying items that have a hierarchical relationship. The topmost item acts as the "trunk" of the tree, second-level items are the main branches, third-level items are subbranches, and so on. For example, the Folders list in Windows Explorer is a tree view, with a drive's root folder as the trunk, the root's folders as the branches, and so on.

NOTE

Some SharePoint sites (such as a blog) don't have hierarchical content by default, so adding the tree view won't do anything.

Here are the steps to follow to add a tree view control to your site:

1. In the Site Settings page, click the Tree View link.

   2. Activate the Enable Tree View check box.

   3. Click OK to put the new setting into effect.

Click the site's home page to see the tree view. Figure 13.17 shows a top-level site with a tree view added to the left side of the page.

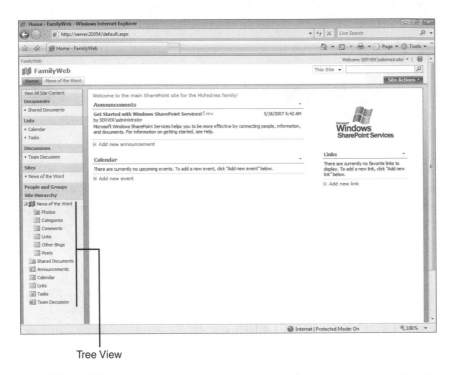

Tree View

FIGURE 13.17   Use the Site Settings page to customize all aspects of a site.

Changing the Site Theme

The overall look of a site is determined by the site theme, which governs all of the following visual factors in the site's design:

   ▶ The color of the regular page text

   ▶ The color of the page headings

   ▶ The color of the links

   ▶ The background color of the page

   ▶ The background color of the top link bar

   ▶ The color of the Quick Launch headings

   ▶ The background color of the entire Quick Launch

SharePoint defines 18 different themes to offer a variety of looks for your site. Here are the steps to follow to select a new theme:

1. In the Site Settings page, click the Site Theme link.

NOTE

The Site Theme link is available to group members who have at least Design permission.

2. Click the theme you want to use. (The Preview section gives you an idea what the theme looks like.)
3. Click OK to apply the theme to the site.

Adding Links to the Top Link Bar

As you know, the top link bar displays the Home tab, which represents the top-level SharePoint site, as well as tabs for each subsite. However, you can also add your own links to the top link bar. This is convenient because the top link bar is visible from any page in any SharePoint site, so you can put your favorite sites a mere mouse click away.

Here are the steps to follow to add a link to the top link bar:

1. In the Site Settings page, click the Top Link Bar link to open the Top Link Bar page.

NOTE

The Top Link Bar link is available to group members who have at least Design permission.

2. Click New Link.
3. Use the Type the Web Address text box to enter the URL of the site. If you'd rather see text instead of the URL in the top link bar, enter a name or short description in the Type the Description box.
4. Click OK to return to the Top Link Bar page.
5. Repeat steps 2–4 to add more links.
6. If you want to modify the order in which the links appear, click Change Order, specify the order for each link, and then click OK.
7. Click OK to put the new settings into effect.

NOTE

To remove a link from the top link bar, open the Site Settings page and click the Top Link Bar link. Click the Edit icon that appears beside the link you want to remove, click Delete, and then click OK when SharePoint asks you to confirm.

Customizing Quick Launch

Quick Launch is a useful area that gives you quick access to the main areas of a SharePoint site. However, you can make Quick Launch even more useful by deleting links and sections you never use, reordering the headings and links, and adding your own headings and links. Follow these steps:

1. In the Site Settings page, click the Quick Launch link.

NOTE

The Quick Launch link is available to group members who have at least Design permission.

---

2. Use one or more of the following techniques to customize Quick Launch:

   ▶ To delete a link, click the Edit icon to the right of the link, click Delete, and then click OK.

   ▶ To delete a heading (and all of its links), click the Edit icon to the right of the heading, click Delete, and then click OK.

   ▶ To change the order of the headings, click Change Order, use the numerical lists beside each heading to set the order, and then click OK.

   ▶ To change the order in which the links appear within a particular heading, click Change Order, use the numerical lists beside each link to set the order, and then click OK.

   ▶ To create a new heading, click New Heading, type the address that you want the heading to link to, the heading description (this is the name that appears in Quick Launch), and then click OK.

   ▶ To add your own links to a heading, click New Link, type the address of the link, the link description (this is the link text that appears in Quick Launch), choose the heading under which you want the link to appear, and then click OK.

3. Click OK.

Working with Users

Unlike a typical website where any user can browse anything on the site, a SharePoint site is restricted to just those Windows Home Server users who have been granted access to the site. So, it's important not only that you grant access to the appropriate users, but also that you apply the appropriate permissions to those users. You learned earlier how to add users to a top-level SharePoint site (see "Adding Users to the Top-Level SharePoint Site"). You use the same technique to add users to a subsite, except that you navigate to the subsite before adding the users.

However, SharePoint has user-related features behind basic site access. You can record user information such as the person's real name, picture, and email address; you can use the email address to send a message to a user, and more. The next few sections take you through some of these features.

Editing User Information

When you add a user to a SharePoint site, the only bit of information you supply is the user's account name. However, SharePoint can record quite a bit more data for each user, as the following steps show:

1. Log on to the top-level SharePoint as an administrator.
2. If you want to work with a user in a subsite, navigate to that subsite.
3. Select Site Actions, Site Settings.
4. Click the People and Groups link.
5. In the Quick Launch Groups header, click the group that contains the user (or click All People to see a list of all the users associated with the site).
6. Click the name of the user you want to edit.
7. Click Edit Item. SharePoint displays the User Information page, shown in Figure 13.18.

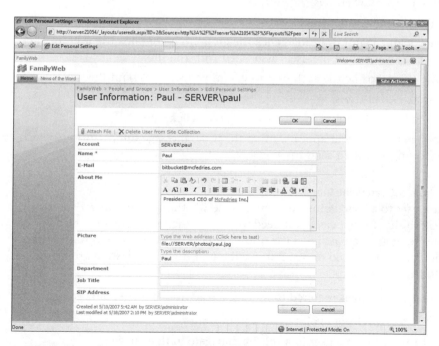

FIGURE 13.18   Use the User Information page to add to or edit the user's data.

8. Add or edit the data in the editable fields.
9. Click OK.

> **TIP**
>
> You're not restricted to just the fields (or *columns*, as SharePoint calls them) that you see in the User Information page. You can add your own custom columns to record data such as birthdays, MySpace or Facebook addresses, cell phone numbers, and so on. Log on to the top-level SharePoint as an administrator, and then select Site Actions, Site Settings, People and Groups. In any group list, select Settings, List Settings to open the Customize User Information List page, and then click the Create Column link. Type the Column Name and select a data type (such as Single Line of Text, Number, or Date and Time). Fill in the other settings, as necessary (these vary depending on the data type you selected), and then click OK.

Sending an Email to Users

In the previous section, you saw that SharePoint includes an E-Mail field in the user information. If you fill in that field for one or more users, you can send an email message to some or all of those users. Here are the steps to follow:

1. Log on to the top-level SharePoint as an administrator.
2. If you want to work with a user in a subsite, navigate to that subsite.
3. Select Site Actions, Site Settings.
4. Click the People and Groups link.
5. In the Quick Launch Groups header, click the group that contains the user (or click All People to see a list of all the users associated with the site).
6. Activate the check box beside each user to whom you want to send the message.
7. Select Actions, E-Mail Users.
8. If you see the Internet Explorer Security dialog box, click Allow.
9. In the message window that appears, fill in the usual message information (subject, body, and so on), and then send the message.

Deleting a User from a SharePoint Group

If you've added a user to a SharePoint site, you may decide that you no longer want that person to access the site. In that case, you need to remove the user from whatever SharePoint group to which you assigned the user originally. Similarly, if you want to move a user to another group, you need to first remove the user from the existing group and then add him to the other group.

In either case, here are the steps required to remove a user from a SharePoint group:

1. Log on to the top-level SharePoint as an administrator.
2. If you want to work with a user in a subsite, navigate to that subsite.
3. Select Site Actions, Site Settings.
4. Click the People and Groups link.

5. In the Quick Launch Groups header, click the group that contains the user.

6. Activate the check box beside each user you want to remove from the group.

7. Select Actions, Remove Users from Group. SharePoint ask you to confirm.

8. Click OK.

Working with Groups

Like the security groups in Windows Home Server, the groups in a SharePoint site serve to simplify user management and user permissions. You've seen how to add a user to one of the three predefined groups—Visitors, Members, or Owners; see "Adding Users to the Top-Level SharePoint Site"—but SharePoint offers several other group features. For example, you can change group settings, such as the group name and permissions; you can create your own custom groups, and you can apply different groups to visitors, members, and owners. The next few sections take you through these useful features.

Modifying Group Settings

For each group, SharePoint maintains settings such as the group name and description, the user or group that owns the group, who can view and edit the group membership, and the permissions applied to the group's users.

You can modify all of these settings and more by following these steps:

1. Log on to the top-level SharePoint as an administrator.

2. If you want to work with a group in a subsite, navigate to that subsite.

3. Select Site Actions, Site Settings.

4. Click the People and Groups link.

5. In the Quick Launch Groups header, click the group you want to work with.

6. Select Settings, Group Settings. The Change Group Settings page appears, as shown in Figure 13.19.

7. Use the Name and About Me boxes to edit the group's name and description.

8. Use the Group Owner list to select the group's owner. (This can be a user or a group.)

9. Under Who Can View the Membership of the Group, select either Group Members or Everyone.

10. Under Who Can Edit the Membership of the Group, select either Group Owner or Group Members.

NOTE

Ignore the options in the Membership Requests section. These options require that an email server be configured on the system, and Windows Home Server doesn't come with an email server.

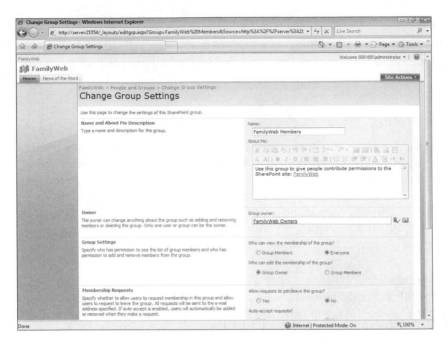

FIGURE 13.19   Use the Change Group Settings page to modify a group's settings.

11. In the Give Group Permissions to This Site section, use the check boxes to specify the permissions for the group membership: Full Control, Design, Contribute, or Read.

12. Click OK to put the new settings into effect.

Creating a New Group

If none of SharePoint's predefined groups has exactly the settings you want (and you don't want to reconfigure an existing group), you can add your own custom group to the SharePoint site. Follow these steps:

1. Log on to the top-level SharePoint as an administrator.

2. If you want to work with a group in a subsite, navigate to that subsite.

3. Select Site Actions, Site Settings.

4. Click the People and Groups link.

5. Select New, New Group. SharePoint displays the New Group page, which has the same controls as the Change Group Settings page, shown earlier in Figure 13.19.

6. Fill in the settings you want for your new group.

7. Click Create to add the group to the site.

Setting Up Groups for a Site

SharePoint defines three types of users who can access a SharePoint site:

▶ **Site visitors**—These users can only view the contents of the site.

▶ **Site members**—These users can view, change, add, and delete site content.

▶ **Site owners**—These users have full control over the site.

In a default site configuration, these users are automatically placed in the site's Visitors, Members, and Owners groups, respectively. However, you can change this, if you like. Here's how:

1. Log on to the top-level SharePoint as an administrator.
2. If you want to work with a group in a subsite, navigate to that subsite.
3. Select Site Actions, Site Settings.
4. Click the People and Groups link.
5. Select Settings, Set Up Groups. SharePoint displays the Set Up Groups for This Site page, as shown in Figure 13.20.

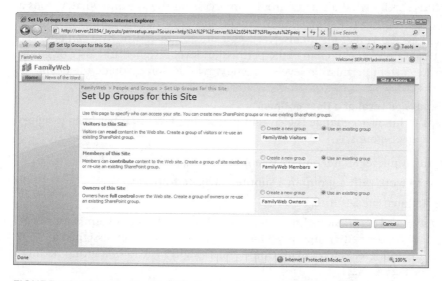

FIGURE 13.20   Use the Set Up Groups for This Site page to associate groups with each type of user.

6. For each type of user—Visitors to This Site, Members of This Site, and Owners of This Site—you have two choices:

   ▶ **Use an Existing Group**—To apply a predefined group, select this option and then use the list to select the existing group.

   ▶ **Create a New Group**—To apply a custom group, select this option and then enter a group name and select the group membership.

7. Click OK to put the new settings into effect.

Deleting a Group

If a SharePoint site has a group that you no longer need, you should delete it to reduce clutter in the Quick Launch Groups header. Follow these steps to delete a group:

1. Log on to the top-level SharePoint as an administrator.

2. If you want to work with a group in a subsite, navigate to that subsite.

3. Select Site Actions, Site Settings.

4. Click the People and Groups link.

5. In the Quick Launch Groups header, click the group you want to work with.

6. Select Settings, Group Settings to open the Change Group Settings page.

7. Click Delete. SharePoint asks you to confirm.

8. Click OK.

Working with Permissions

A site's permissions specify what a user or group can access on the site and what actions a user or group can perform to the site's content and other items that are part of the site (such as users and even permissions themselves). As a site administrator, you can alter permissions in two ways: You can change the permission level assigned to a user or group, and you can create custom permission levels. The next two sections provide the details.

Changing the Permission Level of a User or Group

Here are the steps to follow to change the current permission level that has been assigned to one or more users or groups:

1. Log on to the top-level SharePoint as an administrator.

2. If you want to work with a group in a subsite, navigate to that subsite.

3. Select Site Actions, Site Settings.

4. Click the Advanced Permissions link. SharePoint displays the site's Permissions page. This page lists the defined groups as well as any user who has been assigned a specific permission level (such as Full Control or Design) instead of a group permission level; see Figure 13.21.

5. Click the group or user you want to work with. SharePoint displays the Edit Permissions page for the group or user.

6. Activate the check box beside each permission level you want to apply to the group or user.

7. Click OK.

Creating a Custom Permission Level

SharePoint's predefined permission levels—Full Control, Design, Contribute, and Read—should satisfy most of your needs. However, if none of these levels gives you exactly the permissions you want, you can create your own level. The following steps show you how it's done:

NOTE

SharePoint actually defines a fifth permission level called Limited Access. This level is used to give users permission to view specific lists, libraries, and other content.

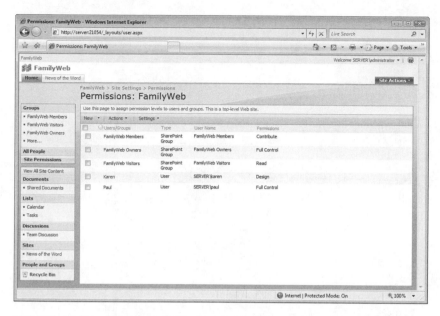

FIGURE 13.21   Use the Permissions page to modify the permission level for a user or group.

1. Log on to the top-level SharePoint site as an administrator.
2. If you want to work with permissions in a subsite, navigate to that subsite.
3. Select Site Actions, Site Settings.
4. Click the Advanced Permissions link.
5. Select Settings, Permission Levels to open the Permission Levels page.
6. Click Add a Permission Level.
7. Type a name and description for the new permission level.
8. Activate the check box beside each type of permission you want to apply to this level, as shown in Figure 13.22.
9. Click Create.

Deleting a Site

If you have a site that you no longer use, you should delete it to save disk space and, in the case of subsites, reduce clutter on the top link bar and Quick Launch. Follow these steps:

1. Log on to the top-level SharePoint site as an administrator.
2. If you want to delete a subsite, navigate to that subsite.
3. Select Site Actions, Site Settings.
4. Under Site Administration, click the Delete This Site link.
5. In the Delete This Site page, click Delete. SharePoint asks you to confirm.
6. Click OK. SharePoint deletes the site.

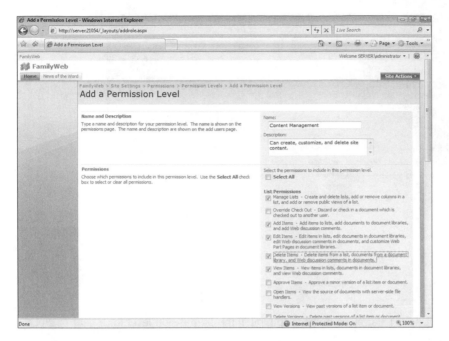

FIGURE 13.22   Use the Add a Permission Level page to create a custom permission level for your site.

Creating Content for a SharePoint Site

Administering even a small SharePoint site is a reasonably big responsibility, which is why I've devoted so much of this chapter to administrative chores. However, the value of any SharePoint site is always found in its content. SharePoint is designed for business users, so most of its content categories have a business feel to them, but there is plenty for families to enjoy. The next few sections take you through four content types that you might want to add to your site: a picture library, a calendar, a contacts list, and a links list.

Storing Images in a Picture Library

A SharePoint picture library is a storage area for images. You can use the library to view an image slide show, and you can also edit the images if your computer has an image-editing program installed. If you have Office installed on the client computer, you can also email images via Outlook and edit and download images to your computer using the Microsoft Office Picture Manager.

To create a picture library, follow these steps:

1. Log on to the top-level SharePoint site using the primary (or secondary) site collection administration account.

2. Click Site Actions and then click Create to display the Create page.

3. Under Libraries, click the Picture Library link.

4. Type a name and description for the new library.

5. In the Navigation section, click Yes if you want to include a link to the picture library on Quick Launch.

6. If you want SharePoint to keep track of versions of pictures as they're editing in the library, click Yes in the Picture Version History section.

7. Click Create. SharePoint builds the new library and (if you clicked Yes in the Navigation section) adds a link to the picture library in the Pictures heading of Quick Launch. Figure 13.23 shows an example picture library. Here's a summary of the most useful commands available in a picture library:

   ▶ **Upload Picture**—(Upload menu) Displays the Add Picture page, which you use to upload an image from your computer or network to the library.

   ▶ **Delete**—(Action menu) Deletes those library images that have their check box activated.

   ▶ **View Slide Show**—(Action menu) Displays the library images in a separate slide window.

   ▶ **Open with Windows Explorer**—(Action menu) Opens the picture library in Windows Explorer. This enables you to click and drag images from another folder window and drop them inside the picture library.

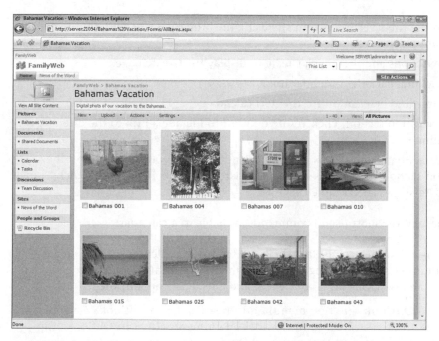

FIGURE 13.23   A SharePoint picture library.

If you have Microsoft Office installed, you also get the following commands:

▶ **Upload Multiple Pictures**—(Upload menu) Displays the Microsoft Office Picture Manager's Uploading Selected Pictures window, which enables you to select and upload multiple images to the library.

▶ **Edit**—(Action menu) Displays the Microsoft Office Picture Manager's Editing Selected Pictures window, which enables you to modify image properties such as brightness, contrast, and color, as well as to crop, rotate, and resize the image.

▶ **Download**—(Action menu) Enables you to select and download multiple images from the library to your computer using the Microsoft Office Picture Manager program.

▶ **Send To**—(Action menu) Attaches the selected images to an Outlook email message.

Tracking Appointments with a Calendar

A SharePoint calendar, similar to the Outlook Calendar, is a special list that keeps track of your appointments and events. It can even synchronize with Outlook so that you don't have to maintain two separate lists of appointments.

SharePoint includes a calendar by default in many site templates. If your site doesn't have a calendar, or if you want to add another calendar to your site, follow these steps:

1. Log on to the top-level SharePoint site using the primary (or secondary) site collection administration account.
2. Click Site Actions and then click Create to display the Create page.
3. Under Tracking, click the Calendar link.
4. Type a name and description for the new calendar.
5. In the Navigation section, click Yes if you want to include a link to the calendar on Quick Launch.
6. Click Create. SharePoint builds the new calendar and (if you clicked Yes in the Navigation section) adds a link to the calendar in the Lists heading of Quick Launch. Figure 13.24 shows an example calendar.

Here's a summary of the most useful commands available in a calendar:

▶ **New Item**—(New menu) Displays the New Item page, which you use to create a new appointment by specifying the appointment title, location, start time, and end time. You can also create an all-day event and a recurring appointment.

▶ **Connect to Outlook**—(Action menu) Adds the calendar to Outlook's Calendar folder. You can then create and work with appointments either in Outlook or in SharePoint. Note, however, that you need Outlook 2003 or later for this to work.

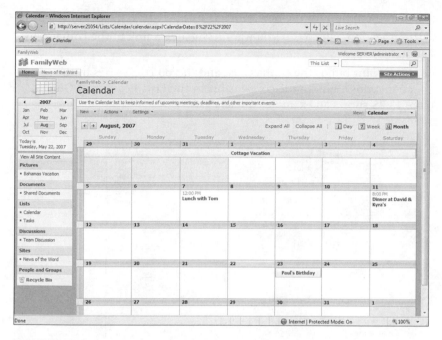

FIGURE 13.24   A SharePoint calendar.

> **TIP**
>
> It's easy to keep the SharePoint and Outlook calendars synchronized. If you change the data in Outlook, refresh the SharePoint window (by pressing F5) to see the new data; if you change the data in SharePoint, select the calendar in Outlook and then select Tools, Send/Receive, This Folder (or press Shift+F9).

Maintaining a List of Contacts

A SharePoint contacts list keeps track of your appointments and events. It's similar to the Outlook Calendar and can even synchronize with Outlook so that you don't have to maintain two separate lists of appointments.

SharePoint includes a calendar by default in many site templates. If your site doesn't have a calendar, or if you want to add another calendar to your site, follow these steps:

1. Log on to the top-level SharePoint site using the primary (or secondary) site collection administration account.

2. Click Site Actions and then click Create to display the Create page.

3. Under Communications, click the Contacts link.

4. Type a name and description for the new contacts list.

5. In the Navigation section, click Yes if you want to include a link to the contacts list on Quick Launch.

6. Click Create. SharePoint builds the contacts list and (if you clicked Yes in the Navigation section) adds a link to the contacts list in the Lists heading of Quick Launch. Figure 13.25 shows an example contacts list.

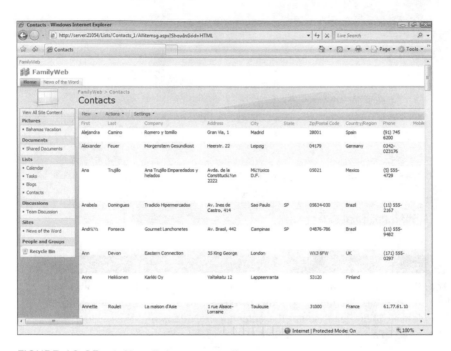

FIGURE 13.25   A SharePoint contacts list.

Here's a summary of the most useful commands available in a contacts list:

▶ **New Item**—(New menu) Displays the New Item page, which you use to create a new contact. The Last Name field is required, but you can also enter a first name, email address, and company name, as well as the person's address and phone number.

▶ **Edit in Datasheet**—(Action menu; Office only) Displays the contacts in an Access datasheet for easier editing.

▶ **Connect to Outlook**—(Action menu; Office only) Adds the contacts folder to Outlook's Contacts folder. You can then create and work with contacts either in Outlook or in SharePoint.

TIP

Unfortunately, SharePoint doesn't offer a command for importing contacts from other programs. You can work around this by using Microsoft Access, if you have it. If your contacts are in a program other than Outlook, use the program's Export feature to export the contacts to a comma-separated values (CSV) text file. In Access, open or create a database, select the External Data tab, and then, in the Import group, select either More, Outlook Folder (to import Outlook's Contacts folder) or Text File (to import the CSV file). When the import is complete, select the table containing the contacts data, and then select External Data, SharePoint List in the Export group. You then specify and log on to your SharePoint site and export the contacts.

Keeping a List of Web Page Links

You can use your SharePoint site as a handy repository for links to your favorite or most-often-viewed websites. SharePoint often includes a list of links by default in many site templates, and you view and work with the links on the site's home page. If your site doesn't have a links list, or if you want to add another links list to your site, follow these steps:

1. Log on to the top-level SharePoint site using the primary (or secondary) site collection administration account.
2. Click Site Actions and then click Create to display the Create page.
3. Under Tracking, click Links.
4. Type a name and description for the new library.
5. In the Navigation section, click Yes if you want to include a link to the list of links on Quick Launch.
6. Click Create. SharePoint builds the links list and (if you clicked Yes in the Navigation section) adds a link to the list in the Lists heading of Quick Launch.

Here's a summary of the most useful commands available in a links list:

- ▶ **New Item**—(New menu) Displays the New Item page, which you use to create a new link. You specify the link URL, as well as an options description and notes.

- ▶ **New Folder**—(New menu) Enables you to create a subfolder for storing related links.

- ▶ **Change Order**—(Action menu) Displays the Change Item Order page, which enables you to specify the order the links appear in the list.

- ▶ **Edit in Datasheet**—(Action menu; Office only) Displays the contacts in an Access datasheet for easier editing.

Managing Permissions for Content

What users can do with the content on a SharePoint site depends on the permissions they've been assigned, either indirectly through membership in a permission group (such as Visitors or Owners) or directly by being assigned a permission level (such as Full Control or Contribute). By default, the permissions apply to the entire site. However, you might want to customize this. For example, you might want to give a user Read permission to the entire site, but Contribute permission to a particular list or library.

Here are the steps to follow to override the site's permissions and set specific permissions on site content:

1. Log on to the top-level SharePoint as an administrator.
2. If you want to work with content in a subsite, navigate to that subsite.
3. Open the content you want to work with.
4. Select Settings, *Content* Settings (where *Content* is the type of content: List, Document Library, and so on).
5. In the Permissions and Management section, click the Permissions for This *Content* link (again, where *Content* is the type of content).
6. Select Actions, Edit User Permissions. SharePoint warns you that you are about to create unique permissions for the content.
7. Click OK.
8. Activate the check box beside the group or user you want to change.

> **NOTE**
>
> If you want to apply the same permission level to two or more groups or users, activate the check box beside each of those groups or users.

9. Select Actions, Edit User Permissions to open the Edit Permissions page.
10. Activate the check box beside each permission level you want to apply.
11. Click OK.

Deleting Content from a Site

If you no longer use a particular list or library, you should delete it to recapture the disk space and make Quick Launch navigation easier. Here are the steps required:

1. Log on to the top-level SharePoint as an administrator.
2. If you want to delete content from a subsite, navigate to that subsite.
3. Select Site Actions, Site Settings.
4. Under Site Administration, click the Site Libraries and Lists link.

5. Click the Customize *Name* link, where *Name* is the name of the content you want to delete.

6. Under Permissions and Management, click Delete This *Content*, where *Content* is the type of content you're deleting (list, picture library, and so on). SharePoint asks you to confirm.

7. Click OK. SharePoint deletes the content.

From Here

▶ For Internet access to your SharePoint site, you need a static IP address for your server so that you can forward to the SharePoint port; **see** "Configuring Windows Home Server with a Static IP Address," **P. 9.**

▶ SharePoint uses the Windows Home Server user account database for permissions and site access; to learn how to create more accounts, **see** "Adding a New User," **P. 38.**

▶ To keep SharePoint secure, it's important to use strong passwords; **see** "Building a Strong Password," **P. 41.**

▶ For Internet access to SharePoint, it helps to use a dynamic DNS service to map a domain name to the dynamic IP address supplied by your ISP; **see** "Using a Dynamic DNS Service," **P. 198.**

▶ For dynamic DNS, you can also set up a Windows Live Custom Domain; **see** "Obtaining a Domain Name from Microsoft," **P. 199.**

▶ For the details on setting up a general website on Windows Home Server, **see** Chapter 14, "Setting Up a Windows Home Server Website."

Tuning Windows Home Server Performance

How hard Windows Home Server works depends on many different factors, but it mostly depends on how you and the others on your network use the server. If you mostly use Windows Home Server for nightly backups and nobody on the network generates tons of content each day, Windows Home Server's workload will always be fairly light (particularly after every client has been backed up at least once). In this kind of situation, server performance is not a big issue. However, if you use Windows Home Server not only for backups, but for file storage; recording TV shows directly to the server; streaming music, video, and other media; remote access; running several websites; and perhaps even running a SharePoint site, Windows Home Server's workload becomes decidedly heavy. In this case, you definitely want not only a fast computer as the server, but you also want to monitor and tweak Windows Home Server's performance to eke out every ounce of horsepower in the machine.

This chapter shows you a number of different methods for monitoring performance. Some of these will no doubt seem like overkill for a home network, but you can always just pick out the ones that give you the information you require. The rest of the chapter takes you through specific techniques for improving the overall performance of Windows Home Server.

Monitoring Performance

Performance optimization is a bit of a black art in that every user has different needs, every configuration has different operating parameters, and every system can react in a unique and unpredictable way to performance tweaks.

What this means is that if you want to optimize your system, you have to get to know how it works, what it needs, and how it reacts to changes. You can do this by just using the system and paying attention to how things look and feel, but a more rigorous approach is often called for. To that end, the next few sections take you on a tour of Windows Home Server's performance monitoring capabilities.

Monitoring Performance with Task Manager

The Task Manager utility is excellent for getting a quick overview of the current state of the system. To get it onscreen, press Ctrl+Alt+Delete. If the Windows Security dialog box appears, click the Task Manager button.

TIP

To bypass the Windows Security dialog box, either press Ctrl+Shift+Esc or right-click an empty section of the taskbar and then click Task Manager.

Monitoring Processes

The Processes tab, shown in Figure 14.1, displays a list of the programs, services, and system components that are currently running on your system. The processes appear in the order in which they were started, but you can change their order by clicking the column headings. (To return to the original, chronological order, you must close and restart Task Manager.)

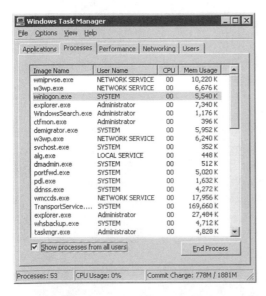

FIGURE 14.1   The Processes tab lists your system's running programs and services.

NOTE

A *process* is a running instance of an executable program.

NOTE

In the list of processes, you'll likely see several instances of `svchost.exe`. This is a program that acts as a host process for services that run from dynamic-link libraries (DLLs) instead of from executable files. To see which services the various instances of `svchost.exe` are running, start a command prompt session and enter the following command:

`tasklist /svc`

This displays a list of all the running processes and includes a column that displays the services that are hosted in each process.

In addition to the name of each process and the user who started the process, you also see two performance measures:

CPU   The values in this column tell you the percentage of CPU resources that each
         process is using. If your system seems sluggish, look for a process that is consum-
         ing all or nearly all of the CPU's resources. Most programs will monopolize the CPU
         occasionally for short periods, but a program that is stuck at 100 (percent) for a
         long time most likely has some kind of problem. In that case, try shutting down the
         program. If that doesn't work, click the program's process and then click End
         Process. Click Yes when Windows Home Server asks whether you're sure that you
         want to do this.

Mem   This value tells you approximately how much memory the process is using. This
Usage   value is less useful because a process might genuinely require a lot of memory to
         operate. However, if this value is steadily increasing for a process that you're not
         using, it could indicate a problem, and you should shut down the process.

TIP

You can control how often Task Manager refreshes its data. Select View, Update Speed and then select High (Task Manager refreshes the data twice per second), Normal (Task Manager refreshes the data every two seconds; this is the default), or Low (Task Manager refreshes the data every four seconds). If you want to freeze the current data, select Paused. You can also refresh the data at any time by selecting View, Refresh Now.

The four default columns in the Processes tab aren't the only data available to you. Select the View, Select Columns command. As you can see in Figure 14.2, the Select Columns dialog box that Task Manager opens has a long list of values that you can monitor. To add a value to the Processes tab, activate its check box and click OK.

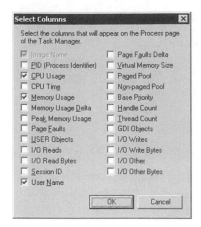

FIGURE 14.2   Use the Select Columns dialog box to choose which values you want to monitor using the Processes tab.

Here's a summary of the columns you can add:

Image Name	This is the name (usually the executable filename) of the process. This is the only column that must be displayed. (Task Manager disables this check box.)
PID (Process Identifier)	This is a unique numerical value that Windows Home Server assigns to the process while it's running.
CPU Usage	This is the CPU value discussed earlier in this section.
CPU Time	This column shows the total time (in hours, minutes, and seconds) that the process has used the CPU since the process was launched. Because most computers (including Windows Home Server) don't access the processor constantly, the CPU is usually idle, which means the System Idle Process almost always shows the lion's share of the CPU Time value. However, if you see another process that seems to have used an inordinate amount of CPU time (for example, hours of CPU time, when all other processes have used only minutes or seconds of CPU time), it could mean that the process is frozen or out of control and should be shut down.
Memory Usage	This is the Mem Usage value discussed earlier in this section.

Memory Usage Delta	This value tells you how much the Memory Usage value changed (in kilobytes) since the last time Task Manager updated the processes. You see a positive value when memory use increases and a negative value when memory usage decreases. Under normal conditions, a program might show gradually increasing memory usage as more resources are used, and gradually decreasing memory usage as files and other objects are closed. If you see a process that has a constantly positive Memory Usage Delta value, particularly when it's not obvious that the process is being used, it might be the sign of a memory leak in the process.
Peak Memory Usage	This value shows the highest Memory Usage value (in kilobytes) that the process has achieved since it was started.
Page Faults	This value tells you how often each process has requested a page from virtual memory and the system couldn't find the page. (A *page* is an area of virtual memory used to transfer data between virtual memory and a storage medium, usually the hard disk.) The system then either retrieves the data from another virtual memory location (this is called a *soft page fault*) or from the hard disk (this is called a hard page fault). Lots of hard page faults can slow down overall system performance and may be a sign that your system doesn't have enough memory or that the virtual memory paging file isn't big enough.

NOTE

Unfortunately, Task Manager doesn't give you any way to differentiate between soft page faults and hard page faults. For this, you need to use System Monitor, as described later in the "Monitoring Performance with System Monitor" section.

NOTE

If you display the Page Faults column, you may notice that the Windows shell process (explorer.exe) seems to constantly accumulate page faults. (To see this, it helps to display the Page Faults Delta column, described a bit later.) In fact, the Page Fault value increases every two seconds. Does this mean explorer.exe has a problem? Not at all. The page faults are caused by Task Manager, which causes an explorer.exe page fault every time it updates the CPU Usage value. Because that happens every two seconds (assuming that Task Manager's update speed is set to Normal), the explorer.exe Page Faults value also increases every two seconds.

USER
Objects

This value tells you the number of interface objects (which are part of User, a core system component used by applications and other processes that impact the user) that the process is using. Interface objects include windows, menus, cursors, icons, monitors, keyboard layouts, and other internal objects. If performance is slow, look for the process that has the highest USER Objects value and close it. (The exception here is the explorer.exe process, which usually has a high number of USER objects, but because it represents the Windows Home Server shell you should never close it.)

I/O Reads

This value shows the total number of input/output operations that the process has used to read data since the process was started. The total includes reads from local files, network files, and devices, but not reads from the console input object, which includes the keyboard. Some processes generate tens or even hundreds of thousands of I/O reads, so this value isn't very useful in monitoring performance.

I/O Read
Bytes

This value shows the total number of bytes generated by the read in input/output operations since the process was started. Again, because you often see I/O Ready Bytes values in the hundreds of millions or even billions, this value isn't much use for performance monitoring.

Session ID

This is a unique numerical value that Windows Home Server assigns to the process while it's running within a Terminal Services session (such as if a user is running Windows Home Server Console or has logged on to Windows Home Server via Remote Desktop).

TIP

To see the Session ID values, activate the Show Processes from All Users check box.

User Name

This value tells you the name of the user or service that launched the process.

Page Faults
Delta

This value tells you how much the Page Faults value changed since the last time Task Manager updated the processes. Because the total number of page faults can never decrease, this will always be either 0 or a positive number. A process that shows a consistently high Page Faults Delta value might not have enough memory to run properly. Consider shutting down the process and starting it again.

Virtual Memory
Size

This value shows the total amount of virtual memory, in kilobytes, that Windows Home Server has allocated to each process. If page faults are high, it could be due to a process using a large amount of virtual memory. Consider ending and restarting that process.

Paged Pool	This value is the amount of virtual memory, in kilobytes, that Windows Home Server has allocated to the process in the paged pool—the system memory area that Windows Home Server uses for objects that can be written back to the disk when the system doesn't need them. The most active processes have the largest paged pool values, so it's normal for this value to increase over time. However, it's unusual for any one process to have a significantly large paged pool value. You can improve performance by shutting down and restarting such a process.
Non-Paged Pool	This value is the amount of virtual memory, in kilobytes, that Windows Home Server has allocated to the process in the nonpaged pool—the system memory area that Windows Home Server uses for objects that must remain in memory and so can't be written back to the disk when the system doesn't need them. Because the nonpaged pool takes up physical RAM on the system, if memory is running low, processes that require a lot of nonpaged pool memory could generate lots of page faults and slow down the system. Consider closing some programs to reduce memory usage.
Base Priority	This value shows you the priority level used by each process. For more on this, see "Setting the Program Priority in Task Manager," later in this chapter.
Handle Count	This value shows you the number of object handles in the object table associated with each process. An object handle is an index that points to an entry in a table of available objects, and it enables programs to interface with those objects. Handles take up memory, so a process with an inordinately large handle count could adversely affect system performance.
Thread Count	This value tells you the number of threads that each process is using. A thread is a program task that can run independently of and (usually) concurrently with other tasks in the same program (in which case, the program is said to support multithreading). Multithreading improves program performance, but programs that have an unusually large number of threads can slow down the server because Windows has to spend too much time switching from one thread of execution to another.
GDI Objects	This value shows the number of graphics device interface (GDI) objects that each process is currently using. The GDI is a core Windows component that manages the operating system's graphical interface. It contains routines that draw graphics primitives (such as lines and circles), manage colors, display fonts, manipulate bitmap images, and interact with graphics drivers. A process that uses an unusually large number of GDI objects can slow down the system.

I/O Writes	This value shows the total number of input/output operations that the process has used to write data since the process was started. The total includes writes to local files, network files, and devices, but not writes to the console input object, which includes the monitor. Some processes generate tens or even hundreds of thousands of I/O writes, so this value isn't very useful in monitoring performance.
I/O Write Bytes	This value shows the total number of bytes generated by the write input/output operations since the process was started. Because you often see I/O Write Bytes values in the hundreds of millions or even billions, this value isn't much use for performance monitoring.
I/O Other	This value shows the total number of non-read and non-write input/output operations that the process has used since the process was started. Examples include starting another process, stopping a running process, requesting the status of a device, and other control functions.
I/O Other Bytes	This value shows the total number of bytes generated by non-read and non-write input/output operations since the process was started.

Monitoring System Performance

The Performance tab, shown in Figure 14.3, offers even more performance data, particularly for that all-important component: your system's memory.

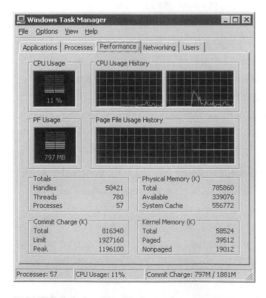

FIGURE 14.3   The Performance tab lists various numbers related to your system's memory components.

The graphs show you both the current value and the values over time for the CPU Usage (the total percentage of CPU resources that your running processes are using) and the Page File Usage. If you also want to monitor the amount of CPU time used by the system files (the kernel), select View, Show Kernel Times. Windows Home Server adds red line graphs to each chart to represent the kernel time usage.

NOTE

If your server has multiple CPUs (or a multicore processor), the CPU Usage History section shows a separate graph for each processor (as shown in Figure 14.3). If you prefer to see a single graph for all the processors, select View, CPU History, One Graph, All CPUs.

What is a paging file? Your computer can address memory beyond what is physically installed on the system. This nonphysical memory is called *virtual memory*, and it's implemented by using a piece of your hard disk that's set up to emulate physical memory. This hard disk storage is actually a single file called a *paging file* (or sometimes a *swap file*). When physical memory is full, Windows Home Server makes room for new data by taking some data that's currently in memory and swapping it out to the paging file. The PF Usage graph shows the current size of the paging file, and the Paging file Usage History graphs shows the relative size of the paging file over time.

Below the graphs are various numbers. Here's what they mean:

NOTE

The memory values are listed in kilobytes. To convert to megabytes, divide by 1,024.

Totals–Handles	The total number of object handles that the running processes are using.
Totals–Threads	The total number of threads that the running processes are using.
Totals–Processes	The total number of running processes.
Physical Memory–Total	The total amount of physical RAM in your system.
Physical Memory–Available	The amount of physical RAM that Windows Home Server has available for your programs. Note that Windows Home Server does not include the system cache (see the next item) in this total.
Physical Memory–System Cache	The amount of physical RAM that Windows Home Server has set aside to store recently used programs and documents.
Commit Charge–Total	The combined total of physical RAM and virtual memory that the system is using.
Commit Charge–Limit	The combined total of physical RAM and virtual memory available to the system.

Commit Charge–Peak	The maximum combined total of physical RAM and virtual memory that the system has used so far in this session.
Kernel Memory–Total	The total amount of RAM used by the Windows Home Server system components and device drivers.
Kernel Memory–Paged	The amount of kernel memory that is mapped to pages in virtual memory.
Kernel Memory–Nonpaged	The amount of kernel memory that cannot be mapped to pages in virtual memory.

Here are some notes related to these values that will help you monitor memory-related performance issues:

▶ If the Physical Memory Available value approaches 0, your system is starved for memory. You might have too many programs running or a large program is using lots of memory.

▶ If the Physical Memory System Cache value is much less than half the Physical Memory Total value, your system isn't operating as efficiently as it could because Windows Home Server can't store enough recently used data in memory. Because Windows Home Server gives up some of the system cache when it needs RAM, close down programs you don't need.

▶ If the Commit Charge Total value remains higher than the Physical Memory Total value, Windows Home Server is doing a lot of work swapping data to and from the paging file, which greatly slows performance.

▶ If the Commit Charge Peak value is higher than the Physical Memory Total value, Windows Home Server had to use the paging file at some point in the current session. If the Commit Charge Total value is currently less than Physical Memory Total value, the peak value might have been a temporary event, but you should monitor the peak over time, just to make sure.

In all of these situations, the quickest solution is to reduce the system's memory footprint either by closing documents or by closing applications. For the latter, use the Processes tab to determine which applications are using the most memory, and then shut down the ones you can live without for now. The better, but more expensive, solution is to add more physical RAM to your system. This decreases the likelihood that Windows Home Server will need to use the paging file, and it enables Windows Home Server to increase the size of the system cache, which greatly improves performance.

TIP

If you're not sure which process corresponds to which program, display the Applications tab, right-click a program, and then click Go to Process. Task Manager displays the Processes tab and selects the process that corresponds to the program.

Monitoring Network Performance

If your network feels sluggish, it could be that the server or node you're working with is sharing data slowly or that network traffic is exceptionally high. To see whether the latter situation is the cause of the problem, you can check out the current *network utilization* value, which is the percent of available bandwidth that your network adapter is currently using.

To check network utilization, open Task Manager and then display the Networking tab, shown in Figure 14.4. If you have multiple adapters, click the one you want to check in the Adapter Name list. Now use the graph or the Network Utilization column to monitor the current network utilization value. Notice that this value is a percentage. This means that the utilization is a percentage of the bandwidth shown in the Link Speed column. So, for example, if the current network utilization is 10 percent and the Link Speed value is 1Gbps, the network is currently using about 100Mbps bandwidth.

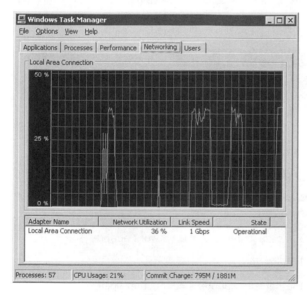

FIGURE 14.4   Use Task Manager's Networking tab to check the current network utilization percentage.

The Network Utilization value combines the data sent by the server and the data received by the server. If the utilization is high, it's often useful to break down the data stream into the separate sent and received components. To do that, select View, Network Adapter History, and then select Bytes Sent (which displays as a red line on the graph) or Bytes Received (which displays as a yellow line on the graph).

As with the Processes tab, you can view much more information than what you see in the default Networking tab. Select the View, Select Columns command. As shown in Figure 14.5, the Select Columns dialog box offers a long list of networking measures that you can monitor. To add a value to the Networking tab, activate its check box and click OK.

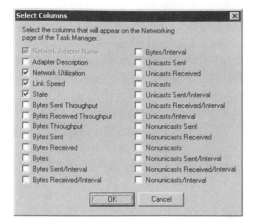

FIGURE 14.5   Use the Select Columns dialog box to choose which values you want to monitor using the Networking tab.

TIP

By default, the Networking tab doesn't collect data when you're viewing some other Task Manager tab. If you prefer that the Networking tab always collects data, select Options, Tab Always Active.

Here's a summary of the columns you can add:

Network Adapter Name	This is the name of the network adapter associated with the network connection. This is the only column that must be displayed. (Task Manager disables this check box.)
Adapter Description	This column shows the description of the network adapter.
Network Utilization	This is the network utilization value.
Link Speed	This value shows the network adapter's connection speed.
State	This column displays the general state of the adapter.
Bytes Sent Throughput	This value shows the percentage of connection bandwidth used by traffic sent from Windows Home Server.
Bytes Received Throughput	This value shows the percentage of connection bandwidth used by traffic received by Windows Home Server.
Bytes Throughput	This value shows the percentage of connection bandwidth used by traffic both sent from and received by Windows Home Server.
Bytes Sent	This column tells you the total number of bytes sent from Windows Home Server over the network adapter during the current session (that is, since the last boot).

Bytes Received	This column tells you the total number of bytes received by Windows Home Server over the network adapter during the current session.
Bytes Total	This column tells you the total number of bytes sent from and received by Windows Home Server over the network adapter during the current session.
Bytes Sent/Interval	This value shows the total number of bytes sent from Windows Home Server over the network adapter during the most recent update interval. (For example, if the Update Speed value is set to Low, the display updates every four seconds, so the Bytes Sent/Interval value is the number of bytes sent during the most recent four-second interval.)
Bytes Received/ Interval	This value shows the total number of bytes received by Windows Home Server over the network adapter during the most recent update interval.
Bytes/Interval	This value shows the total number of bytes sent from and received by Windows Home Server over the network adapter during the most recent update interval.
Unicasts Sent	This column tells you the total number of unicasts sent from Windows Home Server over the network adapter during the current session (that is, since the last boot). A unicast is a packet exchanged between a single sender and a single receiver.
Unicasts Received	This column tells you the total number of unicasts received by Windows Home Server over the network adapter during the current session.
Unicasts Total	This column tells you the total number of unicasts sent from and received by Windows Home Server over the network adapter during the current session.
Unicasts Sent/ Interval	This value shows the total number of unicasts sent from Windows Home Server over the network adapter during the most recent update interval.
Unicasts Received/ Interval	This value shows the total number of unicasts received by Windows Home Server over the network adapter during the most recent update interval.
Unicasts/Interval	This value shows the total number of unicasts sent from and received by Windows Home Server over the network adapter during the most recent update interval.
Nonunicast Sent	This column tells you the total number of nonunicast packets sent from Windows Home Server over the network adapter during the current session (that is, since the last boot). A nonunicast is a packet exchanged between a single sender and multiple receivers.

Nonunicast Received	This column tells you the total number of nonunicasts received by Windows Home Server over the network adapter during the current session.
Nonunicast Total	This column tells you the total number of nonunicasts sent from and received by Windows Home Server over the network adapter during the current session.
Nonunicast Sent/Interval	This value shows the total number of nonunicasts sent from Windows Home Server over the network adapter during the most recent update interval.
Nonunicast Received/Interval	This value shows the total number of nonunicasts received by Windows Home Server over the network adapter during the most recent update interval.
Nonunicast/Interval	This value shows the total number of nonunicasts sent from and received by Windows Home Server over the network adapter during the most recent update interval.

Monitoring Performance with System Monitor

For more advanced performance monitoring, Windows Home Server offers the System Monitor tool, which you can get to by selecting Start, Run, typing **perfmon**, and clicking OK. The System Monitor appears, as shown in Figure 14.6.

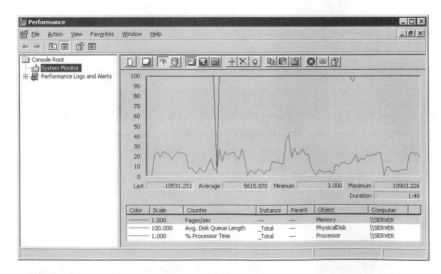

FIGURE 14.6   Use System Monitor to keep an eye on various system settings and components.

System Monitor's job is to provide you with real-time reports on how various system settings and components are performing. Each item is called a *counter*, and the displayed counters are listed at the bottom of the window. Each counter is assigned a different colored line, and that color corresponds to the colored lines shown in the graph. Note, too, that you can get specific numbers for a counter—the most recent value, the average, the minimum, and the maximum—by clicking a counter and reading the boxes just below the graphs.

The idea is that you should configure System Monitor to show the processes you're interested in (paging file size, free memory, and so on) and then keep System Monitor running while you perform your normal chores. By examining the System Monitor readouts from time to time, you gain an appreciation of what is typical on your system. Then, if you run into performance problems, you can check System Monitor to see whether you've run into any bottlenecks or anomalies.

TIP

By default, System Monitor samples the performance data every second. To change the sample interval, right-click System Monitor and then select Properties. (You can also press Ctrl+Q or click the Properties button in the toolbar.) In the System Monitor Properties dialog box, display the General tab, and modify the value in the Sample Automatically Every *X* Seconds text box. Click OK to put the new sample interval into effect.

Adding Performance Counters

By default, System Monitor shows the following three counters:

Pages/Sec	This value shows the number of pages per second that are retrieved from or written to disk to resolve hard page faults. A consistently large number here (say, more than 2,500 pages per second) probably means that the server doesn't have enough memory.
Avg. Disk Queue Length	This value tells you the average number of read and write requests queued for the system's hard disks during the sample interval. If this value is consistently 2.0 or higher, it probably means that at least one of your hard disks is too slow to keep up with the demand being placed on it. You might want to replace the disk with a faster one.

NOTE

The default Avg. Disk Queue Length counter shows the total for all your hard disks. To narrow down which disk is causing the problem, display separate counters for each instance of the Avg. Disk Queue Length value, as described in the steps that follow. (In this case, each instance is a separate hard disk on the server.)

% Processor Time	This is the percentage of time the processor is busy. A consistently high value (say, over 80%) probably indicates a rogue program that needs to be shut down. However, it may also indicate that the Windows Home Server CPU is too slow to keep up with the network demand (although this is unlikely on a home network).

To add another setting to the System Monitor window, follow these steps:

1. Right-click a counter and then click Add Counters. (You can also press Ctrl+I or click the Add button in the toolbar.) The Add Counters dialog box appears, as shown in Figure 14.7.

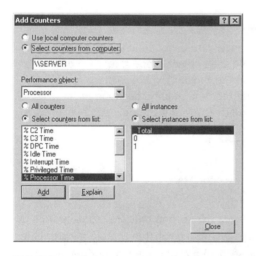

FIGURE 14.7   Use the Add Counters dialog box to add more counters to System Monitor.

2. Use the Performance Object list to select a counter category.

3. Activate the Select Counters from List option.

4. Select the counter you want. If you need more information about the item, click the Explain button.

5. If the counter has multiple instances, select the instance you want from the Select Instances from List. (For example, if you choose Processor as the performance object and your system has either multiple processors or a multiple-core processor, you need to choose which processor you want to monitor. You can also usually select _Total to monitor the total of all the instances.)

6. Click Add.

7. Repeat steps 2–6 to add any other counters you want to monitor.

8. Click Close.

> **TIP**
>
> The graph is only useful if you can see the results properly. Unfortunately, sometimes the scale of the graph isn't appropriate for the numbers generated by a particular counter. The default scale is from 0 to 100, so if a counter regularly generates numbers larger than 100, all you'll see is a straight line across the top of the graph. Similarly, if a counter regularly generates very small numbers, the counter's graph will be a straight line across the bottom of the graph.
>
> To fix this, you can change the scale used by the System Monitor graph. Right-click System Monitor and then select Properties. (You can also press Ctrl+Q or click the Properties button in the toolbar.) In the System Monitor Properties dialog box, display the Graph tab and modify the values in the Maximum and Minimum text boxes. I also find that activating the Horizontal Grid check box helps you to interpret the graph. Click OK to put the new settings into effect.

Understanding Performance Counters

In the Add Counters dialog box, the Performance Object list has dozens of objects, and each object can have dozens of counters. Explaining each one would require another book this size (and would require a level of patience that I don't have). Fortunately, only a few of the performance objects are truly useful for your Windows Home Server network, and in most situations, you need only track a few counters to monitor the server and network performance. Table 14.1 presents my list of the most useful performance objects and counters.

TABLE 14.1   Useful System Monitor Counters for Monitoring Server and Network Performance

Object/Counter	Description
Cache	This performance object represents Windows Home Server's file system cache, which it uses to hold frequently used bits of data. The more data Windows Home Server can read from the cache, the faster the system's performance. See also the Memory\Cache Bytes and Memory\Cache Faults/Sec counters.
Cache\Copy Reads/Sec	This counter tells you the number of times per second that Windows Home Server attempts to locate data in the cache instead of on the disk. Use this counter in conjunction with Copy Read Hits %.
Cache\Copy Read Hits %	This counter tells you the percentage of cache read requests that successfully retrieved data from the cache instead of from the disk. The higher the percentage (anything over 80% is very good), the better the system performance.
Cache\Data Flush Pages/Sec	This counter monitors the number of cache pages that are written back (flushed) to disk per second. If this value is steadily increasing, it might mean that Windows Home Server is having to reduce the size of the cache because memory is getting low.

TABLE 14.1   Useful System Monitor Counters for Monitoring Server and Network Performance

Object/Counter	Description
Memory	This performance object represents Windows Home Server's memory, which includes both physical RAM and virtual memory.
Memory\Available MBytes	This counter tracks the number of megabytes that are currently available for processes. As this number gets lower, system performance slows because Windows Home Server must reduce the size of the system cache and so read more data from the disk. Windows Home Server may also reduce the memory used by services, which can also slow performance. If this number drops below 4MB, your system is seriously low on memory. Use the Task Manager to see if a process is using excessive amounts of memory. Otherwise, you may need to add RAM to your system.
Memory\Cache Bytes	This counter tells you the size, in bytes, of the system cache. If the system cache size is falling, it may indicate that Windows Home Server is running low on memory (so it reduces the cache size to free up memory for processes). For content, examine the Memory\Cache Bytes Peak value to see the largest value of the cache size since the system was last booted.
Memory\Cache Faults/sec	This counter monitors the number of times per second that the system looked for data in the system cache but didn't find it. A steady increase in this value may indicate that the system cache is too small.
Memory\Committed Bytes	This counter measures the number of bytes of physical and virtual memory that the system has committed to running processes. If this value is always close to the value of the Memory\Commit Limit counter—which measures the total amount of physical and virtual memory that can be assigned to processes—it means that either your paging file's maximum value is too small (see "Customizing the Paging File Size," later in this chapter), or your system doesn't have enough physical RAM.*
Memory\Page Faults/Sec	This counter tells you the average number of page faults that occur per second. This value combines soft page faults and hard page faults.
Memory\Pages Input/Sec	This counter tells you the average number of pages per second that the system is reading to resolve hard page faults. A large number of hard page faults degrades performance because the system must retrieve data from the relatively slow hard disk. You need to either shut down some running programs or services, or add RAM. Note, too, that the difference between this value and the Memory\Page Faults/Sec value tells you the number of soft page faults per second.

TABLE 14.1   Useful System Monitor Counters for Monitoring Server and Network
Performance

Object/Counter	Description
Memory\Page Reads/Sec	This counter monitors the number of read operations per second that the system is performing to resolve hard page faults. This doesn't tell you all that much by itself. However, if you divide the Memory\Pages Input/Sec value by Memory\Page Reads/Sec, you learn how many pages the system is retrieving per read operation. A large number of pages per read operation is a sign that your system is low on physical memory.
Memory\Pages Output\Sec	This counter tells you the number of times per second the system writes data to the disk to free up memory. If this value is increasing, your system doesn't have enough physical RAM.
Memory\Pool Nonpaged Bytes	This counter tracks the number of bytes allocated to the nonpaged pool.
Memory\Pool Paged Bytes	This counter tracks the number of bytes allocated to the *paged pool*, the system memory area that Windows Home Server uses for objects that can be written back to the disk when the system doesn't need them. (The current size of the paged pool is given by the Memory\Pool Paged Resident Bytes value.) The nonpaged pool and paged pool take memory away from other processes, so if these values are large relative to the total amount of physical memory, you should add more RAM to the system.
Network Interface	This performance object represents Windows Home Server's network adapter and its connection to the network. For the object instances, select the network adapter you want to monitor (if your system has more than one).
Network Interface\Current Bandwidth	This counter tells you the current network bandwidth, in bits per second.
Network Interface\Bytes Total/Sec	This counter tells you the total number of bytes received and bytes sent over the network connection per second. (This is the sum of the Network Interface\Bytes Received/Sec and Network Interface\Bytes Sent/Sec values.) Multiply this value by 1,024 to calculate the number of bits per second that are passing through the adapter. Under load (say, while streaming media), the result should be close to the Network Interface\Current Bandwidth value. If it's substantially less, you have a network bottleneck.
Paging File	This performance object represents Windows Home Server's paging file.
Paging File\% Usage	This counter tracks the current size of the paging file as a percentage of the maximum paging file size. If this value is consistently high—say, 70 percent or more—you either need to increase the maximum size of the paging file, or you need to add more RAM to the system.

TABLE 14.1   Useful System Monitor Counters for Monitoring Server and Network Performance

Object/Counter	Description
Paging File\% Usage Peak	This counter tells you the maximum size of the Paging File\% Usage value in the current session.
PhysicalDisk	This performance object represents Windows Home Server's hard disks. For the object instances, you can monitor individual hard disks or all the hard disks combined. See also the System\Processor Queue Length counter."
PhysicalDisk\% Disk Time	This counter tracks the percentage of the sample interval that the disk spent processing read and write requests. On your home network, this value should be quite small (usually less than 1 percent). If you see a larger value, you may have a hard disk that's too slow.
Processor	This performance object represents Windows Home Server's CPU. If your system has multiple processors or a multiple-core processor, you can select an individual processor or core as an instance.
Processor\% Idle Time	This counter tells you the percentage of time during the sample interval that the processor was idle.
Processor\% Interrupt Time	This counter shows the percentage of time during the sample interval that the processor was processing interrupt requests from devices.
Processor\% Privileged Time	This counter tells you the percentage of time during the sample interval that the processor spent running code in *privileged mode*, a processing mode that gives operating system programs and services full access to system hardware.
Processor\% User Time	This counter tells you the percentage of time during the sample interval that the processor spent running code in user mode. On your Windows Home Server network, this value—as well as the values for Processor\% Idle Time, Processor\% Interrupt Time, and Processor\% Privileged Time—should be at or near 0 most of the time. If any one of these values is consistently high, you might need to upgrade to a faster processor or a processor with more cores, or add a second processor if your system motherboard supports this.
System	This object represents the Windows Home Server system as a whole.
System\Processor Queue Length	This counter tells you the number of threads that are waiting to be executed by the processor (or processors; there is just one queue for all CPUs). If this value is consistently 10 or more, your processor isn't doing its job, and you should consider upgrading it or adding a second processor (if possible).
System\System Up Time	This counter shows the time, in seconds, that Windows Home Server has been running since the most recent boot.

*Rather than comparing the Memory\Committed Bytes value and the Memory\Commit Limit value, you can monitor the Memory\% Committed Bytes in Use counter. System Monitor derives this value by dividing Memory\Committed Bytes by Memory\Commit Limit. The Memory\% Committed Bytes in Use is considered to be too high when it reaches 85 percent or more.

**Windows Home Server's Drive Extender technology does a good job of balancing the load between your system hard disks. Therefore, disk bottlenecks should rarely occur on Windows Home Server systems, so you shouldn't have to monitor the hard disks. The exception is if your Windows Home Server storage pool includes external USB hard drives, which are much slower than internal drives and so could cause bottlenecks.

Optimizing the Hard Disk

Windows Home Server uses the hard disk to fetch application data and documents as well as to temporarily store data in the paging file. Therefore, optimizing your hard disk can greatly improve Windows Home Server's overall performance, as described in the next few sections.

Examining Hard Drive Performance Specifications

If you're looking to add another drive to your system, your starting point should be the drive itself: specifically, its theoretical performance specifications. Compare the drive's average seek time with other drives. (The lower the value, the better.) Also, pay attention to the rate at which the drive spins the disk's platters. A 7,200 RPM (or higher) drive has noticeably faster performance than, say, a 5,400 RPM drive. Most drives today spin at 7,200 RPM, although you can find faster if you're willing to pay a premium. (Beware of so-called "green" hard drives, which are designed to save power but do so at the cost of performance because most of them spin at a measly 5,400 RPM.)

Finally, the drive type can make a big speed difference. For example, USB 2.0 has a theoretical data transfer rate of up to 480Mbps, whereas the data transfer rates for FireWire 400 and FireWire 800 are about 400Mbps and 800Mbps, respectively. However, compare these speeds with the theoretical data transfer rate of eSATA (external SATA) drives, which can achieve up to 2,400Mbps. (Of course, you can only use an eSATA drive if your Windows Home Server computer's motherboard supplies an eSATA connector, or if you add a controller card that offers one or more eSATA ports.)

NOTE

It's worth mentioning here that USB 3.0 (also known as SuperSpeed USB) is ready for primetime, and you should start seeing USB 3.0–compliant devices and operating sys- tem patches in 2010. They'll be worth the wait because USB 3.0 has a theoretical maximum transfer rate of 4,800Mbps.

Performing Hard Drive Maintenance

For an existing drive, optimization is the same as maintenance, so you should implement the maintenance plan discussed in Chapter 15, "Maintaining Windows Home Server." For a hard disk, this means doing the following:

- ▶ Keeping an eye on the disk's free space to make sure that it doesn't get too low
- ▶ Periodically cleaning out any unnecessary files on the disk
- ▶ Uninstalling any programs or devices you no longer use
- ▶ Frequently checking all partitions for errors
- ▶ Regularly defragmenting partitions

Disabling Compression and Encryption

Windows Home Server's partitions use the NTFS file system, which means they support compressing files to save space, as well as encrypting files for security. From a performance point of view, however, you shouldn't use compression and encryption on a partition. Both technologies slow down disk accesses because of the overhead involved in the compression/decompression and encryption/decryption processes.

Turning Off Windows Search

Windows Search is a service that indexes the contents of the Windows Home Server shared folders as well as the contents of %SystemDrive%\Documents and Settings. Windows Search indexes these locations on-the-fly as you add or delete data. This greatly speeds up content-based file searches because Windows Home Server knows the contents of each file. However, if you frequently transfer data to Windows Home Server, you may find that the indexer (it's the searchindexer.exe process in Task Manager) uses a great deal of resources. If you never use the Windows Search Deskbar on Windows Home Server's taskbar, or if you never use the Search box that appears in the Shared Folders tab of the Remote Access website, you should consider turning off the Windows Search service. To do this, follow these steps:

1. Select Start, right-click My Computer, and then click Manage to open the Computer Management snap-in.
2. Open the Services and Applications, Services branch.
3. Double-click the Windows Search service.
4. Click Stop.
5. In the Startup Type list, select Disabled.
6. Click OK.

Enabling Write Caching

You should also make sure that your hard disk has write caching enabled. Write caching means that Windows Home Server doesn't flush changed data to the disk until the system is idle, which improves performance. The downside is that a power outage or system crash means the data never gets written, so the changes are lost. The chances of this happening are minimal, so I recommend leaving write caching enabled, which is the Windows Home Server default.

You can get even more of a performance boost if your system uses a SATA hard drive, because SATA drives include extra cache features. This hard drive performance improvement is theoretical because on most systems Windows doesn't activate write caching. That's because the downside of write caching is that a power outage or system crash means that the data never gets written, so the changes are lost. For regular write caching this isn't a major concern, because changed data is flushed to the hard drive quite frequently. However, the more advanced SATA drive write caching is more aggressive, so losing data is a distinct possibility unless your system is protected by an uninterruptible power supply (UPS) or a battery backup.

To make sure the write caching setting is activated for a hard drive, and to turn on a SATA drive's advanced caching features, follow these steps:

1. Launch the Control Panel's System icon to display the System Properties dialog box.
2. Display the Hardware tab.
3. Click Device Manager to launch the Device Manager window.
4. Open the Disk Drives branch and double-click your hard disk to display its property sheet.
5. In the Policies tab, make sure that the Enable Write Caching on the Disk check box is activated.
6. For maximum performance with a SATA drive, activate the Enable Advanced Performance check box.
7. Click OK.

CAUTION

Let me reiterate here that activating the Enable Advanced Performance option tells Vista to use an even more aggressive write-caching algorithm. However, an unscheduled power shutdown means you will almost certainly lose some data. Activate this option only if your system is running off a UPS or has a battery backup.

Optimizing Virtual Memory

No matter how much main memory your system boasts, Windows Home Server still creates and uses a paging file for virtual memory. To maximize paging file performance, ensure that Windows Home Server is working with the paging file optimally. The next few sections present some techniques that help you do just that.

CAUTION

One common paging file optimization technique is to move the paging file to the drive that has the faster performance. However, you shouldn't try this in Windows Home Server because it could cause problems. Windows Home Server expects that system files will reside on the C drive, and all other drives are used as part of the storage pool. Therefore, in Windows Home Server, place the paging file only on drive C.

Customizing the Paging File Size

By default, Windows Home Server sets the initial size of the paging file to 1.5 times the amount of RAM in your system, and it sets the maximum size of the paging file to 3 times the amount of RAM. For example, on a system with 1GB RAM, the paging file's initial size will be 1.5GB and its maximum size will be 3GB. The default values work well on most systems, but you might want to customize these sizes to suit your own configuration. Here are some notes about custom paging file sizes:

▶ The less RAM you have, the more likely it is that Windows Home Server will use the paging file, so the Windows Home Server default paging file sizes make sense. If your computer has less than 1GB RAM, you should leave the paging file sizes as is.

▶ The more RAM you have, the less likely it is that Windows Home Server will use the paging file. Therefore, the default initial paging file size is too large and the disk space reserved by Windows Home Server is wasted. On systems with more than 1GB RAM, you should set the initial paging file size to half the RAM size, while leaving the maximum size at three times the RAM, just in case.

▶ If disk space on drive C: is at a premium, set the initial paging file size to 16MB (the minimum size supported by Windows Home Server). This should eventually result in the smallest possible paging file, but you'll see a bit of a performance drop because Windows Home Server often has to dynamically increase the size of the paging file as you work with your programs.

▶ You might think that setting the initial size and the maximum size to the same (relatively large; say, two or three times the RAM) value would improve performance because it would mean that Windows Home Server would never resize the paging file. In practice, however, it has been shown that this trick does *not* improve performance, and in some cases, it can actually decrease performance.

▶ If you have a large amount of RAM (at least 1GB), you might think that Windows Home Server would never need virtual memory, so it would be okay to turn off the paging file. This won't work, however, because Windows Home Server needs the paging file anyway, and some programs might crash if no virtual memory is present.

See "Changing the Paging File's Size" to learn how to customize the paging file size.

Watching the Paging File Size

Monitor the paging file performance to get a feel for how it works under normal conditions, where "normal" means while running your usual collection of applications and your usual number of open windows and documents.

Start up all the programs you normally use (and perhaps a few extra, for good measure), and then watch System Monitor's Process\Page File Bytes and Process\Page File Bytes Peak counters.

Changing the Paging File's Size

Here's how to change the paging file sizes that Windows Home Server uses:

1. Select Start, right-click My Computer, and then click Properties to display the System Properties dialog box.
2. Display the Advanced tab.
3. In the Performance group, click Settings to display the Performance Options dialog box.
4. Display the Advanced tab.
5. In the Virtual Memory group, click Change. Windows Home Server displays the Virtual Memory dialog box, shown in Figure 14.8.

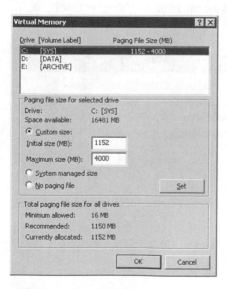

FIGURE 14.8   Use the Virtual Memory dialog box to select a different hard disk to store the paging file.

6. In the Drive list, make sure that drive C: is selected.

7. Make sure the Custom Size option is selected.

8. Use the Initial Size (MB) text box to enter the initial size, in megabytes, that Windows Home Server should use for the paging file.

9. Use the Maximum Size (MB) text box to enter the largest size, in megabytes, that Windows Home Server can use for the paging file.

CAUTION

To ensure that Windows Home Server is able to dynamically resize the paging file as needed, specify a maximum size that's larger than the initial size.

---

10. Click Set.

11. Click OK in all the open dialog boxes. If you decreased either the initial size or the maximum size, Windows Home Server asks if you want to restart the computer.

12. Click Yes.

Defragmenting the Paging File

As Windows Home Server dynamically sizes the paging file, it's possible that it can become fragmented, resulting in a small performance hit. Windows Home Server manipulates the paging file in relatively large blocks, so fragmentation rarely occurs. However, if you're looking to eke out every last drop of performance on your machine, you should probably ensure that the paging file is defragmented.

TIP

To determine whether the paging file is defragmented, run Disk Defragmenter, click drive C:, and then click Analyze. When the analysis is complete, click View Report and, in the Volume Information list, find the Pagefile Fragmentation item. The Total Fragments value tells you the number of fragments that the paging file uses.

Unfortunately, Windows Home Server's Disk Defragmenter tool does *not* defragment the paging file. To accomplish this, you have to temporarily move or disable the paging file. Here are the steps to follow:

1. Display the Virtual Memory dialog box, as described in the previous section.

2. Activate the No Paging File option to disable the paging file.

3. Restart your computer.

4. Defragment drive C.

5. Display the Virtual Memory dialog box and restore the original paging file settings.

6. Restart your computer.

Optimizing Applications

Unless you use Windows Home Server as your main workstation, it's unlikely that you want or need to optimize applications. However, if you do run programs on Windows Home Server, you can do a few things to improve the performance of those applications. The next few sections offer some pointers for improving the performance of applications under Windows Home Server.

Adding More Memory

All applications run in RAM, of course, so the more RAM you have, the less likely it is that Windows Home Server has to store excess program or document data in the paging file on the hard disk, which is a real performance killer. In Task Manager or System Monitor, watch the Available Memory value. If it starts to get too low, you should consider adding RAM to your system.

Optimizing Application Launching

Prefetching is a Windows Home Server performance feature that analyzes disk usage and then reads into memory the data that you or your system accesses most frequently. You can use the prefetcher to speed up booting, application launching, or both. You configure the prefetcher using the following Registry setting:

```
HKLM\SYSTEM\CurrentControlSet\Control\SessionManager\Memory Management\
➥PrefetchParameters\EnablePrefetcher
```

Set this value as follows:

- ▶ 1—Use the value for application-only prefetching.

- ▶ 2—Use this value for boot-only prefetching.

- ▶ 3—Use this value for both application and boot prefetching.

I normally recommend setting this value to 2 for boot-only prefetching (although this is the default on most Windows Home Server systems). This value improves boot performance and, on most systems, has little or no effect on application performance because commonly used application launch files are probably in the RAM cache anyway. However, you can experiment with setting the EnablePrefetcher value to 1 to optimize application launching.

Getting the Latest Device Drivers

If your application works with a device, check with the manufacturer or Windows Update to see whether a newer version of the device driver is available—in general, the newer the driver, the faster its performance. You learn how to update device drivers later in this chapter; see the section titled "Upgrading Your Device Drivers."

Setting the Program Priority in Task Manager

You can improve the performance of a program by adjusting the priority given to the program by your computer's processor. The processor enables programs to run by doling out thin slivers of its computing time to each program. These time slivers are called *cycles* because they are given to programs cyclically. For example, if you have three programs running—A, B, and C—the processor gives a cycle to A, one to B, another to C, and then one back to A again. This cycling happens quickly, appearing seamless when you work with each program.

The *base priority* is a ranking that determines the relative frequency with which a program gets processor cycles. A program given a higher frequency gets more cycles, which improves the program's performance. For example, suppose that you raise the priority of program A. The processor might give a cycle to A, one to B, another to A, one to C, another to A, and so on.

Follow these steps to change a program's priority:

1. Launch the program you want to work with.
2. Open Task Manager, as described earlier in this chapter. (Refer to "Monitoring Performance with Task Manager.")
3. Display the Processes tab.
4. Right-click your application's process to display its shortcut menu.
5. Click Set Priority, and then click (from highest priority to lowest) Realtime, High, or AboveNormal.

TIP

After you've changed the priority of one or more programs, you might forget the values that you have assigned to each one. To help, you can view the priority for all the items in the Processes tab. Click View and then click Select Columns to display the Select Columns dialog box. Activate the Base Priority check box and click OK. This adds a Base Priority column to the Processes list.

More Optimization Tricks

The rest of this chapter takes you through several techniques and tricks for eking out a bit more performance from your system.

Adjusting Power Options

Windows Home Server's power management options can shut down your system's monitor (assuming you're not running Windows Home Server with a headless setup) or hard disk to save energy. Unfortunately, it takes a few seconds for the system to power up these devices again, which can be frustrating when you want to get back to work. You can do two things to eliminate or reduce this frustration:

▶ **Don't let Windows Home Server turn off the monitor and hard disk**—By default, Windows Home Server doesn't turn off the monitor or hard disks, and it doesn't go into a system standby state. To make sure, select Start, Control Panel, Power Options to display the Power Options Properties dialog box. In the Power Schemes tab, use the Power Schemes list to select the Always On item (this is optional), and select Never in the Turn Off Monitor and Turn Off Hard Disks lists. For good measure, you should also make sure that Never is selected in the System Standby list. (If you also see a System Hibernates list, select Never there, as well.)

▶ **Don't use a screensaver**—Again, it can take a few seconds for Windows Home Server to recover from a screensaver. To ensure that you're not using one, select Start, Control Panel, Display, select the Screen Saver tab, and choose (None) in the Screen Saver list. If you're worried about monitor wear and tear, use the Blank screensaver, which is relatively lightweight and exits quickly. Also, if you're not worried about security, you can deactivate the On Resume, Display Welcome Screen check box to avoid having to log on all over again each time you exit the screensaver.

Eliminate the Use of Visual Effects

Unless you use Windows Home Server for day-to-day work, there's no reason for it to be using visual effects. For example, effects such as animating the movement of windows when you minimize or maximize them, fading or scrolling menus and tooltips, and adding shadows under menus and the mouse pointer are all merely cosmetic and are drains on system performance.

NOTE

To keep things in perspective, I should point out that these visual effects only affect system performance slightly, and most modern systems should be able to handle them without slowing noticeably. However, if you're running Windows Home Server on an older system that's already slower than you want it to be, or if you just want every last processor cycle to go to Windows Home Server's core functions, by all means lose the eye candy.

You can use various methods to turn off visual effects:

▶ Select Start, Control Panel, Display to open the Display Properties dialog box. Select the Appearance tab, and click Effects. In the Effects dialog box, deactivate the following check boxes:

Use the Following Transition Effect for Menus and Tooltips

Use the Following Method to Smooth Edges of Screen Fonts

Show Shadows Under Menus

Show Windows Contents While Dragging

▶ While you have the Display Properties dialog box open, select the Settings tab and choose Medium (16 bit) in the Color Quality list. Using fewer colors gives your graphics card less to do, which should speed up video performance. Also, click Advanced, display the Troubleshoot tab, and make sure that the Hardware Acceleration slider is set to Full.

▶ Select Start, Control Panel, System icon, display the Advanced tab, and click Settings in the Performance group. In the Visual Effects tab of the Performance Options dialog box (see Figure 14.9), activate the Adjust for Best Performance option (which deactivates all the check boxes).

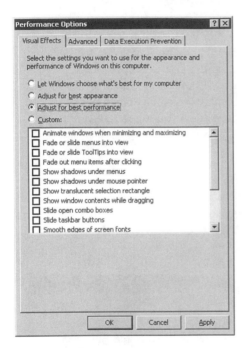

FIGURE 14.9   Turn off the check boxes in the Visual Effects tab to improve performance.

▶ Open the Registry Editor and set the following Registry value to 0:

`HKCU\Control Panel\Desktop\MenuShowDelay`

Optimizing Windows Home Server for Services and the System Cache

You can set up Windows Home Server so that it's optimized to run services and make best use of the system cache. This involves two things:

▶ **Processor scheduling**—This determines how much time the processor allocates to the computer's activities. In particular, processor scheduling differentiates between programs and background services. The latter are the processes that Windows Home Server uses behind the scenes, such as performing backups and monitoring network health. Clearly, background services are what Windows Home Server is all about, so it should be optimized to give more processor cycles to these services.

▶ **Memory Usage**—This determines how Windows Home Server allocates memory resources on the system. You can either optimize memory usage for programs or for the system cache, which is a portion of memory that holds recently used data for faster access:

> ▶ If you optimize for programs, Windows Home Server uses an 8MB system cache, and it allows changed cache pages to remain in memory until the number of available cache pages drops to about 1,000.

> ▶ If you optimize for the system cache, Windows Home Server allows the system cache to expand up to the size of physical RAM, less about 4MB. It also allows changed cache pages to remain in memory until the number of available pages drops to about 250. (This means that data stays in the system cache longer, which improves performance because Windows Home Server spends less time fetching data from the hard disk.)

Optimizing Windows Home Server performance means configuring it to give more CPU time to background services and using a large system cache. This is the default configuration in Windows Home Server, but it's worth your time to make sure that this is still the case on your system. Here are the steps to follow:

1. Select Start, Control Panel, System to display the System Properties dialog box.
2. Display the Advanced Tab.
3. In the Performance group, click Settings to display the Performance Options dialog box.
4. Display the Advanced tab, shown in Figure 14.10.
5. In the Processor Scheduling group, activate the Background Services option.
6. In the Memory Usage group, activate the System Cache option.
7. Click OK.
8. When Windows Home Server tells you the changes require a restart, click OK to return to the System Properties dialog box.
9. Click OK. Windows Home Server asks whether you want to restart your system.
10. Click Yes.

Optimizing Network Data Throughput for File Sharing

When you activate the System Cache option as described in the previous section, Windows Home Server sets the LargeSystemCache Registry setting to 1 in the following key:

HKLM\SYSTEM\CurrentControlSet\Control\Session Manager\Memory Management

It also sets the Size setting to 3 in the following key:

HKLM\SYSTEM\CurrentControlSet\Services\LanmanServer\Parameters

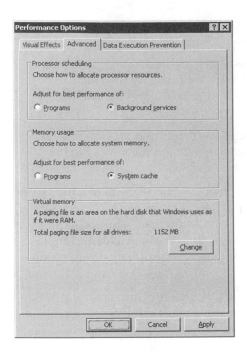

FIGURE 14.10   In the Performance Options dialog box, use the Advanced tab to optimize Windows Home Server for programs.

The Size setting controls how Windows Home Server works with network *data throughput*, which is the collective term for network tasks involving client computers, users, and files. Setting the Size value to 3 tells Windows Home Server to optimize data throughput for file sharing instead of network applications, which makes sense because most Windows Home Server machines spend the majority of their time sharing files instead of running server-based programs.

You can also control the value of the Size setting using the following steps:

1. Select Start, All Programs, Accessories, Communications, Network Connections. Windows Home Server opens the Network Connections window.

TIP

If you have the network icon displayed in the notification area, another way to open the Network Connections window is to right-click the icon and then click Open Network Connections.

▶ **SEE** For details on adding the network icon, **see** "Displaying the Network Icon in the Notification Area," **P. 9**.

2. Right-click the Local Area Connection icon, and then click Properties.

3. Select File and Printer Sharing for Microsoft Networks, and then click Properties to open the property sheet shown in Figure 14.11.

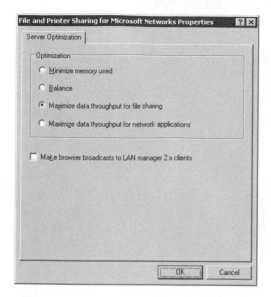

FIGURE 14.11   In the Local Area Connection's property sheet, use the Server Optimization tab to optimize Windows Home Server data throughput for file sharing.

4. Make sure the Maximize Data Throughput for File Sharing option is activated.

5. Click OK in the open dialog boxes.

Upgrading Your Device Drivers

Device drivers that are designed to work with Windows Home Server (or Windows Server 2003) generally load faster than older drivers. Therefore, you should check each of your device drivers to see whether a version exists that's designed to work with Windows Home Server (or Windows Server 2003) and, where available, upgrade to that driver.

The next few sections take you through Windows Home Server's various methods for updating a device driver.

Launching the Hardware Update Wizard

To get started, you need to run the Hardware Update Wizard, as described in the following steps:

1. If you have a disk or CD with the updated driver, insert the disk or CD. If you downloaded the driver from the Internet, decompress the driver file, if necessary.

2. Select Start, right-click My Computer, and then click Manage to open the Computer Management snap-in.

3. Select Device Manager.

4. Locate and select the device you want to upgrade.

5. Select Action, Update Driver, or click the Update Driver toolbar button. (You can also open the device's property sheet, display the Driver tab, and click Update Driver.) The Hardware Update Wizard appears, as shown in Figure 14.12.

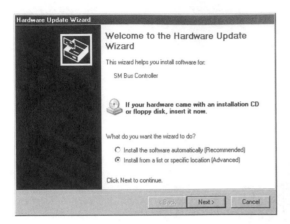

FIGURE 14.12   Use the Hardware Update Wizard to upgrade your device driver.

From here, you can install the driver automatically, install the driver from a disc or downloaded file, or use a built-in Windows Home Server driver. These choices are covered in the next three sections.

Installing the Driver Automatically

If you have a disk or CD that has the updated driver and that driver is Windows Home Server-compatible, you can usually get Windows Home Server to upgrade the driver automatically. Follow these steps:

1. Insert the disk or CD that contains the upgraded driver.

2. In the initial Hardware Update Wizard dialog box, click the Install the Software Automatically option and then click Next. Windows Home Server examines the system's disk drives, locates the driver, and then installs it.

3. If the wizard finds more than one driver, it asks you to choose the one you want from a list. Click the driver you want and then click Next. Windows Home Server installs the driver.

4. Click Finish.

Installing the Driver from a Disc or Download

If the Hardware Update Wizard couldn't find the driver on the disc, or if you've downloaded the driver file, here are the steps to follow to upgrade the driver:

1. If the driver is on a disc, insert the disc.

> **CAUTION**
>
> If the downloaded driver is contained within a compressed file (such as a ZIP file), be sure to decompress the file before moving on to the next wizard step.

2. In the initial Hardware Update Wizard dialog box, click Install from a List or Specific Location, and then click Next. You see the dialog box shown in Figure 14.13.

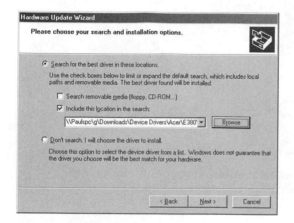

FIGURE 14.13   This dialog box appears if you elected to install the device driver from a list or a specific location.

3. Click the Search for the Best Driver in These Locations option.

4. Activate one of the following check boxes:

   ▶ **Search Removable Media**—Activate this check box if the driver is on a disk or CD.

   ▶ **Include This Location in the Search**—Activate this check box if the driver is on your hard disk or a network share. Enter the full path of the folder that contains the driver.

5. Click Next. Windows Home Server installs the driver from the location you specified.

6. Click Finish.

Installing a Built-In Windows Home Server Driver

If you don't have a disc or download, you can try installing one of Windows Home Server's built-in drivers, although in practice this is more useful for fixing driver problems than it is for improving performance. Follow these steps:

1. In the initial Hardware Update Wizard dialog box, click Install from a List or Specific Location, and then click Next.

2. Click the Don't Search. I Will Choose the Driver to Install option, and then click Next. The Hardware Update Wizard displays a list of compatible drivers for the device.

3. If you don't see an updated (or even a different) driver, you're probably out of luck. If you want, you can deactivate the Show Compatible Hardware check box. The wizard then displays a complete list of its built-in drivers for the device's hardware category, as shown in Figure 14.14.

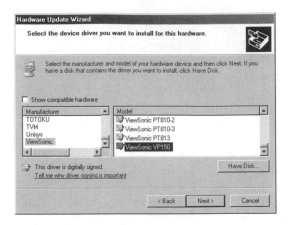

FIGURE 14.14   Deactivate the Show Compatible Hardware check box to see all of the Windows Home Server drivers in the device's hardware category.

4. Use the Manufacturer list to select the manufacturer of your device.

5. Use the Model list to select the device model.

6. Click Next. Windows Home Server installs the driver.

7. Click Finish.

From Here

▶ For details on adding the network icon, **see** "Displaying the Network Icon in the Notification Area," **P. 9**.

▶ To learn about Windows Home Server's new Drive Extender technology, **see** "Understanding Drive Extender," **P. 129**.

▶ To learn how to check for hard disk problems, **see** "Checking Your Hard Disk for Errors," **P. 431**.

▶ For information on checking hard disk free space, **see** "Checking Free Disk Space on the System Drive," **P. 437**.

▶ To learn how to delete files that your system no longer uses, **see** "Deleting Unnecessary Files from the System Drive," **P. 440**.

▶ For details on defragmenting, **see** "Defragmenting the System Drive," **P. 443**.

Maintaining Windows Home Server

Computers are useful beasts that do some pretty amazing tricks. However, one trick they haven't yet mastered is self-maintenance. Most of our other appliances run for years without much tending, but our computer appliances, being much more complex than your average microwave, require near-constant doses of digital TLC to keep them humming and happy. Fortunately, we're starting to see a trend toward self-maintenance in the PC world:

▶ Windows 7 and Windows Vista machines automatically defragment themselves once a week, and a background service monitors hard disk health and reports on problems that it finds.

▶ You learned in Chapter 9, "Backing Up and Restoring Network Computers," that Windows Home Server automatically deletes old backups and installs updates every Sunday.

▶ In this chapter, you learn that Windows Home Server automatically checks for errors on your installed hard drives.

▶ **SEE** For details on Windows Home Server's automatic backup deletions, **see** "Automatic Backup Management," **P. 242.**

These are a good beginning, but we're still an awfully long way from reaching the Holy Grail of self-maintaining computers. For example, if it's no big deal for Windows 7 and Windows Vista machines to defragment themselves regularly, why didn't Microsoft add the same capability to Windows Home Server? Not to worry, though: In this chapter, you learn not only how to perform a few essential maintenance chores in Windows Home Server, but you also learn how to automate most of those chores so that you have a few less things to keep on your to-do list.

Checking System Uptime

In networking parlance, *uptime* refers to the amount of time that some system has been running continuously since the last time the system was started. From the standpoint of Windows Home Server, the longer the uptime the better, because that means the server has been available for clients longer, which means that shared folders, media streaming, and remote access have all been available. Checking the system uptime isn't a crucial system maintenance skill, but it does give you some indication of how the system is running overall. These next few sections take you through various methods for checking the current uptime value.

Displaying Uptime with the SYSTEMINFO Command

The SYSTEMINFO command-line utility gives you a tremendous amount of information about your computer, including data about the manufacturer, processor, and memory, what hotfixes are installed, and what network devices are installed. It also tells you the system uptime:

```
System Up Time:    3 Days, 8 Hours, 55 Minutes, 39 Seconds
```

Unfortunately, the output of the SYSTEMINFO command is quite long, so locating that one line can take some time. To make things faster, pipe the output of SYSTEMINFO through a case-insensitive FIND command, like so:

```
systeminfo | FIND  /i "up time"
```

This forces Windows Home Server to display just the System Up Time line.

▶ **SEE** For details on the SYSTEMINFO command, **see** "SYSTEMINFO: Returning System Configuration Data," **P. 596.**

▶ **SEE** For a discussion of the FIND command, **see** "FIND: Locating a Text String in a File," **P. 579.**

Displaying Uptime with Performance Monitor

In Chapter 14, "Tuning Windows Home Server Performance," you learned how to monitor Windows Home Server's performance using counters that you add to the System Monitor. One of those counters also tells you the current system uptime. Follow these steps to add it:

> ▶ **SEE** "Monitoring Performance with System Monitor," **P. 404.**

1. Select Start, Run, type **perfmon**, and click OK. The System Monitor appears.
2. Right-click the system monitor and then click Add Counters. (Alternatively, press Ctrl+I or click the Add button in the toolbar.) The Add Counters dialog box appears.
3. In the Performance Object list, select System.
4. In Select Counters from List, select the System Up Time counter.
5. Click Add.
6. Click Close.

TIP

The System Up Time counter displays the uptime in seconds. To convert this value to days, divide it by 86,400 (the number of seconds in a day).

If you prefer a command-line solution, you can use the TYPEPERF utility to display performance counters in a Command Prompt window. Here's the command to run:

```
typeperf "\system\system up time" -sc 1
```

The -sc switch specifies the number of samples that you want TYPEPERF to collect and display. We need just one sample in this case.

> ▶ **SEE** For the specifics of using TYPEPERF, **see** "TYPEPERF: Monitoring Performance," **P. 598.**

Displaying Uptime with a Script

The problem with the System Up Time counter (whether you display it in System Monitor or at the command line) is that it displays the uptime in seconds, so you have to convert the value (to, say, days) to get a meaningful number. To avoid that, you can use the script in Listing 15.1, which does the conversion for you.

> **NOTE**
>
> You can download the scripts in this chapter from my website at www.mcfedries.com/HomeServerUnleashed2E/.

LISTING 15.1   A Script That Displays the System Uptime in Days, Hours, and Minutes

```
Option Explicit
Dim objOS, dateLastBoot, nSystemUptime
Dim nDays, nHours, nMinutes
'
' Get the Windows Home Server OS object
'
For Each objOS in GetObject( _
    "winmgmts:").InstancesOf ("Win32_OperatingSystem")
    '
    ' Return the last boot up time and
    ' convert it to a Date object
    '
    dateLastBoot = ConvertToDate(objOS.LastBootUpTime)
    '
    ' Calculate the number of minutes between then and now
    '
    nSystemUptime = DateDiff("n", dateLastBoot, Now)
    '
    ' Convert the total minutes into hours, days, and minutes
    '
    nDays = Int(nSystemUptime / 1440)
    nHours = Int (((nSystemUptime / 1440) - nDays) * 24)
    nMinutes = nSystemUptime Mod 60
    '
    ' Display the result
    '
    Wscript.Echo "Last Boot: " & dateLastBoot & vbCrLf & _
                "System Uptime: " & _
                nDays & " days and " & _
                nHours & " hours and " & _
                nMinutes & " minutes"
Next
'
' This function takes a datetime string and converts
' it to a real date and time object
'
Function ConvertToDate(strDate)
    Dim strYear, strMonth, strDay
```

```
    Dim strHour, strMinute, strSecond
    strYear = Left(strDate, 4)
    strMonth = Mid(strDate, 5, 2)
    strDay = Mid(strDate, 7, 2)
    strHour = Mid(strDate, 9, 2)
    strMinute = Mid(strDate, 11, 2)
    strSecond = Mid(strDate, 13, 2)
    ConvertToDate = DateSerial(strYear, strMonth, strDay) & " " & _
                    TimeSerial(strHour, strMinute, strSecond)
End Function
```

This script references the Win32_OperatingSystem class, which has just one member object: the Windows Home Server operating system, represented in the For Each...Next loop by objOS. The script gets the LastBootUpTime property and converts the resulting string to a Date object using the ConvertToDate function. DateDiff returns the number of minutes between the last boot and Now. (This difference is the raw value for the system uptime.) Then the script converts the total minutes into the corresponding number of days, hours, and minutes and displays the result. Figure 15.1 shows sample output.

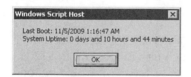

FIGURE 15.1   Sample output from the script in Listing 15.1.

Checking Your Hard Disk for Errors

Our hard disks store our programs and, most importantly, our precious data, so they have a special place in the computing firmament. We ought to pamper and coddle them to ensure a long and trouble-free existence, but that's rarely the case, unfortunately. Just consider everything that a modern hard disk has to put up with:

▶ **General wear and tear**—If your computer is running right now, its hard disk is spinning away at between 5,400 and 10,000 revolutions per minute. That's right—even though you're not doing anything, the hard disk is hard at work. Because of this constant activity, most hard disks simply wear out after a few years.

▶ **Head/platter collisions**—Your hard disk includes *read/write heads* that are used to read data from and write data to the disk. These heads float on a cushion of air just above the spinning hard disk platters. A bump or jolt of sufficient intensity can send them crashing onto the surface of the disk, which could easily result in trashed data. If the heads happen to hit a particularly sensitive area, the entire hard disk could crash. Notebook computers are particularly prone to this problem.

▶ **Power surges**—The current that is supplied to your PC is, under normal conditions, relatively constant. It's possible, however, for your computer to be assailed by massive power surges (such as during a lightning storm). These surges can wreak havoc on a carefully arranged hard disk.

So, what can you do about it? Windows Home Server comes with a program called Check Disk that can check your hard disk for problems and repair them automatically. It might not be able to recover a totally trashed hard disk, but it can at least let you know when a hard disk might be heading for trouble.

Check Disk performs a battery of tests on a hard disk, including looking for invalid filenames, invalid file dates and times, bad sectors, and invalid compression structures. In the hard disk's file system, Check Disk also looks for the following errors:

▶ Lost clusters

▶ Invalid clusters

▶ Cross-linked clusters

▶ File system cycles

The next few sections explain these errors in more detail.

Understanding Clusters

Large hard disks are inherently inefficient. When you format a disk, the disk's magnetic medium is divided into small storage areas called *sectors*, which usually hold up to 512 bytes of data. A large hard disk can contain tens of millions of sectors, so it would be too inefficient for Windows Home Server to deal with individual sectors. Instead, Windows Home Server groups sectors into *clusters*, the size of which depends on the file system and the size of the partition, as shown in Table 15.1.

TABLE 15.1   Default Cluster Sizes for Various File Systems and Partition Sizes

Partition Size	FAT16 Cluster Size	FAT32 Cluster Size	NTFS Cluster Size
7MB–16MB	2KB	N/A	512 bytes
17MB–32MB	512 bytes	N/A	512 bytes
33MB–64MB	1KB	512 bytes	512 bytes
65MB–128MB	2KB	1KB	512 bytes
129MB–256MB	4KB	2KB	512 bytes
257MB–512MB	8KB	4KB	512 bytes
513MB–1,024MB	16KB	4KB	1KB
1,025MB–2GB	32KB	4KB	2KB
2GB–4GB	64KB	4KB	4KB

TABLE 15.1   Default Cluster Sizes for Various File Systems and Partition Sizes

Partition Size	FAT16 Cluster Size	FAT32 Cluster Size	NTFS Cluster Size
4GB–8GB	N/A	4KB	4KB
8GB–16GB	N/A	8KB	4KB
16GB–32GB	N/A	16KB	4KB
32GB–2TB	N/A	N/A	4KB

Still, each hard disk has many thousands of clusters, so it's the job of the file system to keep track of everything. In particular, for each file on the disk, the file system maintains an entry in a *file directory*, a sort of table of contents for your files. (On an NTFS partition, this is called the *Master File Table*, or *MFT*.)

Understanding Lost Clusters

A *lost cluster* (also sometimes called an *orphaned cluster*) is a cluster that, according to the file system, is associated with a file but has no link to an entry in the file directory. Lost clusters are typically caused by program crashes, power surges, or power outages.

If Check Disk comes across lost clusters, it offers to convert them to files in either the file's original folder (if Check Disk can determine the proper folder) or in a new folder named Folder.000 in the root of the %SystemDrive%. (If that folder already exists, Check Disk creates a new folder named Folder.001 instead.) In that folder, Check Disk converts the lost clusters to files with names like File0000.chk and File0001.chk.

You can take a look at these files (using a text editor) to see whether they contain any useful data and then try to salvage the data. Most often, however, these files are unusable, and most people just delete them.

Understanding Invalid Clusters

An *invalid cluster* is one that falls under one of the following three categories:

▶ A file system entry with an illegal value. (In the FAT16 file system, for example, an entry that refers to cluster 1 is illegal because a disk's cluster numbers start at 2.)

▶ A file system entry that refers to a cluster number larger than the total number of clusters on the disk.

▶ A file system entry that is marked as unused but is part of a cluster chain.

In this case, Check Disk asks whether you want to convert these lost file fragments to files. If you say yes, Check Disk truncates the file by replacing the invalid cluster with an *end of file* (*EOF*) marker and then converts the lost file fragments to files. These are probably the truncated portion of the file, so you can examine them and try to piece everything back together. More likely, however, you just have to trash these files.

Understanding Cross-Linked Clusters

A *cross-linked cluster* is a cluster that has somehow been assigned to two different files (or twice in the same file). Check Disk offers to delete the affected files, copy the cross-linked cluster to each affected file, or ignore the cross-linked files altogether. In most cases, the safest bet is to copy the cross-linked cluster to each affected file. This way, at least one of the affected files should be usable.

Understanding Cycles

In an NTFS partition, a *cycle* is a corruption in the file system whereby a subfolder's parent folder is listed as the subfolder. For example, a folder name C:\Data should have C:\ as its parent; if C:\Data is a cycle, C:\Data—the same folder—is listed as the parent instead. This creates a kind of loop in the file system that can cause the cycled folder to "disappear." In this case, Check Disk restores the correct parent folder and all is well again.

Understanding Windows Home Server's Automatic Disk Checking

In Chapter 5, "Setting Up and Using Home Server Storage," you learned how to use the Windows Home Server Console to check hard drive status and, if needed, to repair a hard drive. How does Windows Home Server know when a hard drive needs fixing? It runs a service called Storage Manager that (among many other duties) runs Check Disk (technically, the CHKDSK command-line utility) every six hours to look for problems. To confirm this for yourself, open Event Viewer (select Start, Control Panel, Administrative Tools, Event Viewer; or select Start, Run, type **eventvwr.msc,** and click OK), select the Application log, and look for events where the Source value is Chkdsk. If you have N hard drives on your system, you see N+1 Chkdsk events (one for the system volume, one for the primary data volume, and one each for the secondary volumes). These occur once each day at midnight. Figure 15.2 shows a typical Chkdsk event.

> ▶ **SEE** For details on storage status indicators, **see** "Viewing Storage Status," **P. 137.**

TIP

If you'd like to see the results of these disk checks, first open the following folder on Windows Home Server:

%AllUsersProfile%\Application Data\Microsoft\Windows Home Server\logs

Double-click the qsm*ddmmyy*.txt file (where *ddmmyy* is the date the disk check occurred) to open the log in Notepad. The log is likely huge, so press Ctrl+F and search for chkdsk.

Note in Figure 15.2 that Storage Manager runs Check Disk in read-only mode. This means that Check Disk does not try to repair errors. Instead, if Check Disk reports that a drive is generating errors, it changes the drive's status to Failing, changes the overall network health status to At Risk (orange), and enables the drive's Repair option in Windows Home Server Console.

▶ **SEE** For more on repairing a drive, **see** "Repairing Storage," **P. 138.**

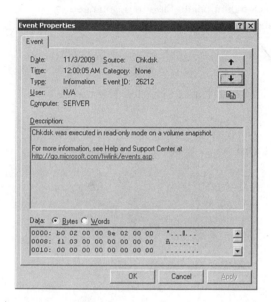

FIGURE 15.2 Windows Home Server's Storage Manager service runs Check Disk on each volume every six hours.

All this means that you probably don't have to run a basic Check Disk by hand very often, particularly if your system is showing no signs of possible hard disk failure (such as intermittent system lock-ups, program crashes, and corrupt documents). However, if you *do* notice any of this behavior, it's always a good idea to run Check Disk as soon as possible, as described in the next section.

What you *will* do with Check Disk is run the more thorough scan that performs a sector-by-sector check of the physical disk. If you do this about once a month, you can give yourself a heads-up about potential problems.

Running Check Disk

Check Disk has two versions: a GUI version and a command-line version. See Chapter 19, "Using Windows Home Server's Command-Line Tools," to learn how to use the command-line version. Here are the steps to follow to run the GUI version of Check Disk:

▶ **SEE** For details on running Check Disk from the command line, **see** "CHKDSK: Checking for Hard Disk Errors," **P. 568.**

NOTE

The GUI version of Check Disk only works with local partitions that have assigned drive letters. In Windows Home Server, this means you can use Check Disk on the system partition (C:) and the primary data partition (D:). However, you can't use Check Disk on secondary data partitions because these exist as mount points in Windows Home Server, so they don't have drive letters. To check mount points for errors, you need to use the CHKDSK command-line utility (again, see Chapter 19).

---

1. Select Start, My Computer. (You can also select Start, Windows Explorer and then click My Computer in the Folders list.)

2. Right-click the drive you want to check and then click Properties. The drive's property sheet appears.

3. Display the Tools tab.

4. Click the Check Now button. The Check Disk window appears, as shown in Figure 15.3.

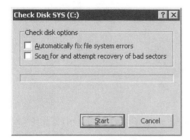

FIGURE 15.3   Use Check Disk to scan a hard disk partition for errors.

5. Activate one or both of the following options, if desired:

   ▶ **Automatically Fix File System Errors**—If you activate this check box, Check Disk automatically repairs any file system errors that it finds. If you leave this option deactivated, Check Disk runs in read only mode and just reports on any errors it finds.

   ▶ **Scan for and Attempt Recovery of Bad Sectors**—If you activate this check box, Check Disk performs a sector-by-sector surface check of the hard disk surface. If Check Disk finds a bad sector, it automatically attempts to recover any information stored in the sector and marks the sector as defective so that no information can be stored there in the future.

CAUTION

A sector-by-sector check can take several hours or more, depending on the size of the partition. Therefore, only run this more intensive check when you won't be using Windows Home Server for a while.

---

6. Click Start.

7. If you activated the Automatically Fix File System Errors check box and are checking a partition that has open system files, Check Disk tells you that it can't continue because it requires exclusive access to the disk. It then asks whether you want to schedule the scan to occur the next time you boot the computer. Click Yes to schedule the disk check.

8. When the scan is complete, Check Disk displays a message letting you know and provides a report on the errors it found, if any.

The AUTOCHK Utility

If you click Yes when Check Disk asks whether you want to schedule the scan for the next boot, the program adds the AUTOCHK utility to the following Registry setting:

    HKLM\SYSTEM\CurrentControlSet\Control\Session Manager\BootExecute

This setting specifies the programs that Windows Home Server should run at boot time when the Session Manager is loading. AUTOCHK is the automatic version of Check Disk that runs at system startup. If you want the option of skipping the disk check, you need to specify a timeout value for AUTOCHK. You change the timeout value by using the AutoChkTimeOut setting in the same Registry key:

    HKLM\SYSTEM\CurrentControlSet\Control\Session Manager\BootExecute

When AUTOCHK is scheduled with a timeout value greater than 0, you see the following the next time you restart the computer:

    A disk check has been scheduled.

    To skip disk checking, press any key within 10 second(s).

You can bypass the check by pressing a key before the timeout expires.

▶ **SEE** You can also use the CHKNTFS command line to set the AUTOCHK timeout value; **see** "CHKNTFS: Scheduling Automatic Disk Checks," **P. 571.**

Checking Free Disk Space on the System Drive

Hard disks with capacities measured in the hundreds of gigabytes are commonplace even in low-end systems nowadays, so disk space is much less of a problem than it used to be. This is particularly true with Windows Home Server and its storage technology that aggregates hard drive capacity into a single storage pool. However, remember that this storage pool is only used for data. Windows Home Server also has a system partition—drive C—and that volume comes with a fixed 20GB size. With Windows Home Server taking up about 6- to 8GB (depending on the size of the paging file), you only have so much space left over to install other programs or store data in the Administrator account's local folders. Therefore, it's a good idea to keep track of how much free space you have on drive C.

One way to check disk free space is to select Start, Windows Explorer and then select My Computer. The Details view (select View, Details to see it) includes columns for Total Size and Free Space, as shown in Figure 15.4. Alternatively, right-click drive C in Windows Explorer and then click Properties. The system partition's total capacity, as well as its current used and free space, appear in the General tab of the property sheet, as shown in Figure 15.5.

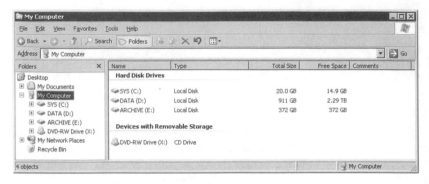

FIGURE 15.4   In Windows Explorer, display My Computer in Details view to see the total size and free space on your system's disks.

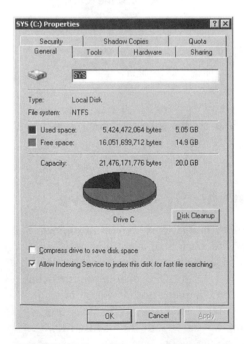

FIGURE 15.5   Right-click drive C and then click Properties to see the system drive's total size and free space.

Listing 15.2 presents a VBScript procedure that displays the status and free space for each drive on your system.

LISTING 15.2   A VBScript Example That Displays the Status and Free Space for the System Drive (C)

```
Option Explicit
Dim objFSO, strMessage

' Create the File System Object
Set objFSO = CreateObject("Scripting.FileSystemObject")

' Start the display string
strMessage = "Status Report for Drive C" & vbCrLf & vbCrLf

' Get the properties of drive C
With objFSO.Drives("C")

    ' Add the volume name to the message
    strMessage = strMessage & "Volume Name: " & .VolumeName & vbCrLf

    ' Check the drive status
    If .IsReady = True Then

        ' If it's ready, add the status, total size,
        ' and the free space to the message
        strMessage = strMessage & "Status: Ready" & vbCrLf
        strMessage = strMessage & "Total space: " & _
                    FormatNumber(.TotalSize / 1073741824, 2) & " GB" & vbCrLf
        strMessage = strMessage & "Free space: " & _
                    FormatNumber(.FreeSpace / 1073741824, 2) & " GB"
        strMessage = strMessage & vbCrLf & vbCrLf
    Else

        ' Otherwise, just add the status to the message
        strMessage = strMessage & "Status: Not Ready" & vbCrLf & vbCrLf
    End If
End With

' Display the message
WScript.Echo strMessage
```

This script creates a FileSystemObject and then uses its Drives collection to return a reference to the system drive: Drives("C"). Then the script checks the Drive object's

IsReady property. If the drive is available (there's no reason why it wouldn't be, but you never know), a series of property values is added to the message: VolumeName, TotalSize, and FreeSpace. (Note that the last two are converted from bytes to gigabytes by dividing the property value by 1,073,741,824.) The script finishes by displaying the drive data as shown in Figure 15.6.

FIGURE 15.6   The script displays the name, status, total space, and free space for the system drive.

Deleting Unnecessary Files from the System Drive

In the previous section, I mentioned that with hard drive capacities now regularly weighing in at several hundred gigabytes (with terabyte—1,000 gigabytes—and larger drives now available), free hard disk is not the problem it once was. Or is it? Just as these massive hard drives became affordable, it also became commonplace to create huge, multi-gigabyte files from DVD rips and recorded TV shows. In other words, no matter how humongous our hard drives are, we always seem to find a way to fill them up.

On your Windows Home Server system, you probably store any large data files in the shared folders, where your storage pool should be large enough to handle them. However, that doesn't mean your system drive (C) is in no danger of filling up. You only get 20GB to play with, and if you install large programs such as SharePoint Services (see Chapter 13, "Running a SharePoint Site on Windows Home Server") and programming tools such as Visual Studio Express, you may find that it doesn't take you all that long to fill up the system drive.

If you find that the system partition is getting low on free space, you should delete any unneeded files and programs. Windows Home Server comes with a Disk Cleanup utility that enables you to remove certain types of files quickly and easily. Before discussing this utility, let's look at a few methods you can use to perform a spring cleaning on your hard disk by hand:

▶ **Uninstall programs you don't use**—If you have an Internet connection, you know it's easier than ever to download new software for a trial run. Unfortunately, that also means it's easier than ever to have unused programs cluttering your hard disk. Use the Control Panel's Add or Remove Programs icon to uninstall these and other rejected applications.

▶ **Delete downloaded program archives**—Speaking of program downloads, your hard disk is also probably littered with ZIP files or other downloaded archives. For those programs you use, you should consider moving the archive files to a removable medium for storage. For programs you don't use, you should delete the archive files.

▶ **Remove Windows Home Server components that you don't use**—If you don't use some Windows Home Server components, use the Control Panel's Add or Remove Programs icon to remove those components from your system.

▶ **Move documents to the shared folders**—Your Administrator account on Windows Home Server has its own My Documents folder, and it's fine to use that folder to store scripts and other local files. However, if you use Windows Home Server to rip audio CDs and DVDs, record TV shows, or work with large database files, your documents can eat up a lot of disk space. If your Windows Home Server storage pool is large, you should probably move some or all of your My Documents contents to the shared folders.

After you've performed these tasks, you should run the Disk Cleanup utility, which can automatically remove some of the preceding file categories, as well as several other types of files. Here's how it works:

1. Select Start, All Programs, Accessories, System Tools, Disk Cleanup. The Select Drive dialog box appears.

2. In the Drives list, select drive C. (It should be selected by default.) Disk Cleanup scans the drive to see which files can be deleted and then displays a window similar to the one shown in Figure 15.7.

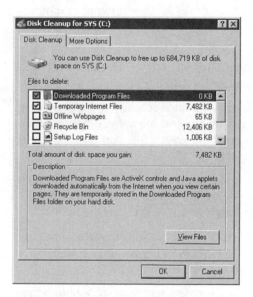

FIGURE 15.7   Disk Cleanup can automatically and safely remove certain types of files from a disk drive.

TIP

Windows Home Server offers two methods for bypassing the Select Drive dialog box. One method is to right-click drive C in Windows Explorer, click Properties, and then click the Disk Cleanup button in the General tab of the drive's property sheet. The other method is to select Start, Run, type `cleanmgr /dc,` and then click OK.

3. In the Files to Delete list, activate the check box beside each category of file you want to remove. If you're not sure what an item represents, select it and read the text in the Description box. Note, too, that for most of these items, you can click View Files to see what you'll be deleting. In most cases, you see the following items in this list:

   ▶ **Downloaded Program Files**—These are ActiveX controls and Java applets used by some web pages. Internet Explorer downloads the objects and stores them on your system.

   ▶ **Temporary Internet Files**—These are copies of web pages that Internet Explorer keeps on hand so that the pages view faster the next time you visit them. Note that deleting these files slows down your web surfing slightly, but you probably won't notice this much if you have a broadband connection.

   ▶ **Offline Webpages**—These are web pages that you've set up as favorites and for which you've activated the "Make available offline" feature. This means that Internet Explorer stores updated copies of these pages on your computer for offline surfing. Deleting them means that you have to go online to view them.

   ▶ **Microsoft Error Reporting Temporary Files**—These are temporary files that the Error Reporting service uses. You can safely delete these files.

   ▶ **Recycle Bin**—These are the files that you've deleted recently. Windows Home Server stores them in the Recycle Bin for a while just in case you delete a file accidentally. If you're sure you don't need to recover a file, you can clean out the Recycle Bin and recover the disk space.

   ▶ **Temporary Remote Desktop Files**—These are temporary files that Windows Home Server uses to make Remote Desktop connections appear faster and more responsive. You can delete these files without causing problems.

   ▶ **Setup Log Files**—These are files that Windows Home Server created while it was installing itself on your computer. If your computer is running well, you'll never need to refer to these logs, so you can toss them.

   ▶ **Temporary Files**—These are files that some programs use to store temporary information. Most programs delete these files automatically, but a program or computer crash could prevent that from happening. You can delete these files at will.

▶ **Compress Old Files**—Windows Home Server can take files that the system hasn't used in a while (the default is 50 days) and compress them so that they take up less disk space, yet remain accessible to you and your programs.

▶ **Catalog Files for the Content Indexer**—These are files that have been left behind by the Windows Home Server Indexing Service. You're unlikely to save much disk space here because Windows Home Server doesn't use the Indexing Service.

4. Click OK. Disk Cleanup asks whether you're sure that you want to delete the files.

5. Click Yes. Disk Cleanup deletes the selected files.

Saving Disk Cleanup Settings

It's possible to save your Disk Cleanup settings and run them again at any time. This is handy if, for example, you want to delete all your downloaded program files and temporary Internet files at shutdown. Select Start, Command Prompt, and then enter the following command:

```
cleanmgr /sageset:1
```

Note that the number 1 in the command is arbitrary: You can enter any number between 0 and 65535. This launches Disk Cleanup with an expanded set of file types to delete. Make your choices and click OK. What this does is save your settings to the Registry; it doesn't delete the files. To delete the files, open the command prompt and enter the following command:

```
cleanmgr /sagerun:1
```

You can also create a shortcut for this command, add it to a batch file, or schedule it with the Task Scheduler.

Defragmenting the System Drive

Windows Home Server comes with a utility called Disk Defragmenter that's an essential tool for tuning your hard disk. Disk Defragmenter's job is to rid your hard disk of file fragmentation.

File fragmentation means that a file is stored on your hard disk in scattered, noncontiguous bits. This is a performance drag because it means that when Windows Home Server tries to open such a file, it must make several stops to collect the various pieces. If a lot of files are fragmented, it can slow even the fastest hard disk to a crawl.

Why doesn't Windows Home Server just store files contiguously? Recall that Windows Home Server stores files on disk in clusters, and these clusters have a fixed size, depending on the disk's capacity. Most NTFS partitions use 4KB clusters, which is a small enough value that it more or less ensures that most files will be stored in multiple clusters.

Suppose, then, that a file requires 100 clusters to store everything. When you go to save that file (or when the system decides to write the file back to disk from memory or the paging file), you might think that Windows Home Server would examine the hard disk and look for a spot large enough to place all 100 clusters in a row. However, that's not the case. Windows Home Server is constantly writing files to disk, and if it took the time to find the perfect disk location every time, your system would feel extremely slow and sluggish.

To speed things up, Windows Home Server stores the first part of the file in the first available cluster, the second part in the next available cluster, and so on. Because available clusters can appear anywhere on the disk (for example, after you delete a file, its clusters become available for use by other files), you almost always end up with bits of the file scattered around the hard disk. That's file fragmentation, and that's what Disk Defragmenter is designed to fix.

Before using Disk Defragmenter on the system drive, you should perform a couple of housekeeping chores:

▶ **Delete any files from drive** C that you don't need, as described in the previous section. Defragmenting junk files only slows down the whole process.

▶ **Check drive** C for errors by running Check Disk, as described earlier in this chapter (refer to "Checking Your Hard Disk for Errors").

Follow these steps to use Disk Defragmenter:

▶ **SEE** You can also defragment a drive from the command line; **see** "DEFRAG: Defragmenting the System Drive," **P. 574.**

1. Select Start, All Programs, Accessories, System Tools, Disk Defragmenter. (Alternatively, in Windows Explorer, right-click the hard drive partition, click Properties, display the Tools tab in the dialog box that appears, and then click the Defragment Now button.) The Disk Defragmenter window appears.

2. Select drive C.

3. Click Analyze. Disk Defragmenter analyzes the fragmentation of the drive and then displays its recommendation (for example, You should defragment this volume, as shown in Figure 15.8). If you want more information, click View Report. If you don't want to defragment the drive, click Close and skip the rest of these steps.

4. Click Defragment. Disk Defragmenter begins defragmenting the drive. As you can see in Figure 15.9, it displays the progress of the defrag in the status bar. As it progresses, you should see less red and more blue in the disk usage bars.

5. When the defrag is done, click Close.

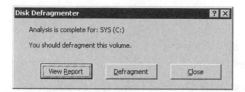

FIGURE 15.8   After analyzing the system drive, Disk Defragmenter tells you whether it needs to be defragmented.

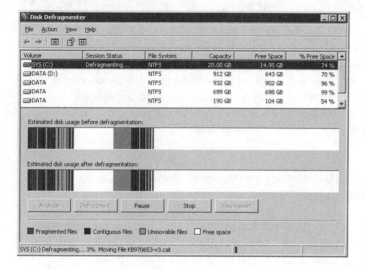

FIGURE 15.9   The Disk Defragmenter window shows you the progress of the defrag.

TIP

In some cases, you can defragment a drive even further by running Disk Defragmenter on the drive twice in a row. (That is, run the defragment, and when it's done, immediately run a second defragment on the same drive.)

Reviewing Event Viewer Logs

Windows Home Server constantly monitors your system for unusual or noteworthy occurrences. It might be a service that doesn't start, the installation of a device, or an application error. These occurrences are called *events*, and Windows Home Server tracks them in four main event logs (most Windows Home Server systems also show a fifth log named Internet Explorer, which I'll ignore here):

Application   This log stores events related to applications, including Windows Home Server programs and third-party applications.

Security   This log stores events related to system security, including logons, user accounts, and user privileges. I discussed this log in detail in Chapter 11, "Implementing Windows Home Server Security."

▶ **SEE** For the specifics of the Security log, **see** "Tracking Auditing Events," **P. 291.**

System	This log stores events generated by Windows and components, such as system services and device drivers.
Windows Home Server	This log stores events related to specific Windows Home Server features, such as the backup service and remote access.

NOTE

The System log catalogs device driver errors, but remember that Windows Home Server has other tools that make it easier to see device problems. As you see in Chapter 17, "Troubleshooting Windows Home Server," Device Manager displays an icon on devices that have problems, and you can view a device's property sheet to see a description of the problem. Also, the System Information utility (`Msinfo32.exe`) reports hardware woes in the System Information, Hardware Resources, Conflicts/Sharing branch and the System Information, Components, Problem Devices branch.

▶ **SEE** For more information on Device Manager's troubleshooting features, **see** "Troubleshooting with Device Manager," **P. 506.**

You should scroll through the Application and System event logs regularly to look for existing problems or for warnings that could portend future problems. The Security log isn't as important for day-to-day maintenance. You need to use it only if you suspect a security issue with your machine, such as if you want to keep track of who logs on to the computer. To examine these logs, you use the Event Viewer snap-in, available via either of the following techniques:

▶ Select Start, Run, type **eventvwr.msc**, and then click OK.

▶ Select Start, Control Panel, Administrative Options, Event Viewer.

Figure 15.10 shows a typical Event Viewer window. Use the tree in the left pane to select the log you want to view: Application, Security, or System.

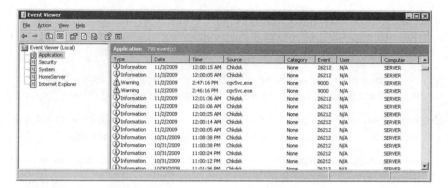

FIGURE 15.10   Use the Event Viewer to monitor events generated by applications and Windows Home Server.

When you select a log, the right pane displays the available events, including the event's date, time, and source; its type (Information, Warning, or Error); and other data. To see a description of an event, double-click it or select it and press Enter.

TIP

Rather than monitoring the event logs by hand, Windows Home Server comes with a couple of tools that can help automate the process. The eventquery.vbs script (it's in the C:\Windows\System32 folder) enables you to query the log files for specific event types, IDs, sources, and more. Search Help and Support for *eventquery* to get the script's command-line syntax. Also, you can set up an *event trigger* to perform some action when a particular event occurs. You do this using the eventtriggers.exe utility (also in C:\Windows\System32). Search Help and Support for *eventtriggers* to get the full syntax for this tool.

Exporting Event Logs to a Database

The Event Viewer gives you various ways to tame the large amount of data found in the event logs:

▶ You can search for the data you want by event source, category, ID, and so on. Select the log you want to search and then select View, Find.

▶ You can filter the data to display on those events that interest you. Select the log you want to filter and then select View, Filter.

▶ You can export the data to a text file for processing in another program. Select the log you want to export and then select Action, Export List. You can export the data to either a tab-delimited or comma-delimited file, using either plain text or Unicode.

The last of these techniques is particularly useful because you can then import the tab- or comma-delimited file into a spreadsheet or database program for analysis. However, if you plan on doing this regularly, the export technique has two large drawbacks:

▶ It requires two separate operations: one to export the event log from Event Viewer and one to import the resulting tab- or comma-delimited file into the other program.

▶ You can also export one log at a time. If you want to analyze multiple logs (or all the logs), you must perform separate export and import operations for each one.

This is clearly time-consuming, so it would be faster and more efficient to automate the process using a script. The rest of this section shows you how to do just that.

Creating a Data Source

Before getting to the script, note that you're going to need access to some kind of database, and you're going to need to create an *Open Database Connectivity*, or *ODBC*, data source for that database. ODBC is a database standard that enables a program or script to connect to and manipulate a data source. An ODBC data source contains three things: a pointer to the file or server where the database resides; a driver that enables a program or script to connect to, manipulate, and return data from the database; and the logon information that the program or script requires to access the database.

Most data sources point to database files. For example, the relational database management programs Access, Visual FoxPro, Paradox, and dBase all use file-based databases. You can also create data sources based on text files and Excel workbooks. Finally, some data sources point to server-based databases, such as SQL Server databases.

Here are the steps to follow to create a data source for an Access database:

1. Log in to Windows Home Server and Select Start, Control Panel, Administrative Tools, Data Sources (ODBC). The ODBC Data Source Administrator window appears.

2. Select the System DSN tab.

3. Click Add to open the Create New Data Source dialog box.

4. Select Microsoft Access Driver (*.mdb) and then click Finish. The ODBC Microsoft Access Setup dialog box appears.

5. Use the Data Source Name text box to enter a name for the data source.

TIP

You use the data source name in your script later on, so a short name with no spaces is best.

6. Click Select to open the Select Database dialog box.

7. Open the folder containing the Access database, select the database file, and then click OK to return to the ODBC Microsoft Access Setup dialog box.

8. If you have to log in to this database, click Advanced, type the login name and password, and then click OK.

9. Click OK. Windows Home Server adds the data source to the System DSN tab.

10. Click OK.

Here are the steps to follow to create a data source for an SQL Server database:

1. Select Start, Control Panel, Administrative Tools, Data Sources (ODBC). The ODBC Data Source Administrator window appears.

2. Select the system DSN tab.

3. Click Add to open the Create New Data Source dialog box.

4. Select SQL Server and then click Finish. The Create a New Data Source to SQL Server dialog box appears.

5. Use the Name text box to enter a name for the data source.

6. Use the Server text box to enter the host or domain name of the SQL Server computer.

7. Click Next.

8. Select an authentication option:

   ▶ **With Windows NT Authentication**—Select this option to log in to the SQL Server database using your Windows Home Server network logon data.

   ▶ **With SQL Server Authentication**—Select this option to specify the login data, which you enter using the Login ID and Password text boxes.

9. Click Next.

10. If you want to log in to a database other than the default master database, activate the Change the Default Database To check box and then use the list to select the database name.

11. Click Next.

12. Click Finish. Windows Home Server displays a summary of the data source information.

> **TIP**
>
> It's a good idea at this point to click the Test Data Source button. Windows Home Server attempts to connect to the data source and then lets you know whether the test was successful. If it wasn't, you need to modify your settings. (For example, you may have typed the wrong login name or password.)

13. Click OK. Windows Home Server adds the data source to the System DSN tab. Figure 15.11 shows the System DSN tab with two data sources added: one for Access and one for SQL Server.

14. Click OK.

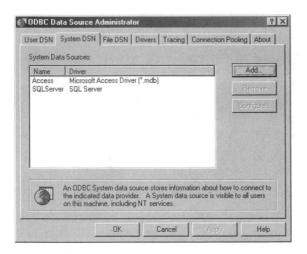

FIGURE 15.11   The System DNS tab with Access and SQL Server data sources added.

Creating a Table for the Event Log Data

Next, you need to access the database and then set up a table that you want to use to store the event log data. These steps vary depending on the database program, so I won't go into the specifics here. Table 15.2 shows a sample table definition, which includes the field name, the field data type, and the corresponding Event Viewer column for each field.

TABLE 15.2   A Sample Definition for a Table to Hold Event Log Data

Field Name	Data Type	Event Viewer Column
EventType	Text	Type
EventTime	Date/Time	Date and Time
EventSource	Text	Source
EventCategory	Text	Category
EventCode	Integer	Event
EventUser	Text	User
EventComputer	Text	Computer
EventLog	Text	N/A
EventRecord	Integer	N/A
EventMessage	Memo	N/A

Exporting the Event Logs with a Script

You're now ready to perform the export operation using a script, which is shown in Listing 15.3.

LISTING 15.3   A Script That Exports Yesterday's Event Logs to a Database

```
Option Explicit
Dim objStartDate, objEndDate
Dim objWMI, objEvents, objEvent
Dim objConn, objRS
Dim strComputer, i
'
' Create a DateTime object for yesterday
'
Set objStartDate = CreateObject("WbemScripting.SWbemDateTime")
objStartDate.SetVarDate Date - 1, True
'
' Create a DateTime object for today
'
Set objEndDate = CreateObject("WbemScripting.SWbemDateTime")
objEndDate.SetVarDate Date, True
'
' Get the collection of events from yesterday's logs
'
strComputer = "localhost"
Set objWMI = GetObject("winmgmts:" _
    & "{impersonationLevel=impersonate}!\\" & strComputer & "\root\cimv2")
```

```
Set objEvents = objWMI.ExecQuery _
    ("SELECT * FROM Win32_NTLogEvent " & _
        "WHERE TimeWritten >= '"  & objStartDate & "' " & _
        "AND TimeWritten < '" & objEndDate & "'")
'
' Create the database objects
'
Set objConn = CreateObject("ADODB.Connection")
Set objRS = CreateObject("ADODB.Recordset")
'
' Connect to the database:
'    -replace DataSourceName with the name of the data source
'    -replace LoginID with your login name
'    -replace Password with your login password
'
objConn.Open "DSN=DataSourceName;UID=LoginID;PWD=Password;"
'
' Open the table to which you want to export the logs
'
objRS.CursorLocation = 3
objRS.Open "SELECT * FROM WHSEvents" , objConn, 3, 3
'
' Run through the collection of events
'
i = 0
For Each objEvent in objEvents
    '
    ' Add a new record
    '
    objRS.AddNew
    '
    ' Populate the record's fields
    '
    objRS("EventType") = objEvent.Type
    objRS("EventTime") = ConvertToDate(objEvent.TimeWritten)
    objRS("EventSource") = objEvent.SourceName
    objRS("EventCategory") = objEvent.CategoryString
    objRS("EventCode") = objEvent.EventCode
    objRS("EventUser") = objEvent.User
    objRS("EventComputer") = objEvent.ComputerName
    objRS("EventLog") = objEvent.LogFile
    objRS("EventRecord") = objEvent.RecordNumber
    objRS("EventMessage") = objEvent.Message
    '
    ' Write the new record to the table
```

```
    objRS.Update
    i = i + 1
Next
'
' Close the database objects
'
objRS.Close
objConn.Close
'
' Display the number of events exported
'
WScript.Echo "Exported " & i & " events to the database."

Function ConvertToDate(strDate)
    Dim strYear, strMonth, strDay
    Dim strHour, strMinute, strSecond
    strYear = Left(strDate, 4)
    strMonth = Mid(strDate, 5, 2)
    strDay = Mid(strDate, 7, 2)
    strHour = Mid(strDate, 9, 2)
    strMinute = Mid(strDate, 11, 2)
    strSecond = Mid(strDate, 13, 2)
    ConvertToDate = DateSerial(strYear, strMonth, strDay) & " " & _
                    TimeSerial(strHour, strMinute, strSecond)
End Function
```

This script exports just the events from yesterday's logs. To do that, the script queries the Win32_NTLogEvent database and asks for just those events where the date is greater than or equal to yesterday's date and less than today's date. To set this up, the script first creates a DateTime object named objStartDate to hold the starting date, and this object is set to the Date - 1, which is yesterday. Next, the script creates another DateTime object named objEndDate to hold the ending date, and this object is set to the Date (today's date).

With these date objects defined, the script initializes the WMI object and uses the ExecQuery method to query the Win32_NTLogEvent database with the following WSQL SELECT statement:

```
"SELECT * FROM Win32_NTLogEvent " & _
    "WHERE TimeWritten >= '" & objStartDate & "' " & _
    "AND TimeWritten < '" & objEndDate & "'"
```

The script then creates ADODB Connection and Recordset objects and uses the Connection object's Open method to connect to the data source. If you're connecting to an Access database that doesn't require a login, you can just specify the data source name, like so. (Replace *DataSourceName* with the name of the data source.)

```
objConn.Open "DSN=DataSourceName;"
```

If your database requires login data, you need to specify the login ID and the password in the connection string, like so (replace *DataSourceName* with the name of the data source; replace *LoginID* with the login name; and replace *password* with the login password):

```
objConn.Open "DSN=DataSourceName;UID=LoginID;PWD=password;"
```

Now the script runs through the collection of events. For each one, it runs the `Recordset` object's `AddNew` method, populates the table's fields with data from the event object, and then runs the `Update` method to write the data.

Backing Up Windows Home Server

Windows Home Server does a great job of backing up your network client machines, and, for me, the peace of mind created by those nightly backups more than makes up for the cost of system. However, if there's one thing that might be keeping you up at night, it's the Windows Home Server system itself, which isn't part of the regular backup schedule, so it's ripe for disaster.

Fortunately, Windows Home Server Power Pack 3 changes all that by offering a backup option for the server itself. As you saw in Chapter 5, "Setting Up and Using Home Server Storage," when you add a new hard drive to Windows Home Server, the Add a Drive Wizard asks whether you want to use the new drive for server storage or for backups. If you choose the latter, two things happen:

▶ In the Windows Home Server Console's Server Storage tab, you see a new Server Backup Hard Drives section, which lists the drive (or drives) that you've set up for server backups.

▶ In the Windows Home Server Console's Computers & Backup tab, you see an icon for your Windows Home Server machine.

▶ **SEE** To learn how to set up a drive for backing up Windows Home Server, **see** "Adding a Drive for Windows Home Server Backups," **P. 135.**

The initial status for the Windows Home Server machine is Not Backed Up. To fix that, follow these steps to back up your home server:

1. Launch the Windows Home Server Console.
2. Select the Computers & Backup tab.
3. Click the icon for your Windows Home Server computer.
4. Click Backup Now. The Backup Now dialog box appears, as shown in Figure 15.12.

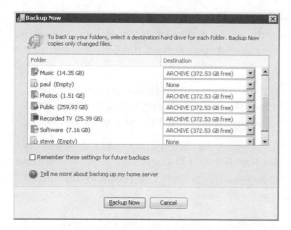

FIGURE 15.12   Use the Backup Now dialog box to choose which Windows Home Server folders you want to back up.

5. For each item in the Folder list, use the Destination drop-down list to select the server backup hard drive you want to use.

6. Click Backup Now. Windows Home Server begins backing up the selected folders and displays the progress of the backup. (You can click Hide if you don't want to see the details of the backup.)

7. When the backup is complete, click Close.

Setting Up a Maintenance Schedule

Maintenance is effective only if it's done regularly, but there's a fine line to be navigated. If maintenance is performed too often, it can become a burden and interfere with more interesting tasks; if it's performed too seldom, it becomes ineffective. So, how often should you perform the maintenance chores I discussed in this chapter? Here's a suggested schedule:

▶ **Check your hard disk for errors**—As I mentioned earlier, Windows Home Server runs automatic disk checks daily, so you only need to run a basic scan when you think your system is having problems that Windows Home Server hasn't noticed yet. Run the more thorough disk surface scan about once a month. The surface scan takes a long time, so run it when you won't be using your computer for a while.

▶ **Check free disk space on the system drive**—Do this about once a month. If the free space on your system drive is getting low, check it weekly.

▶ **Delete unnecessary files on the system drive**—If free disk space isn't a problem on drive C, run this chore once every two or three months.

▶ **Defragment the system drive**—How often you defragment your hard disk depends on how often you use your computer. Your Windows Home Server machine probably gets a pretty good workout every day, so you should run Disk Defragmenter about once a week.

▶ **Review Event Viewer logs**—If your system appears to be working fine, you need only check the Application and System log files weekly or every couple of weeks. If the system has a problem, check the logs daily to look for Warning or Error events.

▶ **Back up Windows Home Server**—How often you back up the server depends on how often you add files to the shared folders. If you add data daily, then you should run a daily backup; if you only add files occasionally, then you probably only need to back up every few days or even once a week.

Remember, as well, that Windows Home Server offers the Task Scheduler (select Start, All Programs, Accessories, System Tools, Scheduled Tasks) to set up a program on a regular schedule. Note that some programs, particularly Disk Defragmenter, can't be scheduled in their GUI form. You need to use the command-line version instead.

From Here

▶ To learn how to set up a drive for backing up Windows Home Server, **see** "Adding a Drive for Windows Home Server Backups," **P. 135**.

▶ For details on storage status indicators, **see** "Viewing Storage Status," **P. 137**.

▶ For more on repairing a drive, **see** "Repairing Storage," **P. 137**.

▶ For details on Windows Home Server's automatic backup deletions, **see** "Automatic Backup Management," **P. 242**.

▶ For the specifics of the Security event log, **see** "Tracking Auditing Events," **P. 291**.

▶ For more information on Device Manager's troubleshooting features, **see** "Troubleshooting with Device Manager," **P. 506**.

▶ For a discussion of the FIND command, **see** "FIND: Locating a Text String in a File," **P. 579**.

▶ You can also run Check Disk from the command line; **see** "CHKDSK: Checking for Hard Disk Errors," **P. 568**.

▶ You can also use the CHKNTFS command-line to set the AUTOCHK timeout value; **see** "CHKNTFS: Scheduling Automatic Disk Checks," **P. 571**.

▶ You can also defragment a drive from the command line; **see** "DEFRAG: Defragmenting the System Drive," **P. 574**.

▶ For details on the SYSTEMINFO command, **see** "SYSTEMINFO: Returning System Configuration Data," **P. 596.**

▶ For the specifics of using TYPEPERF, **see** "TYPEPERF: Monitoring Performance," **P. 598.**

CHAPTER 16

Customizing the Windows Home Server Interface

One of the main assumptions I've made throughout this book is that you're *not* running Windows Home Server as a headless device with no monitor, mouse, and keyboard. I assume that you regularly log on to Windows Home Server locally (or via Remote Desktop) and then use the server's interface to perform tasks such as running websites (see Chapter 12, "Setting Up a Windows Home Server Website"), administering a SharePoint site (see Chapter 13, "Running a SharePoint Site on Windows Home Server"), using third-party programs, or developing Windows Home Server add-ins.

Given these assumptions, it makes sense to consider the interface that you work with when you log on to the Windows Home Server desktop. Microsoft has set up the interface assuming that few users would deal with it very often, and that when users did get to the interface, all they would be doing are tasks directly related to Windows Home Server's core functionality. So, for example, the Windows Home Server Start menu doesn't include icons for Internet Explorer or Outlook Express, it doesn't include a My Recent Documents menu, and it doesn't include a list of frequently used programs. These decisions make sense for users who will have limited access to the Windows Home Server desktop, but they're incredibly restrictive for those of us who also use Windows Home Server as a workstation.

This chapter shows you how to fix these and other Start menu problems, and it takes you through other customizations that I hope will make the Windows Home Server interface more efficient and more productive. (This chapter isn't all business, however. I also show you how to make a few aesthetic improvements to the Windows Home Server interface, with the idea being that a better-looking Windows provides a happier computing experience.)

Making the Start Menu More Efficient

The whole purpose of the Start menu is, as its name implies, to start things, particularly programs and documents. Yes, you can also launch these objects via shortcut icons on the desktop, but that's not a great alternative because the desktop is covered most of the time by windows. So, if you want to get something going in Windows Home Server, the vast majority of the time you're going to have to do it via the Start menu. The good news is that Windows Home Server's Start menu is wonderfully flexible and is geared, in fact, to launching objects with as few mouse clicks or keystrokes as possible. To get to that state, however, you have to work with a few relatively obscure options and settings, which you'll learn about in the next few sections.

Activating the Frequent Programs List

In other versions of Windows, the Start menu includes a section called the *frequent programs list*, which is a collection of shortcuts that represent the programs you've used most often. As you work, Windows Home Server tracks program usage, so it knows those programs that you've started most often.

Unfortunately, Windows Home Server doesn't give you the benefit of this data because, by default, it hides the Start menu's frequent programs list, as you can see in Figure 16.1.

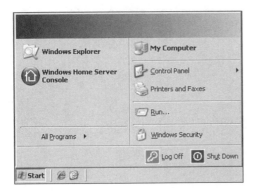

FIGURE 16.1 The default Windows Home Server Start menu doesn't include a frequent programs list.

Fortunately, a quick Registry tweak activates it:

NOTE

Throughout this chapter, I assume that you have logged on to Windows Home Server, either locally or via Remote Desktop.

1. Select Start, Run (or press Windows Logo+R) to open the Run dialog box, type **regedit**, and click OK. Windows Home Server displays the Registry Editor.

2. Navigate to the following key:

   `HKLM\SOFTWARE\Microsoft\Windows\CurrentVersion\policies\Explorer`

3. Double-click the `NoStartMenuMFUprogramsList` setting to open it for editing.

4. In the Value Data text box, change the value of the setting to 0.

5. Click OK.

TIP

While you're in the `Explorer` key, you might also want to change the value of the NoUserNameInStartMenu setting from 1 to 0. This adds your username to the top of the Start menu.

---

6. Log off Windows Home Server and then log back on to put the new setting value into effect, as shown in Figure 16.2.

Pinned Programs

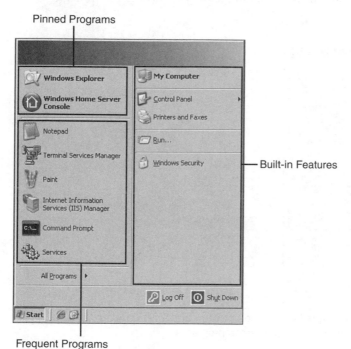

Built-in Features

Frequent Programs

FIGURE 16.2   The Start menu with the frequent programs list activated.

Getting More Favorite Programs on the Start Menu

The list of favorite programs is one of the best features in Windows Home Server because it ensures that the programs you use most often are always just a couple of mouse clicks away. If there's a downside to this feature, it's that it displays a maximum of six icons, so many frequently used programs are left off the list. However, if you have enough room, you can tell Windows Home Server to display up to 30 icons in this area. Here's how:

1. Select Start, Control Panel, Taskbar and Start Menu. The Taskbar and Start Menu Properties dialog box appears.

2. Select the Start Menu tab.

TIP

A quick way to go directly to the Start Menu tab is to right-click either the Start button or an empty section of the Start menu and then click Properties.

3. Make sure that the Start Menu option is activated, and then click the Customize button to its right. The Customize Start Menu dialog box appears, as shown in Figure 16.3.

FIGURE 16.3   Use the Customize Start Menu dialog box to set the maximum number of short-cut icons that appear in the Start menu's list of favorite programs.

4. Use the Number of Programs on Start Menu spin box to specify the number of favorite programs you want to display.

5. If you want to start over with a fresh list of frequent programs, click the Clear List button.

TIP

If you need to get rid of only one or two icons from the Start menu's frequent programs list, display the Start menu, right-click an icon you want to delete, and then click Remove from This List.

6. If you don't think you have enough screen space to display all the icons, activate the Small Icons option. This significantly reduces the amount of space each icon takes up on the Start menu.

7. Click OK.

Adding the Internet and E-Mail Icons

In other versions of Windows, the Start menu includes two icons that are fixed in place:

▶ **Internet**—This icon usually launches the Internet Explorer web browser.

▶ **E-Mail**—This icon usually launches the Outlook Express email client (or Windows Mail in Vista).

However, these icons don't appear in Windows Home Server. Follow these steps to activate these icons and to customize the icons to launch a different program if you have multiple web browsers or email clients installed on Windows Home Server. Here are the steps to follow:

1. Select Start, Control Panel, Taskbar and Start Menu (or right-click the Start button and then click Properties). The Taskbar and Start Menu Properties dialog box appears.

2. In the Start Menu tab, make sure that the Start Menu option is activated and then click the Customize button to its right. The Customize Start Menu dialog box appears.

3. Activate the Internet check box.

4. Use the list to the right of the Internet check box to choose the web browser you want associated with the icon.

5. Activate the E-Mail check box.

6. Use the list to the right of the E-Mail check box to choose the email client you want associated with the icon.

7. Click OK.

Note, too, that it's possible to change the text and the icon used for the Internet item on the Start menu. You do this by first displaying the following key in the Registry Editor:

HKLM\SOFTWARE\Clients\StartMenuInternet*client*\

Here, *client* is the name of the executable file of the program associated with the icon (such as Iexplorer.exe for Internet Explorer). The (Default) setting controls the icon text, and the (Default) setting of the DefaultIcon subkey controls the icon.

Customizing the text and icon for the email item is similar. You'll find the necessary settings here:

`HKLM\Software\Clients\Mail\`*`client`*`\`

Here, *client* is the name of the program associated with the icon (such as Outlook Express). The (Default) setting controls the icon text, and the (Default) setting of the `DefaultIcon` subkey controls the icon. Note that you might have to create this subkey. When you've made your changes, log off and then log back on to Windows Home Server to put the new settings into effect.

Pinning a Favorite Program Permanently to the Start Menu

The Start menu is divided into three sections, as shown earlier in Figure 16.2. Besides the list of frequent programs, the Start menu also includes the following:

▶ **Pinned programs**—This list appears above the frequent programs and includes program shortcuts that are static (that is, they don't move and they don't come and go like the icons on the frequent programs list). If you activated the Internet and E-Mail icons in the previous section, those icons appear at the top of the pinned programs list.

▶ **Built-in features**—This is the right side of the Start menu, which appears by default with a light blue background. It contains icons for various built-in Windows Home Server features.

The Start menu's list of favorite programs is such a time-saving feature that it can be frustrating if a program drops off the list. Another aggravation is that the icons often change position because Windows Home Server displays the programs in descending order of use. When you display the Start menu, this constant shifting of icons can result in a slight hesitation while you look for the icon you want. (This is particularly true if you've expanded the maximum number of icons; see "Getting More Favorite Programs on the Start Menu," earlier in this chapter.) Contrast both of these problems with the blissfully static nature of the icons on the pinned programs list: Windows Explorer and Windows Home Server Console (as well as the Internet and E-Mail icons, if you activated them). These icons are always where you need them, when you need them.

You can get the same effect with other shortcuts by adding—or *pinning*—them to the pinned programs list. To do this, first open the Start menu and find the shortcut you want to work with. Then you have two choices:

▶ Right-click the shortcut and then click Pin to Start Menu.

▶ Drag the shortcut and drop it in the pinned programs list.

You also can use this technique to pin shortcuts residing on the desktop to the pinned programs list. If you decide later on that you no longer want a shortcut pinned to the Start menu, right-click the shortcut and then click Unpin from Start Menu.

TIP

If you're working in Windows Explorer (or on the desktop) and you see a program or document that you'd like to pin to the Start menu, hold down Shift, right-click the file, and then click Pin to Start Menu in the alternative shortcut menu that appears.

TIP

When you display the Start menu, you can select an item quickly by pressing the first letter of the item's name. If you add several shortcuts to the pinned programs list, however, you might end up with more than one item that begins with the same letter. To avoid conflicts, rename each of these items so that they begin with a number. For example, renaming "Command Prompt" to "1 Command Prompt" means you can select this item by pressing 1 when the Start menu is displayed. (To rename a Start menu item, right-click the item and then click Rename.)

Streamlining the Start Menu by Converting Links to Menus

The right side of the Start menu contains a few of the built-in Windows Home Server features. In particular, contrast the My Computer and Control Panel items:

- ▶ The My Computer item is set up as a link—that is, you click the item, and the My Computer window appears in response.

- ▶ The Control Panel item is set up as a menu—that is, when you click the item, you see a list of Control Panel icons, as shown in Figure 16.4.

Having the Control Panel set up as a menu is efficient because it enables you to choose the icon you want right from the Start menu. If the Control Panel item was set up as a link instead, it would open the Control Panel window, and you'd have to double-click the icon you wanted and then close the Control Panel.

One of the nice features in Windows Home Server is that it's easy to convert many of the Start menu links into menus. Here are the required steps:

1. Select Start, Control Panel, Taskbar and Start Menu (or right-click the Start button and then click Properties). The Taskbar and Start Menu Properties dialog box appears.

2. In the Start Menu tab, make sure that the Start Menu option is activated, and then click the Customize button to its right. The Customize Start Menu dialog box appears.

3. Select the Advanced tab.

4. In the Start Menu Items group, find the following items and activate the Display as a Menu option for those items you want to add to the Start menu:

    Control Panel (on by default)

    My Computer

    My Documents

    My Music

    My Pictures

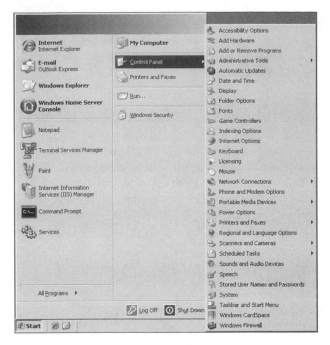

FIGURE 16.4   When you click the Control Panel item in the Windows Home Server Start menu, you see a menu of the Control Panel icons.

5. In the Start Menu Items group, activate the Favorites check box to add a menu of your Internet Explorer favorites to the Start menu.

6. In the Start Menu Items group, find the Network Connections item and activate the Display as Connect to Menu option. This gives you a menu of network connections, and you can launch any connection by selecting it from the menu.

7. In the Start Menu Items group, find the System Administrative Tools item and activate the Display on the All Programs Menu and the Start Menu option. This brings the useful Administrative Tools menu onto the Start menu for easier access.

8. Make sure that the List My Most Recently Opened Documents check box is activated. This adds the My Recent Documents menu to the Start menu, which displays the past 15 documents that you worked with.

9. Click OK to return to the Taskbar and Start Menu Properties dialog box.

10. Click OK.

Adding, Moving, and Removing Other Start Menu Icons

In addition to the main Start menu, the icons on the All Programs menu and submenus can be customized to suit the way you work. Using the techniques I discuss in this section, you can perform the following Start menu productivity boosts:

▶ Move important features closer to the beginning of the All Programs menu hierarchy.

▶ Remove features you don't use.

▶ Add new commands for features not currently available on the All Programs menu (such as the Registry Editor).

Windows Home Server offers three methods for adding and removing Start menu shortcuts, and I explain each of them in the next three sections.

Dragging and Dropping onto the Start Button

The quickest way to add a shortcut is to drag an executable file from Windows Explorer and then do either of the following:

▶ **Drop it on the Start button**—This pins the shortcut to the Start menu.

▶ **Hover over the Start button**—After a second or two, the main Start menu appears. Now hover the file over All Programs until the menu appears, and then drop the file where you want the shortcut to appear.

Working with the Start Menu Folder

The All Programs shortcuts are stored in two places within %SystemDrive%\Documents and Settings\:

▶ The *user*\Start Menu\Programs subfolder, where *user* is the name of the current user. Shortcuts in this subfolder appear only when the user is logged on to Windows Home Server. Because in Windows Home Server you almost always log on using the Administrator account, you'll most often use the Administrator\Start Menu\Programs subfolder, shown in Figure 16.5.

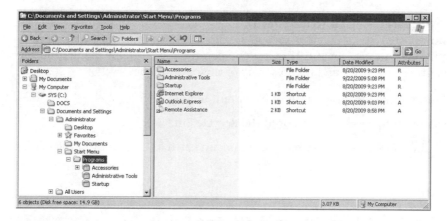

FIGURE 16.5   You can use the Administrator account's Start Menu\Programs subfolder to modify the Start menu shortcuts directly.

▶ The `All Users\Start Menu\Programs` subfolder. Shortcuts in this folder appear to all users. Most of the predefined Start menu shortcuts appear in this folder, so you'll do most of your direct Start menu customizations here.

TIP

A quick way to get to the current user's Start Menu folder is to right-click the Start button and then click Explore.

By working with these folders, you get the most control over not only where your Start menu shortcuts appear, but also the names of those shortcuts. Here's a summary of the techniques you can use:

▶ Within the Programs folder and its subfolders, you can drag existing shortcuts from one folder to another.

▶ To create a new shortcut, drag the executable file and drop it inside the folder you want to use. Remember that if you want to create a shortcut for a document or other nonexecutable file, right-drag the file and then select Create Shortcut(s) Here when you drop the file.

▶ You can create your own folders within the Programs folder hierarchy, and they'll appear as submenus within the All Programs menu.

▶ You can rename a shortcut the same way you rename any file.

▶ You can delete a shortcut the same way you delete any file.

Working with All Programs Menu Shortcuts Directly

Many of the chores listed in the previous section are more easily performed by working directly within the All Programs menu. That is, you open the All Programs menu, find the shortcut you want to work with, and then use any of these techniques:

▶ Drag the shortcut to another section of its current menu.

▶ Drag the shortcut to another menu or to the Recycle Bin.

▶ Right-click the shortcut and then select a command (such as Delete) from the context menu.

Making the Taskbar More Efficient

In Windows Home Server, the taskbar acts somewhat like a mini-application. The purpose of this "application" is to display a button for each running program and to enable you to switch from one program to another. And, like most applications these days, the taskbar has its own toolbars that, in this case, enable you to launch programs and documents.

Displaying the Built-In Taskbar Toolbars

The Windows Home Server taskbar comes with seven default toolbars:

Address	This toolbar contains a text box into which you can type a local address (such as a folder or file path), a network address (a UNC path), or an Internet address. When you press Enter or click the Go button, Windows Home Server loads the address into Windows Explorer (if you entered a local or network folder address), an application (if you entered a file path), or Internet Explorer (if you entered an Internet address). In other words, this toolbar works just like the address bar that Windows Explorer and Internet Explorer use.
Windows Media Player	This toolbar contains controls for playing media. When you activate this toolbar, it appears when you minimize the Windows Media Player window.
Links	This toolbar contains several buttons that link to predefined Internet sites. This is the same as the Links toolbar that appears in Internet Explorer.
Language Bar	This toolbar displays an icon that lets you select a different keyboard language, if you have multiple languages installed on Windows Home Server.
Windows Search Deskbar	With this toolbar, you type a search term into a text box, and Windows Home Server uses Windows Desktop Search to look for files and folders with matching names or content. Windows Desktop Search examines both the Windows Home Server local files and the files in the shared folders. This toolbar is displayed by default in Windows Home Server.
Desktop	This toolbar contains all the desktop icons, as well as an icon for Internet Explorer and submenus for My Documents, My Computer, and My Network Places.
Quick Launch	This is a collection of one-click icons that launch Internet Explorer or Media Player or clear the desktop. Other applications—such as Microsoft Office— also add icons to this toolbar. This toolbar is displayed by default in Windows Home Server.

TIP

To add an icon to the Quick Launch toolbar, drag it from the Start menu or desktop and drop it inside the toolbar.

To toggle these toolbars on and off, you must first right-click an empty spot on the taskbar. In the shortcut menu that appears, click Toolbars and then click the toolbar you want to work with.

Setting Some Taskbar Toolbar Options

Some of the toolbars offer options you can set to customize the look of the toolbar and to make the toolbars easier to work with. Right-click an empty section of the toolbar and then click one of the following commands:

View	This command displays a submenu with two options: Large Icons and Small Icons. These commands determine the size of the toolbar's icons. For example, if a toolbar has more icons than can be shown given its current size, switch to the Small Icons view.
Show Text	This command toggles the icon titles on and off. If you turn on the titles, it makes it easier to decipher what each icon does, but you'll see fewer icons in a given space.
Show Title	This command toggles the toolbar title (displayed to the left of the icons) on and off.

Creating New Taskbar Toolbars

In addition to the predefined taskbar toolbars, you can create new toolbars that display the contents of any folder on your system. For example, if you have a folder of programs or documents that you launch regularly, you can get one-click access to those items by displaying that folder as a toolbar. Here are the steps to follow:

1. Right-click an empty spot on the toolbar, and then click Toolbars, New Toolbar. Windows Home Server displays the New Toolbar dialog box.
2. Use the folder list provided to highlight the folder you want to display as a toolbar (or click Make New Folder to create a new subfolder within the currently highlighted folder).
3. Click OK. Windows Home Server creates the new toolbar.

Creating a Taskbar Toolbar for Launching Programs and Documents

Now that you know how to display, create, and customize taskbar toolbars, you can take advantage of them to get one-click access to large numbers of programs and documents. The basic idea is to create a toolbar, populate its folder with shortcuts to programs and documents, and then display the toolbar on the left side of the screen for easy access. Here's how it's done:

> **NOTE**
>
> Before you begin these steps, make sure that the taskbar isn't locked. Right-click an empty section of the taskbar and then click Lock the Taskbar to deactivate it. Also, make sure that the desktop is visible by minimizing all open windows. (Right-click the taskbar and then click Show the Desktop.)

1. Create a new folder.
2. Create shortcuts in this new folder for your favorite documents and programs.

3. Create a new taskbar toolbar that displays the contents of the new folder.

4. Drag the left edge of the new toolbar and drop it on the desktop. Windows Home Server displays the toolbar as a window.

5. Drag the toolbar window to the left edge of the screen and drop it when the toolbar expands to fill the left edge.

6. Right-click an empty section of the toolbar and activate the Show Title, Show Text, and Always on Top commands. The Always on Top command ensures that the toolbar is always visible, even if other windows are maximized.

As you can see in Figure 16.6, the new toolbar is displayed on the left. Here are some notes about this arrangement:

▶ You can size the toolbar by dragging (in this case) the right edge to the left or right.

▶ If you prefer, you can display the toolbar on the right or top edge of the window. To move it, first drag it from the edge and drop it on the desktop. Then drag the toolbar window and drop it on the edge you want to use.

▶ If you have enough room, you can display multiple toolbars on one edge of the window. For example, you could add the Quick Launch and Links toolbars for easy access to their shortcuts. To do this, display the other toolbar, drag it off the taskbar, drop it on the desktop, and then drag the toolbar window to the edge of the window and drop it on the toolbar that's already in place. You might need to drag the top edge of the toolbar up or down to see its icons.

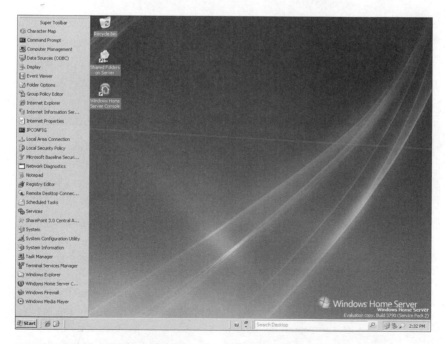

FIGURE 16.6   The new toolbar appears on the left edge of the screen and is visible even when other windows are maximized.

Improving Productivity by Setting Taskbar Options

The taskbar comes with a few options that can help you be more productive either by saving a few mouse clicks or by giving you more screen room to display your applications. Follow these steps to set these taskbar options:

1. Select Start, Control Panel, Taskbar and Start Menu. (Alternatively, right-click the taskbar and then click Properties.) The Taskbar and Start Menu Properties dialog box appears with the Taskbar tab displayed, as shown in Figure 16.7.

FIGURE 16.7   Use the Taskbar tab to set up the taskbar for improved productivity.

2. Activate or deactivate the following options, as required to boost your productivity:

Lock the Taskbar   If you activate this check box, you can't resize the taskbar and you can't resize or move any taskbar toolbars. This is useful if you share your computer with other users and you don't want to waste time resetting the taskbar if someone else changes it.

Auto-Hide the Taskbar   If you activate this check box, Windows Home Server reduces the taskbar to a thin, blue line at the bottom of the screen when you're not using it. This is useful if you want a bit more screen room for your applications. To redisplay the taskbar, move the mouse to the bottom of the screen. Note, however, that you should consider leaving this option deactivated if you use the taskbar frequently; otherwise, auto-hiding it slows you down because it takes Windows Home Server a second or two to restore the taskbar when you hover the mouse over it.

Keep the Taskbar on Top of Other Windows	If you deactivate this option, Windows Home Server hides the taskbar behind any window that's either maximized or moved over the taskbar. To get to the taskbar, you need to either minimize or move the window or press the Windows logo key. This isn't a very efficient way to work, so I recommend leaving this option activated.
Group Similar Taskbar Buttons	See the next section, "Controlling Taskbar Grouping," for more information on this setting.
Show Quick Launch	Activate this check box to display the Quick Launch toolbar, discussed earlier (refer to "Displaying the Built-In Taskbar Toolbars"). Quick Launch is a handy way to access Internet Explorer, the desktop, and Windows Media Player (as well as any other shortcuts you add to the Quick Launch folder), so I recommend activating this option.
Show the Clock	Leave this check box activated to keep the clock displayed in the notification area.
Hide Inactive Icons	If you activate this check box, Windows Home Server hides notification area icons that you haven't used for a while. This gives the taskbar a bit more room to display program buttons, so leave this option activated if you don't use the notification area icons all that often. If you don't use the icons frequently, deactivate this option to avoid having to click the arrow to display the hidden icons.

NOTE

If your notification area is crowded with icons, it's inefficient to display all the icons if you use only a few of them. Instead of showing them all, leave the Hide Inactive Icons check box activated and click Customize. For the icons you use often, click the item's Behavior column and then click Always Show in the list that appears. This tells Windows Home Server to always display the icon in the notification area.

3. Click OK.

Controlling Taskbar Grouping

One of the new things built into the Windows Home Server taskbar is the grouping feature. When the taskbar fills up with buttons, Windows Home Server consolidates icons from the same program into a single button, as shown in Figure 16.8. To access one of these grouped windows, you click the button and then click the window you want.

FIGURE 16.8   When the taskbar gets filled with buttons, Windows Home Server groups similar windows into a single button, as shown here with Windows Explorer and Internet Explorer.

TIP

You can close all of a group's windows at once by right-clicking the group button and then clicking Close Group.

The grouping feature makes it easier to read the name of each taskbar button, but the price is a slight efficiency drop because it takes two clicks to activate a window instead of one. If you don't like this trade-off, you can disable the grouping feature by right-clicking the taskbar, clicking Properties, and then deactivating the Group Similar Taskbar Buttons check box.

TIP

Another way to prevent grouping is to give the taskbar more room to display buttons. The easiest way to do that is to resize the taskbar by dragging up its top edge until the taskbar expands. If this doesn't work, the taskbar is probably locked. Unlock it by right-clicking the taskbar and then clicking Lock the Taskbar.

Alternatively, you can tweak the grouping feature to suit the way you work. To do this, open the Registry Editor and head for the following key:

`HKCU\Software\Microsoft\Windows\CurrentVersion\Explorer\Advanced\`

Add a `DWORD` value called `TaskbarGroupSize` and set it to one of the following values:

- ▶ **0**—When the grouping kicks in (that is, when the taskbar becomes full), Windows Home Server groups the buttons from only the applications that you have used the least.

- ▶ **1**—When the grouping kicks in, Windows Home Server groups the buttons from only the application that has the most windows open. If a second application surpasses the number of open windows in the first application, the second application's windows are grouped as well.

- ▶ *x*—Windows Home Server groups any application that has at least *x* windows open, where *x* is a number between 2 and 99. Note that the grouping occurs even if the taskbar is not full.

Note that you must log off or restart Windows Home Server to put the new setting into effect.

Modifying the Start Menu and Taskbar with Group Policies

Group policies offer unprecedented control over the Windows Home Server interface without having to modify the Registry directly. This is particularly true of the Start menu and taskbar, which boast more than 40 policies that do everything from removing Start menu links such as Run and Help to hiding the taskbar's notification area. It's unlikely that you'll use these policies on Windows Home Server itself, since it's likely that only you or another trusted administrator deal with the Windows Home Server interface directly. However, you can use these policies on other Windows machines to control how other users interact with the Start menu and taskbar.

To see these policies, launch the Group Policy editor (select Start, Run, type `gpedit.msc`, and click OK) and select User Configuration, Administrative Templates, Start Menu and Taskbar.

Most of the policies are straightforward: By enabling them, you remove a feature from the Start menu or taskbar. For example, enabling the Remove Run Menu from Start Menu policy hides the Start menu's Run command for the current user. This is a handy feature if you're trying to restrict a user to using only those programs and documents that appear on the Start menu. Here are a few policies that I think are the most useful:

- **Remove Drag-and-Drop Context Menus on the Start Menu**—Enable this policy to prevent the current user from rearranging the Start menu using drag-and-drop techniques.

- **Prevent Changes to Taskbar and Start Menu Settings**—Enable this policy to prevent the current user from accessing the Taskbar and Start Menu Properties dialog box.

- **Remove Access to the Context Menus for the Taskbar**—Enable this policy to prevent the current user from seeing the taskbar's shortcut (also called *context*) menus by right-clicking the taskbar.

- **Do Not Keep History of Recently Opened Documents**—Enable this policy to prevent Windows Home Server from tracking the current user's recently opened documents.

- **Clear History of Recently Opened Documents on Exit**—Enable this policy to remove all documents from the current user's recent documents list whenever Windows Home Server exits.

- **Remove Balloon Tips on Start Menu Items**—Enable this policy to prevent the current user from seeing the balloon tips that Windows Home Server displays when it prompts you about new hardware being detected, downloading automatic updates, and so on.

- **Remove User Name from Start Menu**—Enable this policy to prevent the current user's name from appearing at the top of the Start menu. This is a good idea if you need more room on the Start menu for the pinned or frequent program lists.

▶ **Hide the Notification Area**—Enable this policy to prevent the current user from seeing the taskbar's notification area.

▶ **Do Not Display Custom Toolbars in the Taskbar**—Enable this policy to prevent the current user from adding custom toolbars to the taskbar.

Customizing the Color Quality and Resolution

How images appear on your monitor and how efficiently you use the monitor's viewable area are a function of two measurements: the color quality and the screen resolution. The *color quality* is a measure of the number of colors available to display images on the screen. Color quality is usually expressed in either bits or total colors. For example, a 4-bit display can handle up to 16 colors (because 2 to the power of 4 equals 16). The most common values are 16-bit (65,536 colors), 24-bit (16,777,216 colors), and 32-bit (16,777,216 colors; this is the same as 24-bit color because 32-bit displays use 24 bits for the colors and 8 bits for the alpha channel to handle transparency effects).

The *screen resolution* is a measure of the density of the pixels used to display the screen image. The pixels are arranged in a row-and-column format, so the resolution is expressed as follows:

`columns by rows`

Here, `columns` is the number of pixel columns and `rows` is the number of pixel rows. For example, a 1024×768 resolution means screen images are displayed using 1,024 columns of pixels and 768 rows of pixels.

How does all this affect productivity?

▶ In general, the greater the number of colors, the sharper your screen image appears. Sharper images, especially text, are easier to read and put less strain on the eyes.

▶ At higher resolutions, individual screen items—such as icons and dialog boxes—appear smaller because these items tend to have a fixed height and width, expressed in pixels. For example, a dialog box that's 400 pixels wide appears half as wide as the screen at 800×600. However, it appears to be only one-quarter of the screen width at 1,600×1,024 (a common resolution for larger monitors). This means that at higher resolutions, your maximized windows appear larger, so you get a larger work area.

The key thing to bear in mind about all this is that there's occasionally a trade-off between color quality and resolution. That is, depending on how much video memory is installed on your graphics adapter, you might have to trade higher resolution for lower color quality, or vice versa. This isn't usually a problem on most modern systems, which almost always have enough memory to display the maximum number of colors at the maximum screen resolution.

To change the screen resolution and color quality, follow these steps:

1. Select Start, Control Panel, Display to get the Display Properties dialog box onscreen.

TIP

You can also open the Display Properties dialog box by right-clicking the desktop and then clicking Properties.

2. Display the Settings tab, as shown in Figure 16.9.

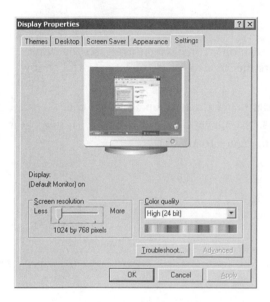

FIGURE 16.9   Use the Settings tab to set the screen resolution and color quality.

3. To set the resolution, drag the Screen Resolution slider left or right.

4. To set the color quality, choose the maximum available number of colors from the Color Quality list.

5. Click OK. Windows Home Server performs the adjustment and then displays a dialog box asking if you want to keep the new setting.

6. Click Yes.

NOTE

If your graphics adapter or monitor can't handle the new resolution or color quality, you end up with a garbled or blank display. In this case, just wait for 15 seconds for Windows Home Server to restore the resolution to its original setting.

Setting the Screensaver

Back in Chapter 8, "Streaming and Sharing Digital Media," I told you about the problems of burn-in and persistence on CRT and LCD monitors, respectively. I also mentioned that the best way to prevent these problems is to set up a screensaver so that no image stays onscreen for any length of time. You don't need to worry about this if you're using a Remote Desktop connection to log on to Windows Home Server, but it might be a concern if you log on locally.

> ▶ **SEE** To learn how to use images from the Photos share as a screensaver, **see** "Using Server Photos as a Screensaver Slideshow," **P. 225.**

Selecting a Screensaver

Unfortunately, Windows Home Server comes with only three screensavers, so you don't get much to choose from. In any case, here are the steps to follow to activate and configure a screensaver:

1. Select Start, Control Panel, Display (or right-click the desktop and then click Properties). The Display Properties dialog box appears.

2. Display the Screen Saver tab, as shown in Figure 16.10.

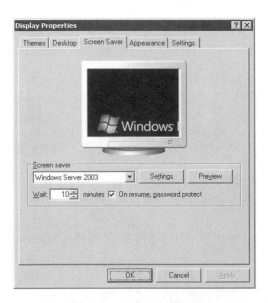

FIGURE 16.10   Use the Screen Saver tab to activate and configure a screensaver.

3. Use the Screen Saver list to select the screensaver you want to use.

CAUTION

Screensavers can sometimes be incredible resource hogs and can eat up processor cycles that may adversely affect the performance of Windows Home Server. To ensure that a screensaver doesn't slow down backups, file transfers, or other network activity, use the Blank screensaver, which only turns off the screen.

4. Use the following controls to configure and test the screensaver:

Settings	Click this button to set various options for the screensaver. The Options dialog box that appears depends on which screensaver you chose.
Preview	Click this button to give the screensaver a trial run. To return to the dialog box, move the mouse or press any key.
Wait	This spinner controls the amount of time your computer must be idle before the screensaver goes to work. You can enter a number between 1 and 9999 minutes.
On Resume, Password Protect	If you activate this check box, Windows Home Server requires you to enter your account password before it shuts down the screensaver and returns the normal screen.

CAUTION

If you're logged on to Windows Home Server using the Administrator account, I highly recommend activating the On Resume, Password Protect check box. The Administrator account is all-powerful, and in the wrong hands, it can do untold damage not only to Windows Home Server but to the network clients, as well.

---

5. Click OK.

Creating an Instant Screensaver

If you deal with sensitive data on Windows Home Server, you probably want to guard against visitors accidentally seeing what's on your screen. Short of always locking your door, an easy way to do this is to create an "instant" screensaver that can be activated using a quick key combination. To try this out, follow these steps:

1. Find your favorite screensaver file (it will have the .scr extension) in the %SystemRoot%\system32 folder.

2. Right-drag the file from Explorer, drop it on the desktop, and click Create Shortcut(s) Here. Windows Home Server creates a desktop shortcut for the file.

3. Right-click the shortcut, and then choose Properties from the context menu.

4. In the properties sheet that appears, activate the Shortcut tab, click inside the Shortcut key box, and press the key you want to use as part of the Ctrl+Alt key combination. (For example, if you press Z, Windows Home Server sets the key combination to Ctrl+Alt+Z.)

5. Click OK.

Now, no matter which application you're working in, you can activate your screensaver immediately simply by pressing the key combination you defined in step 4.

> **TIP**
>
> An alternative is to lock your computer when you leave your desk. Press Windows Logo+L to hide the desktop and display the Computer Locked dialog box. (You also can press Ctrl+Alt+Delete and then click Lock Computer.) The only way to return to the desktop is to press Ctrl+Alt+Delete and then enter your account password.

Customizing the Desktop Colors, Fonts, and Sizes

If you're truly determined to put your personal stamp on the Windows Home Server interface, the Appearance tab in the Display Properties dialog box is a great place to start. Follow these steps to work with this tab:

1. Select Start, Control Panel, Display (or right-click the desktop and then click Properties). The Display Properties dialog box appears.

2. Display the Appearance tab, as shown in Figure 16.11.

FIGURE 16.11   Use the Appearance tab to give the desktop and its objects a makeover.

3. Use the Appearance tab controls (discussed in detail in the next few sections) to customize the Windows Home Server look.

4. Click OK.

The Appearance tab is divided into two sections. The top half shows a fake desktop displaying a few objects; the bottom half contains the various controls you use to alter the appearance. The idea is that as you work with the controls, the fake objects reflect the way your new desktop will look. The rest of this chapter shows you how to work with the Appearance tab controls.

Selecting a Color Scheme

The easiest way to alter the appearance of the Windows Home Server desktop is to select one of the more than 20 predefined color schemes. A *color scheme* is a collection of desktop attributes that includes the color of the desktop and window title bars, the fonts used in dialog boxes and pull-down menus, the size of window borders and desktop icons, and much more.

Use the Color Scheme list to choose a scheme name that sounds interesting, and then check out the fake desktop to see how things look.

Creating a Custom Color Scheme

Some of the color schemes look as though they were created in the Fear Factor House of Design (see, for example, Pumpkin and Wheat). If you think you can do better, it's easy enough to create your own color scheme. First, choose a color scheme as a starting point, and then click the Advanced button to display the Advanced Appearance dialog box shown in Figure 16.12.

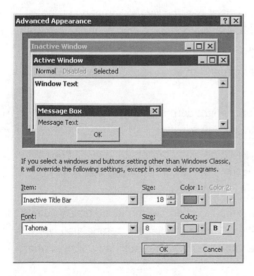

FIGURE 16.12   Use the Advanced Appearance dialog box to customize almost every aspect of the Windows Home Server interface.

The basic procedure is to select an object from the Item drop-down list and then use the other controls—such as Size, Color, and Font—to customize the item. Note that not all the controls are available for each option. (For example, it doesn't make sense to specify a font for the scrollbars.)

TIP

Another way to select some of objects in the Item list is to click the appropriate part of the fake desktop. For example, clicking the title bar of the active window selects the Active Title Bar item.

Here's a rundown of the various objects available in the Item list:

3D Objects	Dialog box command buttons and tabs, caption buttons (see the "Caption Buttons" entry), scrollbars, status bars, taskbar, and window borders. You can set the background color and font color for these objects.
Active Title Bar	The title bar of the window that has the focus. Windows Home Server displays title bar backgrounds as a gradient. To control this gradient, use both the Color 1 and Color 2 palettes. You can also set the size (height) of the title bar, as well as the font, font size, font color, and font style of the title bar text.
Active Window Border	The border surrounding the window that has the focus. You can set the border's width and color. Note that the width setting also controls the width of the taskbar when the Auto-Hide option is activated (as described earlier).
Application Background	Sets the default color for the background of each application window.
Caption Buttons	The buttons that appear in the upper-right corner of windows and dialog boxes. You can set the size of these buttons.
Desktop	The desktop color. Note that this setting also controls the color of the backgrounds used with the desktop icons. You see this background color only if your desktop is covered with either a pattern or wallpaper.
Icon	The icons that appear on the desktop. You can set the icon size as well as the font attributes of the icon titles. Note that this font setting also controls the fonts displayed in Explorer and all open folders (such as Control Panel and My Computer).
Icon Spacing (Horizontal)	The distance allotted (in pixels) between desktop and folder icons on the left and right.
Icon Spacing (Vertical)	The distance allotted (in pixels) between desktop and folder icons on the top and bottom.

Inactive Title Bar	The title bars of the open windows that don't have the focus. You can set the size (height) and gradient colors of the bar, as well as the font, font size, and font color of the title bar text.
Inactive Window Border	The borders surrounding the open windows that don't have the focus. You can set the border's width and color.
Menu	The window menu bar. You can set the size (height) and background color of the menu bar, as well as the font attributes of the menu bar text.
Message Box	Message boxes, such as error messages and information prompts. (Note that this setting doesn't apply to regular dialog boxes.) You can set the font attributes of the message text.
Palette Title	This is the title bar of a floating toolbar. You can set the height of the title bar and the font of the title bar text.
Scrollbar	The scrollbars that appear in windows and list boxes. You can set the width (or height, depending on the orientation) of the scrollbars.
Selected Items	The currently selected menu in a menu bar and the currently selected command in a menu. You can set the height and background color of the selection bar, as well as the font attributes of the item text.
ToolTip	The small banners that appear if you hover the mouse pointer over a toolbar for a couple of seconds. You can set the background color and the font attributes of the ToolTip text. Note that the ToolTip font size also controls the size of a window's status bar text.
Window	The window background and text. You can set the color of these items.

To preserve your color scheme, follow these steps:

1. Display the Themes tab.
2. Click the Save As button to open the Save As dialog box.
3. Enter a name for the theme in the File Name text box.
4. Click OK. Your newly created theme appears in the Theme list.

Creating Custom Colors

You might have noticed that the Color palettes in the Advanced Appearance dialog box have an Other button. You can use this option to pick a different color from Windows Home Server's color palette, or you can create your own color. When you click the Other button, you see the Color dialog box, shown in Figure 16.13.

Color Box

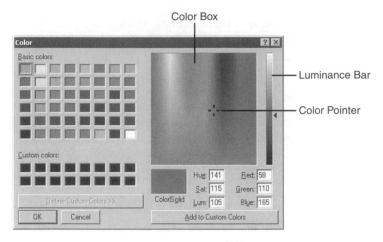

Luminance Bar

Color Pointer

FIGURE 16.13   Use this dialog box to choose or create a different color.

If you want to use one of the colors displayed in the Basic colors area, click it and then click OK.

To create your own color, you can use one of two methods. The first method uses the fact that you can create any color in the spectrum by mixing the three main colors: red, green, and blue. The Color dialog box lets you enter specific numbers between 0 and 255 for each of these colors, by using the Red, Green, and Blue text boxes. A lower number means the color is less intense, and a higher number means the color is more intense.

To give you some idea of how this works, see Table 16.1, which lists eight common colors and their respective red, green, and blue numbers.

TABLE 16.1   The Red, Green, and Blue Numbers for Eight Common Colors

Color	Red	Green	Blue
Black	0	0	0
White	255	255	255
Red	255	0	0
Green	0	255	0
Blue	0	0	255
Yellow	255	255	0
Magenta	255	0	255
Cyan	0	255	255

NOTE

Whenever the Red, Green, and Blue values are equal, you get a grayscale color. Lower numbers produce darker grays, and higher numbers produce lighter grays.

The second method for selecting colors involves setting three attributes: hue, saturation, and luminance.

▶ **Hue**—This number (which is more or less equivalent to the term *color*) measures the position on the color spectrum. Lower numbers indicate a position near the red end, and higher numbers move through the yellow, green, blue, and violet parts of the spectrum. As you increase the hue, the color pointer moves from left to right.

▶ **Sat**—This number is a measure of a given hue's purity. A saturation setting of 240 means that the hue is a pure color. Lower numbers indicate that more gray is mixed with the hue until, at 0, the color becomes part of the grayscale. As you increase the saturation, the color pointer moves toward the top of the color box.

▶ **Lum**—This number is a measure of the color's brightness. Lower numbers are darker, and higher numbers are brighter. The luminance bar to the right of the color box shows the luminance scale for the selected color. As you increase the luminance, the slider moves toward the top of the bar.

To create a custom color, you can either enter values in the text boxes, as just described, or you can use the mouse to click inside the color box and luminance bar. The Color|Solid shows the color based on the current values. (Why is it called Color|Solid? Because if you're using a low-end video driver—that is, one that displays just a few colors—the Color|Solid box shows the selected color on the left and the nearest solid color on the right.) If you think you'll want to reuse the color down the road, click the Add to Custom Colors button to place the color in one of the boxes in the Custom colors area. When you're done, click OK.

Changing the Effects Properties

Finally, Windows Home Server has a number of visual effects that are mostly turned off. Some of these are quite useful and can make text easier to read, make dragging-and-dropping windows more intuitive, and so on. To try out these effects, follow these steps:

1. Select Start, Control Panel, Display (or right-click the desktop and then click Properties). The Display Properties dialog box appears.
2. Display the Appearance tab.
3. Click the Effects button to display the Effects dialog box, as shown in Figure 16.14.

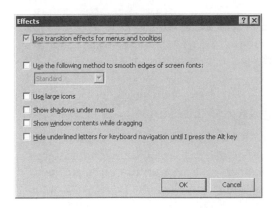

FIGURE 16.14   Use the Effects dialog box to activate the Windows Home Server visual effects.

4. Use the following controls to customize the Windows Home Server look:

Use the Following Transition Effect	Use this list to determine how menus and ToolTips appear and disappear onscreen: Fade Effect or Scroll Effect.
Use the Following Method to Smooth Edges	Activate this check box and then select ClearType in the list. If you read a lot of onscreen text, particularly if you use a notebook or an LCD screen, activating the ClearType feature drastically reduces the jagged edges of screen fonts and makes text super-sharp and far easier to read than regular screen text.
Use Large Icons	Activate this check box to increase the size of the desktop icons (and any other folder) from the default value of 32 pixels on each side to 48 pixels.
Show Shadows Under Menus	If you activate this check box, Windows Home Server displays pull-down menus with a drop shadow effect. This can make the menus stand out from the underlying window text, so it's a good idea to turn on this feature.
Show Window Contents	This check box toggles full-window drag on and off.
While Dragging	When it's deactivated, Windows Home Server shows only the outline of any window you drag with the mouse (by dragging the title bar); if you activate full-window drag, however, Windows Home Server displays the window's contents while you're dragging, which usually makes it easier to position windows.

Hide Underlined Letters   When this check box is deactivated,
                                           Windows Home Server displays the under-
                                           lined accelerator keys in each application's
                                           menu bar (such as the letter F in the File
                                           menu). If you find this distracting, activate
                                           this check box to hide the underlines. When
                                           you need to see the accelerator keys, press
                                           Alt to have Windows Home Server underline
                                           them for you.

5. Click OK to return to the Appearance tab.

6. Click OK.

From Here

▶ For information on customizing the Windows Home Server Remote Access pages, **see** "Customizing the Remote Access Web Pages," **P. 208**.

▶ For the specifics on using images from the Photos share as a screensaver, **see** "Using Server Photos as a Screensaver Slideshow," **P. 225**.

▶ To learn how to customize the Photos share, **see** "Customizing the Photos Share with a Template," **P. 223**.

▶ To learn how to customize the Music share, **see** "Customizing the Music Share with a Template," **P. 230**.

▶ To learn how to customize the Video share, **see** "Customizing the Videos Share with a Template," **P. 233**.

▶ To learn more about the Registry, see Chapter 18, "Working with the Windows Home Server Registry."

▶ For details on group policies, **see** "Using the Group Policy Object Editor," **P. 603**.

Troubleshooting Windows Home Server

One of the most compelling aspects of Windows Home Server is that after it's on your network and your other computers are connected to it, the safety of your data is immediately and dramatically increased:

▶ The Windows 7, Windows Vista, and Windows XP network computers are automatically added to the Windows Home Server backup system and will be completely backed up by the next morning.

▶ If you have two or more hard disk drives, folder duplication is turned on by default, so any data you add to the Windows Home Server shares will not be lost if one of the drives fails.

In short, if you're sleeping better at night these days, it's at least in part because you know Windows Home Server is safeguarding your most important data.

Not that I want to wreck your good night's sleep, but the Achilles' heel in this rosy scenario is Windows Home Server itself: What happens if the server crashes? What happens if the primary hard disk dies? Windows Home Server does an excellent job of backing up the client computers, but it has no way of performing a full backup of itself. Yes, Power Pack 3 enables you to back up the Windows Home Server shared folders, but not the system data. Yes, Windows Home Server comes with the Windows Backup program, but that doesn't help because the Restore feature isn't compatible with Windows Home Server's Drive Extender technology. And, unlike Windows 7, Vista, and XP, Windows Home Server doesn't include System Restore, so you can't restore a broken system to a previous (working) configuration. If you need full backups of Windows Home Server, you must look for third-party backup solutions.

In the meantime, there *are* some techniques you can use to recover from Windows Home Server problems. This chapter shows you a few techniques that are specific to Windows Home Server. It also takes you through some general troubleshooting tips that you can apply to Windows Home Server and to any computer on your network.

Replacing Your System Hard Drive

If you have folder duplication turned on and you lose one of your secondary hard drives—that is, a hard drive that Windows Home Server uses to store a secondary partition—the only real loss you'll feel will be in your bank account when you have to purchase a replacement drive. That's because Windows Home Server always maintains at least one copy of your shared folder data on another drive:

▶ If you have two hard drives, Windows Home Server creates three partitions: the system partition (named SYS) and the primary data partition (named Data) on the first hard drive, and a secondary partition (also named Data) that takes up the entire second hard drive. In this scenario, Windows Home Server stores one copy of each file on the primary partition and a second copy on the secondary partition.

▶ If you have three or more hard drives, Windows Home Server creates N+1 partitions (where N is the number of hard drives): the system partition and the primary data partition on the first hard drive, and secondary partitions on each of the other hard drives. In this scenario, Windows Home Server stores one copy of each file on one of the secondary partitions and a second copy on a different secondary partition.

Note that in both cases, Windows Home Server uses the primary data partition to store tombstones that point to the actual locations of the files (which are called *shadows*).

> ▶ **SEE** For more on tombstones and other Drive Extender information, **see** "Understanding Drive Extender," **P. 129**.

This means that if a secondary hard drive dies, you don't lose any data because Windows Home Server has copies of the files stored either on the main hard drive (in the primary data partition) or another secondary hard drive.

However, what happens if your system hard drive—the drive that stores the system partition and the primary data partition—fails? That's quite a bit more problematic not only because you no longer have access to Windows Home Server, but also because you lose the tombstones that point to the shadow files on the secondary disk (or disks). The good news is that you can replace the hard drive with another one and then use the Windows Home Server DVD to make a partial recovery. Here's what I mean by "partial:"

▶ You can reinstall Windows Home Server on the new drive, and it will re-create the system partition.

▶ Windows Home Server will re-create the primary data partition on the new drive.

▶ Windows Home Server will examine the files on the secondary disk (or disks) and re-create the tombstones in the new primary data partition.

▶ Windows Home Server will *not* reinstate your user accounts or any other Windows Home Server Console settings.

▶ Windows Home Server will *not* reinstate the backup database. That is, any backups you had stored prior to the crash will be gone, and you'll have to start fresh.

It's not the tidiest recovery in the history of computing (losing your stored backups *really* hurts), but you can at least get Windows Home Server back on its feet without much fuss.

Before going any further, if you have multiple internal hard drives installed on your Windows Home Server machine, you do need to know which of them holds the system partition. The easiest way to tell is to use Windows Home Server Console. Start the program and display the Server Storage tab. As you can see in Figure 17.1, one of the drive icons includes a Windows flag logo on it; that's the drive that holds the system partition.

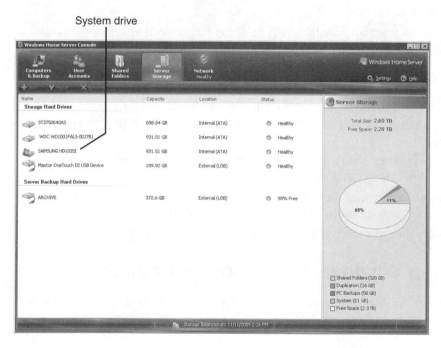

FIGURE 17.1   The hard drive with the Windows flag holds the Windows Home Server system partition.

Here are the steps to follow to replace your system hard drive and reinstate Windows Home Server:

1. Shut down the Windows Home Server computer, if you haven't done so already.

2. Replace the failed system hard drive with a new hard drive.

CAUTION

The order in which the drives' data cables are connected to the motherboard determines the order of the drives on the system. Because your new hard drive must be the first hard drive, be sure to connect the new drive in the same position as the old drive.

3. Turn on the computer, and insert the Windows Home Server installation DVD.

4. Boot from the DVD when your system prompts you. Setup loads the installation files and then displays the Windows Home Server Setup wizard.

5. Click Next.

6. Select the Time and Currency Format as well as the Keyboard or Input Method, and then click Next. Setup displays a list of hard drives.

7. If you don't see your new hard drive, click Load Drivers and then use the dialog box that appears to select the .inf file associated with the new hard drive's device driver, and then click Open.

8. Click Next. The Select an Installation Type dialog box appears.

9. Select Server Reinstallation, and click Next to display the End-User License Agreement dialog box.

10. Click I Accept This Agreement, and then click Next to display the Enter Your Windows Home Server Product Key dialog box.

11. Type your product key and then click Next to display the Name Your Home Server dialog box.

12. Edit the Home Server Name, if desired, and then click Next to display the Ready to Install Windows Home Server dialog box.

13. Click Start. Setup partitions and formats the new drive and then reinstalls Windows Home Server. When it's done, you see the Welcome window.

14. Run through the steps to configure the server.

Restoring a Windows Home Server Backup

If you're running Windows Home Server with Power Pack 3, you can back up some or all of the server's shared folders, as described in Chapter 15, "Maintaining Windows Home Server."

> ▶ **SEE** For details on backing up Windows Home Server's shared folders, **see** "Backing Up Windows Home Server," **P. 454**.

If a hard drive crash or other problem has caused you to lose your shared folder data, you can use your backups to restore that data. Here's how it works:

1. Run the Windows Home Server Console.

2. Select the Computers & Backup tab.

3. Select the icon for your Windows Home Server machine.

4. Click View Backups. Windows Home Server Console displays the View Backups dialog box.

5. If you use more than one hard drive for the server backups, use the drop-down list to select the hard drive that contains the backup you want to use for the restore.

6. Click the backup you want to restore.

7. Click Restore. The Restore Home Server Folders dialog box appears.

8. Activate the check box beside each folder you want to restore.

9. Select a restore option:

   ▶ **Restore Only the Files from the Selected Backup That Are Missing from My Server**—Select this option to have Windows Home Server restore only files that don't exist in the server folder.

   ▶ **Delete All Files in the Selected Folder and Restore Them Exactly as They Were in the Selected Backup**—Select this option to have Windows Home Server restore all files from the selected folders.

10. Click Restore Now. Windows Home Server begins restoring the files.

Understanding Troubleshooting Strategies

One of the ongoing mysteries that all Windows Home Server users experience at one time or another is what might be called the now-you-see-it-now-you-don't problem. This is a glitch that plagues you for a while and then mysteriously vanishes without intervention on your part. (This also tends to occur when you ask someone else to look at the problem. Like the automotive problem that goes away when you take the car to a mechanic, computer problems often resolve themselves as soon as a knowledgeable user sits down at the keyboard.) When this happens, most people just shake their heads and resume working, grateful to no longer have to deal with the problem.

Unfortunately, most computer ills aren't resolved so easily. For these more intractable problems, your first order of business is to track down the source of the glitch. This is, at best, a black art, but it can be done if you take a systematic approach. Over the years, I've found that the best approach is to ask a series of questions designed to gather the required information or to narrow down what might be the culprit. The next few sections take you through these questions.

Did You Get an Error Message?

Unfortunately, most computer error messages are obscure and do little to help you resolve a problem directly. However, error codes and error text can help you down the road, either by giving you something to search for in an online database (see "Troubleshooting Using Online Resources," later in this chapter) or by providing information to a tech support person. Therefore, you should always write down the full text of any error message that appears.

TIP

If the error message is lengthy and you can still use other programs on your computer, don't bother writing down the full message. Instead, while the message is displayed, press Print Screen to place an image of the current screen on the Clipboard. Then open Paint (select Start, All Programs, Accessories, Paint) or some other graphics program, press Ctrl+V to paste the screen into a new image, and save the image. If you think you'll be sending the image via email to a tech support employee or someone else who can help with the problem, consider saving the image as a monochrome or 16-color bitmap or, if possible, a JPEG file, to keep the image size small.

TIP

If the error message appears before Windows Home Server starts, but you don't have time to write it down, press the Pause Break key to pause the startup. After you record the error, press Ctrl+Pause Break to resume the startup.

If Windows Home Server handles the error, it displays a Windows Error Reporting dialog box similar to the one shown in Figure 17.2. It also lets you know that Windows Home Server has generated an error report and asks if you want to send it to Microsoft. (The report includes data about your system and about the error, and these details are stored in a database and are used by Microsoft engineers to help solve problems. Note that you won't receive a reply or any other indication from Microsoft after you send the report.)

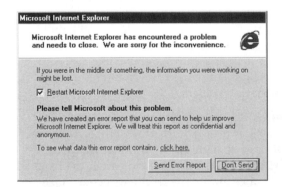

FIGURE 17.2   If Windows Home Server handles a program error, it displays a Windows Error Reporting dialog box similar to this one.

This error report was built by the Dr. Watson debugging tool, which springs into action when an error is detected and then creates an error log in the following folder:

```
%AllUsersProfile%\Application Data\Microsoft\Windows Home Server\logs
```

To see the contents of the error log, either click the `click here` link in the dialog box, or display the preceding folder and open the `drwatsn32.log` text file.

> **TIP**
>
> You can customize the contents of the Dr. Watson error log as well as the operation of the program. Select Start, Run, type **drwtsn32** in the Run dialog box, and then click OK. The dialog box that appears enables you to change the log location, turn log contents on and off, control program options, and view application error logs.

If you're not seeing the Windows Error Reporting dialog box, it may be disabled. Follow these steps to enable it:

1. Select Start, right-click My Computer, and then click Properties to open the System Properties dialog box. (Alternatively, select Start, Control Panel, System.)
2. Display the Advanced tab.
3. Click Error Reporting.
4. Activate the Enable Error Reporting option, as shown in Figure 17.3.

FIGURE 17.3   Activate the Enable Error Reporting option.

5. Use the check box to specify the objects and events you want to report.
6. If you have a program that crashes often, you might prefer not to deal with the Windows Error Reporting dialog box each time. To fix this, click Choose Programs, and then below the Do Not Report Errors for These Programs list, click Add. Use the Add Program dialog box to specify the executable file of the program, and then click OK until you're back in the Error Reporting dialog box.
7. Click OK to return to the System Properties dialog box.
8. Click OK.

Does an Error or Warning Appear in the Event Viewer Logs?

Open the Event Viewer and examine the Application and System logs. In particular, look in the Type column for Error or Warning events. If you see any, double-click each one to read the event description. Figure 17.4 shows an example.

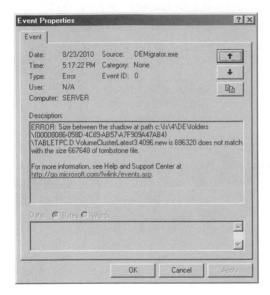

FIGURE 17.4   In the Event Viewer, look for Error events (like the one shown here) or Warning events in the Application and System logs.

> ▶ **SEE** For more information on the Event Viewer, **see** "Reviewing Event Viewer Logs,"
> **P. 445**.

If you see multiple errors or warnings associated with a particular application, consider either repairing or reinstalling the program or check to see if a patch is available from the software vendor. In extreme cases, you may need to uninstall the program. If you see multiple errors or warnings associated with a particular device, see if a device driver upgrade is available.

Does an Error Appear in System Information?

Select Start, All Programs, Accessories, System Tools, System Information to launch the System Information utility. (Alternatively, select Start, Run, type **msinfo32**, and click OK.) In the Hardware Resources, Conflicts\Sharing category, look for device conflicts. Also, see whether any devices are listed in the Components\Problem Devices category, as shown in

Figure 17.5. As with event errors, if you see errors associated with a particular device, your best bet is to check the vendor's website to see if a device driver upgrade is available.

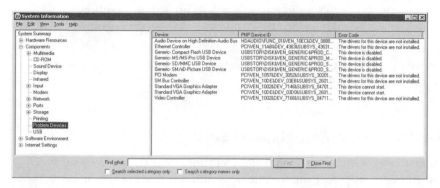

FIGURE 17.5   You can use the System Information utility to look for device conflicts and problems.

Did the Error Begin with a Past Hardware or Software Change?

A good troubleshooting clue is when the onset of an error coincided with a previous hardware or software change. To investigate this possibility, launch the System Information utility (as described in the previous section) and select View, System History. This displays a history of the changes made to your system in each of the main categories: Hardware Resources, Components, and Software Environment, as shown in Figure 17.6. If you know when the problem began, you can look through the history items to see whether a change occurred at the same time and might be the cause of the problem.

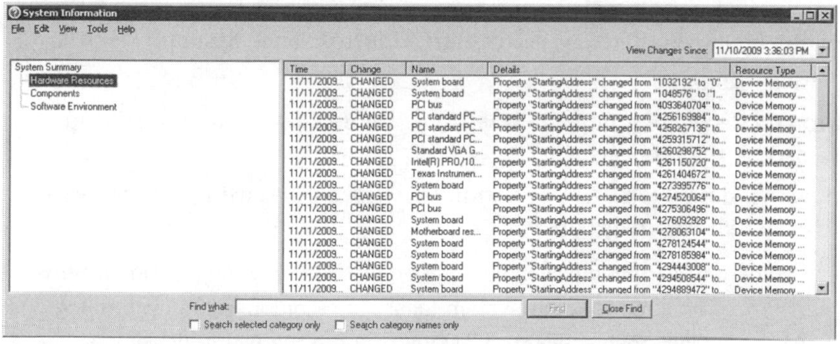

FIGURE 17.6   Use the System Information utility's System History command to examine changes that have been made to your system.

Did You Recently Edit the Registry?

Improper Registry modifications can cause all kinds of mischief. If the problem occurred after editing the Registry, try restoring the changed key or setting. Ideally, if you exported a backup of the offending key, you should import the backup. I show you how to back up the Registry in Chapter 18, "Working with the Windows Home Server Registry."

> ▸ **SEE** For details on backing up the Registry and its keys, **see** "Keeping the Registry Safe," **P. 530**.

Did You Recently Change Any Windows Settings?

If the problem started after you changed your Windows configuration, try reversing the change. Even something as seemingly innocent as activating the screensaver can cause problems, so don't rule anything out. (Actually, if your screen is garbled or the display is frozen, a screensaver should be your prime suspect. There's something about the mode switch from regular video to screensaver video that, at least in my experience, has always been problematic. This shouldn't be an issue if you use the simple Blank screensaver that comes with Windows Home Server, but if you use anything fancier, you may have display troubles.)

Did Windows Home Server "Spontaneously" Reboot?

When certain errors occur, Windows Home Server reboots itself. This apparently random behavior is actually built into the system in the event of a system failure (also called a *stop error* or a *blue screen of death*—BSOD). By default, Windows Home Server writes an error event to the system log, dumps the contents of memory into a file, and then reboots the system. So, if your system reboots, check the Event Viewer to see what happened.

You can control how Windows Home Server handles system failures by following these steps:

1. Select Start, right-click My Computer, and then click Properties to open the System Properties dialog box. (Alternatively, select Start, Control Panel, System.)

2. Display the Advanced tab.

3. In the Startup and Recovery group, click Settings. Figure 17.7 shows the Startup and Recovery dialog box that appears.

4. Configure how Windows Home Server handles system failures using the following controls in the System Failure group:

Write an Event to the System Log	This option (which you can't deactivate in Windows Home Server) ensures that the system failure is recorded in the system log. This enables you to view the event in the Event Viewer.
Send an Administrative Alert	When this option is activated, Windows Home Server sends an alert message to the administrator of the network when the system failure occurs.

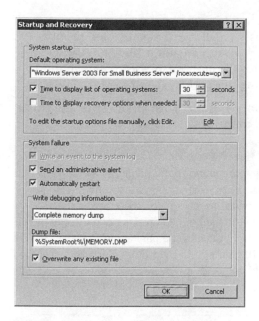

FIGURE 17.7   Use the Startup and Recovery dialog box to configure how Windows Home Server handles system failures.

Automatically Restart   This is the option that, when activated, causes your system to reboot when a stop error occurs. Deactivate this check box to avoid the reboot.

Write Debugging Information   This list determines what information Windows Home Server saves to disk (in the folder specified in the text box below the list) when a system failure occurs. This information—it's called a *memory dump*—contains data that can help a tech support employee determine the cause of the problem. You have four choices:

▶ **None**—No debugging information is written.

▶ **Small Memory Dump (64 KB)**—This option writes the minimum amount of useful information that can be used to identify what caused the stop error. This 64KB file includes the stop error number and its description, the list of running device drivers, and the processor state.

▶ **Kernel Memory Dump**—This option writes the contents of the kernel memory to the disk. (The kernel is the Windows Home Server component that manages low-level functions for processor-related activities, such as scheduling and dispatching threads, handling interrupts and exceptions, and synchronizing multiple processors.) This dump includes memory allocated to the kernel, the hardware abstraction layer, and the drivers and programs that the kernel uses. Unallocated memory and memory allocated to user programs are not included in the dump. This information is the most useful for troubleshooting, so I recommend using this option.

▶ **Complete Memory Dump**—This option writes the entire contents of RAM to the disk.

CAUTION

Windows Home Server first writes the debugging information to the paging file—Pagefile.sys in the root folder of the %SystemDrive%. When you restart the computer, Windows Home Server transfers the information to the dump file. Therefore, you need to have a large enough paging file to handle the memory dump. This is particularly true for the Complete Memory Dump option, which requires the paging file to be as large as the physical RAM, plus one megabyte. The file size of the Kernel Memory Dump is typically about one-third of physical RAM, although it may be as large as 800MB. I showed you how to check and adjust the size of the paging file in Chapter 14, "Tuning Windows Home Server Performance."

▶ **SEE** To learn how to modify the paging file size, **see** "Changing the Paging File's Size," **P. 415**.

▶ **Overwrite Any Existing File**—When this option is activated, Windows Home Server overwrites any existing dump file with the new dump information. If you deactivate this check box, Windows Home Server creates a new dump file with each system failure. Note that this option is enabled only for the Kernel Memory Dump and the Complete Memory Dump (which by default write to the same file: %SystemRoot%\Memory.dmp).

Did You Recently Change Any Application Settings?

If you did just change application settings, try reversing the change to see whether doing so solves the problem. If that doesn't help, check to see whether an upgrade or patch is available. Also, some applications come with a "Repair" option that can fix corrupted files. To try this out, follow these steps:

1. Select Start, Control Panel, Add or Remove Programs.
2. Make sure the Change or Remove Programs tab is displayed.
3. Click the program you're having trouble with.
4. Click the Change button. (You may need to click the Change/Remove button, instead. If you only see a Remove button, it means the program doesn't offer a repair option.) The application's install program launches.
5. Select the Repair option, if one exists. Figure 17.8 shows an example. (In this case, the option you want is called Reinstall or Repair.)
6. Click Next to run the repair.

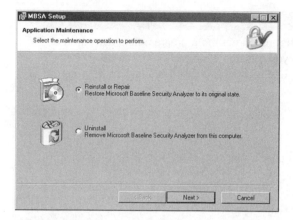

FIGURE 17.8   For some applications, the install program comes with a Repair option that you can use to fix corrupted files or other problems.

If repairing the program doesn't work, try reinstalling the program.

> **NOTE**
>
> If a program freezes, you can't shut it down using conventional methods. If you try, you might see a dialog box warning you that the program is not responding. If so, click End Now to force the program to close. Alternatively, right-click the taskbar and then click Task Manager. When you display the Applications tab, you should see your stuck application listed, and the Status column will likely say Not responding. Click the program and then click End Task.

Did You Recently Install a New Program?

If you suspect that a new program is causing system instability, restart Windows Home Server and try operating the system for a while without using the new program. (If the program has components that load at startup, be sure to deactivate them, as I describe later in this chapter in the section titled "Troubleshooting Startup Using the System Configuration Utility.") If the problem doesn't recur, the new program is likely the culprit. Try using the program without other programs running.

You should also examine the program's readme file (if it has one) to look for known problems and possible workarounds. It's also a good idea to check for a version of the program designed to work with either Windows Home Server or Windows Server 2003. Again, you can also try the program's Repair option, or you can reinstall the program.

Similarly, if you recently upgraded an existing program, try uninstalling the upgrade.

> **TIP**
>
> One common cause of program errors is having one or more program files corrupted because of bad hard disk sectors. Before you reinstall a program, run a surface check on your hard disk to identify and block off bad sectors. I showed you how to do a hard disk surface scan in Chapter 15.

▶ **SEE** To learn how to run a hard disk check, **see** "Checking Your Hard Disk for Errors," **P. 431**.

Did You Recently Install a New Device?

If you recently installed a new device or if you recently updated an existing device driver, the new device or driver might be causing the problem. Check Device Manager to see whether there's a problem with the device. Follow my device troubleshooting suggestions later in this chapter; see the section titled "Troubleshooting Device Problems."

Did You Recently Install an Incompatible Device Driver?

Windows Home Server enables you to install drivers that aren't Windows Home Server–certified, but it also warns you that this is a bad idea. Incompatible drivers are one of the most common sources of system instability, so whenever possible, you should download and install a driver that is designed for Windows Home Server.

▶ **SEE** For information on installing driver updates, **see** "Upgrading Your Device Drivers," **P. 423**.

If you can't find a compatible driver, the next best thing is to roll back the driver you just installed. Here are the steps to follow:

1. Select Start, right-click My Computer, and then click Manage to open the Computer Management snap-in.
2. Select Device Manager.
3. Display the device for the driver that's causing the problem.
4. Double-click the device to open its property sheet.
5. Display the Driver tab.
6. Click Roll Back Driver.

Did You Recently Apply an Update from Windows Update?

If your system becomes unstable after installing an update from Windows Update, in many cases you can uninstall the update. Here are the steps to follow:

1. Select Start, Control Panel, Add or Remove Programs.
2. Make sure the Change or Remove Programs tab is displayed.

3. Activate the Show Updates check box.

4. Select the update you recently installed (see Figure 17.9 for an example).

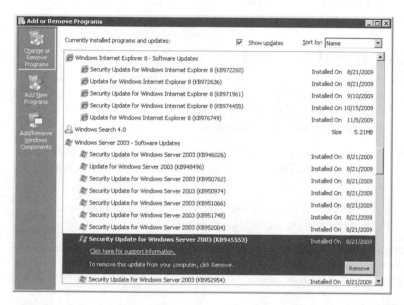

FIGURE 17.9   If you suspect that an update is causing problems, uninstall the update.

5. Click the Remove button. The Software Update Removal Wizard appears.

6. Click Next. The wizard examines Windows Home Server for programs that might be affected by removing the update, and then it displays a list of those programs.

7. Click Yes to confirm that you want to remove the update.

8. Click Finish. In most cases, the wizard restarts the computer to complete the uninstall.

TIP

If you have Windows Home Server set up to perform automatic updating, you can keep tabs on the changes made to your system by going to the Windows Update site. (Select Start, All Programs, Windows Update.) Click the Review Your Update History link.

Did You Recently Install a Windows Home Server Hotfix or Power Pack?

It's ironic that hotfixes and Power Packs that are designed to increase system stability occasionally do the opposite and cause more problems than they fix:

▶ If you've applied a hotfix, you can often remove it using the Control Panel's Add or Remove Programs icon. Look for a Windows Home Server Hotfix entry in the Change or Remove Programs list. If you have multiple hotfixes listed, make sure that you remove the correct one. To be sure, check with either the Microsoft Security site or the Microsoft Knowledge Base, both of which I discuss in the next section. Note, however, that you cannot uninstall many hotfixes.

▶ If you installed a Power Pack and you elected to save the old system files, you can uninstall the Power Pack using the Control Panel's Add or Remove Programs icon. Look for a Windows Home Server Power Pack entry in the Change or Remove Programs list.

General Troubleshooting Tips

Figuring out the cause of a problem is often the hardest part of troubleshooting, but by itself, it doesn't do you much good. When you know the source, you need to parlay that information into a fix for the problem. I discussed a few solutions in the previous section, but here are a few other general fixes you need to keep in mind:

▶ **Close all programs**—You can often fix flaky behavior by shutting down all your open programs and starting again. This is a particularly useful fix for problems caused by low memory or low system resources.

▶ **Log off Windows Home Server**—Logging off clears the RAM and gives you a slightly cleaner slate than merely closing all your programs.

▶ **Reboot the computer**—If there are problems with some system files and devices, logging off won't help because these objects remain loaded. By rebooting the system, you reload it, which is often enough to solve many computer problems.

▶ **Turn off the computer and restart**—You can often solve a hardware problem by first shutting off your machine. Wait for 30 seconds to give all devices time to spin down, and then restart.

▶ **Check connections, power switches, and so on**—Some of the most common (and some of the most embarrassing) causes of hardware problems are the simple physical things: making sure that a device is turned on, checking that cable connections are secure, and ensuring that insertable devices are properly inserted.

Troubleshooting Using Online Resources

The Internet is home to an astonishingly wide range of information, but its forte has always been computer knowledge. Whatever problem you have, there's a good chance that someone out there has run into the same thing, knows how to fix it, and has posted the solution on a website or newsgroup or would be willing to share it with you if asked. True, finding what you need is sometimes difficult, and you often can't be sure how accurate some of the solutions are. However, if you stick to the more reputable sites and if you get second opinions on solutions offered by complete strangers, you'll find the online world to be an excellent troubleshooting resource. Here's my list of favorite online resources:

Microsoft Product Support Services	This is Microsoft's main online technical support site. Through this site, you can access frequently asked questions about Windows Home Server, see a list of known problems, download files, and send questions to Microsoft support personnel: support.microsoft.com/

Microsoft Knowledge Base	The Microsoft Product Support Services site has links that enable you to search the Microsoft Knowledge Base, which is a database of articles related to all Microsoft products including, of course, Windows Home Server. These articles provide you with information about Windows Home Server and instructions on using Windows Home Server features. But the most useful aspect of the Knowledge Base is for troubleshooting problems. Many of the articles were written by Microsoft support personnel after helping customers overcome problems. By searching for error codes or key words, you can often get specific solutions to your problems: support.microsoft.com/search/
Microsoft TechNet	This Microsoft site is designed for IT professionals and power users. It contains a huge number of articles on all Microsoft products. These articles give you technical content, program instructions, tips, scripts, downloads, and troubleshooting ideas: www.microsoft.com/technet/
Windows Update	Check this site for the latest device drivers, security patches, Service Packs, and other updates: windowsupdate.microsoft.com/
Microsoft Security	Check this site for the latest information on Microsoft's security and privacy initiatives, particularly security patches: www.microsoft.com/security/
Windows Home Server Forums	Many Windows Home Server experts prowl this site, and you can usually get help with a problem quickly: social.microsoft.com/Forums/en-US/category/WindowsHomeServer/
Vendor websites	All but the tiniest hardware and software vendors maintain websites with customer support sections that you can peruse for upgrades, patches, workarounds, frequently asked questions, and sometimes chat or bulletin board features.
The Web	Whatever problem you're facing, chances are that someone else has not only faced the same problem, but also created a web page that explains how they fixed it. Use your favorite search engine to search for your problem. This works best if you're getting a specific error message because you can then use some or all of the message as the search text. Google works great for this kind of searching: www.google.com/

Newsgroups	There are computer-related newsgroups for hundreds of topics and products. Microsoft maintains its own newsgroups via the msnews.microsoft.com server, and Usenet has a huge list of groups in the alt and comp hierarchies. Before asking a question in a newsgroup, be sure to search Google Groups to see whether your question has been answered in the past: groups.google.com/

Troubleshooting Device Problems

Windows Home Server has good support for most newer devices, and it's likely that most major hardware vendors will take steps (eventually) to update their devices and drivers to run properly with Windows Home Server. If you use only recent, Plug and Play-compliant devices that are compatible with either Windows Home Server or Windows Server 2003, you should have a trouble-free computing experience (at least from a hardware perspective). Of course, putting *trouble-free* and *computing* next to each other is just asking for trouble. Hardware is not foolproof—far from it. Things still can, and will, go wrong, and, when they do, you'll need to perform some kind of troubleshooting. (That's assuming, of course, that the device doesn't have a physical fault that requires a trip to the repair shop.) Fortunately, Windows Home Server also has some handy tools to help you both identify and rectify hardware ills.

Troubleshooting with Device Manager

Windows Home Server stores all its hardware data in the Registry, but it provides Device Manager to give you a graphical view of the devices on your system. To display Device Manager, first use either of the following techniques:

▶ Select Start, Control Panel, System (or click Start, right-click My Computer, and then click Properties). In the System Properties dialog box that appears, display the Hardware tab and then click Device Manager.

▶ Select Start, right-click Computer, and click Manage. In the Computer Management window, click the Device Manager branch.

> **TIP**
>
> A quick way to go directly to the Device Manager snap-in is to select Start, Run (press Windows Logo+R) to open the Run dialog box, type `devmgmt.msc`, and click OK. Note, too, that you can display the System Properties dialog box quickly by pressing Windows Logo+Pause Break.

Device Manager's default display is a tree-like outline that lists various hardware types. To see the specific devices, click the plus sign (+) to the left of a device type. For example, opening the Network Adapters branch displays all the network adapter drives attached to your computer, as shown in Figure 17.10.

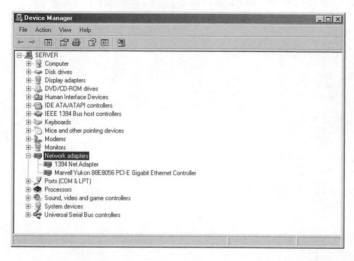

FIGURE 17.10   Device Manager organizes your computer's hardware in a tree-like hierarchy organized by hardware type.

Device Manager not only provides you with a comprehensive summary of your system's hardware data, it also doubles as a decent troubleshooting tool. To see what I mean, check out the Device Manager tab shown in Figure 17.11. See how the icon for the Standard VGA Graphics Adapter device has an exclamation mark superimposed on it? This tells you that there's a problem with the device.

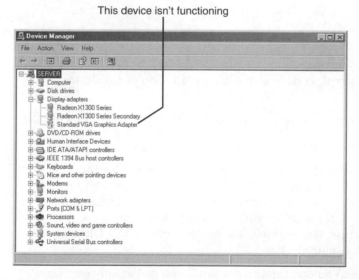

FIGURE 17.11   The Device Manager uses icons to warn you if a device has a problem.

If you examine the device's properties, as shown in Figure 17.12, the Device Status area tells you a bit more about what's wrong. As you can see in Figure 17.12, the problem here is that the device won't start. Either try Device Manager's suggested remedy or click the Check for Solutions button to see whether Microsoft has a fix for the problem.

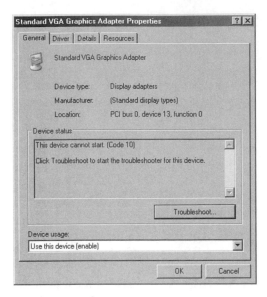

FIGURE 17.12   The Device Status area tells you if the device isn't working properly.

NOTE

Device Manager has several dozen error codes. See the following Microsoft Knowledge Base article for a complete list of the codes, as well as solutions to try in each case: support.microsoft.com/kb/310123.

Device Manager uses three different icons to give you an indication of the device's current status:

▶ A black exclamation mark (!) on a yellow field tells you that the device has a problem.

▶ A red X tells you that the device is disabled or missing.

▶ A blue i on a white field tells you that the device's Use Automatic Settings check box (on the Resources tab) is deactivated and that at least one of the device's resources was selected manually. Note that the device might be working just fine, so this icon doesn't indicate a problem. If the device isn't working properly, however, the manual setting might be the cause. (For example, the device might have a DIP switch or jumper set to a different resource.)

If your system flags a device but you don't notice problems, you can usually get away with just ignoring the flag. I've seen lots of systems that run perfectly well with flagged devices, so this falls under the "If it ain't broke" school of troubleshooting. The danger here is that tweaking your system to try to get rid of the flag can cause other—usually more serious—problems.

Troubleshooting Device Driver Problems

Other than problems with the hardware itself, device drivers are the cause of most device woes. This is true even if your device doesn't have one of the problem icons that I mentioned in the previous section. That is, if you open the device's properties sheet, Windows Home Server may tell you that the device is "working properly," but all that means is that Windows Home Server can establish a simple communications channel with the device. So if your device isn't working right, but Windows Home Server says otherwise, suspect a driver problem. Here are a few tips and pointers for correcting device driver problems:

▶ **Reinstall the driver**—A driver might be malfunctioning because one or more of its files have become corrupted. You can usually solve this by reinstalling the driver. Just in case a disk fault caused the corruption, you should check the partition where the driver is installed for errors before reinstalling (see Chapter 15).

▶ **SEE** For details on running a hard disk check, **see** "Checking Your Hard Disk for Errors," **P. 431**.

▶ **Upgrade to a signed driver**—Unsigned drivers are accidents waiting for a place to happen in Windows Home Server, so you should upgrade to a signed driver, if possible. How can you tell whether an installed driver is unsigned? Open the device's properties sheet, and display the Driver tab. Signed driver files display a name beside the Digital Signer label, whereas unsigned drivers display Not digitally signed instead. See Chapter 14 for the steps on updating a device driver.

▶ **SEE** For information on installing driver updates, **see** "Upgrading Your Device Drivers," **P. 423**.

▶ **Disable an unsigned driver**—If an unsigned driver is causing system instability and you can't upgrade the driver, try disabling the device. Right-click the device, and then click Disable.

▶ **Use the Signature Verification Tool**—This program checks your entire system for unsigned drivers. To learn how it works, see "Verifying Digitally Signed Files," later in this chapter.

▶ **Try the manufacturer's driver supplied with the device**—If the device came with its own driver, try either updating to the manufacturer's driver or running the device's setup program.

▶ **Download the latest driver from the manufacturer**—Device manufacturers often update drivers to fix bugs, add new features, and tweak performance. Go to the manufacturer's website to see whether an updated driver is available. (See "Tips for Downloading Device Drivers," next.)

▶ **Try Windows Update**—The Windows Update website often has updated drivers for downloading. Select Start, All Programs, Windows Update and let the site scan your system. Then click the Driver Updates link to see which drivers are available for your system.

▶ **Roll back a driver**—If the device stops working properly after you update the driver, try rolling it back to the old driver. (Refer to "Did You Recently Install an Incompatible Device Driver?," earlier in this chapter.)

Tips for Downloading Device Drivers

Finding device drivers on the World Wide Web is an art in itself. I can't tell you how much of my life I've wasted rooting around manufacturer websites trying to locate a device driver. Most hardware vendor sites seem to be optimized for sales rather than service, so although you can purchase, say, a new printer with just a mouse click or two, downloading a new driver for that printer can take a frustratingly long time. To help you avoid such frustration, here are some tips from my hard-won experience:

▶ If the manufacturer offers different sites for different locations (such as different countries), always use the company's "home" site. Most mirror sites aren't true mirrors, and (Murphy's Law still being in effect) it's usually the driver you're looking for that a mirror site is missing.

▶ The temptation when you first enter a site is to use the search feature to find what you want. This works only sporadically for drivers, and the site search engines almost always return marketing or sales material first. Note, too, that occasionally these searches are case-sensitive, so bear that in mind when you enter your search text.

▶ Instead of the search engine, look for an area of the site dedicated to driver downloads. The good sites have links to areas called Downloads or Drivers, but it's far more common to have to go through a Support or Customer Service area first.

▶ Don't try to take shortcuts to where you *think* the driver might be hiding. Trudge through each step the site provides. For example, it's common to have to select an overall driver category, and then a device category, and then a line category, and then the specific model you have. This is tedious, but it almost always gets you where you want to go.

▶ If the site is particularly ornery, the preceding method might not lead you to your device. In that case, try the search engine. Note that device drivers seem to be particularly poorly indexed, so you might have to try lots of search text variations. One thing that usually works is searching for the exact filename. How can you possibly know that? A method that often works for me is to use Google (www.google.com), Google Groups (groups.google.com), or some other web search engine to search for your driver. Chances are someone else has looked for your file and will have the filename (or, if you're really lucky, a direct link to the driver on the manufacturer's site).

▶ When you get to the device's download page, be careful which file you choose. Make sure that it's a Windows Home Server driver, and make sure that you're not downloading a utility program or some other nondriver file.

▶ When you finally get to download the file, be sure to save it to your computer rather than opening it. If you reformat your system or move the device to another computer, you'll be glad you have a local copy of the driver so that you don't have to wrestle with the whole download rigmarole all over again.

Troubleshooting Resource Conflicts

On modern computer systems that support the Advanced Configuration and Power Interface (ACPI), use PCI cards, and use external Plug and Play-compliant devices, resource conflicts have become almost nonexistent. That's because the ACPI is capable of managing the system's resources to avoid conflicts. For example, if a system doesn't have enough IRQ lines, ACPI assigns two or more devices to the same IRQ line and manages the devices so that they can share the line without conflicting with each other. (To see which devices share an IRQ line, activate Device Manager's View, Resources by Connection command, and then double-click the Interrupt Request (IRQ) item.)

ACPI's success at allocating and managing resources is such that Windows Home Server doesn't allow you to change a device's resources, even if you'd want to do such a thing. If you open a device's properties sheet and display the Resources tab, you'll see that you can't change any of the settings.

If you use legacy devices in your system, however, conflicts could arise because Windows Home Server is unable to manage the device's resources properly. If that happens, Device Manager lets you know there's a problem. To solve it, first display the Resources tab on the device's properties sheet. The Resource Settings list shows you the resource type on the left and the resource setting on the right. If you suspect that the device has a resource conflict, check the Conflicting Device List box to see whether it lists any devices. If the list displays only No Conflicts, the device's resources aren't conflicting with another device.

If there is a conflict, you need to change the appropriate resource. Some devices have multiple configurations, so one easy way to change resources is to select a different configuration. To try this, deactivate the Use Automatic Settings check box and then use the Setting Based On drop-down list to select a different configuration. Otherwise, you need to play around with the resource settings by hand. Here are the steps to follow to change a resource setting:

1. In the Resource Type list, select the resource you want to change.

2. Deactivate the Use Automatic Settings check box, if it's activated.

3. For the setting you want to change, either double-click it or select it and then click the Change Setting button. (If Windows Home Server tells you that you can't modify the resources in this configuration, select a different configuration from the Setting Based On list.) A dialog box appears that enables you to edit the resource setting.

4. Use the Value spin box to select a different resource. Watch the Conflict Information group to make sure that your new setting doesn't step on the toes of an existing setting.

5. Click OK to return to the Resources tab.

6. Click OK. If Windows Home Server asks whether you want to restart your computer, click Yes.

TIP

An easy way to see which devices are either sharing resources or are conflicting is via the System Information utility. Select Start, Run, type **msinfo32**, and click OK. (Alternatively, select Start, All Programs, Accessories, System Tools, System Information.) Open the Hardware Resources branch and then click Conflicts/Sharing.

Verifying Digitally Signed Files

I mentioned earlier that digitally unsigned drivers are often the cause of system instabilities. To ensure that you don't accumulate unsigned drivers on your system, you should regularly run the Signature Verification tool. This program scans your entire system (or, optionally, a specific folder) for unsigned drivers. Follow these steps to run this tool:

1. Select Start, Run, enter **sigverif**, and click OK. The File Signature Verification window appears.

2. Click Advanced to display the Advanced File Signature Verification Settings dialog box.

3. Activate the Look for Other Files That Are Not Digitally Signed option, as shown in Figure 17.13.

FIGURE 17.13   Use this dialog box to configure the Signature Verification tool.

4. In the Look in This Folder text box, enter **C:\Windows\System32\drivers**.

5. Click OK.

6. Click Start to begin the verification process.

When the verification is complete, the program displays a list of the unsigned driver files, as shown in Figure 17.14. The results for all the scanned files are written to the log file `Sigverif.txt`, which is copied to the `C:\\Windows` folder when you close the window that shows the list of unsigned drivers. In the Status column of `Sigverif.txt`, look for files listed as `Not Signed`. If you find any, consider upgrading these drivers to signed versions.

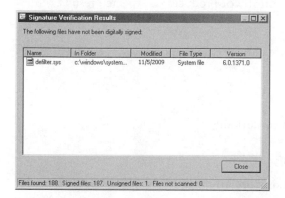

FIGURE 17.14   When the Signature Verification Tool completes its work, it displays a list of the unsigned drivers on your system.

▶ **SEE** For details on installing driver updates, **see** "Upgrading Your Device Drivers," **P. 423**.

Troubleshooting Startup

Computers are often frustrating beasts, but few things in computing are as frustrating as an operating system that won't operate. This section outlines a few common startup difficulties and their solutions.

When to Use the Various Advanced Startup Options

You saw back in Chapter 4, "Configuring Windows Home Server," that Windows Home Server has some useful options on its Advanced Options menu. But under what circumstances should you use each option? That's not such an easy question to answer because there is some overlap in what each option brings to the table, so there are no hard and fast rules. It is possible, however, to lay down some general guidelines.

▶ **SEE** For details on the Advanced Options menu, **see** "Configuring Startup with the Advanced Options Menu," **P. 117**.

Using Safe Mode

You should use the Safe Mode option if one of the following conditions occurs:

▶ Windows Home Server doesn't start after the POST ends.

▶ Windows Home Server seems to stall for an extended period.

▶ Windows Home Server doesn't work correctly or produces unexpected results.

▶ You can't print to a local printer.

▶ Your video display is blank or is distorted and possibly unreadable.

▶ Your computer stalls repeatedly.

▶ Your computer suddenly slows down.

▶ You need to test an intermittent error condition.

Using Safe Mode with Networking

You should use the Safe Mode with Networking option if one of the following situations occurs:

▶ Windows Home Server fails to start using any of the other safe mode options.

▶ The drivers or programs you need to repair a problem exist on a shared network resource.

▶ You need access to email or other network-based communications for technical support.

Using Safe Mode with Command Prompt

You should use the Safe Mode with Command Prompt option if one of the following situations occurs:

▶ Windows Home Server fails to start using any of the other Safe mode options.

▶ The programs you need to repair a problem can be run from the command prompt.

▶ You can't load the Windows Home Server GUI.

Using Enable Boot Logging

You should use the Enable Boot Logging option in the following situations:

▶ The Windows Home Server startup hangs after switching to Protected mode.

▶ You need a detailed record of the startup process.

▶ You suspect (after using one of the other Startup menu options) that a Protected-mode driver is causing Windows Home Server startup to fail.

After starting (or attempting to start) Windows Home Server with this option, you end up with a file named NTBTLOG.TXT in the %SystemRoot% folder. This is a text file, so you can examine it with any text editor. For example, you could boot to the command prompt (using the Save Mode with Command Prompt option) and then use EDIT.COM to examine the file.

Move to the end of the file, and you might see a message telling you which device driver failed. You probably need to reinstall or roll back the driver.

Using Enable VGA Mode

You should use the Enable VGA Mode option in the following situations:

- ▶ Windows Home Server fails to start using any of the safe mode options.
- ▶ You recently installed a new video card device driver, and the screen is garbled or the driver is balking at a resolution or color depth setting that's too high.
- ▶ You can't load the Windows Home Server GUI.

After Windows Home Server has loaded, you can either reinstall or roll back the driver, or you can adjust the display settings to values that the driver can handle.

Using Last Known Good Configuration

Use the Last Known Good Configuration option under the following circumstances:

- ▶ You suspect the problem is hardware related, but you can't figure out the driver that's causing the problem.
- ▶ You don't have time to try out the other more detailed inspections.

Each time Windows Home Server starts successfully in Normal mode, the system makes a note of which *control set*—the system's drivers and hardware configuration—was used. Specifically, it enters a value in the following Registry key:

HKLM\SYSTEM\Select\LastKnownGood

For example, if this value is 1, control set 1 was used to start Windows Home Server successfully:

HKLM\SYSTEM\ControlSet001

If you make driver or hardware changes and then find that the system won't start, you can tell Windows Home Server to load using the control set that worked the last time (that is, the control set that doesn't include your most recent hardware changes). This is called the *last known good configuration*, and the theory is that by using the previous working configuration, your system should start because it's bypassing the changes that caused the problem.

Using Directory Services Restore Mode

The Directory Services Restore Mode option is only for domain controllers. That means you'll never need to use it, because you can't configure Windows Home Server as a domain controller.

Using Debugging Mode

Use the Debugging Mode option if you receive a stop error during startup and a remote technical support professional has asked you to send debugging data.

What to Do If Windows Home Server Won't Start in Safe Mode

If Windows Home Server is so intractable that it won't even start in Safe mode, your system is likely afflicted with one of the following problems:

- ▶ Your system is infected with a virus. You need to run an antivirus program (usually from a bootable disc) to cleanse your system.

- ▶ Your system has incorrect BIOS settings. Run the machine's BIOS setup program to see whether any of these settings needs to be changed or whether the CMOS battery needs to be replaced. (To access the setup program, shut down and then restart the Windows Home Server computer. Look for a message that tells you which key or key combination to press to access the settings.)

- ▶ Your system has a hardware conflict. See "Troubleshooting Device Problems," earlier in this chapter, for hardware troubleshooting procedures.

Troubleshooting Startup Using the System Configuration Utility

If Windows Home Server won't start, troubleshooting the problem usually involves trying various advanced startup options. It's almost always a time-consuming and tedious business.

However, what if Windows Home Server *will* start, but you encounter problems along the way? Or what if you want to try a few different configurations to see whether you can eliminate startup items or improve Windows Home Server's overall performance? For these scenarios, don't bother trying out different startup configurations by hand. Instead, take advantage of Windows Home Server's System Configuration Utility which, as you saw in Chapter 4, gives you a graphical front-end that offers precise control over how Windows Home Server starts.

> ▶ **SEE** To learn more about the System Configuration Utility, **see** "Using the System Configuration Editor to Modify BOOT.INI," **P. 116**.

To launch the System Configuration Utility, select Start, Run (or press Windows Logo+R), type **msconfig**, and then click OK. In the System Configuration Utility windows, display the General tab, which has the following three startup options:

Normal Startup	This option loads Windows Home Server normally.
Diagnostic Startup	This option loads only those device drivers and system services that are necessary for Windows Home Server to boot. This is equivalent to deactivating all the check boxes associated with the Selective Startup option, discussed next.
Selective Startup	When you activate this option, the check boxes below become available, as shown in Figure 17.15. Use these check boxes to select which portions of the startup should be processed.

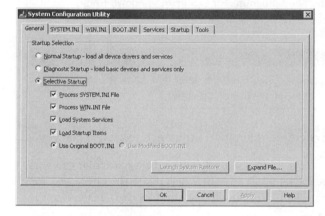

FIGURE 17.15   Use the System Configuration Utility to select different startup configurations.

For a selective startup, you control how Windows Home Server processes items using four categories:

Process SYSTEM.INI File	This file contains system-specific information about your computer's hardware and device drivers. Most hardware data is stored in the Registry, but SYSTEM.INI retains a few set tings that are needed for backward compatibility with older (16-bit) programs. The specific items loaded by SYSTEM.INI are listed in the SYSTEM.INI tab.
Process WIN.INI File	This file contains configuration settings relating to Windows Home Server and to installed Windows applications. Again, the bulk of this data is stored in the Registry, but WIN.INI is kept around for compatibility. The specific items loaded by WIN.INI are listed in the WIN.INI tab.
Load System Services	This category refers to the system services that Windows Home Server loads at startup. The specific services loaded by Windows Home Server are listed in the Services tab.

| Load Startup Items | This category refers to the items in your Windows Home Server Startup group and to the startup items listed in the Registry. For the latter, the settings are stored in one of the following keys: |

`HKCU\SOFTWARE\Microsoft\Windows\CurrentVersion\Run`
`HKLM\SOFTWARE\Microsoft\Windows\CurrentVersion\Run`

The specific items loaded from the Startup group or the Registry are listed in the Startup tab.

> **NOTE**
>
> A *service* is a program or process that performs a specific, low-level support function for the operating system or for an installed program. For example, Windows Home Server's Automatic Updates feature is a service.

> **NOTE**
>
> The Services tab has an Essential column. Only those services that have Yes in this column are loaded when you choose the Selective Startup option.

To control these startup items, the System Configuration utility gives you two choices:

► To prevent Windows Home Server from loading every item in a particular category, activate Selective Startup in the General tab and then deactivate the check box for the category you want. For example, to disable all items in WIN.INI, deactivate the Process WIN.INI File check box.

► To prevent Windows Home Server from loading only specific items in a category, display the category's tab and then deactivate the check box beside the item or items you want to bypass at startup.

Here's a basic procedure you can follow to use the System Configuration Utility to troubleshoot a startup problem (assuming that you can start Windows Home Server by using some kind of Safe mode boot, as described earlier):

1. In the System Configuration Utility, activate the Diagnostic Startup option and then reboot the computer. If the problem did not occur during the restart, you know the cause lies in SYSTEM.INI, WIN.INI, the system services, or the startup items.

2. Activate the Selective Startup option.

3. Activate one of the four check boxes and then reboot the computer.

4. Repeat step 3 for each of the other check boxes until the problem recurs. When this happens, you know that whatever item you activated just before rebooting is the source of the problem.

5. Display the tab of the item that is causing the problem. For example, if the problem recurred after you activated the Load Startup Items check box, display the Startup tab.

6. Click Disable All to clear all the check boxes.

7. Activate one of the check boxes to enable an item, and then reboot the computer.

8. Repeat step 7 for each of the other check boxes until the problem recurs. When this happens, you know that whatever item you activated just before rebooting is the source of the problem.

TROUBLESHOOTING BY HALVES

If you have a large number of check boxes to test (such as in the Services tab), activating one check box at a time and rebooting can become very tedious very fast. A faster method is to begin by activating the first half of the check boxes and rebooting. One of two things will happen:

▶ **The problem won't reoccur**—This means that one of the items represented by the deactivated check boxes is the culprit. Clear all the check boxes, activate half of the other check boxes, and then reboot.

▶ **The problem will reoccur**—This means that one of the activated check boxes is the problem. Activate only half of those check boxes and reboot.

Keep halving the number of activated check boxes until you isolate the offending item.

9. In the System Configuration Utility's General tab, activate the Normal Startup option.

10. Fix or work around the problem:

   ▶ If the problem is an item in SYSTEM.INI or WIN.INI, display the appropriate tab, select the problem item, and then click Disable.

TIP

Another way to edit SYSTEM.INI or WIN.INI is by using the System Configuration Editor. To load this program, select Start, Run, type **sysedit** in the Run dialog box, and then click OK.

   ▶ If the problem is a system service, you can disable the service. Select Start, Control Panel, Administrative Tools, Services. Double-click the problematic service to open its property sheet. In the Startup Type list, select Disabled and then click OK.

   ▶ If the problem is a Startup item, either delete the item from the Startup group or delete the item from the appropriate Run key in the Registry. If the item is a program, consider uninstalling or reinstalling it.

▶ **SEE** For more detailed information on the Registry's Run key, **see** "Launching Items Using the Registry," **P. 121**.

Reinstalling Windows Home Server

Ideally, solving a problem requires a specific tweak to the system: a Registry setting change, a driver upgrade, a program uninstall. But sometimes you need to take more of a "big picture" approach to revert your system to some previous state in hopes of leaping past the problem and getting your system working again. Specifically, if nothing else seems to work, you might be able to fix things by reinstalling Windows Home Server over the existing installation. This doesn't affect your data or any personal settings you've adjusted, but it might cure what's ailing Windows Home Server either by restoring the system to its default settings or by installing fresh copies of corrupted system files. Here are the steps to follow to reinstall Windows Home Server:

1. Shut down the Windows Home Server computer.

2. Insert the Windows Home Server installation DVD.

3. Start the computer and, when prompted, boot from the DVD. After Windows Home Server Setup loads some files, the Welcome to Windows Home Server Setup dialog box appears.

4. Click Next. Setup displays a list of hard drives and volumes. If a hard drive that you know is installed on your system isn't listed, click Load Drivers and then use the dialog box that appears to select the .inf file associated with the hard drive's device driver.

5. Click Next to display the Select an Installation Type dialog box.

6. Make sure that Server Reinstallation appears in the Installation Type dialog box, and then click Next to display the Select Your Regional and Keyboard settings dialog box.

7. Select the Time and Currency Format as well as the Keyboard or Input Method, and then click Next to display the End-User License Agreement dialog box.

8. Click I Accept This Agreement, and then click Next to display the Enter Your Windows Home Server Product Key dialog box.

9. Type your product key and then click Next to display the Name Your Home Server dialog box.

10. Edit the Home Server Name, if desired, and then click Next to display the Ready to Install Windows Home Server dialog box.

11. Click Start.

From Here

- ▶ To learn some network troubleshooting techniques, **see** "Troubleshooting Network Problems," **P. 16.**

- ▶ For information on the System Configuration Utility, **see** "Using the System Configuration Editor to Modify BOOT.INI," **P. 116.**

- ▶ For details on the Advanced Options menu, **see** "Configuring Startup with the Advanced Options Menu," **P. 117.**

- ▶ For more detailed information on the Registry's Run key, **see** "Launching Items Using the Registry," **P. 121.**

- ▶ For more on tombstones and other Drive Extender information, **see** "Understanding Drive Extender," **P. 129.**

- ▶ For information on installing driver updates, **see** "Upgrading Your Device Drivers," **P. 423.**

- ▶ To learn how to modify the paging file size, **see** "Changing the Paging File's Size," **P. 415.**

- ▶ To learn how to run a hard disk check, **see** "Checking Your Hard Disk for Errors," **P. 431.**

- ▶ For details on backing up Windows Home Server's shared folders, **see** "Backing Up Windows Home Server," **p. 454.**

- ▶ For details on backing up the Registry and its keys, **see** "Keeping the Registry Safe," **P. 530.**

Working with the Windows Home Server Registry

The Windows Home Server Registry has come up a fair number of times so far in this book. Here's a quick summary of a few of those instances:

▶ In Chapter 2, "Setting Up and Working with User Accounts," I showed you how to modify a Registry setting to customize Windows Home Server's minimum password length requirement.

   ▶ **SEE** "Customizing the Password Length Requirement," **P. 40.**

▶ In Chapter 4, "Configuring Windows Home Server," you learned how to use the Registry to add your own time servers to the Internet Time tab of Windows Home Server's Date and Time Properties dialog box.

   ▶ **SEE** "Adding Time Servers to the Internet Time Tab," **P. 99**.

▶ In Chapter 4, you also learned how to use the Registry's Run and RunOnce keys to launch a program at startup.

   ▶ **SEE** "Launching Applications and Scripts at Startup," **P. 120**.

▶ In Chapter 16, "Customizing the Windows Home Server Interface," I showed you how to use the Registry to configure Windows Home Server's taskbar grouping feature.

   ▶ **SEE** "Controlling Taskbar Grouping," **P. 473**.

You can do these and many other useful and powerful Windows Home Server tweaks only by modifying the Registry. So just what is the Registry? It's a central repository that Windows Home Server uses to store almost everything that applies to the configuration of your system, including all the following:

- ▶ Information about all the hardware installed on your computer

- ▶ The resources those devices use

- ▶ A list of the device drivers that Windows Home Server loads at startup

- ▶ Settings that Windows Home Server uses internally

- ▶ File type data that associates a particular type of file with a specific application

- ▶ Wallpaper, color schemes, and other interface customization settings

- ▶ Other customization settings for things such as the Start menu and the taskbar

- ▶ Settings for accessories such as Windows Explorer and Internet Explorer

- ▶ Internet and network connections and passwords

- ▶ Settings and customization options for many applications

It's all stored in one central location, and, thanks to a handy tool called the Registry Editor, it's yours to play with (carefully!) as you see fit. No, the Registry doesn't have a pretty interface like most of the other customization options, and many aspects of the Registry give new meaning to the word *arcane*, but it gives you unparalleled access to facets of Windows Home Server that would be otherwise out of reach. This chapter introduces you to the Registry and its structure, and it shows you how to make changes to the Registry by wielding the Registry Editor.

Starting the Registry Editor

As you see a bit later, the Registry's files are binary files, so you can't edit them directly. Instead, you use a program called the Registry Editor, which enables you to view, modify, add, and delete any Registry setting. It also has a search feature to help you find settings, and export and import features that enable you to save settings to and from a text file.

To launch the Registry Editor, follow these steps:

1. Log on to Windows Home Server.
2. Select Start, Run (or press Windows Logo+R) to open the Run dialog box.
3. In the Open text box, type `regedit`.
4. Click OK.

Figure 18.1 shows the Registry Editor window that appears. (Your Registry Editor window might look different if someone else has used the program previously. Close all the open branches in the left pane to get the view shown in Figure 18.1.)

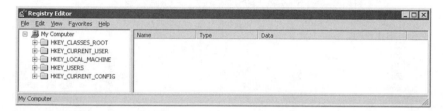

FIGURE 18.1   Running the **REGEDIT** command launches the Registry Editor, a program that enables you to view and edit the Registry's data.

Navigating the Registry

The Registry Editor is reminiscent of Windows Explorer, and it works in basically the same way. The left side of the Registry Editor window is similar to Explorer's Folders pane, except that rather than folders, you see *keys*. In this chapter, I'll call the left pane the *Keys pane*.

> **CAUTION**
>
> The Registry Editor is arguably the most dangerous tool in the Windows Home Server arsenal. The Registry is so crucial to the smooth functioning of Windows Home Server that a single imprudent change to a Registry entry can bring your system to its knees. Therefore, now that you have the Registry Editor open, don't start tweaking settings willy-nilly. Instead, read the section titled "Keeping the Registry Safe," later in this chapter, for some advice on protecting this precious and sensitive resource.

Navigating the Keys Pane

The Keys pane, like Explorer's Folders pane, is organized in a treelike hierarchy. The five keys that are visible when you first open the Registry Editor are special keys called *handles* (which is why their names all begin with HKEY). These keys are collectively referred to as the Registry's *root keys*. I'll tell you what to expect from each of these keys later (see the section called "Getting to Know the Registry's Root Keys," later in this chapter).

All these keys contain subkeys, which you can display by clicking the plus sign (+) to the left of each key, or by highlighting a key and pressing the plus-sign key on your keyboard's numeric keypad. When you open a key, the plus sign changes to a minus sign (–). To close a key, click the minus sign or highlight the key and press the minus-sign key on the numeric keypad. Again, this is just like navigating folders in Explorer.

You often have to drill down several levels to get to the key you want. For example, Figure 18.2 shows the Registry Editor after I've opened the HKEY_CURRENT_USER key, and then the Control Panel subkey, and then clicked the Keyboard subkey. Notice how the status bar tells you the exact path to the current key, and that this path is structured just like a folder path.

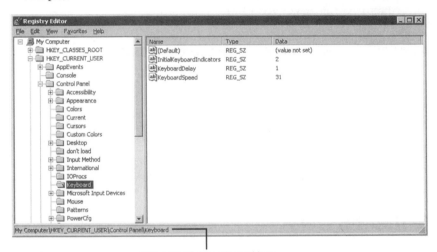

Full path of the selected key

FIGURE 18.2   Open the Registry's keys and subkeys to find the settings you want to work with.

> **TIP**
>
> To see all the keys properly, you likely will have to increase the size of the Keys pane. To do this, use your mouse to click and drag the split bar to the right. Alternatively, select View, Split, use the Right Arrow key to adjust the split bar position, and then press Enter.

Understanding Registry Settings

If the left side of the Registry Editor window is analogous to Explorer's Folders pane, the right side is analogous to Explorer's Contents pane. In this case, the right side of the Registry Editor window displays the settings contained in each key (so I'll call it the *Settings pane*). The Settings pane is divided into three columns:

Name   This column tells you the name of each setting in the currently selected key (analogous to a filename in Explorer).

Type   This column tells you the data type of the setting. There are five possible data types:

   REG_SZ—This is a string value.

   REG_MULTI_SZ—This is a series of strings.

   REG_EXPAND_SZ—This is a string value that contains an environment variable name that gets "expanded" into the value of that variable. For example, the `%SystemRoot%` environment variable holds the folder in which Windows Home Server was installed. So, if you see a Registry setting that includes the value `%SystemRoot%\System32\` (see Figure 18.3 for an example), and Windows Home Server is installed in `C:\Windows`, the setting's expanded value is `C:\Windows\System32\`.

   REG_DWORD—This is a double word value: a 32-bit hexadecimal value arranged as eight digits. For example, 11 hex is 17 decimal, so this number would be represented in `DWORD` form as 0x00000011 (17). (Why "double word"? A 32-bit value represents four bytes of data, and because a *word* in programming circles is defined as two bytes, a four-byte value is a *double word*.)

   REG_BINARY—This value is a series of hexadecimal digits.

Data   This column displays the value of each setting.

Getting to Know the Registry's Root Keys

The root keys are your Registry starting points, so you need to become familiar with what kinds of data each key holds. The next few sections summarize the contents of each key.

HKEY_CLASSES_ROOT

HKEY_CLASSES_ROOT—usually abbreviated as HKCR—contains data related to file extensions and their associated programs, the objects that exist in the Windows Home Server system, as well as applications and their Automation information. There are also keys related to shortcuts and other interface features.

The top part of this key contains subkeys for various file extensions. You see .bmp for BMP (Paint) files, .doc for DOC (Word or WordPad) files, and so on. In each of these subkeys, the Default setting tells you the name of the registered file type associated with the extension. For example, the .txt extension is associated with the txtfile file type.

These registered file types appear as subkeys later in the HKEY_CLASSES_ROOT branch, and the Registry keeps track of various settings for each registered file type. In particular, the shell subkey tells you the actions associated with this file type. For example, in the shell\open\command subkey, the Default setting shows the path for the executable file that opens. Figure 18.3 shows this subkey for the txtfile file type.

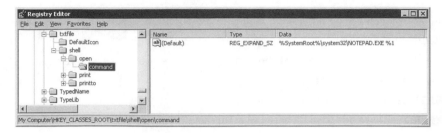

FIGURE 18.3 The registered file type subkeys specify various settings associated with each file type, including its defined actions.

HKEY_CLASSES_ROOT is actually a copy (or an *alias*, as these copied keys are called) of the following HKEY_LOCAL_MACHINE key:

HKEY_LOCAL_MACHINE\Software\Classes

The Registry creates an alias for HKEY_CLASSES_ROOT to make these keys easier for applications to access and to improve compatibility with legacy programs.

HKEY_CURRENT_USER

HKEY_CURRENT_USER—usually abbreviated as HKCU—contains data that applies to the user who's currently logged on (which with Windows Home Server is almost always the Administrator account). It contains user-specific settings for Control Panel options, network connections, applications, and more.

Here's a summary of the most important HKEY_CURRENT_USER subkeys:

AppEvents	Contains sound files that play when particular system events occur (such as maximizing of a window).
Control Panel	Contains settings related to certain Control Panel icons.
Keyboard Layout	Contains the keyboard layout as selected via Control Panel's Keyboard icon.
Network	Contains settings related to mapped network drives.
Software	Contains user-specific settings related to installed applications and Windows.

HKEY_LOCAL_MACHINE

HKEY_LOCAL_MACHINE (HKLM) contains non–user-specific configuration data for your system's hardware and applications. This is by far the most important key, and it's where you'll perform most of your Registry edits. You'll use the following subkeys most often:

`Software`   Contains computer-specific settings related to installed applications. The `Classes` subkey is aliased by `HKEY_CLASSES_ROOT`. The `Microsoft` subkey contains settings related to Windows (as well as any other Microsoft products you have installed on your computer).

`System`   Contains subkeys and settings related to Windows startup.

HKEY_USERS

`HKEY_USERS` (HKU) contains settings that are similar to those in `HKEY_CURRENT_USER`. `HKEY_USERS` is used to store the settings for users with group policies defined, as well as the default settings (in the `.DEFAULT` subkey) that are mapped to a new user's profile.

HKEY_CURRENT_CONFIG

`HKEY_CURRENT_CONFIG` (HKCC) contains settings for the current hardware profile. If your machine uses only one hardware profile, `HKEY_CURRENT_CONFIG` is an alias for `HKEY_LOCAL_MACHINE\SYSTEM\ControlSet001`. If your machine uses multiple hardware profiles, `HKEY_CURRENT_CONFIG` is an alias for `HKEY_LOCAL_MACHINE\SYSTEM\ControlSet`*nnn,* where nnn is the numeric identifier of the current hardware profile. This identifier is given by the *Current* setting in the following key:

`HKLM\SYSTEM\CurrentControlSet\Control\IDConfigDB`

Understanding Hives and Registry Files

The Registry database actually consists of a number of files that contain a subset of the Registry called a *hive*. A hive consists of one or more Registry keys, subkeys, and settings. Each hive is supported by several files that use the extensions listed in Table 18.1.

TABLE 18.1   Extensions Used by Hive Supporting Files

Extension	File Contains
None	A complete copy of the hive data
`log`	A log of the changes made to the hive data
`.sav`	A copy of the hive data as of the end of the text mode portion of the Windows Home Server setup

Table 18.2 shows the supporting files for each hive. (Note that not all of these files might appear on your system.)

TABLE 18.2   Supporting Files Used by Each Hive

Hive	Files
`HKLM\SAM`	`%SystemRoot%\System32\config\SAM`
	`%SystemRoot%\System32\config\SAM.LOG`
	`%SystemRoot%\System32\config\SAM.SAV`
`HKLM\SECURITY`	`%SystemRoot%\System32\config\SECURITY`
	`%SystemRoot%\System32\config\SECURITY.LOG`
	`%SystemRoot%\System32\config\SECURITY.SAV`

TABLE 18.2   Supporting Files Used by Each Hive

Hive	Files
HKLM\SOFTWARE	%SystemRoot%\System32\config\SOFTWARE
	%SystemRoot%\System32\config\SOFTWARE.LOG
	%SystemRoot%\System32\config\SOFTWARE.SAV
HKLM\SYSTEM	%SystemRoot%\System32\config\SYSTEM
	%SystemRoot%\System32\config\SYSTEM.LOG
	%SystemRoot%\System32\config\SYSTEM.SAV
HKU\.DEFAULT	%SystemRoot%\System32\config\DEFAULT
	%SystemRoot%\System32\config\DEFAULT.LOG
	%SystemRoot%\System32\config\DEFAULT.SAV

Also, the Administrator account has its own hive, which maps to HKEY_CURRENT_USER during logon. The supporting files for each user hive are stored in \Documents and Settings\Administrator. The NTUSER.DAT file contains the hive data, and the NTUSER.DAT.LOG file tracks the hive changes.

Keeping the Registry Safe

The sheer wealth of data stored in one place makes the Registry convenient, but it also makes it very precious. If your Registry went missing somehow, or if it became corrupted, Windows Home Server simply would not work. With that scary thought in mind, let's take a moment to run through several protective measures. The techniques in this section should ensure that Windows Home Server never goes down for the count because you made a mistake while editing the Registry.

Backing Up the Registry

Windows Home Server maintains what is known as the *system state*: the crucial system files that Windows Home Server requires to operate properly. Included in the system state are the files used during system startup, the protected system files, and, naturally, the Registry files. The Backup utility has a feature that enables you to easily back up the current system state, so it's probably the most straightforward way to create a backup copy of the Registry.

Here are the steps to follow to back up the system state:

1. Log on to Windows Home Server.
2. Select Start, All Programs, Accessories, System Tools, Backup.
3. If the Backup or Restore Wizard appears, click the Advanced Mode link.
4. Display the Backup tab.
5. In the folder tree, open the Desktop branch and then the My Computer branch, if they're not open already.

6. Activate the System State check box, as shown in Figure 18.4.

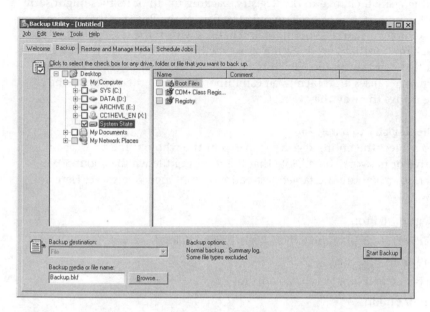

FIGURE 18.4   Select the Backup Utility's System State check box to back up the Windows Home Server Registry.

7. Click Browse and use the Save As dialog box to choose a backup destination.

8. Click Start Backup. The Backup Utility backs up the system state to the selected location.

9. When the backup is complete, click Close.

CAUTION

Make sure the destination resides on a different hard drive, a removable drive, or a network share. Don't back up the system state to the same hard drive on which Windows Home Server is installed.

Also, don't include any data-related Windows Home Server folders in the backup (that is, C:\fs and anything on drive D). Due to the way Windows Home Server's new Drive Extender technology works, you can't restore data from a backup created with the Backup Utility.

CAUTION

Depending on the configuration of your computer, the system state can be quite large—hundreds of megabytes. Therefore, make sure that the destination you choose for the backup has enough free space to handle such a large file.

Protecting Keys by Exporting Them to Disk

If you're just making a small change to the Registry, backing up all of its files might seem like overkill. Another approach is to back up only the part of the Registry that you're working on. For example, if you're about to make changes within the HKEY_CURRENT_USER key, you could back up just that key, or even a subkey within HKCU. You do that by exporting the key's data to a registration file, which is a text file that uses the .reg extension. That way, if the change causes a problem, you can import the .reg file back into the Registry to restore things the way they were.

Exporting the Entire Registry to a .reg File

The easiest way to protect the entire Registry is to export the whole thing to a .reg file on a separate hard drive or network share. Note that the resulting file will be about 50MB, and possibly larger, so make sure the target destination has enough free space. Here are the steps to follow:

1. Open the Registry Editor.
2. Select File, Export to display the Export Registry File dialog box.
3. Select a location for the file.
4. Use the File Name text box to type a name for the file.
5. Activate the All option.
6. Click Save.

Exporting a Key to a .reg File

Here are the steps to follow to export a key to a registration file:

1. Open the Registry Editor and select the key you want to export.
2. Select File, Export to display the Export Registry File dialog box.
3. Select a location for the file.
4. Use the File Name text box to type a name for the file.
5. Activate the Selected Branch option.
6. Click Save.

> **TIP**
>
> You can save time by creating a batch file that uses the REG utility to export one or more keys to a .reg file. Here's the general syntax to use:
>
> ```
> reg export rootkey\subkey destination [/y]
> ```
>
> Here, you replace *rootkey* with one of the following root key values: *HKCR*, HKCU, HKLM, HKU, or HKCC; you replace *subkey* with the path to the key you want to export; and you replace *destination* with the full pathname of the file to which the key should be exported. (Add the /y switch to force Windows Home Server to overwrite the destination file, if one exists.) Here are some examples:
>
> ```
> reg export HKCU \\paulspc\backups\whs_hkcu.reg
>
> reg export HKLM\Software\Microsoft\Windows \\paulspc\backups\whs_hklm.reg
> ```

FINDING REGISTRY CHANGES

One common Registry scenario is to make a change to Windows Home Server using a tool such as the Group Policy editor and then try to find which Registry setting (if any) was affected by the change. However, because of the sheer size of the Registry, this is usually a needle-in-a-haystack exercise that ends in frustration. One way around this is to export some or all the Registry before making the change and then export the same key or keys after making the change. You can then use the file compare (FC) utility at the command prompt to find out where the two files differ. Here's the FC syntax to use for this:

```
FC /U pre_edit.reg post-edit.reg > reg_changes.txt
```

Change *pre_edit.reg* to the name of the registration file you exported before editing the Registry; change *post_edit.reg* to the name of the registration file you exported after editing the Registry; and change *reg_changes.txt* to the name of a text file to which the FC output is redirected. Note that the /U switch is required because registration files use the Unicode character set.

Importing a .reg File

If you need to restore the key that you backed up to a registration file, follow these steps:

1. Open the Registry Editor.
2. Select File, Import to display the Import Registry File dialog box.
3. Find and select the file you want to import.
4. Click Open.
5. When Windows Home Server tells you the information has been entered into the Registry, click OK.

NOTE

You also can import a .reg file by locating it in Windows Explorer and then double-clicking the file.

TIP

You can also import a .reg file using the REG utility:

```
reg import file
```

Here, you replace *file* with the full pathname of the .reg file that you want to import. Here's an example:

```
reg import \\paulspc\backups\whs_hklm.reg
```

> **CAUTION**
>
> Many applications ship with their own `.reg` files for updating the Registry. Unless you're sure that you want to import these files, avoid double-clicking them. They might end up overwriting existing settings and causing problems with your system.

Working with Registry Entries

Now that you've had a look around, you're ready to start working with the Registry's keys and settings. In this section, I'll give you the general procedures for basic tasks, such as modifying, adding, renaming, deleting, and searching for entries, and more.

Changing the Value of a Registry Entry

Changing the value of a Registry entry is a matter of finding the appropriate key, displaying the setting you want to change, and editing the setting's value. Unfortunately, finding the key you need isn't always a simple matter. Knowing the root keys and their main subkeys, as described earlier, will certainly help, and the Registry Editor has a Find feature that's invaluable. (I'll show you how to use it later; see "Finding Registry Entries.")

To illustrate how this process works, let's look at an example: changing your registered owner name and company name. In other versions of Windows, the installation process often asks you to enter your name and, optionally, your company name. These registered names appear in several places as you work with Windows:

- ▶ If you select Help, About in most Windows programs, your registered names appear in the About dialog box.

- ▶ If you install an application, the installation program uses your registered names for its own records (although you usually get a chance to make changes).

Unfortunately, Windows Home Server doesn't ask you for this data. Instead, it uses the generic values `Windows Home Server User` for the owner name and `Family` for the organization name.

With these names appearing in so many places, it's good to know that you can change either or both names. The secret lies in the following key:

`HKLM\SOFTWARE\Microsoft\WindowsNT\CurrentVersion`

To get to this key, you open the branches in the Registry Editor's tree pane: `HKEY_LOCAL_MACHINE`, and then `SOFTWARE`, and then `Microsoft`, and then `Windows NT`. Finally, click the `CurrentVersion` subkey to select it. Here you see a number of settings, but two are of interest to us (see Figure 18.5).

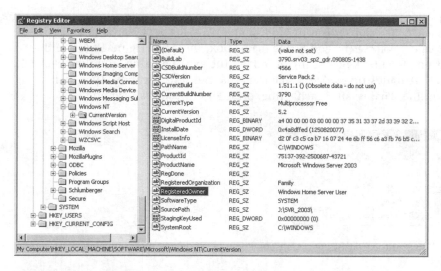

FIGURE 18.5   Navigate to `HKLM\SOFTWARE\Microsoft\Windows NT\CurrentVersion` to see your registered names.

If you have keys that you visit often, you can save them as favorites to avoid trudging through endless branches in the Keys pane. To do this, navigate to the key and then select Favorites, Add to Favorites. In the Add to Favorites dialog box, edit the Favorite Name text box, if desired, and then click OK. To navigate to a favorite key, pull down the Favorites menu and select the key name from the list that appears at the bottom of the menu.

`RegisteredOrganization`	This setting contains your registered company name.
`RegisteredOwner`	This setting contains your registered name.

Now you open the setting for editing by using any of the following techniques:

▶ Select the setting name and either select Edit, Modify or press Enter.

▶ Double-click the setting name.

▶ Right-click the setting name and click Modify from the context menu.

The dialog box that appears depends on the value type you're dealing with, as discussed in the next few sections. Note that edited settings are written to the Registry right away, but the changes might not go into effect immediately. In many cases, you need to exit the Registry Editor and then either log off or restart Windows Home Server.

Editing a String Value

If the setting is a REG_SZ value (as it is in our example), a REG_MULTI_SZ value, or a
REG_EXPAND_SZ value, you see the Edit String dialog box, shown in Figure 18.6. Use the
Value Data text box to enter a new string or modify the existing string, and then click OK.
(For a REG_MULTI_SZ multistring value, Value Data is a multiline text box. Type each string
value on its own line. That is, after each string, press Enter to start a new line.)

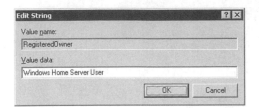

FIGURE 18.6   You see the Edit String dialog box if you're modifying a string value.

Editing a DWORD Value

If the setting is a REG_DWORD, you see the Edit DWORD (32-Bit) Value dialog box shown in
Figure 18.7. In the Base group, select either Hexadecimal or Decimal, and then use the
Value Data text box to enter the new value of the setting. (If you chose the Hexadecimal
option, enter a hexadecimal value; if you chose Decimal, enter a decimal value.)

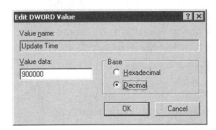

FIGURE 18.7   You see the Edit DWORD Value dialog box if you're modifying a double word
value.

Editing a Binary Value

If the setting is a REG_BINARY value, you see an Edit Binary Value dialog box like the one
shown in Figure 18.8.

For binary values, the Value Data box is divided into three vertical sections:

Starting Byte Number   The four-digit values on the left of the Value Data box tell you the
sequence number of the first byte in each row of hexadecimal numbers.
This sequence always begins at 0, so the sequence number of the first
byte in the first row is 0000. There are eight bytes in each row, so the
sequence number of the first byte in the second row is 0008, and so
on. You can't edit these values.

Hexadecimal Numbers (Bytes)	The eight columns of two-digit numbers in the middle section display the setting's value, expressed in hexadecimal numbers, where each two-digit number represents a single byte of information. You can edit these values.
ANSI Equivalents	The third section on the right side of the Value Data box shows the ANSI equivalents of the hexadecimal numbers in the middle section. For example, the first byte of the first row is the hexadecimal value 48, which represents the uppercase letter H. You can also edit the values in this column.

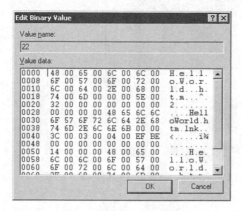

FIGURE 18.8   You see the Edit Binary Value dialog box if you're modifying a binary value.

Editing a .reg File

If you exported a key to a registration file, you can edit that file and then import it back into the Registry. To make changes to a registration file, find the file in Windows Explorer, right-click the file, and then click Edit. Windows Home Server opens the file in Notepad.

TIP

If you need to make global changes to the Registry, export the entire Registry and then load the resulting registration file into WordPad or some other word processor or text editor. Use the application's Replace feature (carefully!) to make changes throughout the file. If you use a word processor for this, be sure to save the file as a text file when you're done. You can then import the changed file back into the Registry.

Creating a .reg File

You can create registration files from scratch and then import them into the Registry. This is a handy technique if you have some customizations that you want to apply to multiple systems. To demonstrate the basic structure of a registration file and its entries, Figure 18.9 shows two windows. The bottom window is the Registry Editor with a key named Test highlighted. The settings pane contains six sample settings: the (Default) value and one each of the five types of settings (binary, DWORD, expandable string, multistring, and string). The top window shows the Test key in Notepad as an exported registration file (Test.reg).

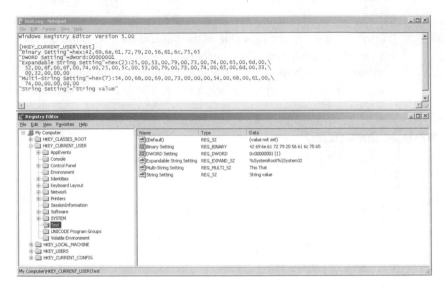

FIGURE 18.9   The settings in the Test key shown in the Registry Editor correspond to the data shown in the Test.reg file in Notepad.

Windows Home Server registration files always start with the following header:

Windows Registry Editor Version 5.00

TIP

If you're building a registration file for a Windows 9x, Me, or NT 4 system, change the header to the following:

REGEDIT4

Next is an empty line followed by the full path of the Registry key that will hold the settings you're adding, surrounded by square brackets:

[HKEY_CURRENT_USER\Test]

Below the key are the setting names and values, which use the following general form:

TIP

If you want to add a comment to a .reg file, start a new line and begin the line with a semicolon (;).

"SettingName"=identifier:SettingValue

SettingName	The name of the setting. Note that you use the @ symbol to represent the key's Default value.
identifier	A code that identifies the type of data. REG_SZ values don't use an identifier, but the other four types do:

dword	Use this identifier for a DWORD value.
hex	Use this identifier for a binary value.
hex(2)	Use this identifier for an expandable string value.
hex(7)	Use this identifier for a multistring value.

SettingValue	This is the value of the setting, which you enter as follows:

String	Surround the value with quotation marks.
DWORD	Enter an eight-digit DWORD value.
Binary	Enter the binary value as a series of two-digit hexadecimal numbers, separating each number with a comma.
Expandable string	Convert each character to its hexadecimal equivalent, and then enter the value as a series of two-digit hexadecimal numbers, separating each number with a comma, and separating each character with 00.
Multistring	Convert each character to its hexadecimal equivalent, and then enter the value as a series of two-digit hexadecimal numbers, separating each number with a comma, and separating each character with 00, and separating each string with space (00 hex).

TIP

To delete a setting using a .reg file, set its value to a hyphen (-), as in this example:

```
Windows Registry Editor Version 5.00

[HKEY_CURRENT_USER\Test]
"BinarySetting"=-
```

To delete a key, add a hyphen to the start of the key name, as in this example:

```
Windows Registry Editor Version 5.00

[-HKEY_CURRENT_USER\Test]
```

Renaming a Key or Setting

You won't often need to rename existing keys or settings. Just in case, though, here are the steps to follow:

1. In the Registry Editor, find the key or setting you want to work with, and then highlight it.
2. Select Edit, Rename, or press F2.
3. Edit the name and then press Enter.

> **CAUTION**
>
> Rename only those keys or settings that you created yourself. If you rename any other key or setting, Windows Home Server might not work properly.

Creating a New Key or Setting

Many Registry-based customizations don't involve editing an existing setting or key. Instead, you have to create a new setting or key. Here's how you do it:

1. In the Registry Editor, select the key in which you want to create the new subkey or setting.
2. Select Edit, New. (Alternatively, right-click an empty section of the Settings pane and then click New.) A submenu appears.
3. If you're creating a new key, select the Key command. Otherwise, select the command that corresponds to the type of setting you want: String Value, Binary Value, DWORD Value, Multi-String Value, or Expandable String Value.
4. Type a name for the new key or setting.
5. Press Enter.

Deleting a Key or Setting

Here are the steps to follow to delete a key or setting:

1. In the Registry Editor, select the key or setting that you want to delete.
2. Select Edit, Delete, or press Delete. The Registry Editor asks whether you're sure.
3. Click Yes.

> **CAUTION**
>
> Again, to avoid problems, you should delete only those keys or settings that you created yourself. If you're not sure about deleting a setting, try renaming it instead. If a problem arises, you can return the setting to its original name.

Finding Registry Entries

The Registry contains only five root keys, but they contain hundreds of subkeys. The fact that some root keys are aliases for subkeys in a different branch only adds to the confusion. If you know exactly where you're going, the Registry Editor's treelike hierarchy is a reasonable way to get there. If you're not sure where a particular subkey or setting resides, however, you could spend all day poking around in the Registry's labyrinthine nooks and crannies.

To help you get where you want to go, the Registry Editor has a Find feature that enables you to search for keys, settings, or values. Here's how it works:

1. In the Keys pane, select Computer at the top of the pane (unless you're certain of which root key contains the value you want to find; in this case, you can highlight the appropriate root key instead).

2. Select Edit, Find or press Ctrl+F. The Registry Editor displays the Find dialog box, shown in Figure 18.10.

FIGURE 18.10   Use the Find dialog box to search for Registry keys, settings, or values.

3. Use the Find What text box to enter your search string. You can enter partial words or phrases to increase your chances of finding a match.

4. In the Look At group, activate the check boxes for the elements you want to search. For most searches, you want to leave all three check boxes activated.

5. If you want to find only those entries that exactly match your search text, activate the Match Whole String Only check box.

6. Click the Find Next button. The Registry Editor highlights the first match.

7. If this isn't the item you want, select Edit, Find Next (or press F3) until you find the setting or key you want.

When the Registry Editor finds a match, it displays the appropriate key or setting. Note that if the matched value is a setting name or data value, Find doesn't highlight the current key. This is a bit confusing, but remember that the current key always appears at the bottom of the Keys pane.

From Here

▶ To learn how to modify a Registry setting to customize Windows Home Server's minimum password length requirement, **see** "Customizing the Password Length Requirement," **P. 40**.

▶ For information on adding your own time servers to the Internet Time tab of Windows Home Server's Date and Time Properties dialog box, **see** "Adding Time Servers to the Internet Time Tab," **P. 99**.

▶ To learn how to use the Registry's Run and RunOnce keys to launch a program at startup, **see** "Launching Applications and Scripts at Startup," **P. 120**.

▶ For details on using the Registry to configure Windows Home Server's taskbar grouping feature, **see** "Controlling Taskbar Grouping," **P. 473**.

▶ Many of the Registry values are generated by Windows Home Server's customization features; **see** Chapter 16, "Customizing the Windows Home Server Interface."

▶ To learn how to read, add, and modify Registry entries programmatically, **see** "Working with Registry Entries," **P. 682**.

Using Windows Home Server's Command-Line Tools

All versions of Windows have at their core a basic premise: It's easier, faster, and more intuitive to work and play using a graphical user interface (GUI) than using an old-fashioned command-line interface, such as the kind we saw way back in the days when MS-DOS and its variants ruled the PC world. Few, if any, people today would dispute that premise; the last of the Windows versus MS-DOS battles was fought a long time ago.

However, that doesn't mean that a GUI is the *only* way to operate a PC. All versions of Windows still come with a command prompt utility that gives you access to the command line. That's not surprising, but what *is* surprising is that the command line is a source of tremendous power and flexibility. After you have that blinking cursor in front of you, a huge and potent arsenal of commands, tools, and utilities becomes available. With these features at your disposal, you can perform amazing tricks in the areas of disk and file management, performance monitoring, network administration, system maintenance, and much more. This chapter introduces you to the Windows Home Server command line and takes you through quite a few of the available command-line tools.

Getting to the Command Line

To take advantage of the command line and all of its many useful commands, you need to start a command-line session.

Windows Home Server offers a number of different ways to get to the command prompt:

▶ Select Start, All Programs, Accessories, Command Prompt.

▶ Press Windows Logo+R (or select Start, All Programs, Accessories, Run), type **cmd** in the Run dialog box, and click OK.

▶ Create a shortcut for %SystemRoot%\system32\cmd.exe on your desktop (or some other convenient location, such as the taskbar's Quick Launch toolbar), and then launch the shortcut.

▶ Reboot your computer, press F8 to display Windows Home Server's Advanced Options menu, and select the Safe Mode with Command Prompt item.

> ▶ **SEE** To learn more about the Advanced Options menu, **see** "Configuring Startup with the Advanced Options Menu," **P. 117**.

NOTE

It's also possible to configure Windows Home Server's Folder file type to open the command prompt in Windows Explorer's current folder. To see how, refer to the "Opening a Folder in a Command Prompt Session" section, later in this chapter.

Running CMD

For the methods that use the CMD executable, you can specify extra switches after the cmd.exe filename. Most of these switches aren't particularly useful, so let's start with the simplest syntax that you'll use most often:

```
CMD [[/S] [/C ¦ /K] command]
```

/S   Strips out the first and last quotation marks from the *command*, provided that the first quotation mark is the first character in *command*.

/C   Executes the *command* and then terminates.

/K   Executes the *command* and remains running.

command   The command to run.

For example, if your ISP provides you with a dynamic IP address, you can often solve some connection problems by asking the IP for a fresh address. You do that by running the command ipconfig /renew at the command line. In this case, you don't need the Command Prompt window to remain open, so you can specify the /C switch to shut down the command-line session automatically after the IPCONFIG utility finishes:

```
cmd /c ipconfig /renew
```

On the other hand, you often either want to see the results of the command, or you want to leave the Command Prompt window open so that you can run other commands. In those cases, use the /K switch. For example, the following command runs the SET utility (which displays the current values of the Windows Home Server environment variables) and then leaves the command-line session running:

```
cmd /k set
```

Here's the full syntax of cmd.exe:

```
CMD [/A ¦ /U] [/Q] [/D] [/T:bf] [/E:ON ¦ /E:OFF] [/F:ON ¦ /F:OFF]
➥[/V:ON ¦ /V:OFF] [[/S] [/C ¦ /K] command]
```

/Q   Turns off command echoing. If command is a batch file, you won't see any of the batch file commands as they're executed. This is the same as adding the statement @ECHO OFF at the beginning of a batch file.

/D   Disables the execution of AutoRun commands from the Registry. These are commands that run automatically when you start any command-line session. You can find the settings here:

```
HKLM\Software\Microsoft\Command Processor\AutoRun
HKCU\Software\Microsoft\Command Processor\AutoRun
```

TIP

If you do not see an AutoRun setting in one or both keys, select the key, select File, New, String Value, type **AutoRun**, and press Enter.

TIP

The AutoRun Registry settings are handy if you always run a particular command at the beginning of each command-line session. If you run multiple commands to launch a session, you can add those commands to either AutoRun setting. In that case, you must separate each command with the command separator string: &&. For example, to run the IPCONFIG and SET utilities at the start of each command-line session, change the value of an AutoRun setting to the following:

```
ipconfig&&set
```

/A   Converts the output of internal commands to a pipe or file to the ANSI character set.

/U   Converts the output of internal commands to a pipe or file to the Unicode character set.

/T:bf   Sets the foreground and background colors of the Command Prompt window, where f is the foreground color and b is the background color. Both f and b are hexadecimal digits that specify the color as follows:

0	Black	8	Gray
1	Blue	9	Light Blue
2	Green	A	Light Green
3	Aqua	B	Light Aqua
4	Red	C	Light Red
5	Purple	D	Light Purple
6	Yellow	E	Light Yellow
7	White	F	Bright White

TIP

You can also set the foreground and background colors during a command-line session by using the COLOR *bf* command, where *b* and *f* are hexadecimal digits specifying the colors you want. To revert to the default command prompt colors, run COLOR without the *bf* parameter.

/E:ON   Enables *command extensions*, which are extra features added to the following commands. (At the command line, type the command name followed by a space and /? to see the extensions.)

ASSOC	IF
CALL	MD or MKDIR
CD or CHDIR	POPD
COLOR	PROMPT
DEL or ERASE	PUSHD
ENDLOCAL	SET
FOR	SETLOCAL
FTYPE	SHIFT
GOTO	START

/E:OFF   Disables command extensions.

/F:ON   Turns on file and directory name completion, which enables you to
               press special key combinations to scroll through a list of files or subdi-
               rectories in the current directory that match the characters you've
               already typed. For example, suppose that the current directory contains
               files named budget2006.doc, budget2007.doc, and budget2008.doc.
               If you type start budget in a command-line session started with /F:ON,
               pressing Ctrl+F tells Windows Home Server to display the first file (or
               subfolder) in the current folder with a name that starts with budget.
               Pressing Ctrl+F again displays the next file with a name that starts
               with budget, and so on. You can do the same thing with just subfolder
               names by pressing Ctrl+D instead.

TIP

You don't need to start the command prompt with the /F:ON switch to use file and
directory name completion. The command prompt offers a similar feature called
AutoComplete that's turned on by default. At the prompt, type the first letter or two of
a file or subfolder name, and then press the Tab key to see the first object that matches your text in the current folder. Keep pressing Tab to see other matching objects. If,
for some reason, you prefer to turn off AutoComplete, pull down the Command Prompt
window's control menu (right-click the title bar), select Defaults, and then deactivate the
AutoComplete check box in the Options tab.

/F:OFF   Turns off file and directory name completion.

/V:ON   Enables delayed environment variable expansion using ! as the delimiter: !*var*!,
               where *var* is an environment variable. This is useful for batch files in which you
               want to delay the expansion of an environment variable. Normally, Windows Home
               Server expands all environment variables to their current values when it reads the
               contents of a batch file. With delayed expansion enabled, Windows Home Server
               doesn't expand a particular environment variable within a batch file until it executes
               the statement containing that variable.

/V:OFF   Disables delayed environment expansion.

/S   Strips out the first and last quotation marks from *command*, provided the first quota-
               tion mark is the first character in *command*.

/C   Executes the *command* and then terminates.

/K   Executes the *command* and remains running.

command   The command to run.

Opening a Folder in a Command Prompt Session

When you're working in Windows Explorer, you might find occasionally that you need to do some work at the command prompt. For example, the current folder might contain multiple files that need to be renamed—a task that's most easily done within a command-line session. Selecting Start, Command Prompt starts the session in the %USERPROFILE% folder, so you have to use one or more CD commands to get to the folder you want to work in.

An easier way is to create a new action for the Folder file type that launches the command prompt and automatically displays the current Windows Explorer folder. To do this, follow these steps:

1. Select Start Run (or press Windows Logo+R), type **regedit**, and then click OK to open the Registry Editor.

2. Navigate to the following key:

   HKCR\Folder\shell

3. Select Edit, New, Key. Type **Open with Command Prompt**, and press Enter.

4. Make sure that the key you created in step 3 is selected, and then select Edit, New, Key. Type **command**, and press Enter.

5. With the new command key selected, double-click the Default value to open the Edit String dialog box.

6. Type the following:

   cmd.exe /k cd "%L"

> **NOTE**
>
> In the command string, cd represents the command prompt's internal CD (change directory) command, which changes the prompt to another folder. The %L placeholder represents the full pathname of the current folder.

7. Click OK.

Figure 19.1 shows two windows. The top window is the Registry Editor showing the new Open with Command Prompt action added to the HKCR\Folder\shell key; in the bottom window, I right-clicked a folder. Notice how the new action appears in the shortcut menu.

Working at the Command Line

When you have your command-line session up and running, you can run commands and programs, create and launch batch files, perform file maintenance, and so on. If you haven't used the command prompt since the days of DOS, you'll find that the Windows

Home Server command prompt offers a few extra command-line goodies. The next few sections highlight some of the more useful ones.

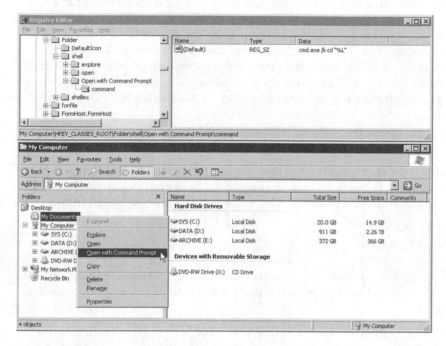

FIGURE 19.1   After you add the new action to the `HKCR\Folder\shell` key, the action appears in the folder file type's shortcut menu.

CAUTION

When you're working in the command prompt, be warned that any files you delete aren't sent to the Recycle Bin but are purged from your system.

Running Commands

Although many of the Windows Home Server accessories provide more powerful and easier-to-use replacements for nearly all commands, a few commands still have no Windows Home Server peer. These include the `REN` command, as well as the many Command Prompt-specific commands, such as `CLS`, `DOSKEY`, and `PROMPT`.

NOTE

Command-line commands that exist as separate executable files—such as `CHKDSK`, `DEFRAG`, and `XCOPY`—are called *external commands*; all other command-line commands—such as `DIR`, `CD`, and `CLS`—are part of the CMD shell and are known as *internal commands*.

How you run a command depends on whether it's an internal or external command and on what you want Windows Home Server to do after the command is finished. For an internal command, you have two choices: You can either enter the command in the command prompt, or you can include it as a parameter with CMD. As you saw earlier, you can run internal commands with CMD by specifying either the /C switch or the /K switch. If you use the /C switch, the command executes, and then the command-line session shuts down. This is fine if you're running a command for which you don't need to see the results. For example, if you want to redirect the contents of drive C:'s root folder in the text file root.txt, entering the following command in the Run dialog box (for example) will do the job:

```
cmd.exe /c dir c:\ > root.txt
```

On the other hand, you might want to examine the output of a command before the Command Prompt window closes. In that case, you need to use the /K switch. The following command runs DIR on drive C:'s root folder and then drops you off in the command prompt:

```
cmd.exe /k dir c:\
```

For an external command, you have three choices: Enter the command in the command prompt, enter the command by itself from within Windows Home Server, or include it as a parameter with CMD.

Entering a command by itself from within Windows Home Server means launching the command's file in Explorer, entering the command in the Run dialog box, or creating a shortcut for the command. For the latter two methods, you can embellish the command by adding parameters and switches. The problem with this method is that Windows Home Server automatically closes the Command Prompt window when the command completes. To change this behavior, follow these steps:

> **NOTE**
>
> When you use the command prompt or the Run dialog box to start an external command prompt command, you don't need to use the command's full pathname. For example, the full pathname for mem.exe is %SystemRoot%\System32\mem.exe, but to run this command, you need to only enter mem. The reason is that the %SystemRoot%\System32 subfolder is part of the PATH statement for each command-line session.

1. Find the command's executable file in the %SystemRoot%\System32 folder.
2. Right-click the executable file and then click Properties to display the command's properties sheet.
3. Display the Program tab. (Note that this tab doesn't appear for all commands.)
4. Deactivate the Close on Exit check box.
5. Click OK.

Working with Long Filenames

If you want to use long filenames in a command, you need to be careful. If the long filename contains a space or any other character that's illegal in an 8.3 filename, you need to surround the long name with quotation marks. For example, if you run the following command, Windows Home Server tells you this: `The syntax of the command is incorrect:`

```
copy Fiscal Year 2010.doc Fiscal Year 2011.doc
```

Instead, you need to enter this command as follows:

```
copy "Fiscal Year 2010.doc" "Fiscal Year 2011.doc"
```

Long filenames are, of course, long, so they tend to be a pain to type in the command prompt. Fortunately, Windows Home Server offers a few methods for knocking long names down to size:

- ▶ In Explorer, drag a folder or file and drop it inside the Command Prompt window. Windows Home Server pastes the full pathname of the folder or file to the end of the prompt.

- ▶ In Windows Explorer, navigate to the folder you want to work with and then select and copy the folder path in the address bar. Return to the Command Prompt window, type the command up to the point where you want the path to appear, right-click the title bar, and then select Edit, Paste.

- ▶ If you're trying to run a program that resides in a folder with a long name, add the folder to the PATH. This technique enables you to run programs from the folder without having to specify the full pathname.

TIP

To edit the PATH environment variable, you have two choices. At the command line, enter the following command (where *folder* is the path of the folder you want to add to the PATH variable):

```
path %path%;folder
```

Alternatively, select Start, Control Panel, System (or select Start, right-click My Computer, and then click Properties) to open the System Properties dialog box. Display the Advanced tab and then click Environment Variables. In the System Variables list, click Path, click Edit, and then append the folder to the end of the Variable Value string. Be sure to separate each folder path with a semicolon (;).

Use the SUBST command to substitute a virtual drive letter for a long pathname. For example, the following command substitutes drive S: for the Start menu's `System Tools` folder:

```
subst s: "%AllUsersProfile%\Start Menu\Programs\Accessories\System Tools"
```

Changing Folders Faster

I mentioned earlier that you use the CD command to change to a different folder on the current drive. However, the command prompt has a few short forms you can use to save time.

You might know that both the command prompt and Windows Home Server use the dot symbol (.) to represent the current folder, and the double-dot symbol (..) to represent its parent folder. You can combine the CD command and the dot notation to jump immediately to a folder's parent folder, or even higher.

To make this more concrete, suppose that the current folder is C:\Animal\Mammal\Dolphin. Table 19.1 demonstrates the techniques you can use to navigate to this folder's parent, grandparent (two levels up), and great-grandparent (three levels up) folders.

TABLE 19.1   Combining the CD Command with Dot Notation

Current Folder	Command	Command
C:\Animal\Mammal\Dolphin	Cd..	C:\Animal\Mammal
C:\Animal\Mammal\Dolphin	Cd..\..	C:\Animal
C:\Animal\Mammal\Dolphin	Cd..\..\..	C:\
C:\Animal\Mammal\Dolphin	Cd..\Baboon	C:\Animal\Mammal\Baboon

> **TIP**
>
> If you want to return to the root folder of any drive, type **cd** and press Enter.

Taking Advantage of DOSKEY

Windows Home Server loads the DOSKEY utility by default when you start any command-line session. This useful little program brings a number of advantages to your command-line work:

▶ You can recall previously entered commands with just a keystroke or two.

▶ You can enter multiple commands on a single line.

▶ You can edit commands instead of retyping them.

The next few sections take you through the specifics.

Recalling Command Lines

The simplest DOSKEY feature is command recall. DOSKEY maintains a *command history buffer* that keeps a list of the commands you enter. To scroll through your previously entered commands in reverse order, press the up-arrow key; when you've done that at least once, you can change direction and run through the commands in the order you entered them by pressing the down-arrow key. To rerun a command, use the arrow keys to find it and then press Enter.

TIP

If you don't want to enter commands from the history buffer, press Esc to get a clean command line.

Table 19.2 lists all the command-recall keys you can use.

TABLE 19.2 DOSKEY Command-Recall Keys

Press	To
Up arrow	Recall the previous command in the buffer.
Down arrow	Recall the next command in the buffer.
Page Up	Recall the oldest command in the buffer.
Page Down	Recall the newest command in the buffer.
F7	Display the entire command buffer.
Alt+F7	Delete all commands from the buffer.
F8	Have DOSKEY recall a command that begins with the letter or letters you've typed on the command line.
F9	Have DOSKEY prompt you for a command list number. (You can see the numbers with the F7 key.) Type the number and press Enter to recall the command.

TIP

The command history buffer holds 50 commands by default. If you need a larger buffer, run DOSKEY with the /LISTSIZE=*buffers* switch, where *buffers* is the number of commands you want to store. You also need to include the /REINSTALL switch to install a new copy of DOSKEY, which puts the new history buffer setting into effect. For example, to change the buffer size to 100, enter the following command:

```
doskey /listize=100 /reinstall
```

Entering Multiple Commands on a Single Line

DOSKEY enables you to run multiple commands on a single line. To do this, insert the characters && between commands. For example, a common task is to change to a different drive and then run a directory listing. Normally, you'd do this with two separate commands:

```
e:
dir
```

With DOSKEY, however, you can do it on one line, like so:

```
e:&&dir
```

> **TIP**
>
> You can enter as many commands as you like on a single line, but just remember that the total length of the line can't be more than 8,191 characters (which should be plenty!).

Editing Command Lines

Rather than simply rerunning a previously typed command, you might need to run the command again with slightly different switches or parameters. Rather than retyping the whole thing, DOSKEY enables you to edit any recalled command line. You use various keys to move the cursor to the offending letters and replace them. Table 19.3 summarizes DOSKEY's command-line editing keys.

TABLE 19.3   DOSKEY Command-Line Editing Keys

Press	To
Left arrow	Move the cursor one character to the left.
Right arrow	Move the cursor one character to the right.
Ctrl+left arrow	Move the cursor one word to the left.
Ctrl+right arrow	Move the cursor one word to the right.
Home	Move the cursor to the beginning of the line.
End	Move the cursor to the end of the line.
Delete	Delete the character over the cursor.
Backspace	Delete the character to the left of the cursor.
Ctrl+Home	Delete from the cursor to the beginning of the line.
Ctrl+End	Delete from the cursor to the end of the line.
Insert	Toggle DOSKEY between Insert mode (your typing is inserted between existing letters on the command line) and Overstrike mode (your typing replaces existing letters on the command line).

Redirecting Command Output and Input

Windows Home Server is always directing things here and there. This generally falls into two categories:

▶ Directing data into its commands from a device called *standard input*

▶ Directing data out of its commands to a device called *standard output*

A device called *CON* (*console*) normally handles standard input and standard output, which is your keyboard and monitor. Windows Home Server assumes that all command input comes from the keyboard and that all command output (such as a DIR listing or a system message) goes to the screen. Redirection is just a way of specifying different input and output devices.

Redirecting Command Output

To send command output to somewhere other than the screen, you use the *output redirection operator* (>). One of the most common uses for output redirection is to capture the results of a command in a text file. For example, you might want to use the report produced by the SYSTEMINFO command as part of a word-processing document. (For the details on this command, see "SYSTEMINFO: Returning System Configuration Data," later in this chapter.) You could use the following command to first capture the report as the file systeminfo.csv:

```
systeminfo /fo csv > c:\systeminfo.csv
```

When you run this command, the usual SYSTEMINFO data doesn't appear onscreen. That's because you directed it away from the screen and into the systeminfo.csv file.

You can use this technique to capture DIR listings, CHKDSK reports, and more. One caveat: If the file you specify as the output destination already exists, Windows Home Server overwrites it without warning. To avoid this, you can use the *double output redirection symbol* (>>). This tells Windows Home Server to append the output to the end of the file if the file exists. For example, suppose you used the following command to output the results of the CHKDSK C: command to chkdsk.txt:

```
chkdsk c: > c:\chkdsk.txt
```

If you then want to append the results of the CHKDSK D: command to chkdsk.txt, you'd enter the following command:

```
chkdsk d: >> c:\chkdsk.txt
```

You can also redirect output to different devices. Table 19.4 lists the various devices that Windows Home Server installs each time you start your system.

TABLE 19.4   Devices Installed by Windows Home Server When You Start Your System

Device Name	Device
AUX	Auxiliary device (usually COM1)
CLOCK$	Real-time clock
COMn	Serial port (COM1, COM2, COM3, or COM4)
CON	Console (keyboard and screen)
LPTn	Parallel port (LPT1, LPT2, or LPT3)
NUL	NUL device (nothing)
PRN	Printer (usually LPT1)

For example, you can send a `DIR` listing to the printer with the following command. (Of course, you need to be sure that your printer is on before doing this. Also note that this only works for a printer attached to a parallel port; it doesn't work for USB printers.)

```
dir > prn
```

The `NUL` device usually throws people for a loop when they first see it. This device (affectionately known as the *bit bucket*) is, literally, nothing. Batch files normally use it to suppress the usual messages Windows Home Server displays when it completes a command. For example, Windows Home Server normally says `1 file(s) copied` when you copy a file. However, the following command sends that message to *NUL*, so you wouldn't see it onscreen:

```
copy somefile.doc \\server\users\paul\ > nul
```

TIP

Unfortunately, Windows Home Server gives you no way to redirect output to a USB port. However, there's a workaround you can use if you're trying to redirect output to a USB printer. Assuming that the printer is shared and that no other device is using the port LPT2, run the following command:

```
NET USE LPT2 \\server\printer
```

Here, replace *server* with the name of your Windows Home Server computer and *printer* with the share name of the USB printer. Now, when you redirect output to LPT2, Windows Home Server sends the output to the USB printer.

Redirecting Input

The *input redirection operator* (<) handles getting input to a Windows Home Server command from somewhere other than the keyboard. Input redirection is almost always used to send the contents of a text file to a Windows Home Server command. The most common example is the `MORE` command, which displays one screen of information at a time. If you have a large text file that scrolls off the screen when you use `TYPE`, the following command, which sends the contents of `BIGFILE.TXT` to the `MORE` command, solves the problem:

```
more < bigfile.txt
```

When you run this command, the first screen of text appears, and the following line shows up at the bottom of the screen:

```
— More —
```

Just press any key, and `MORE` displays the next screen. (Whatever you do, don't mix up < and > when using `MORE`. The command `more > bigfile.txt` erases `BIGFILE.TXT`!) `MORE` is an example of a *filter* command. Filters process whatever text is sent through them. The other Windows Home Server filters are SORT and FIND, which I discuss in a moment.

Another handy use for input redirection is to send keystrokes to Windows Home Server commands. For example, create a text file called enter.txt that consists of a single press of the Enter key, and then try this command:

```
date < enter.txt
```

Windows Home Server displays the current date, and instead of waiting for you to either type in a new date or press Enter, it just reads enter.txt and uses its single carriage return as input. (For an even easier way to input the Enter key to a command, check out the next section.)

One common recipient of redirected input is the SORT command. SORT, as you might guess from its name, sorts the data sent to it and displays the results onscreen. So, for example, here's how you would sort a file called JUMBLED.TXT:

```
sort < jumbled.txt
```

Instead of merely displaying the results of the sort onscreen, you can use > to redirect them to another file.

> **TIP**
>
> SORT normally starts with the first column and works across. To start with any other column, use the /+*n* switch, where *n* is the number of the column you want to use. To sort a file in reverse order (that is, a descending sort—Z to A, then 9 to 0—instead of an ascending sort—0 to 9, then A to Z), use the /R switch.

Piping Commands

Piping is a technique that combines both input and output redirection. Using the pipe operator (¦), the output of one command is captured and sent as input to another command. For example, the SYSTEMINFO command displays about five screens of data, so you usually need to scroll back to see the data you're looking for. However, you can pause the output by piping it to the MORE command:

```
systeminfo ¦ more
```

The pipe operator captures the SYSTEMINFO output and sends it as input to MORE, which then displays the SYSTEMINFO results one screen at a time.

> **NOTE**
>
> Piping works by first redirecting the output of a command to a temporary file. It then takes this temporary file and redirects it as input to the second command. A command such as SYSTEMINFO ¦ MORE is approximately equivalent to the following two commands:
>
> ```
> SYSTEMINFO > tempfile
> MORE < tempfile
> ```

I showed you in the preceding section how to use input redirection to send keystrokes to a Windows Home Server command. But if you have to send only a single key, piping offers a much nicer solution. The secret is to use the ECHO command to echo the character you need and then pipe it to the Windows Home Server command.

For example, if you use the command DEL *.*, Vista always asks whether you're sure that you want to delete all the files in the current directory. This is a sensible precaution, but you can override it if you do things this way:

```
echo y ¦ del *.*
```

Here, the y that would normally be echoed to the screen is sent to DEL instead, which interprets it as a response to its prompt. This is a handy technique for batch files in which you want to reduce or even eliminate user interaction.

> **TIP**
>
> You can even use this technique to send an Enter keypress to a command. The command ECHO. (that's ECHO followed by a period) is equivalent to pressing Enter. So, for example, you could use the following command in a batch file to display the time without user input:
>
> ```
> ECHO. ¦ TIME
> ```

Understanding Batch File Basics

As you've seen so far, the command line is still an often-useful and occasionally indispensable part of computing life, and most power users will find themselves doing at least a little work in the Command Prompt window. Part of that work might involve writing short batch file programs to automate routine chores, such as performing simple file backups and deleting unneeded files. And if you throw in any of the commands that enhance batch files, you can do many other interesting and useful things.

When you run a command in a command-line session, the command prompt executes the command or program and returns to the prompt to await further orders. If you tell the command prompt to execute a batch file, however, things are a little different. The command prompt goes into *Batch mode*, where it takes all its input from the individual lines of a batch file. These lines are just commands that (in most cases) you otherwise have to type in yourself. The command prompt repeats the following four-step procedure until it has processed each line in the batch file:

1. It reads a line from the batch file.
2. It closes the batch file.
3. It executes the command.
4. It reopens the batch file and reads the next line.

The main advantage of Batch mode is that you can lump several commands together in a single batch file and tell the command prompt to execute them all simply by typing the name of the batch file. This is great for automating routine tasks such as backing up the Registry files or deleting leftover .tmp files at startup.

Creating Batch Files

Before getting started with some concrete batch file examples, you need to know how to create them. Here are a few things to bear in mind:

▶ Batch files are simple text files, so using Notepad (or some other text editor) is probably your best choice.

▶ If you decide to use WordPad or another word processor, make sure that the file you create is a text-only file.

▶ Save your batch files using the .bat extension.

▶ When naming your batch files, don't use the same name as a command prompt command. For example, if you create a batch file that deletes some files, don't name it Del.bat. If you do, the batch file will never run! Here's why: When you enter something at the prompt, CMD first checks to see whether the command is an internal command. If it's not, CMD then checks for (in order) a .com, .exe, .bat, or .cmd file with a matching name. Because all external commands use a .com or .exe extension, CMD never bothers to check whether your batch file even exists!

After you've created the batch file, the rest is easy. Just enter any commands exactly as you would at the command line, and include whatever batch instructions you need.

TIP

If you find yourself creating and using a number of batch files, things can get confusing if you have the files scattered all over your hard disk. To remedy this, it makes sense to create a new folder to hold all your batch files. To make this strategy effective, however, you have to tell the command prompt to look in the batch file folder to find these files. To do that, you need to add the batch file folder to the PATH variable, as described earlier (see "Working with Long Filenames").

REM: Adding Comments to a Batch File

The first of the batch file-specific commands is REM (which stands for *remark*). This simple command tells the command prompt to ignore everything else on the current line. Batch file mavens use it almost exclusively to add short comments to their files:

```
REM This batch file changes to drive C
REM folder and starts CHKDSK in automatic mode.
C:
CHKDSK /F
```

Why would anyone want to do this? Well, it's probably not all that necessary with short, easy-to-understand batch files, but some of the more complex programs you'll be seeing later in this chapter can appear incomprehensible at first glance. A few pithy REM statements can help clear things up (not only for other people, but even for you if you haven't looked at the file in a couple of months).

CAUTION

It's best not to go overboard with REM statements. Having too many slows a batch file to a crawl. You really need only a few REM statements at the beginning to outline the purpose of the file and one or two to explain each of your more cryptic commands.

ECHO: Displaying Messages from a Batch File

When it's processing a batch file, Windows Home Server normally lets you know what's going on by displaying each command before executing it. That's fine, but it's often better to include more expansive descriptions, especially if other people will be using your batch files. The ECHO batch file command makes it possible for you to do just that.

For example, here's a simple batch file that deletes all the text files in the current user's Cookies and Recent folders and courteously tells the user what's about to happen:

```
ECHO This batch file will now delete all your cookie text files
DEL "%UserProfile%\Local Settings\Temporary Internet Files\cookie*"
ECHO This batch file will now delete your Recent Documents list
DEL "%UserProfile%\Recent\*.lnk"
```

The idea here is that when Windows Home Server stumbles on the ECHO command, it simply displays the rest of the line onscreen. Sounds pretty simple, right? Well, here's what the output looks like when you run the batch file:

```
C:\>ECHO This batch file will now delete all your cookie text files
This batch file will now delete all your cookie text files
C:\>DEL "%UserProfile%\Local Settings\Temporary Internet Files\cookie*""
C:\>ECHO This batch file will now delete your Recent Items list
This batch file will now delete your Recent Documents list
C:\>DEL "%UserProfile%\Recent\*.lnk"
```

What a mess! The problem is that Windows Home Server is displaying the command and ECHOing the line. Fortunately, Windows Home Server provides two solutions:

▶ To prevent Windows Home Server from displaying a command as it executes, precede the command with the @ symbol:

```
@ECHO This batch file will now delete all your cookie text files
```

▶ To prevent Windows Home Server from displaying any commands, place the following at the beginning of the batch file:

```
@ECHO OFF
```

Here's what the output looks like with the commands hidden:

```
This batch file will now delete all your cookie text files
This batch file will now delete your Recent Documents list
```

TIP

You might think that you can display a blank line simply by using ECHO by itself. That would be nice, but it doesn't work. (Windows Home Server just tells you the current state of ECHO: on or off.) Instead, use ECHO. (that's ECHO followed by a period).

PAUSE: Temporarily Halting Batch File Execution

Sometimes you want to see something that a batch file displays (such as a folder listing produced by the DIR command) before continuing. Or, you might want to alert users that something important is about to happen so that they can consider the possible ramifications (and bail out if they get cold feet). In both cases, you can use the PAUSE command to halt the execution of a batch file temporarily. When Windows Home Server comes across PAUSE in a batch file, it displays the following:

```
Press any key to continue . . .
```

To continue processing the rest of the batch file, press any key. If you don't want to continue, you can cancel processing by pressing Ctrl+C or Ctrl+Break. Windows Home Server then asks you to confirm:

```
Terminate batch job (Y/N)?
```

Either press Y to return to the prompt or N to continue the batch file.

Using Batch File Parameters

Most command-line utilities require extra information such as a filename (for example, when you use COPY or DEL) or a folder path (such as when you use CD or MD). These extra pieces of information—they're called *parameters*—give you the flexibility to specify exactly how you want a command to work. You can add the same level of flexibility to your batch files. To understand how this works, first look at the following example:

```
@ECHO OFF
ECHO.
ECHO The first parameter is %1
ECHO The second parameter is %2
ECHO The third parameter is %3
```

As you can see, this batch file doesn't do much except ECHO four lines to the screen (the first of which is just a blank line). Curiously, however, each ECHO command ends with a percent sign (%) and a number. Type and save this batch file as Parameters.bat. Then, to see what these unusual symbols mean, enter the following at the command line:

parameters A B C

This produces the following output:

```
C:\>parameters A B C


The first parameter is A
The second parameter is B
The third parameter is C
```

The following ECHO command in Parameters.bat produces the first line in the output (after the blank line):

```
ECHO The first parameter is %1
```

When Windows sees the %1 symbol in a batch file, it examines the original command, looks for the first item after the batch filename, and then replaces %1 with that item. In the example, the first item after parameters is A, so Windows uses that to replace %1. Only when it has done this does it proceed to ECHO the line to the screen.

NOTE

If your batch file command has more parameters than the batch file is looking for, it ignores the extras. For example, adding a fourth parameter to the parameters command line has no effect on the file's operation. Note, too, that you can't use more than nine replaceable parameters in a batch file (%1 through %9). However, a tenth replaceable parameter (%0) holds the name of the batch file.

TIP

If the replaceable parameter is a string that includes one or more spaces, surround the parameter with quotation marks (for example, "%1").

FOR: Looping in a Batch File

The FOR command is a batch file's way of looping through an instruction:

```
FOR %%parameter IN (set) DO command
```

%%*parameter*   This is the parameter that changes each time through the loop. You can use any single character after the two % signs (except 0 through 9). There are two % signs because Windows deletes single ones as it processes the batch file.

IN (*set*)   This is the list (it's officially called the *set*) of choices for %%*parameter*. You can use spaces, commas, or semicolons to separate the items in the set, and you must enclose them in parentheses.

DO *command*   For each item in the set, the batch file performs whatever instruction is given by *command*. The %%*parameter* is normally found somewhere in *command*.

Here's an example of the FOR command in a simple batch file that might help clear things up:

```
@ECHO OFF
FOR %%B IN (A B C) DO ECHO %%B
```

This batch file (call it Parameters.bat) produces the following output:

```
C:\BATCH>parameters2
A
B
C
```

All this does is loop through the three items in the set (A, B, and C) and substitute each one for %%B in the command ECHO %%B.

GOTO: Jumping to a Line in a Batch File

Your basic batch file lives a simple, linear existence. The first command is processed, and then the second, the third, and so on to the end of the file. It's boring, but that's all you need most of the time.

However, sometimes the batch file's usual one-command-after-the-other approach breaks down. For example, depending on a parameter or the result of a previous command, you might need to skip over a line or two. How do you do this? With the GOTO batch command:

```
...
... (the opening batch commands)
...
GOTO NEXT
...
... (the batch commands that get skipped)
...
```

```
:NEXT
...
... (the rest of the batch commands)
...
```

Here, the GOTO command is telling the batch file to look for a line that begins with a colon and the word NEXT (this is called a *label*) and to ignore any commands in between.

GOTO is useful for processing different batch commands depending on a parameter. Here's a simple example:

```
@ECHO OFF
CLS
GOTO %1
:A
ECHO This part of the batch file runs if A is the parameter.
GOTO END
:B
ECHO This part of the batch file runs if B is the parameter.
:END
```

Suppose that this file is named GOTOTest.BAT and you enter the following command:

gototest a

In the batch file, the line GOTO %1 becomes GOTO A. That makes the batch file skip down to the :A label, where it then runs the commands (in this example, just an ECHO statement) and skips to :END to avoid the rest of the batch file commands.

IF: Handling Batch File Conditions

Batch files sometimes have to make decisions before proceeding. Here are a few examples of what a batch file might have to decide:

▶ If the %2 parameter equals /Q, jump to the QuickFormat section. Otherwise, do a regular format.

▶ If the user forgets to enter a parameter, cancel the program. Otherwise, continue processing the batch file.

▶ If the file that the user wants to move already exists in the new folder, display a warning. Otherwise, proceed with the move.

▶ If the last command failed, display an error message and cancel the program. Otherwise, continue.

For these types of decisions, you need to use the IF batch command. IF has the following general form:

```
IF condition command
```

condition   This is a test that evaluates to a yes or no answer ("Did the user forget a parameter?").

command   This is what is executed if the *condition* produces a positive response ("Cancel the batch file").

For example, one of the most common uses of the IF command is to check the parameters that the user entered and proceed accordingly. From the previous section, the simple batch file that used GOTO can be rewritten with IF as follows:

```
@ECHO OFF
CLS
IF "%1"=="A" ECHO This part of the batch file runs if A is the parameter.
IF "%1"=="B" ECHO This part of the batch file runs if B is the parameter.
```

The condition part of an IF statement is a bit tricky. Let's look at the first one: "%1"=="A". Remember that the condition is always a question with a yes or no answer. In this case, the question boils down to the following:

```
Is the first parameter (%1) equal to A?
```

The double equal sign (==) looks weird, but that's just how you compare two strings of characters in a batch file. If the answer is yes, the command executes. If the answer is no, the batch file moves on to the next IF, which checks to see whether the parameter is "B".

NOTE

Strictly speaking, you don't need to include the quotation marks ("). Using %1==A accomplishes the same thing. However, I prefer to use them for two reasons: First, it makes it clearer that the IF condition is comparing strings; second, as you'll see in the next section, the quotation marks enable you to check whether the user forgot to enter a parameter at all.

CAUTION

This batch file has a serious flaw that will prevent it from working under certain conditions. Specifically, if you use the lowercase "a" or "b" as a parameter, nothing happens because, to the IF command, "a" is different from "A". The solution is to add extra IF commands to handle this situation:

```
IF "%1"=="a" ECHO This part of the batch file runs if a is the parameter
```

Proper batch file techniques require you to check to see not only what a parameter is, but also whether one exists. This can be vital because a missing parameter can cause a batch file to crash and burn. For example, here's a batch file called DontCopy.bat designed to copy all files in the current folder to a new destination (given by the second parameter) except those you specified (given by the first parameter):

```
@ECHO OFF
CLS
ATTRIB +H %1
ECHO.
ECHO Copying all files to %2 except %1:
ECHO.
XCOPY *.* %2
ATTRIB -H %1
```

What happens if the user forgets to add the destination parameter (%2)? Well, the XCOPY command becomes XCOPY *.*, which terminates the batch file with the following error:

```
File cannot be copied onto itself
```

The solution is to add an IF command that checks to see whether %2 exists:

```
@ECHO OFF
CLS
IF "%2"=="" GOTO ERROR
ATTRIB +H %1
ECHO.
ECHO Copying all files to %2 except %1:
ECHO.
XCOPY32 *.* %2
ATTRIB -H %1
GOTO END
:ERROR
ECHO You didn't enter a destination!
ECHO Please try again...
:END
```

The condition "%2"=="" is literally comparing %2 to nothing (""). If this proves to be true, the program jumps (using GOTO) to the :ERROR label, and a message is displayed to admonish the user. Notice, too, that if everything is okay (that is, the user entered a second parameter), the batch file executes normally and jumps to the :END label to avoid displaying the error message.

Another variation of IF is the IF EXIST command, which checks for the existence of a file. This is handy, for example, when you're using COPY or MOVE. First, you can check whether the file you want to copy or move exists. Second, you can check whether a file with the same name already exists in the target folder. (As you probably know, a file that has been copied over by another of the same name is downright impossible to recover.)

Here's a batch file called `SafeMove.bat`, which uses the MOVE command to move a file but first checks the file and then the target folder:

```
@ECHO OFF
CLS
IF EXIST %1 GOTO SO_FAR_SO_GOOD
ECHO The file %1 doesn't exist!
GOTO END
:SO_FAR_SO_GOOD
IF NOT EXIST %2 GOTO MOVE_IT
ECHO The file %1 exists on the target folder!
ECHO Press Ctrl+C to bail out or, to keep going,
PAUSE
:MOVE_IT
MOVE %1 %2
:END
```

To explain what's happening, I'll use a sample command:

```
safemove moveme.txt "%userprofile%\documents\moveme.txt"
```

The first IF tests for the existence of %1 (MOVEME.TXT in the example). If there is such a file, the program skips to the :SO_FAR_SO_GOOD label. Otherwise, it tells the user that the file doesn't exist and then jumps down to :END.

The second IF is slightly different. In this case, I want to continue only if MOVEME.TXT doesn't exist in the current user's My Documents folder, so I add NOT to the condition. (You can include NOT in any IF condition.) If this proves true (that is, the file given by %2 doesn't exist), the file skips to :MOVE_IT and performs the move. Otherwise, the user is warned and given an opportunity to cancel.

Working with the Command-Line Tools

The real power of the command line shines through when you combine the techniques you've learned so far with any of Windows Home Server's dozens of command-line tools. I don't have enough space to cover every tool (that would require a book in itself), so the rest of this chapter takes you through the most useful and powerful command-line tools in three categories: disk management, file management, and system management.

Working with Disk Management Tools

Windows Home Server comes with a large collection of command-line disk management tools that enable you to check disks or partitions for errors, as well as defragment, format, partition, and convert disks. Table 19.5 lists the disk management tools that you can use with Windows Home Server.

> **NOTE**
>
> In this section, I'll use the word *volume* to refer to any disk, partition, or mount point.

TABLE 19.5   Windows Home Server's Command-Line Disk Management Tools

Tool	Description
CHKDSK	Checks a specified volume for errors.
CHKNTFS	Configures automatic disk checking.
CONVERT	Converts a specified volume to a different file system.
DEFRAG	Defragments a specified volume.
DISKCOMP	Compares the contents of two floppy disks. (This tool does not compare hard disks or other types of removable media, such as memory cards.)
DISKCOPY	Copies the contents of one floppy disk to another. (This tool does not copy hard disks or other types of removable media, such as memory cards.)
DISKPART	Enables you to list, create, select, delete, and extend disk partitions.
EXPAND	Extracts one or more files from a compressed file such as a .cab file found on some installation discs.
FORMAT	Formats the specified volume.
FREEDISK	Checks a local or remote drive to see if it has a specified amount of free space available. This command is most often used before installing a program or copying data to a drive.
FSUTIL	Performs a number of file system tasks.
LABEL	Changes or deletes the name of a specified volume.
MOUNTVOL	Creates, displays, or deletes a mount point.
VOL	Displays the name and serial number of a specified volume.

The next four sections give you more detailed coverage of the CHKDKS, CHKNTFS, DEFRAG, and FSUTIL tools.

CHKDSK: Checking for Hard Disk Errors

In Chapter 15, "Maintaining Windows Home Server," you learned how to use the Check Disk utility to check a hard disk for errors. Check Disk also comes with a command-line version called CHKDSK that you can run in a Command Prompt window.

▶ **SEE** For information on Check Disk and the types of errors it looks for, **see** "Checking Your Hard Disk for Errors," **P. 431**.

Here's the syntax for CHKDSK:

```
CHKDSK [volume [filename]] [/F] [/V] [/R] [/X] [/I] [/C] [/L:[size]]
```

`volume`	The drive letter (followed by a colon) or mount point.
`filename`	On FAT16 and FAT32 disks, the name of the file to check. Include the path if the file isn't in the current folder.
`/F`	Tells CHKDSK to automatically fix errors. This is the same as running the Check Disk GUI with the Automatically Fix File System Errors option activated.
`/V`	Runs CHKDSK in verbose mode. On FAT16 and FAT32 drives, CHKDSK displays the path and name of every file on the disk; on NTFS drives, CHKDSK displays cleanup messages, if any.
`/R`	Tells CHKDSK to scan the disk surface for bad sectors and recover data from the bad sectors, if possible. (The /F switch is implied.) This is the same as running the Check Disk GUI with the Scan for and Attempt Recovery of Bad Sectors option activated.
`/X`	On NTFS nonsystem disks that have open files, forces the volume to dismount, invalidates the open file handles, and then runs the scan. (The /F switch is implied.)
`/I`	On NTFS disks, tells CHKDSK to check only the file system's index entries.
`/C`	On NTFS disks, tells CHKDSK to skip the checking of cycles within the folder structure. This is a rare error, so using /C to skip the cycle check can speed up the disk check.
`/L:[size]`	On NTFS disks, tells CHKDSK to set the size of its log file to the specified number of kilobytes. The default size is 65,536, which is big enough for most systems, so you should never need to change the size. Note that if you include this switch without the size parameter, Check Disk tells you the current size of the log file.

For example, to run a read-only check—that is, a check that doesn't repair errors—on drive C:, you enter the following command:

```
chkdsk c:
```

Note that when you use the /F switch to fix errors, CHKDSK must lock the volume to prevent running processes from using the volume during the check. If you use the /F switch on drive C:, which is the Windows Home Server system drive, CHKDSK can't lock the drive, and you see the following message:

```
Cannot lock current drive.
```

```
Chkdsk cannot run because the volume is in use by another
process. Would you like to schedule this volume to be
checked the next time the system restarts? (Y/N)
```

If you press Y and Enter, CHKDSK schedules a check for drive C: to run the next time you reboot Windows Home Server.

In Chapter 15, you learned that you can use the Check Disk program to check for errors on any volume that has a drive letter, such as the C: and D: drives in Windows Home Server. Unfortunately, Check Disk doesn't work with mount points, so you can't use it to check for errors on your Windows Home Server secondary partitions, which are set up as mount points in the C:\fs folder. Fortunately, you can check these mount points for errors using CHKDSK. You do that by specifying the mount point folder as the volume parameter. For example, if a secondary drive is mounted in the C:\fs\E folder, the following command checks the drive for errors:

```
chkdsk c:\fs\E
```

How do you know where a secondary drive is mounted? You can use the Computer Management snap-in, as described in the following steps:

1. Select Start, right-click My Computer, and then click Manage. The Computer Management snap-in appears.

2. Select Storage, Disk Management.

3. Select View, Drive Paths to display the Drive Paths dialog box, which shows the complete listing of the mounted drives and their paths. (Alternatively, you can right-click a secondary drive and then click Change Drive Letter and Paths.)

NOTE

In the Disk Management section, your main hard drive—the drive that Windows Home Server uses for the system partition and the primary data partition—is listed as Disk 0. Your secondary hard drives are listed as Disk 1, Disk 2, and so on. (If your Windows Home Server computer includes one or more drives for memory cards, these also appear as Disk n, where n is a number greater than or equal to the number of hard drives in your system. These drives include the word Removable in their description.)

4. In the dialog box that appears, the list box shows the mount point. For example, in Figure 19.2, the mount point for this drive is C:\fs\E. Make a note of the location and click OK.

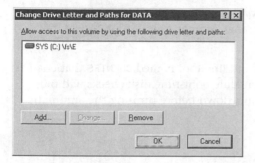

FIGURE 19.2 Your Windows Home Server computer's secondary drives are mounted to a folder in C:\fs.

Windows Home Server is constantly moving files around and balancing storage on the data partitions, which means that these partitions almost always have open file handles. Therefore, if you use the /F switch with a secondary partition mount point (or with drive D:, the primary data partition), CHKDSK will rarely be able to lock the volume. In that case, it displays the following message:

```
Chkdsk cannot run because the volume is in use by another
process. Chkdsk may run if this volume is dismounted first.
Would you like to force a dismount on this volume? (Y/N)
```

Press Y and Enter to dismount the volume and continue with the check. When the check is complete, CHKDSK remounts the volume.

If, instead, you press N and Enter, CHKDSK asks if you want to schedule the mount point to be checked the next time the system boots (as described earlier in this section).

To bypass the dismount prompt and have CHKDSK dismount the volume automatically, run CHKDSK with the /X switch, as in this example:

```
chkdsk c:\fs\E /x
```

CHKNTFS: Scheduling Automatic Disk Checks

You saw in the previous section that CHKDSK prompts you to schedule an automatic disk check during the next reboot in two circumstances:

▶ You run CHKDSK /F on the system drive (drive C: in Windows Home Server).

▶ You run CHKDSK /F on any data partition in Windows Home Server (drive D: or the secondary drive mount points) and elect not to dismount the volume.

If you press Y and Enter at these prompts, CHKDSK adds the AUTOCHK utility to the following Registry setting:

```
HKLM\SYSTEM\CurrentControlSet\Control\Session Manager\BootExecute
```

This setting specifies the programs that Windows Home Server should run at boot time when the Session Manager is loading. AUTOCHK is the automatic version of CHKDSK that runs at system startup.

Windows Home Server also comes with a command-line tool named CHKNTFS that enables you to cancel pending automatic disk checks, schedule boot-time disk checks without using CHKDSK, and set the time that AUTOCHK counts down before running the automatic disk checks.

Here's the syntax for CHKNTFS:

```
CHKNTFS [volume ][/C volume:] [/X volume:] [/D] [/T:[time]]
```

volume	A drive letter (followed by a colon) or mount point.
/C *volume*	Tells CHKNTFS to schedule an automatic startup disk check for the specified volume. You can specify multiple volumes (separated by spaces).
/X *volume*	Tells CHKNTFS to exclude the specified volume from an automatic startup disk check. You can specify multiple volumes (separated by spaces).
/D	Tells CHKNTFS to exclude all volumes from an automatic startup disk check.
/T:[*time*]	Specifies the time that AUTOCHK counts down before starting the automatic disk checks.

When you run CHKNTFS with just a volume name, you see one of the following:

▶ If the volume is not scheduled for a startup disk check, you see the volume's file system:

```
The type of the file system is NTFS.
```

▶ If the volume is scheduled for a startup disk check, you see the following message:

```
Chkdsk has been scheduled manually to run on next reboot.
```

▶ If Windows Home Server's Storage Manager has detected an error on the volume, it marks the volume as *dirty*, so in this case, you see the following message (using drive C: as an example):

```
C: is dirty. You may use the /C option to schedule chkdsk for this drive.
```

This last message is confusing because Windows Home Server *always* performs an automatic startup disk check of any volume that's marked as dirty. What you can do with

CHKNTFS is bypass the automatic startup disk check of any volume that is marked as dirty. To do that, run CHKNTFS with the /X switch, as in this example:

```
chkntfs /x c:
```

NOTE

To manually mark a volume as dirty, use the FSUTIL DIRTY SET *volume* command, where *volume* is the drive you want to work with. (This command doesn't work with mount points.) For example, the following command marks drive C: as dirty:

```
fsutil dirty set c:
```

If you're not sure whether a drive is dirty, either run CHKNTFS *volume* or run FSUTIL DIRTY QUERY *volume*, as in this example:

```
fsutil dirty query c:
```

Note, however, that FSUTIL doesn't give you any way to unmark a drive as dirty.

If a volume isn't already marked as dirty, you can force CHKDSK to check a volume at startup by running CHKNTFS with the /C switch. For example, the following command sets up an automatic start check for drive D:

```
chkntfs /c d:
```

Note that the /C switch is cumulative, meaning that if you run it multiple times and specify a different volume each time, CHKNTFS adds each new volume to the list of volumes to check at startup. Instead of running multiple commands, however, you can specify multiple volumes in a single command, like so:

```
chkntfs /c c: d: c:\fs\E
```

If you know that a volume has been scheduled for a startup check, but you want to cancel that check, run CHKNTFS with the /X switch, as in this example:

```
chkntfs /x d:
```

You can also specify multiple volumes, if needed:

```
chkntfs /x c: d:
```

If you know that multiple volumes are scheduled for automatic startup checks, you can cancel all the checks by running CHKNTFS with the /D switch:

```
chkntfs /d
```

If you've scheduled a startup check for one or more volumes, or if a volume is marked as dirty, the next time you reboot Windows Home Server, you see a message similar to the following (which uses drive C: as an example):

```
Checking file system on C:
The type of the file system is NTFS.
Volume label is SYS.

One of your disks needs to be checked for consistency. You
may cancel the disk check, but it is strongly recommended
that you continue.
To skip disk checking, press any key within 10 second(s).
```

The number of seconds in the last line counts down to 0. If you press a key before the countdown ends, Windows Home Server skips the disk check; otherwise, it continues with CHKDSK.

CAUTION

Pressing any key to skip the disk check usually only works with wired keyboards. On most wireless keyboards, pressing a key has no effect.

You can change the initial countdown value by running CHKNTFS with the /T switch, followed by the number of seconds you want to use for the countdown. For example, the following command sets the countdown to 30 seconds:

```
chkntfs /t:30
```

Note that if you run the command CHKNTFS /T (that is, you don't specify a countdown value), CHKNTFS returns the current countdown value.

DEFRAG: Defragmenting the System Drive

In Chapter 15, you learned how to defragment a volume using Windows Home Server's Disk Defragmenter program. If you want to schedule a defragment or perform this chore from a batch file, you have to use the DEFRAG command-line tool. Here's the syntax:

```
DEFRAG volume [-a] [-f] [-v]
```

volume	Specifies the drive letter (followed by a colon) of the disk or the folder path of the mount point that you want to defragment.
-a	Tells DEFRAG only to analyze the disk.
-f	Forces DEFRAG to defragment the disk, even if it doesn't need defragmenting or if the disk has less than 15% free space. (DEFRAG normally requires at least that much free space because it needs an area in which to sort the files.)
-v	Runs DEFRAG in verbose mode, which displays both the analysis report and the defragmentation report.

CAUTION

The DEFRAG switches are case sensitive. So, for example, the following command will work properly:

```
defrag c: -a
```

However, this command will not:

```
defrag c: -A
```

For example, to get an analysis report of the fragmentation of drive C:, enter the following command:

```
defrag c: -a
```

If the volume isn't too fragmented, you see a report similar to this:

```
Windows Disk Defragmenter
Copyright (c) 2003 Microsoft Corp. and Executive Software International, Inc.

Analysis Report
    20.00 GB Total, 6.23 GB (31%) Free, 4% Fragmented (9% file fragmentation)
```

```
You do not need to defragment this volume.
```

However, if the drive is quite fragmented, you see a report similar to the following:

```
Windows Disk Defragmenter
Copyright (c) 2003 Microsoft Corp. and Executive Software International, Inc.

Analysis Report
    190 GB Total, 17.84 GB (9%) Free, 32% Fragmented (65% file fragmentation)
```

```
You should defragment this volume.
```

In the latter example, notice that the volume only has 9 percent free disk space. If you try to defragment this volume, DEFRAG displays the following message:

```
Volume DATA has only 9% free space available for use by Disk Defragmenter.
To run effectively, Disk Defragmenter requires at least 15% usable free space.
There is not enough disk space to properly complete the operation.
Delete some unneeded files on your hard disk, and then try again.
```

If you can't delete files from the volume (for example, if this is a Windows Home Server data partition), you can try running DEFRAG with the -f switch to force the operation:

```
defrag d: -f
```

> **NOTE**
>
> Forcing the defrag operation shouldn't cause problems in most cases. With less free space in which to work, DEFRAG just takes quite a bit longer to defragment the volume, and there may be parts of the volume that it simply can't defragment.

Working with File and Folder Management Tools

Windows Explorer is the GUI tool of choice for most file and folder operations. However, Windows Home Server comes with an impressive collection of command-line file and folder tools that let you perform all the standard operations such as renaming, copying, moving, and deleting, as well as more interesting chores such as changing file attributes and comparing the contents of two files. Table 19.6 lists the file management tools that you can use with Windows Home Server.

TABLE 19.6   Windows Home Server's Command-Line File and Folder Management Tools

Tool	Description
ATTRIB	Displays, applies, or removes attributes for the specified file or folder.
CD or CHDIR	Changes to the specified folder.
COMP	Compares the contents of two specified files byte by byte.
COMPACT	Displays or modifies the compression settings for the specified file or folder (which must be located on an NTFS partition).
COPY	Creates a copy of the specified file or folder in another location.
DEL	Deletes the specified file or folder.
DIR	Displays a directory listing for the current folder or for the specified file or folder.
FC	Compares the content of two specified files.
FIND	Searches for and displays all the instances of a specified string in a file.
FINDSTR	Uses a regular expression to search for and display all the instances of a specified string in a file.
FTYPE	Displays or modifies file types.
INUSE	Specifies a file that you want to use to replace an existing system file. Windows Home Server performs the replacement the next time you restart the computer.
MD or MKDIR	Creates the specified folder.
MOVE	Moves the specified file or folder to another location.

TABLE 19.6   Windows Home Server's Command-Line File and Folder Management Tools

Tool	Description
REN	Changes the name of the specified file or folder.
REPLACE	Replaces files in the destination folder with files in the source folder that have the same name.
RD or RMDIR	Deletes the specified folder.
SORT	Sorts the specified file and then displays the results.
SFC	Runs the System File Checker, which scans and verifies the protected Windows Home Server files.
TAKEOWN	Enables an administrator to take ownership of the specified file.
TREE	Displays a graphical tree diagram showing the subfolder hierarchy of the current folder or the specified folder.
WHERE	Searches for and displays all the files that match a specified pattern in the current folder and in the PATH folders.
XCOPY	Creates a copy of the specified file or folder in another location. This tool offers many more options than the COPY command.

The next few sections take a closer look at a half dozen of these tools: ATTRIB, FIND, REN, REPLACE, SORT, and XCOPY.

Before getting to the tools, I should mention that most of the file and folder management tools work with the standard wildcard characters: ? and *. In a file or folder specification, you use ? to substitute for a single character, and you use * to substitute for multiple characters. Here are some examples:

File Specification	Matches
Budget201?.xlsx	Budget2010.xlsx, Budget2011.xlsx, and so on
Memo.doc?	Memo.doc, Memo.docx, Memo.docm, and so on
*.txt	ReadMe.txt, log.txt, to-do.txt, and so on
*201?.pptx	Report2010.pptx, Budget2011.pptx, Conference2012.pptx, and so on
.	Every file

ATTRIB: Modifying File and Folder Attributes

A file's *attributes* are special codes that indicate the status of the file. There are four attributes you can work with:

Archive   When this attribute is turned on, it means the file has been modified since it was last backed up.

Hidden   When this attribute is turned on, it means the file doesn't show up in a DIR listing and isn't included when you run most command-line tools. For example, if you run DEL *.* in a folder, Windows Home Server deletes all the files in that folder, except the hidden files.

Read-   When this attribute is turned on, it means the file can't be modified or erased.
only

System   When this attribute is turned on, it means the file is an operating system file (that is, a file that was installed with Windows Home Server).

The ATTRIB command lets you turn these attributes on or off. Here's the syntax:

ATTRIB [+A ¦ -A] [+H ¦ -H] [+R ¦ -R] [+S ¦ -S] *filename* [/S [/D]]

+A   Sets the archive attribute.

-A   Clears the archive attribute.

+H   Sets the hidden attribute.

-H   Clears the hidden attribute.

+R   Sets the read-only attribute.

-R   Clears the read-only attribute.

+S   Sets the system attribute.

-S   Clears the system attribute.

filename The file or files you want to work with.

/S   Applies the attribute change to the matching files in the current folder and all of its subfolders.

/D   Applies the attribute change only to the current folder's subfolders. You must use this switch in conjunction with /S.

For example, if you'd like to hide all the DOC files in the current directory, use the following command:

```
attrib +h *.doc
```

As another example, if you've ever tried to delete or edit a file and got the message Access denied, the file is likely read-only. You can turn off the read-only attribute by running ATTRIB with the -R switch, as in this example:

```
attrib -r readonly.txt
```

> **NOTE**
>
> If you want to check out a file's attributes, use the DIR command's /A switch. Use /AA to see files with their archive attribute set, /AH for hidden files, /AR for read-only, and /AS for system files.

You can also use ATTRIB for protecting important or sensitive files. When you hide a file, it doesn't show up in a listing produced by the DIR command. Out of sight is out of mind, so someone taking a casual glance at your files won't see the hidden ones and, therefore, won't be tempted to display or erase them.

Although a hidden file is invisible, it's not totally safe. Someone who knows the name of the file can attempt to modify the file by opening it with the appropriate program. As an added measure of safety, you can also set the file's read-only attribute. When you do this, the file can't be modified. You can set both attributes with a single command:

```
attrib +h +r payroll.xlsx
```

FIND: Locating a Text String in a File

You use the FIND command to search for a string inside a file. Here's the syntax:

```
FIND [/C] [/I] [/N] [/V] [/OFF[LINE]] "string" filename
```

/C	Displays the number of times that *string* appears in *filename*.
/I	Performs a case-insensitive search.
/N	Displays each match of *string* in *filename* with the line number in *filename* where each match occurs.
/V	Displays the lines in *filename* that don't contain *string*.
/OFF[LINE]	Searches *filename* even if the file's offline attribute is set.
string	The string you want to search for.
filename	The file you want to search in. (Note that you can't use wildcards with the FIND command.) If the filename contains one or more spaces, surround it with double quotation marks.

> **NOTE**
>
> The FIND command doesn't work with the new Office 2007 file formats. However, it works fine with most documents created in earlier versions of Office.

For example, to find the string *DVD* in a file named WishList.txt, you use the following command:

```
find "DVD" WishList.txt
```

If the string you want to find contains double quotation marks, you need to place two quotation marks in the search string. For example, to find the phrase *Dave "The Hammer" Schultz* in the file players.doc, use the following command:

```
find "Dave ""The Hammer"" Schultz" players.doc
```

> **TIP**
>
> The FIND command doesn't accept wildcard characters in the *filename* parameter. That's too bad, because it's often useful to search multiple files for a string. Fortunately, you can work around this limitation by using a FOR loop where the command you run on each file is FIND. Here's the general syntax to use:
>
> ```
>     FOR %f IN (filespec) DO FIND "string" %f
> ```
>
> Replace *filespec* with the file specification you want to use, and *string* with the string you want to search for. For example, the following command runs through all the .doc files in the current folder and searches each file for the string Thanksgiving:
>
> ```
>     FOR %f IN (*.doc) DO FIND "Thanksgiving" %f
> ```
>
> If the file specification will match files with spaces in their names, you need to surround the last %f parameter with quotation marks, like so:
>
> ```
>     FOR %f IN (*.doc) DO FIND "Thanksgiving" "%f"
> ```

One of the most common uses of the FIND command is as a filter in pipe operations (see "Piping Commands," earlier in this chapter). In this case, instead of a filename, you pipe the output of another command through FIND. In this case, FIND searches this input for a specified string and, if it finds a match, it displays the line that contains the string.

For example, the last line of a DIR listing tells you the number of bytes free on the current drive. Rather than wade through the entire DIR output just to get this information, use this command instead:

```
dir | find "free"
```

You'll see something like the following:

```
2 Dir(s) 28,903,331,184 bytes free
```

FIND scours the DIR listing piped to it and looks for the word *free*. You can use this technique to display specific lines from, say, a CHKDSK report. For example, searching for bad finds the number of bad sectors on the disk.

REN: Renaming a File or Folder

You use the REN (or RENAME) command to change the name of one or more files and folders. Here's the syntax:

```
REN old_filename1 new_filename
```

old_filename   The original filename

new_filename   The new filename

For example, the following command renamed Budget 2010.xlsx to Budget 2011.xlsx:

```
ren "Budget 2010.xlsx" "Budget 2011.xlsx"
```

A simple file or folder rename such as this probably isn't something you'll ever fire up a command-line session to do because renaming a single object is faster and easier in Windows Explorer. However, the real power of the REN command is that it accepts wildcards in the file specifications. This enables you to rename several files at once, something you can't do in Windows Explorer.

For example, suppose you have a folder full of files, many of which contain 2010 somewhere in the filename. To rename all those files by changing 2010 to 2011, you'd use the following command:

```
ren *2010* *2011*
```

Similarly, if you have a folder full of files that use the .htm extension and you want to change each extension to .asp, you'd use the following command:

```
ren *.htm *.asp
```

Note that for these multiple-file renames to work, in most cases the original filename text and the new filename text must be the same length. For example, digital cameras often supply photos with names such as img_1234.jpg and img_5678.jpg. If you have a number of related photos in a folder, you might want to give them more meaningful names. If the photos are from a vacation in Rome, you might prefer names such as Rome_Vacation1234.jpg and Rome_Vacation5678.jpg. Unfortunately, the REN command can't handle this. However, it can rename the files to Rome1234.jpg and Rome5678.jpg:

```
ren img_* Rome*
```

The exception to the same length rule is if the replacement occurs at the end of the file-names. For example, the following command renames all files with the `.jpeg` extension to `.jpg`:

```
ren *.jpeg *.jpg
```

REPLACE: Smarter File Copying

If there was such a thing as a Most Underrated Command award, `REPLACE` would win it hands down. This command, which you almost never hear about, can do three *very* useful (and very different) things:

- ▶ It copies files, but only if their names match those in the target directory.

- ▶ It copies files, but only if their names don't exist in the target directory.

- ▶ It copies files, but only if their names match those in the target directory and the matching files in the target directory are older than the files being copied.

Here's the syntax:

```
REPLACE source_files target /A /U /P /R /S /W
```

source_files	The path and file specification of the files you want to copy.
target	The folder to which you want to copy the files.
/A	Copies only new files to the *target* folder. You can't use this switch in conjunction with /S or /U.
/U	Copies files that have the same name in the *target* folder and that are newer than the matching files in the target folder. You can't use this switch in conjunction with /A.
/P	Prompts you for confirmation before replacing files.
/R	Replaces read-only files.
/S	Replaces files in the *target* folder's subfolders. You can't use this switch in conjunction with /A.
/W	Waits for you to insert a disk before starting.

If you don't specify switches, `REPLACE` copies a file from the source folder to the target folder if and only if it finds a file with a matching name in the target.

More useful is the `REPLACE` command's updating mode, where it copies a file from the source folder to the target folder if and only if it finds a file with a matching name in the target and that target file is older than the source file. A good example where updating comes in handy is when you copy some files to a disk or memory card so you can use them on another machine (such as taking files from your computer at work to use them at home). When you need to copy the files back to the first machine, the following `REPLACE` command does the job (this assumes the disk or memory card is in drive G:):

```
replace g:*.* %UserProfile% /s /u
```

For each file on drive G:, REPLACE looks for matching filenames anywhere in the %UserProfile% folder and its subfolders (thanks to the /S switch) and replaces only the ones that are newer (the /U switch).

What if you created some new files on the other computer? To copy those to the first machine, use the /A switch, like so:

```
replace g:*.* %UserProfile%\Documents /a
```

In this case, REPLACE only copies a file from G if it doesn't exist in the %UserProfile%\Documents folder. (You have to specify a target folder because you can't use the /S switch with /A.)

SORT: Sorting the Contents of a File

When you obtain a file from the Internet or some other source, the data in the file may not appear in the order you want. What I usually do in such cases is import the file into Word or Excel and then use the program's Sort feature. This sometimes involves extra steps (such as converting text to a table in Word), so it's not always an efficient way to work.

If the file is text, it's often easier and faster to run the SORT command-line tool. By default, SORT takes the content of the file, sorts it in ascending alphanumeric order (0 to 9, then a to z, and then A to Z) starting at the beginning of each line in the file, and then displays the sorted results. You can also run descending order sorts, write the results to the same file or another file, and more. Here's the syntax:

```
SORT [input_file] [/+n] [/R] [/L locale] [/M kilobytes] [/REC characters] [/T
temp_folder] [/O output_file]
```

input_file	The file you want to sort.
/+n	Specifies the starting character position (n) of the sort. The default is 1 (that is, the first character on each line in the file).
/R	Sorts the file in descending order (Z to A, then z to a, and then 9 to 0).
/L locale	Specifies a locale for sorting other than the default system locale. Your only choice here is to use "C" to sort the file using the binary values for each character.
/M kilobytes	Specifies the amount of memory, in kilobytes, that SORT uses during the operation. If you don't specify this value, SORT uses a minimum of 160KB and a maximum of 90 percent of available memory.
/REC characters	Specifies the maximum length, in characters, of each line in the file. The default value is 4,096 characters, and the maximum value is 65,535 characters.
/T temp_folder	Specifies the folder that SORT should use to hold the temporary files it uses during the sort.
/O output_file	Specifies the file that SORT should create to store the results of the sort. You can specify a different file or the input file.

For example, the following SORT command sorts the data in records.txt and stores the results in sorted_records.txt:

sort records.txt sorted_records.txt

XCOPY: Advanced File Copying

The XCOPY command is one of the most powerful of the file management command-line tools, and you can use it for some fairly sophisticated file copying operations.

Here's the syntax for XCOPY:

```
XCOPY source destination [/A ¦ /M] [/C] [/D[:mm-dd—yyyy]]
[/EXCLUDE:file1[+file2[+file3]]] [/F] [/G] [/H] [/I] [/K] [/L] [/N]
[/O] [/P] [/Q] [/R] [/S [/E]] [/T] [/U] [/V] [/W] [/X] [/Y ¦ -Y] [/Z]
```

source	The path and names of the files you want to copy.
destination	The location where you want the source files copied.
[/A]	Tells XCOPY to only copy those source files that have their archive attribute turned on. The archive attribute is not changed. If you use /A, you can't also use /M.
[/M]	Tells XCOPY to only copy those source files that have their archive attribute turned on. The archive attribute is turned off. If you use /M, you can't also use /A.
[/C]	Tells XCOPY to ignore any errors that occur during the copy operation. Otherwise, XCOPY aborts the operation if an error occurs.
[/D[:*mm-dd-yyyy*]]	Copies only those source files that changed on or after the date specified by *mm-dd-yyyy*. If you don't specify a date, using /D tells XCOPY to copy those source files that are newer than destination files that have the same name.
[/EXCLUDE:*file1* [+*file2* [+*file3*]]]	Tells XCOPY to not copy the files or file specification given by *file1*, *file2*, *file3*, and so on.
[/F]	Displays the source and destination filename during the copy operation.
[/G]	Creates decrypted copies of encrypted source files.
[/H]	Tells XCOPY to include in the copy operation any hidden and system files in the *source* folder.
[/I]	Tells XCOPY to create the destination folder. For this to work, the *source* value must be a folder or a file specification with wildcards.

[/K]	For each *source* file that has its read-only attribute set, tells XCOPY to maintain the read-only attribute on the corresponding *destination* file.
[/L]	Displays a list of the files that XCOPY will copy. (No files are copied if you use /L.)
[/N]	Tells XCOPY to use 8.3 filenames in the *destination* folder. Use this switch if the *destination* folder is a FAT partition that doesn't support long filenames.
[/O]	Tells XCOPY to also copy ownership and discretionary access control list data to the *destination*.
[/P]	Prompts you to confirm each file copy.
[/Q]	Tells XCOPY not to display messages during the copy.
[/R]	Includes read-only files in the copy.
[/S]	Tells XCOPY to also include the *source* folder's subfolders in the copy.
[/E]	Tells XCOPY to include empty subfolders in the copy if you specify the /S or /T switch.
[/T]	Tells XCOPY to copy the *source* folder subfolder structure. (No files are copied, just the subfolders.)
[/U]	Only copies those *source* files that exist in the *destination* folder.
[/V]	Tells XCOPY to verify that each *destination* copy is identical to the original *source* file.
[/W]	Displays the message `Press any key to begin copying file(s)` before copying. You must press a key to launch the copy (or press Ctrl+C to cancel).
[/X]	Tells XCOPY to also copy file audit settings and system access control list data to the *destination*. (This switch implies /O.)
[/Y]	Tells XCOPY not to ask you whether you want to overwrite existing files in the *destination*.
[/-Y]	Tells XCOPY to ask you whether you want to overwrite existing files in the *destination*. Use this switch if you've set the %COPYCMD% environment variable to /Y, which suppresses overwrite prompts for XCOPY, COPY, and MOVE.
[/Z]	If you're copying to a network *destination*, this switch tells XCOPY to restart to the copy if the network connection goes down during the operation.

In its basic form, XCOPY works just like COPY. So, for example, to copy all the .doc files in the current folder to a folder called Documents in drive G:, use the following command:

```
xcopy *.doc g:\documents
```

Besides being faster, XCOPY also contains a number of features not found in the puny COPY command. Think of it as COPY on steroids. (The X in XCOPY means that it's an extended COPY command.) For example, suppose you want to copy all the .doc files in the current folder and all the .doc files in any attached subfolders to G:\Documents. With COPY, you first have to create the appropriate folders on the destination partition and then perform separate COPY commands for each folder, which is not very efficient, to say the least. With XCOPY, all you do is add a single switch:

```
xcopy *.doc g:\documents /s
xcopy *.bat d:\batch /s
```

The /S switch tells XCOPY to copy the current folder and all non-empty subfolders, and to create the appropriate folders in the destination, as needed. (If you want XCOPY to copy empty subfolders, include the /E switch, as well.)

Another useful feature of XCOPY is the ability to copy files by date. This is handy for performing incremental backups of files that you modified on or after a specific date. For example, suppose you keep your word processing documents in %UserProfile%\Documents and you want to make backup copies in your Windows Home Server user share of all the .doc files that have changed since August 23, 2010. You can do this with the following command:

```
xcopy %userprofile%\documents\*.doc \\server\users\%Username%\ /d:08-23-2010
```

It's common to use XCOPY in batch files, but take care to handle errors. For example, what if a batch file tries to use XCOPY, but there's not enough memory? Or what if the user presses Ctrl+C during the copy? It might seem impossible to check for these kinds of errors; yet it is not only possible, it's really quite easy.

When certain commands finish, they always file a report on the progress of the operation. This report, or *exit code*, is a number that specifies how the operation went. For example, Table 19.7 lists the exit codes that the XCOPY command uses.

TABLE 19.7   XCOPY Exit Codes

Exit Code	What It Means
0	Everything's okay; the files were copied.
1	Nothing happened because no files were found to copy.
2	The user pressed Ctrl+C to abort the copy.
4	The command failed because there wasn't enough memory or disk space or because there was something wrong with the command's syntax.
5	The command failed because of a disk error.

What does all this mean for your batch files? You can use a variation of the IF command—IF ERRORLEVEL—to test for these exit codes. For example, here's a batch file called CheckCopy.bat, which uses some of the XCOPY exit codes to check for errors:

```
@ECHO OFF
XCOPY %1 %2
IF ERRORLEVEL 4 GOTO ERROR
IF ERRORLEVEL 2 GOTO CTRL+C
IF ERRORLEVEL 1 GOTO NO_FILES
GOTO DONE
:ERROR
ECHO Bad news! The copy failed because there wasn't
ECHO enough memory or disk space or because there was
ECHO something wrong with your file specs . . .
GOTO DONE
:CTRL+C
ECHO Hey, what gives? You pressed Ctrl+C to abort . . .
GOTO DONE
:NO_FILES
ECHO Bad news! No files were found to copy . . .
:DONE
```

As you can see, the ERRORLEVEL conditions check for the individual exit codes and then use GOTO to jump to the appropriate label.

> **NOTE**
>
> How does a batch file know what a command's exit code was? When Windows Home Server gets an exit code from a command, it stores it in a special data area set aside for exit code information. When Windows Home Server sees the IF ERRORLEVEL command in a batch file, it retrieves the exit code from the data area so that it can be compared to whatever is in the IF condition.

One of the most important things to know about the IF ERRORLEVEL test is how Windows Home Server interprets it. For example, consider the following IF command:

```
IF ERRORLEVEL 2 GOTO CTRL+C
```

Windows Home Server interprets this command as "If the exit code from the last command is equal to or greater than 2, jump to the CTRL+C label." This has two important consequences for your batch files:

▶ The test IF ERRORLEVEL 0 doesn't tell you much because it's always true. If you simply want to find out whether the command failed, use the test IF NOT ERRORLEVEL 0.

▶ To get the correct results, always test the *highest* ERRORLEVEL first and then work your way down.

Working with System Management Tools

System Management is one of those catch-all terms that encompasses a wide range of tasks, from simple adjustments such as changing the system date and time to more complex tweaks such as modifying the Registry. Windows Home Server's command-line system management tools also enable you to monitor system performance, shut down or restart the computer, and even modify the huge Windows Management Instrumentation (WMI) interface. Table 19.8 lists the system management command-line tools that apply to Windows Home Server.

TABLE 19.8   Windows Home Server's Command-Line System Management Tools

Tool	Description
BOOTCFG	Displays or modifies the Boot.ini startup file.
CHCP	Displays or changes the number of active console code pages.
DATE	Displays or sets the system date.
EVENTCREATE	Creates a custom event in an event log.
EVENTQUERY.VBS	Queries the events and event properties from an event log. This is a VBScript file.
EVENTTRIGGERS	Creates or displays event triggers, which are programs that run in response to the occurrence of a particular event.
GETTYPE	Returns information about the current operating system, including the name of the OS, the version number, the build number, and the role of the computer (domain controller, member server, or workgroup client).
PAGEFILECONFIG.VBS	Configures the system's paging file. This is a VBScript file.
REG	Adds, modifies, displays, and deletes Registry keys and settings.
REGSVR32	Registers dynamic link library (DLL) files as command components in the Registry.
SHUTDOWN	Shuts down or restarts Windows Home Server or a remote computer.
SYSTEMINFO	Displays a wide range of detailed configuration information about the computer.
TIME	Displays or sets the system time.
TYPEPERF	Monitors a performance counter.
WHOAMI	Displays information about the current user, including the domain name (not applicable to Windows Home Server), computer name, username, security group membership, and security privileges.
WMIC	Operates the Windows Management Instrumentation command-line tool that provides command-line access to the WMI interface.

The next few sections take more detailed looks at five of these command-line tools: REG, SHUTDOWN, SYSTEMINFO, TYPEPERF, and WHOAMI.

REG: Working with Registry Keys and Settings

In Chapter 18, "Working with the Windows Home Server Registry," you learned how to view, add, and modify Registry keys and settings using the Registry Editor. That's the easiest and safest way to make Registry changes. However, there may be some settings that you change quite often. In such cases, it can become burdensome to be frequently launching the Registry Editor and changing the settings. A better idea is to create a shortcut or batch file that uses the REG command-line tool to make your Registry changes for you.

REG actually consists of 11 subcommands, each of which enables you to perform different Registry tasks:

REG ADD   Adds new keys or settings to the Registry. You can also use this command to modify existing settings.

REG QUERY   Displays the current values of one or more settings in one or more keys.

REG COMPARE   Compares the values of two Registry keys or settings.

REG COPY   Copies Registry keys or settings to another part of the Registry.

REG DELETE   Deletes a key or setting.

REG EXPORT   Exports a key to a .reg file.

REG IMPORT   Imports the contents of a .reg file.

REG SAVE   Copies Registry keys or settings to a hive (.hiv) file.

REG RESTORE   Writes a hive file into an existing Registry key. The hive file must be created using REG SAVE.

REG LOAD   Loads a hive file into a new Registry key. The hive file must be created using REG SAVE.

REG UNLOAD   Unloads a hive file that was loaded using REG LOAD.

I won't go through all of these commands. Instead, I'll focus on the three most common Registry tasks: viewing, adding, and modifying Registry data.

To view the current value of the Registry setting, you use the REG QUERY command:

```
REG QUERY KeyName [/V SettingName ¦ /VE] [/C] [/D] [/E] [/F data] [/K ¦ [/S]
➥[/SE separator] [/T type] [/Z]
```

KeyName	The Registry key that contains the setting or settings that you want to view. The *KeyName* must include a root key value: HKCR, HKCU, HKLM, HKU, or HKCC. Place quotation marks around key names that include spaces.
/V ValueName	The Registry setting in *KeyName* that you want to view.
/VE	Tells REG to look for empty settings (that is, settings with a null value).
/F data	Specifies the data that REG should match in the *KeyName* settings.
/C	Runs a case-sensitive query.
/E	Returns only exact matches.
/K	Queries only key names, not settings.
/S	Tells REG to query the subkeys of *KeyName*.
/SE separator	Defines the separator to search for in REG_MULTI_SZ settings.
/T type	Specifies the setting type or types to search: REG_SZ, REG_MULTI_SZ, REG_EXPAND_SZ, REG_DWORD, REG_BINARY, or REG_NONE.
/Z	Tells REG to include the numeric equivalent of the setting type in the query results.

For example, if you want to know the current value of the RegisteredOwner setting in HKLM\Software\Microsoft\Windows NT\CurrentVersion, you'd run the following command:

```
reg query "hklm\software\microsoft\windows nt\currentversion" /v registeredowner
```

The Registry Editor has a Find command that enables you to look for text within the Registry. However, it would occasionally be useful to see a list of the Registry keys and settings that contains a particular bit of text. You can do this using the /F switch. For example, suppose you want to see a list of all the HKLM keys and settings that contain the text *Drive Extender*. Here's a command that will do this:

```
reg query hklm /f "Drive Extender" /s
```

To add a key or setting to the Registry, use the REG ADD command:

```
REG ADD KeyName [/V SettingName ¦ /VE] [/D data] [/F ¦ [/S separator] [/T type]
```

KeyName	The Registry key that you want to add or to which you want to add a setting. The *KeyName* must include a root key value: HKCR, HKCU, HKLM, HKU, or HKCC. Place quotation marks around key names that include spaces.
/V *ValueName*	The setting that you want to add to *KeyName*.
/VE	Tells REG to add an empty setting.
/D *data*	Specifies the data that REG should use as the value for the new setting.
/F	Modifies an existing key or setting without prompting to confirm the change.
/S *separator*	Defines the separator to use between multiple instances of data in a new REG_MULTI_SZ setting.
/T *type*	Specifies the setting type: REG_SZ, REG_MULTI_SZ, REG_EXPAND_SZ, REG_DWORD, REG_BINARY, or REG_NONE.

For example, the following command adds a key named MySettings to the HKCU root key:

```
reg add hkcu\MySettings
```

Here's another example that adds a setting named CurrentProject to the new MySettings key and sets the value of the new settings to WHS Unleashed:

```
reg add hkcu\MySettings /v CurrentProject /d "WHS Unleashed"
```

If you want to make changes to an existing setting, run REG ADD on the setting. For example, to change the HKCU\MySettings\CurrentProject setting to Windows Home Server Unleashed, you run the following command:

```
reg add hkcu\MySettings /v CurrentProject /d "Windows Home Server Unleashed"
```

Windows Home Server responds with the following prompt:

```
Value CurrentProject exists, overwrite (Yes/No)?
```

To change the existing value, press Y and press Enter.

TIP

To avoid being prompted when changing existing settings, add the /F switch to the REG ADD command.

SHUTDOWN: Shutting Down or Restarting a Computer

You can use the SHUTDOWN command to restart or shut down either the Windows Home Server computer or a remote computer on your network. Here's the syntax:

```
SHUTDOWN [[/R] ¦ [/S] ¦ [/L] ¦ [/H] ¦ [/I] ¦ [/P] ¦ [/E] ¦ [/A]] [/F¦
➥[/T seconds] [/D [P:]xx:yy] [/M \\ComputerName] [/C "comment"]
```

/R	Restarts the computer.
/S	Shuts down the computer.
/L	Logs off the current user immediately.
/H	Puts the computer into hibernation, if the computer supports hibernation mode.
/I	Displays the Remote Shutdown dialog box, which enables you to specify many of the options provided by these switches.
/P	Turns off the local computer immediately (that is, without the usual warning interval).
/E	Enables you to document the reason for an unexpected shutdown. (Note that this switch does not work in Windows Home Server.)
/A	Cancels the pending restart or shutdown.
/F	Forces all running programs on the target computer to shut down without warning. This, obviously, is dangerous and should only be used as a last resort.
/D [P:]*major:minor*	Specifies the reason for the shutdown. Include P: to indicate the shutdown is planned. Use values between 0 and 255 for *major* and between 0 and 65535 for *minor*. Windows Home Server also defines a number of predefined values for the *major* and *minor* parameters:

major	*minor*	Reason
0	0	Other (Planned)
0	5	Other Failure: System Unresponsive
1	1	Hardware: Maintenance (Unplanned)
1	1	Hardware: Maintenance (Planned)
1	2	Hardware: Installation (Unplanned)
1	2	Hardware: Installation (Planned)
2	3	Operating System: Upgrade (Planned)

2	4	Operating System: Reconfiguration (Unplanned)
2	4	Operating System: Reconfiguration
2	16	Operating System: Service Pack (Planned)
2	17	Operating System: Hot Fix (Unplanned)
2	17	Operating System: Hot Fix (Planned)
2	18	Operating System: Security Fix
2	18	Operating System: Security Fix (Planned)
4	1	Application: Maintenance (Unplanned)
4	1	Application: Maintenance (Planned)
4	2	Application: Installation (Planned)
4	5	Application: Unresponsive
4	6	Application: Unstable
5	15	System Failure: Stop Error
5	19	Security Issue
5	19	Security Issue
5	19	Security Issue
5	20	Loss of Network Connectivity (Unplanned)
6	11	Power Failure: Cord Unplugged
6	12	Power Failure: Environment
7	0	Legacy API Shutdown

/M *ComputerName*   Specifies the remote computer you want to shut down.

/T *seconds*   Specifies the number of seconds after which the computer is shut down. The default is 30 seconds, and you can specify any number up to 600.

/C *"comment"*   The *comment* text (which can be a maximum of 127 characters) appears in the dialog box and warns the user of the pending shutdown. This *comment* text also appears in the shutdown event that is added to the System log in Event Viewer. (Look for an Event ID of 1074.)

For example, to restart the local computer in 60 seconds, use the following command:

```
shutdown /r /t 60
```

When you enter the SHUTDOWN command, a System Shutdown dialog box appears and counts down to the shutdown time (see Figure 19.5, later in this section).

To document the shutdown, add the /D and /C switches, as in this example:

```
shutdown /s /d p:1:2 /c "Installing internal hard drive"
```

The reason code given by the /D switch and the comment specified by the /C switch appear in the event that Windows Home Server generates for the shutdown. You can see this event by launching Event Viewer (select Start, Control Panel, Administrative Tools, Event Viewer), opening the System log, and looking for a recent item with Event ID of 1074. Figure 19.3 shows an example.

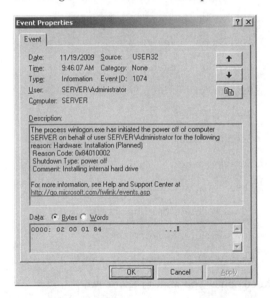

FIGURE 19.3 A shutdown event records the reason and comment that you specified with the SHUTDOWN command's /P and /C switches.

To shut down or restart a remote computer, you must run SHUTDOWN using the *remote* computer's Administrator account. This requires you to use the RUNAS command-line tool:

```
RUNAS /user:ComputerName\UserName cmd
```

ComputerName	The name of the remote computer.
UserName	The name of the account under which you want to run cmd.
cmd	The command you want to run.

For running SHUTDOWN with the /M switch, *UserName* will be Administrator and *cmd* will be the SHUTDOWN command, enclosed in quotation marks. Here's an example that shuts down a remote computer named OFFICEPC in 120 seconds:

```
runas /user:officepc\administrator "shutdown /s /m \\officepc /t 120"
```

When you enter the RUNAS command, Windows Home Server prompts you for the account password:

```
Enter the password for officepc\administrator:
```

Type the password (it doesn't appear onscreen) and press Enter.

> **TIP**
>
> If you need to embed a quotation mark in the *cmd* portion of RUNAS, precede it with a backslash (\). Here's an example:
>
> ```
> runas /user:officepc\administrator "shutdown /s /m \\officepc /c \"Comment\""
> ```

This works fine on XP machines but not on Windows 7 and Vista PCs, because the Administrator account is disabled by default on Windows 7 and Vista systems. Here are the steps to follow to enable this account and set its password:

1. On the Windows 7 or Vista machine, press Windows Logo+R (or select Start, All Programs, Accessories, Run) to open the Run dialog box, type **lusrmgr.msc**, and click OK.

2. If you see the User Account Control dialog box, enter your credentials to continue.

3. In the Local User and Groups snap-in, click Users.

4. Double-click the Administrator account to open its property sheet.

5. Deactivate the Account Is Disabled check box, and then click OK.

6. Right-click the Administrator account, and then click Set Password. Windows warns you that changing an account password can cause problems.

7. You can ignore the warning in this case, so click Proceed to open the Set Password for Administrator dialog box.

8. Type the password in the New Password and Confirm Password text boxes, and then click OK.

Figure 19.4 shows an example of the dialog box that Windows Vista users see when the shutdown event is launched. Figure 19.5 shows the XP dialog box, which is also what the dialog box looks like on Windows Home Server. (Notice that the XP/Home Server dialog box has the courtesy to tell the user how much time he has before the shutdown. No such luck on the Vista box.)

FIGURE 19.4   This is what a Windows Vista user sees when you start the shutdown process from a remote computer.

FIGURE 19.5   This is what a Windows XP user sees when you start the shutdown process from a remote computer.

If you need to cancel a pending shutdown on a remote computer, run SHUTDOWN with the /A switch before the timeout interval is over:

```
runas /user:officepc\administrator "shutdown /a /m \\officepc"
```

SYSTEMINFO: Returning System Configuration Data

If you want to get information about various aspects of your computer, a good place to start is the SYSTEMINFO command-line tool, which displays data about the following aspects of your system:

- ▶ The operating system name, version, and configuration type

- ▶ The registered owner and organization

- ▶ The original install date

- ▶ The system uptime

  - ▶ **SEE** For details on viewing system uptime with SYSTEMINFO, **see** "Displaying Uptime with the SYSTEMINFO Command," **P. 428**.

- ▶ The computer manufacturer, make, and model

- ▶ The system processors

- ▶ The BIOS version

- ▶ The total and available physical memory

- ▶ The paging file's maximum size, available size, in-use value, and location

- ▶ The installed hotfixes

- ▶ The network interface card data, such as the name, connection, DHCP status, and IP address (or addresses)

You can see all this data (and more), as well as control the output, by running SYSTEMINFO with the following syntax:

```
SYSTEMINFO [/S ComputerName] [/U [Domain]\UserName] [/P Password]
➥[/FO Format] [/NH]
```

/S ComputerName	The name of the remote computer for which you want to view the system configuration.
/U [Domain]\UserName	The username and, optionally, the domain, of the account under which you want to run the SYSTEMINFO command.
/P Password	The password of the account you specified with /U.
/FO Format	The output format, where format is one of the following values:
	table—The output is displayed in a row-and-column format, with headers in the first row and values in subsequent rows.
	list—The output is displayed in a two-column list, with the headers in the first column and values in the second column.
	csv—The output is displayed with headers and values separated by commas. The headers appear on the first line.
/NH	Tells SYSTEMINFO not to include column headers when you use the /FO switch with either table or csv.

The output of SYSTEMINFO is quite long, so pipe it through the MORE command to see the output one screen at a time:

```
systeminfo ¦ more
```

If you want to examine the output in another program or import the results into Excel or Access, redirect the output to a file and use the appropriate format. For example, Excel can read .csv files, so you can redirect the SYSTEMINFO output to a .csv file while using csv as the output format:

```
systeminfo /fo csv > systeminfo.csv
```

TYPEPERF: Monitoring Performance

In Chapter 14, "Tuning Windows Home Server Performance," you learned how to use the System Monitor utility to track the real-time performance of counters in various categories, such as processor and memory.

> ▶ **SEE** To learn how to use System Monitor, see "Monitoring Performance with System Monitor," **P. 404**.

You can get the same benefit without the System Monitor GUI by using the powerful TYPEPERF command-line tool. Here's the syntax:

```
TYPEPERF [counter1 [counter2 ...]] [-CF file] [-O file] [-F format]
➥[-SI interval] [-SC samples] [-Q [object]] [-QX [object]]
➥[-CONFIG file] [-S computer]
```

counter1 [counter2 ...]	Specifies the path of the performance counter to monitor. If you want to track multiple counters, separate each counter path with a space. If any path includes spaces, surround the path with quotation marks.
-CF *file*	Loads the counters from *file*, where *file* is a text file that lists the counter paths on separate lines.
-O *file*	Specifies the path and name of the file that will store the performance data.
-F *format*	Specifies the format for the output file format given by the /O switch, where *format* is one of the following values:
	csv—The output is displayed with each counter separated by a comma and each sample on its own line. This is the default output format.
	tsv—The output is displayed with each counter separated by a tab and each sample on its own line.
	bin—The output is displayed in binary format.
	sql—The output is displayed in SQL log format.
-SI *interval*	Specifies the time interval between samples. The *interval* parameter uses the form [mm:]ss. The default interval is 1 second.
-SC *samples*	Specifies the number of samples to collect. If you omit this switch, TYPEPERF samples continuously until you press Ctrl+C to cancel.
-Q [*object*]	Lists the available counters for *object* without instances.
-QX [*object*]	Lists the available counters for *object* with instances.

-CONFIG *file*	Specifies the pathname of the settings file that contains the TYPEPERF parameters you want to run.
-S *computer*	Specifies that the performance counters should be monitored on the PC named *computer* if no computer name is specified in the counter path.
-Y	Answers yes to any prompts generated by TYPEPERF.

The official syntax of a counter path looks like this:

`[\\Computer]\Object([Parent/][Instance][#Index])\Counter`

Computer	The computer on which the counter is to be monitored. If you omit a computer name, TYPEPERF monitors the counter on the local computer.
Object	The performance object—such as Processor, Memory, or PhysicalDisk—that contains the counter.
Parent	The container instance of the specified *Instance*.
Instance	The instance of the *Object*, if it has multiple instances. For example, in a two- (or dual-core) processor system, the instances are 0 (for the first processor), 1 (for the second processor), or _Total (for both processors combined). You can also using an asterisk (*) to represent all the instances in *Object*.
Index	The index number of the specified *Instance*.
Counter	The name of the performance counter. You can also use an asterisk (*) to represent all the counters in *Object* (*Instance*).

In practice, however, you rarely use the *Computer*, *Parent*, and *Index* parts of the path, so most counter paths use one of the following two formats:

`\Object\Counter`
`\Object(Instance)\Counter`

For example, here's the path for the Memory object's Available MBytes counter:

`\Memory\Available MBytes`

Here's a TYPEPERF command that displays five samples of this counter:

`typeperf "\Memory\Available Mbytes" -sc 5`

Similarly, here's the path for the Processor object's % Processor Time counter, using the first processor instance:

`\Processor(0)\% Processor Time`

Here's a TYPEPERF command that displays 10 samples of this counter every 3 seconds, and saves the results to a file named ProcessorTime.txt:

```
typeperf "\Processor(0)\% Processor Time" -sc 10 -si 3 -o ProcessorTime.txt
```

To use the -CONFIG parameter with TYPEPERF, you need to create a text file that stores the command line parameters you want to use. This configuration file consists of a series of parameter/value pairs that use the following general format:

```
[Parameter]
Value
```

Here, *Parameter* is text that specifies a TYPEPERF parameter—such as F for the -F parameter and S for the -S parameter. Use C to specify one or more counter paths—and *Value* as the value you want to assign to the parameter.

For example, consider the following command:

```
typeperf "\PhysicalDisk(_Total)\% Idle Time" -si 5 -sc 10 -o idletime.txt
```

To run the same command using the -CONFIG parameter, you first need to create a file with the following text:

```
[c]
\PhysicalDisk(_Total)\% Idle Time
[si]
5
[sc]
10
[o]
idletime.txt
```

If this file is named IdleTimeCounter.txt, you can run it at any time with the following command (assuming IdleTimeCounter.txt resides in the current folder):

```
typeperf -config IdleTimeCounter.txt
```

WHOAMI: Getting Information About the Current User

The WHOAMI command gives you information about the user who is currently logged on to the computer:

```
WHOAMI [/UPN ¦ /FQDN ¦ LOGONID] [/USER ¦ /GROUPS ¦ /PRIV] [/ALL] [/FO format]
```

/UPN	(Domains only) Returns the current user's name using the user principal name (UPN) format.
/FQDN	(Domains only) Returns the current user's name using the fully qualified domain name (FQDN) format.
/LOGONID	Returns the current user's security identifier (SID).
/USER	Returns the current username using the *computer\user* format.
/GROUPS	Returns the groups of which the current user is a member.
/PRIV	Returns the current user's privileges.
/ALL	Returns the current user's SID, username, groups, and privileges.
/FO *format*	The output format, where *format* is one of the following values:

table—The output is displayed in a row-and-column format, with headers in the first row and values in subsequent rows.

list—The output is displayed in a two-column list, with the headers in the first column and values in the second column.

csv—The output is displayed with headers and values separated by commas. The headers appear on the first line.

You probably won't use this command often on the Windows Home Server computer because you'll almost always be logged on as Administrator. However, WHOAMI is useful when you're working on a client computer and you're not sure who is currently logged on.

For example, the following command redirects the current user's SID, username, groups, and privileges to a file named whoami.txt using the list format:

```
whoami /all /fo list > whoami.txt
```

From Here

▶ For details on setting up a time server using the command line, **see** "Specifying the Time Server at the Command Prompt," **P. 99**.

▶ To learn more about the Advanced Options menu, **see** "Configuring Startup with the Advanced Options Menu," **P. 117**.

▶ To learn how to use the CONVERT tool to convert a FAT32 drive to NTFS, **see** "Run the CONVERT Utility," **P. 243**.

▶ To learn how to use System Monitor, **see** "Monitoring Performance with System Monitor," **P. 404**.

▶ For details on viewing system uptime with SYSTEMINFO, **see** "Displaying Uptime with the SYSTEMINFO Command," **P. 428**.

▶ For information on Check Disk and the types of errors it looks for, **see** "Checking Your Hard Disk for Errors," **P. 431**.

Using Other Windows Home Server Power Tools

One of the main themes of this book has been that getting the most out of Windows Home Server often means eschewing the Windows Home Server Console program and getting your hands on the operating system itself, particularly because that OS is really just Windows Server 2003 in disguise. Throughout the book, I've shown you how to use various OS tools to tweak, improve, and customize your system. These tools have included Device Manager, Event Viewer, Internet Information Services Manager, Network Diagnostics, Registry Editor, Remote Desktop Connection, System Configuration Manager, System Information, System Monitor, Task Manager, and Terminal Services Manager, to name but a few.

That's a long list, but we're not done—not by a long shot. Windows Home Server still has a few other power tools that will be welcome additions to your Windows Home Server workshop, and this chapter shows you how to use them. The chapter begins by taking a closer look at several tools that you've used already in this book: Group Policy Object Editor, Control Panel, and the Microsoft Management Console. You also learn how to control services and configure a fax server.

Using the Group Policy Object Editor

Group policies are settings that control how Windows Home Server works. You can use them to customize the Windows Home Server interface, enable or disable features, specify security settings, and much more.

Group policies are mostly used by system administrators who want to make sure that novice users don't have access to dangerous tools (such as the Registry Editor) or who want to ensure a consistent computing experience across multiple machines. Group policies are also ideally suited to situations in which multiple users share a single computer. However, group policies are also useful on single-user standalone machines, as you've seen in several places in this book. Here are some examples:

▶ In Chapter 4, "Configuring Windows Home Server," you learned how to use group policies to set up programs or scripts to launch at startup.

  ▶ **SEE** "Launching Items Using Group Policies," **P. 122**.

▶ In Chapter 10, "Monitoring Your Network," you learned about a group policy that enables the remote control of the Administrator's desktop on Windows Home Server.

  ▶ **SEE** "Enabling Remote Control Sessions," **P. 279**.

▶ In Chapter 16, "Customizing the Windows Home Server Interface," I took you through a long list of group policies related to customizing the Start menu and taskbar.

  ▶ **SEE** "Modifying the Start Menu and Taskbar with Group Policies," **P. 475**.

In this section, you learn the details of working with group policies using the Group Policy Object Editor, and I take you through a few more useful group policy settings.

Working with Group Policies

You implement group policies using the Group Policy Object Editor, which is a Microsoft Management Console snap-in. To start the Group Policy Object Editor, select Start, Run and then use either of the following methods:

▶ To implement group policies for the local computer, type **gpedit.msc** and click OK.

▶ To implement group policies for a remote computer, type **gpedit.msc /gpcomputer:"name"**, where *name* is the name of the remote machine, and then click OK.

The Group Policy window that appears is divided into two sections:

▶ **Left pane**—This pane contains a treelike hierarchy of policy categories, which is divided into two main categories: Computer Configuration and User Configuration. The Computer Configuration policies apply to all users and are implemented before the logon. The User Configuration policies apply only to the current user and, therefore, are not applied until that user logs on.

▶ **Right pane**—This pane contains the policies for whichever category is selected in the left pane.

The idea, then, is to open the tree's branches to find the category you want. When you click the category, its policies appear in the right pane. For example, Figure 20.1 shows the Group Policy Object Editor window with the Computer Configuration, Administrative Templates, System, Logon category selected.

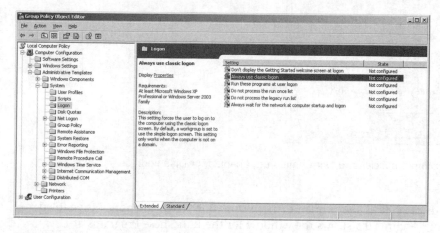

FIGURE 20.1   When you select a category in the left pane, the category's policies appear in the right pane.

TIP

Windows Home Server comes with another snap-in, Local Security Settings, which displays only the policies found in the Group Policy Object Editor's Computer Configuration, Windows Settings, Security Settings branch. To launch the Local Security Settings snap-in, select Start, Run, type **secpol.msc**, and click OK.

In the right pane, the Setting column tells you the name of the policy, and the State column tells you the current state of the policy. Click a policy to see its description on the left side of the pane, as shown in Figure 20.1. To configure a policy, double-click it. The type of window you see depends on the policy:

▶ For simple policies, you see a window similar to the one shown in Figure 20.2. These kinds of policies take one of three states: Not Configured (the policy is not in effect), Enabled (the policy is in effect and its setting is enabled), and Disabled (the policy is in effect but its setting is disabled).

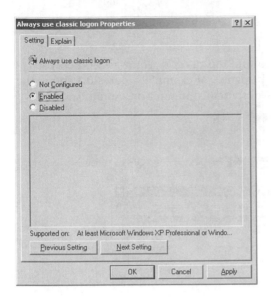

FIGURE 20.2   Simple policies are Not Configured, Enabled, or Disabled.

▶ Other kinds of policies also require extra information when the policy is enabled. For example, Figure 20.3 shows the window for the Run These Programs at User Logon policy. When Enabled is activated, the Show button appears; you use it to specify one or more programs that run when the computer starts.

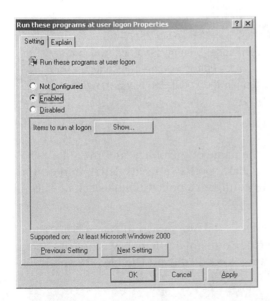

FIGURE 20.3   More complex policies also require extra information such as, in this case, a list of programs to run at logon.

TIP

After you apply some group policies, you may forget which ones you applied, or you may want to see a summary of the applied policies. You can see such a summary by opening the Resultant Set of Policy snap-in: select Start, Run, type rsop.msc, and click OK. The snap-in looks much like the Group Policy Object Editor, except the only sub-branches you see are those that have applied policies.

Customizing the Windows Security Dialog Box

When you press Ctrl+Alt+Delete while logged on to Windows Home Server, you see the Windows Security dialog box, which contains the following buttons, as shown in Figure 20.4:

▶ **SEE** To learn how to use the Windows Home Server Console program to change the Administrator password, **see** "Changing the Windows Home Server Password," **P. 106**.

Lock Computer — Click this button to hide the desktop and display the Computer Locked dialog box. To return to the desktop, you must press Ctrl+Alt+Delete and then enter your Windows Home Server password. This is useful if you're going to leave Windows Home Server unattended and don't want another person accessing the desktop. However, Windows Home Server offers a faster way to lock the computer: Press Windows Logo+L.

Change Password — Click this button to display the Change password dialog box, which enables you to specify a new password for the Administrator account. In Windows Home Server, you're better off doing this through the Windows Home Server Console application.

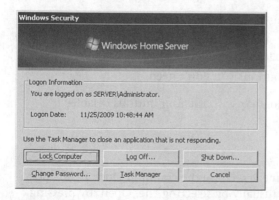

FIGURE 20.4   In Windows Home Server, press Ctrl+Alt+Delete to display the Windows Security dialog box.

Log Off   Click this button and then click Log Off to log off the Administrator account. You
            can also log off by selecting Start, Log Off.

Task   Click this button to open Task Manager. You've seen elsewhere in this book that
Manager   Task Manager is a very useful tool, but Windows Home Server offers two faster
            methods to open it: Press Ctrl+Shift+Esc, or right-click the taskbar and then click
            Task Manager.

> **SEE** For a good example of what Task Manager can do, **see** "Monitoring Performance
with Task Manager," **P. 392**.

Shut   Click this button to display the Shut Down Windows dialog box, from which you
Down   can either restart or turn off Windows Home Server. You can also restart or turn
            off Windows Home Server by selecting Start, Shut Down.

Of these five commands, the first four are customizable using group policies. So if you
find that you never use one or more of those commands, you can use group policies to
disable them in the Windows Security dialog box. Here are the steps to follow:

1. Open the Group Policy Object Editor window, as described earlier in this chapter.
2. Open the User Configuration, Administrative Templates, System, Ctrl+Alt+Del
   Options branch.
3. Double-click one of the following policies:

   > **Remove Task Manager**—You can use this policy to disable the Task Manager
   button in the Windows Security dialog box.

   > **Remove Lock Computer**—You can use this policy to disable the Lock
   Computer button in the Windows Security dialog box.

   > **Remove Change Password**—You can use this policy to disable the Change
   Password button in the Windows Security dialog box.

   > **Remove Logoff**—You can use this policy to disable the Log Off button in the
   Windows Security dialog box.

4. In the policy dialog box that appears, click Enabled and then click OK.
5. Repeat steps 3 and 4 to disable all the buttons you don't need.

Figure 20.5 shows the Windows Security dialog box with the four buttons disabled.

Customizing the Places Bar

Most file-based applications in Windows Home Server use the common Open dialog box
that you use to open a file in an application (usually by selecting File, Open, by pressing
Ctrl+O, or by clicking the Open toolbar button). Figure 20.6 shows an example.

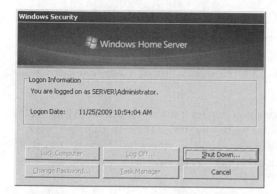

FIGURE 20.5   You can use group policies to disable most of the buttons in the Windows Security dialog box.

Places Bar

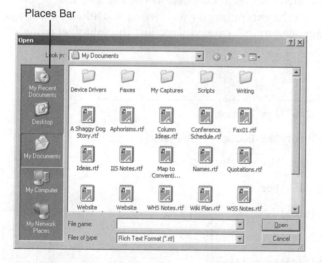

FIGURE 20.6   Most applications display this Open dialog box when you select the File, Open command.

NOTE

The same Places Bar also appears in the common Save As dialog box, which appears when you select File, Save for a new, unsaved document, or File, Save As for any document.

Notice in Figure 20.6 that the left side of the common Open dialog box contains a strip called the Places Bar, which contains icons for five shell folders: My Recent Documents,

Desktop, My Documents, My Computer, and My Network Places. These icons are handy navigation tools, but only if you use the default folders.

Fortunately, if you have other folders that you use more frequently, you can use a group policy to customize the Places Bar icons. You can replace the existing Places Bar icons with up to five of the following items:

▶ A local folder path. For example, someone who writes a lot of scripts for Windows Home Server might set up a `Scripts` folder within `My Documents`. In that case, you could add `%UserProfile%\My Documents\Scripts` to the Places Bar. Note that in this case, only the name of the subfolder appears in the Places Bar. (That is, you don't see the entire folder path.)

▶ A UNC path to a shared network folder. For example, this would be ideal for accessing those Windows Home Server shares that you use most often. In this case, Windows Home Server displays the Places Bar icon with the name *Share* on *Computer*, where *Share* is the name of the shared folder and *Computer* is the name of the computer that's sharing the folder. (The exception to this is when you add a subfolder of the share to the Places Bar. In that case, you see just the subfolder name.)

▶ Here are some of the common shell folders:

Shell Folder	Path
CommonDocuments	`%AllUsersProfile%\Documents`
CommonMusic	`%AllUsersProfile%\Documents\My Music`
CommonPictures	Not available in Windows Home Server
Desktop	`%UserProfile%\Desktop`
MyComputer	`%UserProfile%\`
MyDocuments	`%UserProfile%\My Documents`
MyFavorites	`%UserProfile%\Favorites`
MyMusic	Not available in Windows Home Server
MyNetworkPlaces	`%UserProfile%\NetHood`
MyPictures	Not available in Windows Home Server
Printers	Control Panel, Printers and Faxes
ProgramFiles	`C:\Program Files\`
Recent	`%UserProfile%\Recent`

Follow these steps to use a group policy to customize the Places Bar:

1. Open the Group Policy Object Editor window, as described earlier in this chapter.

2. Navigate to the User Configuration, Administrative Templates, Windows Components, Windows Explorer, Common Open File Dialog branch.

3. Double-click the Items Displayed in Places Bar policy.

4. Activate the Enabled option.

5. Use the text boxes in the Places to Display section to specify the local folders, network paths, or shell folders that you want to include in the Places Bar.

6. Click OK.

Figure 20.7 shows the Items Displayed in Places Bar policy enabled and with some custom items added, and Figure 20.8 shows the resulting Places Bar in the common Open dialog box. (The same customized Places Bar also appears in the common Save As dialog box.)

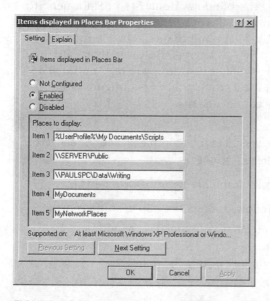

FIGURE 20.7   Use the Items Displayed in Places Bar policy to customize the Places Bar.

FIGURE 20.8   The common Open dialog box showing the custom Places Bar items specified in Figure 20.7.

> **NOTE**
>
> If you don't use the Places Bar at all, you might prefer to hide it to give yourself more room in the Open and Save As dialog boxes. To do that, open the Group Policy Object Editor and navigate to the User Configuration, Administrative Templates, Windows Components, Windows Explorer, Common Open File Dialog branch. Double-click the Hide the Common Dialog Places Bar, click Enabled, and then click OK.

Increasing the Size of the Recent Documents List

In Chapter 16, I showed you how to customize the Windows Home Server Start menu to include the My Recent Documents item. Clicking My Recent Documents displays a list of the 15 documents you worked on most recently. That number should be plenty on any Windows Home Server machine that you use purely as a server. However, if you also use Windows Home Server as a workstation or development platform, you may find that 15 documents isn't enough. In that case, you can use a group policy to configure Windows Home Server to display a higher number of recent documents.

> ▶ **SEE** To learn how to add My Recent Documents to the Start menu, **see** "Streamlining the Start Menu by Converting Links to Menus," **P. 465**.

Here are the steps to follow to customize the size of the My Recent Documents list:

1. Open the Group Policy Object Editor window, as described earlier in this chapter.
2. Navigate to the User Configuration, Administrative Templates, Windows Components, Windows Explorer branch.
3. Double-click the Maximum Number of Recent Documents policy.
4. Click Enabled.
5. Use the Maximum Number of Recent Documents spin box to specify the number of documents you want Windows Home Server to display (see Figure 20.9).
6. Click OK.

> **NOTE**
>
> You can specify a value between 1 and 9999 (!) in the Maximum Number of Recent Documents spin box. If you specify more documents than can fit vertically on your screen, Windows Home Server adds scroll buttons to the top and bottom of the My Recent Documents list.

Enabling the Shutdown Event Tracker

In Windows Home Server, when you select Start, Shut Down (or click the Shut Down button in the Windows Security dialog box as described earlier; see "Customizing the Windows Security Dialog Box"), the Shut Down Windows dialog box appears, as shown in Figure 20.10. From here, you select the action you want the computer to perform—Restart, Shut Down, Log Off, or Stand By—and click OK.

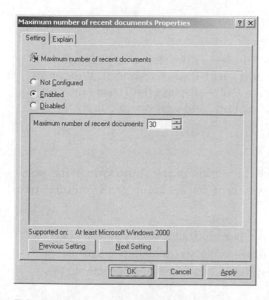

FIGURE 20.9   Use the Maximum Number of Recent Documents policy to customize the size of the My Recent Documents list.

FIGURE 20.10   The default Shut Down Windows dialog box.

If you want to keep track of why you shut down or restart Windows Home Server, you can enable a feature called Shutdown Event Tracker. With this feature, you can document the shutdown event by specifying whether it is planned or unplanned, selecting a reason for the shutdown, and adding a comment that describes the shutdown.

Here are the steps to follow to use a group policy to enable the Shutdown Event Tracker feature:

1. Open the Group Policy Object Editor window, as described earlier in this chapter.
2. Navigate to the Computer Configuration, Administrative Templates, System branch.

3. Double-click the Display Shutdown Event Tracker policy.

4. Click Enabled.

5. In the Shutdown Event Tracker Should Be Displayed list, select either Always or Server Only. (This ensures that the Shutdown Event Tracker appears in Windows Home Server; the third option—Workstation Only—displays the Tracker only on computers running as a client, such as XP or Vista, and so it doesn't apply to Windows Home Server.)

6. Click OK.

Now when you select Start, Shut Down, you see the version of the Shut Down Windows dialog box shown in Figure 20.11. The Shutdown Event Tracker group gives you three new controls to operate:

Planned	Leave this check box activated if this is a planned shutdown. If you didn't plan on shutting down Windows Home Server (for example, you're restarting because a program has crashed or because the system appears unstable), deactivate this check box.
Option	Use this list to select the reason for the shutdown. (Note that the items you see in this list change depending on the state of the Planned check box.)
Comment	Use this text box to describe the shutdown event. If you choose either Other (Planned) or Other (Unplanned) in the Option list, you must add a comment to enable the OK button; for all other items in the Option list, the Comment text is optional.

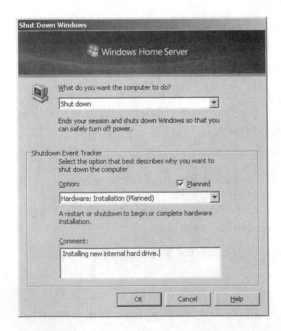

FIGURE 20.11   The Shut Down Windows dialog box with the Shutdown Event Tracker feature enabled.

Getting More Out of Control Panel

Control Panel is a folder that contains a large number of icons—there are 50 or so in the default Windows Home Server setup (including all the Administrative Tools icons). However, more icons could be available on your system depending on the optional Windows Home Server components, applications, and device drivers that you've installed. Each of these icons deals with a specific area of the Windows Home Server configuration: hardware, applications, fonts, printers, multimedia, and much more.

Opening an icon displays (usually) a dialog box containing various properties related to that area of Windows. For example, launching the Add or Remove Programs icon enables you to install or uninstall third-party applications and Windows Home Server components.

To view the Control Panel icons, use any of the following techniques:

- Select Start, Control Panel.

- Select Start, Windows Explorer, and then select the Desktop\My Computer\Control Panel folder.

- Select Start, right-click Control Panel, and then click either Open (see Figure 20.12) or Explore.

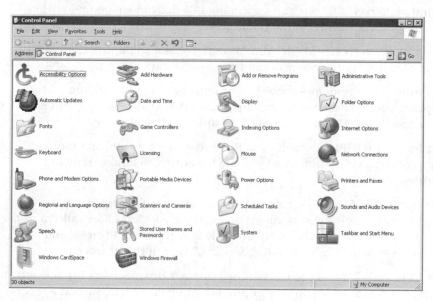

FIGURE 20.12   Windows Home Server's Control Panel folder.

Reviewing the Control Panel Icons

To help you familiarize yourself with what's available in Control Panel, this section offers summary descriptions of the Control Panel icons found in a standard Windows Home Server installation. Note that your system might have extra icons, depending on your system's configuration and the programs you have installed.

▶ **Accessibility Options**—Enables you to customize input—the keyboard and mouse—and output—sound and display—for users with special mobility, hearing, or vision requirements.

▶ **Add Hardware**—Launches the Add Hardware Wizard, which searches for new Plug and Play devices on your system, and can run a more in-depth hardware detection to look for non-Plug and Play devices. You can also use this wizard to install device drivers by hand by choosing the one you want from a list or from a disc that came with your device.

▶ **Add or Remove Programs**—Enables you to install and uninstall applications, and add and remove Windows Home Server components.

▶ **Administrative Tools**—Displays a window with more icons, each of which enables you to administer a particular aspect of Windows Home Server. Many of these apply only to Windows Server 2003 machines operating in a domain environment. Here are the icons that work with Windows Home Server:

  ▶ **Component Services**—Enables you to configure and administer Component Object Model (COM) components and COM+ applications.

  ▶ **Computer Management**—Enables you to manage a local or remote computer. You can examine hidden and visible shared folders, set group policies, access Device Manager, manage hard disks, and much more.

  ▶ **Data Sources (ODBC)**—Enables you to create and work with data sources, which are connection strings that you use to connect to local or remote databases.

  ▶ **Distributed File System**—Enables you to combine multiple shared network folders from multiple network clients under a single logical folder called a *root*. Note that you must start the Distributed File System service to create and manage a DFS root. See "Controlling Services," later in this chapter.

  ▶ **Event Viewer**—Enables you to examine Windows Home Server's list of *events*, which are unusual or noteworthy occurrences on your system, such as a service that doesn't start, the installation of a device, or an application error.

  ▶ **Internet Information Services (IIS) Manager**—Enables you to create and configure websites hosted on Windows Home Server, as described in Chapter 12, "Setting Up a Windows Home Server Website."

▶ **SEE** "Viewing the Default Website with Internet Information Services Manager," **P. 322**.

▶ **Local Security Policy**—Displays the Local Security Settings snap-in, which enables you to set up security policies on your system.

▶ **Performance**—Enables you to monitor the performance of your system using System Monitor, performance logs, and alerts.

▶ **SEE** "Monitoring Performance with System Monitor," **P. 404**.

▶ **Remote Desktops**—Enables you to create Remote Desktop connections to network clients.

▶ **Routing and Remote Access**—Enables you to configure Windows Home Server to accept remote dial-up or virtual private network connections.

▶ **Services**—Displays a list of the system services available with Windows Home Server. See "Controlling Services," later in this chapter.

▶ **Terminal Services Configuration**—Enables you to configure policies for remote connection over Terminal Services.

▶ **Terminal Services Manager**—Enables you to view and manage remote connections to Windows Home Server, as described in Chapter 10.

▶ **SEE** "Monitoring Remote Desktop Sessions," **P. 275**.

▶ **Automatic Updates**—Enables you to configure Windows Home Server's Automatic Updates feature, including setting up a schedule for the download and installation of updates.

▶ **Date and Time**—Enables you to set the current date and time, select your time zone, and set up an Internet time server to synchronize your system time.

▶ **Display**—Offers a large number of customization options for the desktop, screen-saver, video card, monitor, and other display components.

▶ **Folder Options**—Enables you to customize the display of Windows Home Server's folders, set up whether Windows Home Server uses single- or double-clicking, work with file types, and configure offline files.

▶ **Fonts**—Displays the Fonts folder, from which you can view, install, and remove fonts.

▶ **Game Controllers**—Enables you to calibrate joysticks and other game devices.

▶ **Indexing Options**—Enables you to configure the indexing settings used by Windows Desktop Search.

▶ **Internet Options**—Displays a large collection of settings for modifying Internet properties (how you connect, the Internet Explorer interface, and so on).

▶ **Keyboard**—Enables you to customize your keyboard, work with keyboard languages, and change the keyboard driver.

▶ **Licensing**—This is only for Windows Server 2003 computers.

▶ **Mouse**—Enables you to set various mouse options and to install a different mouse device driver.

▶ **Network Connections**—Enables you to create, modify, and launch connections to a network or the Internet.

▶ **Phone and Modem Options**—Enables you to configure telephone dialing rules and to install and configure modems.

▶ **Portable Media Devices**—Displays a list of your system's installed portable media devices, including Flash drives, memory cards, memory card readers, and so on.

▶ **Power Options**—Enables you to configure power management properties for powering down system components (such as the monitor and hard drive), defining low-power alarms for notebook batteries, enabling hibernation, and configuring an uninterruptible power supply.

▶ **Printers and Faxes**—Enables you to install and configure printers and the Windows Home Server Fax service.

▶ **Regional and Language Options**—Enables you to configure international settings for country-dependent items, such as numbers, currencies, times, and dates.

▶ **Scanners and Cameras**—Enables you to install and configure document scanners and digital cameras.

▶ **Scheduled Tasks**—Displays the Scheduled Tasks folder, which you use to set up a program to run on a schedule.

▶ **Sounds and Audio Devices**—Enables you to control the system volume; map sounds to specific Windows Home Server events (such as closing a program or minimizing a window); and specify settings for audio, voice, and other multimedia devices.

▶ **Speech**—Enables you to configure Windows Home Server's text-to-speech feature.

▶ **Stored User Names and Passwords**—Enables you to edit or delete usernames and passwords that you've asked Windows Home Server to remember. You can also add new usernames and passwords.

▶ **System**—Gives you access to a large number of system properties, including the computer name and workgroup; Device Manager and hardware profiles; and settings related to performance, startup, Automatic Updates, Remote Assistance, and Remote Desktop.

▶ **Taskbar and Start Menu**—Enables you to customize the taskbar and Start menu.

▶ **Windows CardSpace**—Enables you to use Microsoft's new CardSpace system to manage your personal online data.

▶ **Windows Firewall**—Enables you to activate and configure Windows Firewall.

Understanding Control Panel Files

Many of the Control Panel icons are represented by Control Panel extension files, which use the .cpl extension. These files reside in the %SystemRoot%\System32 folder. When you open Control Panel, Windows Home Server scans the System32 folder, looking for CPL files, and then displays an icon for each one.

The CPL files offer an alternative method for launching individual Control Panel dialog boxes. The idea is that you run control.exe and specify the name of a CPL file as a parameter. This bypasses the Control Panel folder and opens the icon directly. Here's the syntax:

```
control CPLfile [,option1 [, option2]]
```

CPLfile   The name of the file that corresponds to the Control Panel icon you want to open (see Table 20.1 later in this chapter).

option1   This option is obsolete and is included only for backward compatibility with batch files and scripts that use Control.exe for opening Control Panel icons.

option2   The tab number of a multitabbed dialog box. Many Control Panel icons open a dialog box that has two or more tabs. If you know the specific tab you want to work with, you can use the option2 parameter to specify an integer that corresponds to the tab's relative position from the left side of the dialog box. The first (leftmost) tab is 0, the next tab is 1, and so on.

> **NOTE**
>
> If the dialog box has multiple rows of tabs, count the tabs from left to right and from bottom to top. For example, if the dialog box has two rows of four tabs each, the tabs in the bottom row are numbered 0 to 3 from left to right, and the tabs in the top row are numbered 4 to 7 from left to right.
>
> Also, note that even though you no longer use the option1 parameter, you must still display its comma in the command line.

For example, to open Control Panel's System icon with the Hardware tab displayed, run the following command:

```
control sysdm.cpl,,2
```

Table 20.1 lists the various Control Panel icons and the appropriate command line to use. (Note, however, that you can't access certain Control Panel icons—such as Taskbar and Start Menu—by running Control.exe.)

TABLE 20.1   Command Lines for Launching Individual Control Panel Icons

Control Panel Icon	Command
Accessibility Options	control access.cpl
Add Hardware	control hdwwiz.cpl
Add or Remove Programs	control appwiz.cpl
Administrative Tools	control admintools
Automatic Updates	control wuaucpl.cpl
Data Sources	control odbccp32.cpl
Date and Time	control timedate.cpl
Display	control desk.cpl
Folder Options	control folders
Fonts	control fonts
Game Controllers	control joy.cpl
Internet Options	control inetcpl.cpl
Keyboard	control keyboard
Mouse	control mouse
Network Connections	control ncpa.cpl
Phone and Modem Options	control telephon.cpl
Power Options	control powercfg.cpl
Printers and Faxes	control printers
Regional and Language Options	control intl.cpl
Scanners and Cameras	control scannercamera
Scheduled Tasks	control schedtasks
Security Center	control wscui.cpl
Sounds and Audio Devices	control mmsys.cpl
Stored User Names and Passwords	control keymgr.cpl
System	control sysdm.cpl
Windows CardSpace	control infocardcpl.cpl
Windows Firewall	control firewall.cpl

Alternative Methods for Opening Control Panel Icons

Access to many Control Panel icons is scattered throughout the Windows Home Server interface, meaning that there's more than one way to launch an icon. Many of these alternative methods are faster and more direct than using the Control Panel folder. Here's a summary:

- ▶ **Computer Management**—Click Start, right-click My Computer, and then click Manage.

- ▶ **Date and Time**—Double-click the clock in the taskbar's system tray.

- ▶ **Display**—Right-click the desktop and then click Properties.

- ▶ **Folder Options**—In Windows Explorer, select Tools, Folder Options.

- ▶ **Fonts**—In Windows Explorer, open the %SystemRoot%\Fonts folder.

- ▶ **Internet Options**—In Internet Explorer, select Tools, Internet Options. If you added Internet Explorer to the Start menu as described in Chapter 16, you can also click Start, right-click Internet, and then click Internet Properties.

    ▶ **SEE** "Adding the Internet and E-Mail Icons," **P. 463**.

- ▶ **Network Connections**—In Windows Explorer, right-click My Network Places and then click Properties.

- ▶ **Printers and Faxes**—Select Start, Printers and Faxes.

- ▶ **Scheduled Tasks**—Select Start, All Programs, Accessories, System Tools, Scheduled Tasks. Alternatively, in Windows Explorer, open the %SystemRoot%\Tasks folder.

- ▶ **System**—Click Start, right-click My Computer, and then click Properties.

- ▶ **Taskbar and Start Menu**—Right-click an empty section of the taskbar or Start button and then click Properties.

Putting Control Panel on the Taskbar

For one-click access to the icons, create a new Control Panel toolbar on the taskbar by following these steps:

1. Right-click an empty section of the taskbar and then click Toolbars, New Toolbar. The New Toolbar dialog box appears.
2. Select My Computer, Control Panel.
3. Click OK.

From here, you can customize the Control Panel toolbar to fit all the icons on your screen (for example, by turning off the icon titles). See Chapter 16 to learn how to tweak taskbar toolbars.

▶ **SEE** "Setting Some Taskbar Toolbar Options," **P. 470**.

Displaying Control Panel in My Computer

Technically, the Control Panel folder is part of My Computer. However, if you select Start, My Computer, you don't see an icon for Control Panel in the folder window that appears. (However, you do see Control Panel if you select Start, right-click My Computer, and then click Explorer.)

If you want access to Control Panel from My Computer, follow these steps to set this up in Windows Home Server:

1. Select Start, Control Panel, Folder Options. Windows Home Server displays the Folder Options dialog box.

2. Display the View tab.

3. In the Advanced Settings list, activate the Show Control Panel in My Computer check box.

4. Click OK. An icon for Control Panel now appears in the My Computer window, as shown in Figure 20.13.

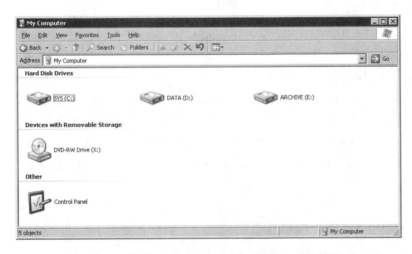

FIGURE 20.13   My Computer with the Control Panel icon displayed.

Removing an Icon from Control Panel

You might find that you don't use some Control Panel icons. For example, if your Windows Home Server computer doesn't have a joystick, you'll never need to use Control Panel's Game Controllers icon. Because Control Panel contains so many icons, it makes sense to remove those you never use. Doing that makes it easier to find the icon you want and faster to navigate the icons.

Here are the steps for using a group policy to remove icons from Control Panel:

1. Open the Group Policy Object Editor window, as described earlier in this chapter.

2. Navigate to the User Configuration, Administrative Templates, Control Panel branch.

3. Double-click the Hide Specified Control Panel applets.

4. Activate the Enabled option.

5. Click Show to display the Show Contents dialog box.

6. Click Add to open the Add Item dialog box.

7. Use the Enter the Item to Be Added text box to specify the Control icon you want to hide. You have two choices:

   ▶ Type the name of the CPL file that corresponds to the Control Panel icon you want to hide (see Table 20.1, earlier in this chapter).

   ▶ Type the icon caption as it appears in Control Panel. For example, to hide the Scanners and Cameras icon, type **Scanners and Cameras**.

NOTE

You can only hide icons that appear in the main Control Panel folder. You can't hide icons that appear in the Control Panel subfolders, such as Administrative Tools.

---

8. Click OK. The Group Policy Object Editor adds the CPL file to the Show Contents dialog box.

9. Repeat steps 6–8 to remove other icons.

10. Click OK.

Showing Only Specified Control Panel Icons

Control Panel is so useful that you'll probably use most of the icons at least some of the time. However, it's possible that you may only use a few of the icons most of the time. In that case, you might want to really streamline the Control Panel view by displaying only those few icons you use. Here's how to do this using a group policy:

1. Open the Group Policy Object Editor window, as described earlier in this chapter.

2. Navigate to the User Configuration, Administrative Templates, Control Panel branch.

3. Double-click the Show Only Specified Control Panel Applets policy.

4. Activate the Enabled option.

5. Click Show to display the Show Contents dialog box.

6. Click Add to open the Add Item dialog box.

7. Use the Enter the Item to Be Added text box to specify the Control Icon you want to show. You have two choices:

   ▶ Type the name of the CPL file that corresponds to the Control Panel icon you want to show (see Table 20.1, earlier in this chapter).

   ▶ Type the icon caption as it appears in Control Panel. For example, to show the Scanners and Cameras icon, type **Scanners and Cameras**.

8. Click OK. The Group Policy Object Editor adds the CPL file to the Show Contents dialog box.

9. Repeat steps 6–8 to show other icons.

10. Click OK.

NOTE

Group policies also enable you to customize the behavior of some Control Panel icons. When you open the User Configuration, Administrative Templates, Control Panel branch, you'll see four sub-branches that correspond to four Control Panel icons: Add or Remove Programs, Display, Printers, and Regional and Language Options. In each case, you use the policies in a particular sub-branch to hide dialog box tabs, specify default settings, and more.

Configuring the Microsoft Management Console

The Microsoft Management Console (MMC) is a system administration program that can act as a host application for a variety of tools. The advantage of MMC is that it displays each tool as a *console*—a two-pane view that has a treelike hierarchy in the left pane (this is called the *tree pane*) and a *taskpad* in the right pane that shows the contents of each branch (this is called the *results pane*). This gives each tool a similar interface, which makes it easier to use the tools. You can also customize the console view in a number of ways, create custom taskpad views, and save a particular set of tools to reuse later. These tools are called *snap-ins*, because you can "attach" them to the console root.

When you work with the MMC interface, what you're really doing is editing a Microsoft Common Console Document, an .msc file that stores one or more snap-ins, the console view, and the taskpad view used by each snap-in branch. You learn how to create custom MSC files in this section, but you should know that Windows Home Server comes with a large number of predefined MSC snap-ins, and I've summarized them in Table 20.2.

TABLE 20.2   The Default Windows Home Server Snap-Ins

Snap-In	File	Description
.NET Framework 1.1 Configuration	mscorcfg.msc	Enables you to configure various aspects of the .NET Framework 1.1.
Active Directory Domains and Trusts	domain.msc	Enables you to manage Active Directory domains and trusts. Windows Home Server doesn't support Active Directory, so this snap-in doesn't work.
Active Directory Sites and Services	dssite.msc	Enables you to manage Active Directory sites and services. Windows Home Server doesn't support Active Directory, so this snap-in doesn't work.

TABLE 20.2   The Default Windows Home Server Snap-Ins (*continued*)

Snap-In	File	Description
Active Directory Users and Groups	`dsa.msc`	Enables you to manage Active Directory users and groups. Windows Home Server doesn't support Active Directory, so this snap-in doesn't work.
Active X Control	N/A	Launches the Insert ActiveX Control Wizard, which enables you to choose an ActiveX control to display as a node. I haven't been able to find a good use for this one yet!
Authorization Manager	`azman.msc`	Used by developers to set permissions on applications.
Certificate Templates	`certtmpl.msc`	Enables you to create and manage certificate templates. This snap-in requires domain access, so it doesn't work with Windows Home Server.
Certificates	`certmgr.msc`	Enables you to browse the security certificates on your system.
Certification Authority	`certsrv.msc`	Enables you to manage Certificate Services. This service is not available in Windows Home Server.
Component Services	`comexp.msc`	Enables you to view and work with Component Object Model (COM) services.
Computer Management	`compmgmt.msc`	Contains a number of snap-ins for managing various aspects of Windows Home Server. You can examine hidden and visible shared folders, set group policies, access Device Manager, manage hard disks, and much more.
Device Manager	`devmgmt.msc`	Enables you to add and manage your system hardware. See Chapter 17, "Troubleshooting Windows Home Server."
Disk Defragmenter	`dfrg.msc`	Enables you to defragment your system hard drives. See Chapter 15, "Maintaining Windows Home Server."
Disk Management	`diskmgmt.msc`	Enables you to view and manage all the disk drives on your system. Changes to hard drives in Disk Management will almost certainly break Windows Home Server's Drive Extender tool, so you should not modify hard drives using this snap-in.
Distributed File System	`dfsgui.msc`	Enables you to combine multiple shared network folders from multiple network clients under a single logical folder called a *root*.

TABLE 20.2   The Default Windows Home Server Snap-Ins (*continued*)

Snap-In	File	Description
Event Viewer	`eventvwr.msc`	Enables you to view the Windows Home Server event logs. See Chapter 15.
Folder	N/A	This item enables you to add a folder node to the root to help you organize your nodes.
Group Policy Object Editor	`gpedit.msc`	Enables you to work with group policies. See "Using the Group Policy Object Editor," earlier in this chapter.
Indexing Service	`ciadv.msc`	Controls the indexing of the contents of the Internet Information Services websites on Windows Home Server. To use this snap-in, you first need to enable and start the Indexing service (see "Controlling Services," later in this chapter.)
Internet Authentication Service (IAS)	`ias.msc`	Enables you to authenticate connections to a network. This snap-in isn't installed by default in Windows Home Server. Use Control Panel's Add or Remove Programs icon to add this component.
Internet Information Services (IIS) Manager	`iis.msc`	Runs the IIS Manager, which I described in detail in Chapter 12, "Setting Up a Windows Home Server Website."
IP Security Monitor	N/A	Enables you to monitor Internet Protocol (IP) security settings.
IP Security Policy Management	N/A	Enables you to create IP Security (IPSec) policies.
Link to Web Address	N/A	Adds a node that displays the contents of a specified web page.
Local Users and Groups	`lusrmgr.msc`	Enables you to add, modify, and delete user accounts. See Chapter 2, "Setting Up and Working with User Accounts."
Performance Logs and Alerts	`perfmon.msc`	Enables you to monitor one or more performance counters. See Chapter 10.
Remote Desktops	`tsmmc.msc`	Enables you to create Remote Desktop connections to network clients.
Removable Storage Management	`ntmsmgr.msc`	Enables you to manage removable media.
Resultant Set of Policy	`rsop.msc`	Shows the applied group policies for the current user.

TABLE 20.2   The Default Windows Home Server Snap-Ins (*continued*)

Snap-In	File	Description
Routing and Remote Access	`rrasmgmt.msc`	Enables you to configure Windows Home Server to accept remote dial-up or virtual private network connections.
Security Configuration and Analysis	N/A	Enables you to open an existing security database, or build a new security database based on a security template you create using the Security Templates snap-in.
Security Templates	N/A	Enables you to create a security template where you enable and configure one or more security-related policies.
Services	`services.msc`	Enables you to start, stop, enable, and disable services. See "Controlling Services," later in this chapter.
Shared Folders	`fsmgmt.msc`	Enables you to monitor activity on the Windows Home Server shared folder. See Chapter 10.
Telephony	`tapimgmt.msc`	Displays the current status of the telephony hardware on your system.
Terminal Services Configuration	`tscc.msc`	Enables you to configure policies for remote connection over Terminal Services.
Wireless Monitor	N/A	Enables you to monitor wireless connections to the home server.
WMI Control	`wmimgmt.msc`	Enables you to configure properties related to Windows Management Instrumentation. See Chapter 21, "Scripting Windows Home Server."

Launching the MMC

To get the MMC onscreen, you have two choices:

▶ To start with a blank console, select Start, Run to open the Run dialog box, type
  mmc, and then click OK.

▶ To start with an existing snap-in, select Start, Run to open the Run dialog box, type
  the name of the .msc file you want to load (see Table 20.2), and then click OK.

Figure 20.14 shows a blank MMC window. I show you how to add snap-ins to the console
in the next section.

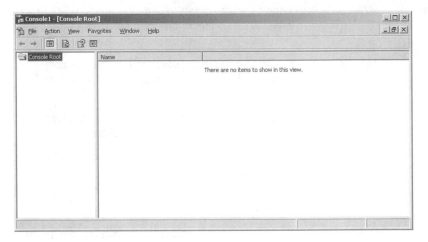

FIGURE 20.14   The Microsoft Management Console ready for customizing.

Adding a Snap-In

You start building your console file by adding one or more snap-ins to the console root,
which is the top-level MMC container. (Even if you loaded the MMC by launching an existing snap-in, you can still add more snap-ins to the console.) Here are the steps to follow:

1. Select File, Add/Remove Snap-In (or press Ctrl+M). The MMC displays the
   Add/Remove Snap-In dialog box.

2. Click Add. The MMC opens the Add Standalone Snap-In dialog box.

3. Select the snap-in you want to use and then click Add.

TIP

You can help organize your snap-ins by adding subfolders to the console root. In the list
of snap-ins, select Folder and then click Add. When you return to the MMC, right-click
the new subfolder and then click Rename to give the subfolder a useful name. To add a
snap-in inside this subfolder, select File, Add/Remove Snap-In (or press Ctrl+M) to open
the Add/Remove Snap-In dialog box, and then choose the subfolder in the Snap-Ins Will
Be Added To list. See Figure 20.16, later in this chapter, for some example subfolders.

---

4. If the snap-in can work with remote computers, you see a dialog box similar to the one shown in Figure 20.15. To have the snap-in manage a remote machine, select Another Computer, type the computer name in the text box, and then click Finish.

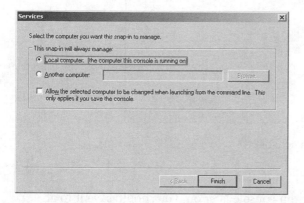

FIGURE 20.15   Some snap-ins can manage remote computers as well as the local machine.

5. Repeat steps 3 and 4 to add other snap-ins to the console.
6. Click Close to return to the Add/Remove Snap-In dialog box, which displays a list of the snap-ins you added.
7. Click OK.

Figure 20.16 shows the MMC with a custom console consisting of several snap-ins and subfolders.

NOTE

In Figure 20.16, the items in the Web Pages subfolder are based on the Link to Web Address snap-in, which is a special snap-in that displays the current version of whatever web page you specify. When you add the snap-in, the MMC runs the Link to Web Address Wizard. Type the web page address (either an Internet URL or a path to a local or network page), click Next, type a name for the snap-in, and then click Finish.

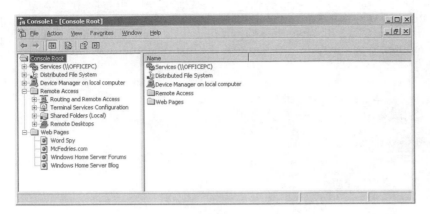

FIGURE 20.16   The MMC with a custom console.

Saving a Console

If you think you want to reuse your custom console later on, you should save it to an
.msc file. Here are the steps to follow:

1. Select File, Save (or press Ctrl+S) to open the Save As dialog box.
2. Type a filename for the console.
3. Select a location for the console file.

TIP

By default, MMC assumes that you want to save your console file in the Administrative
Tools folder. This enables you to launch the console from the Start menu. (Select Start,
All Programs, Administrative Tools, and then click the console name.) However, if you
want to be able to launch your console file from the Run dialog box, you should save it
in the %SystemRoot%\System32 folder, along with the predefined snap-ins.

---

4. Click Save.

NOTE

To make changes to a custom taskpad view, right-click the snap-in and then click Edit
Taskbar View.

Creating a Custom Taskpad View

A taskpad view is a custom configuration of the MMC results (right) pane for a given snap-in. By default, the results pane shows a list of the snap-in's contents—for example, the list of categories and devices in the Device Manager snap-in and the list of installed services in the Services snap-in. However, you can customize this view with one or more tasks that run commands defined by the snap-in, or any program or script that you specify. You can also control the size of the list, whether the list is displayed horizontally or vertically in the results pane, and more.

Here are the steps to follow to create a custom taskpad view:

1. Select a snap-in in the tree pane, as follows:

    ▶ If you want to apply the taskpad view to a specific snap-in, select that snap-in.

    ▶ If you want to apply the taskpad view to a group of snap-ins that use the same snap-in type, specify one snap-in from the group. For example, if you want to customize all the folders, select any folder (such as the Console Root folder); similarly, if you want to customize all the Link to Web Address snap-ins, select one of them.

2. Select Action, New Taskpad View to launch the New Taskpad View Wizard.

3. Click Next to open the Taskpad Style dialog box, shown in Figure 20.17.

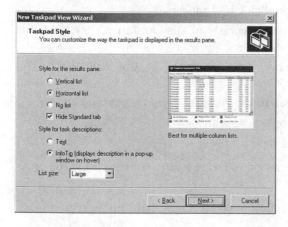

FIGURE 20.17   Use the New Taskpad View Wizard to create your custom taskpad view.

4. Use the following controls to set up the style of taskpad you want:

   ▶ **Style for Results Pane**—Select an option for displaying the snap-in's results: Vertical List (this is best for lists with a large number of items), Horizontal List (this is best for web pages or lists with a large number of columns), or No List (choose this option if you want only tasks to appear in the results pane).

   ▶ **Hide Standard Tab**—After you create the new taskpad view, the MMC displays two tabs in the results pane: The Extended tab shows your custom taskpad view, and the Standard tab shows the default view. To keep the option of displaying the default view, deactivate the Hide Standard Tab dialog box.

   ▶ **Style for Task Descriptions**—When you add descriptions for your tasks later on, you can have the MMC display each description either as text below the task link or as an InfoTip that appears when you hover the mouse over the task link.

   ▶ **List Size**—Choose the size of the list: Small (good if you add lots of tasks), Medium (this is the default), or Large (good if you have few or no tasks).

5. Click Next. The Taskpad Reuse dialog box appears.

6. The wizard assumes that you want to apply the new taskpad view to all snap-ins of the same type. If you only want to apply the taskpad view to the current snap-in, select the Selected Tree Item option.

7. Click Next. The Name and Description dialog box appears.

8. Type a name and optional description for the taskpad view, and then click Next. The final wizard dialog box appears.

9. If you don't want to add tasks to the new view, deactivate the Add New Tasks to This Taskpad After the Wizard Closes check box.

10. Click Finish. If you elected to add tasks to the view, the New Task Wizard appears.

11. Click Next. The Command Type dialog box appears.

12. Select one of the following command types:

    ▶ **Menu Command**—Select this option to create a task that runs an MMC or snap-in menu command.

    ▶ **Shell Command**—Select this option to create a task that runs a program, script, or batch file.

    ▶ **Navigation**—Select this option to create a task that takes you to another snap-in that's in your MMC Favorites list.

NOTE

To add a snap-in to the MMC Favorites list, select the snap-in in the tree pane and then select Favorites, Add to Favorites.

13. Click Next.

14. How you proceed from here depends on the command type you selected in step 12:

> **Menu Command**—In the Menu Command dialog box, first select an item from the Command Source list. Choose Item Listed in the Results Pane to apply the command to whatever item is currently selected in the results pane; choose Node in the Tree to select a command based on an item in the MMC tree pane.

> **Shell Command**—In the Command Line dialog box, use the Command text box to specify the path to the program executable, script, or batch file that you want the task to run. You can also specify startup Parameters, the Start In folder, and a Run window type.

> **Navigation**—In the Navigation dialog box, select the items from the MMC Favorites list.

15. Click Next. The Name and Description dialog box appears.

16. Edit the task name and description, and then click Next. The Task Icon dialog box appears, as shown in Figure 20.18.

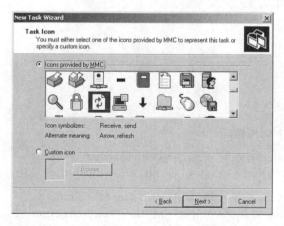

FIGURE 20.18   Use the Task Icon dialog box to choose an icon to display with your task.

17. Click Next. The final New Task Wizard dialog box appears.

18. If you want to add more tasks, activate the When I Click Finish, Run This Wizard Again check box.

19. Click Finish.

20. If you elected to add more tasks, repeat steps 11–19, as needed.

Figure 20.19 shows the MMC with a custom taskpad view applied to a Link to Web Address snap-in.

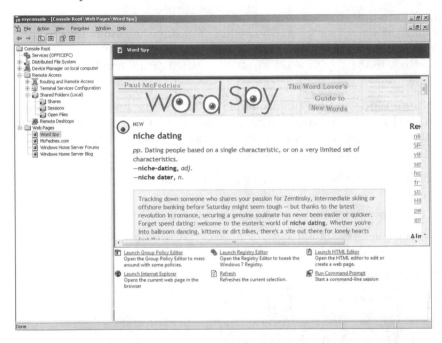

FIGURE 20.19   A custom taskpad view.

Controlling Snap-Ins with Group Policies

If you share Windows Home Server with other people, you can control which snap-ins they're allowed to use, and you can even prevent users from adding snap-ins to the MMC.

The latter is the simpler of the two options, so let's begin with that. The MMC has an *author mode* that enables you to add snap-ins to it. If you prevent the MMC from entering author mode, you prevent users from adding snap-ins. You can do this using a group policy. Note, too, that this policy also prevents users from entering author mode for those snap-ins that can be opened directly (from the Run dialog box, from the command line, from Administrative Tools, and so on). Here are the steps to follow:

1. Open the Group Policy Object Editor window, as described earlier in this chapter.
2. Navigate to the User Configuration, Administrative Templates, Windows Components, Microsoft Management Console branch.
3. Double-click the Restrict the User from Entering Author Mode policy.
4. Activate the Enabled option.
5. Click OK.

Rather than blocking off the MMC entirely, you might prefer to allow users access only to specific snap-ins. Here are the steps to follow:

1. Open the Group Policy Object Editor window, as described earlier in this chapter.
2. Navigate to the User Configuration, Administrative Templates, Windows Components, Microsoft Management Console branch.
3. Double-click the Restrict Users to the Explicitly Permitted List of Snap-Ins policy.
4. Activate the Enabled option.
5. Click OK.
6. Navigate to the User Configuration, Administrative Templates, Windows Components, Microsoft Management Console, Restricted/Permitted Snap-Ins branch.
7. Double-click a snap-in that you want users to access.
8. Activate the Enabled option.
9. Click OK.
10. Repeat steps 7–9 for each snap-in that you want users to access.

Controlling Services

System services are background routines that enable the system to perform tasks such as logging on to the network, managing disks, collecting performance data, and writing event logs. Windows Home Server comes with more than 100 installed services, including the following that are specific to Windows Home Server:

Drive Extender Migrator Service	This service handles Windows Home Server's folder duplication chores. See Chapter 5, "Setting Up and Using Home Server Storage," for the details on duplication.

▶ **SEE** "Safety: Using Duplication to Ensure No Data Is Lost," **P. 128**.

Windows Home Server Archiver	This service archives the server configuration.

| Windows Home Server Computer Backup | This service controls Windows Home Server's backup and restore features. See Chapter 9 "Backing Up and Restoring Network Computers," for information on the backup technology in Windows Home Server. |

▶ **SEE** "Understanding Windows Home Server's Backup Technology," **P. 240**.

| Windows Home Server Drive Letter Service | This service manages the drive letters generated by the Storage Manager service. |
| Windows Home Server Port Forwarding | This service connects with your UPnP router to configure port forwarding settings that enable remote users to connect to the Remote Access pages. See Chapter 7, "Making Connections to Network Computers." |

▶ **SEE** "Letting Windows Home Server Configure the Router," **P. 195**.

| Windows Home Server Storage Manager | This service manages the Windows Home Server storage features. I discuss Windows Home Server storage in Chapter 5. |

▶ **SEE** "Understanding Windows Home Server Storage," **P. 125**.

| Windows Home Server Transport Service | This service manages the connection—the *transport channel*—between Windows Home Server and each computer that has the Connector software installed. For example, this service is responsible for managing the network health icon on each client. |
| Windows Live Custom Domains Service | This service configures a Windows Live subdomain that you can use to connect to the Remote Access pages over the Internet. See Chapter 7 for the details. |

▶ **SEE** "Obtaining a Domain Name from Microsoft," **P. 199**.

Services usually operate behind the scenes. However, you may need to pause, stop, and start services, as well as configure how a service loads at startup. The next few sections show you the various methods you can use to control services.

Controlling Services with the Services Snap-In

The standard interface for the Windows Home Server services is the Services snap-in, which you can load by using any of the following techniques:

▶ Select Start, Control Panel, Administrative Tools, Services.

▶ Select Start, right-click My Computer, click Manage, and then select the Services and Applications, Services branch.

▶ Select Start, Run to open the Run dialog box, type `services.msc`, and click OK.

The Services snap-in that appears displays a list of the installed services, and for each service, it displays the name of the service and a brief description, the current status of the service (Started, Paused, or blank for a stopped service), the service's startup type (such as Automatic or Manual), and the name of the system account that the service uses to log on at startup. When you select a service, the Extended tab of the taskpad view shows the service name and description and offers links to control the service status (such as Start, Stop, or Restart). Figure 20.20 shows an example.

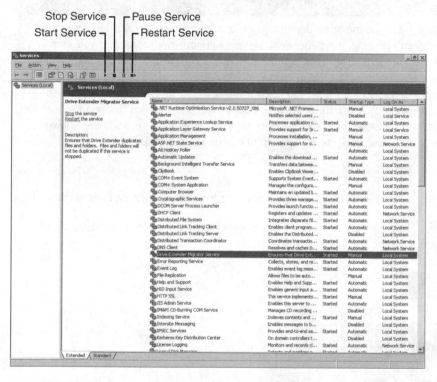

FIGURE 20.20   You can use the Services snap-in to control the Windows Home Server services.

To change the status of a service, select it and then use one of the following techniques:

▶ To start a stopped service, either click the Start link in the taskpad or click the Start Service toolbar button.

▶ To stop a running service, either click the Stop link in the taskpad or click the Stop Service toolbar button.

▶ To pause a running service, either click the Pause link in the taskpad or click the Start Service toolbar button. (Note that only a few services support the Pause task.)

▶ To resume a paused service, either click the Restart link in the taskpad or click the Restart Service toolbar button.

NOTE

If a service is started but it has no Stop link and the Stop toolbar button is disabled, it means the service is essential to Windows Home Server and can't be stopped. Examples of essential services include Event Log, Plug and Play, Remote Procedure Call (RPC), SBCore Service, and Security Accounts Manager.

CAUTION

It's possible that a service might be dependent on one or more other services, and if those services aren't running, the dependent service will not work properly. If you stop a service that has dependent services, Windows Home Server also stops the dependents. However, when you restart the main service, Windows Home Server may not start the dependent services as well. You need to start those services by hand. To see which services depend on a particular service, double-click that service to open its property sheet, and then display the Dependencies tab. Dependent services are shown in a list under "The Following System Components Depend on This Service."

To change the way a service starts when you boot Windows Home Server, follow these steps:

1. Double-click the service you want to work with to open its property sheet. Figure 20.21 shows an example.

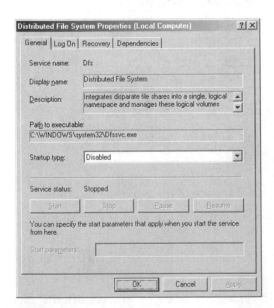

FIGURE 20.21   You use a service's property sheet to control its startup type.

2. Use the Startup Type list to select one of the following types:

Automatic	The service starts automatically when Windows Home Server boots. The service is started before the Welcome to Windows dialog box appears.
Automatic (Delayed Start)	The service starts automatically when Windows Home Server boots. The service does not start until you log on.
Manual	The service does not start when Windows Home Server boots. You must start the service yourself.
Disabled	The service does not start when Windows Home Server boots, and you can't start the service manually.

3. Click OK.

NOTE

If the Startup Type list is disabled, it means the service is essential to Windows Home Server and must be started automatically when the system boots.

NOTE

All the services that Windows Home Server requires to perform its core functions use the Automatic startup type. This explains how Windows Home Server can run on a headless device. When you turn on the headless device, the "boot" only goes as far as the Welcome to Windows prompt. However, all the essential services are started by that point, so Windows Home Server can perform its core duties without the need for a local logon.

TIP

If you make changes to service startup types and you find that your system is unstable or causing problems, the best thing to do is return each service to its default startup type. If you're not sure of the default for a service, open the Services snap-in, select Help, Help Topics, and then select the Services, Concepts, Default Settings for Services branch.

Controlling Services at the Command Prompt

If you regularly stop and start certain services, loading the Services snap-in and manually stopping and then restarting each service can be time-consuming. A better method is to take advantage of the NET STOP and NET START command-line tools, which enable you to stop and start any service that isn't disabled. If a service can be paused and restarted, you can also use the NET PAUSE and NET CONTINUE commands to control the service. Each of these commands uses the same syntax:

```
NET STOP Service
NET START Service
NET PAUSE Service
NET CONTINUE Service
```

Service   The name of the service you want to control. Use the same value that appears in the Name column of the Services snap-in. If the name contains a space, surround the name with quotation marks.

Here are some examples:

```
net start Telephony
net stop "Distributed File System"
net pause "World Wide Web Publishing Service"
net continue "Windows Management Instrumentation"
```

You can combine multiple commands in a batch file to easily control several services with a single task.

TIP

To see a list of the currently running services, open a command-line session and enter the command net start without the Service parameter.

Controlling Services with a Script

If you want to automate service control, but you want to also control the startup type, you need to go beyond the command line and create scripts that manage your services. Windows Management Instrumentation (WMI) has a class called Win32_Service that represents a Windows service. You can return an instance of this class to work with a specific service on Windows Home Server. After you have the service object, you can query its current status with the State property; determine whether the service is running with the Started property; and return the service's startup type with the StartMode property. You can also change the service state using the StartService, StopService, PauseService, and ResumeService methods.

> ▶ **SEE** For details on WMI scripting, **see** "Programming the Windows Management Instrumentation Service," **P. 688**.

Listing 20.1 presents a script that uses most of these properties and methods.

NOTE

You can find this script on my website at www.mcfedries.com/ HomeServerUnleashed2E.

LISTING 20.1   A WMI Script That Toggles a Service's State Between Started and Stopped

```
Option Explicit
Dim strComputer, strServiceName, intReturn
Dim objWMI, objServices, objService
'
' Get the WMI service
'
strComputer = "localhost"
Set objWMI = GetObject("winmgmts:{impersonationLevel=impersonate}!\\" & _
    strComputer & "\root\cimv2")
'
' Specify the service name
'
strServiceName = "Distributed File System"
'
' Get the service instance
'
Set objServices = objWMI.ExecQuery("SELECT * FROM Win32_Service " & _
                "WHERE DisplayName = '" & strServiceName & "'")
For Each objService In objServices
    '
    ' Save the service name
    '
    strServiceName = objService.DisplayName
    '
    ' Is the service started?
    '
    If objService.Started Then
        '
        ' Can it be stopped?
        '
        If objService.AcceptStop Then
            '
            ' Attempt to stop the service
            '
            intReturn = objService.StopService
            '
            ' Check the return value
            '
            If intReturn <> 0 Then
                '
                ' Display the error message
                '
                    WScript.Echo "ERROR: The " & strServiceName & " service " & _
                        "failed to stop. The return code is " & intReturn
```

```
            Else
                '
                ' Display the current state
                '
                WScript.Echo "The " & strServiceName & " service is now " & _
                            objService.State
            End If
        Else
            '
            ' Display the error message
            '
            WScript.Echo "ERROR: The " & strServiceName & " service " & _
                        "cannot be stopped."
        End If
    Else
        '
        ' Attempt to start the service
        '
        intReturn = objService.StartService
        '
        ' Check the return value
        '
        If intReturn <> 0 Then
            '
            ' Display the error message
            '
            WScript.Echo "ERROR: The " & strServiceName & " service " & _
                        "failed to start. The return code is " & intReturn
        Else
            '
            ' Display the current state
            '
            WScript.Echo "The " & strServiceName & " service is now " & _
                        objService.State
        End If
    End If
Next
'
' Release the objects
'
Set objWMI = Nothing
Set objServices = Nothing
Set objService = Nothing
```

This script gets the WMI service object and uses its ExecQuery method to return an instance of the Win32_Service class by using the WHERE clause to look for a specific service name. That name was earlier stored in the strServiceName variable. In the For Each...Next loop, the script first checks to see if the service is currently started by checking its Started property:

▶ If the Started property returns True, the service is running, so we want to stop it. The script then checks the service's AcceptStop property, which returns False for essential Windows Home Server services that can't be stopped. In this case, the script returns an error message. If AcceptStop returns True, the script attempts to stop the service by running the StopService method.

▶ If the Started property returns False, the service is stopped, so we want to start it. The script attempts to start the service by running the StartService method.

The StopService and StartService methods generate the return codes shown in Table 20.3.

TABLE 20.3   Return Codes Generated by the StartService and StopService Methods

Return Code	Description	Return Code	Description
0	Success	13	Service dependency failure
1	Not supported	14	Service disabled
2	Access denied	15	Service logon failed
3	Dependent services running	16	Service marked for deletion
4	Invalid service control	17	Service no thread
5	Service cannot accept control	18	Status circular dependency
6	Service not active	19	Status—duplicate name
7	Service request timeout	20	Status—invalid name
8	Unknown failure	21	Status—invalid parameter
9	Path not found	22	Status—invalid service account
10	Service already stopped	23	Status—service exists
11	Service database locked	24	Service already paused
12	Service dependency deleted		

For both the StopService and StartService methods, the script stores the return code in the intReturn variable and then checks to see if it's a number other than 0. If so, the script displays an error message that includes the return code; otherwise, the script displays the new state of the service (as given by the State property).

Setting Up a Fax Server

Perhaps I'm dating myself, but I still remember when the fax machine (or the *facsimile machine*, as it was called back then) was the hottest thing around—the new kid on the telecommunications block. How amazing it seemed that we could send a letter or memo or even a picture through the phone lines and have it emerge seconds later across town or even across the country. Sure, the fax that came slithering out the other end was a little fuzzier than the original, and certainly a lot slimier, but it sure beat using the post office.

The faxing fad has come and gone, and with so many other ways to share documents nowadays (email, the web, SharePoint sites, and so on), faxing is becoming increasingly rare. But reports of the demise of the fax have been greatly exaggerated, which is why Windows Home Server continues to provide fax services.

Most Windows clients come with some faxing capabilities built in, but Windows Home Server does them one better by enabling you to share a fax with the network and to route incoming faxes to an email address. The rest of this chapter shows you how to configure the Fax service and how to use it to send and receive faxes. Note that I'm assuming here that your Windows Home Server machine either comes with a fax modem built in or you've connected an external fax modem. If you're thinking about purchasing a fax modem for use with Windows Home Server, be sure to get one that's compatible with Windows Server 2003.

Installing the Fax Service

If you want to get into the fax fast lane, look no further than the Fax service. If you don't have this service on your system, follow these steps to install it:

1. Select Start, Control Panel, Add or Remove Programs.
2. Click Add/Remove Windows Components to launch the Windows Components Wizard.
3. Activate the Fax Services check box.
4. Click Next. The wizard asks whether you want to share the fax printer.
5. Select the Share the Fax Printer option, and then click Next.
6. If you're prompted to insert a disc, insert your Windows Home Server DVD and then click OK when the DVD is loaded. The wizard installs the fax services.
7. Click Finish.

Starting the Fax Console

You begin your faxing duties at the Fax Console, which you open by selecting Start, All Programs, Accessories, Communications, Fax, Fax Console. (Alternatively, select Start Printers and Faxes. In the Printers and Faxes window, double-click the Fax icon.) The first time you do this, the Fax Configuration Wizard appears. The next section takes you through this wizard's steps.

Configuring the Fax Service

Follow these steps to configure the Fax service:

1. Select Start, All Programs, Accessories, Communications, Fax, Fax Console. The Fax Configuration Wizard appears.

2. Click Next. The wizard displays the Sender Information dialog box.

3. Use this dialog box to enter your name, fax number, address, and so on. This information will be added automatically to your fax cover pages, so only enter data that you want your fax recipients to see.

4. Click Next. You now see the Select Device for Sending Faxes dialog box.

NOTE

Instead of the Select Device for Sending Faxes dialog box, you might see the final wizard dialog box. When you click Finish, a Windows Security Alert dialog box appears, letting you know that Windows Home Server is blocking the Fax Console program. If this happens, click Unblock. In the Fax Console window, select Tools, Configure Fax to restart the Fax Configuration Wizard. If you see the Location Information dialog box, select your country, type your area code, click OK, and then click OK again.

5. Select the device you want to use for sending faxes, and then click Next. The wizard now prompts you for your *Transmitting Subscriber Identification,* or *TSID.* Type the text (such as your name or your company name) and click Next. The wizard displays the Select Devices for Receiving Faxes dialog box.

NOTE

Windows Home Server assigns a name to your fax machine. This is known in the trade as the TSID—Transmitting Subscriber Identification (or sometimes Transmitting Station Identifier). When the other person receives your fax, your TSID is displayed at the top of each page. If the other person is receiving on a computer, the TSID appears in the TSID line (or some similar field, depending on the program the recipient is using). Unfortunately, the default TSID in Windows Home Server is *Fax,* which redefines the word *uninspiring.* To fix this, edit the TSID as described in step 4. For example, it's common to change it to a name—such as your company name, your department name, or your own name—followed by your fax number.

6. This dialog box has the following controls (click Next when you've made your choices):

Select Devices for Receiving Faxes	This is a list of the fax/modems installed on your computer. If you have more than one, use the list to choose the one you want to perform the fax reception chores.

Manual Answer	Activate this option to answer incoming calls manually (as described in the "Answering Calls Manually" section, later in this chapter).
Automatically Answer After *X* Rings	Activate this option to have the Fax service answer incoming calls automatically (as described in the "Answering Calls Automatically" section, later in this chapter).

7. If you elected to receive faxes, the wizard asks you for your *Called Subscriber Identification*, or *CSID*. This identifies your computer to the fax sender. This isn't as important as the TSID, so enter whatever you like and click Next.

8. If you'll be receiving faxes, the wizard now wonders what you want to do with incoming faxes (click Next when you're done):

Print It On	Activate this check box to have Windows Home Server automatically print any received fax. Use the list that becomes activated to choose the printer you want to use.
Store a Copy in a Folder	Activate this check box to store a second copy of each fax in the folder that you specify. The original copy of the fax is saved in the Fax Console, which you learn about in the next section.

TIP

If you want others to have access to the incoming faxes, create a subfolder called, say, Faxes in Windows Home Server's Public shared folder. For this to work, you also need to add permissions for the Network Service, which is the system account that the Fax service uses. Right-click the new Faxes folder, click Sharing and Security, and then display the Security tab. Click Add, type **Network Service** in the Select Users or Groups dialog box, and then click OK to return to the Security tab. Click Network Service and click Full Control under the Allow column. Click OK. You can now specify the *Server*\Public\Faxes folder in the Store a Copy in a Folder text box.

---

9. Click Finish.

Examining the Fax Console

When the wizard exits, you end up with the Fax Console window onscreen, as shown in Figure 20.22. The Fax Console is where you'll do your fax work in Windows Home Server.

The Fax Console includes four folders that store fax-related things:

Incoming	This folder displays information about the fax that is currently being received. For example, during fax reception, the Status column displays In progress and the Extended Status column displays Answered and then Receiving.

Inbox   This folder stores the incoming faxes that were received successfully. Note that the TSID column shows the name or phone number of the sender.

Outbox   This folder stores data about the fax that is currently being sent. For example, during the send, the Status column displays In progress and the Extended Status column displays Transmitting.

Sent Items   This folder stores a copy of the faxes that you have sent successfully.

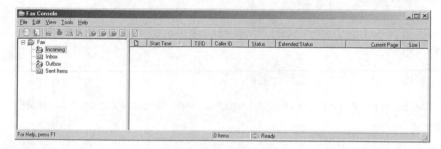

FIGURE 20.22   The Fax Console is your home base for Windows Home Server faxing.

Sending a Fax

To fax something to a friend or colleague (or, heck, even a total stranger), Windows Home Server gives you two ways to proceed:

▶ You can fax a simple note by sending just a cover page.

▶ You can fax a more complex document by sending it to the Windows Home Server fax "printer."

Sending a Cover Page Fax

Let's start with the simple cover page route. This is handled by the Send Fax Wizard, which you can launch by using any of the following methods:

▶ In the Fax Console, select File, Send a Fax.

▶ From the Printers and Faxes window, click the task pane's Send a Fax link. Alternatively, select File, Send Fax.

▶ Select Start, All Programs, Accessories, Communications, Fax, Send a Fax.

Here's what happens when the Send Fax Wizard arrives on the scene:

1. The initial dialog box isn't much use, so just click Next to continue. The Send Fax Wizard displays the Recipient Information dialog box, shown partially completed in Figure 20.23.

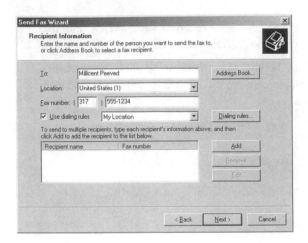

FIGURE 20.23   The Send Fax Wizard takes you through the steps necessary to send a simple cover page fax.

2. Fill in the following fields:

TIP

If the recipient is in your Address Book and you have the Fax field filled in (in either the Business or the Home tab), click Address Book, select the recipient, click To, and then click OK. The Send Fax Wizard adds the person's name and fax number to the recipient list.

To	Type the name of the fax recipient.
Location	If you're calling long distance and you need to start the dialing with a number other than 1, activate the Use Dialing Rules check box and then use the Location list to select the country code for the fax recipient's phone number.
Fax Number	Use these two text boxes to enter the area code (if necessary) and phone number for the fax recipient. Note that you can't enter the area code unless you activate the Use Dialing Rules check box.

3. Click Add. (This isn't necessary if you're sending the fax to a single recipient or if you inserted the recipient via the Address Book.)

4. If you want to send the fax to several people, repeat steps 2 and 3 as necessary.

5. When you're ready to move on, click Next. The Preparing the Cover Page dialog box appears.

6. Fill in the following fields (click Next when you're done):

Cover Page Template	Select the cover page you want to use.
Subject Line	Type the subject of the fax.
Note	Type your cover page message.

7. The wizard now asks you for the time you want the fax sent:

Now	Sends the fax right away.
When Discount Rates Apply	Sends the fax as soon as possible after your discount rates begin.
Specific Time in the Next 24 Hours	Sends the fax at the specified time.

8. Set the fax priority to High, Normal, or Low, and then click Next. The Delivery Notification dialog box appears.

9. If you want the Fax service to send you an email message telling you the status of the sent fax, select the E-Mail Message option and enter your email address. You can also activate the Attach Copy of Sent Fax to include the fax along with the message. Click Next.

10. In the final wizard dialog box, click Preview Fax to check out the fax in the Windows Picture and Fax Viewer.

11. When you're ready to send the fax, click Finish. The Fax Monitor window replaces the wizard so that you can see what's happening with the fax.

Faxing from an Application

The other (and probably more common) method of sending a fax is to send a document directly from an application. You don't need applications with special features to do this, either. That's because when you install the Fax service, it adds a new printer driver to Windows Home Server. This printer driver, however, doesn't send a document to the printer. Instead, it renders the document as a fax and sends it to your modem.

To try this, follow these steps:

1. Create the document that you want to send.

2. Select the program's File, Print command to get to the Print dialog box.

3. Select Fax as the printer and then click Print. The Send Fax Wizard appears.

4. Follow the steps outlined in the previous section to set the fax options. With this method, you don't have to bother with a cover page. If you'd still like to include one, activate the Select a Cover Page Template with the Following Information check box when you get to the Preparing the Cover Page dialog box.

Connecting to the Shared Fax Printer

When you configured the Fax service earlier, you shared the Windows Home Server Fax printer with the network. This means that anyone else on the network can use the Fax printer to send a fax. Here are the steps clients must follow to connect to this printer:

1. Double-click the Shared Folders on *Server* icon on the desktop. (Alternatively, open Windows Explorer and navigate to the *Server* folder.)

2. Right-click the Fax printer and click Connect.

3. In Windows XP, you're asked to confirm. Click Yes.

Windows connects to the Fax printer and adds it to your list of printers. In the Print dialog box of any local application, use the Fax on *SERVER* printer to fax a document.

Receiving Faxes

This section explains how the Fax service handles incoming faxes and shows you how to view those faxes when they're sitting in your Inbox.

Specifying Receive Options

Before getting to the specifics of receiving a fax, let's take a quick look at the various options that the Fax service provides for receiving. To see these options, follow these steps:

1. In the Fax Console, select Tools, Fax Service Manager to display the Fax Service Manager snap-in.

2. Open the Device and Providers, Devices branch.

3. Right-click your modem and then click Properties. The modem's property sheet appears.

4. The General tab has the following options:

Receive Faxes	Activate this check box if you want to receive faxes on Windows Home Server.
CSID	Use this text box to type your Called Subscriber Identification.
Automatic Answer	Activate this option to have the Fax service answer incoming calls automatically (as described later in the "Answering Calls Automatically" section).
Rings Before Answering	Specify the number of rings after which you want Windows Home Server to answer an incoming call.
Manual Answer	Activate this option to answer incoming calls manually (as described later in the "Answering Calls Manually" section).

Answering Calls Automatically

Enabling the Automatic Answer option is the easiest way to handle incoming calls. In this mode, the Fax service constantly polls the modem's serial port for calls. When it detects a call coming in, it waits for whatever number of rings you specified (which can be as few as one ring or as many as 99) and then leaps into action. Without prodding from you, it answers the phone and immediately starts conversing with the remote fax machine. To follow the progress of the transfer, in the Fax Console, select Tools, Fax Monitor to open the Fax Monitor window, as shown in Figure 20.24.

TIP

If you find the Fax service's sounds (such as the ringing associated with an incoming call) annoying, you can disable them. In the Fax Console, select Tools, Fax Printer Configuration, and then display the Tracking tab. Click Configure Sound Settings, and then deactivate the check boxes for each sound you want to silence.

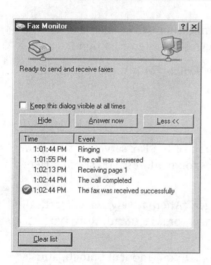

FIGURE 20.24   You can display the Fax Monitor to follow the progress of an incoming fax.

Answering Calls Manually

If you work with the Fax service in Manual Answer mode, when a call comes in, you hear a ringing tone, and the taskbar's notification area pops up a message that says The line is ringing. Click that message to receive the fax. If you happen to have the Fax Monitor open already, click the Receive Now toolbar button, or select File, Receive a Fax Now.

This mode is ideal if you receive both voice calls and fax calls on the same phone line. Here's the basic procedure you need to follow for incoming calls:

1. When the phone rings, pick up the receiver.

2. If you hear a series of tones, you know that a fax is on its way. In this case, click the notification message or the Answer Now button, as described earlier.

3. The Fax service initializes the modem to handle the call. Wait until the Fax service reports Receiving fax in the Fax Monitor window and then hang up the receiver. If you hang up before you see this message, you disconnect the call.

Working with Received Faxes

Depending on the size of the fax transmission, the Fax service takes from a few seconds to a few minutes to process the data. Eventually, though, your fax appears in the Inbox. From there, you can perform the following chores:

▶ **Read the fax**—Double-click the fax in the Fax Console's Inbox folder (or select the fax and then select File, View). This launches the Windows Picture and Fax Viewer, which displays your fax and enables you to annotate it.

▶ **Print the fax**—Select the fax and then select File, Print.

▶ **Save the fax as an image**—Select the fax and then select File, Save As. Use the Save As dialog box to choose a name and location for the file, and then click Save. Note that the fax is saved as a TIF image.

▶ **Email the fax as an attachment**—Select the fax and then select File, Mail To. Use the New Message window to set up the email message, and then click Send.

▶ **Delete the fax**—Select the fax and then select File, Delete (or just press the Delete key).

Routing a Received Fax

One of the nice features in Windows Home Server's version of the Fax service is that you can configure it to automatically route all incoming faxes to an address you specify. Here are the steps to follow to set this up:

1. In the Fax Console, select Tools, Fax Service Manager. (Alternatively, select Start, All Programs, Communications, Fax, Fax Service Manager, or select Start, Run, type fxsadmin.msc, and click OK.)

2. Open the Devices and Providers, Devices branch, open your modem branch, and then click Incoming Methods. You see three methods in the list:

Route Through E-Mail	This is the method we'll use here to send incoming faxes to an email address, as described in the rest of the steps in this section.
Store in a Folder	Use this method to have Windows Home Server store a second copy of each fax in the folder that you specify. (You may have done this earlier; see "Configuring the Fax Service.") To change the folder, double-click this method and use the text box in the Store in Folder tab.
Print	Use this method to have Windows Home Server automatically print any received fax. Double-click this method, display the Print tab, and use the Printer Name list to choose the printer you want to use.

3. Double-click the Route Through E-Mail method.

4. Display the E-Mail tab, type an address in the Mail To text box, and then click OK.

5. In the tree pane, right-click the Fax (Local) item at the top of the tree, and then click Properties.

6. Display the Receipts tab, shown completed in Figure 20.25.

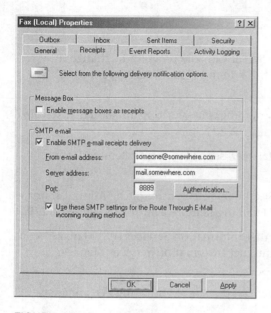

FIGURE 20.25   Use the Receipts tab to configure the routing of incoming faxes to an email address.

7. Activate the Enable SMTP E-Mail Receipts Delivery check box.

8. Fill in the fields for From E-Mail Address and the Server Address, which is the domain name of your ISP's or email host's SMTP server.

9. If your ISP or host requires you to use a port other than 25 for outgoing mail, enter that port number in the Port text box.

10. If your ISP or host requires authentication for outgoing mail, click Authentication, activate the Basic Authentication option, click Credentials, and then enter the username and password (twice) that you use to authenticate outgoing mail. (On most systems, this is the same as the login credentials you use for incoming mail.) Click OK until you return to the Microsoft Fax Service Manager.

11. Right-click the Route Through E-Mail method, and then click Enable.

12. Activate the Use These SMTP Settings for the Route Through E-Mail Incoming Routing Method check box.

13. Click OK.

Now when a fax comes in, the Fax service will use the address you specified in step 9 to send the fax as an attachment to the address you specified in step 4.

From Here

▶ To learn how to use the Windows Home Server Console program to change the Administrator password, **see** "Changing the Windows Home Server Password," **P. 106**.

▶ To learn how to use group policies to set up programs or scripts to launch at startup, **see** "Launching Items Using Group Policies," **P. 122**.

▶ For details on using Terminal Services Manager, **see** "Monitoring Remote Desktop Sessions," **P. 275**.

▶ To learn about a group policy that enables the remote control of the Administrator's desktop on Windows Home Server, **see** "Enabling Remote Control Sessions," **P. 279**.

▶ For details on using Control Panel's Internet Information Services (IIS) Manager icon, **see** "Viewing the Default Website with Internet Information Services Manager," **P. 322**.

▶ For a good example of what Task Manager can do, **see** "Monitoring Performance with Task Manager," **P. 392**.

▶ To learn how to add a shortcut for Internet Explorer to the Windows Home Server Start menu, **see** "Adding the Internet and E-Mail Icons," **P. 463**.

▶ For details on configuring taskbar toolbars, **see** "Setting Some Taskbar Toolbar Options," **P. 470**.

▶ To see descriptions of the group policies related to customizing the Start menu and taskbar, **see** "Modifying the Start Menu and Taskbar with Group Policies," **P. 475**.

Scripting Windows Home Server

You've seen throughout this book that unleashing the power of Windows Home Server involves understanding the technology behind Windows Home Server, getting in-depth explanations of the standard tools and features, and going behind the scenes to explore Windows Home Server's vast bounty of hidden tools, programs, and settings.

I've also helped you unlock Windows Home Server's potential by providing you with sample scripts that automate routine or cumbersome tasks and take advantage of the power that only scripting and programming can provide. This isn't a programming book, so I've tried not to overwhelm you with too many scripts. However, there have been quite a few, as this incomplete list shows:

▶ In Chapter 2, "Setting Up and Working with User Accounts," I showed you a script that disabled all users at once, which might come in handy if you're performing server maintenance.

   ▶ **SEE** "Disabling All User Accounts with a Script," **P. 52**.

▶ In Chapter 11, "Implementing Windows Home Server Security," you saw a script that extracted specific security events from the Windows Home Server Security events log.

   ▶ **SEE** "Viewing Auditing Events with a Script," **P. 293**.

▶ In Chapter 15, "Maintaining Windows Home Server," I showed you a script that displayed the current Windows Home Server uptime.

> ▶ **SEE** "Displaying Uptime with a Script," **P. 429**.

▶ Chapter 15 also provided a script for checking the free space on the Windows Home Server system drive.

> ▶ **SEE** "Checking Free Disk Space on the System Drive," **P. 437**.

▶ Finally, Chapter 15 presented a script that exported Windows Home Server event log items to a database.

> ▶ **SEE** "Exporting the Event Logs with a Script," **P. 451**.

If you're looking to automate a wider variety of tasks in Windows, you need to supplement your knowledge with scripts that can deal with the Registry, shortcuts, files, and network drives, and that can even interact with Windows programs via Automation. The secret to these powerful scripts is the *Windows Script Host* (*WSH*). This chapter introduces you to the Windows Script Host, shows you how to execute scripts, and runs through the various elements in the Windows Script Host object model.

Understanding Windows Script Host

As you might know, Internet Explorer is really just an empty container application that's designed to host different data formats, including ActiveX controls, various file formats (such as Microsoft Word documents and Microsoft Excel worksheets), and several ActiveX scripting engines. A *scripting engine* is a dynamic link library (DLL) that provides programmatic support for a particular scripting language. Internet Explorer supports two such scripting engines: VBScript (`VBScript.dll`) and JavaScript (`JSscript.dll`). This enables web programmers to write small programs—*scripts*—that interact with the user, control the browser, set cookies, open and close windows, and more. Although these scripting engines don't offer full-blown programmability (you can't compile scripts, for example), they do offer modern programming structures such as loops, conditionals, variables, objects, and more. In other words, they're a huge leap beyond what a mere batch file can do.

The Windows Script Host is also a container application, albeit a scaled-down application in that its only purpose in life is to host scripting engines. Right out of the box, the Windows Script Host supports both the VBScript and JavaScript engines. However, Microsoft designed the Windows Script Host to be a universal host that can support any ActiveX-based scripting engine. Therefore, third-party vendors also offer scripting engines for languages such as Perl, Tcl, and Rexx.

The key difference between Internet Explorer's script hosting and the Windows Script Host is the environment in which the scripts run. Internet Explorer scripts are web page-based, so they control and interact with either the web page or the web browser. The Windows Script Host runs scripts within the Windows Home Server shell or from the command prompt, so you use these scripts to control various aspects of Windows Home Server. Here's a sampling of the things you can do:

- ▶ Execute Windows programs.

- ▶ Create and modify shortcuts.

- ▶ Use Automation to connect and interact with Automation-enabled applications such as Microsoft Word, Outlook, and Internet Explorer.

- ▶ Read, add, and delete Registry keys and items.

- ▶ Access the VBScript and JavaScript object models, which give access to the file system, runtime error messages, and more.

- ▶ Use pop-up dialog boxes to display information to the user, and determine which button the user clicked to dismiss the dialog box.

- ▶ Read environment variables, which are system values that Windows Home Server keeps in memory, such as the folder into which Windows Home Server is installed— the %SystemRoot% environment variable—and the name of the computer—the %ComputerName% environment variable.

- ▶ Deal with network resources, including mapping and unmapping network drives, accessing user data (such as the username and user domain), and connecting and disconnecting network printers.

- ▶ Script the Windows Management Instrumentation (WMI) interface.

What about speed? After all, you wouldn't want to load something that's the size of Internet Explorer each time you need to run a simple script. That's not a problem because, as I've said, the Windows Script Host does nothing but host scripting engines, so it has much less memory overhead than Internet Explorer. That means that your scripts run quickly. For power users looking for a Windows-based batch language, the Windows Script Host is a welcome tool.

NOTE

This chapter does not teach you how to program in either VBScript or JavaScript and, in fact, assumes that you're already proficient in one or both of these languages. If you're looking for a programming tutorial, my *VBA for the Office 2007 System* (Que, 2007) is a good place to start. (VBScript is a subset of Visual Basic for Applications, or VBA.) For JavaScript, try my *Special Edition Using JavaScript* (Que, 2001).

Running Scripts

Scripts are simple text files that you create using Notepad or some other text editor. You can use a word processor such as WordPad to create scripts, but you must make sure that you save these files using the program's Text Only document type. For VBScript, a good alternative to Notepad is the editor that comes with either Visual Basic or any program that supports VBA (such as the Office suite). Just remember that VBScript is a subset of VBA (which is, in turn, a subset of Visual Basic), so it does not support all objects and features.

In a web page, you use the <script> tag to specify the scripting language you're using, as in this example:

```
<SCRIPT LANGUAGE="VBScript">
```

With the Windows Script Host, the script file's extension specifies the scripting language:

- For VBScript, save your text files using the .vbs extension (which is registered as the following file type: VBScript Script File).

- For JavaScript, use the .js extension (which is registered as the following file type: JScript Script File).

As described in the next three sections, you have three ways to run your scripts: by launching the script files directly, by using WSscript.exe, or by using CScript.exe.

Running Script Files Directly

The easiest way to run a script from within Windows is to launch the .vbs or .js file directly. That is, you either double-click the file in Windows Explorer or type the file's path and name in the Run dialog box. Note, however, that this technique does not work at the command prompt. For that, you need to use the CScript program described a bit later.

Using WScript for Windows-Based Scripts

The .vbs and .js file types have an open method that's associated with WScript (WScript.exe), which is the Windows-based front-end for the Windows Script Host. In other words, launching a script file named MyScript.vbs is equivalent to entering the following command in the Run dialog box:

```
wscript myscript.vbs
```

The WScript host also defines several parameters that you can use to control the way the script executes. Here's the full syntax:

```
WSCRIPT [filename] [arguments] [//B] [//D] [//E:engine] [//H:host] [//I]
➥[//Job:xxxx] [//S] [//T:ss] [//X]
```

filename   Specifies the filename, including the path of the script file, if necessary.

arguments   Specifies optional arguments required by the script. An *argument* is a data value that the script uses as part of its procedures or calculations.

//B	Runs the script in batch mode, which means script errors and Echo method output lines are suppressed. (I discuss the Echo method later in this chapter.)
//D	Enables Active Debugging. If an error occurs, the script is loaded into the Microsoft Script Debugger (if it's installed), and the offending statement is high-lighted.
//E:*engine*	Executes the script using the specified scripting *engine,* which is the scripting language to use when running the script.
//H:*host*	Specifies the default scripting host. For *host,* use either CScript or WScript.
//I	Runs the script in interactive mode, which displays script errors and Echo method output lines.
//Job:*id*	In a script file that contains multiple jobs, executes only the job with id attribute equal to *id.*
//S	Saves the specified WScript arguments as the default for the current user; uses the following Registry key to save the settings:

HKCU\Software\Microsoft\Windows Script Host\Settings

| //TT:*ss* | Specifies the maximum time in seconds (*ss)* that the script can run before it shuts down automatically. |
| //X | Executes the entire script in the Microsoft Script Debugger (if it's installed). |

For example, the following command runs MyScript.vbs in batch mode with a 60-second maximum execution time:

```
wscript myscript.vbs //B //TT:60
```

CREATING SCRIPT JOBS

A script *job* is a section of code that performs a specific task or set of tasks. Most script files contain a single job. However, it's possible to create a script file with multiple jobs. To do this, first surround the code for each job with the <script> and </script> tags, and then surround those with the <job> and </job> tags. In the <job> tag, include the id attribute and set it to a unique value that identifies the job. Finally, surround all the jobs with the <package> and </package> tags. Here's an example:

```
<package>
<job id="A">
<script language="VBScript">
    WScript.Echo "This is Job A."
```

```
    </script>
    </job>


    <job id="B">
    <script language="VBScript">
        WScript.Echo "This is Job B."
    </script>
    </job>
    </package>
Save the file using the .wsf (Windows Script File) extension.
```

NOTE

If you write a lot of scripts, the Microsoft Script Debugger is an excellent programming tool. If there's a problem with a script, the debugger can help you pinpoint its location. For example, the debugger enables you to step through the script's execution one statement at a time. If you don't have the Microsoft Script Debugger, you can download a copy from msdn.microsoft.com/en-us/library/ms532989(VS.85).aspx. (To install this program on Windows 7 and Vista, right-click the downloaded file and then click Run as Administrator.)

Using CScript for Command-Line Scripts

The Windows Script Host has a second host front-end application called CScript (CScript.exe), which enables you to run scripts from the command line. In its simplest form, you launch CScript and use the name of the script file (and its path, if required) as a parameter, as in this example:

```
cscript myscript.vbs
```

The Windows Script Host displays the following banner and then executes the script:

```
Microsoft (R) Windows Script Host Version 5.6 for Windows
Copyright (C) Microsoft Corporation 1996-2001. All rights reserved.
```

As with WScript, the CScript host has an extensive set of parameters you can specify:

```
CSCRIPT [filename] [arguments] [//B] [//D] [//E:engine] [//H:host] [//I]
➡[//Job:xxxx] [//S] [//T:ss] [//X] [//LOGO ¦ //NOLOGO] [//U]
```

This syntax is almost identical to that of WScript, but it adds the following three parameters:

//LOGO	Displays the Windows Script Host banner at startup.
//NOLOGO	Hides the Windows Script Host banner at startup.
//U	Uses Unicode for redirected input/output from the console.

Script Properties and .wsh Files

In the previous two sections, you saw that the WScript and CScript hosts have a number of parameters you can specify when you execute a script. It's also possible to set some of these options by using the properties associated with each script file. To see these properties, right-click a script file and then click Properties. In the properties sheet that appears, display the Script tab, shown in Figure 21.1. You have two options, as follows:

- **Stop Script After Specified Number of Seconds**—If you activate this check box, Windows shuts down the script after it has run for the number of seconds specified in the associated spin box. This is useful for scripts that might hang during execution. For example, a script that attempts to enumerate all the mapped network drives at startup might hang if the network is unavailable.

- **Display Logo When Script Executed in Command Console**—As you saw in the previous section, the CScript host displays some banner text when you run a script at the command prompt. If you deactivate this check box, the Windows Script Host suppresses this banner (unless you use the //LOGO parameter).

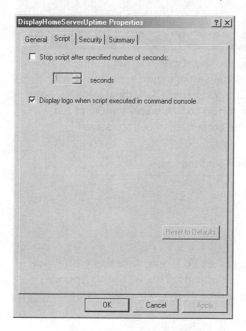

FIGURE 21.1   In a script file's properties sheet, use the Script tab to set some default options for the script.

When you make changes to these properties, the Windows Script Host saves your settings in a new file that has the same name as the script file, except with the .wsh (Windows Script Host Settings) extension. For example, if the script file is MyScript.vbs, the settings are stored in MyScript.wsh. These .wsh files are text files organized into sections, much like .ini files. Here's an example:

```
[ScriptFile]
Path=C:\Documents and Settings\Administrator\My Documents\Scripts\
➥DisplayHomeServerUptime.vbs
[Options]
Timeout=10
DisplayLogo=0
```

To use these settings when running the script, use either WScript or CScript and specify the name of the .wsh file:

```
wscript myscript.wsh
```

NOTE

Rather than setting properties for individual scripts, you might prefer to set global properties that apply to the WScript host itself. Those global settings then apply to every script that runs using the WScript host. To do this, run WScript.exe without parameters. This displays the properties sheet for WScript, which contains only the Script tab shown in Figure 21.1. The settings you choose in the properties sheet are stored in the following Registry key:

    HKLM\Software\Microsoft\Windows Script Host\Settings

Programming Objects

Although this chapter isn't a programming primer per se, I'd like to take some time now to run through a few quick notes about programming objects. This will serve you well throughout the rest of the chapter as I take you on a tour of the Windows Script Host object model.

The dictionary definition of an object is "anything perceptible by one or more of the senses, especially something that can be seen and felt." In scripting, an *object* is an application element that exposes an interface to the programmer, who can then perform the programming equivalent of seeing and feeling:

▶ You can make changes to the object's *properties*. (This is the seeing part.)

▶ You can make the object perform a task by activating a *method* associated with the object. (This is the feeling part.)

Working with Object Properties

Every programmable object has a defining set of characteristics. These characteristics are the object's *properties*, and they control the appearance and position of the object. For example, the WScript object (the top-level Windows Script Host object) has an Interactive property that determines whether the script runs in interactive mode or batch mode.

When you refer to a property, you use the following syntax:

Object.Property

Object   The name of the object.

Property   The name of the property with which you want to work.

For example, the following expression refers to the Interactive property of the WScript object:

WScript.Interactive

Setting the Value of a Property

To set a property to a certain value, you use the following syntax:

Object.Property = value

Here, *value* is an expression that specifies the value to which you want to set the property. As such, it can be any of the scripting language's recognized data types, which usually include the following:

- ▶ A numeric value

- ▶ A string value, enclosed in double quotation marks (such as "My Script Application")

- ▶ A logical value (in VBScript: True or False; in JavaScript: true or false)

For example, the following VBScript statement tells the Windows Script Host to run the script using interactive mode:

WScript.Interactive = True

Returning the Value of a Property

Sometimes you need to store the current value of a property or test that value before changing the property or performing some other action. You can store the current value of a property in a variable by using the following syntax:

variable = Object.Property

Here, *variable* is a variable name or another property. For example, the following statement stores the current script mode (batch or interactive) in a variable named currentMode:

```
currentMode = WScript.Interactive
```

Working with Object Methods

An object's properties describe what the object is, whereas its *methods* describe what the object *does.* For example, the WScript object has a Quit method that enables you to stop the execution of a script.

The way you refer to a method depends on whether the method requires arguments. If it doesn't, the syntax is similar to that of properties:

Object.Method

Object   The name of the object.

Method   The name of the method you want to run.

For example, the following statement shuts down a script:

```
WScript.Quit
```

If the method requires arguments, you use the following syntax:

Object.Method (Argument1, Argument2, ...)

> **NOTE**
>
> In VBScript, the parentheses around the argument list are necessary only if you'll be storing the result of the method in a variable or object property. In JavaScript, the parentheses are always required.

For example, the WshShell object has a RegWrite method that you use to write a key or value to the Registry. (I discuss this object and method in detail later in this chapter; see "Working with Registry Entries.") Here's the syntax:

```
WshShell.RegWrite strName, anyValue[, strType]
```

strName   The name of the Registry key or value.

anyValue   The value to write, if *strName* is a Registry value.

strType   The data type of the value.

ARGUMENT NAMING CONVENTIONS

When presenting method arguments in this chapter, I'll follow Microsoft's naming conventions, including the use of the following prefixes for the argument names:

Prefix	Data Type
any	Any type
b	Boolean
int	Integer
nat	Natural numbers
obj	Object
str	String

For many object methods, not all the arguments are required. In the RegWrite method, for example, the *strName* and *anyValue* arguments are required, but the *strType* argument is not. Throughout this chapter, I differentiate between required and optional arguments by surrounding the optional arguments with square brackets—for example, [strType].

For example, the following statement creates a new value named Test and sets it equal to Foo:

```
WshShell.RegWrite "HKCU\Software\Microsoft\Windows Script Host\Test",
➥"Foo", "REG_SZ"
```

Assigning an Object to a Variable

If you're using JavaScript, you assign an object to a variable using a standard variable assignment:

var *variableName* = *ObjectName*

variableName	The name of the variable.
ObjectName	The object you want to assign to the variable.

In VBScript, you assign an object to a variable by using the Set statement. Set has the following syntax:

Set *variableName* = *ObjectName*

variableName	The name of the variable.
ObjectName	The object you want to assign to the variable.

You'll see later on that you must often use Automation to access external objects. For example, if you want to work with files and folders in your script, you must access the scripting engine object named `FileSystemObject`. To get this access, you use the `CreateObject` method and store the resulting object in a variable, like so:

```
Set fs = CreateObject("Scripting.FileSystemObject")
```

Working with Object Collections

A *collection* is a set of similar objects. For example, `WScript.Arguments` is the set of all the arguments specified on the script's command line. Collections are objects, too, so they have their own properties and methods, and you can use these properties and methods to manipulate one or more objects in the collection.

The members of a collection are *elements*. You can refer to individual elements by using an *index*. For example, the following statement refers to the first command-line argument (collection indexes always begin at 0):

```
WScript.Arguments(0)
```

If you don't specify an element, the Windows Script Host assumes that you want to work with the entire collection.

VBScript: Using For Each...Next Loops for Collections

As you might know, VBScript provides the `For...Next` loop that enables you to cycle through a chunk of code a specified number of times. For example, the following code loops 10 times:

```
For counter = 1 To 10
    Code entered here is repeated 10 times
Next counter
```

A useful variation on this theme is the `For Each...Next` loop, which operates on a collection of objects. You don't need a loop counter because VBScript loops through the individual elements in the collection and performs on each element whatever operations are inside the loop. Here's the structure of the basic `For Each...Next` loop:

```
For Each element In collection
    [statements]
Next
```

element	A variable used to hold the name of each element in the collection.
collection	The name of the collection.
statements	The statements to execute for each element in the collection.

The following code loops through all the arguments specified on the script's command line and displays each one:

```
For Each arg In WScript.Arguments
    WScript.Echo arg
Next
```

JavaScript: Using Enumerators and for Loops for Collections

To iterate through a collection in JavaScript, you must do two things: create a new Enumerator object, and use a for loop to cycle through the enumerated collection.

To create a new Enumerator object, use the new keyword to set up an object variable (where collection is the name of the collection you want to work with):

```
var enum = new Enumerator(collection)
```

Then set up a special for loop:

```
for (; !enumerator.atEnd(); enumerator.moveNext())
{
    [statements];
}
```

enumerator   The Enumerator object you created.

statements   The statements to execute for each element in the collection.

The Enumerator object's moveNext method runs through the elements in the collection, whereas the atEnd method shuts down the loop after the last item has been processed. The following code loops through all the arguments specified on the script's command line and displays each one:

```
var args = new Enumerator(WScript.Arguments);
for (; !args.atEnd(); args.moveNext())
{
    WScript.Echo(args.item());
}
```

Programming the WScript Object

The WScript object represents the Windows Script Host applications (WScript.exe and CScript.exe). You use this object to get and set certain properties of the scripting host, as well as to access two other objects: WshArguments (the WScript object's Arguments property) and WshScriptEngine (accessed via the WScript object's GetScriptEngine method). WScript also contains the powerful CreateObject and GetObject methods, which enable you to work with Automation-enabled applications.

Displaying Text to the User

The WScript object method that you'll use most often is the Echo method, which displays text to the user. Here's the syntax:

```
WScript.Echo [Argument1, Argument2,...]
```

Here, Argument1, Argument2, and so on are any number of text or numeric values that represent the information you want to display to the user. In the Windows-based host (WScript.exe), the information displays in a dialog box; in the command-line host (CScript.exe), the information displays at the command prompt (much like the command-line ECHO utility).

> ▶ **SEE** For more about the ECHO command-line tool, **see** "ECHO: Displaying Messages from a Batch File," **P. 560**.

For example, here's a one-line script that uses the Echo method:

```
WScript.Echo "Hello Scripting World!"
```

Figure 21.2 shows the dialog box that appears when you run this script.

FIGURE 21.2   When you run the Echo method with WScript.exe, the message appears in a dialog box.

Shutting Down a Script

You use the WScript object's Quit method to shut down the script. You can also use Quit to have your script return an error code by using the following syntax:

```
WScript.Quit [intErrorCode]
```

intErrorCode   An integer value that represents the error code you want to return.

You could then call the script from a batch file and use the ERRORLEVEL environment variable to deal with the return code in some way.

> ▶ **SEE** I discuss using ERRORLEVEL in relation to the XCOPY command in Chapter 19; **see** "XCOPY: Advanced File Copying," **P. 584**.

Scripting and Automation

Applications such as Internet Explorer and Word come with (or *expose*, in the jargon) a set of objects that define various aspects of the program. For example, Internet Explorer has an Application object that represents the program as a whole. Similarly, Word has a Document object that represents a Word document. By using the properties and methods that come with these objects, you can programmatically query and manipulate the applications. With Internet Explorer, for example, you can use the Application object's Navigate method to send the browser to a specified web page. With Word, you can read a Document object's Saved property to see whether the document has unsaved changes.

This is powerful stuff, but how do you get at the objects that these applications expose? You do that by using a technology called *Automation*. Applications that support Automation implement object libraries that expose the application's native objects to Automation-aware programming languages. Such applications are *Automation servers*, and the applications that manipulate the server's objects are *Automation controllers*. The Windows Script Host is an Automation controller that enables you to write script code to control any server's objects.

This means that you can use an application's exposed objects more or less as you use the Windows Script Host objects. With just a minimum of preparation, your script code can refer to and work with the Internet Explorer Application object, or the Microsoft Word Document object, or any of the hundreds of other objects exposed by the applications on your system. (Note, however, that not all applications expose objects. Outlook Express and most of the built-in Windows Home Server programs—such as WordPad and Paint—do not expose objects.)

Creating an Automation Object with the CreateObject Method

The WScript object's CreateObject method creates an Automation object (specifically, what programmers call an *instance* of the object). Here's the syntax:

WScript.CreateObject(*strProgID*)

strProgID   A string that specifies the Automation server application and the type of object to create. This string is a *programmatic identifier*, which is a label that uniquely specifies an application and one of its objects. The programmatic identifier always takes the following form:

AppName.ObjectType

Here, *AppName* is the Automation name of the application and *ObjectType* is the object class type (as defined in the Registry's HKEY_CLASSES_ROOT key). For example, here's the programmatic ID for Word:

Word.Application

Note that you normally use CreateObject within a Set statement, and that the function serves to create a new instance of the specified Automation object. For example, you could use the following statement to create a new instance of Word's Application object:

```
Set objWord = CreateObject("Word.Application")
```

You need to do nothing else to use the Automation object. With your variable declared and an instance of the object created, you can use that object's properties and methods directly. Listing 21.1 shows a VBScript example that works with Internet Explorer.

LISTING 21.1   A VBScript Example That Creates and Manipulates an Internet Explorer Application Object

```
Option Explicit
Dim objIE
'
' Create the Internet Explorer object
'
Set objIE = WScript.CreateObject("InternetExplorer.Application")
'
' Navigate to a page
'
objIE.Navigate "http://www.wordspy.com/"
'
' Make the browser window visible
'
objIE.Visible = True
'
' Release the object
'
Set objIE = Nothing
```

This script displays a website in Internet Explorer by working with Internet Explorer's Application object via Automation. The script begins by using the CreateObject method to create a new Internet Explorer Application object, and the object is stored in the objIE variable. From there, you can wield the objIE variable just as though it were the Internet Explorer Application object.

For example, the objIE.Navigate statement uses the Navigate method to navigate to the website given by the URL. Then the object's Visible property is set to True so that we can see the new browser window. Finally, the script sets the objIE object variable to Nothing to release the variable's memory (always a good idea when dealing with Automation objects).

For comparison, Listing 21.2 shows a JavaScript procedure that performs the same tasks.

LISTING 21.2   A JavaScript Example That Creates and Manipulates an Internet Explorer Application Object

```
// Create the Internet Explorer object
//
var objIE = WScript.CreateObject("InternetExplorer.Application");
//
// Navigate to a page
//
objIE.Navigate ("http://www.wordspy.com/");
//
// Make the browser window visible
//
objIE.Visible = true;
//
// Release the object
//
objIE = null;
```

Working with an Existing Object Using the GetObject Method

If you know that the object you want to work with already exists or is already open, the CreateObject method isn't the best choice. In the example in the previous section, if Word is already running, the code starts a second copy of Word, which is a waste of resources. For these situations, it's better to work directly with the existing object. To do that, use the GetObject method:

WScript.GetObject(*strPathname*[, *strProgID*])

strPathname   The pathname (drive, folder, and filename) of the file you want to work with (or the file that contains the object you want to work with). If you omit this argument, you have to specify the *strProgID* argument.

strProgID   The programmatic identifier that specifies the Automation server application and the type of object to work with (that is, the *App Name.ObjectType* class syntax).

Listing 21.3 shows a VBScript procedure that puts the GetObject method to work.

LISTING 21.3   A VBScript Example That Uses the GetObject Method to Work with an Existing Instance of a Word Document Object

```
Option Explicit
Dim objDoc
'
' Get the Word Document object
```

```
'
Set objDoc = WScript.GetObject("C:\Documents and Settings\Administrator\" & _
                               "My Documents\GetObject.doc", "Word.Document")'
' Get the word count
'
WScript.Echo objDoc.Name & " has " & objDoc.Words.Count & " words."
'
' We're done, so quit Word
'
objDoc.Application.Quit
```

The GetObject method assigns the Word Document object named GetObject.doc to the objDoc variable. After you've set up this reference, you can use the object's properties and methods directly. For example, the Echo method uses objDoc.Name to return the filename and objDoc.Words.Count to determine the number of words in the document.

Note that although you're working with a Document object, you still have access to Word's Application object. That's because most objects have an Application property that refers to the Application object. In the script in Listing 21.3, for example, the following statement uses the Application property to quit Word:

```
objDoc.Application.Quit
```

Exposing VBScript and JavaScript Objects

One of the most powerful uses for scripted Automation is accessing the object models exposed by the VBScript and JavaScript engines. These models expose a number of objects, including the local file system. This enables you to create scripts that work with files, folders, and disk drives, read and write text files, and more. You use the following syntax to refer to these objects:

```
Scripting.ObjectType
```

Scripting is the Automation name of the scripting engine, and ObjectType is the class type of the object.

> **NOTE**
>
> This section gives you a brief explanation of the objects associated with the VBScript and JavaScript engines. For the complete list of object properties and methods, please see the following site: msdn.microsoft.com/en-us/library/d1wf56tt(VS.85).aspx.

Programming the FileSystemObject

FileSystemObject is the top-level file system object. For all your file system scripts, you begin by creating a new instance of FileSystemObject.

In VBScript:

```
Set fs = WScript.CreateObject("Scripting.FileSystemObject")
```

In JavaScript:

```
var fs = WScript.CreateObject("Scripting.FileSystemObject");
```

Here's a summary of the file system objects you can access via Automation and the top-level FileSystemObject:

▶ **Drive**—This object enables you to access the properties of a specified disk drive or UNC network path. To reference a Drive object, use either the Drives collection (discussed next) or the FileSystemObject object's GetDrive method. For example, the following VBScript statement references drive C:

```
Set objFS = WScript.CreateObject("Scripting.FileSystemObject")
Set objDrive = objFS.GetDrive("C:")
```

▶ **Drives**—This object is the collection of all available drives. To reference this collection, use the FileSystemObject object's Drives property:

```
Set objFS = WScript.CreateObject("Scripting.FileSystemObject")
Set objDrives = objFS.Drives
```

▶ **Folder**—This object enables you to access the properties of a specified folder. To reference a Folder object, use either the Folders collection (discussed next) or the FileSystemObject object's GetFolder method:

```
Set objFS = WScript.CreateObject("Scripting.FileSystemObject")
Set objFolder = objFS.GetFolder("C:\My Documents")
```

▶ **Folders**—This object is the collection of subfolders within a specified folder. To reference this collection, use the Folder object's Subfolders property:

```
Set objFS = WScript.CreateObject("Scripting.FileSystemObject")
Set objFolder = objFS.GetFolder("C:\Windows")
Set objSubfolders = objFolder.Subfolders
```

▶ **File**—This object enables you to access the properties of a specified file. To reference a File object, use either the Files collection (discussed next) or the FileSystemObject object's GetFile method:

```
Set objFS = WScript.CreateObject("Scripting.FileSystemObject")
Set objFile = objFS.GetFile("c:\Boot.ini")
```

▶ **Files**—This object is the collection of files within a specified folder. To reference this collection, use the Folder object's Files property:

```
Set objFS = WScript.CreateObject("Scripting.FileSystemObject")
Set objFolder = objFS.GetFolder("C:\Windows")
Set objFiles = objFolder.Files
```

▶ **TextStream**—This object enables you to use sequential access to work with a text file. To open a text file, use the FileSystemObject object's OpenTextFile method:

```
Set objFS = WScript.CreateObject("Scripting.FileSystemObject")
Set objTS= objFS.OpenTextFile("C:\Boot.ini")
```

Alternatively, you can create a new text file by using the FileSystemObject object's CreateTextFile method:

```
Set objFS = WScript.CreateObject("Scripting.FileSystemObject")
Set objTS= objFS.CreateTextFile("C:\Boot.ini")
```

Either way, you end up with a TextStream object, which has various methods for reading data from the file and writing data to the file. For example, the following script reads and displays the text from C:\Boot.ini:

```
Set objFS = WScript.CreateObject("Scripting.FileSystemObject")
Set objTS = objFS.OpenTextFile("C:\Boot.ini")
strContents = objTS.ReadAll
WScript.Echo strContents
objTS.Close
```

Programming the WshShell Object

WshShell is a generic name for a powerful object that enables you to query and interact with various aspects of the Windows shell. You can display information to the user, run applications, create shortcuts, work with the Registry, and control Windows' environment variables. The next few sections discuss each of those useful tasks.

Referencing the WshShell Object

WshShell refers to the Shell object exposed via the Automation interface of WScript. Therefore, you must use CreateObject to return this object:

```
Set objWshShell = WScript.CreateObject("WScript.Shell")
```

From here, you can use the objWshShell variable to access the object's properties and methods.

Displaying Information to the User

You saw earlier that the WScript object's Echo method is useful for displaying simple text messages to the user. You can gain more control over the displayed message by using the WshShell object's Popup method. This method is similar to the MsgBox function used in Visual Basic and VBA in that it enables you to control both the dialog box title and the buttons displayed, as well as to determine which of those buttons the user pressed. Here's the syntax:

```
WshShell.Popup(strText[, nSecondsToWait][, strTitle][, intType])
```

WshShell	The WshShell object.
strText	The message you want to display in the dialog box. You can enter a string up to 1,024 characters long.
nSecondsToWait	The maximum number of seconds the dialog box will be displayed.
strTitle	The text that appears in the dialog box title bar. If you omit this value, Windows Script Host appears in the title bar.
intType	A number or constant that specifies, among other things, the command buttons that appear in the dialog box (see the next section). The default value is 0.

For example, the following statements display the dialog box shown in Figure 21.3:

```
Set objWshShell = WScript.CreateObject("WScript.Shell")
objWshShell.Popup "Hello Popup World!", , "My Popup"
```

TIP

For long messages, VBScript wraps the text inside the dialog box. If you prefer to create your own line breaks, use VBScript's Chr function and the carriage return character (ASCII 13) between each line:

```
WshShell.Popup "First line" & Chr(13) & "Second line"
```

You can also use the vbCrLf constant, which does the same thing:

```
WshShell.Popup "First line" & vbCrLf & "Second line"
```

For JavaScript, use \n:

```
WshShell.Popup("First line" + "\n" + "Second line");
```

FIGURE 21.3   A simple message dialog box produced by the Popup method.

Setting the Style of the Message

The default Popup dialog box displays only an OK button. You can include other buttons and icons in the dialog box by using different values for the intType parameter. Table 21.1 lists the available options.

TABLE 21.1   The Popup Method's intType Parameter Options

VBScript Constant	Value	Description
Buttons		
vbOKOnly	0	Displays only an OK button. This is the default.
vbOKCancel	1	Displays the OK and Cancel buttons.
vbAbortRetryIgnore	2	Displays the Abort, Retry, and Ignore buttons.
vbYesNoCancel	3	Displays the Yes, No, and Cancel buttons.
vbYesNo	4	Displays the Yes and No buttons.
vbRetryCancel	5	Displays the Retry and Cancel buttons.
Icons		
vbCritical	16	Displays the Critical Message icon.
vbQuestion	32	Displays the Warning Query icon.
vbExclamation	48	Displays the Warning Message icon.
vbInformation	64	Displays the Information Message icon.
Default Buttons		
vbDefaultButton1	0	The first button is the default (that is, the button selected when the user presses Enter).
vbDefaultButton2	256	The second button is the default.
vbDefaultButton3	512	The third button is the default.

You derive the intType argument in one of two ways:

▶ By adding the values for each option

▶ By using the VBScript constants separated by plus signs (+)

The script in Listing 21.4 shows an example, and Figure 21.4 shows the resulting dialog box.

LISTING 21.4   A VBScript Example That Uses the Popup Method to Display the Dialog Box
Shown in Figure 21.4

```
Option Explicit
Dim strText, strTitle, intType, objWshShell, intResult
'
' First, set up the message
'
strText = "Are you sure you want to copy" & vbCrLf
strText = strText & "the selected files to the server?"
strTitle = "Copy Files"
intType = vbYesNoCancel + vbQuestion + vbDefaultButton2
'
' Now display it
'
Set objWshShell = WScript.CreateObject("WScript.Shell")
intResult = objWshShell.Popup(strText, ,strTitle, intType)
```

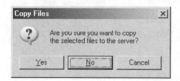

FIGURE 21.4   The dialog box that's displayed when you run the script.

Here, three variables—strText, strTitle, and intType—store the values for the Popup
method's strText, strTitle, and intType arguments, respectively. In particular, the
following statement derives the intType argument:

```
intType = vbYesNoCancel + vbQuestion + vbDefaultButton2
```

You also could derive the intType argument by adding up the values that these constants
represent (3, 32, and 256, respectively), but the script becomes less readable that way.

Getting Return Values from the Message Dialog Box

A dialog box that displays only an OK button is straightforward. The user either clicks OK
or presses Enter to remove the dialog from the screen. The multibutton styles are a little
different, however; the user has a choice of buttons to select, and your script should have
a way to find out which button the user chose, which enables it to decide what to do
next, based on the user's selection. You do this by storing the Popup method's return value
in a variable. Table 21.2 lists the seven possible return values.

TABLE 21.2   The Popup Method's Return Values

VBScript Constant	Value	Button Selected
vbOK	1	OK
vbCancel	2	Cancel
vbAbort	3	Abort
vbRetry	4	Retry
vbIgnore	5	Ignore
vbYes	6	Yes
vbNo	7	No

To process the return value, you can use an If...Then...Else or Select Case structure to test for the appropriate values. For example, the script shown earlier used a variable called intResult to store the return value of the Popup method. Listing 21.5 shows a revised version of the script that uses a VBScript Select Case statement to test for the three possible return values.

LISTING 21.5   A Script That Uses a Select Case Statement to Process the Popup Method's Return Value

```
Option Explicit
Dim strText, strTitle, intType, objWshShell, intResult
'
' First, set up the message
'
strText = "Are you sure you want to copy" & Chr(13)
strText = strText & "the selected files to the server?"
strTitle = "Copy Files"
intType = vbYesNoCancel + vbQuestion + vbDefaultButton2
'
' Now display it
'
Set objWshShell = WScript.CreateObject("WScript.Shell")
intResult = objWshShell.Popup(strText, ,strTitle, intType)
'
' Process the result
'
Select Case intResult
    Case vbYes
        WScript.Echo "You clicked ""Yes""!"
    Case vbNo
```

```
        WScript.Echo "You clicked ""No""!"
    Case vbCancel
        WScript.Echo "You clicked ""Cancel""!"
End Select
```

Running Applications

When you need your script to launch another application, use the Run method:

WshShell.Run *strCommand*[, *intWindowStyle*][, *bWaitOnReturn*]

WshShell	The WshShell object.
strCommand	The name of the file that starts the application. Unless the file is in the Windows folder, you should include the drive and folder to make sure that the script can find the file.
intWindowStyle	A constant or number that specifies how the application window will appear:

intWindowStyle	Window Appearance
0	Hidden
1	Normal size with focus
2	Minimized with focus (the default)
3	Maximized with focus
4	Normal without focus
6	Minimized without focus

bWaitOnReturn	A logical value that determines whether the application runs asynchronously. If this value is True, the script halts execution until the user exits the launched application; if this value is False, the script continues running after it has launched the application.

Here's an example:

```
Set objWshShell = WScript.CreateObject("WScript.Shell")
objWshShell.Run "Control.exe Inetcpl.cpl", 1, True
```

This Run method launches the Control Panel's Internet Properties dialog box.

▶ **SEE** To learn more about launching individual Control Panel icons using `Control.exe`, **see** "Understanding Control Panel Files," **P. 619**.

Working with Shortcuts

The Windows Script Host enables your scripts to create and modify shortcut files. When writing scripts for other users, you might want to take advantage of this capability to display shortcuts for new network shares, Internet sites, instruction files, and so on.

Creating a Shortcut

To create a shortcut, use the `CreateShortcut` method:

WshShell.CreateShortcut(*strPathname*)

WshShell   The `WshShell` object.

strPathname The full path and filename of the shortcut file you want to create. Use the `.lnk` extension for a file system (program, document, folder, and so on) shortcut; use the `.url` extension for an Internet shortcut.

The following example creates and saves a shortcut on a user's desktop:

```
Set WshShell = objWScript.CreateObject("WScript.Shell")
Set objShortcut = objWshShell.CreateShortcut("C:\Documents and Settings\" & _
                "Administrator\Desktop\test.lnk")
objShortcut.Save
```

Programming the `WshShortcut` Object

The `CreateShortcut` method returns a `WshShortcut` object. You can use this object to manipulate various properties and methods associated with shortcut files.

This object contains the following properties:

`Arguments`—Returns or sets a string that specifies the arguments used when launching the shortcut. For example, suppose that the shortcut's target is the following:

C:\Windows\Notepad.exe C:\Boot.ini

In other words, this shortcut launches Notepad and loads the Boot.ini file. In this case, the `Arguments` property would return the following string:

C:\Boot.ini

`Description`—Returns or sets a string description of the shortcut.

FullName—Returns the full path and filename of the shortcut's target. This is the same as the `strPathname` value used in the `CreateShortcut` method.

Hotkey—Returns or sets the hotkey associated with the shortcut. To set this value, use the following syntax:

WshShortcut.Hotkey = *strHotKey*

WshShortcut   The WshShortcut object.

strHotKey   A string value of the form *Modifier+Keyname*, where *Modifier* is any combination of Alt, Ctrl, and Shift, and *Keyname* is one of A through Z or 0 through *23*.

For example, the following statement sets the hotkey to Ctrl+Alt+7:

objShortcut.Hotkey = "Ctrl+Alt+7"

IconLocation—Returns or sets the icon used to display the shortcut. To set this value, use the following syntax:

WshShortcut.IconLocation = *strIconLocation*

WshShortcut   The WshShortcut object.

strIconLocation   A string value of the form *Path*, *Index*, where *Path* is the full pathname of the icon file and *Index* is the position of the icon within the file (where the first icon is *0*).

Here's an example:

objShortcut.IconLocation = "C:\Windows\System32\Shell32.dll,21"

TargetPath   Returns or sets the path of the shortcut's target.

WindowStyle   Returns or sets the window style used by the shortcut's target. Use the same values outlined earlier for the Run method's intWindowStyle argument.

WorkingDirectory   Returns or sets the path of the shortcut's working directory.

NOTE

If you're working with Internet shortcuts, bear in mind that they support only two properties: FullName and TargetPath (the URL target).

The WshShortcut object also supports two methods, as follows:

Save   Saves the shortcut file to disk.

Resolve   Uses the shortcut's TargetPath property to look up the target file. Here's the syntax:

       WshShortcut.Resolve = *intFlag*

       WshShortcut   The WshShortcut object.

intFlag	Determines what happens if the target file is not found:
intFlag	**What Happens**
1	Nothing.
2	Windows continues to search subfolders for the target file.
4	Updates the TargetPath property if the target file is found in a new location.

Listing 21.6 shows a complete example of a script that creates a shortcut.

LISTING 21.6   A Script That Creates a Shortcut File

```
Option Explicit
Dim objWshShell, objShortcut
Set objWshShell = WScript.CreateObject("WScript.Shell")
Set objShortcut = objWshShell.CreateShortcut("C:\Documents and Settings\" & _
                "Administrator\Desktop\Edit Boot.ini.lnk")
With objShortcut
    .TargetPath = "C:\Windows\Notepad.exe"
    .Arguments = "C:\Boot.ini"
    .WorkingDirectory = "C:\"
    .Description = "Opens Boot.ini in Notepad"
    .Hotkey = "Ctrl+Alt+7"
    .IconLocation = "C:\Windows\System32\Shell32.dll,21"
    .WindowStyle = 3
    .Save
End With
```

Working with Registry Entries

You've seen throughout this book that the Registry is one of the most crucial data structures in Windows. However, Windows isn't the only software that uses the Registry. Most 32-bit applications use the Registry as a place to store setup options, customization values the user selected, and much more. Interestingly, your scripts can get in on the act as well. Not only can your scripts read the current value of any Registry setting, but they can also use the Registry as a storage area. This enables you to keep track of user settings, recently used files, and any other configuration data that you'd like to save between sessions. This section shows you how to use the WshShell object to manipulate the Registry from within your scripts.

Reading Settings from the Registry

To read any value from the Registry, use the WshShell object's RegRead method:

WshShell.RegRead(*strName*)

| *WshShell* | The WshShell object. |

strName	The name of the Registry value or key that you want to read. If *strName* ends with a backslash (\), RegRead returns the default value for the key; otherwise, RegRead returns the data stored in the value. Note, too, that *strName* must begin with one of the following root key names:

Short Name	Long Name
HKCR	HKEY_CLASSES_ROOT
HKCU	HKEY_CURRENT_USER
HKLM	HKEY_LOCAL_MACHINE
N/A	HKEY_USERS
N/A	HKEY_CURRENT_CONFIG

The script in Listing 21.7 displays the name of the registered owner of this copy of Windows.

LISTING 21.7   A Script That Reads the RegisteredOwner Setting from the Registry

```
Set objWshShell = WScript.CreateObject("WScript.Shell")
strSetting = "HKLM\SOFTWARE\Microsoft\Windows NT\CurrentVersion\
➥RegisteredOwner"
strRegisteredUser = objWshShell.RegRead(strSetting)
WScript.Echo strRegisteredUser
```

Storing Settings in the Registry

To store a setting in the Registry, use the WshShell object's RegWrite method:

WshShell.RegWrite *strName*, *anyValue* [, *strType*]

WshShell	The WshShell object.
strName	The name of the Registry value or key that you want to set. If *strName* ends with a backslash (\), RegWrite sets the default value for the key; otherwise, RegWrite sets the data for the value. *strName* must begin with one of the root key names detailed in the RegRead method.
anyValue	The value to be stored.
strType	The data type of the value, which must be one of the following: REG_SZ (the default), REG_EXPAND_SZ, REG_DWORD, or REG_BINARY.

The following statements create a new key named `ScriptSettings` in the `HKEY_CURRENT_USER` root:

```
Set objWshShell = WScript.CreateObject("WScript.Shell")
objWshShell.RegWrite "HKCU\ScriptSettings\", ""
```

The following statements create a new value named `NumberOfReboots` in the `HKEY_CURRENT_USER\ScriptSettings` key and set this value to 1:

```
Set objWshShell = WScript.CreateObject("WScript.Shell")
objWshShell.RegWrite "HKCU\ScriptSettings\NumberOfReboots", 1, "REG_DWORD"
```

Deleting Settings from the Registry

If you no longer need to track a particular key or value setting, use the `RegDelete` method to remove the setting from the Registry:

WshShell.RegDelete(*strName*)

WshShell	The WshShell object.
strName	The name of the Registry value or key that you want to delete. If *strName* ends with a backslash (\\), RegDelete deletes the key; otherwise, RegDelete deletes the value. *strName* must begin with one of the root key names detailed in the RegRead method.

To delete the `NumberOfReboots` value used in the previous example, you would use the following statements:

```
Set objWshShell = WScript.CreateObject("WScript.Shell")
objWshShell.RegDelete "HKCU\ScriptSettings\NumberOfReboots"
```

Working with Environment Variables

Windows Home Server keeps track of a number of environment variables that hold data, such as the location of the Windows folder, the location of the temporary files folder, the command path, the primary drive, and much more. Why would you need such data? One example would be for accessing files or folders within the main Windows folder. Rather than guessing that this folder is `C:\Windows`, it would be much easier to just query the `%SystemRoot%` environment variable. Similarly, if you have a script that accesses files in a user's My Documents folder, hard-coding the username in the file path is inconvenient because it means creating custom scripts for every possible user. Instead, it would be much easier to create just a single script that references the `%UserProfile%` environment variable. This section shows you how to read environment variable data within your scripts.

The defined environment variables are stored in the Environment collection, which is a property of the WshShell object. Windows Home Server environment variables are stored in the "Process" environment, so you reference this collection as follows:

```
WshShell.Environment("Process")
```

Listing 21.8 shows a script that runs through this collection, adds each variable to a string, and then displays the string.

LISTING 21.8   A Script That Displays the System's Environment Variables

```
Option Explicit
Dim objWshShell, objEnvVar, strVariables
Set objWshShell = WScript.CreateObject("WScript.Shell")
'
' Run through the environment variables
'
strVariables = ""
For Each objEnvVar In objWshShell.Environment("Process")
    strVariables = strVariables & objEnvVar & vbCrLf
Next
WScript.Echo strVariables
```

Figure 21.5 shows the dialog box that appears. (The environment variables in your version of Windows Home Server may be different.)

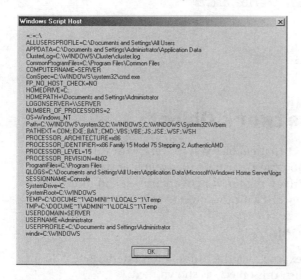

FIGURE 21.5   A complete inventory of a system's environment variables.

If you want to use the value of a particular environment variable, use the following syntax:

`WshShell.Environment("Process")("strName")`

WshShell	The WshShell object.
strName	The name of the environment variable.

Listing 21.9 shows a revised version of the script from Listing 21.6 to create a shortcut. In this version, the Environment collection is used to return the value of the %UserProfile% variable, which is used to contrast the path to the current user's Desktop folder.

LISTING 21.9   A Script That Creates a Shortcut File Using an Environment Variable

```
Option Explicit
Dim objWshShell, strUserProfile, objShortcut
Set objWshShell = WScript.CreateObject("WScript.Shell")
strUserProfile = objWshShell.Environment("Process")("UserProfile")
Set objShortcut = objWshShell.CreateShortcut(strUserProfile & _
                "\Desktop\Edit BOOT.INI.lnk")
With objShortcut
    .TargetPath = "C:\Windows\Notepad.exe"
    .Arguments = "C:\Boot.ini"
    .WorkingDirectory = "C:\"
    .Description = "Opens BOOT.INI in Notepad"
    .Hotkey = "Ctrl+Alt+7"
    .IconLocation = "C:\Windows\System32\Shell32.dll,21"
    .WindowStyle = 3
    .Save
End With
```

Programming the WshNetwork Object

WshNetwork is a generic name for an object that enables you to work with various aspects of the Windows network environment. You can determine the computer name and username, enumerate the mapped network drives, map new network drives, and more. The next couple of sections show you how to work with this object.

Referencing the WshNetwork Object

WshNetwork refers to the Network object exposed via the Automation interface of WScript. This means you use CreateObject to return this object, as shown next:

`Set objWshNetwork = WScript.CreateObject("WScript.Network")`

From here, you use the WshNetwork variable to access the object's properties and methods.

WshNetwork Object Properties

The WshNetwork object supports three properties:

ComputerName   Returns the network name of the computer.

UserDomain   Returns the network domain name of the current user.

UserName   Returns the username of the current user.

Mapping Network Printers

The WshNetwork object supports several methods for working with remote printers. For example, to map a network printer to a local printer resource, use the WshNetwork object's AddWindowsPrinterConnection method:

WshNetwork.AddPrinterConnection *strPrinterPath*

WshNetwork   The WshNetwork object.

strPrinterPath   The UNC path to the network printer.

Here's an example:

```
Set objWshNetwork = WScript.CreateObject("WScript.Network")
objWshNetwork.AddWindowsPrinterConnection "\\SERVER\printer"
```

To remove a remote printer mapping, use the WshNetwork object's RemovePrinterConnection method:

WshNetwork.RemovePrinterConnection *strPrinterPath* [, *bForce*] [, *bUpdateProfile*]

WshNetwork   The WshNetwork object.

strPrinterPath   The UNC path to the network printer.

bForce   If True, the resource is removed even if it is currently being used.

bUpdateProfile   If True, the printer mapping is removed from the user's profile.

Here's an example:

```
Set objWshNetwork = WScript.CreateObject("WScript.Network")
objWshNetwork.RemovePrinterConnection "\\SERVER\inkjet"
```

Mapping Network Drives

The WshNetwork object supports several methods for mapping network drives. To map a shared network folder to a local drive letter, use the WshNetwork object's MapNetworkDrive method:

WshNetwork.MapNetworkDrive *strLocalName*, *strRemoteName*
➥[, *bUpdateProfile*][, *strUser*][, *strPassword*]

WshNetwork   This is the WshNetwork object.

strLocalName   This is the local drive letter to which the remote share will be mapped (for example, F:).

strRemoteName   This is the UNC path for the remote share.

bUpdateProfile   If True, the drive mapping is stored in the user's profile.

strUser   Use this value to enter a username that might be required to map the remote share (if you're logged on as a user who doesn't have the proper permissions, for example).

strPassword   Use this value to enter a password that might be required to map the remote drive.

Here's an example:

```
Set objWshNetwork = WScript.CreateObject("WScript.Network")
objWshNetwork.MapNetworkDrive "Z:", "\\SERVER\Music"
```

To remove a mapped network drive, use the WshNetwork object's RemoveNetworkDrive:

WshNetwork.RemoveNetworkDrive *strName*[, *bForce*][, *bUpdateProfile*]

WshNetwork   The WshNetwork object.

strName   The name of the mapped network drive you want removed. If you use a network path, all mappings to that path are removed; if you use a local drive letter, only that mapping is removed.

bForce   If True, the resource is removed even if it is currently being used.

bUpdateProfile   If True, the network drive mapping is removed from the user's profile.

Here's an example:

```
Set objWshNetwork = WScript.CreateObject("WScript.Network")
objWshNetwork.RemoveNetworkDrive "Z:"
```

Programming the Windows Management Instrumentation Service

Windows Management Instrumentation (WMI) is a powerful tool that gives you access to just about every aspect of Windows Home Server and of remote computers, as well. With WMI, your scripts can manage applications, systems, devices, networks, and much more. WMI consists of a series of classes that implement various properties and methods that you can access using your scripts. For example, the Win32_OperatingSystem class represents the computer's operating system. Its properties include `InstallDate`, the date and time the OS was installed, and `LastBootUpTime`, the date and time when the OS was last started; its methods include `Reboot` for restarting the computer and `SetDateTime` for setting the system's date and time.

> **NOTE**
>
> WMI is massive. It has hundreds of classes that you can use, although you'll mostly use the Win32 classes, which enable you to manage the operating system, hardware, and applications, and to monitor performance. For the complete WMI reference, see msdn.microsoft.com/en-us/library/aa394582(VS.85).aspx.

Referencing the WMI Service Object

Your WMI scripts will always begin by setting up a variable for the WMI service object. One way to do that is to create an `SWbemLocator` object and use it to connect to the WMI service. Here's the code:

```
strComputer = "localhost"
Set objLocator = CreateObject("WbemScripting.SWbemLocator")
Set objWMI = objLocator.ConnectServer(strComputer, "root\cimv2")
objWMI.Security.ImpersonationLevel = 3
```

That works fine, but most scripts use a shortcut method that reduces to just a couple of statements:

```
strComputer = "localhost"
Set objWMI = GetObject("winmgmts:{impersonationLevel=impersonate}!\\" & _
            strComputer & "\root\cimv2")
```

> **TIP**
>
> I like to use `localhost` to reference the local computer because it's straightforward and easy to read. However, you can also use just dot (.) to refer to the local machine:
>
> ```
> strComputer = "."
> Set objWMI = GetObject("winmgmts:{impersonationLevel=impersonate}!\\" & _
>             strComputer & "\root\cimv2")
> ```

Returning Class Instances

After you have your WMI service object, you can use it to access a class. Each class is really a collection of instances, or actual implementations of the class. For example, the `Win32_UserAccount` class consists of all the user accounts defined on the computer. Each user account is an instance of the `Win32_UserAccount` class. To access the instances of a class, you can use either of the following WMI object methods: `ExecQuery` or `InstancesOf`.

The ExecQuery method executes a SELECT query using the WMI Query Language (WQL). In general, this method uses the following form:

object.ExecQuery("SELECT * FROM *class*")

object   A variable that references the WMI object.

class   The WMI class you want to work with.

For example, the following method assumes that the WMI object is referenced by the objWMI variable, and the query returns all the instances of the Win32_UserAccount class:

objWMI.ExecQuery("SELECT * FROM Win32_UserAccount")

The InstancesOf method uses the following syntax:

object.InstancesOf("*class*")

object   A variable that references the WMI object.

class   The WMI class you want to work with.

For example, the following method assumes the WMI object is referenced by the objWMI variable, and the code returns all the instances of the Win32_UserAccount class:

objWMI.InstancesOf("Win32_UserAccount")

Which method should you use? If you want to work with all instances of a particular class, either method is fine, and you may gravitate to the InstancesOf method only because it's slightly shorter. However, if you only want to work with a subset of the instances, the ExecQuery method is better because you can add a WHERE clause to the WQL statement. For example, if you just want to work with the account named Administrator, the following code returns just that instance from the Win32_UserAccounts class:

```
objWMI.ExecQuery("SELECT * FROM Win32_UserAccount " & _
            "WHERE Name = 'Administrator'")
```

Both ExecQuery and InstancesOf return a collection object that contains the class instances. You usually store that collection in a variable, as in this example:

```
Set objUsers = objWMI.ExecQuery("SELECT * FROM Win32_UserAccount")
```

You could then use a For Each...Next loop to run through the collection and perform some action on each instance. For example, Listing 21.10 presents a script that runs through all the instances of the Win32_UserAccount class, stores the Name and Fullname properties for each user in a string, and then displays the string.

LISTING 21.10   A Script That Runs Through the Instances of the Win32_UserAccount Class

```
Option Explicit
Dim strComputer, strUserInfo
```

```
Dim objWMI, objUsers, objUser
'
' Work with the local computer
'
strComputer = "localhost"
'
' Get the WMI service
'
Set objWMI = GetObject("winmgmts:{impersonationLevel=impersonate}!\\" & _
                       strComputer & "\root\cimv2")
'
' Store the instances of the Win32_UserAccount class
'
Set objUsers = objWMI.ExecQuery("SELECT * FROM Win32_UserAccount")
'
' Initialize the display string
'
strUserInfo = ""
'
' Loop through the instances
'
For each objUser in objUsers
    strUserInfo = strUserInfo & objUser.Name & " (" & _
                                objUser.FullName & ")" & vbCrLf
Next
'
' Display the string
'
WScript.Echo strUserInfo
'
' Release the objects
'
Set objWMI = Nothing
Set objUsers = Nothing
Set objUsers = Nothing
```

In many cases, the class only returns a single instance, either because the class only has one instance or because you used the WQL WHERE clause to restrict the class to a particular instance. Either way, you still need to use a For Each...Next loop to extract the data from the instance.

As an example, consider the script in Listing 21.11.

LISTING 21.11   A Script That Displays BIOS Data

```
Option Explicit
Dim strComputer, strBIOS
Dim objWMI, objBIOS, objItem
'
' Get the WMI service
'
strComputer = "localhost"
Set objWMI = GetObject("winmgmts:{impersonationLevel=impersonate}!\\" & _
            strComputer & "\root\cimv2")
'
' Get the BIOS instance
'
Set objBIOS = objWMI.ExecQuery("SELECT * FROM Win32_BIOS " & _
                            "WHERE PrimaryBIOS = true")
'
' Initialize the display string
'
strBIOS = "BIOS Data for " & UCase(strComputer) & ":" & vbCrLf & vbCrLf
'
' Collect the BIOS data
'
For Each objItem in objBIOS
        strBIOS = strBIOS & _
            "BIOS Name:" & vbTab & objItem.Name & vbCrLf & _
            "Manufacturer:" & vbTab & objItem.Manufacturer & vbCrLf & _
            "BIOS Version:" & vbTab & objItem.Version & vbCrLf & _
            "SMBIOS Version:" & vbTab & objItem.SMBIOSBIOSVersion & vbCrLf & _
            "BIOS Date:" & vbTab & ConvertToDate(objItem.ReleaseDate)

Next
'
' Display the string
'
WScript.Echo strBIOS
'
' Release the objects
'
Set objWMI = Nothing
Set objBIOS = Nothing
Set objItem = Nothing
'
' This function takes a datetime string and
' converts it to a real date object
'
Function ConvertToDate(strDate)
```

```
    Dim strYear, strMonth, strDay
    strYear = Left(strDate, 4)
    strMonth = Mid(strDate, 5, 2)
    strDay = Mid(strDate, 7, 2)
    ConvertToDate = DateSerial(strYear, strMonth, strDay)
End Function
```

This script uses ExecQuery to return the instance of the Win32_BIOS class that represents the computer's primary BIOS (that is, where the PrimaryBIOS property equals true). Then a For Each...Next loop runs through the single instance and uses a string variable to store the values of five properties: Name, Manufacturer, Version, SMBBIOSBIOSVersion, and ReleaseDate. The last of these is converted to a proper date object using the ConvertToDate function. The script then uses the Echo method to display the results, as shown in Figure 21.6.

FIGURE 21.6   A computer's BIOS data displayed by the script in Listing 21.11.

From Here

▶ For a script that disables all users, **see** "Disabling All User Accounts with a Script," **P.** 52.

▶ For a script that extracts specific security events from the Windows Home Server Security events log, **see** "Viewing Auditing Events with a Script," **P.** 293.

▶ For a script that displays the current Windows Home Server uptime, **see** "Displaying Uptime with a Script," **P.** 429.

▶ For a script that checks the free space on the Windows Home Server system drive, **see** "Checking Free Disk Space on the System Drive," **P.** 437.

▶ For a script that exports Windows Home Server event log items to a database, **see** "Exporting the Event Logs with a Script," **P.** 451.

▶ For more about the ECHO command-line tool, **see** "ECHO: Displaying Messages from a Batch File," **P.** 560.

▶ I discuss using ERRORLEVEL in relation to the XCOPY command in Chapter 19; **see** "XCOPY: Advanced File Copying," **P.** 584.

▶ To learn more about launching individual Control Panel icons using Control.exe, **see** "Understanding Control Panel Files," **P.** 619.

Glossary

accelerator key
The underlined letter in a menu name or menu command.

active partition
A disk drive's bootable partition. Its boot sector tells the ROM BIOS at startup that this partition contains the operating system's bootstrap code. The active partition is usually the same as the primary partition.

ADC
See *analog-to-digital converter*.

Address Resolution Protocol
A network protocol that handles the conversion of an IP address to a MAC address of a network interface card.

ad hoc wireless network
A wireless network configuration that allows for direct wireless NIC-to-NIC communication. See also *infrastructure wireless network*.

Advanced Power Management
A specification developed by Microsoft and Intel that lets the operating system, applications, BIOS, and system hardware work cooperatively to manage power and extend battery life.

allocation unit
See *cluster*.

analog-to-digital converter
A chip in a sound card that converts analog sound waves to the digital audio format. See also *digital-to-analog converter*.

API
See *application programming interface*.

APM

See *Advanced Power Management*.

application programming interface

A set of procedures and other code that higher-level programs can call to perform lower-level functions.

archive bit

An attribute of a file or folder that is activated when the file or folder is created, when it's modified, or when it's renamed.

ARP

See *Address Resolution Protocol*.

ARP cache

A memory location that improves network performance by temporarily storing addresses that have been resolved by the Address Resolution Protocol.

auditing

Tracking Windows Home Server events such as logon failures and privilege use failures.

bitmap

An array of bits (pixels) that contains data that describes the colors found in an image.

bps

Bits per second. The rate at which a modem or other communications device transmits data.

burn-in

Permanent damage to areas of a CRT monitor caused by continuously displaying a particular image over a long period. See also *persistence*.

client

In a client/server network, a computer that uses the services and resources provided to the network by a server.

client/server network

A network model that splits the computing workload into two separate but related

areas. On the one hand, you have users working at intelligent "front-end" systems called clients. In turn, these client machines interact with powerful "back-end" systems called servers. The basic idea is that the clients have enough processing power to perform tasks on their own, but they rely on the servers to provide them with specialized resources or services, or access to information that would be impractical to implement on a client (such as a large database). See also *peer-to-peer network*.

Clipboard

A memory location used to store data that has been cut or copied from an application.

cluster

The basic unit of storage on a hard disk or floppy disk. On most systems, clusters are 4KB.

cluster chain

The sequence of clusters that defines an entire file.

codec

A compressor/decompressor device driver. During playback of audio or video data, the codec decompresses the data before sending it to the appropriate multimedia device. During recording, the codec decompresses the raw data so that it takes up less disk space. Most codecs offer a variety of compression ratios.

color quality

A measure of the number of colors available to display images on the screen. Color quality is usually expressed in either bits or total colors. For example, a 4-bit display can handle up to 16 colors (because 2 to the power of 4 equals 16). The most common values are 16-bit (65,536 colors; see *High Color*), 24-bit (16,777,216 colors; see *True Color*), and 32-bit (16,777,216 colors).

color scheme
A collection of desktop attributes that includes the color of the desktop and window title bars, the fonts used in dialog boxes and pull-down menus, the size of window borders and desktop icons, and much more.

command extensions
Extra features added to commands such as DEL, MD, and SET.

compress
To reduce the size of a file by replacing redundant character strings with tokens.

concentrator
See *hub*.

connection-oriented protocol
See *transport layer protocol*.

connectionless protocol
See *network layer protocol*.

context menu
A menu that appears when you right-click an object. The context menu gives you access to the properties and actions associated with that object.

covert reinstall
When a malicious program surreptitiously reinstalls a fresh version of itself when the computer is idle.

cross-linked cluster
A cluster that has somehow been assigned to two different files or that has two FAT entries that refer to the same cluster.

DAC
See *digital-to-analog converter*.

data source
A file that contains a pointer to the file or server where a database resides; a driver that enables a program or script to connect to, manipulate, and return data from the database; and the logon information that is required to access the database. See also *Open Database Connectivity*.

data throughput
The collective term for network tasks involving client computers, users, and files.

datagram
An IP packet. The datagram header includes information such as the address of the host that sent the datagram and the address of the host that is supposed to receive the datagram.

DE
See *Drive Extender*.

demodulation
The conversion into digital data of an analog wave (a series of tones) transmitted over a telephone line. This conversion is performed by a modem. See also *modulation*.

device driver
A small software program that serves as an intermediary between hardware devices and the operating system. Device drivers encode software instructions into signals that the device understands, and, conversely, the drivers interpret device signals and report them to the operating system.

Device Manager
A tab in the System properties sheet that provides a graphical outline of all the devices on your system. It can show you the current configuration of each device (including the IRQ, I/O ports, and DMA channel used by each device). It even lets you adjust a device's configuration (assuming that the device doesn't require you to make physical adjustments to, say, a DIP switch or jumper). The Device Manager actually gets its data from, and stores modified data in, the Registry.

DHCP

See *Dynamic Host Configuration Protocol*.

DHCP lease

An agreement from a DHCP server that allows a client computer to use a specified IP address for a certain length of time, typically 24 hours.

DHCP server

A computer or device that dynamically assigns IP addresses to client computers.

digital-to-analog converter

A sound card chip that converts digitized audio back into an analog wave so that you can hear it. See also *analog-to-digital converter*.

digital media receiver

A device that can access a media stream being sent over a wired or wireless network connection and then play that stream through connected equipment such as speakers, audio receivers, or a TV.

directory entry

See *file directory*.

Display Power Management Signaling

A specification that lets a device driver use the video adapter to send a signal to the monitor that can either blank the screen (standby mode) or turn off the monitor entirely.

DMA

Direct Memory Access. See also *DMA channel*.

DMA channel

A connection that lets a device transfer data to and from memory without going through the processor. A DMA controller chip coordinates the transfer.

DMR

See *digital media receiver*.

DNS

See *Domain Name System*.

Domain Name System

On the Internet, a hierarchical distributed database system that converts hostnames into IP addresses.

dotted-decimal notation

A format used to represent IP addresses. The 32 bits of the address are divided into quads of 8 bits, which are then converted into their decimal equivalent and separated by dots (for example, 205.208.113.1).

dotted-quad notation

See *dotted-decimal notation*.

double output redirection operator (>>)

A command-line operator that redirects the output of a command, program, or batch file to a location other than the screen. If the output is redirected to a file, the output is appended to the end of the file. See also *output redirection operator*.

DPMS

See *Display Power Management Signaling*.

Drive Extender

A Windows Home Server technology that combines all hard drives into a single storage pool with no drive letters, supports multiple hard drive types (internal Serial ATA and external USB 2.0 and FireWire), and implements folder duplication.

Drive Extender Migrator

A Windows Home Server application and service that implements the distribution of data files among the system's hard drives.

drive-by download

The download and installation of a program without a user's knowledge or consent. See also *pop-up download*.

Dynamic Host Configuration Protocol

A system that manages the dynamic allocation of IP addresses.

environment

A small memory buffer that holds the DOS environment variables.

environment variables
Settings used to control certain aspects of DOS and DOS programs. For example, the PATH, the PROMPT, and the values of all SET statements are part of the environment.

extended partition
The hard disk space that isn't allocated to the primary partition. For example, if you have a 1.2GB disk and you allocate 300MB to the primary partition, the extended partition will be 900MB. You can then subdivide the extended partition into logical drives.

extensible markup language
See *XML*.

extension
In a filename, the part to the right of the period. Windows uses extensions to determine the type of a file.

FAT
See *File Allocation Table*.

File Allocation Table
A built-in filing system that is created on every formatted disk. The FAT contains a 16-bit entry for every disk cluster that specifies whether the cluster is empty or bad, or points to the next cluster number in the current file.

file directory
A table of contents for the files on a disk that is maintained by the File Allocation Table. The entries in the file directory specify each file's name, extension, size, attributes, and more.

File Transfer Protocol
An Internet protocol that defines file transfers between computers. Part of the TCP/IP suite of protocols.

folder duplication
The creation of redundant copies of data files spread across multiple physical hard drives so that if one hard drive fails, no data is lost. See also *Drive Extender*.

font
A unique set of design characteristics that is common to a group of letters, numbers, and symbols.

forehead install
An installation so simple that theoretically you could run through each step by just hitting the spacebar with your forehead.

frequent programs list
The section of the Start menu that displays a collection of shortcuts representing the programs you've used most often.

FTP
See *File Transfer Protocol*.

Full access
Gives a user read/write permissions on a shared folder, meaning that the user can traverse subfolders, run programs, open documents, make changes to documents, create new files and folders, and delete files and folders. See also *None access* and *Read access*.

gateway
A network computer or other device that acts as a middleman between two otherwise-incompatible systems. The gateway translates the incoming and outgoing packets so that each system can work with the data.

GDI
See *graphical device interface*.

graphical device interface
A core Windows component that manages the operating system's graphical interface. It contains routines that draw graphics primitives (such as lines and circles), manage colors, display fonts, manipulate bitmap images, and interact with graphics drivers. See also *kernel* and *User*.

graphics adapter
The internal component in your system that generates the output you see on your monitor.

handle
See *object handle*.

hard page fault
A type of page fault where the system must retrieve the data from the hard disk. See also *soft page fault*.

High Color
A color quality of 16 bits, or 65,536 colors.

hostname
The unique name of a network or Internet computer expressed as an English-language equivalent of an IP address.

HTTP
See *Hypertext Transport Protocol*.

hub
A central connection point for network cables. They range in size from small boxes with six or eight RJ-45 connectors to large cabinets with dozens of ports for various cable types.

hypertext
In a World Wide Web page, an underlined word or phrase that takes you to a different website.

Hypertext Transport Protocol
An Internet protocol that defines the format of Uniform Resource Locator addresses and how World Wide Web data is transmitted between a server and a browser. Part of the TCP/IP suite of protocols.

infrastructure wireless network
A wireless network configuration that uses a wireless access point to receive and transmit signals from wireless computers. See also *ad hoc wireless network*.

input redirection operator (<)
A command-line operator that redirects input to a command, program, or batch file from somewhere other than the keyboard. See also *output redirection operator*.

Internet protocol
A network layer protocol that defines the Internet's basic packet structure and its addressing scheme, and also handles routing of packets between hosts. See also *TCP/IP* and *transmission control protocol*.

internetwork
A network that combines two or more LANs by means of a special device, such as a bridge or router. Internetworks are often called internets for short, but they shouldn't be confused with the Internet, the global collection of networks.

interrupt request
An instruction to the CPU that halts processing temporarily so that another operation (such as handling input or output) can take place. Interrupts can be generated by either hardware or software.

intranet
The implementation of Internet technologies such as TCP/IP and World Wide Web servers for use within a corporate organization rather than for connection to the Internet as a whole.

invalid cluster
A cluster that falls under one of the following three categories:

▶ A FAT entry that refers to cluster 1. This is illegal, because a disk's cluster numbers start at 2.

▶ A FAT entry that refers to a cluster number larger than the total number of clusters on the disk.

▶ A FAT entry of 0 (which normally denotes an unused cluster) that is part of a cluster chain.

I/O port
A memory address that the processor uses to communicate with a device directly. Once a device has used its IRQ line to catch the processor's attention, the actual exchange of data or commands takes place through the device's I/O port address.

IP
See *Internet protocol*.

IP address
The unique address assigned to every host and router on the Internet. IP addresses are 32-bit values that are usually expressed in dotted-decimal notation. See also *hostname*.

IPX/SPX
Internet Packet eXchange/Sequenced Packet eXchange. IPX is a network layer protocol that addresses and routes packets from one network to another on an IPX internetwork. SPX, on the other hand, is a transport layer protocol that enhances the IPX protocol by providing reliable delivery. IPX/SPX is used by NetWare networks.

IRQ line
A hardware line over which peripherals and software can send interrupt requests.

Kbps
One thousand bits per second (bps).

kernel
A core Windows component that loads applications (including any DLLs needed by the program), handles all aspects of file I/O, allocates virtual memory, and schedules and runs threads started by applications. See also *graphical device interface* and *User*.

LAN
See *local area network*.

lazy write
A file write process that waits until the CPU is free before copying or moving data to a disk. This process is used by Drive Extender Migrator.

local area network
A network in which all the computers occupy a relatively small geographical area, such as a department, office, home, or building. All the connections between computers are made via network cables.

local resource
Any peripheral, file, folder, or application that is either attached directly to your computer or resides on your computer's hard disk. See also *remote resource*.

logical drive
A subset of an extended partition. For example, if the extended partition is 300GB, you could create three logical drives, each with 100GB, and they would use drive letters D:, E:, and F:. You can assign up to 23 logical drives to an extended partition (letters D: through Z:).

lost cluster
A cluster that, according to the File Allocation Table, is associated with a file but has no link to any entry in the file directory. Lost clusters are typically caused by program crashes, power surges, or power outages.

MAC address
The Media Access Control address, which is the unique physical address assigned to a device such as a network interface card or router.

malware
The generic term for malicious software such as viruses, Trojan horses, and spyware.

master boot record
The first 512-byte sector on your system's active partition (the partition your system boots from). Most of the MBR consists of a

small program that locates and runs the core operating system files.

Mbps
One million bits per second (bps).

MBR
See *master boot record*.

Media Access Control address
See *MAC address*.

MIDI
See *Musical Instrument Digital Interface*.

mini-driver
A small device driver that augments the functionality of a universal driver by providing the commands and routines necessary to operate a specific device.

miniport driver
A device driver supplied by a SCSI controller manufacturer that provides support for device-specific I/O requests. See also *mini-driver*.

modem
A device used to transmit data between computers via telephone lines. See also *modulation* and *demodulation*.

modulation
The conversion, performed by a modem, of digital data into an analog wave (a series of tones) that can be transmitted over a telephone line. See also *demodulation*.

Moore's Law
Processing power doubles every 18 months (from Gordon Moore, cofounder of Intel).

motherboard
The computer's main circuit board, which includes connectors for the CPU, memory chips, hard drives, ports, expansion slots, controllers, and BIOS.

multimedia
The computer-based presentation of data using multiple modes of communication, including text, graphics, sound, animation, and video.

Multiple Document Interface
A Windows programming interface that lets applications display several documents at once, each in its own window.

multithreading
A multitasking model in which multiple threads run simultaneously.

Musical Instrument Digital Interface
A communications protocol that standardizes the exchange of data between a computer and a musical synthesizer.

name resolution
A process that converts a hostname into an IP address. See *Domain Name System* and *Windows Internet Name Service*.

NAS
See *network attached storage*.

NetBIOS
An API that handles the conversion between the network names of computers and their IP addresses.

NetBIOS name cache
A memory location used to improve network performance by storing names resolved by NetBIOS.

network
A collection of computers connected via special cables or other network media (such as infrared) to share files, folders, disks, peripherals, and applications.

network adapter
See *network interface card*.

network attached storage
A device that contains one or more hard drives that plugs into a switch or router to enable computers on the network to store files on the device instead of on a network share.

network health notification
A fly-out message displayed by the Windows Home Server Status icon that tells you why the network health status has recently changed.

network interface card
An adapter that usually slips into an expansion bus slot inside a client or server computer. (There are also external NICs that plug into parallel ports or PC Card slots, and internal NICs that are integrated into the system's motherboard.) The NIC's main purpose is to serve as the connection point between the PC and the network. The NIC's backplate (the portion of the NIC that you can see after the card is installed) contains one or more ports into which you plug a network cable.

network layer protocol
A protocol in which no communications channel is established between nodes. Instead, the protocol builds each packet with all the information required for the network to deliver each packet and for the destination node to assemble everything. See also *transport layer protocol*.

network name
The unique name by which a computer is identified on the network.

Network News Transport Protocol
An Internet protocol that defines how Usenet newsgroups and postings are transmitted. Part of the TCP/IP suite of protocols.

network operating system
Operating system software that runs on a network server and provides the various network services for the network clients.

network redirector
A virtual device driver that lets applications find, open, read, write, and delete files on a remote drive.

network utilization
The percent of available bandwidth that the computer's network interface card is currently using.

NIC
See *network interface card*.

NNTP
See *Network News Transport Protocol*.

node
A computer on a network.

None access
Prevents a user from accessing a shared folder. See also *Full access* and *Read access*.

nonpaged pool
The system memory area that Windows Home Server uses for objects that must remain in memory and thus can't be written back to the disk when the system doesn't need them. See also *paged pool*.

nonunicast
A network packet exchanged between a single sender and multiple receivers. See also *unicast*.

NOS
See *network operating system*.

notification area
The box on the right side of the taskbar that Windows uses to display icons that tell you the current state of the system.

object
A separate entity or component that is distinguished by its properties and methods.

object handle
An index that points to an entry in a table of available objects and enables programs to interface with those objects.

ODBC
See *Open Database Connectivity*.

OOBE
See *out-of-box experience*.

Open Database Connectivity
A database standard that enables a program or script to connect to and manipulate a data source.

out-of-box experience
What you must do to get a computer running after you take it out of the box.

output redirection operator (>)
A command-line operator that redirects the output of a command, program, or batch file to a location other than the screen. If the output is redirected to a file, that file is overwritten without warning. See also *double output redirection operator* and *input redirection operator*.

packet
The data transfer unit used in network and modem communications. Each packet contains not only data, but also a "header" that contains information about which machine sent the data, which machine is supposed to receive the data, and a few extra tidbits that let the receiving computer put all the original data together in the correct order and check for errors that might have cropped up during the transmission.

page
An area of virtual memory used to transfer data between virtual memory and a storage medium, usually the hard disk.

page fault
An error that occurs when a running process requests data from a page in virtual memory and the system can't find the page in the requested memory location. See also *soft page fault* and *hard page fault*.

paged pool
The system memory area that Windows Home Server uses for objects that can be

written back to the disk when the system doesn't need them. See also *nonpaged pool*.

paging file
A special file used by the Memory Pager to emulate physical memory. If you open enough programs or data files that physical memory becomes exhausted, the paging file is brought into play to augment memory storage. Also called a swap file.

Parkinson's Law of Data
Data expands to fill the space available for storage (from the original Parkinson's Law: Work expands to fill the time available).

peer-to-peer network
A network in which no one computer is singled out to provide special services. Instead, all the computers attached to the network have equal status (at least as far as the network is concerned), and all the computers can act as both servers and clients. See also *client/server network*.

permissions
Attributes applied to a user or security group that define the actions the user can take in a specified folder, usually a network share. See also *Full access*, *None access*, and *Read access*.

persistence
A faint and usually temporary version of an image that has been continuously displayed on an LCD monitor over a long period. See also *burn-in*.

phishing
Creating a replica of an existing web page to fool a user into submitting personal, financial, or password data.

pipe operator (¦)
A command-line operator that captures the output of one command and sends the data as input to another command.

pop-up download

The download and installation of a program after the user clicks an option in a pop-up browser window, particularly when the option's intent is vaguely or misleadingly worded. See also *drive-by download*.

port driver

A device driver that provides complete functionality for working with devices such as hard disk controllers.

port number

A 16-bit number that uniquely identifies each running process on a computer. See also *socket*.

POST

At system startup, the POST detects and tests memory, ports, and basic devices such as the video adapter, keyboard, and disk drives. If everything passes, your system emits a single beep.

Power-On Self Test

See *POST*.

primary name

In a filename, the part to the left of the period.

primary partition (non-WHS)

The first partition (drive C:) on a hard disk. See also *active partition* and *extended partition*.

primary partition (Windows Home Server)

A partition (drive D:) created on the main hard drive and used by Drive Extender to store either data from the Windows Home Server shared folders (if the system has only one hard drive) or tombstones that point to the actual data files on one or more secondary partitions.

process

A running instance of an executable program.

Process Scheduler

The Windows component that doles out resources to applications and operating system processes. In particular, the Process Scheduler organizes running applications so that they take advantage of multitasking and multithreading.

property sheet

A dialog box with controls that let you manipulate various properties of the underlying object.

protocol

A set of standards that defines the way information is exchanged between two systems across a network connection. See also *transport layer protocol* and *network layer protocol*.

Read access

Gives a user read-only permissions on a shared folder, meaning that the user can traverse subfolders, run programs, and open documents, but he cannot make changes to the shared folder or any of its contents. See also *Full access* and *None access*.

redirector

A networking driver that provides all the mechanisms needed for an application to communicate with a remote device, including file reads and writes, print job submissions, and resource sharing.

Registry

A central repository that Windows Home Server uses to store anything and everything that applies to your system's configuration. This includes hardware settings, object properties, operating system settings, and application options.

remote resource

Any peripheral, file, folder, or application that exists somewhere on the network. See also *local resource*.

reparse point
An NTFS technology that associates a kind of tag or marker with a file system object and implements a custom function that the file system runs when you access the object. Drive Extender uses reparse points on the primary disk to distribute data among multiple secondary disks.

repeater
A device that boosts a network cable's signal so that the length of the network can be extended. Repeaters are needed because copper-based cables suffer from attenuation—a phenomenon in which the degradation of the electrical signal carried over the cable is proportional to the distance the signal has to travel.

resolution
See *screen resolution*.

router
A device that makes decisions about where to send the network packets it receives. Unlike a switch, which merely passes along any data that comes its way, a router examines the address information in each packet and then determines the most efficient route that the packet must take to reach its eventual destination.

routing
The process whereby packets travel from host to host until they eventually reach their destination.

Safe mode
A Windows Home Server startup mode that loads a minimal system configuration. Safe mode is useful for troubleshooting problems caused by incorrect or corrupt device drivers.

screen resolution
A measure of the density of the pixels used to display the screen image and usually expressed as rows by columns, where rows is the number of pixel rows and columns is the number of pixel columns (for example, 1024 by 768).

secondary partition
A partition created from an extra hard drive and used by Drive Extender to store data from the Windows Home Server shared folders. See also *primary partition*.

security group
A security object that is defined with a specific set of permissions, and any user added to the group is automatically granted that group's permissions.

server
In a client/server network, a computer that provides and manages services (such as file and print sharing and security) for the users on the network.

shadow
An actual file stored on a secondary partition and pointed to by a tombstone.

shortcut
A pointer to an executable file or a document. Double-clicking the shortcut starts the program or loads the document.

Simple Mail Transport Protocol
An Internet protocol that describes the format of Internet email messages and how those messages are delivered. Part of the TCP/IP suite of protocols.

Single Instance Storage
The storage technology used by Windows Home Server's backup feature, where backups are tracked at the cluster level, and only a single instance of a particular cluster—even if that cluster appears in multiple folders and multiple computers—is included in the backup.

SMTP
See *Simple Mail Transport Protocol*.

snap-in
A Microsoft Management Console tool that is wrapped in a Microsoft Common

Console Document (.msc) file and can be added to the MMC interface.

socket
In the transmission control protocol, a communications channel between two hosts that consists of their IP addresses and port numbers.

soft page fault
A type of page fault where the system is able to retrieve the data from another virtual memory location. See also *hard page fault*.

spyware
Any malware program that surreptitiously monitors a user's computer activities—particularly the typing of passwords, PINs, and credit card numbers—or harvests sensitive data on the user's computer, and then sends that information to an individual or a company via the user's Internet connection without the user's consent.

subnet
A subsection of a network that uses related IP addresses.

subnet mask
A 32-bit value, usually expressed in dotted-decimal notation, that lets IP separate a network ID from a full IP address and thus determine whether the source and destination hosts are on the same network.

swap file
See *paging file*.

switch
A network device that forwards data from one part of the network to another, or across multiple network segments.

TCP
See *transmission control protocol*.

TCP/IP
Transmission control protocol/Internet protocol. TCP/IP is the underlying language of most UNIX systems and the

Internet as a whole. However, TCP/IP is also an excellent choice for other types of networks because it's routable, robust, and reliable.

thread
A program task that can run independently of other tasks in the same program. In a spreadsheet, for example, you might have one thread for recalculating, another for printing, and a third for accepting keyboard input. See also *multithreading*.

tombstone
An NTFS reparse point that resides on the Windows Home Server primary partition and serves to redirect file system calls to the actual file—called the shadow—located on a secondary partition.

topology
Describes how the various nodes that comprise a network—which include not only the computers, but also devices such as hubs and bridges—are connected.

transmission control protocol
A transport layer protocol that sets up a connection between two hosts and ensures that data is passed between them reliably. If packets are lost or damaged during transmission, TCP takes care of retransmitting the packets. See also *Internet protocol* and *TCP/IP*.

transport layer protocol
A protocol in which a virtual communications channel is established between two systems. The protocol uses this channel to send packets between nodes. See also *network layer protocol*.

True Color
A color quality of 24 bits, or 16,777,216 colors.

unicast
A network packet exchanged between a single sender and a single receiver. See also *nonunicast*.

uniform resource locator
An Internet addressing scheme that spells out the exact location of a Net resource. Most URLs take the following form:

protocol://host.domain/directory/file.name

- ▶ *protocol* – The TCP/IP protocol to use for retrieving the resource (such as HTTP or FTP).

- ▶ *host.domain* – The domain name of the host computer where the resource resides.

- ▶ *directory* – The host directory that contains the resource.

- ▶ *file.name*—The filename of the resource.

universal driver
A device driver that incorporates the code necessary for the devices in a particular hardware class to work with the appropriate Windows operating system component (such as the printing subsystem). See also *mini-driver*.

uptime
The amount of time that some system has been running continuously since the last time the system was started.

URL
See *uniform resource locator*.

User
A core Windows component that handles all user-related I/O tasks. On the input side, User manages incoming data from the keyboard, mouse, joystick, and any other input devices that are attached to your computer. For "output," User sends data to windows, icons, menus, and other components of the Windows user interface. User also handles the sound driver, the system timer, and the communications ports. See also *graphical device interface* and *kernel*.

virtual memory
Memory created by allocating hard disk space and making it look to applications as though they are dealing with physical RAM.

WAN
See *wide area network*.

wardriving
An activity where a person drives through various neighborhoods with a portable computer or another device set up to look for available wireless networks.

web application
An object that acts as a container for one or more SharePoint sites.

website headline
Text that identifies the Windows Home Server website. This text appears in several places, including the Remote Access logon page (above the Username text box) and the upper-right corner of the Remote Access pages.

wide area network
A network that consists of two or more local area networks or internetworks that are spaced out over a relatively large geographical area, such as a state, a country, or the entire world. The networks in a WAN typically are connected via high-speed fiber-optic phone lines, microwave dishes, or satellite links.

Windows Internet Name Service
A service that maps NetBIOS names (the names you assign to computers in the Identification tab of the Network properties sheet) to the IP addresses assigned via DHCP.

WINS
See *Windows Internet Name Service*.

wireless access point

A device that receives and transmits signals from wireless computers to form a wireless network.

wireless gateway

A wireless access point that has a built-in router to provide Internet access to all the computers on the network.

wireless range extender

A device used to boost signals going to and from a wireless access point.

XML

A markup language that creates a universal data format for defining complex documents and data structures using custom tags and text.

Windows Home Server Keyboard Shortcuts

If Windows Home Server is just another appliance in your home—that is, it's a headless device (no keyboard, no mouse, no monitor) that you rarely interact with directly or via Remote Desktop—then you have no reason to learn any keyboard shortcuts because they simply don't apply. However, this book assumes that you're regularly interacting directly with Windows Home Server, so the keyboard comes into play. Fortunately, like all versions of Windows, Home Server is loaded with keyboard shortcuts that you can take advantage of to speed up your work and reduce the risk of "mouse elbow," a painful malady most often caused by excessive mouse use. This appendix presents you with a complete list of the Windows Home Server keyboard shortcuts.

TABLE B.1   General Windows Home Server Shortcut Keys

Press	To Do This
Ctrl+Esc	Open the Start menu.
Ctrl+Shift+Esc	Open Task Manager.
Windows Logo	Open the Start menu.
Ctrl+Alt+Delete	Display the Windows Security dialog box (Windows Home Server Pro) or the Task Manager (Windows Home Server Home).
Print Screen	Copy the entire screen image to the Windows Clipboard.
Alt+Print Screen	Copy the active window's image to the Windows Clipboard.
Alt+double-click	Display the Properties dialog box for the selected item.
Alt+Enter	Display the Properties dialog box for the selected object.
Shift	Prevent an inserted CD from running its AutoPlay application. (Hold down Shift while inserting the CD.)
Shift+F10	Display the shortcut menu for the selected object. (This is the same as right-clicking the object.)
Shift+right-click	Display the shortcut menu with alternative commands for the selected object.

TABLE B.2   Shortcut Keys for Working with Program Windows

Press	To Do This
Alt	Activate or deactivate the program's menu bar.
Alt+Esc	Cycle through the open program windows.
Alt+F4	Close the active program window.
Alt+spacebar	Display the system menu for the active program window.
Alt+Tab	Cycle through icons for each of the running programs.
F1	Display context-sensitive help.
F10	Activate the application's menu bar.

TABLE B.3   Shortcut Keys for Working with Documents

Press	To Do This
Alt+- (hyphen)	Display the system menu for the active document window.
Alt+Print Screen	Copy the active window's image to the Clipboard.
Ctrl+F4	Close the active document window.
Ctrl+F6	Cycle through the open documents within an application.
Ctrl+N	Create a new document.
Ctrl+O	Display the Open dialog box.
Ctrl+P	Display the Print dialog box.
Ctrl+S	Save the current file. If the file is new, display the Save As dialog box.

TABLE B.4   Shortcut Keys for Working with Data

Press	To Do This
Backspace	Delete the character to the left of the insertion point.
Ctrl+C	Copy the selected data to memory.
Ctrl+F	Display the Find dialog box.
Ctrl+H	Display the Replace dialog box.
Ctrl+X	Cut the selected data to memory.
Ctrl+V	Paste the most recently cut or copied data from memory.
Ctrl+Z	Undo the most recent action.
Delete	Delete the selected data.
F3	Repeat the most recent Find operation.

TABLE B.5   Shortcut Keys for Moving the Insertion Point

Press	To Do This
Ctrl+End	Move the insertion point to the end of the document.
Ctrl+Home	Move the insertion point to the beginning of the document.
Ctrl+left arrow	Move the insertion point to the next word to the left.
Ctrl+right arrow	Move the insertion point to the next word to the right.
Ctrl+down arrow	Move the insertion point to the end of the paragraph.
Ctrl+up arrow	Move the insertion point to the beginning of the paragraph.

TABLE B.6   Shortcut Keys for Selecting Text

Press	To Do This
Ctrl+A	Select all the text in the current document.
Ctrl+Shift+End	Select from the insertion point to the end of the document.
Ctrl+Shift+Home	Select from the insertion point to the beginning of the document.
Ctrl+Shift+left arrow	Select the next word to the left.
Ctrl+Shift+right arrow	Select the next word to the right.
Ctrl+Shift+down arrow	Select from the insertion point to the end of the paragraph.
Ctrl+Shift+up arrow	Select from the insertion point to the beginning of the paragraph.
Shift+End	Select from the insertion point to the end of the line.
Shift+Home	Select from the insertion point to the beginning of the line.
Shift+left arrow	Select the next character to the left.
Shift+right arrow	Select the next character to the right.
Shift+down arrow	Select the next line down.
Shift+up arrow	Select the next line up.

TABLE B.7　Shortcut Keys for Working with Dialog Boxes

Press	To Do This
Alt+down arrow	Display the list in a drop-down list box.
Alt+underlined letter	Select a control.
Ctrl+Shift+Tab	Move backward through the dialog box tabs.
Ctrl+Tab	Move forward through the dialog box tabs.
Enter	Select the default command button or the active command button.
Spacebar	Toggle a check box on and off; select the active option button or command button.
Esc	Close the dialog box without making changes.
F1	Display help text for the control that has the focus.
F4	Display the list in a drop-down list box.
Backspace	In the Open and Save As dialog boxes, move up to the parent folder when the folder list has the focus.
Shift+Tab	Move backward through the dialog box controls.
Tab	Move forward through the dialog box controls.

TABLE B.8　Shortcut Keys for Drag-and-Drop Operations

Press	To Do This
Ctrl	Copy the dragged object.
Ctrl+Shift	Display a shortcut menu after dropping a left-dragged object.
Esc	Cancel the current drag.
Shift	Move the dragged object.

TABLE B.9   Shortcut Keys for Working in a Folder Window

Press	To Do This
Alt+D	Select the address bar text.
Alt+left arrow	Navigate backward to a previously displayed folder.
Alt+right arrow	Navigate forward to a previously displayed folder.
Backspace	Navigate to the parent folder of the current folder.
Ctrl+A	Select all the objects in the current folder.
Ctrl+C	Copy the selected objects.
Ctrl+V	Paste the most recently cut or copied objects.
Ctrl+X	Cut the selected objects.
Ctrl+Z	Undo the most recent action.
Delete	Delete the selected objects.
F2	Rename the selected object.
F5	Refresh the folder contents.
F6	Cycle between the address bar, the Folders list, and the folder contents.
letter	In the Folders list or folder contents, select the next item that begins with *letter*.
Shift+Delete	Delete the currently selected objects without sending them to the Recycle Bin.
Tab	Cycle between the address bar, the Folders list, and the folder contents.

TABLE B.10   Shortcut Keys for Working with Internet Explorer

Press	To Do This
Alt	Display the Classic menu bar (Internet Explorer 7 and 8).
Alt+Home	Go to the home page.
Alt+left arrow	Navigate backward to a previously displayed web page.
Alt+right arrow	Navigate forward to a previously displayed web page.
Ctrl+A	Select the entire web page.
Ctrl+B	Display the Organize Favorites dialog box.
Alt+C	Display the Favorites Center (Internet Explorer 7 and 8).
Ctrl+Shift+J	Pin the Feeds list (Internet Explorer 7 and 8).

Press	To Do This
Ctrl+N	Open a new window.
Ctrl+T	Open a new tab (Internet Explorer 7 and 8).
Ctrl+W	Close the current tab (Internet Explorer 7 and 8).
Ctrl+Q	Display the Quick Tabs (Internet Explorer 7 and 8).
Ctrl+O	Display the Open dialog box.
Ctrl+P	Display the Print dialog box.
Ctrl+Tab	Cycle forward through the open tabs (Internet Explorer 7 and 8).
Ctrl+Shift+Tab	Cycle backward through the open tabs (Internet Explorer 7 and 8).
Ctrl++	Zoom in on the current web page.
Ctrl+–	Zoom out on the current web page.
Esc	Stop downloading the web page.
F4	Open the Address toolbar's drop-down list.
F5	Refresh the web page.
F11	Toggle between Full Screen mode and the regular window.
Spacebar	Scroll down one screen.
Shift+spacebar	Scroll up one screen.
Shift+Tab	Cycle backward through the Address toolbar and the web page links.
Tab	Cycle forward through the web page links and the Address toolbar.
Ctrl+D	Add the current page to the Favorites list.
Ctrl+E	Activate the Instant Search box (Internet Explorer 7 and 8).
Ctrl+F	Display the Find dialog box.
Ctrl+H	Display the History list.
Ctrl+Shift+H	Pin the History list (Internet Explorer 7 and 8).
Ctrl+I	Display the Favorites list.
Ctrl+Shift+I	Pin the Favorites list (Internet Explorer 7 and 8).
Ctrl+J	Display the Feeds list (Internet Explorer 7 and 8).

TABLE B.11   Shortcut Keys for DOSKEY

Press	To Do This
Command Recall Keys	
Alt+F7	Delete all the commands from the recall list.
Arrow keys	Cycle through the commands in the recall list.
F7	Display the entire recall list.
F8	Recall a command that begins with the letter or letters you've typed on the command line.
F9	Display the Line number prompt. You then enter the number of the command (as displayed by F7) that you want.
Page Down	Recall the newest command in the list.
Page Up	Recall the oldest command in the list.
Command-Line Editing Keys	
Backspace	Delete the character to the left of the cursor.
Ctrl+End	Delete from the cursor to the end of the line.
Ctrl+Home	Delete from the cursor to the beginning of the line.
Ctrl+left arrow	Move the cursor one word to the left.
Ctrl+right arrow	Move the cursor one word to the right.
Delete	Delete the character over the cursor.
End	Move the cursor to the end of the line.
Home	Move the cursor to the beginning of the line.
Insert	Toggle DOSKEY between Insert mode (your typing is inserted between existing letters on the command line) and Overstrike mode (your typing replaces existing letters on the command line).
Left arrow	Move the cursor one character to the left.
Right arrow	Move the cursor one character to the right.

TABLE B.12   Windows Logo Key Shortcut Keys

Press	To Do This
Windows Logo	Open the Start menu.
Windows Logo+D	Minimize all open windows. Press Windows Logo+D again to restore the windows.
Windows Logo+E	Open Windows Explorer in My Computer.
Windows Logo+F	Display the Search Companion.
Windows Logo+Ctrl+F	Find a computer.
Windows Logo+L	Lock the computer.
Windows Logo+M	Minimize all open windows, except those with open modal windows.
Windows Logo+Shift+M	Undo minimize all.
Windows Logo+R	Display the Run dialog box.
Windows Logo+U	Display the Utility Manager.
Windows Logo+F1	Display Windows Help.
Windows Logo+Break	Display the System Properties dialog box.
Windows Logo+ spacebar	Scroll down one page (supported only in certain applications, such as Internet Explorer).
Windows Logo+ Shift+spacebar	Scroll up one page (supported only in certain applications, such as Internet Explorer).
Windows Logo+Tab	Cycle through the taskbar buttons.

Windows Home Server Online Resources

When Microsoft first announced Windows Home Server at the Consumer Electronics Show in January of 2007, it seemed like only minutes later that the web was awash in blogs, reviews, forums, and other online sites dedicated to Windows Home Server. I'm exaggerating, of course, but it's true that it didn't take long for Windows Home Server to have a significant presence on the web, and that presence has continued to grow. Lists of websites are always fraught with peril for a book author, because no sooner has the book rolled off the presses than some sites go belly-up (or *sneakers-up*, in the vernacular) and others spring up to take their places. But fortune favors the bold, or something like that, so this appendix offers a list of my favorite Windows Home Server sites and blogs.

Windows Home Server Websites

Here are some general websites devoted to Windows Home Server:

Windows Home Server—Microsoft's home page for Windows Home Server. It includes general information about the product and its features, links to other Windows Home Server sites, links to Windows Home Server resources, and more:

www.microsoft.com/windows/products/winfamily/windowshomeserver/

Windows Home Server Forums—This Microsoft site offers several different groups for discussing all aspects of Windows Home Server. There's a Windows Home

Server frequently asked questions list (FAQ), and you can discuss Windows Home Server software, hardware, and more:

forums.microsoft.com/windowshomeserver/

Doug Knox on Windows Home Server—This site has lots of links to good Windows Home Server content:

www.dougknox.com/whs/index.htm

Windows Home Server Add-ins—A comprehensive list of add-ins available for Windows Home Server:

www.whsaddins.com/

Windows Home Server Unleashed—The home page for this book on my website, which includes all the sample code used in the book:

www.mcfedries.com/HomeServerUnleashed2E/

Windows Home Server Blogs

Name a topic, and there's almost certainly a blog devoted to it—probably more than one. Windows Home Server is no exception:

Windows Home Server Team Blog—The official Windows Home Server blog featuring posts directly from the Windows Home Server management and development teams:

blogs.technet.com/homeserver/

cek.log—This blog is run by Charlie Kindel, who was the original general manager of Windows Home Server at Microsoft:

kindel.com/blogs/charlie/

Home Server Hacks—This blogs offers lots of great tips and tricks for Windows Home Server:

www.homeserverhacks.com

We Got Served—This blog includes lots of great Windows Home Server info, hardware and software reviews, and more:

www.wegotserved.com

Ramblings of a Home Server Tester—A high-quality blog run by a Windows Home Server enthusiast:

homeserver.wordpress.com/

Windows Home Server for Developers

If you're interested in writing add-ins for Windows Home Server and accessing Windows Home Server objects in your VB.NET or C# code, here are some resources to help you get started:

Windows Home Server Software Development Kit (SDK) Documentation—This Microsoft Developer Network (MSDN) site has the documentation you need to get started writing code for Windows Home Server:

msdn.microsoft.com/en-us/library/bb425866.aspx

Windows Home Server Developers Forum—Use this section of the Windows Home Server forums to ask and answer questions about developing for Windows Home Server:

forums.microsoft.com/WindowsHomeServer/ShowForum.aspx?ForumID=1407&SiteID=50

Index

SYMBOLS

A

C

How can we make this index more useful? Email us at indexes@samspublishing.com

How can we make this index more useful? Email us at indexes@samspublishing.com

E

F

How can we make this index more useful? Email us at indexes@samspublishing.com

H

J - K

How can we make this index more useful? Email us at indexes@samspublishing.com

How can we make this index more useful? Email us at indexes@samspublishing.com

How can we make this index more useful? Email us at indexes@samspublishing.com

V

How can we make this index more useful? Email us at indexes@samspublishing.com

How can we make this index more useful? Email us at indexes@samspublishing.com

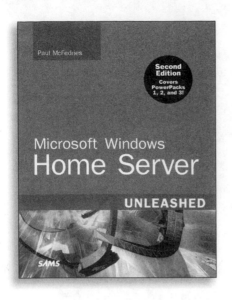

FREE Online Edition

Your purchase of **Microsoft Windows Home Server Unleashed** includes access to a free online edition for 45 days through the Safari Books Online subscription service. Nearly every Sams book is available online through Safari Books Online, along with more than 5,000 other technical books and videos from publishers such as Cisco Press, Exam Cram, IBM Press, O'Reilly, Prentice Hall, Que, and Addison-Wesley Professional.

SAFARI BOOKS ONLINE allows you to search for a specific answer, cut and paste code, download chapters, and stay current with emerging technologies.

Activate your FREE Online Edition at
www.informit.com/safarifree

> **STEP 1:** Enter the coupon code: RFHJPXA.

> **STEP 2:** New Safari users, complete the brief registration form.
> Safari subscribers, just log in.

If you have difficulty registering on Safari or accessing the online edition, please e-mail customer-service@safaribooksonline.com